DR. FRANK MAST.

DEVELOPMENTAL PSYCHOPATHOLOGY
From Infancy through Adolescence

DEVELOPMENTAL PSYCHOPATHOLOGY
From Infancy through Adolescence

Second Edition

Charles Wenar

Ohio State University

McGraw-Hill Publishing Company

New York   St. Louis   San Francisco   Auckland   Bogotá   Caracas
Hamburg   Lisbon   London   Madrid   Mexico   Milan   Montreal   New Delhi
Oklahoma City   Paris   San Juan   São Paulo   Singapore   Sydney
Tokyo   Toronto

DEVELOPMENTAL PSYCHOPATHOLOGY
FROM INFANCY THROUGH ADOLESCENCE

2 3 4 5 6 7 8 9 0   **DOH DOH**   9 4 3 2 1 0

ISBN 0-07-069269-6

This book was set in Serif by Monotype Composition Company.
The editors were Rochelle Diogenes and Elaine Rosenberg;
the designer was Amy E. Becker;
the production supervisor was Valerie A. Sawyer.
The cover illustrator was Wiktor Sadowski.
R. R. Donnelley & Sons Company was printer and binder.

Library of Congress Cataloging-in-Publication Data

Wenar, Charles.
    Developmental psychopathology from infancy through adolescence /
Charles Wenar.—2nd ed.
        p.   cm.
    Rev. ed. of: Psychopathology from infancy through adolescence. 1st ed. c. 1983.
    Includes bibliographical references.
    ISBN 0-07-069269-6
    1. Child psychopathology.   2. Adolescent psychopathology.
I. Wenar, Charles. Psychopathology from infancy through adolescence.   II. Title.
RJ499.W396   1990
    618.92'89—dc20   89-12794

About the Author

Charles Wenar is professor emeritus of psychology at The Ohio State University. He headed both the developmental area and the clinical child program in the department of psychology there. A graduate of Swarthmore College and Iowa State University, Dr. Wenar was both a clinician and a researcher at Michael Reese Hospital, the Illinois Neuropsychiatric Institute, and the University of Pennsylvania. His two previous books and numerous articles, as well as his research on autism and on negativism in healthy toddlers, attest to his long-standing interest in both normal and disturbed children. In 1986, Dr. Wenar received the Distinguished Professional Contribution Award of the Section on Clinical Child Psychology of Division 12 of the American Psychological Association for his meritorious contribution to the advancement of knowledge and service to children.

To Solveig—still the light of my life.

Contents

Preface to the Second Edition

Since the publication of the first edition there have been three noteworthy changes in regard to understanding childhood disturbances. First, *developmental psychopathology* has come into its own. In the first edition, we remarked on the "painfully slow" progress toward the acceptance of childhood psychopathology as a field in its own right rather than being adult psychopathology applied to children. The progress is no longer slow. In fact, it has been so rapid that the battle has been all but won. The similarity between adult and child psychopathology has to be demonstrated rather than assumed, while the many distinctive disturbances in early development are clearly recognized as such.

Not that there is agreement on how developmental psychopathology should be conceptualized. For many, it involves locating disturbances within the traditional developmental periods of infancy, preschool, middle childhood, and adolescence and then trying to discover the necessary and sufficient conditions for producing the abnormality. Others add a developmental dimension by searching for etiologic factors in previous periods as well as addressing the issue of prognosis with and without remedial interventions. Our own orientation, which is that psychopathology is *normal development gone awry*, is still not widely accepted. While many books on psychopathology begin with a discussion of normal development, it is largely ignored subsequently. By contrast, we maintain that all development is one; that is, developmental psychology is a unitary field of inquiry. Whether one chooses to study its normal or deviant path is a matter of preference. Moreover, the quest to understand how the two paths are related enriches the understanding of both. The present edition, like the previous one, was written to illustrate this thesis.

The second significant change is in regard to the *determinants* of psychopathology. In the past, there was a tendency to search for a single cause that would be the key to understanding a particular disturbance. The cause might be organic or cognitive or parental behavior or stress, and so on. Now there is a shift away from this so-called linear model to a multiple causal one. A disturbance is the result not only of a number of factors but also of the interaction among such factors. We presented such a model in the first edition, and we continue to advocate it. However, there is a tendency at present to regard the shift in models as a solution to the problem of etiology when, in fact, it vastly complicates the search. We will pay particular attention to the few investigators who are actually using the multicausal approach rather than merely referring to it in a general way.

Finally, and most gratifyingly, in the past few years there has been an *expansion of data* on childhood psychopathology. The present revision contains more than 250 new references for example, which represents a significant expansion in total number of references over the first edition. This enlarged data base is reflected in a number of ways.

1. There are new sections on *sexual abuse, pediatric psychology,* and *social skills training.*

2. A new chapter is devoted to *minority children.* Ethnic minority groups make up an estimated 20 percent of our population. To evaluate and understand the children they see, it is essential for clinicians to be familiar with these children's different cultural backgrounds.

3. A number of topics have been significantly expanded, including *autism, depression, attention deficit–hyperactivity disorder, learning disabilities, phobias, schizophrenia,* and *physical abuse.*

4. There are also important new data concerning *anorexia* and *bulimia, homosexuality,* and the *effectiveness of psychotherapy.*

In fact, with the exception of the neuroses or anxiety disorders, in which interest continues to languish, the information on every psychopathology has been updated.

One final point: the discussion of *methodological* problems has been expanded to include those involved in studying children at risk for becoming schizophrenic and sexually abused children, as well as the special problems involved in doing prevalence surveys. In certain instances, the reader follows an investigator's reasoning as he or she successively generates and then tests hypotheses concerning confounds or alternative explanations in order to find the necessary and sufficient conditions for producing the disturbance at hand. Finally, in this edition we continue to present in detail particularly successful solutions to methodological problems. The overall goal is to acquaint the reader not only with findings but also with problems researchers face in designing studies and how they go about solving them.

Acknowledgments

I am grateful to a number of editors for their unfailing helpfulness, advice, and expertise. From Random House, I would like to thank Mary Falcon and, from McGraw-Hill, Rochelle Diogenes, Barry Fetterolf, Elizabeth Greenspan, and Elaine Rosenberg. My colleague Felicisima Serafica reviewed the chapter on ethnic minority children and served as a general sounding board for my ideas. Allison Dodge is the kind of copyeditor every author should have but few are so lucky as I.

Charles Wenar

1

The Developmental Approach

YOU ARE a clinical child psychologist.[1] A mother telephones your office frantic over the sudden personality change in her boy. "He used to be so sweet and then, out of the clear blue sky, he started being sassy and sulky and throwing a fit if anybody asked him to do the least little thing. What really scared me was last night he got so mad at his brother, he ran at him and started hitting him with all his might. His brother was really hurt and started screaming, and my husband and I had to pull them apart. I don't know what would have happened if we hadn't been there. I just never saw anybody in a rage like that before."

What is the first question you ask?

YOU ARE at a cocktail party and, after learning that you are a clinical child psychologist, a former star-quarterback-turned-successful-business-executive takes you aside. After some rambling about "believing in sexual equality as much as the next fellow," he comes to the point. "Last week my son turned to my wife and announced that when he got old enough, he was going to become a girl. When my wife asked him where he got a crazy idea like that, he said that he thought boys were too rough, and he liked to be with girls more. I know he's always been

---

[1] This and subsequent sections will concern the experiences of a hypothetical clinical child psychologist. However, the experiences themselves might apply to any professional who is involved with the mental health of children. All names are fictitious.

a 'mama's boy,' but I'll be damned if I want any son of mine to have one of those sex changes done on him."

What is the first question you ask?

YOU ARE a clinical child psychologist conducting an initial interview with a mother who has brought her daughter to a child guidance clinic. "She has always been a sensitive child and a loner, but I thought she was getting along all right—except that recently she has started having some really strange ideas. The other day we were driving on the highway to town, and she said, 'I could make all these cars wreck if I just raised my hand.' I thought she was joking, but she had a serious expression on her face and wasn't even looking at me. Then, another time she wanted to go outside when the weather was bad, and she got furious at me because I didn't make it stop raining. And now she's started pleading and pleading with me every night to look in on her after she has gone to sleep to be sure her leg isn't hanging over the side of the bed. She says there are some kind of crab creatures in the dark waiting to grab her if her foot touches the floor. What worries me is that she believes all these things can really happen. I don't know if she's crazy or watching too much TV or what's going on."

What is the first question you ask?

The first question is the same in all three cases: *How old is your child?*

OVERVIEW

Our general concern is with time—or, more precisely, with change over time.

Our specific charge is to understand psychopathological disturbances of childhood.

Our procedure will involve placing various psychopathologies within a developmental context and examining them as instances of *normal development gone awry.*

The three vignettes illustrate this procedure. Whether the described behaviors are regarded as normal or pathological depends upon when they occur in the developmental sequence. All three are to be expected in toddlers and preschoolers but would be suspect at later ages. It is not unusual for a docile infant to become a willful, negativistic, temperamental tyrant during the "terrible twos." If the child were 10, however, his attack on his brother may well represent a serious lapse in self-control. In a like manner it is not unusual for preschool boys to believe that they can grow up to be women because they have not grasped the fact that sex remains constant throughout life. If an adolescent boy seriously contemplated a sex change, this would be cause for parental concern and professional attention. And finally, ideas of omnipotence and a failure to clearly separate fantasy from reality are part of normal cognitive development in toddlers and preschoolers; their presence from middle childhood on suggests the possibility of a serious thought disturbance and an ominous lack of reality contact.

The vignettes also provide us with our first clue to understanding child psychopathology as normal development gone awry: psychopathology is behavior which once was but no longer can be considered appropriate to the child's level of development. This was one of Freud's most brilliant and influential insights. The general thesis that adult disturbances have their roots in childhood continues to be a pervasive etiological hypothesis accepted even by those who reject all other aspects of Freudian theory. We shall make use of the same developmental hypothesis but apply it within childhood itself. As we examine various psychopathologies, we shall discover that there are many variations on this theme of psychopathology as developmentally inappropriate behavior; therefore we shall constantly be seeking the specific developmental model that best fits the data at hand. We shall also come across some unexpected exceptions for which the model itself does not seem to hold.

At the applied level, the developmental approach underlies the child clinician's deceptively simple statement, "There's nothing to worry about—most children act that way at this age, and your child will probably outgrow it"; or its more ominous version, "The behavior is unusual and should be attended to, since it might not be outgrown." A considerable amount of information concerning normal development must be mastered before one can judge whether the behavior at hand is age appropriate, as well as whether a suspect behavior is likely to disappear in the course of a child's progress from infancy to adulthood. In addition, the child clinician must know which frankly psychopathological behaviors stand a good chance of being outgrown with or without therapeutic intervention and which are apt to persist.

Incidentally, to state that behavior is outgrown is not as much an explanation as a label for ignorance. While certain psychopathologies tend to disappear with time, exactly what happens developmentally to cause their disappearance is not known. In fact, the phenomenon has rarely been investigated. The best we can do is to recognize that "outgrown" is a nonexplanation.

Before we set out to understand child psychopathology as normal development gone awry, there are a number of preliminary matters to be attended to. First, we must present a *general developmental model* in order to examine various characteristics of development itself. Then we must select those *variables* that are particularly important to the understanding of childhood psychopathology and trace their normal developmental course. Our vignettes, for example, suggest that the

variables of self-control, sex, and cognition should be included in the list. We shall also have to select the *theories* that will contribute most to the developmental approach. Next, we shall turn to a descriptive account of the *behaviors comprising childhood psychopathology*, since these are the behaviors we must understand in terms of our developmental perspective. And, finally, we must examine *longitudinal studies* that have followed groups of normal and disturbed children into adulthood, since these studies will provide a general guide as to which psychopathologies are apt to persist and which are likely to be outgrown.

Developmental Model

Our general developmental model includes the time dimension along with intrapersonal, interpersonal, superordinate, and organic variables. These five categories will be referred to as *contexts*. They are represented schematically in Figure 1.1.

TIME Since our general concern is with change over time, our task would be simpler if there were agreement as to how change should be conceptualized. There is not.

Some psychologists anchor change in chronological time. Gesell is a prime exemplar, since he links crucial behavioral changes to chronological age. In tracing the child's relation to the parents, for example, he describes age 6 as a time of high ambivalence toward the mother, cravings for affection being followed by tantrums and rebellion. Age 7 is calm and inward, the child being companionable, sympathetic, anxious to please. Age 8 is stormy again, with the child demanding the mother's attention while being exacting, rude, and "fresh," while 9 marks a return to self-sufficiency, eagerness to please, and affectionate behavior. And so it goes (Gesell et al., 1946).

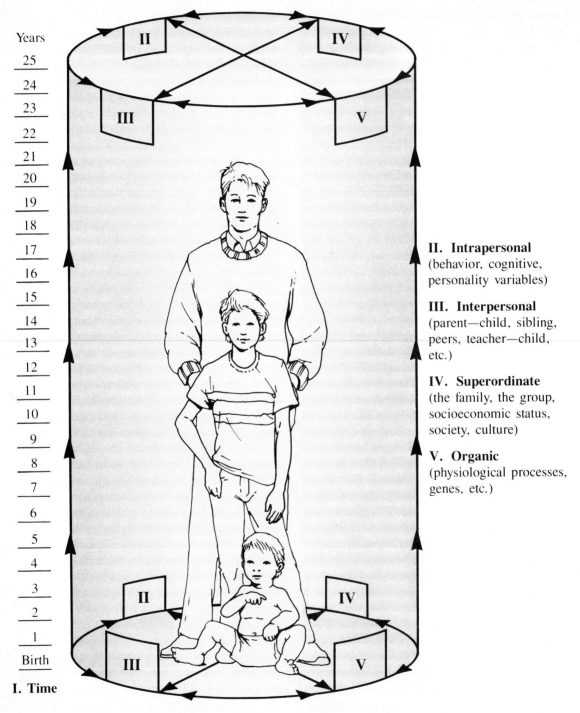

Contexts II-V interact at all points in time as well as over time.

The labels within the figure read:

Years
25
24
23
22
21
20
19
18
17
16
15
14
13
12
11
10
9
8
7
6
5
4
3
2
1
Birth

I. Time

II. Intrapersonal
(behavior, cognitive,
personality variables)

III. Interpersonal
(parent—child, sibling,
peers, teacher—child,
etc.)

IV. Superordinate
(the family, the group,
socioeconomic status,
society, culture)

V. Organic
(physiological processes,
genes, etc.)

A different way to conceptualize change is in terms of *stages* of development, Piaget's cognitive theory and Freud's psychosexual theory being two prominent examples. Stage theories are more concerned with change itself than with chronological age. Typically they make two assumptions: stages represent qualitative reorganizations of behavior rather than "more of the same"; and the sequence of stages is unalterable. Thus, something new emerges at each stage, and the order of emergence is fixed. For both Piaget and Freud, the question "How old is the child?" is not as important as "What stage is the child in?" Fortunately for the clinician, the stages they depict can be assigned chronological age guidelines.

The conceptualization of change over time is of more than academic interest. A characteristic of stage theories is that they often regard the transition between stages as a time of increased tension, unrest, and even reversion to less mature behaviors. The psychosexual stages have this characteristic, while Piaget describes the child's return to immature ways of thinking during cognitive transitions. Even Gesell, whose maturational theory does not include specific stages, describes development in terms of periods of unstable expansion alternating with ones of stable consolidation. All such conceptualizations stand in contrast to radical environmentalism, which claims that stability or instability is primarily the consequence of the experiences the child is having. The important point for us is that normal development may entail built-in times of stress and upset; the transitions from infancy to the preschool period and from middle childhood to adolescence, for example, are two potentially stressful periods. Knowing when disturbed behavior is part of normal growth helps the clinician decide whether to tell a parent, "Most children act like that, and yours is likely to outgrow it."

There is another aspect of the time dimension. Our developmental approach implies that, in order to evaluate the meaning and import of an event in a child's life, it is essential to know not only *what* happened but also *when* it happened. To illustrate: a lengthy separation from the mother may have few adverse effects in early infancy before an attachment to her has developed but may trigger a dramatic reaction of protest and extreme withdrawal after an attachment has been formed. Being hospitalized becomes progressively less upsetting between 2 and 12 years of age and also may have different meanings, the younger children being distressed over separation, the 4- to 6-year-olds fearing mutilation or death or viewing hospitalization as punishment. Whether obese adults regard their body with disgust or not depends, among other things, on whether they were obese during adolescence, a period when body consciousness is at a height.

It is also widely believed that events happening in the first few years of life have a more lasting effect on development than events happening subsequently. However, this so-called critical-period or sensitive-period hypothesis has not gone unchallenged and is viewed with a certain amount of skepticism (see Clarke and Clarke, 1977). While the controversy over the critical or sensitive period will play only a minor role in our presentations, we will not accept either hypothesis as a universally valid principle of human development. Rather we prefer to test its validity in regard to the particular aspect of development under discussion.

THE INTRAPERSONAL CONTEXT   The intrapersonal context will figure most prominently in our discussions of psychopathology, since it contains the greatest amount of developmental data. However, here, as with the context of time, we are confronted by the problem of how best to conceptualize the individual child. Once past the obvious variables of age and sex, in what direction should we go? Traditional behaviorists would persuade us to deal exclusively with manifest behavior and to avoid all mentalistic or inferential concepts; Freudians urge us to examine the child's ego strength and monitor the battles between id and superego; Piaget reminds us not to neglect egocentrism and the balancing act between assimilation and accommodation; Erikson points to the centrality of ego identity; and Werner insists on the importance of differentiation and hierarchical integration. (The technicalities of the various theories need not concern us here. However, it would be helpful to have the kind of general familiarity with the major developmental theories to be found in introductory texts in child development. See, for example, Hetherington and Parke, 1986.)

The choice among conceptualizations has important clinical implications. The behavioral viewpoint leans toward a statistical and social approach to psychopathology. Since there is nothing in behavior itself which designates it as abnormal, the judgment must be based on its infrequency or on the fact that a given society chooses to label certain behaviors as psychopathological. In another society the same behavior might go unnoticed or even be regarded as a special gift.

The psychoanalysts, on the contrary, maintain that behavior is important only as it furnishes clues to the child's inner life; psychopathology is not a matter of behavior per se, but of the meaning of such behavior. The frequency of masturbation in adolescence, for example, is not as important as the stage-appropriateness of the fantasies which accompany masturbation.

Because our primary goal is to understand rather than to champion a particular conceptualization of the intrapersonal context, we shall utilize various theories only as they throw light on the psychopathology at hand.

Such eclecticism assumes that no one theory offers a satisfactory account of all of childhood psychopathology, while various individual theories are apposite in accounting for specific disturbances.

THE INTERPERSONAL AND SUPERORDINATE CONTEXTS   Interpersonal variables are concerned with the interaction of individuals—of child with parents, of child with siblings, and so on. Superordinate variables deal with aggregates of individuals taken as a unit—the family, the adolescent clique, the middle class, the industrialized society, and so on. Superordinate variables are primarily the province of social psychologists, sociologists, and cultural anthropologists. We shall refer to such variables only on occasion, since we shall be concerned primarily with psychological ones. Our neglect should not be taken to imply that the superordinate context is unimportant; rather it represents a different approach to psychopathology from the one we are adopting.

THE ORGANIC CONTEXT   The psychological representation of the body should be distinguished from the purely organic body. The two clearly cannot be equated: many physiological processes do not and cannot have any representation in consciousness; most people have only a sketchy and inaccurate image of how their bodies look; in the case of phantom limbs, pain is still felt in a toe which has been amputated; and severe psychopathology may be marked by somatic delusions, such as believing that one's bowels are turning to stone.

The effects of psychological disturbances on the organic body will be central to our examination of obesity and anorexia nervosa in chapter 6, and, reversing the direction of influence, the behavioral consequences of blindness and of certain brain psychopathologies will be explored in chapter 12. The organic context also includes genes, which, as transmitters of hereditary characteristics, will figure in our discussion of the etiology of schizophrenia (see chapter 10). Aberrations in an individual's genetic structure itself produce Down's syndrome, the specific kind of mental retardation we shall study in detail in chapter 11.

Interaction

We have been discussing the contexts as static entities. In reality, they are constantly interacting. An emergency appendectomy may arouse anxiety not only in the child but in parents and siblings as well, just as a stellar performance in soccer may elevate self-esteem while raising status among parents, peers, and teachers.

More important, interactions among contexts change with time. While we are accustomed to thinking of the child as changing, all the other contexts are changing also. Parents who are 25 years old when their infant daughter is born are not at the same stage in their development as they will be at 40 when she is entering adolescence. Nor is the single-child family the same after other children are added, while the casual, improvised peer group of the preschool period differs from the adolescent clique, which is the arbiter of taste in clothes, music, language, and social deportment. Being a member of the lower class in the socially stable 1950s had a different meaning than it did in the 1960s when riots and protests made the plight of the urban poor a matter of national concern. The social ferment of the 1960s has had other effects as well. The family as a social institution is being markedly changed by the willingness of parents to place toddlers and preschoolers in day-care facilities, by the increasing number of working mothers, by the emphasis on negotiable rather than assigned parental roles, and by the increase in divorce and single-parent families. Our society has become increasingly tolerant of early sexual experiences and of couples living together without being married, while the emphasis on doing "your own thing" has broadened the spectrum of acceptable behavior. All these changes have an impact on our concern with differentiating normal from deviant development.

The changes described above are well known. Not so well known is the fact that the concept of childhood itself is changing. In the pioneer days, children were workers and miniature adults; since they were born into sin, their parents were advised—often by the clergy—to beat the devil out of them. Quite a different image from our present one, with its emphasis on the uniqueness of childhood and the importance of child-centeredness on the part of the parents. (For a more detailed account, see Abramowitz, 1976.) To cite another example: in 1874 a brutally abused, starving, and mutilated child named Mary Ellen received legal protection from her parents only after she had been legally defined as an animal so that the laws against animal cruelty could be applied to her. This is a far cry from the current concern for children's rights; in Sweden, for example, corporal punishment is against the law and a child has the right to have a parent arrested for spanking him or her.

Just as the concept of childhood is changing, so is the concept of childhood psychopathology. Some changes have come from within the profession, such as Kanner's delineation of early infantile autism in 1943; others have resulted from social forces, such as the elimination of homosexuality as a psychiatric disturbance in 1974 when the members of the American Psychiatric Association voted to eliminate homosexuality from the list of psychiatric disturbances found in the Diagnostic and Statistical Manual of Mental Disorders. The social ferment of the 1960s forced professionals to recognize that poverty vastly increases the risk of a variety of psychopathologies, thereby changing the course of the mental health movement from an individual to a community orientation. (See chapter 16. For a comprehensive historical account, see H. E. Rie, 1971.) Thus, there is nothing final about the list of psychopathologies that will be introduced in chapter 3. The list has changed and will continue to change in response both to theoretical and empirical progress within the profession and to social pressures and values outside the profession. In fact, a consistent application of our developmental model requires that this be so.

It is worthwhile to examine in some detail the history of childhood psychopathology. After tracing its roots, we shall turn to current conceptualizations of psychopathology and the diverse methods by which understanding of abnormal behavior of children has been advanced.

CHILDHOOD PSYCHOPATHOLOGY: THE HISTORICAL CONTEXT

Before the twentieth century "one could not confidently point to disordered behavior in children as a field of study, or . . . identify a body of knowledge. The virtual absence of proposed treatment of the described conditions is [also] significant" (Rie, 1971, p. 26). By contrast, the twentieth century has witnessed major advances in all aspects of child psychopathology. Spearheaded by the psychoanalytic movement and later by behaviorism, along with Adolph Meyer's common sense psychiatry, William Healy's study of juvenile delinquents, and Lightner Witmer's clinic for psychoeducational problems, the scientific investigation of childhood disorders

came into its own. With the advent of the psychometric movement, behavior descriptions could be supplemented by measuring instruments, while professionals concerned with diagnosis strove for a comprehensive accounting of the entire range of childhood disorders. On the professional front, the mental hygiene movement was launched, child psychotherapies and residential treatment centers for children proliferated, child guidance clinics—typically staffed with an interdisciplinary team of psychiatrist, psychologist, and social worker—came into being, and targets for remediation were extended down the age span to infancy and outward from the child to include parents, entire families, and the community. As a sign of the vitality of the field, scientific and professional organizations and publications devoted to childhood psychopathology appeared at an accelerated rate.

We shall have time only to sample this rich fare, highlighting the developments most germane to our interests.

The Psychoanalytic Movement

The landmark event in the scientific study of childhood psychopathology was the publication of Sigmund Freud's "Three Essays on the Theory of Sexuality" (1905). Freud's thesis that early development held the key to understanding adult neurosis moved the study of childhood from the periphery to the center of inquiry. Moreover, the psychosexual theory provided a detailed model whereby developments in the first six years of life could be related to subsequent adult disturbances. Finally, Freud was explicit in attributing a sexual drive to children, in regarding conflict over sexuality as the etiologic factor in neurosis, and in postulating repression and the unconscious as two factors crucial to the production of a neurosis: "An alertness for the unconscious, the sexual and the infantile may be called the psychoanalytic point of view" (Waelder, 1960). (We shall present the psychoanalytic theory of neurosis in detail in chapter 8.)

Freud and his followers continued to elaborate upon and revise psychoanalytic theory. Freud himself was most interested in exploring the motivational aspects of his theory, in particular the sexual and aggressive drives and the workings of the unconscious. His followers, notably Heinz Hartman and Ernst Kris, expanded his concept of the ego or the reality-oriented, adaptive functions of the psyche (Hartman, 1964), the superego, or conscience (Jacobson, 1964), and the defense mechanisms (A. Freud, 1946), while enlarging the interpersonal context from the nuclear family to society (Erikson, 1950). The initial emphasis on a single trauma as the origin of neurosis concomitantly shifted to a consideration of the complex interaction among intra- and interpersonal variables.

Freud never studied children. His famous psychoanalysis of a phobic boy, little Hans, was conducted through Hans's father and led Freud to conclude that he had learned little he had not already known through his investigation of adults! It remained for Melanie Klein and Anna Freud to study children directly. Through such studies, the mother–infant relationship came into prominence, play came to be viewed not as a trivial pastime but as a disguised expression of unconscious wishes and conflicts, psychoanalytic concepts were applied to the entire array of childhood disorders from psychosis to situational disturbances, and the traditional psychosexual variables were expanded to include self-reliance, companionship, and work (A. Freud, 1965). (For a more detailed account of the psychoanalytic movement, see Rie, 1971.)

Of the many disciples who broke with Freud, often over the issue of the central role of sexuality, Adler was one who made major contributions to the understanding of childhood psychopathology. Adler regarded human nature as basically social rather than sexual and the striving for superiority as more important than the need for sexual gratification. Because of their social nature, children should be viewed within the context of the entire family rather than within the narrow triangle of the oedipal situation, and both siblings and peers play a central role in children's development. The striving for superiority, as Adler came to view it in his later writings, is a striving for mastery, for fulfillment, for growth. This striving can be undermined by excessive parental indulgence or excessive discipline, either of which paves the way to psychopathology. Far from using discipline to "break the child's will," for example, parents should strive to preserve the child's sense of autonomy, confidence, and expansiveness. (A detailed presentation of the Adlerian approach can be found in Ansbacher and Ansbacher, 1956.)

The Behavioral Movement

The behavioral movement was formally launched in 1913 by John B. Watson's paper, "Psychology as the Behaviorist Views It." In defiance of the current tradition, Watson proclaimed that the study of overt behavior, not consciousness, was the sole basis for a scientific psychology. Just as we need not trouble ourselves with the thoughts and introspections of animals in order to predict and control their behavior, neither should we trouble ourselves with those of human beings. While allowing for the importance of hereditary equipment, Watson championed a radical environmentalism in which it was possible to produce any kind of behavior one wished, given the proper learning conditions. The learning model itself, involving the building up of habits through stimulus–response connections, had a refreshing simplicity, especially in contrast to the complexities of the

Freudian theory. And if one could mold human behavior as one wished, one could both prevent psychopathology from occurring and change it to normality after it had taken place. This mixture of simplicity and unbounded optimism was a heady brew.

Specifically in regard to children, Watson prescribed rigid schedules for child rearing which would mold children to be independent, require little affection, have no unnecessary fears, and fit comfortably into a socially prescribed niche. Laboratory experiments, especially with little Albert (the behavioral counterpart of little Hans) indicated that fears could be both acquired and eliminated utilizing learning principles. However, Watson's contribution to childhood psychopathology was rather like a promissory note that has been redeemed only in recent years.

Subsequently, the behavioral tradition has undergone both a narrowing and a broadening. B. F. Skinner goes Watson one better in rejecting not only mentalism but also physiological explanations of the link between stimulus and response. And just for good measure, he eschews theory construction and hypothetical constructs as aids to explaining behavior. His learning model relies heavily on the simple principles of reinforcement, extinction, generalization, and discrimination to account for a large spectrum of normal and disordered behavior. Like Watson, Skinner enthusiastically champions a cradle-to-grave environment in which scientifically proven learning principles would be utilized to produce an ideally adjusted society. (The best-known statement of Skinner's environmental engineering is *Walden Two*, 1948. For a general statement of his position, see *Science and Human Behavior*, 1953.)

The behavioral tradition has been broadened by social-learning theorists who insist that imitation or modeling must be added to the list of learning principles responsible for behavioral change. The thesis was defended by Miller and Dollard (1941) and subsequently by Bandura and Walters (1963). The learning theorists are "social" because they are primarily concerned with learning that takes place in a social context, such as between parent and child or among peers.

Among social-learning theorists, Bandura has been one of the most venturesome in making "private events," such as ideas, plans, wishes, and feelings, compatible with the scientific tenets of behaviorism. The study of private events, he argues, need not involve a return to the mentalism of the past, since these events can be operationally defined in terms of antecedents and consequences. The time-honored concept of a "mental" image, for example, can be anchored in behavioral antecedents, such as instructions to "Imagine you are lifting a weight," and measurable consequences, such as changes in muscle potential in the arms. Moreover, having the concept of an image accounts for the observed behavior better than if the concept were excluded. Thus the requirements of objective inquiry are satisfied. In general, Bandura argues that a host of cognitive variables, such as symbolic representations of experiences, expectancies, and problem solving, can be encompassed within the social-learning framework with no loss of rigor and with significant gains in explanatory scope. Rejecting Skinner's exclusive emphasis on observable antecedents and consequences, Bandura maintains that external events affect behavior through intermediary cognitive processes which "partly determine which external events will be observed, how they will be perceived, whether they leave any lasting effects, what valence and efficacy they have, and how the information they convey will be organized for future use" (Bandura, 1977, p. 160).

Bandura also counters the charge that behaviorism makes the individual into a mere recipient of environmental events. He has his own version of initiative which he calls *self-efficacy*. In the initial stages, observing the differential effect of one's actions enables individuals to respond appropriately to various situations; for example, a preschool boy learns that playing in a day-care center will be rewarding and fighting will be punished, and behaves appropriately. Next, individuals come to anticipate not only that a given behavior will produce a given outcome, but more important, they also come to estimate whether they can successfully execute such a behavior. This conviction of success is called an efficacy expectation. Such an expectation of mastery affects both the initiation and persistence of coping behavior. Thus people fear and avoid situations they believe exceed their coping skills, and they behave assuredly in those which they believe themselves capable of handling. Therefore, self-efficacy influences both the choice of activities and persistence in the face of obstacles. It is important to note that Bandura's concept of self-efficacy is not merely speculative but also buttressed by empirical data (Bandura, 1977).

One final development in the behavioral movement may prove the most significant in regard to the study of childhood psychopathology. It is the appearance of a cluster of remedial techniques called *behavior therapies*. The behavior therapies have taken a number of behaviorists out of the rarefied atmosphere of the laboratory and challenged them to apply their scientific principles to the complexities of social interactions. In the process these therapies have firmly secured a place for the behavioral movement in the clinical arena while raising searching issues concerning the adequacy of a simple learning model to account for the therapeutic changes that take place within individuals. (We shall take up this thread in chapter 16.)

OTHER CONTRIBUTORS   The *psychometric tradition* began auspiciously in 1905 when Alfred Binet, a French psychologist, together with Theophile Simon, developed the first test for differentiating feebleminded children from other students in the Paris school system. The test was designed to serve the practical purpose of providing a relatively objective procedure for determining whether a given child's intellectual functioning was sufficiently below average to justify special education. Binet clearly regarded his intelligence test as an estimate of current functioning rather than an evaluation of some hypothetical potential or some fixed intellectual level. He also realized that test results provided no information as to the reasons a child was functioning at a given level, such as heredity or environment. (For a translation of the original article, see Binet and Simon, 1916.) Unfortunately, these crucial insights tended to be ignored as the testing movement gained in popularity and the IQ score began to be perceived as having an immutability which was never intended.

As school attendance became mandatory and as children with academic and emotional problems came increasingly to the attention of professionals charged with evaluating them, tests became diversified to include abilities, achievement, personality, social maturity, and psychopathology itself.

The rise of the *child study movement* is particularly relevant to our interest in understanding psychopathology as normal development gone awry. The pivotal figure was G. Stanley Hall, the first promoter of the psychological study of children in the United States. He was concerned with understanding, within an evolutionary framework, how individuals develop and adapt to their environment. Because of this interest in origins or genesis, his is called a genetic psychology. In his research, for example, he distributed questionnaires to parents, teachers, and children to obtain developmental data on thinking, fears, motor abilities, dreams, and prayers. His most famous book was on adolescence (1904); its thesis, that this is a period of inherent turmoil, is still being debated.

The subsequent history of the child study movement up until World War II is largely a history of child development institutes. (Our presentation follows Sears, 1975, chap. 1—a chapter which deserves to be read in its entirety.) In 1906, Mrs. Cora Bussey Hillis reasoned that, if agricultural colleges in Iowa could study ways to improve livestock and disseminate the information efficiently to farmers, why couldn't a similar model be set up to research, teach, and disseminate information about children? The idea was difficult to sell because, although the "agricultural public believed in science for hogs . . . children were another matter. . . . Could the human soul be subjected to Science?" (Sears, 1975, p. 19). In 1917 the Iowa legislature finally appropriated funds for the Iowa Child Welfare Research Station at the State University of Iowa. After World War I had sensitized the public to the deplorable state of literacy in the male population, the Rockefeller interests followed suit by dedicating approximately $12 million for research, teaching, and dissemination of knowledge in the field of child development. The era of the institutes had been launched. The research conducted in such settings in large measure defined the content of the study of child development.

Thus, during the interwar period there was a giant leap forward in terms of factual information and research methodology, while physical, mental, and personality development were explored from infancy to adulthood. World War II almost decimated the child development movement, which was rescued only by massive federal funding. While institutes continued to exist, child development moved into departments of psychology. The move was mutually beneficial; general psychology was enriched by the ad-

dition of a developmental dimension and child development profited from the scientific advances in general psychology. The combination of financial support and intellectual challenges has produced the current state of widespread interest and high productivity. We will not cover the current substantive issues (see Sears, 1975) because we are more concerned with current models of psychopathology. However, before examining these, we need to summarize one more important historical trend—the mental hygiene movement.

The *mental hygiene movement* for children began in 1896 when Lightner Witmer established the first clinic for children in this country at the University of Pennsylvania. He also coined the terms "clinical psychology" and "psychological clinic." (Our presentation again follows Rie, 1971.) Witmer's initial presentation of clinical psychology to the American Psychological Association was received with cool indifference, but, undaunted, he went on to found both a journal, *Psychological Clinic,* and an orthogenic school for prolonged observation and training. During this period, William Healy was pioneering a tridisciplinary clinic for juvenile delinquents in which psychiatrists, psychologists, and psychiatric social workers joined in a team approach to deal with problems of diagnosis and remediation. In 1921 the Commonwealth Fund, together with the National Committee of Mental Hygiene, sponsored a conference on the prevention of juvenile delinquency, which resulted in the launching of a five-year demonstration program of child guidance clinics. This "may well have been the single most important step toward the goal of the definition, prevention and remediation of behavior disorders in children" (Rie, 1971, p. 33). The clinics were basically atheoretical and eclectic, learning primarily from firsthand experience. The contributions to childhood psychopathology were numerous. The addition of mild and moderate disorders to the list of disturbances expanded the range of psychopathologies and countered the tendency to concentrate only on the severely disturbed child. Early influences, rather than heredity, came to be viewed as the major determinants of behavior disorders. However, there was also evidence that, instead of a one-to-one correspondence between childhood experiences and subsequent disturbance, similar situations could be followed by dissimilar behavior patterns in adults, while dissimilar early experiences might eventuate in similar adult behavior. There was little evidence to support the old belief that disturbances were due to the impact of a single traumatic event; rather, they resulted from the cumulative weight of untoward events. Undoubtedly buttressed by the team approach, interest shifted from symptom to the "whole-child" approach, requiring a comprehensive evaluation of the children's current functioning, their interactions at home and at school, and their histories—what we have called the intra- and interpersonal contexts and the context of time.

As for the clinics themselves, they expanded from a handful in 1922 to 285 exclusively serving children and 350 serving children and adults by 1946 (see Rie, 1971). This growth was accompanied by an expansion of organizations and journals devoted to clinical and professional issues.

The Interplay of Ideas

Before bringing the historical context up to the present, it is worth noting that the trends discussed were described separately only for convenience in presentation. In reality, interest in childhood psychopathology was vitalized by the continual interaction among the various trends. The desire to help went hand in hand with the desire to learn and to teach; the basic and the applied, the labora-

tory and the clinic, were in constant interaction. Psychoanalysis was at once a therapeutic technique and a device for exploring personality. To celebrate Clark University's twentieth anniversary, Hall invited Freud to speak and to receive an honorary degree. John B. Watson dedicated *Psychology from the Standpoint of the Behaviorist* (1919) to an academic psychologist, J. McKeen Cattell, and to a clinician, Adolph Meyer, and established the pattern of applying findings from laboratory experiments to the practical problems of preventing and remedying disturbed behavior. Finally, the child guidance clinics, while carrying out their service mission, uncovered valuable leads as to the nature and etiology of childhood psychopathologies. It is this same picture of diversity with component elements overlapping, complementing, and conflicting with one another which continues to lend a special excitement to the quest for understanding and, ultimately, eradicating childhood psychopathology.

CHILDHOOD PSYCHOPATHOLOGY: CURRENT MODELS

There are, at present, a variety of models of childhood psychopathology, most of which are rooted in the historical developments we have just examined. While having distinctive features, the models are not necessarily incompatible. Some share common features. Others are complementary or tangential. Still others represent irreconcilable differences. Each has merit; none is totally satisfactory. Moreover, few efforts have been made to integrate them all, as there is tacit agreement that such a unification lies far in the future. Therefore we must reconcile ourselves to living with diversity and partial truths. (For a more comprehensive coverage of models of psychopathology than we shall give, see Bootzin and Acocella, 1988.)

The term "model" is best interpreted as a frame of reference, since it has little of the precision and explanatory potency of models in the physical sciences, such as a model for the structure of the atom or the DNA molecule. Each model has its own concepts, often couched in terms of a specialized vocabulary, its own assumptions concerning which are relevant variables, its own view of etiology and remediation, and its own stand on the nature of scientific inquiry. In addition to its expected functions of organizing existing facts and generating new ones, a model of psychopathology must also serve the pragmatic function of being useful to the professionals concerned with understanding and remedying childhood disturbances.

The Medical Model

The medical model is the present-day version of the organic emphasis, which, by replacing the demonology of the Middle Ages, was a step forward in the scientific study of psychopathology but which, in its exclusion of all other etiological factors in the nineteenth century, became a roadblock to progress. Currently, the organic emphasis is more temperate and buttressed by a more substantial body of empirical findings than it was 100 years ago. The present-day medical model consists of two components. The first involves the general etiological hypothesis that certain psychopathologies result from organic dysfunctions. The second involves classifying and interpreting psychopathological behavior in the same way as physical diseases, namely, in terms of diagnostic entities.

ORGANIC ETIOLOGY There is evidence that organic factors play a major role in certain kinds of adult schizophrenia and depression, and in certain kinds of mental retardation

and schizophrenia in children. Organic factors have also been implicated in the etiology of autism and in certain kinds of antisocial acting-out behaviors, hyperactivity, and learning disabilities in children, although the evidence varies in definitiveness. Thus, the list of psychopathologies having a possible organic etiology continues to be impressive. Note the modifier "certain kinds of," however: a given psychopathology—adult depression, for example—may have an organic basis in some cases while being psychogenic in others.

There are three specific models of organic etiology. In the first, *genetic* factors are responsible for the appearance of a given psychopathology. Research has centered around three related areas of inquiry. The first of these concerns which psychopathologies have a significant genetic component; for example, there is compelling evidence for the inheritance of certain kinds of schizophrenia. The second area concerns the mode by which a genetic abnormality is transmitted. This involves tracing the path from gene to behavior and understanding all the mediators involved. The third area concerns the extent of hereditability in a given psychopathology. Extremists maintain that genes per se determine the abnormal behavior; moderates counter that only vulnerability to a psychopathology is inherited, while its actual appearance depends on environmental conditions. For example, one child may become schizophrenic because of a genetic vulnerability interacting with a series of traumatic life experiences, while another child with the same genetic vulnerability may make an adequate adjustment because of a sympathetic, benign environment.

Proponents of the *biochemical model* seek to discover the biochemical agents that may contribute to the etiology of psychopathological behavior. Again, schizophrenia has been the most frequently targeted disturbance, each new advance in medical science leading to new hope that the psychotoxic agent has been discovered. When bacteria were found to cause physical disease, it was also suggested that they were involved in mental illness; then attention shifted to viruses and, most recently, to alterations in the metabolism of certain brain chemicals, or neurochemicals, particularly a group of naturally occurring neurochemical substances called mono-amines. Despite promising leads, the gap between chemistry and behavior, as between genes and behavior, is far from closed—and the assumption of a direct causal relation is a highly oversimplified one.

The *neurophysiological model* assumes that abnormal behavior is due to inherited, congenital, or acquired brain pathology. Obviously, it overlaps with the genetic and biochemical models but includes other etiological agents such as intrauterine disease, premature birth, or traumatic brain insult. What this model does is make brain functioning the key to understanding psychopathological conditions.

At the most general level, the medical model is part of the quest to build a bridge between human behavior and human physiology. The quest is an ancient one and is currently being facilitated by astonishing advances in modern technology. However, to claim at this point that psychopathology is "nothing but" organic dysfunctioning would be as erroneous as to claim that it is "nothing but" a problem in adjustment. The organic context interacts with the intra- and interpersonal contexts, and knowledge of this interaction is necessary if progress is to be made in understanding the etiology of psychopathology. (For further details concerning the organic basis of psychopathological behavior, see Werry, 1986.)

THE MEDICAL MODEL OF DIAGNOSIS At one level, diagnosis can be viewed as a variation on the age-old scientific exercise of classification. Psychopathologies, like insects and flowers, are so diverse that viewing each separately would be overwhelming. In order to simplify their task, therefore, investigators assume that there are classes in nature and that keen observation will reveal what these classes are.

To classify psychopathologies according to the medical model, we must first answer two basic questions. First, what is the rationale for regarding the behaviors as abnormal rather than normal? Second, are the specific classifications valid or true to nature? The first question establishes the general criteria for inclusion and exclusion and, among classifications utilizing the medical model, has been answered in a variety of ways. The least satisfactory is based on an analogy of mental health and illness to physical health and illness. An analogy is not an acceptable rationale and can be both incorrect and misleading. Yet it is the analogy which has crept into and dominates the very vocabulary we have used in dealing with psychopathology—mental illness, mental health, mental hygiene, syndrome, patient, treatment, cure, and, indeed, psychopathology itself all derive from medicine.

Whether a classification is really there in nature involves validation, with diverse professionals and investigators putting the classification to empirical and statistical tests which either affirm or cast doubt upon its soundness. As we shall see, some classifications, such as autism, have met the test of subsequent validation; others, such as minimal brain damage, have not.

But the medical model has always entailed more than a descriptive classification; the classifications themselves are called diagnoses, and these have both etiological and prognostic implications. It is the former which is most troublesome. Emil Kraepelin, who published the landmark classification of adult psychopathologies in 1833, set the stage by assuming an organic etiology for each class of psychopathology. While it is an erroneous overgeneralization, the equation "classification = diagnosis = organic etiology" lingers on, particularly in the ceaseless professional skirmishes between psychiatrists and other mental health professionals. The former claim that their medical background makes them the ultimate arbiters of diagnosis and therapy in mental as well as physical illness. Psychologists are particularly incensed by this stand, and heated legal battles are being fought over what constitutes the legitimate province of each professional.

There is another problem with medical terminology, involving the use of the word "symptom." To designate a given psychopathology, say, a phobia, as a symptom means that there is an underlying cause, just as in medicine a virus may be the underlying cause of the symptoms of the flu. The underlying cause need not be organic, however; it might just as well be psychological. Thus an 8-year-old boy may be obstreperous in class because he is afraid to express his defiance of his mother and displaces it onto the teacher. In this case the behavior in school is symptomatic of an underlying problem in the home. The issue of underlying causes is a complex and controversial one which will occupy us later (see chapter 8). Suffice it to say at this point that the evidence is too inconclusive to resolve the controversies satisfactorily, but the word itself remains a bone of contention.

Since the term "medical model" has become so affect-laden among professionals, it is important to disentangle relevant from irrelevant issues. Purely as a classification system, one based on the medical model should stand or fall on the basis of proven validity and clinical utility—that is, on independent evidence that clusters of symptoms do, in fact, exist in nature, that etiology and

prognosis are, in fact, what the system claims them to be, and on practitioners' reports of the fit between described classifications and observed behavior. Currently, there are two dangers. One is that classifications based on the medical model will be used as a vehicle for making unwarranted assumptions concerning organic etiology and for extending the province of psychiatrists into childhood disturbances which have little or nothing to do with medical training and expertise. The second danger is that nonmedical professionals and researchers will reject the classification out of hand because of the label "medical model," thus turning their backs on its empirical merits and clinical utility.

The Behavioral Model

Three characteristics distinguish behavioral psychology. First is the assertion that *observable behavior* comprises the basic data of a scientific psychology. The more radical theorists would limit psychology to the response organisms make to environmental stimuli, excluding all mentalistic and inferential variables such as thoughts, images, drives, and memory traces. More moderate theorists admit inferential concepts under two conditions: that such terms can be defined behaviorally and that their introduction facilitates the fundamental goals of predicting and controlling behavior. Next, behaviorists favor *research conducted under highly controlled conditions,* the laboratory experiment being the technique par excellence for establishing the necessary and sufficient conditions for producing the behavior being investigated. Measurement and quantification are highly valued as part of the overall emphasis on precision. Third, behaviorists assume that a limited number of *learning principles* can account for a wide array of behavior in animals and humans. True, there are other forces at work—genetic, instinctual, maturational, temperamental—but the acquisition, maintenance, change, or elimination of much behavior can be adequately and concisely accounted for in terms of learning principles.

PRINCIPLES OF LEARNING The three principles of learning which form the basis of the behavioral approach are *classical conditioning* (also called respondent or Pavlovian conditioning), *operant conditioning* (also called instrumental conditioning), and *imitation* (also called modeling or observational learning).

In classical conditioning a stimulus (the conditioned stimulus, or CS) which initially is incapable of eliciting a response (the unconditioned response, UR) is successively paired with a stimulus (the unconditioned stimulus, US) which is the UR's uniform or innate elicitor. After a given number of pairings, the previously neutral stimulus (the CS) comes to elicit the response (the UR) which is now known as the conditioned response, or CR. To vary the well-known example of a dog being conditioned to salivate to the sound of a bell, a tone (the CS) that is successively paired with a puff of air to the eyelid (the US)—a stimulus which naturally elicits a blinking response (the UR)—will, with time, itself come to elicit the blinking response (now called the CR), even when the air puff is omitted.

Two other principles derived from classical conditioning have proved useful in accounting for the development and elimination of psychopathological behavior. *Stimulus generalization* is the tendency for stimuli similar to the conditioned stimulus also to elicit the conditioned response; the greater the degree of similarity, the more vigorous the response. In the above example, the blinking response can be elicited by tones similar to the CR. The increase in efficiency is obvious since the organism does not have to learn to respond anew to each variation in the stimulus. *Discrimination learning* is the opposite of gener-

alization in that it involves learning to distinguish among stimuli and to respond only to the appropriate one. Typically, the discrimination is established through nonreinforcement or punishment. Thus a preschooler who has learned that a dog is a wolf-wolf might label a number of animals wolf-wolf until the parent supplies another, more appropriate label.

In *operant conditioning* the organism operates upon or does something to the environment in order to achieve a given result. In essence, it is a process by which an organism learns to associate certain results with certain actions it has taken. These results may serve either to increase or decrease the likelihood of the behavior's being repeated. The term used to designate an increase in the likelihood of occurrence is reinforcement. Reinforcement can be positive or negative. In *positive reinforcement* behavior is followed by a reward; for example, the father of an 8-year-old treats his son's soccer team to ice cream after a victory. In *negative reinforcement* an aversive stimulus is removed; for example, a 10-year-old girl is excused from washing dishes for a week after improving her grade in history.

The two terms used to designate a decrease in the likelihood of a behavior's being repeated are extinction and punishment. In *extinction* the reinforcement maintaining a response is removed; for example, upon her therapist's advice, a mother no longer gives in to her 4-year-old's demands every time he has a temper tantrum, and the tantrums disappear. In *punishment* a response is followed by an aversive stimulus; for example, a 3-year-old's hand is slapped as he reaches out to touch a flame on the stove.

A distinction is also made between *primary* and *secondary reinforcers*. The first are unlearned, having a biological base: primary positive reinforcers include food, water, warmth, and sex, while primary negative reinforcers include pain, extremes of heat and cold, and intensely loud sounds. Most reinforcers are learned in association with primary reinforcers and are called secondary or conditioned reinforcers; the cuddly blanket which provided the infant with warmth becomes a security blanket during the toddler and preschool years, just as mother's harsh voice preceding punishment becomes feared in its own right. Subsequently words, the mere symbols of reinforcement, acquire great potency, and much of the child's behavior is regulated by the value judgments of "Good" and "Bad."

One consequence of punishment is particularly relevant to our interest in psychopathology. Once exposed to an aversive stimulus, an organism will try in the future to avoid reexposure, a process which is called *avoidance learning*. Avoidance learning is a two-edged sword. It protects the organism from a repeated encounter with a possibly harmful situation; for example, once burned, a 2-year-old does not continually touch the burner of a stove. But avoidance learning can also lead to unrealistic avoidance of situations after they are no longer noxious; for example, an adult may be terrified of his reasonable, benevolent boss because, as a child, he was brutally beaten by his father. Thus avoidance prevents the individual from adopting new behaviors which are appropriate to changed circumstances.

The final concept which will be useful in subsequent discussions is *shaping*. Operant conditioning depends on the natural occurrence of the operant response. Yet, some of these responses have a very low rate of occurrence or, indeed, do not occur at all. In such instances the response must be shaped by reinforcing successive approximations to the desired one; for example, young children are progressively taught to swim by first getting them accustomed to the water, teaching them to float, then to kick their legs or tread water while floating, and so on, until the basic skill of swimming has been mastered.

The third in the triad of learning principles is *imitation*, which involves learning a new behavior by observing and imitating another person's performance of that behavior. Thus, without any direct parental tutelage preschoolers will pretend to clean the house or hammer a nail as their parents do or will answer the phone with the exact words and intonation they have heard adults use. While learning theorists have devoted a good deal of attention to studying the possible mechanisms involved in imitation, their research and theorizing will not be relevant to our discussions.

NORMAL AND ABNORMAL DEVELOPMENT   The behaviorists' credo is that all behavior is one and—once allowance has been made for genetic, maturational, and temperamental factors—all behavior conforms to the basic principles of learning just described. Of course, one may divide behavior into categories, such as infant or adolescent, normal or abnormal, but this is done only to stake out territory of special interest to the investigator. The basic task is to discover how the principles of learning can be utilized to account for the special behaviors one has chosen.

According to the behaviorists, some children grow up with the kinds of learning experiences that maximize their chances of making a successful adaptation to environmental demands, while others have experiences that minimize such an outcome. In the latter instance, behaviorists prefer to talk in terms of "maladaptive" rather than "abnormal" behavior to avoid any suspicion of a qualitatively different developmental outcome. Implicit in their stand is also a cultural relativism: What would be adaptive in one society may be maladaptive in another.

In addition to being cultural relativists, behaviorists have a penchant for quantification which leads them to define psychopathology as deviations in the frequency or intensity of behavior. Note A. O. Ross's definition of a psychological disorder as behavior which "deviates from an arbitrary and relative social norm in that it occurs with a frequency or intensity that authoritative adults . . . judge . . . to be either too high or too low" (Ross, 1980, p. 9).

According to such a definition, psychopathologies can be grouped in terms of behavioral deficit or excess. In *behavior deficit,* behaviors occur at a lower frequency or intensity than is expected within society so that the child's social, intellectual, or practical skills are impaired. Autism, learning disabilities, mental retardation, and even juvenile delinquency are examples, the last resulting from deficient behavioral controls. In *behavior excess,* behavior occurs at a higher frequency or intensity than is adaptive to the standards of society. The hyperactive child who is in a continual state of excitement, the compulsive child who repeatedly washes his hands, and the anxious child who is constantly terrified by real and imagined dangers all show signs of behavior excess.

However, other kinds of deviations are also recognized, one being the appropriateness of the stimulus–response relationships. In *inappropriate stimulus control,* either a response occurs in the absence of any appropriate stimulus, or a stimulus fails to elicit the appropriate response. A psychotic boy's delusion that his therapist will bite his head off if he enters the therapy room is an example, as is the anorectic girl's conviction that she is still too fat when she is on the verge of starving herself to death.

In addition to categorizing types of maladaptations, behaviorists have also conceptualized traditional psychopathologies in terms of learning principles. A phobia, for example, could readily be regarded as an example of maladaptive avoidance behavior, in which

the child is too terrified to learn how harmless the feared object really is; depression may be interpreted as the result of extinction, in which significant positive reinforcements are withdrawn, and the person becomes passive and hopeless; while autism, with its imperviousness to the human environment, may result from a failure of parents to acquire secondary reinforcing value.

The Psychodynamic Model

The psychodynamic school of thought was founded by Freud and his followers, some of whom subsequently rebelled against the Freudian tenets of psychoanalysis. What they all shared was an interest in discovering the dynamics—the basic motives, the prime movers—of human behavior. This concern with intrapersonal forces immediately sets them apart from the behaviorists, with their concern for the environmental factors that shape behavior. As with the other two approaches discussed so far, our coverage of the psychodynamic approach will not be comprehensive; instead, we shall concentrate on the two aspects of Freudian theory most relevant to understanding childhood psychopathology—the structural and genetic theories. (For more extensive coverage, see Bootzin and Acocella, 1988.)

THE STRUCTURAL THEORY Freud arrived at a tripartite conceptualization of the human psyche: the id, the ego, and the superego.

According to classical Freudian theory, the id is the source of all psychic energy, which in turn derives from biological drives. Among these, the sexual drive is prepotent in its import for personality development. (Freud subsequently added the death instinct, which included aggression as the other primary motivating force, but its conceptualization was unsatisfactory and its status remains controversial.) The drives of the id are alogical, demanding immediate and complete satisfaction, or what Freud called discharge. Freud coined the term the *pleasure principle* for the id's ceaseless striving for immediate discharge. Ideation in the id is also at the service of the pleasure principle, resembling the irrational images and sequencing of events in dreams. Freud called such ideation *primary process thinking* to distinguish it from rational thought. Developmentally speaking, the infant is an id-dominated creature, concerned only with reducing the tensions generated by physiological needs, having no capacity for delay and no awareness of the realistic parameters of the world he or she has entered.

In the classical formulation, the ego arises from the id's need for maximal gratification. Unlike the id, the ego is endowed with functions such as perception, memory, and reasoning which enable it to learn realistic means of satisfying the id. A 2-year-old's ego may advise, "You can do anything you want with your teddy bear when you're mad; but when you get mad at your baby brother, better wait until no one is around or else the pain of punishment will outweigh the pleasure of hitting him." Thus the ego functions on what Freud called the *reality principle*; he called the rational thinking which is in tune with the parameters of reality *secondary process thinking*. Note that the ego requires the id to postpone immediate gratification, although postponement is inimical to its nature, and that secondary process thinking both delays and guides behavior. Subsequently, the ego psychologists made a major revision in the classical theory by postulating that the ego initially is endowed with its own energy and can function autonomously rather than being subservient to the id. Important as this change is, it will not bear directly on our discussions.

The ego begins to emerge at about 6 months of life, and the third structure, the superego, comes into its own at about 5 to 6 years of age. It contains the moral standards of right and wrong which the preschooler takes over from his or her parents and which become an internalized judge of the moral rectitude of the child's behavior. In case of transgression, the superego punishes the child with guilt feelings. The superego is comparable to the conscience, but it is an absolutistic, implacable conscience and demands continual obedience to its standard of proper behavior.

From middle childhood on, then, the ego must find ways of obtaining as much id gratification as reality will allow without arousing the superego, which in its way is as irrational in its demands as the id itself. The image of the beleaguered ego contending with inevitable conflict between irreconcilable intrapersonal forces has been regarded as stern and heroic by some, bleak and dour by others. It certainly has little of the behaviorist's belief in the malleability and therefore the potential perfectability of human behavior and none of the humanist's belief that humans inherently desire to grow and maximize themselves.

While Freud's structural theory is relevant to our concern with psychopathology, his genetic theory of psychosexual development will figure more prominently in subsequent discussions.

THE PSYCHOSEXUAL THEORY Freud's psychosexual theory assumes that eroticized intimacy exists throughout the life span, adult sexuality being only the culmination of a process begun in earliest infancy. Our bodies themselves are so constituted that stimulation of certain areas arouse exquisitely pleasurable sensations. Once having experienced them, we are forever driven to obtain the maximum bodily pleasures which society will allow. Freud called this biologically determined drive to obtain erotic bodily sensations *libido*. Furthermore, the body is constituted so that the mouth, the anus, and the genitals are particularly rich in erotic sensations when stimulated. Freud assumed that there is an inevitable progression, whereby first the mouth, then the anus, and finally the genitals predominate as sources of pleasure. Equally important, each progression of libido is accompanied by a psychological change in the intimate relations with the parents or primary caretakers. The label *psychosexual* epitomizes the complementary relation between psychological and erotic development.

The three specific stages of psychosexual development are called the oral, the anal, and the phallic. These are true stages in that their sequencing is unalterable and each represents a qualitative change in personality. The Oedipus complex, which is the climax of the psychosexual stages, occurs toward the end of the preschool period. Finally, Freud stated that progression is never complete; even in normal development, residuals of prior stages can be found. Such residuals are called *fixations*. We will briefly describe both the stages themselves and their normal residuals.

In the *oral stage* the infant derives pleasure first from sucking and, after teeth appear, from biting. In the context of being fed, the first emotional attachment or, to use the Freudian term, the first *object relation* is formed. This initial intimacy is particularly potent in setting the tone for all future intimacies. Sensitive, loving caretaking engenders a positive image both of mother and of being mothered; caretaking marked by distress and frustration will engender an image in which love is mixed with anxiety and rage. And at a primitive level, being loved and being fed are forever equated.

Normal fixations include pleasure in sucking candy and chewing gum as well as smoking and kissing. In religion, the Madonna preserves the image of the all-loving, all-powerful mother figure, while in literature the witch epitomizes the angry, destructive mother, the poisoned apple or poison in general representing love contaminated by the destructiveness of hostility. "There's no apple pie like mother's apple pie" and "The way to a man's heart is through his stomach" derive from the basic equation: being well loved equals being well fed.

In the *anal stage* the toddler achieves erotic gratification from retaining and evacuating feces or from manual manipulation of the anus. For the first time, the toddler also has control of the source of pleasure: whereas the infant is totally dependent on the caretaker for feeding, the toddler alone can decide when, where, and how to have a bowel movement. Toilet training requires the relinquishing of this pleasurable autonomy. For such a sacrifice the toddler should be adequately compensated by love. If training is punitive, unloving, or coercive, the toddler becomes rebellious and stubbornly resistive or anxious and overly compliant.

One normal residual of the anal stage is the cult of regularity; laxatives always sell well, and there are adults whose daily mood is contingent upon a daily evacuation. Preschoolers call one another "you old BM" or "you old pooh-pooh," and adult cursing continues the tradition by substituting adult for childhood equivalents of feces. The preschooler's fascination with mud and clay derive from the earlier interest in feces. In addition, any number of behaviors can be categorized as being "clean" or "dirty"— being personally clean, neat, orderly, being clean minded and clean living as contrasted with being messy and slovenly, being a dirty dealer, having a dirty mind, and telling dirty jokes, dirt being only a thin disguise for feces.

In the *phallic stage* masturbation and curiosity about anatomical differences are at their height, so that the desire to peek and to show, to look and to exhibit, run high. The period is also marked by expansiveness, assertiveness, and an intoxicating sense of power as the child feels that he or she is now—or soon will be—"big" and "grown up." Normal residuals include an abiding interest in the human body, sexual techniques, and intercourse evidenced in scholarly descriptions, pinup magazines and pornography alike. The desire to show off also harks back to the phallic stage and is evident in the "sex symbol," the muscle man on the beach, the actress who tries to captivate the audience, the physicist who tries to dazzle the scientific community, or even the conspicuous sufferer who proclaims that no one else has ever known such misery.

The *Oedipus complex* and *castration anxiety* climax early psychosexual development for boys, the girls experiencing a variation called the *Electra complex*. The preschool boy is incapable of feeling generous about his attachment to his mother; he feels possessive and jealous. In the exuberance of the phallic stage he wants to be the only person in his mother's life. This passionate attachment makes him his father's rival, which in turn leads to a wish that the father would disappear. The desire to possess the mother and destroy the father is called the Oedipus complex.

The Oedipus complex precipitates a crisis because of the boy's terrifying fantasy that the rivalrous, retaliatory father will cut off his penis. Freud claimed that castration anxiety is inevitable, even with the most benevolent of fathers, since it is essentially of the child's own making. Remember that we are dealing with the 4- to 5-year-old who is still in the egocentric stage of assuming that others feel as he does. Thus the boy reasons that if he wants to destroy the father, the father must have similar wishes toward him. It is the projection of his own hostility which makes castration anxiety inevitable. The typical resolution of the oedipal conflict is for the boy to renounce his sexual feelings and his claim

on the mother and identify with the powerful father. In essence he says, "I am not your rival, I am like you."

The boy's relations with the mother during the Oedipus complex set the tone of his future heterosexual strivings. If the relationship is positive, he will unconsciously seek to replicate it at the adult level; if the relationship is mixed with anxiety and/or anger, other kinds of relationships will prove attractive. Fear of physical injury, operations, or vigorous contact sports as well as a negative attitude toward same-sex competition may be a residual of castration anxiety. "I'm afraid to stick my neck out because someone will cut it off" is a thinly disguised expression of the preschooler's castration terror that assertiveness will lead to destruction by a powerful rival.

Freud regarded middle childhood as a period of diminished sexual activity caused by the repression that resolved the Oedipus complex along with an inherent decrease in the libidinal drive. Physiological maturation at puberty revives all the difficulties of psychosexual development in the first six years, which once again must be dealt with and mastered. However, Freud's contributions to understanding both the middle years and adolescence have been minor. More relevant to our subsequent discussion of homosexuality is the Freudian concept of normal and deviant sexuality in adulthood.

Adult sexuality remains a psychosexual development. Sexually, all the erotic elements of the first six years of life are revived as components of foreplay, except that oral, anal, and genital stimulation along with exhibition of the body serve the function of heightening the pleasure of the ultimate goal of mature sexuality, which is genital union. It may be that the idiosyncratic reactions of pleasure, indifference, and disgust in regard to specific aspects of foreplay are rooted in comparable experiences during the first three stages of psychosexual development. Sexual *perversions* result when elements of foreplay become goals in themselves; for example, the psychopathology called exhibitionism involves an irresistible desire to display one's genitals in public, while voyeurism involves Peeping Tom activities or the irresistible urge to view nude bodies. Both pathologies result from a failure to develop beyond the phallic period.

Mature sexuality is a psychological achievement as well. It too involves components of the early stages of psychological development: from the oral period comes the need for and ability to provide tender care, along with trust that the partner will be there in times of distress; from the anal period comes a willingness to negotiate the many areas of adult responsibility and decision making, such as how money will be spent, work loads apportioned, or discipline enforced; from the phallic period comes pride in those achievements that make the partner proud, whether it be a bowling trophy or a PhD; from the oedipal period comes confidence that one is as good as the next person. However, maturity entails a mutuality, a givingness, and an appreciation of the partner's point of view which counteracts the basic egocentricism (using the term in the Freudian sense) of the early psychosexual stages.

And, just as is true of the sexual act, the psychological relationship is immature if any one of the initial psychosexual stages becomes a goal in itself—a woman who is primarily seeking someone to protect her from feeling helpless and to pamper and baby her, a man whose primary purpose is to impose his will and crush the autonomy of his partner, or an adult who only wants an audience to admire him or her for real or imagined achievements. Note that the psychosexual theory maintains that sexual maturity is only incidentally related to the performance of the sexual act. A man who has intercourse five times a week just to prove his prowess or three times a week because he read that this is the average for a person his age, is fixated or, quite literally, childlike in his behavior. Maturity is a matter of the psychological qualities one brings to the sexual experience itself and to the intimacy it entails.

PSYCHOPATHOLOGY The title of one of Freud's books, *The Psychopathology of Everyday Life*, (1971), succinctly states his thesis that normality imperceptibly blends into psychopathology. The difference between the two is quantitative rather than qualitative.

In structural terms, psychopathology is a matter of a significant imbalance between id, ego, and superego. If the id is excessively strong, either because of innate endowment or a weak ego and superego, the result is impulsive aggressive or sexual behavior. If the superego is excessively strong, the result is overly inhibited behavior in which the child is tortured by guilt feelings for the slightest transgression, real or imagined.

Psychosexual theory contains a rich source of clues as to both the nature and form of psychopathology. While fixations are normal, as we have seen, excessive fixations lay the groundwork for psychological disturbances, either because they hamper further development or because they increase the possibility that, having progressed, the child will return to the fixated, less mature stage. This latter process is called *regression*. The greater the fixation, the more vulnerable the child to regression. Excessive fixations can result either from inadequate libidinal gratification, such as inadequate love during the oral period, or excessive gratification, such as an oversolicitous, overprotective mother during the oedipal phase. The psychosexual stage of fixation determines both the severity and the kind of psychopathology. In general, the earlier the fixation, the more severe the psychopathology, so that a child who is either fixated at or regresses to the oral stage is more disturbed than one who is fixated at or regresses to the anal stage. In addition, each stage is apt to produce a particular kind of disturbance: the Oedipus complex is associated with hysterical and phobic disturbances, the anal stage with obsessive-compulsive disorders, and the oral stage with psychosis. (These classifications will be discussed in chapter 3.) Thus, for example, the bizarre ideation of the schizophrenic, which is determined more by idiosyncratic needs, longings, and fears than by a desire to communicate intelligibly, marks a return to the primary process thinking of the id-dominated oral stage.

As a developmental theory of psychopathology, the psychodynamic model has no peer. Yet it is also mentalistic, inferential, exceedingly complex, peppered with contingencies, and lacking just those clear behavioral referents and accessibility to tightly controlled research which behaviorists claim are essential to a scientific psychology. It is also true that neither the preferred method of investigation, namely psychoanalysis or psychoanalytically oriented psychotherapy, nor the data it produces are available to the general scientific community. But to conclude, as some have done, that psychodynamic concepts are unscientific because they cannot be tested by the usual controlled procedures is unjustified. Psychodynamic theory has generated more research than any other personality theory, and while older reviews claimed that the theory was totally lacking in scientific credibility, a more recent review found it to be faring surprisingly well (Fisher and Greenberg, 1977). It is also true that a number of psychodynamic concepts are either taken for granted by the general scientific community or regarded as tenable hypotheses: that adult psychopathologies have their roots in early childhood; that anxiety may be conceptualized as the anticipation of pain, and that defense mechanisms are uti-

lized to reduce it; that early conscience is the internalization of parental values by means of identification; that the infantile conscience is particularly absolutistic and punitive; that frustration is one of the conditions leading to aggression; that behavior may be determined by ideas and impulses which are unconscious; that there is a cognitive progression from irrational to rational thinking in the first eight years of life; that adequate maternal care during infancy is essential to subsequent healthy personality development; and even the once shocking idea that sexuality is present throughout childhood. Like all other models, the psychodynamic one has its advantages and limitations, but the charge that it lies beyond the pale of science or that it has been discredited by controlled studies is false.

The Cognitive Models

Strictly speaking, there is no cognitive model of childhood psychopathology. This is a puzzling state of affairs in light of the fact that since mid-century interest has shifted from motivation to cognition and Piaget has been the towering figure in developmental psychology. While a number of researchers have utilized Piagetian concepts to account for specific psychopathological phenomena, there has been no attempt to integrate all the relevant aspects of Piagetian theory with the psychopathological thinking and behavior of children. Consequently the current situation resembles a patchwork more than a comprehensive frame of reference. However, we shall be referring to Piaget with sufficient frequency to justify a review of some of his major concepts.

GENERAL REMARKS   Newborns know practically nothing about the world they have entered. In particular, they do not know that they are individuals and that they are entering a world composed of animate and inanimate objects. All they know is the stream of sensations they are experiencing. There is nothing about the sensation of hunger which informs infants, "I am coming from your stomach"; there is nothing in two vaguely seen dots which says, "I am your mother's eyes"; nor does a sound announce itself as coming from a rattle. The infant must learn to distinguish experiences comprising "me" from those comprising "not-me," and among the latter he or she must learn to distinguish things from people. Depending upon what aspect of cognitive development one studies, evidence of this kind of learning can be found until middle childhood.

Cognitive development is not a simple matter of accumulating increasingly large pieces of correct information until a comprehensive understanding of the self and the environment is achieved. On the contrary, initial understandings are erroneous and must be revised in light of experience, and these revisions, in turn, must be further revised, until an accurate grasp of reality is achieved. Since erroneous understandings contain the seeds of psychopathology, it is essential that the child remain open to growth so that, by constant testing, the validity of erroneous beliefs can be revised and corrected.

PIAGET'S STAGE THEORY In addition to the above picture of cognitive development, Piaget makes the assumption that successive modifications in thinking occur in orderly, fixed stages. Each stage of cognitive development is qualitatively distinct, and no higher type of thinking can evolve until the child has gone through all the preceding stages. The timetable may differ from child to child, but the order can never vary. It is these stages and the significant cognitive advances within each which will concern us next. (One of the most succinct and clearest expositions of Piaget's theory is found in chapters 1 and 2 of Piaget, 1967.)

The *sensorimotor stage* lasts for approximately the first two years of life and is so called because the vehicle for intellectual growth is the sensory and motor apparatus. Incapable of symbolization, except toward the end of the period, infants and toddlers must explore and learn by acting directly upon the environment motorically and by watching and listening.

For our purposes, the significant development in this period is that of the *object concept,* or *object permanence.* For the first few months, infants give no evidence of missing an object they can no longer see or hold. Thus the world exists only when they are acting upon it or perceiving it. Out of sight not only means out of mind but out of existence as well. Only gradually, through a succession of cognitive steps, do they come to realize that objects exist regardless of their own actions or perceptions—objects exist "out there" as part of the environment, while actions exist "in here" as part of the self. Instead of being the center or even the creator of the universe, toddlers grasp the fact that they are only one of the many furnishings of the world. A giant step has been taken toward separating me from not-me.

The *preoperational stage* lasts from approximately 2 to 7 years of age and marks the appearance of symbolic functions. The most obvious but by no means the exclusive manifestation of symbolization is language, which develops rapidly in this period. However, the preschooler tends literally to believe what he or she sees. Consequently, something that looks different is different. Piaget's well-known documentation of this thesis dazzled the psychological world. If, before their very eyes, water is poured from a wide squat glass into a tall narrow glass or a ball of clay is rolled out into an elongated snake, children will claim that there is now more water or more clay. It looks like more, so it must be more. Piaget calls such literal thinking *intuitive,* to contrast it with thinking based on reason.

The *concrete-operational stage* extends from approximately 7 to 11 years of age. The triumph of middle childhood is that the children are capable of understanding the world in terms of reason rather than in terms of naive perception. They grasp the notion that an object remains the same despite perceptual variations. Piaget's term for this achievement is *conservation,* denoting that objects conserve or maintain their identity in the face of manifold changes in appearance. Although realistic, the child's thinking is still tied to concrete reality, however, and bound to the here and now.

The *formal-operational stage* begins around the twelfth year and lasts into adulthood. It is in this period that general ideas and abstract constructions flourish. The ability to draw conclusions from hypotheses rather than relying totally on actual observation is called *hypothetic-deductive thinking.* Adolescents can go wherever their thoughts lead them. They discuss, they write, they ruminate. They create a philosophy of life and explain the universe. They are also capable of being truly self-critical for the first time because they can reflect on and scrutinize their own ideas.

We have emphasized Piaget's cognitive theory because it best suits our purposes. However, it is not the only theory we shall use, e.g., when discussing mental retardation, we shall refer to an information-processing model (see chapter 11).

The Developmental Model

Any theory of human behavior can contain a developmental component and can attempt to account for both normal and psychopathological development. In this sense there is

no developmental model that is somehow different from other models of abnormal behavior. It is just a historical fact that few theories have accepted the developmental challenge and fewer still have generated a body of empirical findings which would take them out of the category of the merely speculative. The three models we have discussed in detail are the exceptions. The medical model is best exemplified by the number of eminent child psychiatrists who have distinguished themselves as diagnosticians, investigators, and textbook writers, Leo Kanner and his classic *Child Psychiatry* (1977) being among the most notable. Development lies at the heart of the psychodynamic model and is indispensable. Its adherents were the first to grasp the meaning of a developmental psychopathology, and it has evolved into the most comprehensive theory extant. For behaviorists, concerned as they are with general laws applicable to all living organisms at any age, childhood psychopathology is one of many areas of interest rather than one occupying a special status; thus behaviorists are relative latecomers, although vigorous ones. They bring with them a clear-eyed view of psychology as a science and a pragmatic orientation to clinical practice, which serve to correct the tendency toward obscurity and the infatuation with complexity that can become roadblocks to progress.

In sum, there is no satisfactory comprehensive theory of psychopathological development, but there are three models that have significantly advanced our understanding. In addition, there is a body of nontheoretically aligned research which furnishes valuable data concerning childhood disturbances. In light of the current situation we have adopted a loose conceptualization—psychopathology as normal development gone awry—whose very openness allows us to select from any model and from any body of data what we need in order to understand the psychopathology at hand. The question of how well our conceptualization has fared will be raised in each of our discussions.

Other Models

There are sundry models of psychopathology which we will do little more than catalog, since they have not addressed themselves extensively to child psychopathology or have not generated sufficient empirical evidence to be considered anything more than speculative. (For a more detailed presentation see Bootzin and Acocella, 1988.) At times the models overlap one another as well as the three we have already presented.

The *deviance model* takes many forms, but they all share the definition of abnormal as a deviation from the norm. In its most precise form, the norm is a *statistical* one epitomized by the bell-shaped curve that results from measuring a particular trait, such as intelligence. Deviance itself is defined in terms of scores that lie a certain number of standard deviations above and below the mean. However, the statistical model lacks criteria for differentiating between desirable and undesirable behavior and so considers the creative genius as abnormal as the severe retardate. The model also implies that as infrequent behaviors such as learning disabilities and violent crimes become more frequent, they become normal, and it makes conformity the primary goal of treatment. Both ideas are obviously unacceptable. Next, there are *cultural* norms, which are approved standards of behavior a given society establishes for its members. Particular deviations from these norms are considered psychopathological. Certain of these deviations are culture-specific, while others, such as delusions, hallucinations, phobias, and sexual deviations, seem to be universal. The cultural model belongs in the superordinate context and, as we have stated, will not be our concern.

However, the final category, deviations from *developmental* norms, will play a central role in our discussions.

The *humanistic model* is based on an image of humanity as innately good, capable of growth, and striving for self-actualization. It emphasizes the uniqueness of each individual, the potential for fulfilling capabilities, freedom of choice, and responsibility for one's own destiny. It follows that psychopathology is the inability to accept or express one's true nature, to take responsibility for one's actions, and to make self-generated choices. Because the model has been more influential in the area of child psychotherapy than child psychopathology, we shall postpone further discussion of it until we take up Carl Rogers's nondirective therapy (see chapter 16).

SOME COMMENTS ABOUT METHODOLOGY

In discussing research, Meehl (1978) referred to the five "noble traditions" in clinical psychology that he speculates will be around long after current fads have faded: descriptive clinical psychiatry; psychometric assessment; behavior genetics; behavior modification (with its remarkable technical power); and psychoanalytic theory (with its unsurpassed level of interest). Two relative newcomers that seem to merit addition to this list are the cognitive theories of Piaget and information processing, whose impact on developmental psychopathology is just beginning to be felt. We shall have many encounters with all of these noble traditions, for they make up the rich and varied foundation on which clinical psychology rests.

Meehl's point concerning traditions is equally applicable to methodologies. The three giants of psychology—Pavlov, Freud, and Piaget—utilized quite different research methodologies. Thus the progress of psychology as a science has taken place by means of diverse investigatory strategies. Note that we said "as a science." Science is defined as the search for knowledge. Different sciences have found different methodologies to be most fruitful in this quest: astronomy, the oldest science, advanced through observation of naturally occurring events, while physics and chemistry advanced through highly controlled laboratory experiments. Psychology, in contrast, has not settled on a method of choice. What is true of psychology in general is doubly true of developmental psychopathology, which owes as much to the Darwinian tradition of *natural observation* as it does to the *laboratory experiment*. The research of choice is the research which is clearly conceived and elegantly executed, regardless of the methodology.

Instead of looking at methodology in the abstract, we shall approach it through research that has actually advanced our understanding of childhood psychopathology. (For a more formal discussion, see Achenbach, 1978.) We shall use illustrations taken from studies that we shall discuss in detail in subsequent chapters. These illustrations are set apart from the main text. The first words are in bold type and the format is a single, wide column.

The Naturalistic Tradition

THE CLINICAL EYE　In developmental psychopathology, the naturalistic tradition in pure culture is carried on by individuals with a clinical eye, which is at the opposite extreme from the innocent eye. "The Emperor's New Clothes" notwithstanding, inexperienced individuals quite literally see very little of the behavior occurring around them. As Piaget has taught us, current stimuli, in order to register, must be assimilated into organized bodies of meaningful concepts, which in turn have grown out of meaningful observations

in the past. Thus the clinical eye requires, first, sensitive and disciplined observation with the intent of maximizing understanding. The challenge may well last a lifetime. But observation is not enough: the clinical eye must nourish a conceptualizing mind. A vast quantity of accumulated clinical wisdom goes no further than the application of past experience to present problems. To make the leap from the applied to the conceptual is rare among clinicians, but it marks the transition from personal experience to embryonic scientific knowledge.

Naturalistic observation aims at describing and understanding naturally occurring behavior. It maximizes the chances of obtaining ecologically valid ("true to life") data and of capturing the multiplicity of variables which may be responsible for producing such behavior. By selecting comparative and contrasting populations and settings, the researcher takes a step toward disentangling relevant from irrelevant and confounding variables. However, there are practical limits to the extent to which such disentangling can be done. Limitations in the degree of control over the data should not be equated with a lessening of investigatory rigor, however. There is no reason to claim, for example, that Darwin and Piaget were less rigorous than Pavlov just because they chose to examine naturally occurring behavior rather than to work in a laboratory. Or in the research we are about to cite it would be unthinkable to view the investigators as lacking in rigor (see Shakow, 1953).

Our two examples of the use of the clinical eye represent two successive levels of understanding. Kanner's delineation of autism (chapter 4) is a model of *descriptive classification,* in which the entity is clearly and accurately described in its own right while also being differentiated from other disturbances that resemble and therefore could be mistaken for it. Redl (chapter 9), through his keen observation of a small group of impulsive, acting-out boys, was able to analyze their behavior according to a number of separate psychological functions, such as memory, anticipation, and social perspective-taking, and to discover how each function deviated from normal.

OBJECTIVE PROCEDURES   The clinical eye has undoubtedly made major contributions to our science.   But like all research procedures, it has its disadvantages.   What if one observer fails to verify what another has reported? What if two observers disagree as to what has occurred? Behavior such as guilt or anxiety is not objectively "out there" like a fossil or a plant.   To correct for the possible error involved in individual observation, objective procedures have been devised.   Such procedures have two advantages: their reliability can be tested, and they can be used by all members of the scientific community.   In certain instances, naturally occurring behavior still comprises the basic data; for example, observers can be trained reliably to record the number of friendly overtures made to normally achieving and learning disabled fourth-graders during recess.   In other instances, special instruments may be used that measure naturally occurring behavior indirectly: standardized interviews, behavioral checklists, and personality tests are examples.   These instruments must be shown to be reliable and valid, so that there is evidence that they do, indeed, measure the behavior they purport to evaluate.

We shall encounter studies that use objective procedures both for descriptive purposes and for hypothesis testing.   Rutter is a master at testing hypotheses by means of objective measures of various naturally occurring events.   In chapter 9 we shall follow his line of reasoning as he attempts to tease out the relation between schooling on the one hand and conduct disorders on the other.

Olweus, in his research on bullies, used procedures ranging from teachers' reports to projective techniques to eliminate hypotheses concerning the contribution of various superordinate, interpersonal, and intrapersonal variables before concluding that the aggression in these boys most likely resulted from an innate predisposition (see chapter 9).

The Laboratory Tradition

While it is possible to introduce objective procedures and control of variables into naturalistic research, it takes considerable ingenuity (and often good luck) to do so (see Wenar, 1976).   Both objectivity and control are built into laboratory studies.   The instruments are objective and available to the scientific community, while the actual conduct of the research is explicitly described so others may replicate it.   The investigators' control of the situation allows them systematically to manipulate the variable or variables being studied, while holding all others constant. The result is a powerful tool for disentangling crucial from confounding and tangential variables as well as for revealing processes responsible for the psychopathological behavior being investigated.

Of the many admirable examples of controlled studies we shall encounter, we shall select only three.   A series of interrelated investigations provided evidence that mental retardation is not synonymous with a slow rate of learning but may be, in part, due to a failure to generate appropriate hypotheses for learning and remembering or—and this is the most intriguing puzzle—a failure to utilize potentially efficient strategies even when they are available (see chapter 11).   Controlled studies of autism are separating mental retardation as a confounding variable and isolating other variables that seem specific to the psychopathology: difficulty with processing patterned information and a deficiency in imitation being two of the most important (see chapter 4). Finally, Douglas's elegant programmatic research is exploring hyperactivity as the product of a defect in sustaining attention. Douglas has also isolated a variable of impulsivity, which undermines the hyperactive child's ability to stop, look, listen—and think (see chapter 7).

Along with its many assets, the laboratory study has a potential disadvantage which is the mirror image of that of the naturalistic study—the maximizing of control might result in artificial data. Instead of being a paradigm of reality, the findings may have little ecological validity, being applicable only to the highly rarefied setting of the laboratory (see Bronfenbrenner, 1977).

In general, naturalistic studies rate high on ecological validity and, in certain instances, on objectivity of procedures, but controlling variables is exceedingly difficult. Laboratory studies rate high on objectivity and control but are marred by the question of ecological validity. In actuality, the subjective, uncontrolled naturalistic study has taught us as much about childhood psychopathology as the highly controlled, objective laboratory study. While particular psychologists may stoutly defend one methodology as being scientific, science itself is capricious. So far at least, it has no favorites.

A RETURN TO OUR MODEL

It will be interesting to view the medical, behavioral, and psychodynamic models of psychopathological development in terms of the variables of our own developmental model. In doing so, we will have to oversimplify them somewhat for the sake of emphasizing their distinctive features, since each is more broadly based than we shall allow.

The medical model is concerned primarily with the interaction between the organic and the intrapersonal contexts. The genetic, biochemical, and neurophysiological components all aim at relating organic variables to specific intrapersonal abnormalities, such as schizophrenia and hyperactivity. When interpersonal variables enter, for example, as stressors aggravating the basic physiological vulnerability, typically they are not explored in depth. The conservative behaviorists hew closely to the interpersonal context, allowing only for observable responses to observable stimuli. The more venturesome behaviorists and social-learning theorists, however, are exploring the intrapersonal context, admitting both "private events" and variables connected with the self, such as self-efficacy, under the strict condition that they be objectively defined and enhance prediction and control. The psychodynamic advocates are most at home in the intrapersonal realm and the limited interpersonal context of the nuclear family. The drama of id–ego–superego is acted out on the intrapersonal stage, while psychosexual development is closely tied to the transactions between parents and child. Although some notable efforts have been made to broaden the interpersonal scope and to introduce the superordinate context of societal values, they have not become part of the mainstream of psychodynamic thought.

If each of these models is complex, our own model, which embraces all three, might seem to raise complexity to the point of unworkability. Indeed, the image of multiple variables in diverse interactions which change over time boggles the mind. But remember, this is only a model, an ideal that suggests what we should know to give a comprehensive accounting of psychopathological development. In reality, we know very little—a fragment here, a tag end there. Far from being overwhelmed by the complexity of the field of childhood psychopathology, we will more frequently be impressed by how much more there is to learn. The field has suffered from neglect in the past and is just now coming into its own. With the aid of our comprehensive model, we will be able to see which details of the total picture have been filled, thereby putting the present stage of knowledge into proper perspective. Knowing the important variables will also serve to organize our thinking in regard to a given psychopathology, the model serving as a topical guide to areas that might be explored as the clinician attempts to answer the two simplest but most baffling questions: Is this child disturbed? And, if so, how disturbed is he or she?

Having outlined our general developmental model, we are now ready to describe the normal development of the intra- and interpersonal variables that will have a bearing on our subsequent discussions of the various childhood psychopathologies. Then, in chapter 3, we shall be able to build a bridge to the psychopathologies themselves and learn which ones tend to persist and which ones tend to disappear with time.

2

Normal Development

We are now in something of a quandary. If we are to understand childhood psychopathology as normal development gone awry, obviously we must first chart normal development. But having decided not to follow any one of the current models in favor of a looser, more inclusive framework, we still need a conceptual guide for selecting variables to discuss. Fortunately, it is still possible to draw up a list of variables crucial to a child's well-being so that, if anything went radically wrong with any one of them, we would be willing to regard the child as disturbed.

First there is a group of variables binding the child to the human environment. Prominent in this group is the bond of love that develops between infant and mother in the first year of life, which we shall call *attachment*. Throughout childhood and throughout life the ability to feel deeply about and become attached to another individual lies at the core of the human experience. Attachments may become erotic, resulting in *sexual* relationships, or at a more moderate and diffuse level, the human bond may be expressed in friendships and companionableness, which we shall call *social feelings*. If something goes radically awry with any of these bonds—if, for example, the loving overtures of a parent are met with rage or profound indifference, if sexual intimacy is a source of terror rather than pleasure, if the child is socially isolated and friendless—we would rightfully be concerned.

Another basic variable involves *initiative* or self-reliant expansiveness. The bright-eyed infant scanning the environment for new and interesting sights epitomizes this urge to explore and to master. In many of their ventures children are free to follow their own interests; but increasingly with age they are required to stay with a task whether or not they want to. We shall call this combination of initiative and necessity *work*, the special setting for work during childhood being the classroom. If, instead of having initiative and the capacity for work, the child is apathetic or distracted or fearful of any kind of venturing out, or if there is a persistent, self-defeating rebelliousness at being told what to do no matter how benign and reasonable, again we have cause to be concerned about the child.

Perhaps the most obvious variable for us to examine is *self-control,* the control of *aggression* looming particularly large in the public mind. Socializing children often involves curbing their preferred behaviors; with time, children take over this monitoring, controlling function themselves, eventually adding another mechanism specifically concerned with judging the moral content of behavior, the *conscience.* Self-control also involves the generation of *anxiety*, which serves as one of the principle deterrents to performing socially disapproved actions. Having "everything under control" is a sign of healthy growth, while both excessive and deficient control are deviations; the child who is plagued by anxiety and guilt as well as the violently destructive child concern parent and clinician alike.

Finally, it is essential for the child to understand the physical and social environment as well as him- or herself, a variable we shall call *cognition.* Reality can be distorted by magical ideas in the first few years of life because of cognitive immaturity. Therefore it is essential that these distortions be replaced by realistic understanding; the persistence of

bizarre, magical ideas, such as a 10-year-old believing he can hear through his "belly button" and can control television pictures by merely thinking about them, is generally recognized as a sign of disturbed development.

In sum, the ten variables we have selected in our developmental approach to childhood psychopathology are: attachment, initiative, self-control, conscience, cognition, anxiety, sex, aggression, social relations, and work.

ATTACHMENT

The bond of love between parents and child is one of the pivotal variables determining the course of development throughout childhood. We shall refer to it in many of our discussions of psychopathology—the failure of the bond to develop in infancy, the rupture of the bond by death or divorce, the contamination of the bond with excessive anger or anxiety, the atrophy of the bond through neglect. It is essential, therefore, to understand how this bond is established in infancy and how it develops throughout childhood. While labeled differently in various theories, we shall call the bond *attachment.* (For a discussion of various conceptualizations, see Ainsworth, 1969.)

The Formation of Attachment

Two reminders are in order before we begin our descriptive account. First, neonates have practically no knowledge of the world of people or the world of things; they even lack knowledge of themselves as a separate entity. They do not know who their mother is or how she differs from a rattle or a stomachache. Their experience consists of various sensations, out of which they must grasp the fundamental distinction between people, things, and self. How they go about doing this is discussed in the section on cognitive development.

The second point is that human beings have the longest period of helpless infancy of any species. In order to survive they must be cared for by more mature human beings for many years. Thus attachment takes place in the caretaking situation; the kind of care infants receive determines, to a significant degree, the kind of attachment they form. While most of our information comes from the infant's attachment to the mother, psychologists have begun to recognize and investigate the importance of father–infant attachment as well. (For a summary of research on mother–infant attachment, see Rosenblith and Sims-Knight, 1985.)

The development of attachment to the mother or primary caretaker (for convenience, the two terms will be used synonymously) follows a reasonably predictable course. Neonates are no more or less interested in the caretaker than in any other object that comes their way. However, by two weeks of age they prefer the human voice over other sounds and, by four weeks, prefer the mother's voice over other human voices. In the second month, eye contact is established. Between the third and fourth months, these precursors of attachment reach a cognitive and emotional climax: the pattern of stimuli comprising the human face is perceived with sufficient cohesiveness and detail to be distinguished from other patterns of stimuli and, equally important, is a source of special delight. The percept "people" and the affect "pleasure" are fused into what is called the *social smile*. The social smile is indiscriminate and hedonistic: infants light up when anyone hits upon that combination of grimacing and vocalizing and bouncing and tickling which delights them. On their part, adults will go through all kinds of absurd antics to elicit such a smile. The simple fact that delighting the infant is highly rewarding to the adult is

one of the strongest guarantees that an attachment will be formed.

Between the sixth and ninth month, indiscriminate responsiveness gives way to selectivity as infants show a strong preference for the mother and other special caretakers. This inner circle of caretakers can elicit greater delight than anyone else and can most readily comfort the infant in times of distress. In addition, two negative affects come to the fore. The first is *separation anxiety* when the mother leaves. Despite the label, the distress is not akin to fear, as are most anxieties, but is better described as anguish—that painful blend of protest and despair which wells up when a crucial source of pleasure disappears and one is helpless to bring it back. Thus separation anguish is more closely related to depression than to terror. *Stranger anxiety*, or the fear of unfamiliar persons, is not as prevalent as it was once believed to be. However, the indiscriminate pleasure that marked the era of the social smile is replaced with a more cautious, wary response to unfamiliar adults.

Separation anxiety has implications for many aspects of normal and deviant development. First, intense anxiety is part of normal development. Indeed, there are those who claim that the absence of such anxiety is suggestive of deviant development; for example, some children reared in impersonal institutions will subsequently respond to anyone who shows them affection (like the infant during the stage of the indiscriminate social smile) while failing to form an enduring relationship and being unaffected by loss (see chapter 4). We also learn that, from the beginning, intense affection and intense anguish over loss go hand in hand. Dare I love deeply and risk abandonment? is a question that comes up throughout life and that each individual must answer in his or her own way. Certain delinquents are difficult to help because they fear that if they let themselves become emotionally attached to their therapist, the therapist will desert them as other adults have done in the past.

Hostility is also a consequence of attachment, although it has received less attention than anxiety. In reunions after separations, such as hospitalization, it is not unusual for infants and toddlers first to ignore their parents and then become unusually angry and touchy for the next few days or even weeks. Infants and toddlers are cognitively incapable of grasping the reality of the situation, such as the fact that the separation was for good reason and unavoidable; all they can understand is that they needed the mother and she was not there. In their eyes she becomes a "bad" mother and the target for anger (see Bowlby, 1973).

Thus we see that attachment, even in its normal manifestations, is never purely positive; it is inevitably a mixture of love and anguish and fear and anger. It is when the negative components begin to dominate that the chances for deviant development are increased.

Caretaking

A few comments concerning *caretaking* are relevant to the discussions to come. The traditional image has been that of the mother caring for a totally helpless, passive infant, who is capable only of responding to environmental inputs. However, there is now convincing evidence that infants are never merely passive recipients. From the beginning they are actively taking in and trying to cope with their environment (see Appleton, Clifton, and Goldberg, 1975). They also have their special temperament—their individualized tempo and activity level, their characteristic mood and adaptability, their special set of vulnerabilities and resiliencies, their preferences and dislikes. Psychologists have verified what mothers have known for many

years—namely, that certain infants are temperamentally easy to care for while others are difficult, regardless of the kind of care they receive. Thus caretaking is now viewed as an interaction between mother and infant in which each has to accommodate to the other. If all goes well, the result is a mutual enhancement of development in which not only the infant grows but also the mother in terms of her caretaking skills, feelings of competence, and sources of gratification. This interdependence of mother and infant has sometimes been called *symbiosis;* when we discuss symbiotic psychosis, we shall see the devastating consequences to certain toddlers when it fails to exert its growth-promoting influence (chapter 6.)

Caretaking itself is conceptualized as a combination of *comforting* and *stimulation.* Comforting and relieving the infant's distress has been the traditional view of mothering. More recently, attention has turned to the mother as stimulator. The very fact that she is human means she is a source of fascinating and delightful visual and auditory stimuli, since infants seem to be preprogrammed to respond most intensely to stimuli characteristic of the human. The mother is also a mediator of stimulation, bringing the infant in contact with a variety of interesting sights and sounds such as rattles and rings and mobiles. Hers is a dual role of comforter and stimulator, so her sensitivity to the infant's needs and the promptness and appropriateness with which she responds to them are more important than the sheer amount of time she spends with the infant. And through her comforting and stimulation, the mother provides both the emotional security and the varied environmental input necessary to normal development.

Attachment has two important consequences. If the mother is sensitive in her caretaking, that is, if she is alert to the infant's needs and reacts quickly and appropriately, the infant will develop a *secure* attachment. Securely attached infants are responsive to the mothers' stimulation and comfort and can explore the environment confidently. If the mother is intrusive or distant and angry, infants will be insecurely attached. In the first instance they will be *resistant* or ambivalent toward the mother, demanding attention and affection but petulant when they receive it. In the second instance infants will be *avoidant*, ignoring the mother in a kind of psychological armed truce.

When caretaking is consistently and sensitively administered, therefore, the infant develops a *loving, trusting* relationship. Those who accept the critical-period hypothesis would say that this relationship sets the infants to view future closeness in terms of love and trust; they can subsequently reveal intimate thoughts and feelings without fear of betrayal, and they know that their cry for help will be answered, however this cry may be expressed. Well-cared-for infants are also apt to develop a positive self-image and confidence in their ability to cope successfully with problems as they arise. There is evidence, for example, that the securely attached infant becomes the effective problem solver as a toddler and the flexible, resourceful, and curious preschooler who is enthusiastically involved with school tasks and peers (Bretherton, 1985).

Second, attachment is a prerequisite for successful *socialization*. Infants and toddlers have no natural desire to be neat and clean or to respect property; quite to the contrary, they want to explore and mess and possess at will. Why, then, should they ever give up the pleasure of immediate gratification? Because the love of the parents is at stake. The behavior that the parents regard as good is rewarded with love; the behavior that they regard as bad is punished by the withdrawal of love. In normal development, toddlers and preschoolers for the most part acquiesce,

because the love they receive compensates for the autonomy they lose. But already we can sense the possibilities for abuse of parental love. Suppose parental demands are excessive and entail total subjugation, as may have happened during childhood in someone who became anorectic (see chapter 6)? Or suppose demands are made with inadequate compensations of love, as may have happened during the childhood of someone who became a juvenile delinquent (see chapter 9)? We would rightly suspect that chances of deviant development would be increased.

Attachment and the Older Child

With regard to attachment, the developmental picture grows dim in middle childhood. Gesell's previously summarized account of the relationship of the 6- to 9-year-old child to the parents is one of the most complete descriptions (see chapter 1). In adolescence, however, the issue of attachment comes again to the fore. Adolescence is a time of major revolutions: a biological revolution brought about by sexual maturation, an interpersonal revolution involving a shift away from the family and toward the peer group, an identity revolution involving a search for a fulfilling adult role. While we now know that the picture of adolescence as necessarily a time of "storm and stress" is exaggerated and that there are significant continuities between the generations alongside the more highly publicized alienation and rebelliousness of youth, the cultural expectation of independence still marks the period as a time of significant change in the relation between parent and child. Attachment is caught up in this change. Parental expressions of affection become an embarrassment, offers of comfort and help are apt to be met with the standard outcry, "I'm not a baby any more!" (To a clinician, the vigorousness of the protest suggests that the underlying longing for love and comfort and help might still be a strong but unacceptable one.) If the adolescent is having problems with growing up and becoming independent, however, parents are also having problems with growing older and no longer being needed. A change in status and function is occurring in all parties involved in the interaction, as the interpersonal context of our developmental model would indicate.

While adolescence can go relatively smoothly, it still stands as a time of increased vulnerability for those whose relations with their parents make the challenge of independence an exceptionally threatening one. In examining schizophrenia, for example, we shall be dealing with an instance in which the stresses cannot be managed and contribute to the production of a severe psychological breakdown (chapter 10).

Independence from parents is not the ultimate or necessary fate of attachment. While adulthood is not our concern, we should note that it often brings with it a rapprochement between parent and child if a rift had taken place in adolescence. The ability to express love for parents without embarrassment or guilt over being close marks the return of an old theme in a mature variation. By the same token, the adult who must continue to protest vigorously against any show of parental affection or any sign of closeness gives the impression of being inappropriately adolescent.

INITIATIVE

If attachment is central in the first year of life, initiative is central in the second, toddlers literally and figuratively standing on their own two feet and turning their backs on their mothers. Intoxication with a newfound sense of power propels them into a stage of willfulness and negativism. The selfsame 2-year-

old who, a few months ago, was terrified at the mother's departure, now counters her every request with an imperious "No!" For her part, the mother finds that she must increasingly restrict her child, who is into everything and all over the place. Thus begins the conflict between freedom to do what one wants and conformity to the requirements of society, a conflict that will last a lifetime. We will take a closer look at the toddler's self-reliant venturing forth, which we call *initiative*, tracing its roots in infancy and commenting further on some of its manifestations during the "terrible twos."

Origins and Nature

Initiative in the toddler period has a number of roots in infancy, primary ones being curiosity and exploration. The old image of the infant's life as totally dominated by physiological needs such as hunger, thirst, and sleep is erroneous. (The landmark article is White, 1959.) As soon as there are periods of alert wakefulness, neonates begin exploring their environment. Their searching eyes and receptive ears lead the way, followed increasingly by motoric exploration as they outgrow their body's initial clumsiness. In the first month of life exploratory behaviors are remarkably mature, characterized by orientation, concentration, perseverance, gratification with success, or annoyance at failure. Infants are as hungry for stimulation as they are for food, their endless fascination undergirding the giant steps taken in comprehending their environment in the first year (Appleton, Clifton, and Goldberg, 1975).

But infants not only want to take in the environment; they want actively to control it as well. When eight-week-old infants who were placed in a specially designed crib discovered they could make a mobile move by turning their head, they repeatedly did so with great glee (Watson and Ramey, 1972).

Around 20 weeks of age infants begin to take the initiative in establishing, sustaining, and renewing contact and interaction with the mother, lifting their arms in greeting her, clinging to her, following her when they are able to crawl. By the end of the first year they may be so adept and insistent in their demands for attention that some mothers become resentful (Sander, 1964). Other evidence of an early need to control is the many "battles" between mother and infant: 8-month-olds who have had the experience of holding the bottle, thereby taking feeding "into their own hands," may strongly resist attempts to make them drink from a cup (Spock, 1963). The "battle of the bottle" is subsequently replaced by the "battle of the spoon," as 1-year-olds insist on feeding themselves, although their ineptness results in bringing the oatmeal to their nose or ear or hair as often as to their mouth. The mother who cannot stand the ensuing mess and tries to take the spoon away by sheer force might be met with a tenacious determination to hold onto it and a rage reaction when the infant is overpowered. Just over the horizon—during the toddler period—lies the "battle of the potty."

There is an important cognitive component to this desire to control the environment. Neonates are too immature cognitively to grasp the relation between their actions and environmental events. By the middle of the first year the connection has been established, but—and this is the important point—it is an unrealistic, magical one. After discovering that their vigorous, jerky movements can make a mobile on their crib dance, they proceed to repeat these movements and look at the television set or the clock or other familiar objects, expecting them to dance also. Again, infants whose attentive mothers come when they cry initially believe that their cry actually produces the mother's presence. But how could it be otherwise? How could infants grasp the reality of the sequence—that the mother was in another room, that she heard the cry, that she could decide to ignore it or come to the infant, and that she chose the latter? While unable to grasp reality, infants can make sense of their immediate experience, which is, "I make jerky movements, objects dance; I cry, mother appears; *ergo* my actions alone cause environmental events to happen." In short, infants have an *omnipotent* concept of causality. While such thinking would be a sign of severe psychopathology in adolescence, it is not only developmentally appropriate but represents a significant advance over the prior period when the notion of causality itself was not grasped (see Piaget, 1967).

The desire to venture out in infancy continues into the toddler period, locomotion opening up a whole new world for the toddler to explore and master. It is important to underscore the spontaneous, *intrinsically rewarding* nature of this exploration, in contrast to the socializing parents' directives and prohibitions, many of which go against the grain. Also, as toddlers explore they continue to develop the concept of the *self-as-agent*, and as their explorations are successful and pleasurable, they develop *self-confidence* and a healthy self-pride. This self-reliant venturing out, which we call initiative, has variously been labeled autonomy, mastery, competence, and independence by others. While the definitions may vary, all the terms share an emphasis on the self-as-agent and on expansiveness.

We now have a better appreciation of why anything that impedes the toddler's self-reliant exploration is apt to be resented and resisted. Typically such resistance takes the form of negativism, which may be an active noncompliance (shouting "I won't" or throwing a tantrum) or a passive noncompliance (ignoring the parent or doing nothing). And typically, impediments take the form of the socializing adult's "No" and "Don't." Evidence indicates that the toddler will bridle no matter how sweetly reasonable the parent is (Wenar, 1982). Just as the self-centered infant knew only, "Mother is not here when I need her," the self-centered toddler knows only, "My parents are preventing me from doing what I want to do." The terrible twos are, by and large, of the toddler's own making. By the same token, exasperated parents can take comfort in the fact that, while nothing they do will prevent or shorten its reign, negativism is usually "outgrown" in a couple of years.

We have emphasized the toddler's physical venturing forth because it sets the stage for the conflict between compliance and defiance which will figure so prominently in our discussion of psychopathology. However, not all initiative is physical. Producing varied sounds seems to have an intrinsic appeal, and the toddler soon learns that certain sounds, made either fortuitously or in imitation of adult speech, have the magical property of eliciting responses of great delight from parents. "Baby's first word" typically becomes the occasion for rejoicing. The toddler also learns that words as well as gestures can be used to communicate, subsequently realizing that they are also more versatile and require less effort. In addition to their communicative value, words and language play an important role in self-control and cognition. Subsequently, when we turn to the psychopathologies, we shall learn that the absence or breakdown of communicative speech plays a crucial role in two of the most severe childhood disturbances—autism and schizophrenia (see chapters 4 and 10).

Developmental Course of Initiative

The toddler's fascination with objects continues throughout childhood. "What is it?" and "How does it work?"—questions first asked about ordinary household objects—are asked about objects in the wider physical environment and, eventually, in outer space. In the realm of tools, the toy hammer is replaced by the tool kit, the blunt scissors by the sewing machine; ahead lies the computer. The 10-word vocabulary of the 19-month-old increases to the 80,000-word vocabulary of the high school freshman. In the social realm, playing house with the preschoolers next door develops into the complex gangs and cliques of adolescence.

We could go on, but we are not as interested in areas of self-reliant expansion as in certain consequences of initiative for the self. First, discovering what one can do plays a central role in *self-definition*. The 3-year-old who announces excitedly, "I can jump" and the high school sophomore who says, "I was elected class treasurer," have defined themselves through their various ventures. As they succeed, they are accruing a sense of *self-worth* and pride. Such healthy self-love can be as important as a healthy love relation with another person. Finally, enterprising individuals are developing a sense of being in charge of their own destinies, which psychologists have studied under the heading of *locus of control*. Individuals who perceive events as contingent on their own behavior or some characteristic of themselves have an *internal* locus of control; individuals who believe that events are the result of factors other than themselves, such as luck or chance or fate, have an *external* locus of control. Thus initiative affects the individual's perception of personal responsibility for events. Such perceptions have been shown to be significantly correlated with academic achievement; for example, children who believe that education does not matter because they will never have a chance to make anything of themselves do poorly compared to children who believe they can use education to make a difference to their future (Phares, 1976).

Adolescence may be a period that presents

special problems in regard to initiative, as it does for attachment. The adolescent must negotiate the transition from dependent child to independent adult, a transition made difficult by conflicts at many levels. Parents, for their part, want their adolescent to take on responsibilities, earn money, date, and be popular, but they also want to retain their role as guides to proper conduct and as decision makers. And adolescents themselves are ambivalent about independence. Physically, sexually, and intellectually they are young adults, not children; they have the capacity to work and devote themselves to an ideal; they are socially sensitive and can form meaningful friendships. For the first time the adult world is within their grasp. Yet they also sense that they might lack the experience, judgment, and psychological maturity to use such assets appropriately. They cannot become adults overnight; finding a niche in a complex society and mastering the intricacies of vocational and sexual relations are often a matter of trial and error. Setbacks are apt to bruise their egos and remind them that, if they are no longer children, they are also not quite adults. When all the conflicts within and between family members boil over, the last of the normal battles of childhood is fought—the battle of the generations. The adolescent is viewed as wild, disrespectful, and amoral, the parents are seen as old-fashioned, self-centered, and lacking in understanding.

Like attachment, initiative is fundamental to normal development. A significant diminution of initiative is an ominous sign, while a lack of initiative, as evidenced in autism, indicates severe psychopathology. Curiosity, which lies at the heart of initiative from earliest infancy, requires the ability to focus attention on interesting stimuli or the task at hand. When there is a deficit in this ability to pay attention, healthy initiative is replaced by the scattered behavior of the hyperactive

child (chapter 7). We shall see how certain bleak institutional settings can crush initiative so that normal infants and mentally retarded children are no longer motivated to use their abilities and skills (chapters 11 and 13). A special kind of loss of initiative called learned helplessness may underlie the defeatist attitude that characterizes depression (chapter 5). Both the normal negativism of the terrible twos and the normal transitional problems of adolescence can become exaggerated to the point where they block further growth (chapter 6) or in the case of adolescence eventuate in drug use and abuse (chapter 10).

SELF-CONTROL

In a number of psychopathologies, self-control figures more prominently than any other single variable. In early childhood, control of bodily functions is a basic aspect of self-control. Toddlers may fail to learn to control their bladders and continue to wet their beds at night or, less frequently, their pants during the day. Eating may get out of control, leading to obesity at one extreme or self-starvation even to the point of death at the other (chapter 6). When self-control is excessive in middle childhood, the groundwork for neurosis is laid; when self-control is weak, acting-out behavior such as aggression and juvenile delinquency may result (chapters 7 and 8). Therefore, it is essential that we understand the development of self-control from infancy to adulthood and the factors that enable the child to achieve normal self-control. In the subsequent sections we shall examine that special kind of control exercised by the conscience, the role cognition and anxiety play in achieving self-control, and finally, the two most important behaviors the child must learn to control—sex and aggression.

Factors Involved in Self-Control

Descriptively, the situation could not be simpler. The exploring toddler reaches for a vase on the living room table. Her mother rushes in, says "No," and slaps her hand. She withdraws. She may reach again, and again be punished. The pattern is repeated many times. Eventually, however, as the toddler approaches the vase and begins reaching for it, she suddenly stops, shakes her head, and even slaps her own hand. Then she withdraws. She never again reaches for the forbidden vase. She has achieved self-control. However, teasing out the factors involved in this achievement and understanding how they work is far from simple (Wenar, 1971). Let us examine certain important ingredients.

As our example clearly suggests, there is *reward and punishment*. These may be physical: a toddler who puts his toy away at mother's request may get to lick the chocolate-pudding bowl, while another toddler who pokes a finger into the light socket may get slapped or spanked. Rewards and punishments may also be psychological. As we have just seen, attachment enables parents to bestow love for conformity to their directives; it also enables them to withdraw love when disobeyed, thus creating a situation akin to separation anguish in the child. Thus the child's concern about being love-worthy is a major force in the motivation to seek parental approval and avoid parental disapproval by complying with socializing directives.

In rewarding and punishing the child, parents convey more meaning than they intend, since they are also serving as a model of either controlled or uncontrolled behavior. Children are adept imitators. A parent can be taken aback on hearing a toddler, during a pretend telephone conversation, turn around and shout, "Be quiet! Can't you see I'm on the phone?" in an exact duplication of the parent's own words and tone of voice. Children imitate spontaneously; no reward and punishment is necessary, and at times the imitated behavior appears full-blown. In certain instances, *modeling* or *imitation* may serve to undermine socialization; a father who punishes aggression by losing his temper and beating the child is simultaneously serving as a model of uncontrolled behavior.

A host of *cognitive* variables are involved in self-control. At the simplest level, toddlers must be able to grasp cause-and-effect relations and remember what behavior leads to reward or punishment; only then will they be able to apply past experiences to the situation at hand. They must then be able to integrate fragmentary experiences into guiding principles of behavior, so that "I should not take that toy" will eventually become "I should not take anything that belongs to somebody else." Words play a pivotal role in this process of achieving higher levels of self-control. The simple "No" becomes, "Mustn't touch," and then, "That's Jimmy's truck, not yours," and finally, "You shouldn't take other people's things without asking them first." As the directives become increasingly complex, they guide behavior in an increasingly wide variety of situations. And as the cognitively developing child can both verbalize these directives and grasp their meaning, built-in controls become increasingly effective. Since "saying things to oneself" is one aspect of thinking, we can see why *thinking* is regarded as the ally of control: the very fact that the child must stop and think serves to check immediate action, while the content of the thought itself serves to guide behavior into socially acceptable channels. As thinking serves its *delaying* and *guiding* functions, control is enhanced.

However, thought is not the only aid to counteracting impulsivity; interpersonal *trust* is equally important. Socialization consists not only of prohibitions but also of delayed gratification. The child's capacity to wait is enhanced if the promised rewards are consistently forthcoming. If parents are unreliable or if the environment is disorganized and unpredictable, children are less likely to tolerate the tensions of delay and more apt to seize upon the pleasures of the moment. Finally, the availability of *substitute gratifications* helps the child master the frustration of being forbidden to pursue a desired goal. The sensitive parent who has prohibited a toddler from touching a treasured vase may then present the child with a favorite set of pots and pans to play with. As children grow older, they become increasingly capable of redirecting their own activities into acceptable substitutes. Note that some substitutes involve the relinquishing of the original goal, as with our toddler; others provide alternate, socially acceptable ways of achieving or partially achieving the goal; a boy who is forbidden to fight with a peer can defeat him in athletics, for example. One function of play and fantasy is to provide safe substitutes for achieving forbidden goals; the girl recently punished by her mother can spank her doll for being a "mean old mommy," while adults continue to fantasize victories and glories in situations too threatening to undertake in real life (Mischel, 1974). Our discussion of a group of impulse-ridden boys will illustrate what happens when many of these factors involved in self-control fail to develop adequately (chapter 9).

Parental Discipline

There are three dimensions to parental discipline. First is the specific technique used, or what the parent does. Next is the affect accompanying the technique, such as warmth, anger, or coldness. Finally, there is the degree of control the parent exerts, which can range from total neglect to total domination. Ideally, we should know the effects on children of all possible combinations of these three variables, but we do not. What we do know can be summarized as follows.

Some techniques have been conceptualized as *love-oriented* in that they involve either praise and reasoning (*induction*) or the threat of *love withdrawal*. Induction involves explanation together with appeals to pride, to a desire to grow up, and to a concern for others. It tends to produce children who are responsible, cooperative, concerned with their own role in events, introspective, and guilty. In the preschool period, induction often must be accompanied by some intense affect or forcefulness for it to be effective because the children are still too young to respond to sweet reasonableness alone. In love withdrawal, the parent conveys the implicit message, "If you do X, I temporarily will not love you." The results are quite different from induction. The children tend to comply immediately, but also to become anxious, conforming, and to have low self-esteem.

The *authoritarian* or power-oriented parent is demanding, controlling, and unreasoning. The implicit message is, "Do what I say because I say so." If parents discipline in a punitive, rejecting manner, their children tend to become aggressive, uncooperative, fearful of punishment, and prone to blame others. They are low on initiative, self-esteem, and competence with peers. Authoritarian parents do not have to be punitive, however; they can discipline out of concern and respect for the child. Unfortunately, this kind of stern but fair parent has not been studied.

The *permissive* parent can be either indulgent or neglectful. In the former instance the parent is undemanding, accepting, and child-centered and makes few attempts to control. The result is a selfish, dependent, irresponsible, aggressive, "spoiled" child. The neglectful parent is indifferent, uninvolved, or self-centered. Lax, unconcerned parenting is the breeding ground for antisocial aggression and juvenile delinquency. Self-centeredness on the parents' part is associated with self-centeredness in the children, along with impulsivity, moodiness, truancy, lack of long-term goals, and early drinking and smoking.

Authoritative parents set standards of mature behavior and expect the child to comply, but they are also highly involved, consistent, loving, communicative, willing to listen to the child, and respectful of the child's point of view. Their children tend to be self-reliant, self-controlled, secure, popular, and inquisitive. (For a comprehensive review of parental discipline, see Maccoby and Martin, 1983.)

The literature on parental discipline furnishes several leads as to which kinds are detrimental. Extremes of rejection, brutality, neglect, and permissiveness should be avoided. An inconsistent alternation between neglect and harsh punishment is apt to result in antisocial behavior; the child receives no love to make self-control worthwhile, while parental punitiveness foments rebellion and serves as a model of impulsive hostility. Excessive indulgence with few restrictions is apt to produce children who are impudent, demanding, disrespectful tyrants at home, are bossy and uncooperative with peers, and have few friends.

There is no one discipline ideally suited to all children, because healthy growth itself can take many forms. One parent may value assertiveness and creativity, another conformity and docility; a sensitive, introspective child may have advantages in certain settings, a tough-skinned scrapper in another. In other words, there are stylistic differences in normal development which are not a matter of healthy versus unhealthy adjustment. If there is no absolute answer to the question which discipline is best, such absolutism does not seem necessary in light of the diversity of healthy personality development itself.

We shall return to this theme of diversity when discussing minority children in chapter 14.

Developmental Trends

To tell infants to wait a minute when they cry or to punish them for having a bowel movement makes no sense. It is only in the toddler period that requirements for self-control begin to be developmentally appropriate. Such requirements are apt to precipitate the angry storms, the temper tempests, the shouts of defiance of the terrible twos and threes. Gradually, however, the storm subsides. Not only are controls being strengthened but affective investments are being diversified, the intense involvement with parents and siblings now being supplemented by extrafamiliar adults and peers. Diversification aids modulation so that the preschooler is increasingly capable of managing feelings that are becoming increasingly manageable.

The period between 6 and 9 years of age is the high point of self-control. The early anxieties and jealousies within the nuclear family, the accommodation to peer groups, and the transition from home to school have all been weathered, and no comparably dramatic new adjustments need to be made. Children of this age are variously described as conforming, practical, industrious, self-motivated, and self-controlled. They have more insight into their own behavior and the behavior of others than they did formerly and are more orderly, organized, and persistent. They are less aggressive and possessive than before, while the tendencies to blame and ridicule, to be greedy and possessive, or to snatch and steal are all on the wane. There is also a general tendency to be more inward rather than acting on the feelings and impulses of the moment.

The calm of middle childhood is shattered

by the physiological changes and explosive growth of puberty. The period between 12 and 14 years of age may be marked by turmoil: some preadolescents are confused, touchy, negativistic and solitary, aggressive, deliberately provocative, and resistant to authority. Little wonder that some developmentalists have seen a similarity between this period and the terrible twos, even while recognizing that the preadolescent is vastly more complex. Adolescence itself is not so dramatically unstable, although, as we have seen, the many problems involved in the transition to adulthood still make it a time of vulnerability rather than stability in regard to self-control.

At this point we can anticipate a question which bedevils the clinician: If adolescence is a period of "normal upset" for some individuals, at what point does moody or impulsive behavior become psychopathological? This issue will have to be faced squarely in the discussion of drug abuse in chapter 10; as we shall see, there is no clear answer. Rather, there is a large gray area in which the normal shades into the deviant and even the experts disagree as to where a given adolescent stands.

CONSCIENCE

Self-control evolves from parental prohibitions epitomized by "No" and "Wait." Conscience develops from parental evaluations typified by "good boy" or "good girl," "bad boy" or "bad girl." It is this added element of evaluation which makes conscience a special kind of control mechanism. Because conscience is a complex psychological creation, we had best describe it before discussing its development.

Description

Conscience grows out of evaluations of the child's behavior. "Evaluation" suggests that conscience is intimately connected with *values*. Typically we think of moral values as residing in the conscience and rightfully so. But the human conscience contains values from many other sources: some, such as success, achievement, and self-reliance, are cultural values; some, such as cleanliness and an unwillingness to waste food, derive from the family's style of living and parental idiosyncrasies; some, such as fair play and cooperativeness, come from peers. To various degrees, such values exist in harmony, conflict, and isolation. Their psychological potency is not determined by their moral weight; a man who is unconcerned over beating his children may suffer a pang of conscience over having forgotten to send his mother a birthday card.

Next, conscience involves *thinking, feeling,* and *behaving*—understanding what is morally right or wrong, feeling appropriate satisfaction or guilt, and acting in a moral manner. But this is the description of the ideal, integrated conscience. In reality, one element can overshadow the other two: the Devil can quote Scripture, people can feel righteous or guilty over acts that have nothing to do with morality, and moral behavior can serve immoral or amoral ends.

A special word should be said about the feelings originating in the conscience. Interestingly, we have a ready label for the negative affect accompanying transgressions, which is *guilt:* but we have no such label for the positive affect accompanying obedience, so we will arbitrarily call it *self-satisfaction.* Both affects derive from the parental evaluations "good boy" or "good girl," "bad boy" or "bad girl"; the former implies that the child is worthy of love, the latter that he or she is not. Because of the bond of love, being loveworthy is a source of one of the greatest pleasures of early childhood, while not being loveworthy subjects the child to intense anguish. As toddlers and preschoolers develop, they begin to internalize these two judgments; they judge their own behavior as good or bad. And as they say "good boy" or "good girl," "bad boy" or "bad girl" to themselves, they also experience the same pleasure and anguish that accompanied parental evaluations. The pleasure becomes self-satisfaction, the anguish becomes guilt.

Already we can sense the importance and potential dangers of guilt. Certainly guilt is essential to normal development, but the preschooler's negative self-judgment enters the scene long before it can be employed judiciously. And this raises the possibility of all kinds of problems. It is time for us to look at the developmental picture and find out why.

The Development of Conscience

Freud, in trying to understand the childhood origins of adult psychopathology, and Piaget, in trying to understand the cognitive development of children, arrived at a similar picture of the early conscience as an absolutistic, punitive, irrational tyrant. They hypothesized different but complementary reasons why the early conscience was such a monster; Freud emphasized the emotional turmoil created by the Oedipus complex, whereas Piaget emphasized the cognitive immaturity that characterizes the preschool period. But they both believed that the early conscience is the child's own creation. It is not necessarily a reflection of rigid, punitive socialization on the parents' part.

The punitiveness of the early conscience has been documented in preschoolers, who, for example, might believe that if they are naughty, God will drown the world or they will be killed or starved or shut out of their homes or pursued and eaten by large animals. Piaget (1932) provided the richest documentation of the cognitive distortions that characterize moral judgment in the preschool period and the beginning of middle childhood. He demonstrated that the seriousness of a transgression is judged by its physical consequences; breaking five cups is worse than breaking one cup, for example, even if the former were accidental and the latter intentional. Wrongdoing must be punished unconditionally, and in certain cases, the more severe the punishment the better. Punishment is an end in itself, and there is little concern that it fit the crime or help the child avoid similar misdeeds in the future. In regard to justice, the child believes that what the adult in authority does is, by its very nature, justified; if a child is punished when there is no evidence of wrongdoing, for example, then the child must have done something wrong anyway. The next stage in the development of conscience is marked by an inflexible egalitarianism: the child believes in "an eye for an eye" in regard to retaliation and, in regard to altruism, believes that one does something nice for someone else so he or she will do something nice in return! Even in nonmoral areas such as playing marbles, the child believes that rules are absolute and immutable, that they always existed and never can be broken. In short, the absolutistic, unconditional, punitive nature of the child's thinking is clear. It is only during the latter part of middle childhood that children begin to take intentions into account and consider degrees of punishment which match the seriousness of the transgression. Punishment itself serves a constructive purpose. Children begin to realize that people in authority can be wrong, that rules exist for social regulation and can be altered by common consent, and that fairness requires that an issue be considered from the points of view of all parties involved.

Piaget (1932) calls the early stages of thinking *moral realism,* which might seem a strange term except that by realism Piaget means literalness rather than rationality. Just as infants literally believe their cries produce the mother's presence, preschoolers literally believe what they see and hear. They can see a broken cup, but they cannot see an intention, so naughtiness is manifested by its physical consequences. A father can carry a tool box that his son cannot budge, a mother can read books that do not even have pictures; how could such omnipotent and omniscient parents be wrong? And parents unwittingly cater to the child's literalism. When they tell their toddler or preschooler that he is a "bad boy" or that she is a "bad girl," they have two perspectives that the child lacks: they know that what their child is doing is no worse than what other children his or her age do and that the behavior is only temporary. But the child is incapable of thinking, "This is just a phase and I will outgrow it"; instead, "bad" takes on an absolute connotation. Piaget would add that, even if the parent tried to provide reasons and perspective, the child's immature mind could not grasp them.

Elaborating and expanding on Piaget, Kohlberg (1976) reconstructs the stages of moral development in the following manner. At the *preconventional* level the child is concerned only with the reward or punishment an act will lead to. During the *conventional morality* stage, the child adopts the conventional standards of "good boy" or "good girl" behavior to maintain the approval of others or conform to some moral authority such as religion. In the *postconventional or principled stage,* children judge behavior in terms of the morality of contract and democratically accepted law, of universal principles of ethics and justice, and of individual conscience, holding themselves personally accountable for moral decisions. Between 6 and 16, the preconventional level gradually declines while the other two levels increase, although only about one-quarter of 16-year-olds have achieved the highest level.

Although we know that the tyrannical conscience changes, we do not know why. Piaget emphasized the importance of the cognitive give and take during peer interaction as counteracting the rigid authoritarianism of early moral reasoning, but the evidence has not been clearly supportive. The parent who confronts the child with such simply stated challenges as, "How would you feel if someone did that to you?" may help the child think of transgressions in terms of all the parties involved. Dramatic play requiring children to assume various roles, such as those involved in playing house or grocery store or space travel, may also help the child realize that the same situation can be seen from different perspectives depending on the individual's role, thus counteracting the rigidity of absolutist thinking. Social learning theorists emphasize the importance of parents as models of moral behavior, of their reinforcing moral behavior in their children, and of their combining punishment with reasoning, very much as is done in inductive disciplining. When the mystery concerning the agents of change has been solved, we will be in a better position than we now are to insure that normal children "outgrow" their primitive conscience and to help disturbed children who continue to suffer needlessly from its tyranny.

This would be a good place to emphasize a point that has come up in previous sections: there is a significant gap between reality and the young child's understanding of reality. Separation anxiety is an unrealistic fear in most instances, as is the infant's anger with the mother for not being there when needed regardless of the reason for her absence; the toddler can throw a tantrum in response to the most reasonable request from the most loving mother; and now we see a conscience developing that has little resemblance to the values the parent is trying to teach, no matter how simply those values are presented and how patiently they are explained. One implication is that good parenting cannot protect the child from the inevitable distresses and distortions of early childhood; however, good parenting can prevent such distresses and distortions from being magnified and, equally important, can maximize the corrective forces inherent in continued growth. For the child clinician, the implication is that the child's view of family and friends and school is just that, rather than an accurate report of reality; age-appropriate distortions can result in an attentive mother being perceived as a "mean old witch," while a competent father may be seen as a destructive giant. Especially before middle childhood, the child is capable of creating a chamber of horrors out of personal needs and cognitive distortions.

To return to conscience: up to this point we have been dealing with the thinking aspect of conscience, not with feeling or acting. Fortunately for the child, there is no evidence that primitive ideas of wrongdoing are inevitably accompanied by guilt. Unfortunately for our interests, the developmental picture of guilt itself is incomplete. Clinical reports indicate that guilt can exist in the preschool period; however, studies that rely on older children's verbal responses present a different picture. Young school-age children are concerned primarily with punishment rather than with guilt over transgressions; they think an act is wrong because it entails the pain of physical punishment, and their main worry is being caught. Thus they have an *externally oriented* conscience. Subsequently the theme of confession increases and is a kind of halfway house between externally oriented fear of punishment and internally oriented guilt. Children are inwardly troubled and driven to confession, even if they could get away with the transgression, because of what others might think of them. However, confession can also be used manipulatively by children learning the trick of saying "I'm sorry" in

order to forestall punishment. It is only in the preadolescent period that true guilt in the sense of an *internal judgment* and self-criticism appears. Punishment or even the love and opinion of others are not central; rather, preadolescents are concerned with the damage done to their own self-image and self-respect.

Conscience, like self-control, can be either too strong or too weak. Excessive guilt has been implicated particularly in the obsessive-compulsive neurosis and in depression, while antisocial children with acting out behavior may have an externally oriented conscience concerned only with getting caught and being punished. We shall deal with these deviations in chapters 8 and 9.

COGNITION

The aspect of cognitive development most pertinent to understanding the relation between normal and psychopathological development is the separation of the self from the social and physical environment—what has been called the separation of the "me" from the "not-me." Within this general domain, we shall explore the development of causal thinking and the concept of egocentrism, both of which will figure in future discussions.

Causality

An adolescent girl who will not speak for fear that feces would come out of her mouth, or a young man who always sleeps on his back in the belief that, if he did not, he would turn into a woman, would be regarded as psychopathologically disturbed, because they are convinced that they can cause events which, in reality, are beyond their control. This magical notion is called *omnipotence*. Yet omnipotence is not the creation of the mature mind—many concepts of causality are initially magical. Piaget tells us that, between 5 and 8 months of age, the infant is beginning to grasp the idea that events, rather than being discrete, are related to one another: if A happens, then B is likely to follow. Yet infants mistakenly believe causal relations are dependent on their own activity. We have already seen two examples of such omnipotent thinking: infants who believe their cries produce the mother's presence and those who believe their bodily movements can cause any object in the room to jiggle and dance. Their thinking is omnipotent because it has not become *spatialized:* while they can understand their motor activity affecting an object (such as the motion of their hand causing a rattle to make noise), they cannot grasp the idea of causal relations among objects (such as a ball knocking a tower of blocks down). Understanding that objects in space can affect one another, thereby causing change, does not occur until the middle of the second year of life (Piaget, 1954).

Why, then, does not magical thinking disappear from the scene? Because the arena of cognitive development shifts from action, where it was during the sensorimotor stage, to verbal symbols or words, where it remains from the preschool period on. Instead of being able to transfer the insights of the earlier period, preschoolers once again revert to magical notions of causality when they think and reason with verbal symbols.

As in infancy, preschoolers revive the error of viewing all causality in terms of human activity. They conceptualize the physical environment in terms of animism— objects have life and consciousness—and the world becomes conscious, purposeful, and industrious, just as preschoolers themselves are. Piaget calls this thinking *precausal.* When asked to explain natural phenomena, such as the movement of clouds, the child may respond in terms of a humanized God who,

for example, pushes the clouds with his hands or pulls them by a string or presses a button to make them move. The child can also cause natural events to happen so that, for example, the clouds move because the child moves. This last example is particularly interesting because when the child walks, clouds and the entire landscape do seem to move. Because children in the preoperational stage literally believe what they see, they distort the physical environment, just as did the medieval astronomers who believed the sun went around the earth.

Let us now consider the implications of magical thinking for early development. The first six years are unmatched in terms of intense affect and fateful beginnings: attachment brings with it anxieties over loss and jealousy over competition; socialization requires the control of initiative, anger, and sexual behavior; evaluations in terms of good and bad are internalized and become sources of self-satisfaction and guilt; and as we shall soon see, peers place their special demands on social participation. All of these momentous events occur at a time when the child is cognitively incapable of fully understanding the reality of what is happening. Distortions are highly likely to occur. If, for example, a 5-year-old girl's parents are going through a stormy period in their marriage marked by quarreling and accusations, the child might not understand the reality of the situation (indeed, how could she?) but instead distort it in terms of her own "badness" causing the disharmony. Or if a father is drafted when his preschool son happens to be angry with him, there is a chance that the boy will blame himself for the father's disappearance from the family group. Thus omnipotence can create fears and guilts that have no basis in reality. As we shall see, it is just such highly charged distortions of reality which may block development and eventuate in a childhood neurosis (chapter 8).

Egocentrism

Piaget defines egocentrism as conceiving the physical and social world exclusively from one's own point of view. Consequently, characteristics of the self are used to define or interpret characteristics of the objective environment: the "me" is confused with the "not-me."

Egocentric thinking appears at all stages of cognitive development. The infant believes the very existence of objects depends on its actions, while from the toddler period to middle childhood physical causation is interpreted in terms of the child's activities or humanlike agents. Egocentrism has an important social consequence in that it prevents the preschooler from understanding that other people not only have an independent existence but also their own point of view. The ability to view the same situation from multiple vantage points—for example, to see an episode of classroom cheating from the viewpoint of the boy who cheated, the boy who was pressured into helping him cheat, and the teacher responsible for disciplining the classroom—represents a giant step forward in cooperative social interactions. In fact, a lively research interest has sprung up around what is called *social-perspective taking* and its consequences for social behavior. We will have an opportunity to explore some of this literature when we discuss impulsive and delinquent behavior in chapter 9. (For a review of the literature, see Shantz, 1975.)

Egocentrism makes its last childhood stand in early adolescence. Piaget assumed that times of cognitive transition are times when primitive modes of thought are apt to reappear. One aspect of egocentrism may be expressed as self-consciousness; if someone laughs on the bus while the adolescent boy is fumbling to find the correct change for the fare, he is certain that he is being laughed at. Another aspect of the adolescent's egocentrism is the belief that ideas alone will win the day and that their ideas hold the key to solving the world's problems—if only the world would listen! Such egocentrism is overcome by the realities of adult life. Adolescents discover that they cannot impose their answers on the world, but that they must moderate their idealism if it is to have any effect. They realize that the purpose of reflection is not to reorder experience but to interpret it and to offer realistic guides for future conduct.

Recent research has cast doubt on many of Piaget's findings concerning egocentrism. It has been shown, for example, that preschoolers will adjust their language according to whether they are speaking to younger or older children. (For an extensive critique, see Gelman and Baillargeon, 1983.) Thus they are not as locked into egocentric thinking as Piaget would have us believe; rather, they shift back and forth, at times being able to see a situation from the viewpoint of others, at times not. Psychologists are puzzled by this cognitive duality and have not solved the mystery of what conditions produce one kind of thinking rather than the other. Piaget's cognitive theory is valuable to clinicians because psychopathology is often marked by irrational thinking in regard to causality and interpersonal relations, and he offers the fullest account of the developmental origins of such irrationality.

Reality Testing

No one knows for certain how cognitive growth takes place. However, many theories postulate a progressive change as the child tests faulty ideas against reality. The psychoanalysts in fact call this process *reality testing*. When faulty ideas fail to serve their function as guides to realistic behavior, they are modified to bring them in line with reality. Healthy growth requires that reality testing be kept vigorously alive. If not, stagnation with the possibility of deviant development may occur.

Failure to correct irrational thinking is not the only source of irrational behavior, however. Another source is anxiety, the topic that will concern us next.

ANXIETY

While anxiety has diverse definitions, its conceptualization as anticipation of pain is most relevant for our purposes. The concept itself originated with Freud, who used the term *signal anxiety* to designate the moderately painful anticipation of a noxious situation which warns, "Danger ahead!" Forewarned, the child can take steps to avoid reexposure to the situation. As we have seen in our discussion of self-control, anxiety lies at the heart of socialization, the child forgoing various pleasures to avoid the pain of parental discipline.

The Developmental Picture

We will be discussing the development of fear in detail in chapter 8, and so we will only outline it here. Certain fears, such as fear of loud noise and of unexpected movement, seem to be innate, while the fear of strangeness enters the picture in the second half of the first year. Such primitive fears decline in the preschool period as other, experientially based ones appear. Here we find the fear of doing "bad" things and of failure, of traffic accidents and fires. However, unrealistic fears, such as of imaginary animals and characters, also appear for the first time.

In middle childhood the trend toward realistic fears continues so that fear of bodily injury and failure increases while fear of

ghosts declines. However, irrational fears—such as fear of snakes and mice, of nightmares and fictional characters—are still present. Adolescence brings with it new, age-appropriate fears, such as sexual fears, concerns over money and work, and concerns over war. The fear of failure is heightened, again as would be expected. Irrational fears are now infrequent but do not altogether disappear; adolescents can be afraid of the dark, of storms, of mice and snakes, or of cemeteries.

In sum, the development of fears reflects the increased realism of children's thinking and their developmentally appropriate concerns along with the gradual decline in irrationality, although the latter never completely releases its hold.

Defense Mechanisms

The major features of defense mechanisms are so well known that they need be only briefly reviewed. Freud stated that signal anxiety can itself become so painful that certain maneuvers are undertaken to defend the individual against it. The basic defense is *repression*, in which both the dangerous impulse and the ideas and fantasies associated with it are banished from consciousness. In essence, the child says, "What I am not aware of does not exist"; for example, a girl who is frightened of being angry with her mother no longer is aware of such ideas and feelings after repression. If repression is insufficient, *reaction formation* might be called into play so that the child thinks and feels in a manner diametrically opposed to the anxiety-provoking impulse; continuing our example, the girl now feels particularly loving toward her mother and would not dream of being angry. In *projection*, the forbidden impulse is both repressed and attributed to others, so that the little girl might be upset that "all of the other girls" she knows are so sassy and disrespectful of their mothers. In *displacement*, the impulse is allowed expression but is directed toward a different object; for example, our little girl becomes angry with her older sister or with a teacher.

We would like to call attention to certain *congnitive* and *developmental* implications of defense mechanisms. Defense mechanisms inevitably persuade the individual that a distorted image of reality is an accurate reflection. The child who claims to have no hostility toward her parents on the basis of repression is as convinced as if, in reality, the relationship were an unusually congenial one. The point illustrates the Freudian thesis that if affect is sufficiently intense, it can readily twist reason into endless distortions, which are then mistaken for the truth.

But also recall that, in discussing cognition, we stressed the importance of continual reality testing in order for development to proceed along acceptable lines. If defense mechanisms prevent this process from taking place by protecting the child from his or her fear of facing a given reality, are they not pathogenic by their very nature? In answering this question we must rely on the clinical wisdom of Anna Freud (1965), who has been studying children all her professional life within a psychoanalytic framework. While acknowledging their potential danger, Anna Freud sees no inherent incompatibility between defense mechanisms and the general goals of socialization. Neatness and orderliness, which might be a reaction formation against the messiness of the toddler period, can be an adaptive, serviceable defense through adulthood; a political activist who is displacing anger toward parents onto anger toward entrenched political corruption still has a useful and meaningful direction to his life. In addition, the healthy child can use defenses flexibly, relying on them to manage a particularly painful episode in development but discarding them when they are no longer needed. It is when defenses become rigid, pervasive, and extreme and when the child's repertoire of defenses becomes unduly narrow that they are in danger of jeopardizing future growth.

The Dual Nature of Anxiety

Anxiety, like other variables we have discussed, can either promote or block development. On the positive side, it prevents constant reexposure to painful and destructive situations, it raises the level of motivation, enabling the child to make maximal use of abilities, and it engenders defenses that may be socially adaptive and growth promoting. However, anxiety can also perpetuate inappropriate, self-defeating defenses and can bizarrely distort both thought and action; an individual may cling to the most extreme form of deviant behavior out of sheer terror over what might happen if it were relinquished. Clearly, anxiety will figure prominently in our discussions of psychopathologies and of psychotherapies as well (chapter 16).

SEX

Sexuality has been approached from a learning-cognitive point of view and from an affective point of view; both will be relevant to the subsequent exploration of homosexuality (chapter 10). Infants, lacking innate knowledge, must learn to classify themselves as "boys" or "girls." This sex classification of humans is called *gender identity*. In addition, society prescribes which behaviors and feelings are appropriate to boys and which to girls, and children must learn such appropriate *sex-role behavior*. Finally, sexuality involves intense *erotic pleasures* which, at the very least, must be controlled through socialization or which, if psychoanalytic theory is correct, form the leading edge of major personality developments and changes in interpersonal relations.

Gender Identity

The typical 2- to 3-year-old male child has grasped the idea that "boy" applies to him and can correctly answer the question, "Are you a boy or a girl?" However, he does not comprehend the real meaning of the label, nor has he grasped the principle of categorizing people by sex, except by relying on external cues of size, clothing, and hairstyle. Remember that the preschooler is still cognitively in the preoperational stage, literally believing what he sees, so his categorizations by sex are on the basis of manifest differences. Because children this age are incapable of conservation (understanding that objects remain the same even when their appearance changes), they also believe that as appearances change so do essences—things that look different are different. Consequently, it is perfectly possible that boys change into girls and vice versa just by altering their clothes, hairstyle, and behavior to that of the opposite sex. And, referring to our vignette in chapter 1, it is perfectly possible for a child to grow up to be a "mommy" or a "daddy" regardless of his or her present status. It is only around 6 or 7, when conservation is cognitively possible, that children grasp the idea that gender is permanent and immutable. They also come to realize that the genitals are the crucial factor determining gender (McConaghy, 1979).

Sex Role

Every society prescribes behaviors and feelings appropriate and inappropriate to each sex. Traditionally in our society, boys should be dominant, aggressive, unsentimental, stoic in the face of pain, pragmatic, and work-oriented; girls should be nurturing, sociable, nonaggressive, emotionally expressive, and concerned with domestic and child-care pursuits. The message is inescapable: parents know it, advertisers know it, television directors know it, gym teachers and car sales people know it. And now that there is a strong movement afoot to change the traditional stereotypes and foster equality between the sexes, the same social forces are being mobilized to send the new message. Society is never subtle about an issue so important as sex role. Along with the image go rewards for conforming to and punishments for deviation from the prescribed role. In fact, it was society's punitiveness toward women who deviated from their traditionally prescribed role which eventually led to the rebellion against the narrowness of the prescriptions themselves.

It is too early to tell the effects of the movement toward sexual equality on child development. However, the literature on traditional sex roles shows how pervasive the influence of such roles can be. Children as young as 3 years of age can classify toys, clothes, household objects, and games according to social stereotypes, and preschoolers do the same with adult occupations. As thinking becomes less concrete and more inferential in middle childhood, psychological characteristics such as assertiveness and nurturance are added to the list. While awareness of stereotypes increases, acceptance declines, as can be seen in adolescents' pursuit of gender atypical vocations.

So far we have been dealing primarily with knowledge of stereotypes. Very early in development there is also a preference for sex stereotypical behavior. Two- to three-years-olds prefer sexually stereotyped toys (trucks for boys, dolls for girls) and would rather play with same-sex peers. In middle childhood boys increasingly prefer sex-typed behavior and attitudes, while girls shift to more masculine activities and traits. This is just one of many examples of boys being more narrowly sex-typed than girls. "Sissies" are teased; "tomboys" are tolerated.

Social learning theorists point to the many ways culturally prescribed behavior according to gender is reinforced. Fathers play more vigorously with their infant sons than with their infant daughters. In the toddler and preschool periods boys receive more physical punishment, are rewarded for playing with sex-typed toys, and are encouraged to manipulate objects and to climb. In middle childhood parents interact more with the same-sex child, boys are reinforced for investigating the community and being independent, while girls are supervised more and rewarded for being compliant. In general fathers are more narrowly stereotyped in their behavior than are mothers, which is one reason boys are punished for deviations more than girls are.

Another reason boys' behavior is narrowly prescribed is that social stereotypes change slowly. The feminist movement has not altered the image of masculine superiority, which is part of Western culture and which is still present in the media and advertisements. Nor has it changed our society's differential monetary rewards for men and women. Thus there is no mystery about the fact that girls wish to be boys more frequently than boys wish to be girls. (For further details concerning sexual development, see Shaffer, 1985.)

Erotic Pleasure

In addition to learning gender and sex roles, children also have erotic experiences of intense pleasure when stimulating their genitals and are curious about anatomic differences and intercourse. Having already discussed psychosexual development (see chapter 1),

we shall focus here on the literature describing the development of erotic pleasure.

An infant's erect penis unmistakably points to the presence of at least one precursor of adult sexuality in the first year of life. The toddler may derive sporadic pleasure from genital stimulation, and by the preschool period the child is frequently practicing masturbation as a source of pleasurable sensations, looking at the genitals of adults and peers, and asking questions concerning anatomic sex differences and the origin of babies. Erotic feelings may be aroused by the tickling and teasing and generally pleasurable excitement of caretaking during the toddler period. A mother may become concerned when her preschooler wants to masturbate while lying in bed with her, or a father may realize that his little girl is becoming too excited by "riding horsy" on his foot (Gesell and Ilg, 1949).

While informed parents no longer react to sexual behavior with threats to cut the boy's penis off or with terrifying visions of the insanity and depravity that will be his certain fate, even the most enlightened ones must inevitably require a certain amount of self-control. Typically, the parent wants to curb socially disapproved expressions of sexual behavior without alienating the child from natural feelings and curiosities. Instead of judging the child as bad, the parent conveys the message that there is a proper time and place for sexual behavior. Without such socialization, there might well be an increase in heterosexual activity throughout middle childhood, as there is in cultures with different sexual taboos. As it is, boys during middle childhood talk and joke about sex in their gangs, sometimes experimenting with mutual masturbation, while girls talk more about love and have powerful sexual fantasies, although engaging less in actual experimentation. Sexual curiosity is evidenced by an interest in peeking, seeking pornographic or sex-education books, and exchanging sex information with same-sex friends. Middle childhood is also the time of sex cleavage between boys and girls in regard to peer relations (Gesell and Ilg, 1949).

Puberty ushers in physiological maturity, the period extending from around 11 to 15 years of age for girls and from around 12 to 16 years of age for boys. The complexities of sexuality now clearly occupy the center of the stage. At the simplest level, there is the matter of obtaining accurate information. Because society rarely provides ready access to factual material, the adolescent is apt to accumulate both correct and incorrect information and to have areas of uncertainty and ignorance. In the search for personally gratifying sexual techniques, however, instructions in lovemaking are of limited value. Sexual techniques are intrinsically interpersonal, each partner having idiosyncratic sources of erotic arousal and having to adapt to those of the other partner. Thus adolescents are dealing not merely with the awkwardness of inexperience, but also with individual differences that make the same technique exquisitely pleasurable to one partner and deeply repugnant to another. And because intense pleasures are at stake, frustration readily becomes rage, insensitivity touches off anxiety or disgust. In addition, each sexual venture involves the question, What kind of sexual being am I? Adolescents know that society will judge them, and they in turn will judge themselves in terms of the success or failure of their ventures. Most important of all, sexuality is part of the questions, "Whom can I love?" and "With whom can I share my life?" Such questions transcend those of information, technique, and social criteria of adequacy. In sum, the adolescent is searching for a physically and psychologically fulfilling relationship with a person of the opposite sex under the pressure of irresistible demands for periodic sexual gratification.

AGGRESSION

While there has been a notable relaxation of controls on sexual behavior, as evidenced by earlier sexual experiences for both boys and girls and the increase in unmarried couples living together, concern over the control of aggression may well have increased. It is not clear whether there has been a quantitative increase in violence, but certainly the possibility for massive destruction has vastly accelerated. Among the psychopathologies, uncontrolled aggression is a much more serious problem from a prognostic point of view than is excessive inhibition and neurosis, although, ironically, it is receiving insufficient attention from the professional community and from society at large (chapter 9).

As with sex, there is no consensus concerning the definition of aggression. It is defined here as behavior that has injury or destruction as its goal, and anger or hatred as its accompanying affect.

The Developmental Picture

INFANCY   Anger can be differentiated from general distress in the 6-month-old baby and is marked by crying, random and overall body movements such as kicking, flailing of arms and legs, and arching of the back. (For details of this developmental picture, see Wenar, 1971.)

THE TODDLER/PRESCHOOL PERIOD   The period between 1 and 4 years of age is the high-water mark for unvarnished expressions of rage, the developmental trend being from explosive, undirected outbursts of temper to directed attacks, and from physical violence to symbolic expression of aggression. Thus temper tantrums that include kicking, biting, striking, and screaming peak around 3½ years of age and gradually decline. The more directed expressions of aggression, such as retaliation, are negligible in the first year but increase, until about one-third of the outbursts of 4- and 5-year-old children are of this nature. Concomitantly, verbal forms of aggression such as name calling, arguing, and refusals also increase. Self-aggression is not uncommon in this early period, children hitting themselves, pulling their hair, or even occasionally biting themselves during a tantrum.

The descriptive picture makes sense in light of what we have learned about development. The infant cannot be angry *at* anyone because the independent existence of others has not been grasped; directed anger becomes possible only after the object concept is understood. While the toddler can intend to aggress, the idea that an attack actually hurts does not register until around the third year of life. Thus only from 3 years of age on is the child capable of meeting all the criteria of our definition of aggression. Subsequently, attack becomes less physical and more verbal and "psychological." While it would be comforting to believe the transition from physical to verbal aggression represents an intrinsic diminution in aggression rather than merely a change in form, this does not appear to be the case. A blow to self-esteem can be as painful as a blow to the face; a humiliation can be more destructive than a beating.

The situations likely to evoke aggression also follow a developmentally meaningful trend: frustrations in relation to feeding, sleeping, and receiving attention in the first year; toileting in the second year, particularly being forced to remain on the toilet when the toddler is ready to leave. Thwarting of initiative, either by an authoritarian caretaker's refusal to permit an activity or, to a much less extent, by the child's own ineptness in achieving a goal, also begins to trigger aggression in the toddler period and continues to do so through the preschool period. Anger

over having to share or not being able to appropriate an object belonging to another child peaks in the 3- to 4-year-old. Typically, aggressive episodes are brief, preschool quarrels lasting less than half a minute.

The meaning of aggressive behavior itself changes according to the intra- and interpersonal context. In certain emotionally unstable children, extremes of aggression alternate with extremes of withdrawal and fearfulness. On the other hand, vigorous social participation and the formation of mutual friendships also increase the incidence of aggressive behavior. Thus while aggression solely as a desire to harm and destroy may be undesirable and aggression accompanied by withdrawal and fearfulness may be part of a general emotional instability, aggression that results from a high level of sociability may be regarded as innocuous or even healthy.

MIDDLE CHILDHOOD After the preschool period, aggression in the form of a crude physical attack in reaction to the immediate situation declines, and children's behavior becomes progressively more intentional, retaliatory, and symbolic. Children are concerned with getting even and paying back in kind, while their aggressive repertoire proliferates: bickering, quarreling, teasing, and swearing abound, along with bullying, prejudice, and cruelty. Their increased cognitive sophistocation enables them to differentiate intentional from accidental provocations and respond less aggressively to the latter. In keeping with the development of conscience, children now can be troubled by their outbursts. To counterbalance this gain, their increased time perspective also enables them to hold a grudge and have both more delayed and sustained aggression than was possible in the preschool period.

The situations provoking anger continue to reflect the situations that are of great concern to the child.   Anger over other children's cheating, lying, teasing and bossing as well as over adults' lecturing, unjust punishment, and neglect, and over their own ineptness and poor grades in school reflect children's concern with strict justice, their growing desire for independence, their need to be valued in their own right, and resentment over being ignored. On the other hand, their pride dictates that they should not be pushed around or mocked or treated as less than they are.   From the earlier period they retain irritation over their own shortcomings and jealousy of siblings, especially when siblings take their property and when parents hold them up as models.

In general, then, anger is developmentally appropriate in middle childhood, unlike anxiety, which is a mixture of realistic and unrealistic fears.   Thus the developmentally oriented clinician knows it is "normal" for an 8- or 9-year-old boy to have an unrealistic fear of nightmares, but it is not normal for him to have a tantrum when he is told to finish all the food on his plate or when his mother continues talking on the phone after he asks her a question.

ADOLESCENCE   The early phase of adolescence, often called preadolescence, is a generally unstable time.   The more infantile modes of expressing anger, such as stamping feet, throwing objects, and crying, may reappear for a while and disappear subsequently.   In adolescence verbal expressions of anger predominate, such as sarcasm, name calling, swearing, ridiculing, and humiliating.   Sulking frequently follows an angry outburst. The situations evoking anger resemble those of middle childhood—unfair treatment, encroachment on rights, refusal of privileges, being treated as a child, and being incapable of achieving a goal.

Further Characteristics of Aggression

Societies and classes within societies differ in the amount and kinds of aggressive behavior they consider acceptable.   In our society, boys are uniformly more aggressive and more physically aggressive than girls, who rely more on verbal aggression.   A child is more likely to behave aggressively in a crowded playroom than in an uncrowded one and when ill and tired rather than when well and rested.   Thus variables ranging from situation-specific to societal all have an effect on aggression.

More important for our purposes are the multiform variations of aggressive behavior. First let us consider the effect of certain defense mechanisms on the expression of aggression.   In *displacement*, changing the object of anger reduces the fear of retaliation. The familiar example is the parent who, after failing to get a raise at work, comes home and punishes his child.   In the turbulent 1960s, adolescent anger toward "the establishment" might well have been displaced anger toward parents in certain instances. Next, aggression can be *sublimated;* that is, both the affect and the destructive intent are sufficiently modified so as to become socially acceptable.   Competitive athletics are a prime example: anger is sublimated into a "fighting spirit," and the intent to destroy becomes a determination to defeat; the cheerleaders shout, "Yea team, fight, fight, fight!" and the following day, sportswriters describe the home team as having been "slaughtered" or "annihilated."

Aggression can assume *passive* disguises. Dawdling, or complying with parental demands in slow motion, is an exquisite form of revenge that both exasperates the parents and robs them of their right to punish the child for open defiance.   Underachievement in school may represent a child's unconscious revenge on parents who have demanded too much intellectually and given too little emotionally. In general, the clinician must be aware of the possibility that an unrealistic ineptness in an area highly valued by parents (such as physical awkwardness in a healthy boy whose father wants him to be an outstanding athlete) may at least be partly motivated by unconscious hostility.

Finally, aggressive behavior itself can serve nonaggressive goals. The toddler who realizes that her genuine temper tantrum always monopolizes parental attention may soon learn to use anger as a highly effective manipulative behavior. The adolescent, experiencing the loneliness of becoming independent of the family, may adopt the face-saving tactic of maintaining contact through contrived confrontations. Certain acting-out children—toddlers and juvenile delinquents alike—are not so much angry as in desperate need of being loved and valued; despairing of that, they settle for getting attention. "It is better to be wanted for murder than not to be wanted at all."

The many disguises and uses of aggression give us our first taste of the complexity that lies ahead. Aggression may or may not appear as aggressive behavior, may or may not be appropriate to the target, may motivate constructive as well as destructive behavior, and may be serving needs in addition to the one to destroy. Yet complexities such as these are inherent in human behavior, and oversimplification would lead to distortion of the very psychopathologies we are trying to understand.

The Management of Aggression

Generally, parents should be affectionate and serve as models of self-control. Love-oriented discipline and consistently prescribed standards of behavior favor control of aggression, while punitiveness, rejection, neglect, and inconsistency undermine it. The heightened arousal characterizing aggression should be channeled into alternate, constructive behaviors; it can motivate the sprinter, the satirist, the social reformer, as well as the delinquent. Attention should be paid to the problems underlying aggressive behavior—the feeling of being unloved, the humiliating sense of insignificance, the self-loathing. The aggressive child, in turn, should be helped to find constructive ways of coping with anger and to focus on its source (Berkowitz, 1973).

We have now finished our discussion of self-control and the major behaviors the child is required to control. However, we have not exhausted our list of important developmental variables. In concentrating on socialization and on the socializing parents we have neglected peer relations as well as school, work, and occupational choice. These are the topics that will concern us next.

SOCIAL RELATIONS

A number of factors have conspired to prevent peer relations from receiving the attention they deserve. The impact of Freudian theory riveted attention on parents as the prime determiners of personality development, with peers occupying a tertiary role at best. The Freudian orientation was congruent with American societal values, which emphasize the primacy of the parents in charting the course of the child's development at least until adolescence. This neglect of peer relations is being corrected from two sources: the increased interest in peer interaction in the early years and—of direct concern to us—the finding that peer relations are a potent predictor of subsequent psychopathology.

In our discussion we shall distinguish a general interest in peers, which we shall call *sociability,* from *friendship,* which represents a more intense involvement with particular peers—both of which differ from *groups,* which are organizations of individuals possessing norms or values regulating the behavior of the individual. In interpreting the significance of social relations we shall refer to Sullivan (1953), one of the few authorities on child development who fully appreciated their significance. (For a more empirically oriented review and evaluation, see Hartup, 1983.)

The Early Years

There is no lack of dramatic developments in the first six years, but we shall treat such developments summarily, because they have yet to be linked with psychopathology. (For details, see Wenar, 1971.) Two-month-old infants are interested in looking at one another, and by 10 months of age there is a more varied and sustained reaction expressed in mimicking, patting, hitting, and imitation of laughing. By 15 months of age affection appears, and by 2 years there is participation in games, although the toddler's short attention span and limited ability to communicate and to control the behavior of others gives sociability a fleeting, improvisational quality. However, toddlers have been observed to select one member of the group to be an object of attention, concern, or affection, the relationship suggesting the intensity and focus of a friendship, except that it is often not reciprocated.

Clearly, all early social behaviors are less stable and intense than attachments, and for good reason. Peers have no interest in assuming the caretaking role of relieving distress and providing stimulation; nor do they have the caretaker's skill in responding quickly and appropriately to needs. However, they have one inherent advantage over adults in that, being at comparable developmental levels, they are naturally attracted to one another's activities. A parent may love a child for what he or she is; peer attraction is based on interest. Peer relations are important not because they represent diluted versions of attachment, but because they add a new dimension to development.

A number of changes take place in the preschool period. Positive exchanges such as attention and approval increase, although sharing and sympathy do not. Competition and rivalry are also on the rise, while quarrels are fewer but longer. More important, immature or inefficient social actions are becoming more skilled; for example, there is greater speaker-listener accommodation so that the child begins to talk *to* rather than *at* another child, while collaboration begins to emerge in social problem solving (see Hartup, 1983). Cooperativeness, respect for property, constructiveness, and adaptability are the basis of general social attraction; the child who is highly aggressive, quarrelsome, or dictatorial, who refuses to play with others or is dependent on adults for attention and affection rates low on attractiveness and sociability.

Friendships now have that combination of sharing and quarreling which will characterize them throughout childhood. They are unrelated to general sociability, as will also be true into adulthood. Finally, under special circumstances, such as having no adult caretaker in a concentration camp, preschoolers can form remarkably cohesive groups, caring for one another with great warmth and sharing responsibilities with a total lack of the jealousy, possessiveness, and competition that so often mark peer and sibling relations (Freud and Dann, 1951).

Friendship

According to Sullivan (1953) friendships in middle childhood and adolescence are essential for the transition from the egocentrism of the preschool period to the mutuality, sharing, and concern for the partner which mark mature heterosexual relations. We can see the beginnings of that shift in middle childhood. Anger does not lead to disruption of the relationship as it did in the preschool years, but friendship is now sufficiently important to be sustained in the face of difficulties. The child is also beginning to want his or her friend to be happy and is concerned about the friend's attitude toward himself or herself. Thus the concept of a friend as an independent individual is beginning to register. What is more, being with a friend is rewarding in its own right, whereas formerly the pleasure of friendship was limited to sharing specific activities. However, the readiness with which friends are shifted and the dependence of friendship on propinquity, along with a tendency to make a public show of friendship, attest to the superficiality of the relationship.

In adolescence friendships become even more sustained and personalized. Being together rather than doing together is now paramount and is apt to involve the sharing of forbidden and disturbing feelings, especially sexual feelings and problems with parents. In the process, the friend can gain support, relieve guilt, and check reality with a trusted confidante. However, adolescents are also more frank and critical of their friends than they were as children or than they will be as adults. Anyone who knows adolescents is aware of their ability to be pitiless critics, to epitomize faults with a nickname, while all the virtues and extenuations, all the overlooking and covering up of shortcomings vanish. Finally, friendship teaches the adolescent the responsibility and respect of intimacy—tolerance of others, a balance of giving and receiving, knowing the limits to expression and confession. (For a summary of the empirical literature, see Hartup, 1983.)

Such a developmental progression through middle childhood and adolescence fits nicely with Sullivan's concept of friendship as a prelude to adult intimacy, in which sexuality is united with mutuality, sharing, intimate exchange, concern for the partner, and steadfastness. Finally, Sullivan states that friendship increases self-knowledge. The critical confrontations in adolescence are particularly valuable because parents have difficulty with playing the role of critic or are either too involved with or too isolated from their adolescent to play the role constructively.

Sociability

The qualities making for sociability in the preschool years continue to hold sway in middle childhood. The child who is accepted by others is resourceful, intelligent, emotionally stable, dependable, cooperative, and sensitive to the feelings of others. Popular boys are strong, agile, active, aggressive, daring; popular girls traditionally have been sociable, neat, and docile, although toward preadolescence they are more assertive, vigorous, and given to fair play. The child low on social acceptability is retiring, nonadaptive to others, negativistic, individualistic, insensitive, and overbearing. Boys who run counter to the masculine stereotype by being effeminate or "sissies" suffer greater ridicule than girls who run counter to the traditional stereotype by being tomboys.

The characteristics that make for peer acceptance or rejection are not as important for our purposes as the psychological significance of peer relations. Sullivan claims that the shift from "me" to "we" is highly unlikely in the parent-child relationship and highly likely among peers. The child literally and figuratively looks up to parents as the source of love and of socializing directives that must be obeyed because of parental authority. By contrast, the child can look peers in the eye, literally and figuratively. The word "peer" itself means "equal." Consequently, the possibility of mutuality is greatly enhanced. As we have seen, shared interests form one of the primary bonds among peers. In this context of sharing, children learn what Sullivan calls *accommodation:* instead of thinking of themselves as unique or special, as they might at home, they begin to learn how to get along with others.

There is another important dimension that sociability adds to the child's development. At home the child has to be *loveworthy* because affection and obedience lie at the heart of the parent-child relationship. With peers the child must be *respect-worthy*, which is a matter of proven competence. Children must expose themselves to comparisons with other children in regard to athletic ability, manual skills, resourcefulness in suggesting and implementing interesting activities, and so on. They are valued in terms of their actual contributions to the activities that peers themselves value.

In sum, sociability prepares the child to live in the adult world of peers, just as friendship is preparation for adult heterosexuality.

The Group

MIDDLE CHILDHOOD   The insubstantial, play-oriented groups of the preschool period become the middle childhood *gang,* which, by the time children are 8 to 10 years of age, is sufficiently potent to compete with the family in terms of interest, loyalty, and emotional involvement. The child begins to subordinate personal interests to the goals of the group, tries to live up to group standards, and criticizes those who do not. Thus, "we" becomes more important than "I." The gang no longer needs to rely on stereotyped games and activities such as hopscotch or jump rope but is sufficiently autonomous to respond to general suggestions such as, "Let's make a

clubhouse," or "Let's give a party." Names, insignia, and secret passwords help give the gang a special identity. In addition to being identifiable social units, gangs traditionally have been segregated by sex, boys being action-oriented, girls being sociable in their interests.

Just as friendship advances mutuality, the gang advances the sense of belonging. It offers training in interdependent behavior, ventures out further than the individual could go alone, and through its cohesiveness buttresses the individual member's self-control. Sullivan notes that by being able to test one's feelings against those of the group, the individual is less apt to exaggerate them, either positively or negatively.

ADOLESCENCE   Group involvement reaches a high point in adolescence . The adolescent group is an autonomous social organization with purposes, values, standards of behaviors, and means of enforcing them. In its stability and differentiation it resembles adult groups rather than those of middle childhood. Conformity peaks in 11- to 13-year-olds and gradually declines; it is greatest in those adolescents low in status among their peers and high in self-blame.

Adolescent groups vary in structure and nature. There is the small, close-knit *clique* whose members are bound together by a high degree of personal compatibility and mutual admiration. The *crowd* is a larger aggregate than the clique, is concerned with social activities such as parties and dances, and does not demand the same high personal involvement. Crowds vary in status; being a member of a high-status crowd is one of the surest ways of gaining popularity. An important function is that of providing a transition from unisexual to heterosexual relations. The *gang* still survives and requires more loyalty than the crowd. It is often hostile to adult society and has a specific goal—sexual, athletic, delinquent. It retains its emphasis on adventure and excitement as well as on the formal trappings of organization, such as name, dress, and initiation ritual.

These groups serve as the adolescent's primary bridge to the future. They provide a sense of belonging, which is especially important during this period of transition between being a child and being an adult. They help adolescents master uncertainty by prescribing behavior down to what clothes to wear, what music to listen to, and what language to use. They provide both provocation and protection in changing from a same-sex to a heterosexual orientation. Finally, they support individuals in their opposition to their parents. This does not imply that the majority of adolescents are rebellious and alienated; the battle of the generations is fought only fitfully and the values of the group, such as cooperation, self-control, and dependability, are congruent with or even reflections of parental values (Coleman, 1980).

What mars adolescent groups is their rigidity and demands for conformity. Adolescence is a high-water mark for group prejudice, when caste and class lines are sharply drawn, and inclusions and exclusions are absolute. For all their rebelliousness against adult society, adolescents are more slavishly conforming to the group than they have been before or will be in the future. In short, in middle childhood and especially in adolescence there is a narrow group centeredness, which is the counterpart of the child's earlier egocentrism. Perspective and flexibility, evaluation of individuals in terms of personal worth, loyalty without chauvinism, social commitments that transcend immediate group interests—all these lie in the future.

As we shall see, peer relations play an important role in both juvenile delinquency and drug abuse. However, there is a ques-

tion whether they play a leading etiological role. Does the juvenile gang force its members to defy the law whether they want to or not? Or do angry, defiant youths seek out juvenile gangs? While peer pressure is a potent force in drug abuse, does it also *cause* drug abuse? Or are the adolescents who become addicted those who are particularly disturbed to begin with? These questions will be discussed in chapters 9 and 10.

WORK

Why discuss work? Work is what adults do. It is important to the adult's self-esteem and self-definition, the question who is X usually being answered in terms of what X does. Work both expresses and determines personal values while playing a central role in determining friends, social activities, and conduct. The decision to enter the labor market on a full-time basis marks the end of childhood as much as any single decision can. What children do is play. So why not discuss play? The principal reason is that while there are no psychopathologies of play, there are psychopathologies of work as it is conceptualized here (Wenar, 1971).

Work and Requiredness in Middle Childhood

Work derives from initiative. Watch toddlers exploring the environment and you will see embryonic workers. They are totally absorbed in what they are doing, distracted neither by extraneous inner needs nor by external events; they experiment, construct, and solve problems within the limits of their intelligence and skill; they persist in the face of frustration. Note that we have described an *embryonic* worker, not a miniature one. A host of developments lies ahead. The one that concerns us now is *requiredness.*

Initiative in pure culture is the toddlers' paradise. They can do what they want just because they want to do it. As we have seen, socialization, with its "no," "wait," "good boy" and "bad girl," is an intrusion, although sensitive parents try to preserve initiative while requiring self-control. The next major development in regard to initiative is school. As with socialization, children cannot choose *not* to go to school, nor can they choose not to learn what they are supposed to. With the introduction of requiredness, initiative takes on an important characteristic of adult work—work is something you do whether you want to or not. Ideally, work will be intrinsically rewarding and pleasurable, but these are not of the essence.

Interestingly, disagreements among educators concerning requiredness echo disagreements among parents concerning socialization. Some educators, like some parents, favor giving the child's spontaneous interests free rein, capitalizing on natural curiosity and the ability to learn through discovery. Other educators, like other kinds of parents, emphasize formal instruction, along with the adult's ability to guide wisely and to serve as models of disciplined thinking. Good teachers from both camps share a concern with keeping spontaneous curiosity alive while enabling children to master the content of their intellectual heritage. And good teachers are concerned when children fail to live up to their potential. A special group of such children, the learning disabled, will be discussed in chapter 7.

There are other aspects of school which make it a halfway house between the free exercise of initiative and the constraints of adult occupation. School is often the child's first encounter with an extrafamilial organization empowered to make significant decisions concerning the regulation of his or her

daily life. The boy entering kindergarten, for example, is among children he has not chosen to be with; he is also with an adult on whom he has no special claim and who feels obliged to show him no favoritism. His physiological needs cannot be gratified at will since neither the refrigerator nor the toilet is available on demand. Rather, there are schedules and rules that apply to all. Thus school is an *impersonal* environment compared to home.

What is more, the products of children's efforts are valued as never before. Children are with an adult whose principle function is to scrutinize what they do and help them do even better. Grades introduce an element of public evaluation so that not only the teacher but parents and peers as well have knowledge of the quality of the children's products. "Right" and "wrong" enter the picture and take a place alongside "good" and "bad" as preconditions for adult approval or disapproval. In sum, school is *product-oriented.* Schoolchildren add "student" to the list of self-characterizations, and their success or failure in this new role contributes significantly to their self-esteem.

While school has many influences on personality development, we are interested primarily in the requiredness, impersonality, and product evaluation it brings to initiative, thereby placing initiative in a context resembling the adult work situation. (For a review of literature on school as socializing agent, see Minuchin and Shapiro, 1983.)

School failure figures prominently in discussions of psychopathology. Both the future delinquent and the future schizophrenic might be variously described as disruptive and inattentive in class, defiant and truant, for example, while the devaluing of achievement in school is an important factor determining drug use in adolescence (see chapters 9 and 10). Thus the ability to harness and direct initiative into the work-oriented demands of school takes its place alongside other facets of self-control as a determinant of normality or psychopathology.

Vocational Choice and Identity in Adolescence

In addition to being students, adolescents begin to think of themselves as potential workers. The complexities of vocational choice are such that exploring them will continue into young adulthood. The job market itself is complicated and constantly changing, and today's adolescents probably are as poorly prepared for a vocation as they are for mature sexual behavior. The world of work has its own structure of class- and sex-appropriate occupations, its hierarchy of prestige, its requirements for occupational preparation. But work is not only doing a job; it is relating to others as well. In fact, more jobs are lost for interpersonal reasons than for lack of skill and inadequate preparation. Fellow workers have different needs—to dominate and protect, to destroy and seduce, to expand and conserve, to placate and manipulate. Finding a congenial interpersonal setting introduces an unpredictable element into the adolescent quest because there is no sure way of knowing how their idiosyncratic needs will mesh with those of fellow workers.

Along with interpersonal factors, intrapersonal factors are important in choosing a vocation. Ideally, adolescents' interests, values, and talents should all find full expression in the work they choose. Yet development itself decreases the probability of such a harmonious outcome. Vocational self-knowledge lags behind other cognitive developments, and most high school seniors make important choices concerning education or work on the basis of little accurate information concerning their aptitudes. Fortunately, they have progressed in other areas, so that the unrealistic idealism of middle childhood, such as an airy dedication to "helping others," has been replaced by a realistic set of vocational values.

In sum, adolescents must engage in a long period of trying to define their vocational as well as sexual selves. In a special form of reality testing, they set out to discover the most rewarding fit between their peculiar set of ideals, values, and talents and the world of work. Because the work they do will be an important aspect of self-definition and self-esteem, more is at stake than just finding a "good job."

Interestingly, the adolescent's search for a vocation in the broad sense has much in common with Erikson's (1968) well-known concept of the adolescent *search for identity* (see also Marcia, 1980). For Erikson, the adolescent's question, Who am I? is closely related to the question, What can I do that will be fulfilling? Similar intra- and interpersonal variables are involved. Adolescents bring with them a unique constellation of aptitudes, interests, values, and personality traits, which are their heritage from the past. Their occupation must offer an opportunity to continue and fulfill this special heritage, so that what they value most will be valued by others, whether such "others" are the nation, an industry, the neighborhood, or a handful of close friends.

The instability of the adolescent period makes this search for identity a difficult period of trial and error with two inherent dangers: at one extreme there may be premature occupational choice, the adolescent latching on to a stereotyped image of the "successful executive" or "prestigious doctor" only to be trapped in meaningless activities. At the other extreme, uncertainty becomes pervasive and immobilizing, so that the adolescent bogs down in what Erikson calls role diffusion. In fact, identity disorder has recently been added to the list of childhood psychopathologies (see chapter 3). However, such untoward outcomes need not be discussed now. In successful vocational choice, as in successful socialization, the individual wants to do what is required by maturity. If he or she can no longer live in the toddler's paradise, it does not matter; finding fulfillment in the adult world is far better.

RECAP OF KEY POINTS

This review of normal development has taught us a number of lessons that will stand us in good stead as we discuss childhood psychopathology.

First, we have seen the importance of *context* to the understanding of behavior. The context of time is essential; *when* a behavior or an event occurs is as vital to understanding it as *what* it is (see chapter 1). The intra- and interpersonal contexts are equally important. We saw, for example, that aggressive behavior may alienate a preschooler from the group or might be part of sociability and friendship. Other examples anticipate the discussion of psychopathology: enuresis is different in a 6-year-old boy whose negligent parents have not troubled to toilet-train him than in a child whose parents have trained him "according to the books"; juvenile delinquency can represent an impulsive lashing out at society, a desperate bid to be noticed, or a need to be accepted by a delinquent gang; homosexuality can be the most fulfilling or the most terrifying of sexual impulses.

The emphasis will again be on context when we discuss psychological assessment in chapter 15. There we will discuss what kinds of information are needed to make the crucial decision concerning the deviance of a given behavior or the chances of it being outgrown, and what techniques are available that can provide data relevant to making such decisions.

Next, we have seen the *complexity of growth patterns* characterizing normal development.

Some patterns conform to a simple incremental model: just as children become taller and heavier, they become more intelligent with age. Other variables follow different patterns. Self-control is low during the terrible twos, increases to a high point during middle childhood, declines dramatically during preadolescence, and recovers again during adolescence, although still remaining on the unstable side. Piagetian egocentrism is conquered during the first eighteen months of life but reappears in the preschool period to distort the verbalized concepts of causality, and returns again in the self-referent thinking of the adolescent. Negativism peaks in the early preschool period, only to vanish from the developmental scene except for a brief return during preadolescence.

As was noted in chapter 1, the professional must be mindful of the many complexities of development in making a judgment concerning the possibility of psychopathology. But even more is needed. Knowledge of norms does not in and of itself answer the question whether a child's behavior is pathological. Knowing that most children behave in such and such a way does not mean that this particular child is developing normally, and the child clinician is typically concerned with a given child. To return to the opening clinical vignettes in chapter 1: if the child is a toddler or preschooler rather than an adolescent, it is significantly more likely that his furious attack on his sibling or his desire to change sex or her magical thinking is normal. However, the possibility still remains that this particular toddler or preschooler is severely disturbed. The conscientious clinician proceeds to examine the context variables of history, general personality, interpersonal relations, and physiological intactness before coming to a final decision.

While we have not quite finished with normal development, we are now at a point where we can begin to make a bridge to psychopathology. We shall need to know the kinds of behaviors that have been designated pathological so we can understand what we have to account for in our quest to view psychopathology as normal development gone awry. Finally, we need a general overview as to which psychopathologies are apt to be outgrown and which are apt to continue into adulthood. All these matters will occupy us next.

3

The Bridge to the Psychopathologies

W̲e now have a general developmental model and a working knowledge of the variables we shall use in understanding psychopathology as normal development gone awry. It is time to focus on the psychopathologies themselves. First, we will discuss the way normality shades imperceptibly into psychopathology both conceptually and empirically; then the major psychopathologies of childhood will be described; finally, longitudinal studies of normal and disturbed children will be summarized so that we can learn which psychopathologies tend to persist and which tend to be outgrown. Then, in chapters 4 to 12 selected psychopathologies will be explored.

THE CONCEPTUAL BRIDGE

Again and again in our previous discussion we have seen that the same variables that facilitate development have the potential to impede its course. Attachment goes hand in hand with separation anguish, which, if exaggerated, may undermine the preschooler's self-reliant expansiveness; initiative can become a self-defeating negativism in which the child strikes out at all authorities, even those who can be genuinely helpful; self-control can become a prison and conscience a punitive inquisitor;

realistic anxiety can become unrealistic terror; peer groups can mercilessly torment the outsider; schoolwork can become drudgery. This affinity between growth and failure to grow is our first, tentative support for viewing psychopathology as normal development gone awry. Note the word "tentative," since we have yet to put the view to the test in regard to specific psychopathologies.

In fact, one of the major unresolved issues in the study of psychopathology concerns the continuity or discontinuity between normal and disturbed behavior, which at times is referred to as the *quantity versus quality* debate. Is all pathological behavior on a continuum with normal behavior so that, for example, a phobia is just an exaggeration of normal fearfulness, delinquency is just an exaggeration of minor antisocial acts (such as the mischievous stealing of hubcaps), or the sexual perversion of exhibitionism is just an exaggeration of "streaking"? Or do we find, particularly among the severe psychopathologies, certain kinds of behaviors or certain patterns of development that have little or no counterpart in normal behavior and normal development? We are in no position to debate the issue now, but we should keep it in mind as we examine specific psychopathologies.

THE DIAGNOSTIC BRIDGE

Classification Systems

There is no agreed upon classification of childhood psychopathologies. Some derive from a single theory (such as the psychoanalytic or behavioral); others are in the psychiatric tradition of accurate descriptions of symptoms; others stress the statistical manipulation of readily observed behaviors, while still others are a grab bag from sundry traditions. However, there are characteristics

all classification systems should share. There should be a *rationale* for regarding behaviors as psychopathological rather than normal, and the rationale should be appropriate to the population being studied. There should be a reason for including bed-wetting as a psychopathology, for example, while excluding unpopularity. The classifications should be more than variations of adult categories because, as we have seen, pathological adult behavior can be developmentally appropriate in children, while a number of childhood psychopathologies, such as autism, enuresis, learning disabilities, truancy, and certain types of hyperactivity, have little or no counterpart in adulthood.

Next, the range of psychopathologies should be *comprehensive;* each category should be *clearly delineated* in terms of its behavioral characteristics and *differentiated* from other categories it may resemble. Ironically, at present, there is an inverse relation between a detailed coverage of the various psychopathologies and the reliability of the categories themselves: specific disturbances such as school phobias or compulsions tend to have low reliability as measured by agreement among experts as to diagnosis, while broadgauged classifications, such as neurotic versus psychotic behavior, fare better.

One purpose classification systems serve is to parcel an unwieldy mass of information into meaningful and manageable units. However, they do more than help place a given child in a given category: they are points of departure for exploring *etiology* on the one hand, *prognosis* on the other. Thus the diagnosis of adolescent schizophrenia should carry with it implications as to causative factors and prognosis, both in regard to the chances of outgrowing the disturbance and the effectiveness of therapeutic intervention. At present, we are far from realizing such an ideal goal.

While classification may be essential, children rarely fit neatly into a single diagnostic category. Consequently, *multiple diagnoses* are often preferable to a single diagnostic label. The clinician should take into account *acuteness* or *chronicity* based on the history of the disturbance, evaluate the *severity* of disturbance, specify the *developmental period* the child is in, and describe the *specific behaviors* that comprise the psychopathology. Thus a child's diagnosis might read: a severe, acute reactive disorder of middle childhood, with phobic and compulsive features, manifested by persistent restlessness, irritability, fitful sleep, along with occasional panic while waiting for the school bus and a frequent need to retrace his paper route to make sure each paper was properly delivered.

In many classifications the categories themselves carry connotations concerning severity of disturbance. Reactive disorders are regarded as the least severe because of their close relation to realistic events. Severity increases as the disturbance becomes progressively more internalized in the sense of being self-perpetuating and independent of reality, more pervasive and more disruptive of normal functioning. Psychoneurotic disorders, for example, are regarded as more serious than reactive disorders because the problem is internalized to a greater degree; for example, an adolescent girl may realize that her bus phobia is irrational, since there is little chance of her being killed in an accident, yet the terror persists. A personality disorder is more serious still, since the problem affects a wider range of behavior than is affected in the psychoneurosis. Psychotic disorders represent the extreme of disturbance because the behavior is more bizarre and further removed from normal functioning than in the other classifications.

Most classifications differentiate disturbances that are psychological, or—to use the technical term—*functional,* in origin from those that are *organic* in origin. In "pure cases" of

brain syndrome, for example, organic brain pathology is established and affects behavior in characteristic ways; in "pure cases" of psychophysiological disorders, an otherwise healthy body begins to malfunction because of some psychological distress. In actuality, pure cases are all too rare; a number of disorders may have an organic and a functional component. Mental retardation is a case in point: organic and functional factors, either singly or in combination, may play a major etiological role, while subnormal intellectual functioning itself may place a child at risk for developing psychological problems.

Finally, a number of specific psychopathologies can be ordered along a dimension of *internalization–externalization* of children's problems. When children themselves suffer, they are regarded as internalizers. Neurotic children, for example, generally are well behaved but are tormented by fears or guilt. Delinquents, on the other hand, engage in antisocial behavior; the form their disturbance takes differs from that of internalizers in that they act out their problems in relation to society. Thus they are called externalizers. Internalization–externalization is a dimension of behavior, not a typology; while a certain percent of children fall at either extreme, many of them are mixtures of both elements; that is, they can be both anxious and aggressive or have a "nervous stomach" and steal.

The current scene in regard to classifying childhood psychopathologies is a lively one. The appearance of a new revision of a widely used diagnostic manual has occasioned a rethinking of the traditional questions: What are the basic requirements of a diagnostic system that relies on clinical observation? How well does the present revision meet such requirements? At the same time, a classification based on the statistical manipulation of discrete behavioral items is coming into prominence and promises to be an alternative to traditional clinical diagnosis. It is worthwhile to examine both of these developments in detail.

A TRADITIONAL APPROACH: DSM-III

The *Diagnostic and Statistical Manual of Mental Disorders,* third edition, or DSM-III (American Psychiatric Association, 1980) and its subsequent revision, DSM-III-R (1987), are the latest in the tradition of classification based on naturalistic observations. The tradition has primarily been carried on by psychiatrists and relies heavily on the observational skills of clinicians. After describing the goals of DSM-III, we shall see how well it has met certain specific standards for judging the adequacy of a diagnostic system. (The criteria are based on Cantwell, 1980, and Spitzer and Cantwell, 1980.) The revision, or DSM-III-R, primarily changed some of the criteria for certain diagnostic categories, eliminated some of these categories, and added others. The nature of these changes need not concern us. Later, however, when we describe the various diagnoses of childhood disturbances we will follow DSM-III-R.

Goals

The goals of DSM-III are to provide a clinically useful, reliable set of diagnostic categories that will be valid for treatment and management decisions, acceptable to clinicians and researchers of different theoretical persuasions, and consistent with research findings. The categories should be suitable for describing subjects in research studies while also serving an educational function for health professionals. Finally, the diagnoses should be comparable with the current International Classification of Diseases ICD-9.

Evaluation

We shall now present five standards for evaluating diagnostic classifications and see how DSM-III has fared. Our presentation will be primarily in terms of DSM-III because it has been more extensively evaluated than DSM-III-R.

RATIONALE The rationale for singling out behavior as abnormal is typically embodied in a definition of psychopathology. In reality, there is no generally accepted definition, as our survey of models has shown. The authors of DSM-III do not pretend to resolve the knotty issue but are content merely to state their own criteria: clinically significant pain or impairment in one or more important areas of functioning with the inference that there is a behavioral, psychological, or biological dysfunction. In short, *distress* and *dysfunction* are basic.

There is one other point worth noting. The authors are careful to state that disorders, not individuals, are being classified. Thus, the manual never refers to "a schizophrenic" or "an alcoholic," as if the psychopathology were the person; instead it uses "a child with schizophrenia" or "an adult with alcoholic dependency." The point itself is simple but basic and easily lost sight of.

OBJECTIVITY OF DESCRIPTION The diagnostic categories should be objectively described and operationally defined. There is now convincing evidence that reliability is directly related to behavioral specificity and declines as terms become more general, more inferential, and more theoretical. Thus "Fights more frequently than age-mates" is more satisfactory than "Is aggressive" or "Has destructive impulses." In respect to objectivity, DSM-III is quite behavior-specific and a significant improvement over its predecessor, DSM-II. To take only one example, Separation Anxiety Disorder is defined in terms of nine behavioral criteria, such as unrealistic worry about possible harm befalling major attachment figures, repeated nightmares involving the theme of separation, persistent reluctance or refusal to go to school in order to stay with major attachment figures. As additional aids, specific information is furnished as to age of onset, course, degree and kind of impairment, prevalence, sex ratio, familial pattern, and differential diagnosis.

While being applauded for their behavioral emphasis, the authors of DSM-III have also been scored for their failure to have their criteria conform to current research findings in given instances (Rutter and Shaffer, 1980). The diagnosis Reactive Attachment Disorder of Infancy, for example, states that the onset is always before 8 months "since attachments are formed by eight months if there has been adequate caretaking" (APA, 1980, p. 38). Such a statement ignores the fact that attachment is a process that develops over time, and the issue of when it is formed depends on what criteria one uses. In addition, it fails to recognize the marked individual differences among infants, which invalidate most absolute age criteria.

RELIABILITY   Realiability refers to the consistency of results obtained from using a diagnostic instrument. An instrument that would place the same child in different categories when used by two different clinicians would not be very useful. One criterion of reliability is the consistency with which a diagnostic instrument functions at two points in time, or *test-retest reliability*. More frequently, however, diagnostic systems utilize *interobserver agreement*, in which two experts are asked to evaluate the same child at the same point in time. In the field-testing of DSM-III, eighty-four clinicians evaluated 126 child and adolescent patients, two clinicians typically evaluating four cases, utilizing the same material

such as case records, nursing notes, and family informants. The study was done in two phases, and, while the reliabilities in Phase I were quite satisfactory, those in Phase II were unaccountably lower. The overall conclusion is that the reliability of DSM-III is only fair.

Critics of DSM-III often overlook the fact that reliability studies were conducted in an unusual manner because the clinicians were given no preliminary training in using this particular instrument. Even to evaluate simple behavior such as toddlers' exploration of the environment, raters must be trained initially and, ideally, should be given periodic retraining sessions to make sure they still agree on how the behavior should be rated. Training is necessary to insure that observers understand the categories to be rated and the behaviors that are and are not to be included in these categories. To expect clinicians with no preliminary training to agree on an instrument as complex as DSM-III, therefore, is unrealistic. It is more reasonable to conclude that the reliability of DSM-III has yet to be evaluated fairly than to state that it has been shown to be low.

VALIDITY   *Validity* is the extent to which a test measures what it claims to measure or, in this case, the extent to which a diagnostic system does, in fact, correctly classify disturbed children. The concept has proved a troublesome one and has spawned a variety of definitions. There is *content* or *face* validity, which is the degree to which the content of a diagnostic category has an obvious relation to what is being evaluated. In the case of Separation Anxiety Disorder, the three behavioral criteria mentioned make sense on the face of it. Ideally, the criteria should also be analyzed statistically to test whether they do, in fact, cluster together. *Predictive* validity compares current evaluations with some future criterion; for example, children diagnosed as schizophrenic in middle childhood should continue to be more disturbed as young adults than children diagnosed as having a school phobia. *Concurrent* validity compares the current evaluation with some other contemporary criterion; the diagnosis of a reading disability based on parental report could be compared with scores on a reading achievement test, for example. Note that the difference between predictive and concurrent validity concerns whether the outside criterion lies in the future or is current. *Construct* validity is the relationship between a diagnostic category and other variables that should be related to it theoretically; for example, children classified as violently antisocial should do poorly on measures of self-control, such as the ability to delay gratification. And, finally, *discriminative* validity is the extent to which clinical features are unique to the disorder in question and differentiate it from other similar disorders. It corresponds to the traditional clinical task of differential diagnosis.

Admittedly, DSM-III has only face validity. This is about as good a showing as reality allows, however. There are few independent criteria that can be used for predictive or concurrent validation studies, and many of the relations between diagnostic categories and other variables either have not been investigated or have yielded controversial findings. Practically speaking, the clinician cannot indefinitely postpone the task of diagnosing children until the desired validation studies have been done (Spitzer and Cantwell, 1980). Now that the pace of research on childhood psychopathology is accelerating, however, periodic revisions and updating, as was done in DSM-III-R, are highly desirable.

COMPREHENSIVENESS A diagnostic system should be comprehensive in its coverage of psychopathologies. In this respect, DSM-III is a significant improvement over DSM-II, containing twice as many categories for children and adolescents as its predecessor. The major areas of disturbance that DSM-III covers are intellectual (for example, mental retardation), behavioral (for example, conduct disorders), emotional (for example, anxiety disorders), physiological (for example, eating disorders), and pervasive and specific developmental disorders (for example, autism for the former, reading disabilities for the latter). Not that all the additions have been immune to criticism. Oppositional Disorder, defined in terms of disobedient, negativistic, and provocative opposition to authority figures for at least six months' duration, has been singled out as sounding more like "the kid down the block" than a psychopathologically disturbed one (Rutter and Shaffer, 1980).

A New Feature

A significant departure from the past is the use of a *multiaxial* classification system. Instead of being classified in terms of a single dimension as has been the custom, each child is classified along five dimensions. For many years clinicians have realized that diagnosis is multifaceted, so that a single label often fails to do justice to a child's disturbance. In addition, some of the diagnostic dimensions involve different frames of reference. It makes sense to ask if a child is autistic or schizophrenic because the question involves a discrimination between two kinds of psychopathologies. However, to ask if a child is mentally retarded or diabetic makes as little sense as to ask if he walks to school or carries his lunch. The multiaxial approach represents one solution to the problems of multiple psychopathologies and independent dimensions.

Axes I and II contain the classifications of all the mental disorders. Axis I includes the clinical syndromes, such as mental retardation, conduct disorders, infantile autism, anxiety disorders, and eating disorders. Axis II includes specific developmental disorders such as reading, arithmetic, language, and articulation disorders. This separation ensures that consideration is given to the less spectacular developmental disorders, which might be overlooked when the clinician concentrates on the presenting symptoms. Axis III includes any current physical disorder or condition that is potentially relevant to understanding or management, such as neurological damage or a chronic debilitating illness. Axes I through III comprise the official diagnosis.

The remaining axes are used in specific research and clinical settings. Axis IV, labeled Psychosocial Stressors, rates the severity of such stressors on a 7-point scale from None to Catastrophic (for example, multiple family deaths). The dimension is important, because a psychopathology that occurs in the absence of stress is more ominous than the same one occurring in the presence of great stress.

Axis V, Highest Level of Adaptive Functioning during Past Year, rates a child's social relations, functioning as a student or worker, and use of leisure time on a 7-point scale from Superior to Grossly Impaired. The axis has prognostic import, because individuals tend to return to their previous level of adaptive functioning after the psychopathological episode is over.

Critique

DSM-III has been justifiably praised for its assets and criticized for certain shortcomings. The increased specificity of its diagnostic criteria, its atheoretical, behavioral orientation, its added scope in regard to children and adolescence, and its venturing into a multiaxial approach are generally admired. Its definition of psychopathology and reliance

on face validity are probably as good as reality allows, although far from satisfactory. Its reliability remains to be determined. In certain instances it has been out of step with research findings in its diagnostic criteria; in addition, the wisdom of its choices for including and excluding specific categories has been questioned. Its encouragement of continued research and revision is commendable.

But DSM-III has generated more controversy than would seem warranted in light of this balancing of assets and liabilities. The basis of some of the more biting attacks is an assumption that DSM-III conforms to the medical model. In fact, it does not. While it classifies in terms of categories of disorders as is done in medicine, such classification is common in the natural sciences, where animals are separated from vegetables, felines from canines. In addition, the authors recognize that these categories should not be regarded as discrete, qualitatively different entities, because the issue of continuity and discontinuity among categories is an unsettled one. While the medical terminology of "symptom" and "diagnosis" are retained, they are consistently translated into behavioral terms. The implications that a symptom is a sign of some underlying disorder or that the majority of the diagnoses have an organic etiology are explicitly denied; symptoms are nothing more than behaviors, and etiology in the majority of cases is unknown.

However, the medical terminology remains, together with the fact that the manual is the product of physicians; with feelings of resentment running high among health care professionals, this is enough for DSM-III to stand accused of adhering to the medical model. Nor is the situation helped when individuals involved in DSM-III publish articles stating that its mental disorders are a subset of medical disorders (Schacht and Nathan, 1977). More is involved here than mere conceptual confusion, however; at stake are issues of territoriality (which profession or professions have the final authority over psychopathologically disturbed children?) and livelihood (which professions have the right to bill for their services directly?). If, indeed, mental disorders are a subset of medical disorders, then the medical profession in general—and psychiatrists in particular—preempt both territory and livelihood.

There are those who maintain that DSM-III should be evaluated solely in terms of its successes and failures in achieving its stated goals (Rutter and Shaffer, 1980). Its authors are in no way responsible for its misuse. As a descriptive classification, it says nothing concerning who should diagnose and treat, and this neutrality should exempt it from involvement in interprofessional squabbles. On the other hand, there are those who claim that DSM-III is part of a social context marked by interprofessional rivalries and emotionally charged legal battles. Whether intentionally or not, both its form and its content serve to extend the medical domain far beyond justifiable limits. What we have in these opposing views is a variation of the old question: To what extent is science answerable only to itself, and to what extent is it answerable to society? It is an issue each individual must wrestle with and decide on his or her own.

THE MULTIVARIATE STATISTICAL APPROACH

Until recently there has been a perfect inverse relation between reliability and utility in classification. The traditional diagnostic systems had low reliabilities, while the reliable categories, such as internalizer versus externalizer or neurotic versus psychotic, were too gross to be useful to the clinician. However, just as the authors of DSM-III have been concerned with improving the precision of their diagnostic categories, advocates of precision show promise of devising a more finely differentiated set of classifications.

Progress in science, so the argument goes, often involves a change from description to measurement and quantification. In the realm of diagnosis, quantification has often involved a multivariate statistical approach. (For a review of the studies, see Quay, 1986.) The basic format is simple. Collect specific behaviors used in describing psychopathologically disturbed children, eliminate the infrequent, redundant, and obscure ones, and subject the rest to statistical techniques designed to determine which are highly related. The statistical technique frequently employed is called *factor analysis* and the related behavioral items are called factors. After examining the content of the interrelated items, the investigator assigns each factor a label. Such labels may resemble those used in traditional diagnosis, such as delinquent or hyperactive; however, they should not be regarded as equivalent until empirical evidence has shown them to be.

To illustrate the multivariate statistical approach we shall concentrate on the work of Achenbach, who is currently advancing it further than his predecessors (Achenbach, 1979; Edelbrock and Achenbach, 1980). Achenbach's first step was to collect descriptions of pathological behavior from psychiatric case histories and from the literature. Through a series of preliminary studies these were reduced to 118 items that formed the Child Behavior Checklist (CBCL). Examples of items are: the child argues a lot, complains of loneliness, does not eat well, runs away from home, has strange ideas. Another set of items concerned competencies and were used to construct additional scales, but they will not concern us now.

Next, the CBCL was filled out by parents of 1,800 children referred for mental health services, and the results were factor-analyzed. The analyses yielded both *wide-band* and *nar-*

row-band factors. Wide-band factors included the now familiar categories of externalizing and internalizing behaviors, or conflicts with the environment and problems with the self. The narrow-band factors included specific syndromes or behavior problems, such as depressed, obsessive-compulsive, somatic complaints, hyperactive, aggressive, and delinquent.

To give two illustrations of narrow-band syndromes: the Schizoid scale contained the behavioral items of clinging to adults, fretting, fear of school, auditory and visual hallucinations, nightmares, shy and timid, while the Delinquent scale contained the behavioral items of destroys own and others' things, disobedient in school, has bad friends, lies, cheats, runs away, sets fires, steals, truants, and swears. As so often happens in multivariate studies, the majority of the narrow-band scales could be subsumed under either the internalizing or externalizing scales.

The data were analyzed separately for boys and girls and for the age groups 4 to 5 years, 6 to 11 years, and 12 to 16 years so that sex and age differences in syndromes could be detected. It was found, for example, that, while 6- to 11-year-old boys and girls shared the syndromes of Delinquent, Aggressive, and Hyperactive, the girls had the additional syndromes of Sex Problems and Cruel; 12- to 16-year-olds shared the syndromes of Somatic Complaint and Schizoid, with the boys having the added syndromes of Uncommunicative, Immature, and Obsessive-Compulsive, and the girls having the added syndromes of Anxious-Obsessive and Depressed Withdrawal.

To obtain norms, the CBCL was next administered to 1,400 nonclinical children matched for age, sex, race, and socioeconomic status with the clinical population, and percentiles were calculated for the scores in the various narrow- and wide-band syndromes. With data from the normal and clinical populations it was possible to determine cutoff scores, below which the child would be considered within the normal range and above which the child would be considered disturbed. These cutoff scores were at the ninety-eighth percentile of scores for the total population. Thus a boy with a score of 1 on the Schizoid scale would be at a point equivalent to 69 percent of the population and therefore within normal limits; however, the same boy's score of 26 on the Aggressive scale would be higher than 99 percent of the population and might well be cause for concern. After scoring all eight or nine narrow-band scales (the number depending on the child's age and sex), one can obtain a profile indicating which scales are within normal limits and which exceed them. A hypothetical child might be within the normal limits for the internalizing scales of Schizoid, Depressed, Uncommunicative, Obsessive-Compulsive, and Somatic Complaint, while exceeding the norm in the externalizing scales of Delinquent, Aggressive, and Hyperactive.

Because using computers to generate syndromes is quite different from using clinicians, it is interesting to compare Achenbach's (1980) factors with the diagnostic categories of DSM-III. Overall, DSM-III is more differentiated in the sense of having more classifications, but there is general agreement between the two approaches in regard to the categories of psychopathologies such as Aggressive, Anxious, Socially Withdrawn, Obsessive-Compulsive, Depressed, Somatic Complaint, and sex problems. However, the DSM-III has certain diagnostic classifications not found among Achenbach's syndromes, such as Autism, Anorexia Nervosa, and specific learning disabilities. Achenbach uncovered syndromes of Immaturity and Cruelty, which are missing from the DSM-III's categories for children.

It is easy to understand the appeal of the statistical approach for those who value precision. Test-retest reliabilities are characteristically satisfactory, while the behavioral nature of the basic data gives them a palpability the more inferential diagnostic systems lack. As an added bonus, the CBCL and similar instruments are great time-savers compared with the traditional diagnostic procedures.

Yet one should not make the mistake of assuming that the combination of behavioral specificity and statistical manipulation guarantees precision. To begin with, objectivity in behavioral evaluation is a matter of degree. While it is true that the statement "Is disobedient at home" is more objective than "Has a problem with authority figures," the former still requires a judgment. Thus the same behavior a mother might regard as disobedience in her son might be dismissed by the father as "just the way boys are." Behavioral ratings depend on who does the rating and the situation in which the behavior occurs: parents, teachers, and professionals may all disagree in rating a particular child either because they evaluate the same behavior differently, or because the child behaves differently in different settings, or because of a combination of both factors. In point of fact, Achenbach, McConaughy, and Howell (1987) found that, while agreement within the same category of informants—specifically, parents, teachers, mental health workers, peers, and the child himself—was reasonably high, agreement among these categories of informants was low. To cite one example, the mean correlation between parents was .59, but the mean correlation between parents and teachers, mental health workers, peers, and the children's self ratings ranged from .24 to .27. While the latter correlations were statistically significant, they were too low to have clinical utility.

In discussing clinical applications, Achenbach and McConaughy (1987) recommend that the CBCL and its different adaptations for parents, teachers, and peers be used in conjunction with an interview designed to provide historical and current information relevant to the child's disturbance, and with results from intelligence tests and other tests which would aid the clinician in understanding the child's problems and in making appropriate treatment recommendations. Achenbach and McConaughy regard disagreements among different informants as due to the fact that behavior varies with the situation; e.g., a child's problems might be evident only in school and not at home, or only with the mother and not the father. Unaccountably, the authors make almost no mention of the fact that an adequately functioning child may be rated as having problems by a disturbed parent. According to Kazdin (1989), "Parent perception of deviance and evaluations of their children on standardized rating scales is significantly related to their own symptoms of psychopathology (especially depression and anxiety), marital discord, expectations for child behavior, parental self-esteem, and reported stress in the home" (p. 182). Consequently, therapy may focus on changing the child's behavior when it should be directed to the parent's behavior instead.

THE CLASSIFICATIONS: HEALTH AND NORMAL PROBLEM BEHAVIOR

In our presentation of the classifications we shall draw on both DSM-III-R and the so-called GAP Report (Group for the Advancement of Psychiatry, 1966). The latter is less behavioral and explicit than DSM-III-R, more theoretically oriented, and, consequently, less reliable. However, it has features that make it a valuable complement to DSM-III-R. To begin with, the GAP Report contains two categories that are important in understanding childhood psychopathology—Healthy Responses and Developmental Crises—neither of which appears in DSM-III-R. The GAP Report retains certain traditional designations, such as Psychotic Disorders, which are more in keeping with our presentations than are the revisions of DSM-III. When adult and childhood disturbances are essentially the same, DSM-III-R gives only the adult criteria, while the GAP Report description is more child-oriented and therefore preferred. Finally, DSM-III-R has categories that are at variance with our approach to understanding psychopathology; e.g., it singles out autism, learning disabilities, and mental retardation as developmental disorders while, to our way of thinking, all the classifications are developmental disorders. In sum, a combination of DSM-III-R and the GAP Report will be more relevant to our subsequent discussions than either one alone.

Healthy Responses

The GAP Report sensitizes us to the importance of evaluating the healthy features in a child's personality. In the past, clinicians have focused exclusively on the psychopathological elements, almost as if it were their professional obligation to ferret them out. Experience has shown that such a narrow focus, which fails to do justice to strengths and assets, distorts both the current picture and the prognosis. We have already noted that aggression in the context of sociability and friendship differs from aggression that isolates the child from his or her peers. Now, however, we can explicitly recognize the evaluation of health as central to the clinician's charge of deciding whether a child is disturbed and the degree of disturbance. (The issue of evaluating growth-promoting and growth-inhibiting behavior will be discussed again when we examine the neuroses in chapter 8.)

The GAP Report states that there is no single criterion for health; rather, a number of functions are involved. In *intellectual* functioning, health involves "adequate use of capacity, intact memory, reality-testing ability, age-appropriate thought processes, some degree of inquisitiveness, alertness, and imagination" (p. 220). Healthy *social functioning* involves an adequate balance between dependence on others and autonomy, a reasonably comfortable and appropriately loving relation with adults and other children, and an age-appropriate capacity to share and empathize with peers. The emphasis on age appropriateness makes an understanding of normal development essential. Healthy *emotional functioning* involves an adequate degree of emotional stability, some capacity for self-perspective, some degree of frustration tolerance and sublimation potential, along with some capacity to master anxiety and cope with conflicting emotions. Healthy *personal and adaptive functioning* requires a degree of flexibility, a drive toward mastery, an integrative capacity, a degree of self-awareness, the existence of a self-concept, and the capacity to use fantasy in play constructively.

Note that the definition makes frequent use of the qualifying phrases "a certain degree of" or "some capacity for." As clinicians we would prefer more exact statements so that our evaluations would be less subjective. Such objective criteria for health lie in the future; the definition reflects current reality. On the positive side, the GAP Report does not present an idealized picture of the "normal, well-rounded child," with the implication that any deviation from such an ideal is suspect. Indeed, what is impressive about normal children is how much "deviance" they can take in stride!

Finally, the GAP Report emphasizes the importance of stage appropriateness—which they prefer to age appropriateness—of development. There should also be a general "smoothness" of development, as contrasted with alternating periods of exceptionally slow and rapid growth. And finally, there should not be excessive discrepancies in growth among the components of health, as is seen in the pseudomature 6-year-old whose adult behavior effectively blocks peer participation.

Developmental Crises

In line with earlier discussions of the context of time, the GAP Report recognizes that there are inherent crises in normal development itself. It lists separation anxiety, which accompanies attachment in the first year of life; the subsequent variation of separation anxiety that comes as the toddler turns away from the mother to explore the environment; the fearfulness that marks the transition from the preschool to the school-age periods; ritualistic behaviors such as excessive neatness and propriety which are part of the conformity of middle childhood; and the search for identity that underlies some of the erratic behavior of the adolescent.

While we prefer the term "stress" to "crises," this category is congruent with our contention that normal development involves stresses that increase the likelihood of problem behavior. Evidence for this contention comes from the Berkeley Growth Study (Macfarlane, Allen, and Honzik, 1954). Enuresis, food finickiness, and thumb sucking were found to be prevalent in the age group from 21 months to 3 years, a time when toddlers are being pressured to control their urination and appetite and take refuge in one of the earliest and most readily available of solaces— thumb sucking. Except for a brief reappearance of food finickiness, all three problems vanished from the developmental scene. As might be expected, negativism characterized the preschool period and also disappeared subsequently. Certain problems marked transition periods: the 5- to 6-year-olds tended to have disturbing dreams and loss of appetite, to be finicky eaters, and to become somber, while preadolescents tended to be troubled by disturbing dreams, moodiness, and shyness.

Thus, paradoxical as it sounds, there is such a thing as normal problem behavior. It would be a mistake either to expect a normal child to be problem-free or to assume that the existence of problem behavior per se is a sign that development has gone awry.

Situational crises are also part of normal development. These are events that are not inherent in the developmental process itself, but that the child may well encounter: a severe illness or accident, being transferred from a favored to an unfavored school because of integration, family disruption owing to the father being drafted or the mother returning to work, and so forth. In situational crises there are no ominous preludes to the event, such as a mother going to work because she finds caring for her children intolerable. Although the children may be upset, their overall development is not blocked, nor is their behavior excessively age-inappropriate. Once again, a knowledge of normal development is essential in evaluating the appropriateness of the behavior.

With situational crises, the bridge from normal development is complete. Now the psychopathologies themselves will be presented.

THE CLASSIFICATIONS: THE PSYCHOPATHOLOGIES

Adjustment Disorders (DSM-III-R) or Reactive Disorders (GAP Report)

Adjustment disorders comprise the first class of psychopathologies to take us out of the realm of normal development while still partaking of some of the qualities of normality, particularly of situational crises. (This description is based on the GAP Report, rather than DSM-III-R, since it is more specifically concerned with children.) As in a situational crisis, the child's behavior is in reaction to a specific event or set of events. In addition, the untoward behavior patterns have not become internalized; that is, they have not become relatively autonomous, tending to persist long after the precipitating event has passed. While not as "self-corrective" as situational crises, in which the natural intra- and interpersonal forces making for growth are usually sufficient to enable the child to achieve mastery, the majority of the reactive disorders tend to be transitory; appropriate advice to the parents or a few psychotherapeutic sessions with the child usually suffice in eliminating the troublesome behavior. In general, then, reactive disorders represent a more extreme version of situational crises; the reactions are more intense and may block growth to a greater degree or involve the return of more developmentally inappropriate behaviors. Consequently the risk of the reactive disorder becoming a more serious form of psychopathology is greater than in the case of situational crises.

While certain situations may be potentially traumatic for most children, such as the loss of a loved parent, the GAP Report emphasizes the variability among children, so that an event that overwhelms one might be only temporarily distressing to another. The behaviors themselves may vary depending on the developmental level of the child: an infant deprived of parenting may react with apathy or eating and sleeping disturbances; the preschooler may become aggressive or withdraw into self-stimulation such as thumb sucking or masturbation for solace; the early school-age child may start wetting or soiling or retreat into excessive daydreaming.

In rare instances, the children may seem to be severely disturbed only because they are living with severely disturbed parents and modeling parental behavior; thus a child's bizarre ideas, for example, that people are out to kill her or that it is unsafe to eat food away from home, may not be evidence of primitive, omnipotent thinking but a reflection of parental fears. The psychopathology that appears so serious is, in fact, reactive. Once again we see the importance of viewing a behavior in context.

Anxiety Disorders (DSM-III-R) or Psychoneurotic Disorders*[1] (GAP Report)

The GAP Report retains the time-honored classification and its conceptualization, while DSM-III-R prefers the purely descriptive label, Anxiety Disorders. Psychoneurotic disorders are conceptualized as resulting from internalized conflicts between the child and significant people in the environment, most frequently the parents. Because of their internalized character, they tend to be more chronic than reactive disorders. However, there is no marked personality disorganization and the child's reality testing is not grossly disturbed. There are a number of specific types of psychoneuroses, as follows:

OVERANXIOUS DISORDER (DSM-III-R) OR ANXIETY TYPE* (GAP REPORT) The picture here is of excessive or unrealistic anxiety or worry about the future, about past behavior, or about competence in one or more areas, such as athletics or school. There may be marked feelings of tension or self-consciousness and an excessive need for reassurance. There also may be somatic complaints such as headaches or stomachaches with no physical basis.

[1] An asterisk (*) indicates psychopathologies that will be discussed in chapters 4 through 12.

PHOBIC DISORDERS (DSM-III-R) OR PHOBIC TYPE* (GAP REPORT)　A phobia is an intense, persistent, irrational fear of an animate or inanimate object or of a situation. The list of phobias is extensive: spiders, school,* dirt, high places, germs, airplanes, and so on. Unlike free-floating anxiety, the anxiety here can be managed as long as the child can avoid the specific eliciting stimulus.

SEPARATION ANXIETY DISORDER (DSM-III-R) This disturbance is marked by excessive anxiety upon separation from major attachment figures, from home or other familiar surroundings; for example, the child may experience anxiety to the point of panic when sleeping overnight in a friend's home or attending camp. Children are unrealistically worried about what harm might befall the loved adult or themselves during separation.

CONVERSION DISORDERS (DSM-III-R) OR CONVERSION TYPE* (GAP REPORT)　In this disorder, conflicts are dealt with through disturbances in bodily function. There may be disturbances in motor functions, such as tics or paralysis; in sensory perception, such as blindness or deafness; or in awareness, as in convulsionlike phenomena. Certain instances of vomiting and hyperventilation may be evidence of a conversion reaction. Conversion reactions must be distinguished from symptoms of physical illness, one clue being that the dysfunction may follow the child's naive concepts of the body rather than anatomic lines of distribution.

OBSESSIVE-COMPULSIVE DISORDER (DSM-III-R) OR OBSESSIVE-COMPULSIVE TYPE* (GAP REPORT)　An obsession is a persistent, recurring idea, usually of an unpleasant nature, which the child is unable to control. A religious adolescent, for example, may be bedeviled by "dirty" words that intrude upon his thoughts during prayer time, while another

may have recurrent thoughts of plunging a knife into her breast. Compulsions are persistent, irresistible, irrational behaviors. The classic example is the need to wash one's hands over and over in a futile attempt to counteract a feeling of being dirty.

DYSTHYMIA (DSM-III-R) OR DEPRESSIVE TYPE* (GAP REPORT)　Neurotic depression is more intense and persistent than the transitory feelings of depression in healthy children undergoing developmental or situational crises. There is a greater loss of self-esteem, more intense feelings of self-deprecation and guilt, along with a depressed mood. Eating and sleeping disturbances and even agitation may also be part of the picture.

Personality Disorders

While psychoneurotic disturbances affect only limited areas of the child's functioning, personality disorders represent ingrained traits that pervade a good deal of the child's life. From what we have learned about the development of control, we can understand why personality disorders are uncommon until the later school-age period when the organization of the child's personality begins to stabilize. DSM-III-R and the GAP Report are essentially in agreement on this classification.

There are many personality disorders, but our coverage will be selective because only one (Oppositional Disorders) will figure in our subsequent discussions of psychopathologies.

COMPULSIVE PERSONALITY AND ANXIOUS PERSONALITY　In these disorders, neurotic behaviors have become pervasive personality traits. Thus the compulsive personality is excessively concerned with orderliness, cleanliness, and conformity, is relatively rigid and inflexible, and cannot relax. Ordinarily such a child performs well and may have a kind of pseudomaturity that adults may mistake for healthy childhood behavior. Children with an anxious personality are chronically tense and apprehensive over new situations and perceive their environment as threatening, although their anxiety is not as intense and crippling as in an anxiety neurosis. After an initial fearfulness, they are able to deal adequately with new situations.

OVERLY DEPENDENT PERSONALITY   Children in this category are chronically helpless and clinging, indicating their great difficulty in achieving autonomy and taking initiative. They may also be markedly controlling and passively aggressive, using demandingness and helplessness as means of tormenting and antagonizing adults. DSM-III-R specifically designates these latter children as having a Passive-Aggressive Personality Disorder.

OPPOSITIONAL DISORDER* These children defy or refuse adult requests and rules, deliberately do things that annoy others, are argumentative, touchy, spiteful, or vindictive. At times, persistent stubbornness, dawdling, and procrastination are passive disguises for their underlying hostility.

Conduct Disorders* (DSM-III) or Tension Discharge Disorders (GAP Report)

Children in this category directly act out their feelings or impulses toward others in an antisocial or destructive fashion. Many labels have been given to such children, including antisocial personality, psychopathic personality, and impulsive character, but the essential feature is the persistent violation of the rights of others or of major societal norms and rules. The GAP Report is more congruent than DSM-III-R with our discussion. We will also use DSM-III because DSM-III-R only differentiates group and solitary types,

which is at variance with our discussion and with research findings as well (Quay, 1986a).

UNDERSOCIALIZED, AGGRESSIVE TYPE* (DSM-III) OR IMPULSE-RIDDEN PERSONALITY (GAP REPORT)   These children have great difficulty controlling their aggressive and sexual impulses, which are acted out immediately and impulsively, often without regard for the consequences. Their relationships with adults or other children are shallow, and they have little anxiety or guilt. They tend to project their hostile feelings onto adults and society and to rationalize their own behavior. Stealing, fire setting, vandalism, aggressive attack, and other antisocial acts may occur frequently.

NEUROTIC PERSONALITY DISORDER (GAP REPORT)   While superficially resembling the impulse-ridden personality, children in this category have reached a higher level of personality development: relationships are warmer and more meaningful, self-control and conscience are stronger, as manifested in a greater amount of anxiety and guilt. Rather than acting out on the spur of the moment and engaging in a variety of antisocial acts, they behave in a repetitive manner suggestive of a specific conflict; for example, a child may steal every time a favored younger sibling receives special attention from parents and teachers. This category is discussed under the label neurotic conduct disorder.*

SOCIALIZED, AGGRESSIVE TYPE* (DSM-III) OR SOCIOSYNTONIC PERSONALITY DISORDER (GAP REPORT)   This category was created in recognition of the fact that aggressive and antisocial behavior may not result from poor impulse control but from conformity to familial or group standards that deviate from those of society. For example, a boy may steal because his embittered, impoverished family believes that the poor have a right to take everything they can get from the rich. Thus antisocial behavior arises from antisocial socialization.

Attention-Deficit Hyperactivity Disorder* (DSM-III-R)

The essential feature is developmentally inappropriate inattention. The disorder has been variously called the Hyperkinetic Syndrome, the Hyperactive Child Syndrome,* or Minimal Brain Damage or Dysfunction.* The GAP Report regards hyperactivity primarily as a manifestation of chronic brain dysfunction, an idea that is more dated and less congruent with research findings than is the DSM-III-R classification. Hyperactivity in the young is manifested by gross motor activity such as excessive running or climbing; in older children it typically takes the form of extreme restlessness and fidgeting. Behavior has a haphazard, poorly organized quality.

Psychoactive Substance Dependence (DSM-III-R)

Psychoactive Substance Dependence is usually known as Drug Abuse.* Abuse, as contrasted with use, is marked by a significant impairment of social or occupational functioning caused by a pattern of pathological use (such as a need for daily use and an inability to cut down or stop despite repeated effort or serious physical damage) lasting at least one month.

Gender Identity Disorders (DSM-III-R) or Sexual Deviations (GAP Report)

This category should be employed only when the personality disturbance is sufficiently chronic and pervasive as to dominate the individual's orientation toward social life, since behaviors considered perversions in adults

may be part of normal development. Of the many deviations, we shall be discussing homosexuality* in detail. DSM-III-R defines Gender Identity Disorder as a persistent, intense distress about being one's own sex and a strong desire to be the opposite sex. There is a repudiation of one's own anatomic structures and a preoccupation with a stereotypic dress and activities of the opposite sex.

Disturbances Related to Bodily Functions

Both classifications address the disturbances related to bodily functions. We shall only sample the list from DSM-III-R.

Among Eating Disorders DSM-III-R lists anorexia nervosa,* which is an intense fear of becoming obese eventuating in a weight loss of at least 25 percent of original body weight; bulimia nervosa,* or recurrent episodes of binge-eating accompanied by an awareness of the abnormality of the eating pattern, fear of being unable to stop eating voluntarily, and a depressed mood; and pica, in which nonnutritive substances such as sand, bugs, leaves, or hair are persistently eaten. Under the heading Other Disorders with Physical Manifestations DSM-III-R lists functional enuresis,* or involuntary voiding of urine during the day or night after the child is 5 years of age; functional encopresis, or the repeated voluntary or involuntary passage of feces in inappropriate places after the child is 4 years of age; and sleeping terror disorder, or repeated episodes of abrupt awakening in a state of intense anxiety, which is relatively unresponsive to efforts of others to comfort the child.

Psychotic Disorders (GAP Report)

The GAP Report includes all the severe disturbances of childhood under the traditional classification of psychoses. DSM-III-R argues that because severe disturbances are so distinctive and—especially in the case of autism—have so little counterpart in adult psychopathology, it would be misleading to include them all under a classification derived from adult psychopathology. While agreeing with DSM-III-R, we shall follow the GAP Report as a matter of convenience, with the caveat that the term psychotic be interpreted as meaning a severe psychopathology.

In psychotic disorders there are marked, pervasive deviations in interpersonal relationships, thought, affect, perception, motility, speech, and individuation; for example, there may be severe and continued impairment of emotional relationships with others, associated with aloofness and a tendency toward preoccupation with inanimate objects; loss of speech or failure in its development; bizarre or stereotyped behavior; outbursts of intense, unpredictable panic; absence of a sense of personal identity; and a blunted, uneven, or fragmented intellectual development. The specific categories of psychoses are presented in order of their chronological appearance, since the nosological formulation is heavily predicated on developmental considerations.

The following constitute psychoses of infancy and early childhood.

INFANTILE AUTISM* (DSM-III-R) OR EARLY INFANTILE AUTISM (GAP REPORT)   This disorder has its onset during the first thirty months of life. The child is extremely aloof, shows little apparent awareness of other human beings, and is preoccupied with inanimate objects. Speech is delayed, absent, or not used for communication. There is a strong need to maintain sameness and resist change, temper outbursts or acute anxiety resulting from alterations in routine. Stereotyped and bizarre motor patterns are frequent.

INTERACTIONAL PSYCHOTIC DISORDER (GAP REPORT)   Many of these children have developed adequately in the first year or two of life but subsequently show unusual dependence on the mother, evidenced by intense separation anxiety and clinging, together with other regressive behaviors including the giving up of communicative speech. This category includes symbiotic psychosis.*

The psychoses of later childhood include:

SCHIZOPHRENIFORM PSYCHOTIC DISORDER (GAP REPORT)   This disturbance usually is not seen until the child is between 6 and 12 years of age. The clinical picture may include marked withdrawal, intense involvement in fantasy, low frustration tolerance. Intellectually there may be inappropriately concrete thinking, looseness of association, and a breakdown of reality testing. Bizarre behavior and stereotyped motor patterns such as whirling are present. True hallucinations are not common until the later school-age period. Onset may be gradual, or there may be a sudden, acute eruption marked by intense anxiety, uncontrollable phobias, marked withdrawal, and distorted reality testing. This disturbance will be discussed under the heading Childhood Schizophrenia.*

The psychoses of adolescence include:

ACUTE CONFUSIONAL STATE (GAP REPORT)   This disorder is characterized by a rather abrupt onset, with acute, intense anxiety, depressive trends, and confused thinking. The adolescent's sense of identity is disturbed, but there is not the kind of bizarre ideation that would indicate a breakdown of reality testing. The adolescent can also maintain meaningful emotional relationships and adaptive capacities, although both may be unstable. The prognosis for a relatively quick recovery is good.

SCHIZOPHRENIC DISORDER, ADULT TYPE* (GAP report and DSM-III)   The traditional adult classifications of disorganized (or hebephrenic), catatonic, and paranoid schizophrenia can be seen in adolescents.

Disorganized (Hebephrenic) Schizophrenia is characterized by giggling, grimacing, or flat affect, absurd posturing, incoherent speech such as neologisms and word salads (a jumbling of words and phrases in a meaningless manner), delusions, and hallucinations. Because the behavior is both blatantly bizzare and disorganized, it conforms to the popular stereotype of being "crazy."

There are two types of Catatonic Schizophrenia. The first is marked by stupor, mutism, negativism, and/or waxy flexibility, in which the individuals may leave their limbs in positions imposed by another person for long periods of time as if they were a flexible, wax doll. The catatonic individual may be huddled in a painfully awkward position in a corner for long periods of time or may be standing rigid and immobile, staring blankly ahead. Catatonic excitement is marked by incessant, highly excited, driven activity, at times spilling over into violent behavior.

The Paranoid Schizophrenic is characterized by systematized delusions and hallucinations. There may be persecutory delusions or delusions of grandiosity; for example, the individual believes he is Napoleon or Christ or some other famous figure. Hallucinations may consist of faces in the dark or voices that complement the individual's delusional systems.

Other Disorders of Infancy, Childhood, and Adolescence (DSM-III-R)

REACTIVE ATTACHMENT DISORDER OF INFANCY OR EARLY CHILDHOOD (DSM-III-R) This psychopathology is characterized by markedly disturbed social relatedness, either in the form of disinterest or indiscriminate sociability, such as excessive familiarity with relative strangers. The disturbance is due to grossly pathogenic care which may take the form of neglect or privation,* brutal treatment or physical abuse,* or sexual abuse.*

IDENTITY DISORDER (DSM-III-R) This adolescent disturbance is characterized by severe distress because of uncertainty about long-term goals, career choice, sexual orientation, friendship patterns, moral values, and group loyalties. Social, academic, and occupational functioning are significantly impaired. We will be dealing with the topic under the heading Identity Diffusion.*

Psychological Factors Affecting Physical Condition (DSM-III-R) or Psychophysiological Disorders (GAP Report)

More popularly termed psychosomatic disorders, psychophysiological disorders result from the interaction between somatic and psychological components. Psychophysiological disorders may be precipitated and perpetuated by psychological stress. Unlike the simple physiological concomitants of emotion involved in "fight or flight," psychophysiological disorders involve structural changes continuing to the point of being irreversible or even life-threatening. There is no specific personality type or interpersonal interaction characteristic of individual psychophysiological disorders, such as "the ulcer type" of child; rather, diverse psychological as well as physiological factors play varying roles. The more common psychophysiological disorders are neurodermatitis, "tension" headaches, bronchial asthma, essential hypertension, peptic ulcer, and ulcerative colitis. Psychological factors may be minimally implicated in some disorders while playing a major role in others. It would therefore be a mistake to regard these disorders as exclusively psychogenic; rather, the relative role of psychological and somatic factors must always be considered. This interplay will be discussed under the topic of Pediatric Psychology.*

Organic Mental Syndrome (DSM-III-R) or Brain Syndrome* (GAP Report)

The disorders included here are caused by impairment of brain tissue, particularly that of the cerebral cortex. They are characterized by impairment of orientation and cognitive functions, such as judgment, discrimination, learning, and memory, as well as by lability of affect. In addition, there may be personality disturbances associated with the basic syndrome, such as psychotic or neurotic manifestations. The child's age and personality prior to the brain impairment are important in determining the kind and degree of disturbance as well as the prognosis.

Mental Retardation* (DSM-III-R and GAP Report)

Mental retardation involves both significantly subaverage general intellectual functioning and deficits in adaptive behavior. There are three major groups of retardates.

The biological group includes conditions of known etiologic factors affecting brain function, such as prenatal infections and toxic influences, birth trauma, metabolic disturbances, and congenital abnormalities such as Down's syndrome (mongolism).*

The environmental group includes retardation primarily owing to sociocultural factors, such as inadequate intellectual stimulation in economically and educationally deprived families and retardation resulting from psychological disturbances, such as severe anxiety or significant emotional deprivation.

The intermediate group includes retardation arising from both biological and environmental factors.

Specific Developmental Disorders (DSM-III-R) or Developmental Deviations (GAP Report)

Because individuals differ, we should expect children to vary both in their overall rates of development and in their progress through the components of personality delineated in chapter 2. The image of the well-rounded child is an ideal; most normal children are advanced in some areas, while lagging in others. However, beyond a certain difficult-to-define point, the range of normal variation is exceeded. The child may then be classified as having a developmental deviation. Biological factors such as heredity, constitution, or maturation play an important but not an exclusive etiologic role, since environmental influences may also be involved. The child does not have the kinds of brain damage delineated in the section on brain syndrome nor is there the generalized developmental lag characteristic of the mentally retarded. Finally, the deviations are not predominantly physical in nature, such as those found in delayed growth or precocious puberty.

Some of the developmental disorders are: deviations in motor development, such as poor coordination or significant delays in motor milestones such as walking; deviations in language and speech development, including both infantile speech and marked limitations in expressing oneself verbally or understanding the verbal communications of others; and deviations in cognitive functions, or what we shall call learning disabilities,* which hamper academic progress in reading,* arithmetic, and spelling.

Our coverage of the DSM-III-R and the GAP Report has not been exhaustive since we have concentrated on the disorders relevant to our developmentally oriented viewpoint. The original publications should be consulted for a comprehensive account as well as for richer descriptive pictures than have been presented here. However, we are now sufficiently acquainted with the nature and range of childhood psychopathologies to turn to the issue of their persistence over time.

Table 3.1 presents a summary of the psychopathologies in relation to the context of time and the development of relevant personality variables.

LONGITUDINAL STUDIES

Because the best evidence concerning persistence comes from longitudinal studies, we need to learn about the methodological issues involved in collecting such data. In the process we shall gain a better understanding than we now have of what it means for a child to outgrow or not to outgrow disturbed behavior.

The Continuity of Behavior

The issue of the persistence of psychopathology is one aspect of the general problem of continuity of behavior, which lies at the heart of developmental psychology (see Hetherington and Parke, 1986). The discussion of personality variables in chapter 2 demonstrated that continuity is not a simple matter of the constant recurrence of a specific behavior. Developmental forces reshape manifestations of the same variable so that, for example, the toddler's temper tantrum becomes the highly organized vengeance of rival street gangs. At the very least, manifest behaviors must be organized into *categories* relevant to psychopathology, and the developmental course of these categories charted.

Such a model is still too simple, however, because it only allows room for categories of pathological behavior to continue or to disappear over time. In reality, one kind of psychopathology may be replaced by another: an enuretic preschooler may become a depressed underachiever in middle childhood; a truant from school may turn to drug abuse; or a psychotic adolescent may pull together and become an adequately functioning obsessive-compulsive neurotic. Thus we must be on the lookout for *systematic relationships* among psychopathologies within the developmental context and, if possible, evaluate how such relationships affect the child's prognosis in terms of making it more favorable or unfavorable.

Finally, continuity must be evaluated with and without *therapeutic intervention*. As we shall see, certain psychopathologies are responsive to remedial measures, others are not. Understandably, the more severe the disturbance, the more difficult it is to alter its course.

Research Strategies

THE RETROSPECTIVE STRATEGY A time-honored method of gathering developmental data is the *interview* in which a disturbed adult or the parents of a disturbed child are systematically questioned for historical information; the origins of the psychopathology are subsequently reconstructed from such data. Despite its popularity among clinicians and researchers alike, much retrospective data are of questionable reliability and validity. In order for a parent to be a satisfactory informant, he or she must accurately observe the behaviors a clinician will deem important (without foreknowledge of what behaviors these might be), preserve the observations in memory over a considerable period of time, and recall them intact on being questioned. Such an image befits a computer better than it does a human being, who is apt to distort

Chronological time	The Context of Time						
	Developmental periods	Piagetian stages	Freudian stages	Eriksonian stages	Attachment	Initiative and Work	Self-co
Birth	Infancy: 0–12 months	Sensorimotor: 0–2 years	Oral	Trust *vs.* mistrust	Social smile, 3–4 months Attachment: separation anguish, hostility, 6–9 months	Exploration; self-as-agent; battle of bottle and spoon	Not requi
— 1 year —	Toddlerhood: 1–2½ years						
— 2 years —		Preoperational: 2–6 years	Anal	Autonomy *vs.* shame, doubt		Willful, negativistic; battle of the potty	Low: "terrible t
— 3 years —	Preschool age: 2½–6 years					Expansion of skills: verbal, social, intellectual, etc.	Increasing
— 4 years —							
— 5 years —			Phallic Oedipal	Industry *vs.* inferiority			
— 6 years —	Middle childhood: 6–11 years	Concrete operations: 6–11 years	Latency	Initiative *vs.* guilt	Fluctuation	School: requiredness, impersonality, product orientation	High
— 7 years —							
— 8 years —							
— 9 years —							
— 10 years —							
— 11 years —	Preadolescence: 11–13 years	Formal operations: 11 years on			Vigorous denial		Low
— 12 years —							
— 13 years —	Adolescence: 13–18 years		Genital	Identity *vs.* role diffusion	Emancipation	Vocational choice; identity	Increasing
— 14 years —							
— 15 years —							
— 16 years —							
— 17 years —							
— 18 years —	Young adulthood: 18–20 years			Intimacy *vs.* isolation	Rapprochement		High
— 19 years —							
— 20 years —							

Personality Variables *

Conscience		Cognition		Anxiety	Sex		
tive	Affective	Causality	Social, Self		Gender	Erotic Feelings	Psychosexual Developments
		Omnipotence of action		Innate			Mouth libidinized; object relation
			Egocentrism				Anus libidinized; autonomy
ealism: , rigid, entional	Guilt (Freudian theory)	Omnipotence of words; precausal thinking		Innate declines Dark, imaginary creatures, etc.; defense mechanisms (timetable uncertain)	Determined by external clues; changeable	Masturbation; sexual curiousity	Genitals libidinized; exhibitionism; castration anxiety; Oedipus complex
of tion; ional	Punishment is sole concern		Social perspective taking; cooperation; communication; reflection	Realistic and imaginary, supernatural dangers	Determined by genitals; immutable		Diminution of sexuality
	Troubled; confesses; others' reactions are important						
	Guilt: self-oriented regardless of others	Realistic grasp of physical causality		Age-appropriate: prestige, sex, responsibility, etc. Some unrealistic fears		Central concerns: information, techniques, adequacy, love	Revival of earlier conflicts
pted inciples							
							Integration of previous stages into mature love

*Each entry marks the *beginning* of a continuous developmental process.

Chronological time	Personality Variables (continued) *			
	Aggression	Social Relations		
		Sociability	Friendship	Groups
Birth	Rage differentiated from distress (6 months)	Interest in peers		
— 1 year —	Peak for uncontrolled aggression; age-appropriate provocations		Unreciprocated "friendships"	
— 2 years —				
— 3 years —	Intentional attack, tantrums, retaliation			
— 4 years —		Cooperative play	Insubstantial, activity oriented	Insubstantial play group
— 5 years —				
— 6 years —	Increasingly verbal-symbolic, intentional, retaliatory; age-appropriate provocations	Accommodation to others; respectworthiness	More sustained, other oriented; superficial	Gangs: identifiable unit
— 7 years —				
— 8 years —				
— 9 years —				
— 10 years —				
— 11 years —	Immature modes reappear, e.g., tantrums			
— 12 years —				
— 13 years —	Verbal expressions predominate: name calling, sarcasm, etc.; age-appropriate provocations		Sustained; personalized; sharing, frank, critical	Stable groups with pote control: clique, crowd, gang
— 14 years —				
— 15 years —				
— 16 years —				
— 17 years —				
— 18 years —				
— 19 years —				
— 20 years —				

*Each entry marks the *beginning* of a continuous developmental process.

Onset of Psychopathologies†

tism: 0–30 months

Depression: any age
Brain syndrome: any age
Mental retardation: any age

a: 1–2 years

mbiotic psychosis:
years

tention-deficit — Oppositional disorder: 3 years; more common
peractivity disorder: in middle childhood and adolescence
dler/preschool period

opresis: 4 years — Sleep terrors: 4 years

uresis: 5 years
paration anxiety disorder:
school period

hool phobia: Learning disabilities: — Schizophreniform psychotic
years   beginning school years   disorders: 6 years

sonality disorders: middle — Psychoneurotic disorders:
dhood and adolescence   middle childhood, but more
       — usual in adolescence

version symptoms:
dle childhood, but more
ically in adolescence

nduct disorders: ———— Homosexuality: ———— Drug abuse:
eadolescence   early adolescence   early adolescence

———————————— Suicide: increases in —— Substance abuse:
choses of adolescence   adolescence   adolescence

orexia nervosa: ———— Bulimia: adolescence
lescence

ntity disorder: late ——— Anorexia nervosa:
lescence   adolescence

†Our entries follow DSM-III-R. Special qualifications are noted following specific psychopathologies.

information at all three stages even when the parent and child are psychologically sound—let alone if they are disturbed. While *retrospective data* may contain initial leads as to which intra- and interpersonal variables may be fruitful to study, they are currently considered an inadequate basis for understanding the origins and developmental course of childhood psychopathologies (Yarrow, Campbell, and Burton, 1970).

The reaction against retrospective data has spurred an interest in techniques that evaluate the child at two different points in time, Time 1 and Time 2. The interval should be sufficient to capture general developmental trends, while the evaluations should be independently conducted by individuals who are more objective than parents. Two of the most popular strategies are the *follow-back* and the *follow-up* study, both of which eliminate a number of the deficiencies of retrospective data, although they have limitations of their own.

THE FOLLOW-BACK STRATEGY   Like the retrospective approach, the follow-back study begins with a population of disturbed children or adults but obtains Time 1 data from records kept by observers other than parents: school records, teachers' assessments, child guidance case studies, court records, and so forth. A control group should also be selected, say, from the next name in the list of classmates or clinic patients, in order to narrow the variables relevant to the psychopathology being studied. For example, one might find that parental death, while hypothetically an important precursor of a given pathology, occurred no more frequently in disturbed children than in a control group.

In the follow-back study, not only can the investigator immediately focus on the target population, but also the strategy has a flexibility that allows the pursuit of new etiologic leads as they emerge. As we shall soon see,

the follow-up strategy has neither advantage. However, the follow-back strategy has a number of limitations. The *data* may be uneven in quality, some being comprehensive and reflecting a high degree of professional competence, others being skimpy and distorted by conceptual or personality biases. The data also tend to be gross—for example, number of arrests, decline in school grades, intact or broken family, number of job changes—lacking both the detail and the interrelatedness of variables found in an in-depth evaluation.

Other problems concern design and *population bias* in particular. Clinical populations may not be representative of disturbed children in general. To take one example: parents who seek professional help for a child with a school phobia may be different from those who do not, so findings from a clinical population cannot be generalized to all parents of phobic children. Or again, children who are arrested may not be a representative sample of all youthful offenders, because police officers have their own biases as to whom they arrest and whom they let go.

More important, reliance on child guidance and court records bias the data in terms of accentuating pathology and exaggerating relationships found at Time 1 and Time 2. To illustrate: one follow-back study indicated that 75 percent of alcoholics had been truants, compared with 26 percent of healthy individuals—a highly significant difference; yet, a follow-up study revealed that only 11 percent of truants became alcoholics, compared with 8 percent of the nontruant population that became alcoholic. Thus truancy can have a variety of outcomes, its particular association with alcoholism being too weak for predictive purposes. In general, follow-up studies, which capture the variability of development, show fewer relations among Time 1 and Time 2 variables than do follow-back studies, which select especially disturbed individuals.

THE FOLLOW-UP STRATEGY What could be a more ideal method of charting children's development than the follow-up strategy? The resulting longitudinal data should reveal which children develop what psychopathologies, together with the fate of the population with and without intervention. The children may be evaluated at Time 1 and Time 2 only, or at regular intervals as was done in the Berkeley Growth Study. Instead of being at the mercy of extant records as with follow-back studies, the investigator can insure that data will be gathered by well-trained investigators using the best available evaluative techniques.

Yet the follow-up study has a number of disadvantages. It is extremely *costly* in terms of time, money, and expenditure of effort. Investigators are bedeviled with the problem of *attrition;* not only do they lose track of subjects, but they may do so selectively, the most disturbed, unstable families or children tending to move around, move away, or be uncooperative. Thus researchers may be faced with a dwindling number of people in the very population they are most interested in studying. Population *selectivity* is another problem. Because most psychopathologies are rare, large numbers of children must be evaluated at Time 1 to insure a reasonable number of disturbed ones at Time 2. As one solution, many investigators begin with a disturbed population or with a population at risk for developing a given psychopathology, such as infants of schizophrenic mothers, who have a greater likelihood of becoming schizophrenic than do infants from an unselected population. However, such selectivity may introduce the same population bias we noted in the follow-back design.

Moreover, the follow-up study is *rigid.* Once having selected variables to study, the design does not allow the investigator to drop some and add others as results from relevant studies come in or as new theories and concepts come to the fore. Moreover, new measurement techniques may be devised which are superior to the ones in use but cannot be substituted for them.

One final problem with follow-up studies is the so-called *cohort effect;* one cannot assume that groups born at different times are equivalent, since the time of birth may significantly affect development. Children born in times of war or depression are not necessarily comparable to those born in times of peace and prosperity, just as children born before television or the sexual revolution or the feminist movement grew up in a different environment than those born afterward. Thus the results of a twenty-year longitudinal study may or may not be applicable to the current population of children.

The cohort effect may confound the *cross-sectional* approach to gathering developmental data, which consists of studying different age groups at one point in time. Although these groups may be equated for all the variables thought to be important, they cannot be equated for differential experiences which they might have had because of their time of birth. For example, the parent-child relationship of a group of 14-year-old boys who grew up during the Vietnam war might differ significantly from a group of 7-year-old boys who grew up after the war.

One solution to the confounding of developmental with cohort effects is the so-called *longitudinal, cross-sectional approach.* In this design children at different ages are studied as in the cross-sectional approach but are subsequently followed until the children in the younger groups are the same age as those in the next older groups; for example, groups of 3-, 6-, and 9-year-olds can be followed for three years, so that the 3-year-olds are now 6 and the 6-year-olds are 9. Such a design allows one to compare the age trends obtained cross-sectionally with longitudinal data. The saving in time is obvious; a longitudinal study that would have had to follow the 3-year-olds for six years can now be accomplished in half the time. As with any design, this one is not foolproof, because problems in equating groups and in selective loss of subjects remain. (For an example of the longitudinal, cross-sectional study, see Klausmeier and Allen, 1978.)

EVALUATION While the follow-up and follow-back strategies are an improvement over the retrospective approach, neither is a panacea. Because of its flexibility, the follow-back strategy is most suited to generating hypotheses. Leads as to possible significant antecedents can subsequently be accepted or rejected as they are put to further tests. However, follow-up studies, because of their ability to monitor the child's development while it actually occurs, provide the most convincing data concerning change. This strategy also comes closest to testing causal relations among variables, although because it is basically naturalistic rather than experimental, it cannot provide the kind of manipulation and control of variables essential to the establishment of causation. (For a more detailed presentation of longitudinal strategies, see Garmezy and Streitman, 1974.)

One final cautionary note: the design of follow-up and follow-back studies has only recently received the attention it deserves. Consequently, our review of longitudinal research will include studies of varying degrees of methodological sophistication and results with varying degrees of conclusiveness. While containing the most important leads as to the developmental course of childhood psychopathology, the findings reviewed should be regarded as tentative.

The Findings

First, the continuities among psychopathologies will be examined, including those that are behaviorally consistent or consistent within categories of behavior, and those that change from one classification of psychopathology to another. Then the discontinuities or the psychopathologies which the child "grows out of" or "grows into" by adulthood will be presented. The primary concern will be with long-range predictions from childhood into adulthood, although occasionally developmental trends within childhood itself will be dealt with. (This presentation is based on Gelfand, Jenson, and Drew, 1988, and Robins, 1979.)

THE CONTINUITIES The three deviations with the greatest degree of continuity from childhood to adulthood are the psychotic disorders, undersocialized, aggressive behavior, and severe mental retardation.

The *psychoses* of infancy and early childhood have a gloomy prognosis, although even here one-quarter to one-third of the children make an adequate adult adjustment with or without treatment. The deviant behavior of those who do not recover may well change while still remaining in the psychotic category; for example, an autistic preschooler may no longer evidence the classic signs as an adult, but may be diagnosed as a simple or undifferentiated schizophrenic. More provocative is the finding that around one-quarter of the psychotics who fail to recover develop clear evidence of organic brain pathology, even though none was present earlier. Finally, the prognosis for schizophrenia in adolescence is as poor as it is for the early psychoses.

Undersocialized, aggressive behavior after 6 years of age becomes predictive of subsequent aggressive-antisocial behavior in the adolescent period; specifically, disobeying the teacher, cheating, unpopularity because of fighting and quarreling, poor school work, and truanting are predictive of what is popularly called juvenile delinquency. Neurotic symptoms such as "nervousness," nail biting, bed-wetting, and thumb sucking are unrelated but not incompatible with becoming a delinquent; some delinquents rate high on the anxiety-withdrawal dimension.

Undersocialized, aggressive behavior in adolescence, in turn, is predictive of a host of acting-out behaviors affecting every area of the adult's life—criminality, vagrancy, excessive drinking, marital friction, promiscuity, and gambling. About half the children evidencing undersocialized, aggressive behavior will continue such behaviors into adulthood, although there is no way of predicting which children will do so. Robins (1979) concludes that "if one could successfully treat the antisocial behavior of childhood, the problems of adult crime, alcoholism, divorce, and chronic unemployment might be significantly diminished" (p. 509). The implicit irony is that there is relatively little interest in or funding for helping undersocialized, aggressive children.

An interesting example of continuity of disturbance but discontinuity of behavior is *adult schizophrenia,* which is characterized by emotional withdrawal, anxiety, and thought disturbances in the form of delusions and hallucinations. None of the characteristics are found in children destined to become schizophrenic as adults. The prevalent belief to the contrary, there is no evidence that the shy, withdrawn child is apt to develop schizophrenia—or any other adult psychopathology for that matter. On the contrary, the at-risk child evidences both acting-out and withdrawal behaviors and is characterized as unstable, irritable, aggressive, resistant to authority, seclusive, friendless, and given to daydreaming. The conceptual bridge between such behaviors and adult schizophrenia remains to be built (Ledingham, 1981).

School adjustment, which includes both academic achievement and attendance, is moderately related to adult adjustment, although, obviously, the specific behaviors involved are different. On the positive side, absence of both underachievement and serious truancy predicts a high level of adult success in slum-dwelling children; on the negative side, the presence of these problems in similar populations predicts problems with the police, sexual misbehavior, and problem drinking. Sadly, truancy in both sexes predicts having children who will also be truant.

The limited data on *sexual behavior* present a mixed picture in regard to the continuity-discontinuity dimension. There is no evidence that the sexually deviant boy will grow up to become the adult who engages in sex crimes. Thus there is discontinuity in regard to specific sexual behavior. However, to the extent that sexually deviant behavior is evidence of poor self-control and a tendency to act out, it is predictive of adult antisocial behaviors, which may include sex crimes along with other criminal, irresponsible behavior (Kohlberg, LaCrosse, and Ricks, 1972). Thus self-control rather than sexuality per se becomes the predictive variable. The same findings hold true of girls, except that in addition to antisocial behavior the sexually deviant girl is also likely to become the hysterical woman. This relation between sexual problems and hysterically determined body dysfunctions has been noted from the time of the Greeks to Freud.

Finally, there is a relation between the sheer quantity of problems and subsequent disturbance even if each problem taken alone is not sufficiently potent to be predictive. Thus if children have nine or more specific problems, they are at risk for developing some form of psychopathology in the future.

THE DISCONTINUITIES Aside from the early psychoses and severe mental retardation, problem behavior in the toddler/preschool period tends not to be a good prognosticator of subsequent disturbances, although the evidence is not wholly consistent on this point. Such unpredictability is congruent with the fluidity of early development. Around 6 or 7 years of age predictability increases, children with many symptoms at one age tending to have many symptoms later as well.

In contrast with undersocialized, aggressive behavior, a wide range of *neurotic behaviors* tends to be "outgrown" by adulthood, since anxiety-withdrawal disorders have a good prognosis. Not only is the shy, withdrawn, inhibited child unlikely to become a neurotic adult, but adult adjustment is likely to be as good as that of a random sample of the normal population. Other behaviors that tend not to persist are nervous habits such as nail biting, sleep disturbances, and eating problems such as food pickiness and refusal to eat (but not obesity and anorexia). The only cloud in this sunny picture is the finding that preadolescent boys (aged 11 to 13) who are introverted, shy, and somber and preadolescent girls who are excessively modest, dependent, and finicky eaters tend to be maladjusted adults.

The findings from a recent follow-up study of 200 adults seen ten to fifteen years earlier at a child guidance clinic underscore and elaborate on the summary just presented. Except for the extreme deviation of psychoses and excessive antisocial behavior, there was little continuity between child and adult disturbances. Childhood neurosis, which comprised the largest category of children, did not portend severe maladjustment in adulthood, with or without therapy. It was easier to predict health than maladjustment, since the healthier children were likely to continue to be so while the children with severe problems might either remain disturbed or improve. Severity of disturbance, social class, and IQ were significantly related to the degree of adult maladjustment. Sex was another predictive variable, withdrawn girls and aggressive, antisocial boys rating low on adult adjustment. In regard to age, the data indicated that problems in the preadolescent period (11- to 12-year-olds) and very early in life (before age 5) foreshadowed later maladjustment. In general, children receiving outpatient therapy failed to show a better social adjustment than those equally disturbed children who received no therapy. (For further details and an extensive discussion of the problems involved in follow-up research, see Cass and Thomas, 1979).

NORMAL CHILDREN   Even psychotic and antisocial, aggressive children who have the gloomiest prognosis are not all fated to become disturbed adults. But if disturbed children can "outgrow" their psychopathology, can normal children "grow into" disturbances as adults? The evidence suggests that this possibility exists. While the Berkeley Growth Study did not specifically address the issue of psychopathology, it was concerned with the kind of adjustment children made as adults. One investigator found that a group of able, confident, well-adjusted children turned out to be brittle, restless, puzzled adults (MacFarlane, 1964). A more statistically elegant analysis of the same data uncovered a type of gregarious, vigorous, cheerful adolescent boy who became a tense, touchy, hostile man, as well as a type of bright, driving, relatively mature adolescent girl who grew to be an isolated, rigid, pushy, depressive woman (Block and Haan, 1971). When aggressive behavior is discussed in chapter 9, data will be presented indicating that children rated as extremely high on adjustment in early childhood can be rated very aggressive or withdrawn a few years later.

The thought that certain well-functioning children are at risk for becoming disturbed is a tantalizing one. Just what are the telltale signs indicating that all is not as well as it appears to be? And even if we know these signs, what are the implications of informing the parents that such a child is at risk and needs help, as our concern with prevention would require? Such questions are so far from being answered as to be almost hypothetical. However, the developmental approach requires an equal concern with "growing into" as with "outgrowing" psychopathology. It may even be that understanding the former will provide important clues to understanding the latter.

INCIDENCE VERSUS DURATION   Robins (1979) makes an important distinction between variables that predict the incidence or likelihood of occurrence of various childhood psychopathologies and those that predict their duration. Let us take a brief look at the former.

Low socioeconomic status and broken homes have frequently been found to be associated with the now familiar constellation of antisocial, aggressive behavior and underachievement in school, although they are not related to anxiety, psychoneurosis, and psychophysiological (psychosomatic) symptoms. Closer scrutiny has revealed that it is parental behavior rather than socioeconomic status or broken homes per se which is highly correlated with psychopathology. Specifically, *antisocial parents* who quarrel, separate, and work at low-level occupations when they work at all are apt to have acting-out, low-achieving children. Such parents are more frequently found in the lower classes and in broken homes. Finally, having a large number of siblings has also been found to be associated with both antisocial behavior and poor school achievement and adjustment.

Psychiatric illness in parents increases the incidence of psychopathology in children. While it is difficult to disentangle the contribution of genetic from environmental factors, the passing on of problems from one generation to the next occurs at a rate well beyond chance for hyperactivity, school problems, delinquency, schizophrenia, and mental retardation. Genetic factors have been most clearly established in the cases of the last two disturbances. However, the generational picture is complicated by the fact that disorders other than the one exhibited by the parents also appear in their children more frequently than in the general population. A schizophrenic mother, for example, is more apt to have not only a schizophrenic child but one with various kinds of antisocial, acting-out behaviors such as convictions for felony, alcoholism, and drug abuse. Why this should be is not clear.

The above information concerning incidence or likelihood of occurrence is essential to the clinician and researcher concerned with *prevention* of psychopathology. However, the variables predicting incidence do not predict the duration of the psychopathology once it has occurred. Information concerning duration of psychopathology is crucial to the issue of *treatment* when a decision must be reached regarding whether therapeutic intervention is warranted and, if so, what measures can be taken to shorten the natural course of the psychopathology.

CONCLUDING REMARKS

This overview of diagnostic categories and longitudinal studies helps us appreciate the special fund of information a professional must have to make knowledgeable statements concerning *diagnosis* and *prognosis* epitomized by the statement, "Most children act like this and your child will outgrow it," or its more ominous version, "The behavior is unusual and your child should receive special help." We now have at least a working idea of what the psychopathologies are, when they are apt to appear, and the chances of their continuing, changing into other psychopathologies, or disappearing with time.

We have also ventured in a preliminary way into the realm of *prevention* and *treatment*. The longitudinal data suggest that special efforts should be directed toward eliminating or ameliorating the early psychoses, severe acting-out behavior, and mental retardation. Ironically, these are the very disturbances that are only fitfully responsive to even the most heroic therapeutic efforts and can be prevented only in special instances.

Equally as troublesome as the inadequacy of therapeutic techniques for children who need help most is the ethical issue of providing psychotherapy for that large group of anxious-withdrawn children who are apt to "outgrow" such behavior without treatment. Certainly the conscientious professional cannot recommend remedial measures on the basis that they will forestall even greater and more intractable trouble in the future—one of the bedrock reasons for treating children. Rather, the clinician must find other grounds for recommending treatment, such as a humanitarian concern that children should not suffer unduly, even if such suffering is temporary. Parents also have the right to be informed before treatment that the chances are in favor of the child's outgrowing his or her disturbance. They should also know that a probability statement is not a guarantee because there is always the possibility that a particular child will continue to be disturbed.

With such information parents can make an in formed decision whether to agree to treatment for their child.

The longitudinal overview has also dispelled any notion we might have had that children are easier to treat than adults. As with adults, some children respond readily to treatment, others are highly resistive. The decision to become a professional helper should be made on the basis of wanting to help children and finding such help intrinsically rewarding, not on the basis of an expectation that somehow the task will be an easy one.

We are now ready for a detailed exploration of selected psychopathologies. As much as possible we will take them in chronological order, using the information about normal development provided in chapter 2 to answer the question, How can this psychopathology be understood in terms of normal development gone awry? How deviations from normality at one point in time affect future development will also be discussed. This dual concern requires reconstructing the natural history of the psychopathology. Finally, the issue of the efficacy of psychotherapeutic measures in curtailing further deviance will be addressed. However, a systematic examination of psychotherapy will come only after our exploration of the psychopathologies is concluded.

4

Severe Deviations in Infancy: The Undermining of Normal Development

What lies at the heart of human development in the first two years of life? The establishment of the bond of love, surely, and curiosity, and symbolic communication culminating in speech. And what if all were wrenched from their normal course? One would rightly predict severe psychopathology. In fact, a number of such psychopathologies have been described under the general category of psychoses. Here, only two will be discussed: autism and childhood schizophrenia. First, their behavioral manifestations and effects on subsequent development will be outlined. Then, the knotty and unanswered etiologic question will be discussed, namely, What causes these deviant behaviors?

AUTISM

▄▄▄▄▄

YOU ARE a clinical child psychologist approaching a group of disturbed preschoolers in a play yard. From a distance they look surprisingly like any healthy, intelligent youngsters. You particularly notice a little girl on a swing. Her face is pensive. She has an ethereal beauty. You go up to greet her and start a friendly conversation. She does not look at you, nor does she look away. Rather, she looks through you

97

as if you did not exist. You are face to face, and she looks through you. If you were to put her on your lap, her body would not accommodate to yours, but she would sit as if you were a chair. If she needed you to do something, say, open a door, she would take your hand (rather than taking *you* by the hand) and bring it in contact with the doorknob. As a person you would not exist. ▬▬▬

The initial encounter with autistic children can be a shattering experience. Other disturbed children might ignore you or defy you or call you names or strike out or kick and bite, all of which are forms of relating. But to be impervious is different; it runs counter to the basic responsiveness of one human being to another.

In his classic paper, Kanner (1943) delineated the three essential features of early infantile autism. The first is *extreme isolation* and an inability to relate to people, as we have just seen. The second is a pathological *need for sameness*. This need applies both to the child's own behavior and to the environment. Often the child's activities are simple, such as sitting on the floor and rocking back and forth for long periods of time, or twirling his or her shoelaces, or running up and down a hall. Sometimes the activities resemble complex rituals, such as a 5½-year-old who takes a toy truck, turns it on its side, spins a wheel while making a humming noise, goes over to the window, looks out while drumming his fingers on the sill, and then returns to the truck, only to repeat the exact same sequence over and over. The need for environmental sameness can be expressed in a number of ways; for example, the child must have the exact same food and plate and utensils, or wear the same article of clothing, or have the same arrangement of furniture. The intensity of the need is evidenced not only by the rigidity of the behavior but also by the child's panic and rage when attempts are made to alter the environment even in

minor ways, such as providing a different food or moving a chair to a different part of the room. (For an example of such rigidity in a laboratory study, see Ferster and DeMyer, 1962.)

The third characteristic of autism is either *mutism or noncommunicative speech*. The latter may include echolalia, phrases or sentences that are irrelevant to the situation (for example, while repeatedly flushing the toilet, an autistic girl suddenly said, "The hamburgers are in the refrigerator!"), extreme literalness (when taught to say "Please" to get a cookie, an autistic boy would use the word only when he wanted a cookie, as if "please" and "cookie" had become inseparably linked), and personal-pronoun reversals, typically the child referring to himself as "you." Kanner (1946–1947) presents evidence that, in certain instances, seemingly irrelevant remarks are meaningful from the child's point of view. A 5-year-old would frequently say "Fifty-five," which seemed nonsensical until it was learned that his favorite grandmother was 55 years old and the number was his way of referring to her. Another autistic child said, "Don't throw the dog off the balcony," which again was seemingly irrelevant but referred to the fact that, three years previously, his mother had angrily said this when he was throwing a toy dog off the balcony. The first child was recalling a loving image that represented comfort to him; the second child was checking an impulse to throw something. Both children were not communicating because, instead of taking their listeners into account, they were living in and expressing a world of private meanings. Unless children can take the viewpoint of others, thereby relinquishing their egocentrism, they cannot communicate.

There are other behaviors that may be present in the autistic child, but not necessarily. Autistic children are frequently healthy and appear intelligent, judging by their facial expression. They also may have excellent rote memory and may perform remarkable feats of remembering names or tunes or pic-tures. Finally, they are at home and content in the world of physical objects rather than in the interpersonal world.

Kanner's 1943 paper is a prime example of the *naturalistic tradition* as implemented by means of the *clinical eye*. The descriptions remain vivid and fresh and can be read with profit many decades after they were written. As any good naturalist should, Kanner also took care to differentiate infantile autism from other conditions that might resemble it, schizophrenia in particular. But many clinicians share Kanner's keen eye for detail; what distinguishes him is his ability to organize these richly detailed clinical pictures into categories of behavior that define the psychopathology. Thus the clinical eye nourished a conceptualizing intellect. If today we can say, "of course" there is aloneness, sameness, and mutism, it is because Kanner opened our eyes to the "obvious." After all, autism has probably been in existence for centuries and had gone unnoticed, just as the cognitive developments in the sensorimotor stage had before Piaget. Kanner's *descriptive classification* of early infantile autism remains a scientific achievement of the first order.

Subsequent research has added important new information concerning autism while generally confirming Kanner's three defining characteristics (Prior and Werry, 1986). Although autistic behavior may be noted in early infancy, it can also appear after a period of up to thirty months of normal development. Oddly enough, its appearance is not necessarily associated with any particular precipitating event. The clinical impression of average or above average intelligence, based on the child's facial expression and feats of memory, has not been confirmed. Initially it was thought that the child's unrelatedness prevented the utilization of innate intelligence, but subsequent research found that retardation tends to persist over time when progress is made in social relations. Only one-fifth to one-quarter of autistic children have normal to borderline intelligence, the majority being moderately to severely retarded (Prior and Werry, 1986). Whether the thinking characteristic of retarded autistic children is peculiar to them or resembles that of comparably retarded, nonpsychotic children is not known. DeMyer (1976) found few meaningful differences in intellectual functioning between autistic and nonpsychotic subnormal 5- to 6-year-olds whose mean IQ scores were between 61 and 65. Admittedly, the findings are preliminary. While it was also initially thought that autism existed only in the middle class and was not inherited, subsequent studies showed it is found in all classes and that there is a genetic component not for autism per se, but for a predisposition to language and cognitive difficulties that form a part of autism (Rutter and Garmezy, 1983). Finally, autism can coexist with known organic brain pathologies. Out of 243 children who had been infected with congenital rubella (German measles) in utero, 10 had symptoms of autism along with organic defects such as visual, auditory, and neurological handicaps (Chess, 1971). In addition, both grand mal and psychomotor seizures develop in roughly one-quarter or more autistic children, compared with a 7 percent rate among children in general. Typically, the seizures do not appear until adolescence, and up until then there is no evidence of a neurological disorder (Rutter and Garmezy, 1983).

That autism can coexist with both mental retardation and known organic brain pathologies complicates, rather than solves, the task of understanding etiology. It would be unwarranted to claim that either one causes autism, because the majority of mentally retarded and organically damaged children do not evidence the full-blown syndrome described by Kanner (although individual behaviors that constitute the syndrome—such as social isolation—might appear separately in specific cases). The discovery of coexisting pathology means we must understand not only the etiology of "pure" cases of autism but also the special role mental deficiency and organic brain damage play in producing autism in given instances.

Developmental Course

One would correctly predict that so severe and pervasive a disturbance occurring so early in life would have ominous implications for future development. In summarizing eight follow-up studies of 474 autistic children, Lotter (1978) found that between two-thirds and three-quarters had poor outcomes, in that they continued to be severely disturbed, roughly 40 percent being institutionalized. The prognosis is worse than that of other severe childhood disturbances, such as borderline psychosis or mental deficiency. Speech, IQ scores, and severity of disturbance are the most potent predictors of future development—children who have not developed communicative speech by 5 years of age, who are untestable or have an IQ score below 60, and who are evaluated as being

severely disturbed will remain severely handicapped through life; those who achieve communicative speech by 5 years and have average intelligence stand only a fifty-fifty chance of making an adequate social adjustment as adults (Rutter and Garmezy, 1983). On the other hand, socioeconomic status, mental illness in the family, age of onset of autism, and the development of seizures are unrelated to outcome.

It is also possible to sketch a more differentiated developmental picture than is found in outcome studies (Miller, 1974; Rutter, 1978). Based on retrospective accounts of infancy, the following behaviors are absent, delayed, or qualitatively impaired: eye contact, posturing anticipatory to being picked up, smiling in recognition of a familiar person, vocalization, stranger anxiety, interest in early games such as peekaboo, pointing, and response to sound. The infant's body may be rigid and therefore difficult to cuddle, or flaccid to the point of "collapsing" or "melting" into the mother's body.

Autistic toddlers and preschoolers show few positive social responses. They do not follow or greet parents, or kiss and cuddle, or go to parents for comfort when hurt; but neither do they physically withdraw and avoid. Rather, they seem profoundly detached. Not only is language delayed, but babbling may also lack the richness and variety found in normal development. Understanding of language is also impaired; the child may follow a simple command if it is accompanied by a gesture, but not one that contains two ideas such as, "Go to your room and get your toy." There is no delight in "chatting" or in give-and-take conversation, and there is no infatuation with the magic of verbal communication. The child is deficient in social imitation (for example, waving bye-bye), in meaningful exploration of objects (being content to spin a wheel on a toy car or mouth it, for example), and in dramatic play such as "house" or "tea party." Play patterns tend to be limited and rigidly repeated.

In middle childhood the lack of social relatedness abates somewhat, but the children tend to be friendless, noncooperative, and lacking in empathy. While no longer impervious, their social responses are odd and inappropriate. In a like manner, they do not speak in a communicative way but talk *at* rather than *with* a person. What they say is often confined to the immediate situation. (Of course, certain children remain mute or have no intelligible speech.) Activities continue to be ritualistic, with adherence to strict routines and marked distress at slight deviations. Special preoccupations might appear, such as memorizing timetables.

Adolescence is a time of dramatic developments. Seizures appear in about one-quarter to one-third of the children, predominantly those with IQ scores below 65. At the other extreme, Kanner et al. (1972) found that the period could be one of significant improvement. Certain adolescents seem to realize that their behavior is deviant and make a conscious effort to act in an appropriate manner. Between 5 and 15 percent of autistic children achieve a satisfactory social and occupational adjustment, with or without therapy (Lotter, 1978). Typically, they cope with life by scrupulously sticking to the rules of acceptable behavior. Their speech, for example, may resemble that of certain foreigners who use flawless English but still sound rather stilted. Work and play have the same quality of being learned by rote without the freedom to vary and improvise which comes with full understanding. Adequately functioning adults know the letter of the law, but the spirit eludes them. They can be devoid of empathy and, significantly, seem generally indifferent to sexuality. On the positive side, their slavish devotion to rules and regulations can fit nicely into the demands of a bureaucratic society.

One final point: while the majority of autistic children continue to be severely disturbed, they do not become classically schizophrenic in the sense of having delusions and hallucinations. Whether there is a basic difference between autism and schizophrenia is a hotly debated issue to which we shall return.

Underlying Causes

There is a simple way to understand the primary features of autism: the major pleasures and interests of normal infants are aversive to autistic ones. In the first weeks of life a multitude of factors conspire to make the adult human the most attractive and pleasurable stimulus for the normal infant; e.g., the human voice quickly becomes preferred over all other sounds, and the patterning of the face, particularly the eyes, holds a special fascination; moreover the infant learns to adjust his or her body to that of the caretaker when held and to anticipate relief from distress when the caretaker comes into view. In addition, the need for variable stimulation lies at the heart of exploration of the environment, the infant being nicely constituted to seek ever more complex challenges as the simple ones are mastered. In autism, the very basis of cognitive and affective development is undermined so that avoidance and repetition replace approach and expansion.

In a most general way we have accounted for autism. Yet scientists are rarely satisfied with such generalities and continue to ask, "Yes, but why?" What has gone wrong to produce this negative image of normal development? At present the answers are legion, everything from blood platelets to social class being implicated. (For a review of these etiological hypotheses, see Schwartz and Johnson, 1985.)

Laboratory studies of etiology provide some of the best illustrations of the advantage of the *control of relevant variables* inherent in this research methodology. The discovery that a considerable number of autistic children might also be mentally retarded casts doubt on previous research by raising the question, Which aspects of these children's behavior are the result of autism per se and which are shared with the general population of retardates? The question, in turn, is part of the quest to find the psychological defects or deficiencies specific to autism. It can be answered by adding a control group of nonautistic retardates matched for mental age with the low-functioning autistic children. A further question can also be raised: To what extent is the behavior of low-functioning autistic children shared with a younger, normal population? In other words, does the observed behavior of the autistic group represent developmental delay or fixation, or does it represent a qualitatively distinct behavior having no counterpart in normal development? This question can be answered by adding a control group of normal children whose chronological age is matched with the mental age of the autistic children. Thus a study might be designed as shown in Table 4.1.

Table 4.1   Research Design Comparing Autistic, Mentally Retarded, and Normal Children

	Autistic Children	Mental Retardates	Normal Children
Chronological age	8	8	5
Mental age	5	5	5

One such study was conducted by Hermelin (1976), using 10- to 15-year-old autistic children with a mental age of about 5 years, matched with mental retardates with similar chronological and mental ages, and with normally developing 5-year-olds. In the first experiment, the children were presented with a card on which were two black rectangles, one large and one small. Then they were presented with a series of cue cards with either a large or small rectangle of the same size as the ones on the original card. The task was to match the rectangle on the cue card with the one on the original card. In this task the autistic children performed as well as the mentally retarded and normal children. Even when the cue card was first shown, then removed, so that the children had to match from memory, the autistic children performed as well as the normals and were superior to the retardates. Therefore there is nothing faulty in their basic ability to discriminate size. However, when a series of five black rectangles of differing sizes were presented in random order and the children were asked to arrange them from smallest to largest, the autistic children's performance was inferior to that of both other groups. This is only one of many instances in which the autistic child is capable of responding appropriately to simple stimuli but is hamstrung when dealing with complex patterning or ordering of stimuli.

The control the laboratory affords also allows the kind of highly refined exploration of a given psychological function that would be next to impossible using any other research methodology. Let us take memory, for example, since one could hypothesize that the autistic children's difficulty in coping with the physical and social environment might be owing to a memory defect. The laboratory approach allows the investigator systematically to vary many parameters of memory: the kind of material to be remembered, such as meaningful or nonsense; the interval of time for remembering the material, from immediate recall to varying periods of delay; and the mode of presentation of the material to be remembered, such as visual or auditory. Even more important, a laboratory approach can separate a memory defect from a defect in the initial intake of information; for example, an apparent deficiency in the recall of a list of words may be because the autistic children were able to take in fewer words than the other groups. Only when there is evidence that the groups are similar in the amount of information they can initially process can one properly attribute an inferior recall to a memory deficiency.

Prior and Chen's study (1976) illustrates this last point. The investigators made sure the autistic, mentally retarded, and normal groups were equally adept in the acquisition phase of the task before testing for recall. The study involved nine children in each group, all of whom had mental ages between 4½ and 5 years of age, with the autistic and retarded groups being approximately 10 years of age, the normal children around 4 years of age. The test material consisted of hollow blocks of various sizes, shapes, and colors. The blocks were presented two at a time, and the children were to guess which was the "correct" one. (The "correct" choice was arbitrarily determined before-hand by the researchers.) If they succeeded, they would receive a bit of candy hidden in the hollow. To illustrate: for a given child a small white pyramid might be the correct choice. This block would be paired with other blocks, such as a large white cube or a small black cylinder. Each child had to solve a number of such puzzles. In the initial phase of their research, the investigators demonstrated that the autistic children were as adept as the other children in learning the correct choices. Only then did the researchers vary the time between presentation of pairs from 30 to 60 to 120 seconds to test the effect of the length of interval on memory. They found that, while delay did significantly affect performance—the longer time intervals making it more difficult for the children to remember the correct responses—it affected all groups of children equally. Mental age rather than autism was the significant determiner of memory.

One final general point: laboratory research with any severely disturbed population, such as autistic or retarded or hyperactive children, presents special problems that do not arise in studies of less disturbed and normal children. It is essential that the investigator make sure that the disturbed children attend to the task, that they are motivated to perform it, and that they understand its nature. Without such safeguards, there is the danger that an inferior performance would be interpreted in terms of a psychological deficit or deviation when it may represent nothing more than a disinterest in or a resistance to performing the task at hand.

QUANTITATIVE   VERSUS   QUALITATIVE DIFFERENCE   The question whether psychopathology represents a quantitative or a qualitative difference from normality is a perennial one.   Generally speaking, the quantitative view is more prevalent: phobias are regarded as extremes of normal fears, delinquency is viewed as an exaggeration of normal adolescent rebelliousness.   The three major developmental models of psychopathology—fixation, regression, and developmental delay—are quantitative.   Yet DSM-III describes autism in terms of "severe qualitative abnormalities which are not normal for any stage of development" (American Psychiatric Association, 1980, p. 86).   This could mean that autistic behavior has no counterpart even in the behavior of younger, normal children and that the developmental sequencing of behavior does not follow that charted for normal children.

To evaluate the quantitative versus qualitative issue, Wenar et al. (1986) compared the development of 41 autistic children between 5 and 11 years of age with that of 195 normal children between 3 months and 5 years of age, using a standardized observational technique called the Behavior Rating Instrument for Autistic and other Atypical Children (BRIAAC).   The investigators found that severely autistic children's obliviousness to caretaking adults, their minimal expressiveness, their disinterest in or fleeting exploration of objects, their unresponsiveness or negative reaction to sound, and their indifference to social demands all indicated an imperviousness to the social and physical environment that had little counterpart in normal behavior and development.   How

ever, such qualitative differences were present only in the most severely disturbed autistic children; less disturbed ones and normal 2- to 3-year-olds shared the same developmental sequence but progressed at different rates so that autism could be regarded as "normal development in slow motion."

ATTENTION AND PERCEPTION   Autistic children do well on standard tests of hearing and vision and are capable of sustained attention. Thus they are not like deaf children, although they are sometimes mistaken for deaf because of their unresponsiveness; nor are they like hyperactive children, who have a specific deficit in sustaining attention.   Also, like normal children, they prefer looking at complex stimuli rather than simple ones.   Because autistic children can see and hear and attend to the environment, some other process must have gone wrong.

Unlike normal toddlers, who can modulate their responses to environmental stimulation, autistic children may be *extreme* and *erratic* in their reactions.   As infants they may be hyperirritable or too placid; as toddlers their bodies may be excessively rigid and their actions may have a driven quality, or they may be limp and inert like a sack of flour. They may scream in distress when a vacuum cleaner goes on, but then at another time prefer a louder sound than a normal child. They may be impervious to the speech of the adult standing next to them while listening intensely to the sound of a garbage truck two blocks away.   In a fit of rage a child may bite his arm and then look with detached wonder at the blood, showing no evidence of pain.

Some authors conceptualize this responsiveness in terms of a faulty *arousal mechanism*. (For a detailed presentation of the arousal hypothesis, see Schwartz and Johnson, 1985.) Others prefer to theorize in terms of an *imbalance between excitation and inhibition* in the brain (Miller, 1974). The insufficiently aroused child is comfortable assimilating only a small portion of available stimulation and gravitates toward simple activities that do not tax the meager supply of energy. If arousal or excitation is excessive, the child is readily overwhelmed by novel and complex stimuli; as a protection, many of the sights and sounds of the everyday environment are defensively blotted out through inattention or through clinging to the safety of simple repetitive activities. This latter hypothesis of hypersensitivity is the more popular one.

In their review of attention and perception, Prior and Werry (1986) conclude that "autistic children, like other groups with a variety of handicapping conditions, do not orient, focus, control, or sustain their attention effectively" (p. 170). Thus while not specific to autism, peculiarities in perception and attention play an important role in the overall picture of deviancy.

MEMORY Autistic children's short-term memory is intact, with regard to both visual and auditory material; for example, their ability to repeat a series of digits is age-appropriate. Until recently, it was believed that autistic children's long-term memory was deficient owing to their inability to use meaning so that, for example, a sentence would not be recalled any better than a list of random words. However, Fyffe and Prior (1978) showed that the ability to use meaning was not impaired in higher functioning autistic children and was at a lower level, rather than being absent, in lower functioning children. In general, there is little evidence of a memory-specific deficiency in autism.

LEARNING There is evidence that autistic children respond to reward and punishment, success and failure in operant conditioning experiments as do normal children. They also become more noncompliant or withdrawn as tasks become too difficult. However, stimulus overselectivity greatly restricts their progress as it does with retarded children, while their failure to generalize beyond the immediate learning situation may be even greater than in the retarded. Consequently, although autistic children do respond to operant techniques, their resistance to new learning is a pervasive one (Prior and Werry, 1986).

The research evidence clearly points to a deficit in *imitation* in autistic children regardless of their mental age level. Lovaas et al. (1979) vividly describe autistic children's failure to imitate even after each child had 1,000 trials of hearing a teacher say "phone" and observing a model pick up the phone. The children would learn only part of the response, such as merely touching the phone, or they would pick it up regardless of when the teacher gave the command. When we recall that imitation, along with classical and operant conditioning, is one of the three basic principles of learning, we can appreciate the magnitude of this particular deficit.

HIGHER-ORDER THINKING A number of hypotheses have been generated to account for the autistic child's higher-order thinking (Miller, 1974). One is that the children can take in information but cannot relate it to past experience; to use Piaget's term they cannot *assimilate*. Autistic children tend to echo rather than understand. One consequence is that thinking is concrete and situation-specific; for example, once a girl has learned that "ride" means leaving the house and getting into a particular car, she will be unable to grasp the idea that "going for a ride" can mean leaving from any place in any car.

Another hypothesis addresses itself to the autistic child's difficulty with comprehending verbal and nonverbal *symbols* and using them to communicate. One important function of symbolization is to release the child from his or her bondage to action; for example, the act of walking upstairs can be represented by the thought, "I can walk upstairs." Symbols can replace trial-and-error behavior as well; for example, the child can think, "My ball is not in the kitchen or the playroom but upstairs in my room, so I will go upstairs to get it," thus saving himself the necessity of going from one room to the next. Finally, symbols open the door to abstractions that have no specific referent in concrete reality, such as "right" and "wrong," "good" and "bad." For the autistic child, however, the basic idea that a sound or gesture can represent an object or activity does not fully register. Recall that the autistic infant will not imitate bye-bye gestures, the autistic toddler does not pretend to sweep the floor and set the table, and finally, symbolic play is impoverished in the autistic child's preschool period.

Another specific problem autistic children have is in *coding* and *organizing* stimuli in terms of patterns and rules. The amount of information from the social and physical environment impinging on any individual at any given time is prodigious. What prevents normal children from being overwhelmed is the fact that the information is not random, but patterned and meaningfully organized. While normal children are particularly adept at reducing information to manageable proportions by organizing it according to patterns and classes of events, autistic children are deficient in this respect. One can speculate that their repetitious, stereotyped behavior is an attempt to establish islands of predictability and stability in a potentially overwhelming environment.

LANGUAGE   Many of the perceptual, cognitive, and social deficiencies we have explored converge in the autistic child's acquisition and use of language, which is one reason it is so potent prognostically. In addition, autistic children do more poorly in certain aspects of language development than do retarded children, suggesting that something more than a cognitive delay is involved. Autistic children may go about mastering the various components of language in idiosyncratic ways, and these components may also be acquired in a disjointed manner, rather than in the synchronistic manner observed in normal children. (For a detailed account of autistic language as normal development gone awry and of treatment implications, see Schopler and Mesibov, 1985).

Prosody, according to linguists, is the melody of speech. Normal infants make remarkable progress in discriminating and imitating speech sounds. They may be innately programmed to discriminate human speech from other sounds, and their subsequent babbling will have the rhythm and melody of speech, even though the content is meaningless. Moreover, prosody provides valuable clues to phrases and sentence boundaries, both of which are signaled by a fall/rise pattern in fundamental frequencies. The structure of language would be much more difficult for infants and toddlers to grasp if we spoke in a monotonous, robotlike fashion with each word intoned exactly as the preceding one. Prosody also helps direct attention to the most important elements of an utterance and signals the speaker's attitudes and mood.

While not all autistic children are deviant in the use of prosody, and while such an abnormality in itself would not undercut language development, a number of autistic children do have a deficit that, when taken in conjunction with other deficits, can make language difficult to comprehend. Lacking the clues for analyzing speech into meaningful units, some autistic children are forced to learn whole phrases that are used in a rigid, echolalic manner. The lack of discrimination of units also blocks the flexible recombining of such units into new ways to express new meanings. (For a detailed presentation of prosodic development in normal and autistic children, see Baltaxe and Simmons, 1985.)

Syntax is the way words are combined to produce meaningful sentences. The evidence indicates that while autistic children may lag behind normal children, they are no different from children at a comparable intellectual level. In both production and understanding, autistic children display mastery of a variety of grammatical rules. The girl who said, "The hamburgers are in the refrigerator" while flushing the toilet repeatedly was not communicating, but her sentence was grammatically correct. (See Tager-Flusberg, 1985.)

Semantics involves the meaning of words and sentences, and it is here that the autistic flaws appear. When dealing with concrete objects, autistic children may be developmentally delayed, but no more so than a comparable group of retarded children; for example, they know that the category "fish" includes a bluefish and a shark, might include a seahorse, but would not include a padlock. Thus autistic children do not acquire idiosyncratic word meanings, but show the same pattern of generalization of meaning as children at a comparable developmental level (Tager-Flusberg, 1985). However, words that are not anchored in concrete reality present difficulties. While the normal toddler's vocabulary contains a wide range of experiential and social terms, such as "bye-bye," "all gone," "up," and "dirty," the autistic child's vocabulary typically relates to static aspects of the environment such as inanimate objects and food.

This general difficulty with words that do not refer to concrete objects and the attendant specific difficulty with relational words continues throughout childhood. While the normal preschooler masters such relational words as "big" and "small," the autistic child has great difficulty, tending to treat them as absolute qualities, so that "big" becomes as much a characteristic of a given object as its shape. By the same token, active verbs that refer to some clearly perceived ongoing event, such as eating, are more easily grasped than ones that have no specific physical referent, such as "want," "like," and "believe." While autistic children use the present tense as frequently as normal children do, their use of the past tense is significantly depressed. Prepositions such as "beside" or "in" are troublesome because they are not characteristics of objects but denote relations among objects. "I" and "you" present special problems because they have shifting referents depending on the speaker rather than consistently designating a single person. Even high functioning autistic children have difficulty in double classifications, which involve two people doing two different things at the same time; for example, "I have a ball and am sitting down; you have a bat and are standing up." Each idea can be grasped separately but cannot be entertained simultaneously.

Thus we can see progressively complex steps in learning language. The simplest rule is this: one word, such as "chair," stands for one object. Relational words, such as "on" or "I," are difficult because they do not refer to a single object or person. Multiple classifications of a single object are baffling (for example, a "white chair" presents problems because other objects may be white without being chairs and chairs need not be white), while double classifications are more baffling still. The patterning of words to produce sentences, the ordering of phrases within sentences, and the relations among sentences produce even greater obstacles in terms of analyzing and integrating information (Menyuk, 1978). Finally, it follows that holding a conversation, which requires a constant shift of perspective from self to others, presents extreme difficulties to an autistic child. (For a detailed presentation of semantic problems in autistic children, see Menyuk and Quill, 1985.)

COMMUNICATION   Speaking is more than understanding and ordering verbal symbols, however; it is communication as well. Normal infants are quick to grasp the notion of communication via expressive sounds. Within the first three months they can take turns vocalizing with their caretaker and, by the end of the first year, they can vocalize to indicate needs and feelings as well as to socialize. The socially isolated autistic child has no such need to communicate. It has been noted, for example, that autistic children are impoverished in their use of gestures to communicate even when such gestures are within their repertoire (Prior and Werry, 1986). Thus the cognitive problem of symbolization is compounded by a motivational problem of disinterest. Moreover, even when children have mastered the basic rules of combining words into meaningful sentences, they still may have trouble with *pragmatics*, the social context of language, which involves learning when to say what to whom to communicate effectively and to achieve an underlying objective. In fact, pragmatic deficits are found even in high functioning autistic children, suggesting that they are specific to the disturbance; autistic children have been described as talking *at* others rather than talking *to* them in the sense of engaging in reciprocal exchanges, and they do not explain matters well. Objective studies indicate that they have significantly less socialized speech and significantly more egocentric speech than matched groups of normal, retarded, and aphasic children (Swisher and Demetras, 1985).

What is specific to autism—what sets it apart from retardation and language impairments—is a mismatch between syntax and semantics or between syntax and pragmatics. The "echo-box" quality of autistic children's speech means they store in memory and later repeat syntactic structures that have little or no meaning to them. Here syntax is unrelated to semantics. Autistic children also produce sentences that are grammatically impeccable but that have no relation to the social context, such as "Don't throw the dog off the balcony." Such disjointed development is very much at odds with the progression of normal speech, which is characterized by synchrony among the various components, children knowing the meaning of what they say and knowing the rules for using words to communicate to others (Swisher and Demetras, 1985).

LANGUAGE ACQUISITION   Like communication and pragmatics, language comprehension in the first few years depends heavily on social interaction. In normal 8- to 12-month-olds, such comprehension grows out of social exchanges between caretaker and infant. Commands such as "Give me the spoon" are given typically when the infant is handing the parent the spoon, while parents frequently call for attention by saying "Look" and "See" when the child is already attending. When the caretaker names the objects the infant is exploring, he or she uses accompanying gestures and physical manipulation; thus visual attention is as important for the infant as listening. Language comprehension is initially a kind of overlay on already meaningful social behavior. Autistic children, with their social isolation and odd interests, make it difficult for caretakers even to set the stage for language comprehension. This difficulty continues into the toddler and early preschool period since language comprehension continues to be closely tied to the social context. (For an account of the subsequent development of language comprehension, see Lord, 1985.)

SUMMARY Because the above findings concerning causes are complex, an integrative review would be helpful. Most of autistic children's basic psychological functions are intact. They can see and hear, attend and remember, discriminate among stimuli, and can be conditioned by classical and operant techniques. Many but not all of their peculiarities in perception and attention are not specific to autism, but can be found in retarded populations as well. However, their deficits in imitation and their failure to generalize what they have learned may well be specific.

It is in the realm of higher-order thinking and in language that their deficits are most clearly in evidence. Here the children's thinking tends to be concrete, situation-specific, literal, and inflexible. Concrete objects and events can be grasped readily, but relationships, patterns, abstractions, double and multiple classifications are difficult for them to understand. Their concreteness hampers their use of symbols in general and language in particular. They can grasp syntax to the point of using grammatically correct sentences and can understand concrete words, but abstract words and ideas elude them, as does the use of language to communicate. The disjointed nature of language development is as distinguishing a feature of autism as the specific deficits themselves, resulting in grammatically correct utterances that are more like echoes than expressions of ideas and that have little or no communicative value.

Social Relations

Although extreme social aloneness is a core characteristic of autism, just as Kanner described it, it has received scant attention, researchers having bypassed both social cognition (the understanding of social and interpersonal transactions) and its accompany affects. Primarily on the basis of interview data, we know that in autistic children all the major landmarks of the development of attachment in the first year of life are absent: the initial, indiscriminate social response of interest and delight which subsequently focuses on a few caretakers, the facility in developing reciprocal exchanges, and, finally, the use of the caretaker as a source of security in times of distress. From the caretaker's viewpoint, it is difficult to hold an autistic infant or toddler lovingly because they tend to be excessively stiff or flaccid. Also, the infant's relatively expressionless face and minimal gesturing make it difficult for the caretaker to "read" and communicate with him or her. However, systematic research has added little to this general picture.

Empirical investigations have tended to be fragmented. For example, rather than there being an absence of eye contact in autistic children, studies show that eye contact is not used to mediate social interaction; autistic children do not look at people's faces when they want something, and they do not use engagement and aversion of eye contact to regulate the reciprocal to and fro so characteristic of normal social interchange (Rutter, 1985). An exception to this bleak research picture is Hobson's (1982, 1984, 1986a, 1986b) investigation of *empathy* and *perspective taking*. Empathy, defined as the process by which a person responds affectively to another as if he were experiencing the same affect, has been observed in preschoolers (Hoffman, 1978). However, empathy itself depends on the ability to understand the behaviors in others which are characteristic of various affects. Hobson's research (1986a, 1986b) suggests that this ability is impaired in autistic children. Specifically, when compared with a carefully selected sample of retardates, autistic children were inferior in matching facial expressions of various emotions to the appropriate vocal and bodily expressions. Thus the fact that people look and sound and act in special ways when they display the basic emotions of happiness, sadness, anger, and fear is not readily grasped by autistic children.

Perspective taking, or the ability, mentally, to put oneself in someone else's shoes, can be observed in preschoolers; for example, when asked to introduce a new toy to a 2-year-old and to an adult, 4-year-olds adjusted their speech accordingly (Gelman and Schatz, 1977). Hobson (1984) found that autistic children were capable of perspective taking when inanimate objects were involved. They realized, for example, that two miniature figures could not "see" a third figure that was obstructed from the figures' line of vision, although all three figures were in plain sight of the children themselves. As we already know, autistic children are more at home with objects than with people, and their ability to look at the world through the eyes of toys does not transfer to the human environment, as their noncommunicative speech and their difficulty with pragmatics attest.

Incidentally, case histories on adults who are no longer autistic indicate they still are deficient in empathy. At times they may be bewildered when trying to understand how others feel, or they may be socially gauche; for example, they may fail to realize when a tactful glossing over of a painful truth is preferable to embarrassing honesty. Just as their speech rarely becomes completely nor-mal, both their empathy for and sexual interest in others also continue to be impaired.

Interpersonal Hypotheses

Many hypotheses in this area concern the mother who, for a variety of reasons, cannot provide the infant with warm, sensitive care (Miller, 1974). She may be cold, obsessive, and intellectual, or she herself may be disturbed—psychotic, depressed, or immature. Even some behaviorists have speculated in terms of parental failure to attend to and reinforce the infant's early social overtures because the parents are depressed or preoccupied with illness or other concerns. Another hypothesis is that the negative feelings of the caretaker are directed toward the infant and engender a feeling of helplessness; fearing total destruction if he or she acts, the infant seeks safety in inaction and insensitivity to external and internal stimulation. Finally, various patterns of parental and familial interaction have also been implicated; for example, parents can use the child in an attempt to solve their own unconscious conflicts, thus preventing the development of an individualized identity.

In an ingenious variation of the longitudinal approach, home movies of infants who subsequently became autistic were collected and studied in terms of the mother–infant interaction (Massie, 1980). Particular attention was paid to eye contact, touching, clinging, feeding, and vocalizing, behaviors presumed to mediate the bond of love. Certain interactions were marked by insensitive, intrusive stimulation, but in one case, attachment was disrupted for 4 months by maternal illness when the infant was 7 months of age. Of particular interest are cases of maternal failure to respond to the infant's smile, in one instance by gaze aversion, in another by staring blankly at the infant. One is reminded of Brackbill's (1958) classical study of reinforcement, in which she reports that, after being continually rewarded by the experimenter's smiling face, the infants showed a strong aversive reaction to the presentation of her nonsmiling face. More important, when she forced the infants to look at her instead of turning away, they defended themselves by the same kind of impervious "looking through" her that characterizes autistic children. This suggests that an autistic-type defense may be called into play under conditions which, to an adult, seem rather benign.

However, a study of mother-infant interaction in twins, using home movies, provided evidence that autistic children may show deviant behavior even with the most sensitive caretaking (Kubicek, 1980). As it happened, in one case of fraternal twin brothers, one of the boys subsequently became autistic. Analysis of filmed interaction revealed that the future autistic infant failed to establish eye contact with his mother, his face was expressionless, and his head was either turned away from her or held back with his gaze directed toward the ceiling. For most of the interaction his back was arched, his arms rigidly flexed or extended, and his hands were fisted, indicating a high level of overall body tension. Despite the mother's continued attempts to accommodate, the infant avoided her approaches. By contrast, the mother and her normal infant were able to establish a mutually pleasurable interaction by sensitively responding to one another's cues.

On the whole, the hypothesis of mother-engendered autism has not fared well when evaluated by objective studies because such mothers are not significantly different in their personality characteristics and attitudes toward their children from mothers of children with handicaps other than autism (McAdoo and DeMyer, 1978). One consequence of the decline in popularity of the theory of interpersonal relations as a cause of autism is that parents in general and mothers in particular no longer have to blame themselves for their children's psychopathology. Caring for an autistic child is difficult enough without the additional weight of undeserved guilt.

Organic Hypotheses

The decline in the tenability of interpersonal hypotheses concerning etiology has gone hand in hand with an increase in research on possible organic factors. In general, while many abnormalities have been found, none is specific to autism; the bridge from the organic to the behavioral abnormality remains to be built (Rutter and Garmezy, 1983). And, while psychologists may stand in awe of the technological advances in physiological and biochemical research, such advances prove nothing if the basic requirements of a well-designed study have not been met. Specifically, the autistic population must be well defined and clearly differentiated from other disturbed populations, the factor of mental retardation must be controlled for, the reliability of the assessment instrument must be well established, and normative developmental data should be available. Because a number of studies of organic etiology have not been sufficiently rigorous, results are equivocal or fail to be replicated.

NEUROLOGY Autopsies have found either no neuropathology or no consistent pattern of neuropathology in the brains of autistic children. EEG abnormalities have been reported, but none that is unique to autism. The most sophisticated computer-assisted tomography (CT scan), which uses computer-controlled x-rays to produce views of successive layers of brain tissue, indicate brain abnormalities among autistic children, but methodological problems raise questions about the reliability and validity of the findings. Increased brainstem transmission times as determined by auditory-evoked responses suggest brainstem dysfunction, while other studies suggest defective information storage and, consequently, abnormalities in the hippocampus or related structures. Once again, the findings have been inconsistent and inconclusive.

Impairment of *cerebral lateralization* has recently come into prominence as an etiologic explanation because of the interest in hemispheric specialization. The left hemisphere deals with verbal material while the right hemisphere deals with spatial and other nonverbal material. Because autistic children have a language deficit while their spatial abilities are less impaired, it was logical to hypothesize a left hemisphere defect. Initial confirmatory findings were inconclusive, however, because some studies failed to include a group of mentally retarded and a group of language-impaired, nonautistic children and because the tasks used to indicate left or right brain functioning had low reliability and validity. When proper controls were added, autistic children could not be distinguished from normals, while only the language-impaired children showed left hemisphere dysfunction. After reviewing the evidence, Fein et al. (1984) concluded that not only is the left hemisphere hypothesis inadequate to account for many of the cardinal features of autism, but also the heterogeneity in form and severity of major autistic symptoms reflect a corresponding heterogeneity in the timing, locus, and severity of central nervous system insult. While left hemisphere deficits may contribute to specific language problems in individual cases, such deficits should not be regarded as the key that unlocks the etiologic mystery of autism.

Perinatal *brain injury* has also been implicated in autism; for example, neonatal convulsions and other biological hazards carrying the risk of brain damage differentiate autistic children from their nonautistic twins, and unfavorable perinatal factors have been found more frequently in autistic children than in their siblings or in controls. However, no single event or combination of events can account for many cases of autism, nor is there an explanation for why autism should develop rather than, say, mental retardation or cerebral palsy, which also may be due to the same perinatal hazards.

BIOCHEMISTRY   Advances in biochemistry have led to attempts to discover possible abnormalities in autistic children. Particular attention has been paid to serotonin, one of the neurotransmitters or "chemical messengers" responsible for communication between nerve cells. While several studies have found elevated serotonin levels in the blood platelets of autistic children, some nonautistic children have similarly high levels while some autistic children have normal levels. (For a more detailed review of research on the organic hypotheses, see Schwartz and Johnson, 1985.)

Evaluation of Hypotheses

While evidence can be marshaled to support any one particular etiologic hypothesis, in no instance is there an accumulation of positive findings, refutation of alternative explanations, and control for confounding factors which would allow one to choose among rival explanations. Such a situation is understandable in light of the difficulties involved in conducting research. Autism is rare, and the very nature of the disturbance mitigates against the child's understanding and cooperating with the procedures. Until recently there have not even been objective assessment instruments to insure that one population labeled "autistic" was indeed comparable to another one labeled "autistic." Fortunately, researchers can now use a checklist (Rimland, 1971) or a behavior rating scale (Ruttenberg et al., 1978).

Another difficulty with the current situation is the frequent assumption that a single key will unlock all the etiologic mysteries: that understanding the peculiarities of language development, for example, will explain the lack of relatedness and pathological need for sameness. Often the conceptual links from single defect to comprehensive explanation are speculative at best and are not buttressed by research findings. The single-key approach also runs counter to normal development, in which behavior is the result of the interaction of multiple variables.

One more comment: at present, organic explanations are more popular than interpersonal ones—and for good reason. Attachment is rugged; while caretaking may affect the kind of attachment, the bond itself develops under a wide variety of conditions. Neither physical abuse nor extreme neglect produces autism. In addition, the interpersonal hypotheses often sound similar to those found in less severe psychological disturbances, and many champions of a psychogenic explanation admit to an organic vulnerability. Finally, the cold, intellectualized mother described in the clinical literature may be the product of having a child whose development is erratic and baffling. Instead of producing autism, such a mother may be protecting herself from the constant defeats she suffered in the past when she reached out with love and understanding (Escalona, 1948). The effects of the infant on the caretaker are too well established in normal development to be ignored in the case of autism. In sum, it is difficult to avoid the conclusion that autistic children are, in some unknown way, ill equipped to cope with a normal environment.

Yet admitting a constitutional vulnerability to autism does not justify the neglect of caretaking variables, because autism might result from an interaction of organic and environmental factors. To date there are few empirical data concerning the conditions under which the infant is forced to avoid responding to the caretaker. Yet the few hints we have suggest that not only do grossly deviant patterns (such as intrusive, insensitive stimulation) produce temporary imperviousness on the infant's part, but so do very subtle deviations, particularly in regard to face-to-face contact (such as changing from a smiling to a somber face), which would seem rather insignificant to adults. Categorical statements that all autism is due solely to organic factors seem particularly premature at a time when our understanding of the variables influencing the establishment of the bond of love is both more detailed than it was in the past and expanding.

Treatment

The prognostic picture for autism is only slightly altered by psychotherapy. While some improvement may be made, heroic efforts are required to achieve it, progress is slow and fragile, and gains are easily lost. Even the behaviorally oriented therapists, who have been most vigorous and versatile in their remedial efforts—reporting successes in the areas of teaching language, increasing appropriate self-help and social behavior, and decreasing inappropriate behaviors such as self-mutilation and tantrums—write primarily in terms of improving the level of functioning rather than of "curing" autism in the sense of producing a child whose behavior falls within the normal range.

The usual way of presenting therapy with autistic children is to discuss and compare specific kinds of treatment, such as psychotherapy, behavior therapy, or medication. By contrast, Rutter (1985) maps out an integrated goal-directed approach based on what has been learned about autism and then locates specific treatments within this overall model. His approach has the obvious advantages of being comprehensive and empirically based.

Rutter's approach also assumes that, just as there is no one etiologic key to understanding such a pervasive disturbance as autism, there is no one kind of therapy that should be regarded as a treatment of choice.

For overall goals of therapy, Rutter (1985) lists (1) fostering normal cognitive, language, and social development, (2) promoting learning, (3) reducing rigidity and stereotypes, (4) eliminating nonspecific maladaptive behaviors such as tantrums and self-injurious behavior, and (5) alleviating family distress. Because of its relevance to our presentation of the basic deficiencies in autism, the first goal will be discussed in greatest detail.

In promoting *language* development, Rutter (1985) emphasizes the social, communicative aspects as well as the purely linguistic components of speech. In regard to the former, he recommends that parents have a half-hour period each day of uninterrupted play and conversation with their autistic child, when any and all kinds of communication are encouraged, not just speech per se. The goal is to enhance the social usage of language. Direct teaching must be geared to the child's developmental level because there are important individual differences among autistic children.

Although not specifically mentioned by Rutter (1985), one of the most impressive language training programs has been conducted by Lovaas (1977), who uses an operant conditioning model. In children with deficits in observational learning, imitation must be taught through reinforcements. When this is accomplished, the therapist may begin uttering sounds for the child to copy. After being rewarded for vocalizations, the child is reinforced for closer and closer approximations of the therapist's verbal stimuli. Next, through the therapist's modeling and reinforcing of words and phrases, the child gradually acquires a repertoire of language. The meaningful use of language is accomplished

by two of Lovaas's programs. In *expressive discrimination* the child is reinforced for making a verbal response to an object, such as correctly labeling a cup when it is presented. In *receptive discrimination* the stimulus is verbal and response nonverbal, such as correctly responding to "Give me the cup." Sequences are carefully graded so that new ones are based on mastered material. Ideally, language itself becomes self-rewarding so that external reinforces and prompts are eliminated. (For a more detailed account of behavior modification of autistic behavior, see Wicks-Nelson and Israel, 1984.) As often happens, impressive initial reports of improvement led to overoptimism that subsequently had to be tempered. As has been noted, regardless of technique, improvement is painfully slow and fragile.

Other remedial programs, such as TEACCH, are based more on the principles of normal language development than is the behavioral approach. (For a detailed account, see Watson, 1985.) TEACCH views remediation within the context of the many factors that impede language development in autistic children: the impaired social relations, the odd and repetitious involvement in objects which limits the basis for communication, the failure to generalize from one situation to another, the use of nonverbal rather than verbal demands to get another person to do something, along with the language-specific impediments. The motivational, social, and pragmatic aspects of language receive as much attention as developing specific linguistic skills.

Because autistic children vary widely in their language ability, TEACCH requires a detailed assessment of each child. It also involves setting specific goals that are congruent with the child's present level of functioning and that are realistic in terms of what is known about autistic children's openness to learning. The remedial program itself includes a number of teaching strategies and activities. The motivational aspect of teaching is handled by making language relevant to the children's own interests and showing them that words are powerful means for getting people to act in a desired way; e.g., "ride" is taught not as a label to a picture, recognition of which is rewarded with candy, but as a means of obtaining a favored tricycle. While teaching begins in a highly structured situation, every effort is made to transfer what is learned to the children's everyday environment. For example, the child who has learned the request "open" is presented with many objects, such as locked closets and peanut butter jars, which require him or her to use this command. Comprehension is aided by teachers simplifying their language and supplementing it with gestures. And, as is done in the case of normal children, language is integrated into ongoing activities and is supported by as many contextual cues as possible, rather than being taught as an isolated skill.

Although the behavioral and linguistic approaches seem quite different, they have a good deal in common. The linguistic approach uses contingent reinforcement because this is the most effective means of altering the behavior of severely autistic children, while the behavioral approach has become increasingly concerned with the pragmatics of language as shown by Lovaas's (1977) advanced training in expressive and receptive discrimination. In fact, this is only one example of the many instances in which therapeutic approaches that seem different turn out to have a number of common features.

In regard to promoting language, all studies reveal striking individual differences in outcome, the most positive results being achieved when there is evidence of some limited language skills, such as understanding speech or speechlike babbling and echoing of words, before treatment begins. For the mute autistic child, lacking in prelinguistic and linguistic skills, speech training is ineffective (Rutter, 1985).

With regard to *social* development, autistic children need both intensive personal interaction and facilitation of social cognitive capacity. Rutter (1985) recommends deliberate intrusion on the children's solitary pursuits with activities that are pleasurable, individualized, and structured so that they can readily become reciprocal. Ruttenberg (1971), using a psychodynamic framework, described a therapeutic program whose primary goal is that of establishing a close relationship to a single caretaker. These child-care workers have a high degree of "motherliness," that is, they give the children sensitive attention and care and comfort them, but also participate in and facilitate reciprocal and constructive play beginning with patty cake and finger play and advancing to assembling puzzles and coloring. The program does not include promoting social cognition, for example, through direct teaching of social skills, but even Rutter (1985) acknowledges that little is known about this aspect of helping autistic children.

Reducing rigidity and stereotypy may be accomplished through a series of small steps, each of which is acceptable to the child. Stereotyped behaviors may also be reduced by introduction of activities that are incompatible or compete with them. Because there is evidence that stereotyped behaviors are maximized in barren, bleak environments, it is important that the child be provided with toys and activities. Too frequently a vicious cycle is set up whereby the unresponsiveness or peculiarities of autistic behavior discourage adults from interaction; this lack of interaction, in turn, increases the undesirable behavior.

Rutter's (1985) advice concerning *pharmacological interventions* is particularly important because such interventions are regarded as facilitators of a general therapeutic program rather than as a "cure" for autism. He states that while no drug is specific to autism, some drugs may be useful for controlling particular behaviors; for example, tranquilizers may reduce agitation and tension. While claims have been made for the benefits of megavitamin therapy and the pharmacological reduction of raised serotonin levels, each remains in the experimental stage.

Alleviating family distress has two components. The first is helping parents cope with feelings of guilt and anger, as well as with the burden of having to care for a child who often is unresponsive and unrewarding to be with. It is just as important for parents to understand what they can do to be helpful as it is for them to understand the realistic limitations of help. The idea of parents becoming cotherapists is gaining in popularity. Behavioral therapists, in particular, have advocated parental involvement not only to counteract parental feelings of helpless frustration, but also to extend the therapeutic program to the home setting, thereby maximizing chances of generalization to a number of naturalistic settings. (See Wicks-Nelson and Israel, 1984.)

Unlike Rutter, whose comprehensive program involves a variety of treatment approaches, therapists are prone to search for a treatment of choice. Currently, behavioral techniques occupy that position because of their objective documentation of progress. Other psychotherapies too often rely on therapists' narrative accounts of success which are subject to biases and methodological flaws. One of the few studies to compare therapeutic approaches using a standardized instrument and objective observers was done by Wenar and Ruttenberg (1976), who found that psychotherapy was better than mere custodial care, but that no one type of psychotherapy has an advantage if it is sensitively and expertly implemented. This generalization applies to psychoanalytically oriented psychotherapy, behavior modification, educational therapy, and activity therapy. It may be that intrapersonal variables determine therapeutic progress to a greater degree than choice of therapy. There is evidence, for example, that preschool autistic children are both more disturbed and able to make significantly greater gains than autistic children in middle childhood, regardless of the type of therapy (Wenar and Ruttenberg, 1976). Mental age could be another potent determiner of success (Prior, 1979).

The obstacles to therapeutic progress are formidable. Most psychotherapies require at least a minimum of cooperation, while therapeutic progress necessitates change. Yet the very nature of their psychopathology renders autistic children impervious or resistant to responding to the therapist, while causing them to react to any variation in the status quo with panic and rage. In addition, the concreteness of autistic children's thinking results in their learning only what they are specifically taught. They do not *generalize* readily, nor do they *grasp rules*. Teach an autistic boy that a block may be yellow or blue, and you may have to continue teaching him that it can also be red or green or black or white. The idea that a block can be any color comes slowly. To make the point in a different way: in treating neurotic children the therapist can be reasonably sure that the progress such children make during the session will generalize to home or school; with the autistic child such a transfer is far less likely to happen. To compound the problem, there is evidence that what the child learns does not really become part of the self but has to be constantly maintained by environmental stimulation and rewards. In technical terms, the child does not *internalize* advances the way a normal child does.

One of the greatest impediments to therapy is the autistic child's lack of *initiative*. In charting the progress of a large number of autistic children, there is evidence of a predictable sequence: imperviousness and resistance followed by acceptance until the children finally begin to do things on their own. This sequence applies to their relationship to significant adults, their exploration of physical objects, and their learning of social skills (Ruttenberg et al., 1978). It is often the shift from recipient to agent, from willingness to be taught to wanting to learn, that marks a crucial turning point in therapy and that is so difficult to achieve. Lovaas (1977), for example, after citing impressive evidence that mute autistic children can be taught to speak in simple sentences, goes on to state that a major stumbling block is their lack of motivation to practice on their own—so unlike normal toddlers, who are infatuated with talking and practicing not only with others but also by themselves.

Such obstacles not only help us understand the slow progress of autistic children but also sensitize us to the importance of generalization, grasping rules, internalization, and initiative to normal development, all of which happen so naturally that we tend to take them for granted. Thus psychopathology can illuminate normal development as well as the other way around.

In addition, the study of one psychopathology can throw light on another, as will be evident as we examine childhood schizophrenia.

CHILDHOOD SCHIZOPHRENIA

As autism is identified with Kanner, so childhood schizophrenia is identified with Bender, who began working with schizophrenic children in 1935. In all these years she did not modify her basic premise that schizophrenia is an organic pathology of the central nervous system—an encephalopathy that involves the total organism. She never searched for the single key that would explain schizophrenic behavior, because multiple dysfunctions are involved. Bender has also been a thoroughgoing developmentalist; while schizophrenia is a single entity, its expression differs as a function of the child's developmental level. A schizophrenic infant, for example, could not behave like a schizophrenic school-aged child because the infant lacks speech, cognitive sophistication, a complex network of interpersonal relations, and an explicit awareness of self.

If schizophrenia is a pathology that affects behavior at every level and in every area of integration (Bender, 1947), its manifestations are legion. The electroencephalograms of schizophrenic children are dysrhythmic, although they cannot be interpreted as any specific cortical pattern disorder. The children may have faulty *vasovegetative functioning;* for example, they may flush and perspire easily or be colorless and have cold extremities. The *timing of physiological events* is out of joint, causing daily rhythms of sleeping, eating, and elimination to be erratic. Likewise, long-term growth and sexual maturation are erratic, so that the child is too large or too small, obese or underweight.

Disturbances in *motor behavior* and *postural responses* are particularly important. The toddler and preschooler are awkward and insecure in mastering the many motor skills of the period, from walking and climbing stairs to using swings and tricycles. However, primitive behavior can alternate with precocious grace and coordination. *Perceptual difficulties* show the same mixture of primitive and mature performance that characterizes motility; for example, a child may begin copying a rectangle or diamond and then get carried away by whirling, circular motions.

Finally there are a variety of *thought* and *language* disturbances. In the first few years of life there may be mutism. If schizophrenia occurs later, the child's language may be fragmented, dissociated, and bizarre: "It's open in the front but closed behind. I'm open in the front but closed behind. Did you see me today? I think I was here but Mommy wasn't. They don't take it away from Mommy. My dollie won't mind. I won't mind. [Enumerates all the members of the family who won't mind.] I was there yesterday. Was I here today?"

While the pervasiveness of schizophrenia is apparent from the above catalogue, Bender claims that an individual child is not equally damaged in all areas. Quite the contrary. It is the unevenness of development—the juxtaposition of primitive and adequate functioning, of immaturity and precocity—which is so devastating, because it prevents such children from making coherent sense of themselves and their environment, while leaving them chronically vulnerable to intense anxiety. If they were consistently retarded in all areas, as are some mentally defective children, or if only a delimited group of functions were adversely affected, as in some brain damaged children, these children could learn to cope more effectively than they do. Bender's term for this organically determined erratic development within a psychological function and a profound developmental imbalance among psychological functions is *dysmaturation*.

The Developmental Picture

INFANCY   By conducting a prospective study, Fish (1971, 1976) was able to obtain important data on infants who subsequently became schizophrenic, thus avoiding the distortions of retrospective information from mothers and the meagerness of routine medical data.

As early as the first month, Fish found no fixed neurological defect, but rather disorders of timing, integration, and organization with marked acceleration and retardation succeed-

ing one another. For example, in one baby gross motor development was 45 percent behind normal at 9 months and then, with no environmental change, accelerated so that he more than doubled his rate of growth in gross motor skills the next two months. The usual orderly sequence of postural development—from head to feet, from trunk out to extremities—may be disrupted so that an infant is able to stand (which normally happens around 10 to 11 months of age), but unable to roll over from back to stomach (which normally happens at 6 to 7 months), or can roll over but is unable to sit (which normally happens around 5 to 6 months). The same erratic sequencing is evident in the visual-motor sphere; thus an infant that can perform a difficult task fails an easier one.

Fish's findings have been corroborated by other investigators studying schizophrenic infants of schizophrenic mothers, particularly in regard to deficiencies in psychomotor development, although the evidence has not been uniformly supportive (Watt, 1984). In her defense, Fish (1984) rightfully notes that other investigators did not use the same assessment instruments she did and, more important, did not evaluate the discrepancies among functions and erratic rates of development which lie at the heart of her conceptualization.

PRESCHOOL PERIOD   Onset of schizophrenia is most common in this period (Bender, 1947). Emotional instability is evidenced by irritability, excitement, anxiety, unprovoked aggression and temper tantrums, fears, disturbed sleep, and preoccupation with body functions. As is so characteristic of this psychopathology, physical growth and language development may be slow or accelerated.

MIDDLE CHILDHOOD   In middle childhood the clinical picture differs depending on whether the children internalize their problem, in which case they are called *pseudoneurotic*, or externalize their problem and are called *pseudopsychopathic* (Bender, 1947). In the former, traditional neurotic symptoms such as anxiety, phobias, obsessions, and compulsions are present, along with evidence of severe thought disturbances such as hallucinations and delusions of persecution or bizarre preoccupations. Pseudopsychopathic children have a number of typical acting-out symptoms such as stealing, fire setting, truanting, and sexual acting out, but there is also the same underlying picture that characterizes the pseudoneurotic, such as distorted reality perception and intense anxiety. Fish (1976) emphasizes the erratic nature of cognitive functioning; there are isolated areas of intactness seen in the child's ability to do puzzles and to remember word definitions and associations, but such abilities do not become integrated into useful, goal-directed activities. Thus behavior is haphazard or stereotyped and fragmented.

Empirical support for Bender's concept of dysmaturation comes from Fish's (1984) ten-year follow-up of the previously described study of infants of schizophrenic mothers. Of the eight infants who clearly showed evidence of dysmaturation, or what Fish came to call pandysmaturation (PDM), five were severely disturbed and three moderately disturbed in middle childhood. Of the thirteen infants showing no evidence of PDM, four were moderately disturbed, and nine showed mild to no disturbance. Because of the limited number of subjects, Fish's (1984) findings should be regarded as suggestive rather than definitive.

Prognosis

The earlier the onset of schizophrenia, the more severe the disturbance in adulthood. In 34 percent of the early-onset group, organicity dominated the picture, and the life course was one of deterioration, combined with schizophrenia; in 40 percent of the cases, there was a life history of schizophrenia uncomplicated by organicity; only 26 percent of the population was adjusting to the community with the aid of various therapeutic programs and/or tolerant family situations. By contrast, 46 percent of the children with later onset were adjusting to the community, although they needed supportive help from family, social agencies, and mental health facilities.

Interestingly, Bender found that puberty is the most favorable period in many schizophrenic children's development. Spontaneous remissions occur, and some children not only may be symptom-free but also may deny or be unable to remember their former behavior. Kanner made a similar observation concerning autistic children. Yet in normal development, the pre- and early-adolescent periods are often regarded as stormy and disruptive. This may well be so, but the very disruptiveness of adolescence may weaken old, maladaptive patterns in severely disturbed children and offer opportunities for growth which were previously unavailable.

Is All Schizophrenia One?

Is autism a distinct type of psychosis, or is there a single underlying schizophrenic process throughout childhood which may be expressed in autistic behavior during infancy? While the issue has been hotly debated in the past, there now is evidence that autism differs from childhood schizophrenia. The clinical picture of the two psychopathologies is different from middle childhood on. Autism lacks the delusions and hallucinations, the loose associations, and the mood disturbances which characterize schizophrenia. The autistic child is a highly ritualized, very odd outsider; the schizophrenic child's behavior is florid, excessive, and bizarre. In their developmental courses, schizophrenia is marked by progressions and regressions, while autism is highly stable. There are important differences in context factors. Parents of autistic children tend to have average or above average intelligence and do not come from any one socioeconomic group, while parents of schizophrenic children tend to have below average intelligence and come from a low socioeconomic stratum. Schizophrenia in parents of autistic children is no higher than in the normal population, while it is elevated in parents of schizophrenic children. (For a detailed presentation, see Kolvin, Ounsted, Humphrey, and McNay, 1971; Kolvin, Ounsted, Richardson, and Garside, 1971.)

Two Models of Deviation

For our purposes, the most important aspect of the above controversy is that it involves two models of deviant development. In autism, variable stimulation in general and the human caretaker in particular are aversive. Development is marked by slow mastery of and clinging to a limited repertoire of techniques for coping with the physical and social environment. Aloneness, sameness, mutism, or noncommunicative speech all suggest a pathology of extreme encapsulation. Bender's, by contrast, is a model of profound imbalance and instability—retardation, normality, and precocity can exist within and between psychological functions at one point in time, as well as characterizing development over time. The term epitomizing Bender's image of development is dysmaturation. If the autistic child is all too predictable, the schizophrenic is all too unpredictable.

Thus we have taken one step in our quest to understand psychopathology as normal development gone awry, because we now have two specific models of how this can happen. We have seen the bedrock foundation of normal development undermined: in autism, people and objects are aversive rather than sources of interest, delight, and relief from distress, while in schizophrenia, orderly organization no longer marks a given developmental level or the progress to higher levels.

Current Diagnosis and Research

Bender's approach to childhood schizophrenia has been presented in detail because of its developmental orientation. However, with a few notable exceptions such as Fish's (1984) research her concept of dysmaturation has failed to keep pace with progress in clinical child psychology for a number of reasons. The vagueness of some of its terms has hampered the kind of operational definition essential to objective studies, and the multitude of variables subsumed under the general rubric of dysmaturation has made it difficult to generate and test specific hypotheses. Moreover, Bender's mistake in assuming that autism is merely an early version of the schizophrenic process has cast doubt on her general credibility. While the validity of Bender's concept of dysmaturation is in a state of limbo, it has not been replaced by any developmental explanation of comparable scope. Her clinical observations, however, are still cited.

Currently autism is viewed as separate from childhood schizophrenia. And, currently, childhood schizophrenia is thought to be essentially the same as adult schizophrenia in its clinical manifestations, correlates, and etiology. While findings to date support this continuity between childhood and adult schizophrenia, they are preliminary. Research is not only meager but, until recently, much of the research included schizophrenic and autistic children under some general category such as "psychotic children," making the results impossible to interpret in terms of schizophrenia alone. This paucity of research is complicated by the rare occurrence of schizophrenia. We will discuss schizophrenia in more detail in chapter 10 on the adolescent period.

In autism, the normal loving, trusting relation between infant and its caretaker has failed to develop. But what if the bond does develop and is then disrupted? What happens to normal anguish when separation is prolonged or permanent, as in the case of the death of a loved caretaker? Such questions lead us to the topic of the psychology of loss and depression, which will be discussed next.

5

Depression and the Consequences of Loss

Development would be easy to understand—but far less interesting—if it were linear or a matter of "more of the same": if children became progressively more intelligent, self-controlled, conforming, empathetic, and so on, just as they become taller and heavier. In the first chapter, however, we saw that such a linear model does not fit all the facts of development; instead, there are normal progressions and regressions, appearances, disappearances, and reappearances, as well as seemingly magical transformations.

What we discussed abstractly in the beginning can be concretely illustrated by the development of depression. Until recently the two periods in which depression was clearly recognized were infancy and late adolescence. The vast area of middle childhood was disputed territory. One could find claims that depression did not exist and, indeed, that it was developmentally impossible for it to exist during the period. There were equally strong counterclaims that it was present, but masked by other behaviors such as aggression or physiological complaints. Now it is generally recognized that depression can and does exist in middle childhood and that it has many of the features of the adult form.

Yet the recognition of middle childhood depression does not clear up two mysteries. The first mystery is why, instead of reacting with depression as one would expect, the school-aged child might begin to fight with peers or defy parents or fail in school or engage in a host of other behaviors that seem to have nothing to do with depression. It was just such baffling behavior that led to the mistaken notion of masked depression. The second mystery concerns continuity and discontinuity. While experts are divided in their opinion as to whether middle childhood depression is the same as adult depression, it makes no sense to claim that depression in infancy is the same as it is in adults. Are we to assume, then, that there are two kinds of depressions—one for the earliest years and the other for the middle years on? Such appearances, disappearances, and reappearances of behavior are perfectly congruent with the developmental approach. A well-known illustration is that newborn infants can walk soon after birth if properly held; this ability then disappears, only to return some eight to ten months later. However, we shall maintain that the two-appearance model is not necessary in the case of depression. Moreover, we shall maintain that the key to unlocking both mysteries is to regard depression as a reaction to loss but to two different kinds of loss: namely, the *loss of a loved person* in the infant/toddler period and the *loss of self-worth* subsequently. As we shall see, each kind of loss has a distinctly different origin in normal development, and in both cases psychopathological depression can be viewed as an exaggeration of the normal pattern of response. In the process we shall illustrate our general thesis that childhood psychopathology can be understood as normal development gone awry and that exploring the interplay between normal and abnormal development enhances the understanding of both.

First, we shall discuss depression in infancy. Then we shall describe depression in

adults as a background for dealing with its manifestations in middle childhood and adolescence. Finally, we shall integrate the findings in terms of the development of two kinds of loss.

DEPRESSION IN INFANCY

We have seen that adequate mothering in infancy is not a sentimental luxury but an absolute necessity for optimal physiological and psychological development. Being deprived of mothering after the bond of love is forged results in dramatically deviant behavior.

Anaclitic Depression

The classical studies of *maternal deprivation* were conducted by Spitz (1946) and Bowlby (1960). From the beginning, depression was observed as a response to a prolonged loss of contact with the mother. Typically, the infants were studied in settings such as hospitals or orphanages or foundling homes that lacked adequate substitute mothering, even though the infant's physiological needs might have been adequately met.

The descriptive picture of the infant's reaction to maternal deprivation is important to our understanding of depression. Bowlby's (1980) descriptions were based on observations of hospitalized infants. He labels the first stage *protest*. The infant is severely distressed, cries loudly, searches the surrounding area for the mother, shakes the bed, and rejects all substitute caretakers. Agitation and anxiety are both prominent. There may also be generalized anger evidenced by striking out at substitute caretakers, temper tantrums, and destruction of objects. The next phase Bowlby labels *despair*. The infant becomes withdrawn and inactive—for example, lying in bed with face averted, ignoring adults. Attempts to initiate contact produce panic and screaming. Loss of appetite and weight as well as insomnia are present. The facial expression resembles that of a depressed adult. The final phase Bowlby labels *detachment*. The infant once again responds to caretakers, to food, and to toys. However, the infant no longer acts as if he or she were attached to the mother, treating her like any other friendly stranger. Relationships are socially acceptable, but lack depth of feeling.

Bowlby's (1980) conceptualization of the above pattern of responses is based on his theory of *attachment* in infancy. In brief, attachment in the first year of life involves the formation of an affectionate and secure relationship to the caretaker. The temporary loss of the loved caretaker is marked by separation anxiety and anger, while a more prolonged loss is met by sadness and anger. The specific components of the reaction to loss can be meaningfully related to various aspects of attachment. The painful yearning of protest, with its search for the sight and sound of the caretaker, is regarded as an effort to recover her and reestablish the bond of love. The confused agitation, distractability, and overactivity result from the frustration brought on by bond disruption; the innumerable behaviors that constitute attachment continue to be activated but cannot be properly consummated in the absence of the caretaker. Anger in the protest phase is basically directed toward the loved caretaker for not being there when needed, but is displaced onto other people and physical objects in an essentially indiscriminate manner.

During the protest phase the child still has hope that the loved caretaker will return. The phase of despair represents the abandoning of such hope as evidenced by grief, apathy, withdrawal, and somatic symptoms.

In the final phase, detachment, the child protects himself from reexperiencing the pain of loss by denying the existence of the bond of attachment.

Bowlby (1980) claims that the basic pattern of yearning for the lost caretaker, anger, agitation, sadness, and defensive indifference are reactions to loss which can be documented from the toddler period through adolescence, although he also acknowledges that the evidence is meager. We shall return to this claim when we attempt a developmental integration of all the data on depression.

One final point pertains to the conceptualization of anaclitic depression. While the typical explanation is in terms of the rupture of the affective bond between mother and infant, Bibring (1953) regards depression as an expression of *helplessness*. It is the awareness that the heroic efforts to regain the mother during the protest phase are of no avail. In the past such efforts have been effective and now they are not; the ensuing helplessness lies at the heart of despair.

Short-Term Effects of Maternal Deprivation

Spitz and Bowlby's original descriptions of reactions to maternal deprivation have stood the test of time and are still regarded as valid. (Our presentation follows Rutter, 1972, 1979b.) The characteristic behaviors appear if separation occurs after the child is around 6 months old, because this is when attachment has developed; the behavior continues to appear upon separation throughout the first three years of life. Not all infants show such behaviors after separation, though, perhaps because of temperamental differences, perhaps because of prior experiences with separation. Many other factors influence the responses to loss of mother. If the separation is of short duration, if the mother or other familiar figures can be with the infant periodically, if sensitive substitute care is available, then the distress-depression reaction is minimal; it is the extended stay in a strange, bleak, or socially insensitive environment with little or no contact with the mother or other familiar figures that is so devastating. Interestingly, the effect of the prior mother–infant relationship upon reactions to separation is uncertain; some investigators find that a good relationship enables the infant to tolerate the separation reasonably well, while others find that a poor relationship produces less disturbance, presumably because the infant has already experienced various forms of aversive or neglectful caretaking at home.

In sum, maternal deprivation is not an absolute evil to be avoided at all costs, as has sometimes been depicted in the professional and popular literature. Rather, the total interpersonal, intrapersonal, and temporal context must be taken into account (Etaugh, 1980). Intense, prolonged distress and despair appear only under special circumstances and can be avoided under others.

Long-Term Effects of Maternal Deprivation

Tracing the effects of early maternal deprivation on subsequent developments presents certain problems. Few psychologists subscribe to a single-trauma approach, which states that the disruption of the affective bond is a necessary and sufficient condition for producing severe psychopathology. Fortunately, human beings are not that precariously balanced on the edge of disaster. On the other hand, if maternal deprivation is just the first in a series of traumatic events— coming at the beginning of a long stay in a bleak institution, for example, or the first in a series of losses as the child goes from one foster home to another—there is little reason to attribute the resulting pathology exclusively to disrupted attachment.

There are two theoretical reasons for weighing maternal deprivation in infancy more heavily than subsequent deleterious experiences. The first is the widely held notion that traumatic experiences occurring early in development tend to be more damaging than those occurring subsequently. The clearest supporting evidence comes from animal research in which traumatic events can systematically be introduced and their effects on development studied. The second assumption is that the infant's relation to the mother is central, and that attachment to her is the pivotal event in the infant's life. Incidentally, neither assumption has gone unchallenged. There have been objections to extrapolating from animal to human development and attempts to refute empirically the "myth" of early experience (Clarke and Clarke, 1977). Also, there is increasing recognition that the infant often attaches to a number of family members, particularly the father, and there is no reason to give the bond to the mother an exclusive status.

Now let us look at the relation between maternal deprivation and the development of psychopathology in *middle childhood* and *adolescence*. In a comprehensive review Rutter (1972, 1979b) finds no evidence that deprivation, uncomplicated by other stresses, is related to subsequent psychopathology. While hospitalization may produce anaclitic depression in infancy, in and of itself it is not the prelude to psychological disturbances in later childhood. There is a relation between antisocial behavior and broken homes, but the rise in such behavior is greater in homes broken by divorce rather than in homes broken by death, the latter representing the more severe disruption of the affective tie to the parent. Moreover, because there is evidence that antisocial behavior is related to parental disharmony and neglect even in intact homes, it seems that the nature of the family interaction is more important than the disruption of affective bonds by either divorce or death. In sum, Rutter concludes that the evidence suggests that it is a disturbed relationship between parent and child rather than a bond disruption per se which is related to the subsequent development of psychopathology.

The picture in regard to *adult psychopathology* is unclear. Gregory (1966), who conducted one of the more sophisticated studies, found no significant relation between the permanent loss of one or both parents, the age of first permanent parental loss, and a wide variety of psychotic and neurotic disturbances in adults, including depression. On the other hand, certain studies that concentrated exclusively on adult depression did find a relation between parental death and severe—not moderate—depression (Beck et al., 1963; Munro, 1966). Munro found no relation between severe depression and the patient's age at the time of parental death, while Beck et al. found a trend for severely depressed adults to suffer parental loss before 5 years of age. As often happens, we are faced with data that are both contradictory and far from definitive. Perhaps it is best, therefore, to regard the hypothesized relation between early maternal loss and adult depression or other forms of severe adult psychopathology as not proven to date. As we shall soon see, such inconclusive findings are to be expected from studies that predict outcomes from infancy to adulthood while ignoring events in the intervening years.

DEPRESSION IN MIDDLE CHILDHOOD

Because adult depressive disorder has been the point of departure for discussing depression in middle childhood, we should be familiar with its behavioral characteristics.

Behavioral Characteristics of Adult Depression

Depression, like anxiety and anger, is a normal phenomenon experienced by most people. Some individuals are moody "by nature," having a generally gloomy outlook on life. Dejection and despair, loss of appetite and fatigue, viewing oneself as worthless and life as futile are expected reactions to situations such as failure to achieve a crucial goal or loss of a loved one. Thus psychopathology is a matter of intensity, persistence, and poor prognosis in the milder cases along with inappropriate and bizarre behavior in extreme instances. Keep in mind that sadness or depressed affect as a single *symptom* should be distinguished from depression as a *syndrome*, which is a complex of symptoms having a specific etiology, course, outcome, and response to treatment, along with characteristic psychological, familial, and biological correlates.

The syndrome of depression involves changes in four areas: affect, motivation, physical and motor functioning, and cognition.

Affective symptoms include dejection, despair, and loneliness. All pleasures vanish, whether social, vocational, or sexual. The affect may be one of sadness or emptiness.

Motivation declines during episodes of depression, the depressed adult suffering a "paralysis of the will." At worst, the simplest activities, such as getting dressed or reading a book, become overwhelmingly burdensome. Initiative and new ventures are out of the question. While depressed persons become increasingly passive and dependent, they often berate themselves for their helplessness.

Changes in *physical and motor functioning* that accompany the depressed mood include loss of appetite, insomnia (especially waking early in the morning), loss of sexual responsiveness, and fatigability. In a retarded depression, movements are slow and labored, the individual often sitting slumped over and inert. In an agitated depression, the individual is constantly in motion—restless, pacing, moaning, fidgeting.

Cognitive symptoms include immutable feelings of worthlessness, even in the face of manifest competencies and successes. Depressed individuals feel helpless and hopeless, firmly convinced that neither they nor anyone else can bring about any change. They elevate the slightest imperfection to a major defect, and they constantly torture themselves with self-blame.

Depressions vary in severity. In neurotic depression, also called *dysthymic disorders*, the individual can continue to function despite chronic, recurring bouts of depression; Abraham Lincoln is one famous example. *Major depression*, however, is more episodic and socially debilitating. In the most severe cases there are delusions of sinfulness and worthlessness (for example, "I caused my mother to die," when the death was due to natural causes; "I caused Christ to suffer"; "My guts are rotting"; "My flesh stinks"; "I am dead"). Finally, depressive episodes can be precipitated by a traumatic event or can occur without apparent cause. The former are called exogenous, the latter endogenous.

Middle Childhood Depression versus Adult Depression

Until recently it was commonly held that there was no evidence of depression in middle childhood; instead, children displayed a variety of behaviors that were regarded as the equivalent of depression or that masked an underlying depression. A wide range of symptoms were included in the diagnosis of *masked depression*: physical manifestations such as abdominal complaints, anorexia, migraine headaches, and encopresis; delinquent be-

havior and rebelliousness; obsessional activities; restlessness and hyperactivity; and affectionless, psychopathic behavior (Malmquist, 1972). Not only did the list seem excessively long, but also it was not clear on what basis depression could be inferred. Thus the category lacked conceptual clarity and solid empirical verification.

The greatest blow to the credibility of masked depression was the discovery of *neurotic depression* in middle childhood. Kovacs and Beck (1977), for example, concluded that many of the behaviors indicative of adult depression are present in children: emotional (feels sad, cries, looks tearful); motivational (schoolwork declines, shows no interest in play); physical (loss of appetite, vague somatic complaints); and cognitive (anticipates failure, says, "I'm no good").

Research also indicated that depression in middle childhood has the same temporal diversity as adult depression. Thus depression that is part of an adjustment reaction, major depression, and dysthymic depression differ in course and prognosis (Kovacs et al., 1984). Depression with an adjustment disorder and major depression are acute conditions in that their appearance and disappearance are relatively sudden, while dysthymia has an earlier onset and a protracted course. Despite this difference in course, major depressions and dysthymia are alike in that early onset is a poor prognosticator. The rate of "spontaneous" remissions is high in all conditions, but there are differences among the types of depression. Major depressions and dysthymia put children at risk for future depression; adjustment reaction with depression does not. Finally, children with dysthymia are at risk for recurrent major depressive episodes, the course of dysthymia being punctuated by superimposed attacks of major depression during the first five years of the psychopathology. Such findings suggest significant differences among depressed children even though they have the same symptoms. As we shall see when discussing other psychopathologies, treating a heterogeneous group as if it were homogeneous because the children have the same diagnostic label can create and perpetuate confusion.

The discovery of a depressive syndrome has also raised the question whether depression in middle childhood can be regarded as the same as that in adults or whether the child's developmental status necessitates modifications and, if modifications are in order, what kinds and how extensive. (See Carlson and Garber, 1986, for a detailed presentation.) At one extreme there are those who point to the behavioral similarities in the manifestations of depression in children and adults as evidence that depression is essentially the same. Another school of thought acknowledges the similarities but claims that symptoms such as aggression, negativism, conduct problems, separation anxiety, and school phobias may be uniquely characteristic or more characteristic of children than adults. At the other extreme are those who maintain that, while there are behavioral similarities, the child's cognitive, linguistic, and affective status is so different from that of an adult that the syndrome in children is distinct. While a depressed 8-year-old boy and a 30-year-old man may both say, "The future looks hopeless," for example, they mean something quite different because their concept of future time differs, the boy's extending only to the next few months while the man's includes the rest of his life. Advocates of this position raise core questions of developmental psychology: How can one judge similarity across time when the same behaviors have different meanings? And can different behaviors be regarded as basically the same? Answering the question about the similarity between childhood and adult depression will require a more detailed understanding of the syndrome and its correlates than is now available.

The *descriptive picture* presents another problem in that childhood depression is frequently associated with other psychological disturbances. A third of depressed boys have conduct disorders and engage in aggressive, antisocial acts, such as setting fires or stealing, while separation anxiety is common in the general population of depressed children. Moreover, depression can be found in physically abused children, children having a learning disability, and ones suffering from anorexia nervosa (Rutter, 1986a). The pervasiveness of depression in instances of other psychopathologies raises the perennial chicken-and-egg dilemma: for example, is depression a consequence of having a learning disability, or did the decrease in motivation which is part of depression produce the learning disability?

Changes in Frequency of Depression in Middle Childhood

Studies of change in frequency of depression reveal an interesting pattern. Depressive *feelings* increase significantly in adolescence; e.g., while 10 to 15 percent of children 10 to 11 years old evidence depressed mood, more than 40 percent of adolescents report substantial feelings of misery. The rise seems to be a function of puberty in boys (there are no data on girls) rather than of chronological age (Rutter, 1986a).

Depressive disorders are rare in middle childhood and even rarer in the preschool period. However, there is not only a dramatic increase in adolescence but also a reversal of incidence in regard to sex, boys being more depressed than girls before adolescence, girls being more depressed than boys after. Adolescence also marks a significant increase in suicide and attempted suicide, both of which are rare in middle childhood. Immediate grief reactions following bereavement tend to be milder and shorter in young children than in adolescents (Rutter, 1986a).

Continuity with Adult Adjustment

Of those children with depression who go on to be disturbed, the great majority show depression as part of the adult disorder. However, in depressed children and adults, nondepressive symptoms are usually also present, depression being the primary diagnosis in only a minority of cases. Therefore it is not clear what role depression plays—whether it is primarily responsible for the other symptoms or merely one element in a complex or even possibly a consequence of the other disturbances (Rutter and Garmezy, 1983).

Affective Development

Izard and Schwartz (1986) traced the development of depression-related affects subsequent to the protest-despair reactions of the infant/toddler period. Shame enters the developmental picture in the toddler period, although it is not sufficiently stable to be part of the depressive picture until middle childhood, when it may accompany low self-esteem and excessive self-criticism. Guilt as a failure to live up to internalized standards also is not sufficiently stable to play a role in depression until the latter part of middle childhood.

The pattern of depressive emotions in normal and disturbed children and adolescents is similar, suggesting that psychopathology is a matter of degree. More important, depression in these two periods is a *complex pattern* of emotions as it was in earlier developmental periods. For all age groups from middle childhood to adulthood and regardless of severity of depression, the predominant affect is sadness, indicating that dejection, discouragement, and loneliness are the prominent features of the depressive experience. However, there are important age and sex differences in regard to the patterning of affects. In childhood anger plays a prominent role in depression, but not a adolescence and adulthood, and among children, boys evidence more hostility than girls, who in turn are more similar to adolescents and adults in their pattern. Finally, guilt is more prominent in adolescence than in childhood.

Parental Loss

The loss of a loved parent through death or a lengthy separation is the middle childhood counterpart to material deprivation in infancy and raises some questions: What is the expected reaction, particularly to death? What are the criteria for deviant reactions? And what are the developmental consequences of such deviant reactions?

ADULT CONSEQUENCES   As we have already noted, the confusing findings concerning the consequences of parental death may be due to the fact that most investigators have ignored events in the intervening years. By contrast, Brown, Harris, and Bifulco (1986) have developed a model that takes such intervening events into account although, in their research, they deal not only with death but also with a significant period of separation from the mother, rather than with death alone. In its simplest form the model assumes that a depressive episode is due to current adversities or what the investigators call *provoking agents* such as a major disappointment. Next, the chance of such experiences bringing about depression is greatly influenced by the presence of *vulnerability factors* such as lack of social support, lack of intimate ties with a spouse, or having three or more children under the age of 14 living at home. Brown, Harris, and Bifulco (1986) found that loss of the mother before the age of 11, whether by death or separation, was clearly associated with sebsequent depression for adult women in the general population and, to a lesser extent, for women diagnosed as being depressed. Thus it could be considered a vulnerability factor. Loss had no effect in the absence of a provoking agent, however. Incidentally, loss of a father before 11 years of age had no effect on depression regardless of whether there was a provoking agent. Brown, Harris, and Bifulco (1986) further reasoned that because working class women experience more provoking agents and vulnerability factors, the relation between loss of mother and depression should be more common in this class. Analysis of the data showed this to be so.

A subsequent study by the same authors (1986) illustrates how complex the pattern of intervening events can be. The subjects were adult women who lost their mothers before the age of 17 either through death or through a separation of a year or more. One initial finding was that the rate of depression was twice as high in women who had experienced aberrant or traumatic separations, such as being neglected, abused, or abandoned, than it was in women separated by death or by socially accepted causes such as maternal illness, employment, or divorce. A comparison study with similar results was done by Hilgard, Newman, and Fisk (1960), who found that the nature of the mother-child relationship was crucial in determining adjustment after the death of the father. Girls who made a good adjustment as adults had mothers who were strong, responsible, hardworking, and even strict, rather than sweet and loving. Their mothers could also use the support of relatives, the church, or community resources after being widowed. By contrast, the women who did not make a good adjustment had mothers who became extremely dependent on their children after the death of their husbands, making separation particularly dif-

ficult or impossible. Consequently, the child had inadequate opportunities to develop the skills and assurance necessary for successful living as an independent adult. Once again, it was not only parental death but also the subsequent events that determined adult adjustment.

Returning to Brown, Harris, and Bifulco's (1986) data, further analyses revealed further complexities. Depression was significantly increased if the child was placed in an institution after the death or separation, although this held only for lower-class subjects. Lack of care in the form of indifference or lax control following the loss or separation also increased the incidence of depression. Finally, a general feeling of helplessness in coping with life's stresses significantly increased depression. Overall, predictors were more potent in the lower than in the middle class. Of all the variables, the interpersonal one of lack of care was the most crucial; the intraindividual variable of helplessness was also important but to a lesser degree. While the authors did not systematically compare their two studies, they did find that the impact of loss before 11 years of age was greater than loss after 11 years of age.

The findings concerning *father loss* in middle childhood and adolescence have a familiar ring (Herzog and Sudia, 1973). There is no evidence that paternal death is the prelude to subsequent psychopathology. While paternal loss owing to divorce, desertion, and separation does have adverse consequences, such losses are complicated by many added stresses, and there is no evidence that loss per se is prepotent. In fact, the same stresses in intact families are equally likely to produce subsequent psychological disturbances.

The lesson is clear. The idea that if a parent dies, the child subsequently becomes depressed is simplistic and incorrect. Rather, depression is contingent upon the interaction of a host of intrapersonal (such as helplessness), interpersonal (such as lack of social support), and superordinate (such as socioeconomic level) factors, including the developmental factor of the child's age. The task of investigators is to tease out the interactions among variables and the ways such interactions might change as loss occurs at different points in development.

DEVELOPMENTAL INTEGRATION

As we noted at the beginning of this chapter, the findings concerning depression from infancy through adolescence can be integrated if we regard them as the consequence of loss but of two different types of loss—loss of a loved caretaker, typically a parent, and loss of healthy self-love, or what is more commonly called self-worth or self-esteem. We are now ready to consider both kinds of loss in detail.

LOSS OF A LOVED PARENT

If childhood psychopathology can be regarded as normal development gone awry, then what we must do now is search for the normal counterpart of childhood depression. The striking feature of depression in this period is that it is often a complex of affects and behaviors. In the case of masked depression, clinicans were incorrect in stating that depression was absent in middle childhood, but they accurately described the behaviors other than depression that children display in response to loss. The question then becomes, Where in normal development have we seen a similar complex reaction to loss? The answer is obvious—in the pattern of protest and despair that characterizes the infant/toddler's reaction to maternal separation. In fact, if one juxtaposes the clinical descriptions of depression and masked depression in middle childhood with Bowlby's (1980) expanded description of reactions to loss of a loved caretaker in the first five years of life, the overlap is striking, especially when viewed in a developmental context (see Table 5.1).

Dysphoric Reactions

Dysphoric responses form the affective core of bereavement at all ages.

CRYING, GRIEF, AND APATHY Violent or hysterical crying—which Bowlby (1980) calls protest, or the pain of yearning—has been observed from infancy through the preschool period, appearing as tearfulness in adolescence. The affect is constant but the quantity and degree of control change as would be expected. For example, Achenbach and Edelbrock (1981) found that crying, as part of a depressive syndrome, declines significantly between 4 and 16 years of age. The grief and total apathy of the infant/toddler period also moderate, older children being described as sad, withdrawn, listless, and moody. The overall developmental trend is from intense, pervasive expressions of affect to moderation and control.

SELF-COMFORTING Thumb and finger sucking along with cuddling toys serve as solace from infancy through the preschool period, with masturbation appearing in preschoolers. Once again, the change from oral to genital stimulation is developmentally appropriate. Whether such behaviors disappear subsequently, or whether school-aged children and adolescents are more reluctant to admit to them, is an unanswered question. It would not be unreasonable to assume that masturbation would continue, especially in boys.

Table 5.1 Reactions to Loss of Loved Parent

	Dysphoric Reactions		Response to Other Caretakers		Externalizing Reactions	
	1. Pain and despair	2. Self-comforting	1. Dependency	2. Fear of loss	1. Anger	2. Restlessness
Infancy	Anguished crying, grief, apathy	Thumb sucking, cuddling toys	Clinging	Separation anxiety	Indiscriminate tantrums	Agitation
Toddler/ preschooler	Crying (but decreasing), sadness, withdrawal	Masturbation	Clinging, desire to be nursed	Separation anxiety	Playing out anger, tantrums (but decreasing)	Agitation
Middle childhood	Crying (but decreasing), sadness		Clinging, whining, baby talk; independence	School phobias	Disobedience, cheating, truancy, delinquency	Restlessness, schoolwork declines
Adolescence	Tearfulness, sadness, listlessness			School phobias	Rebelliousness, fighting, rudeness, drug abuse, drinking, running away, sexual acting out	Restlessness, schoolwork declines

Response to Other Caretakers

Loss of a loved parent affects the child's relation to the surviving parent and to other caretakers.

DEPENDENCY The infant/toddler period is characterized by clinging to the surviving caretakers and a regressive desire to be nursed again. Clinging, whining, and baby talk reappear as regressive behaviors in middle childhood, along with the more socially appropriate behavior of exaggerated independence, which may well represent a protection against the vulnerability of reexperiencing loss. One would not expect obvious manifestations of dependency in adolescents, who are striving for independence, although an exaggeration of this striving, similar to that observed in middle childhood, might be present.

FEAR OF LOSS Fear of loss seems closely related to dependency: the more one needs the surviving caretakers, the more one is fearful of losing them. Separation anxiety has been noted from infancy through the preschool period and is supplemented by a fear of losing loved pets in preschoolers. While separation anxiety per se disappears from middle childhood through adolescence, school phobias appear. Certainly there are diverse causes for school phobias, but in those instances in which separation is critical, they represent an age-appropriate transfer of the fear of loss from home to school.

Externalizing Reactions

Anger and agitation frequently accompany loss, although the form they take changes as the child develops.

ANGRY REACTIONS A number of behaviors can be conceptualized in terms of anger and follow the well-known developmental progression from intense, raw expressions of affect to more controlled, diverse, and disguised expressions. The arena for expressing anger also expands from home to school to community, as one would expect from a developmental perspective.

In the infant/toddler period one finds temper tantrums and violent temper outbursts. Preschoolers begin to harness such outbursts and express their anger symbolically through words and play. In middle childhood there are many signs of defiance of authority, such as disobedience, delinquent acts, cheating, or truanting from school. While the affective intensity has been tamed, the target has expanded to include not only home but school and society in general. This same trend continues into adolescence, a period in which rebelliousness, fighting, quarrelsomeness, rudeness, and negativism have been noted. Finally, there is a cluster of behaviors specific to adolescence which, while potentially arising from many different motivations, may well represent angry, defiant gestures directed toward authority, the implicit message being, "Nobody is going to tell me how to behave." This constellation includes running away from home, sexual acting out, drug abuse, and drinking.

AGITATION A high state of manifest agitation has been observed from infancy through the preschool period, while school-aged children and adolescents are described as being restless. The primary development here, as it was in anger, is an increase in control, which moderates the expression of the reaction. Decline in the level of schoolwork in middle childhood and adolescence may be due, in given instances, to the difficulty in concentration which accompanies restlessness, although, as has been noted, the decline may also be due to anger directed toward authority figures.

Developmental Trends and Principles

The developments just described conform to general trends and principles. First, there is increased control of affect, seen in the moderation of crying, apathy, agitation, and rage. There is a trend toward expanding the psychological environment from home to school to community seen in the change from separation anxiety to school phobias, and from anger at caretakers to disobedience at school to breaking laws. The change from thumb sucking to masturbation represents an age-appropriate progression from oral to genital autoeroticism. Finally, there is an overall change in terms of increasing differentiation. The protest-despair reaction is a comparatively global one occurring in a short period of time. With development, elements of the pattern become singled out or differentiated, just as the infant comes to use his arms, legs, hands, and fingers as independent units of his body. With differentiation comes independence, so that by middle childhood reactions to loss can contain single elements or any combination of elements.

LOSS OF SELF-WORTH OR SELF-ESTEEM

Not all childhood depression is due to loss of a loved caretaker; more often it is due to a loss of feelings of self-worth or self-esteem. This means the focus of our discussion now shifts from the interpersonal to the intrapersonal context. The shift is partly historical as well because of the widely held but erroneous belief that Freud regarded all depression as due to aggression toward the ambivalently loved parent being turned back upon the self at the parent's death. Thus, it was thought, unconscious anger is transformed into the self-lacerating guilt of depression: "I

hate you" becomes "I hate myself for the anger I felt toward my dead parent." In reality, Freud regarded this formula as applicable only to severe, psychotic depressions. He recognized that other kinds of depressions could be due to what he called a narcissistic blow to the ego, or what we would call loss of the feeling of self-worth (Mendelson, 1975). Subsequent psychoanalysts have taken up the theme of loss of self-worth and have elaborated on it in a manner comparable to that of developmental psychologists. The shift in focus to the self has also entailed a shift of interest to the cognitive depressive triad of worthlessness ("I am no good"), helplessness ("There is nothing I can do about myself"), and hopelessness ("I will always be this way").

Developmental Data

Unlike the reactions to loss of a loved parent, the cognitive triad of worthlessness, helplessness, and hopelessness cannot exist in infancy. As we did before, we must once again turn to research on normal development. The most relevant data involve the development of the self concept in general and of self-esteem in particular, as well as data on the development of affect in general and dysphoric affect and guilt in particular. The data summarized here come from more detailed presentations by Cicchetti and Schneider-Rosen (1986), Digdon and Gotlib (1985), Dweck and Slaby (1983), Kovacs (1986), and Garmezy (1986).

The basic question we must ask is not, At what point do the components of childhood depression appear on the developmental scene? but, At what point do the components of childhood depression become sufficiently stable and potent to produce the characteristic symptom picture? The literature on normal development indicates that depression is not possible in the preschool period but is possible in middle childhood. Even within this latter span, there is suggestive evidence that depression becomes increasingly possible as one moves from 7 to 11 years of age. More specifically, a sustained negative self-image, along with a self-sustained feeling of helplessness and a dysphoric mood, are not consolidated until middle childhood, while hopelessness and guilt do not become firmly established until the preadolescent period. Thus the components comprising the syndrome of depression become stabilized at different points in middle childhood, some appearing early, others not until preadolescence.

The following is a summary of relevant literature (see Table 5.2).

THE SELF CONCEPT The preschooler has a physicalistic idea of the self. He is his body or his possessions or the things he does. In response to the question, "Who are you," he is apt to reply, "I have a baseball and I go to playschool." Such an image is subject to frequent change. Only in middle childhood is the self defined in terms of psychological characteristics and traits, thereby achieving stability and continuity. For example, the child might say of himself, "I'm friendly and have a good sense of humor." However, it is not until adolescence that true self-reflection is possible in the sense of an integration of the components of the self into stable characteristics that can be viewed in terms of both past and future.

SELF-EVALUATION AS WORTHY OR WORTHLESS Preschoolers judge themselves absolutely and globally as "good" or "bad." However, such judgments are inaccurate and vacillate with the situation because they are based on the physicalistic "me." Thus the all-good-me can turn into the all-bad-me as the child behaves now one way and now the other. However, children are aware that others are proud or ashamed of them. In middle childhood the physicalistic "I" gives way to the conceptual "I," as has already been noted. This increased realism is accompanied by more stable personal evaluations so that the children can have sustained feelings of being proud or ashamed of themselves. Thus they can feel either worthy or worthless and unloved, these feelings being due to social evaluations, success or failure in living up to their own standards, or a combination. In adolescence, the judgment of worthlessness is comparable in stability and potency to that found in adults.

SELF-EVALUATION AS COMPETENT OR HELPLESS A good deal of the literature here concerns intellectual achievement. On the positive side, preschoolers have developed to the point where they can set goals, take action to achieve them, evaluate the achievement against inner standards, and feel such positive and negative affects as pride and shame. However, they do not explicitly engage in self-evaluation or relate outcomes to personal attributes. For example, they do not ask what they did right when they succeed or wrong when they fail. Moreover, they may overevaluate themselves ("I am the best") and underestimate task difficulty while maintaining high expectations of success in the face of failure. Thus their view of achievement is unrealistically sunny. Finally, they always find reasons for success or failure no matter how farfetched, such as, "These dumb things [pieces of a puzzle] don't want to fit together."

Two developments take place in middle childhood. The more important of these is school attendance, which introduces positive and negative evaluations by powerful others, the teacher in particular but peers as well. Next, social comparisons are used to evaluate competence, and these social standards are increasingly employed as criteria of success.

Table 5.2　Self-Esteem: Cognitive and Affective Components

	Preschool	Middle Childhood	Adolescence
Self-concept ("I am")	Physical self: actions, body, possessions	Psychological self: traits, characteristics	Adult form: integration of components, stable characteristics, time perspective
Self-evaluation: worthy or worthless	Absolute "good" or "bad" Inconsistent, inaccurate Vacillates with context Knows others are proud or ashamed of him/her	Stable evaluations based on: evaluations of others, self-evaluations Negative self-evaluations, ideas of worthlessness	Adult stability achieved Persistent feelings of worthlessness
Self-evaluation: competent or helpless (especially cognitive competence)	Can set goals, take actions to achieve, evaluate outcome, feel satisfied or dissatisfied But no explicit self-evaluation, no relating outcome to personal attributes May overestimate self, underestimate difficulty Attributes reasons capriciously	Evaluations based on: teachers' judgments, comparison with peers Realistic self-evaluation Pervasive feelings of helplessness possible	Accurate self-evaluation Persistent feelings of helplessness
Self-evaluation: hopeful or hopeless	Limited grasp of time, lives primarily in present	Understanding of time increases	Past and future grasped Hopelessness possible
Affect:			
1. Cognition	In others: distinguishes affects, identifies causes In self: physicalistic identification of situation, body	Distinguishes affects in self Sadness increasingly attributed to internal factors	Accurate grasp
2. Mood	Context-dependent and changeable	Sadness increasingly prolonged and sustained	Intense, persistent dysphoric mood possible
3. Guilt	Temporary guilt over accidental as well as intentional acts	Intentionality necessary	Intense, persistent guilt possible

Thus a realistic, objectively based self-evaluation replaces the former unrealistic optimism. A realistic awareness of reasons for success and failure also makes its appearance. The change in self-appraisal and awareness of one's personal role in success and failure may lead to feelings of helplessness when children are in situations of repeated failure ("No matter what I do, nothing ever works"). One finds a gradual increase in pervasive feelings of helplessness between 7 and 12 years of age.

Seligman's (1975) concept of *learned helplessness* has proven to be a particularly fruitful behavioral translation of the helplessness dimension. The original data came from laboratory studies of dogs. In one study a dog was strapped into a hammock and administered sixty-four electric shocks from which there was no escape. Twenty-four hours later he was put into a box and again shocked, except now he could escape by jumping over a barrier into an adjacent box. Dogs with no previous experience with inescapable shock quickly learn to jump the barrier to safety. However, approximately two-thirds of the dogs who had been shocked failed to escape. After an initial reaction of running around frantically, they lay down and whined, passively accepting the pain. The behavior is not limited to dogs: it has been found in cats, rats, fish, nonhuman primates, and people.

In all the studies subjects learn that noxious events occur independent of their own responses. Therefore, they no longer respond with an effort to avoid pain. Such nonresponsiveness is called learned helplessness. It has a complementary cognitive and motivational component. Cognitively, the individual learns that responding is futile, and this knowledge concomitantly reduces the motivation to respond. In terms of self-conceptualization, the individual is no longer an agent but the recipient of whatever pain happens to come along.

Seligman (1975) draws a number of interesting parallels between extremes of learned helplessness and certain aspects of depression. The parallel between learned helplessness and the depressive sense of futility is obvious: powerlessness and helplessness are rooted in a perceived loss of control over gratification and relief from suffering. In both conditions there is a decline in the initiation of voluntary responses, seen in the depressives' motor sluggishness, their complaints concerning the difficulty in meeting even the routine demands of living, and the decline in the level of intellectual performance. There is a concomitant negative set in which individuals, no matter how capable, believe they are ineffectual, that they will continue to fail, and that they are losers. In both learned helplessness and depression there is a diminution of sexual and aggressive behavior as well as a loss of appetite and weight.

In a subsequent reformulation the variable of *causal attribution* was added to Seligman's learned helplessness model (Abramson, Seligman, and Teasdale, 1978). Three dimensions are involved: attribution must be *internal*, *stable*, and *global* in order to lead to depression. If uncontrollable events are attributed to characteristics of the individual, rather than to external agents, self-esteem will diminish as helplessness increases. If the uncontrollable events are attributed to factors that persist over time, then helplessness is stable. And if uncontrollability is attributed to causes present in a variety of situations, helplessness is global. Depression results from this attributional style in the individual interacting with uncontrollable bad events. Neither style nor uncontrollable events alone result in depression. Subsequent research on elementary school children confirmed the hypothesis that depressive symptoms are correlated with the attribution of bad events to internal, stable, and global causes (Seligman and Peterson, 1986).

Returning to our developmental model,

we would predict that learned helplessness would not be possible in the preschool period. Preschoolers are much too unrealistically sunny, much too unconcerned with their own role in success and failure, much too capricious in improvising explanations for bad things happening, for them to make internal, stable, and global attributions no matter how uncontrollable events are. (For a review of the developmental data on learned helplessness, see Fincham and Cain, 1986.)

HOPELESSNESS   The meager evidence indicates that preschoolers are incapable of hopelessness because they live primarily in the here and now. They can neither abstract a general theme of hopelessness from life nor project it into the future. There is little information concerning middle childhood, but the literature suggests that only the adolescent has a sufficiently realistic grasp of time to make a truly hopeless view of the future possible.

AFFECT: COGNITIVE ASPECTS   Preschoolers distinguish the basic emotions in others and can even identify their causes, but cannot bring the same cognitive sophistication to their own emotions. Instead, they are as physicalistic here as they are in regard to their self, identifying emotions by situational and bodily cues. For example, sadness is bruising a knee; happiness is having a birthday party. Thus others can be sad, but not one's self. School-aged children, by contrast, can distinguish emotions in the self. More specifically, the 7-year-old begins to attribute sadness to emotional factors such as failure, although an external orientation still persists. By 12 years of age, internality is prevalent and stable. As can be expected, adolescents accurately grasp the inner, mentalistic nature of emotions so that, for example, one can act in a way that is different from one's feelings.

AFFECT: MOOD   The preschooler's mood is context-dependent and changeable. There is also some evidence that the prevalent mood is positive. Seven-year-olds can have periods of sadness, but sustained sadness is generally possible only toward the end of middle childhood. The adolescent is capable of sustained dysphoric moods, which increase in frequency during this period and which must be distinguished from abnormal depressions.

AFFECT: GUILT   The preschooler tends to be guilty over accidental and uncontrolled events. In middle childhood, intentionality is necessary for guilt. However, only the adolescent is capable of experiencing intense and prolonged guilt.

Developmental Trends and Principles

As was the case with loss of a loved caretaker, changes in the components of self-esteem follow well-established developmental trends and principles. One trend is from concrete to abstract thinking as exemplified by the change from a physicalistic understanding of the self and its affects to a more abtract conceptualization of both. Abstract thinking, in turn, brings a stability that contrasts with the more environmentally contingent concreteness of the preschool period. A parallel progression is from action to reflection upon action to explicit self-awareness; for example, from a self that consists only of ongoing behavior to monitoring and judging actions to explicit self-characterizations such as "I am worthless." Certain developmental trends and principles are common to both kinds of loss, the expansion in time noted in loss of a loved one, for example, being expressed here in an increased ability to envision a hopeless future.

Complexity of Reaction

If loss of self-esteem becomes a source of depression in middle childhood, does the reaction show the same mixture of affects and behaviors as loss of a loved caretaker? The evidence, while mostly clinical in nature, suggests it does. Thus Glaser (1968) cites cases in which aggression, hyperactivity, and school failure in middle childhood and adolescence are all due to low-self-esteem. In the literature on conduct disorders there is also evidence that certain instances of antisocial acting out are motivated by low self-esteem; for example, children may join a gang and engage in delinquent behavior to achieve a sense of worth they previously lacked (Rosenberg and Rosenberg, 1978). Finally, loss of self-esteem can produce internalizing reactions such as phobias and psychophysiological symptoms.

COMPARISON OF THE TWO KINDS OF LOSS

A case has been made that the response to both kinds of loss is similar, being a mixture of depression, anger, and anxiety. However, the two kinds of loss are distinctly different in origin. The response to the loss of a loved caretaker seems to be one of those behavioral patterns ethologists claim are "wired in" by evolution. This at least is Bowlby's (1980) point of view. It is difficult to see how such a complex sequencing of behaviors and such a predictable patterning could be learned. While the behavior accompanying loss of a loved one appears on the developmental scene full blown, loss of self-esteem, like self-esteem itself, is more the result of extended and diverse experiences. It is multifaceted, each of its components in all probability having different precursors. Feeling helpless, for example, does not necessarily mean that one

feels worthless and, within the realm of helplessness, feeling futile in one's attempt to be loved may have a different impact than feeling futile in one's attempt to be successful academically. (See Harter, 1983, for an exemplary exposition of the complexities of self-esteem.)

In regard to the *developmental model* psychopathology in both instances of loss seems only quantitatively different from normal reactions. At times, the behaviors are exaggerations of age-appropriate reactions, such as an excessively long period of apathy or feelings of worthlessness becoming suicidal gestures in preadolescence. At times, the behaviors may be age-inappropriate regressions, such as clinging, baby talk, enuresis, and separation anxiety in middle childhood.

The final question as to *why* normal development goes awry is only partially answerable. In regard to the loss of a loved caretaker in the first few years of life Bowlby (1980) emphasizes the familial setting as well as the handling of the loss itself. Among important general variables are the amount of love and understanding versus the amount of anger, rejection, and indifference the child experiences before, during, and after the loss. Specific variables include how adults handle the death in regard to the child and, most important, whether the child is allowed to mourn. Research on older children tends to support Bowlby's general thesis as we have seen: the interpersonal context along with certain characteristics of the child, such as coping ability, play an important role in determining the reaction to death.

In regard to self-esteem, the question is, Under what conditions do the growth-promoting factors such as achievement, mastery, pride, and confidence become distorted into feelings of worthlessness, helplessness, and hopelessness? There is no satisfactory answer. One possible source of distortion is the incorporation of others' evaluations: if significant adults label a child "bad" or "stupid," he or she might adopt such labels into the view of the self. A more complex and more developmentally advanced process involves too great a discrepancy between experienced success and perceived potential (Harter, 1983). Depression might also result from overinvestment in unrealistically high standards and overvaluing of ability so that any failure becomes a devastating defeat. As we have seen from our presentation of learned helplessness, noncontingent reinforcement in which rewards and punishments are unrelated to the child's behavior is apt to produce feelings of futility. Finally, in the moral realm, a primitive, punitive conscience can make even trivial transgression a source of shame and guilt.

DEPRESSION IN ADOLESCENCE

There is general agreement that adolescents have developed to the point where they can become depressed as adults do. Emotionally, they are capable of experiencing intense sadness and of sustaining this experience over time. Cognitively, they can think in terms of generalizations and can project into the future. They can consciously evaluate the self and judge it as helpless or inept. In fact, moderate versions of the classical signs of depression may appear in adolescence as part of the expected turmoil of the period. The question is no longer, Can an adolescent be depressed? but, How can one tell normal from pathological depression? This diagnostic task of the clinician need not concern us here, however.

The *reasons* for depression in adolescence are not new, since they involve actual or fantasied loss of a significant personal relation or of self-esteem (I. B. Weiner, 1980). However, the developmental context is different from what it was in middle childhood. In middle childhood, children have the basic security of knowing they are an integral part of the family unit. By contrast, adolescents are faced with the task of giving up their place within the family and developing a new status as an independent adult. Even in healthy adolescence, therefore, one might expect some temporary depressive states when closeness to the family is taboo but mature sources of love have not yet been found. Temporary loss of self-confidence might also be expected during the search for a vocation that would utilize the adolescent's competences. Thus depression is more an exaggeration of normal developments in adolescence, while in middle childhood it is a reaction to the disruption of normal expectations that parental love will always be available when needed.

Adolescent Suicide

Depression is a rather infrequent psychopathology among adolescents. It becomes ominous, however, as a frequent prelude to suicide, which is the third leading cause of death among 15- to 19-year-olds in the United States. (Our presentation follows Hawton, 1986, unless otherwise noted.)

Before reviewing the findings concerning suicide, we must again note that the data frequently are meager or inconclusive. In part this is due to the uncertainty involved in deciding whether a death was an accident or a suicide and in deciding whether an adolescent attempted suicide. There is also ambiguity as to how the last should be defined as well as recognized. In addition, data gathering is difficult because the family may be in a state of distress and dismay in the case of suicide, or the adolescent and the family may tend to minimize the importance of the event in a suicidal attempt. Finally, there is the traditional problem of poorly designed studies with inadequate or no control groups.

Because there are some important differences between adolescents who commit suicide and those who attempt it, both groups will be addressed in the following review.

EPIDEMIOLOGY There has been a dramatic increase in suicides and attempted suicides among adolescents in the past twenty years. Suicides among 15- to 19-year-olds increased from 3.6 per 100,000 in 1960 to 8.7 per 100,000 in 1981, or an annual total of 5,161 deaths in the United States. Whereas boys commit suicide more frequently than girls, girls outnumber boys in suicide attempts. Adolescent males also tend to use more violent means, such as firearms or hanging, while girls tend to use drugs or poisons. Suicide is lower among blacks and higher among married teenagers and individuals in prestigious universities (Hawton, 1986). Both suicide and attempted suicide are rare but not unknown in children under 12, and there are even clinical reports of repeated and apparently serious attempts at suicide among preschoolers (Rosenthal and Rosenthal, 1984).

DEVELOPMENT A classic reconstructive study was conducted by Jacobs (1971), who investigated fifty 14- to 16-year-olds who attempted suicide. A control population of thirty-one subjects, matched for age, race, sex, and level of mother's education was obtained from a local high school. Through an intensive, multitechnique investigation, Jacobs was able to reconstruct a five-step model of suicidal attempts.

1. A long-standing history of problems from early childhood to the onset of adolescence. Such problems included parental divorce, death of a family member, serious illness, parental alcoholism, and school failure. The control group had also experienced such problems, although not quite to the same extent; for example, 72 percent of the experimental group came from broken homes (parental loss, separation, divorce) compared with 53 percent of the control group. No single event or combination of events separated those who attempted suicide from those who did not.

The importance of a control group is clear. Many clinical studies, lacking such a group, point to broken homes and parental disharmony as a prime cause of suicide. Jacobs' study suggests that familial problems should be regarded as a contributing factor rather than a necessary and sufficient condition.

2. An acceleration of problems in adolescence. Far more important than earlier childhood problems was the frequency of distressing events occurring within the last five years for the suicidal subjects; for example, 45 percent of the experimental subjects experienced a broken home while only 6 percent of the control group did. Termination of a serious romance was also much higher among the suicidal group, as were arrests and jail sentences.

3. The progressive failure to cope with the increase in problems leading to isolation from meaningful social relationships. Among coping mechanisms, the suicidal and control groups were equally rebellious in terms of becoming disobedient, sassy, and defiant. However, the suicidal adolescents engaged in much more withdrawal behavior, such as running away, long periods of silence, and a depressed mood. The isolation in regard to talking with parents was particularly striking; for example, while 70 percent of all suicide attempts took place in the home, only 20 percent of those who reported the attempt reported it to their parents. In one instance, an adolescent telephoned a friend who lived miles away, and he, in turn, telephoned the parents, who were in the next room!

4. A dissolution of social relationships in

the days and weeks preceding the attempt, leading to the feeling of hopelessness.

5. A justification of the suicidal act, giving the adolescent permission to make the attempt. This justification was reconstructed from 112 suicide notes of adolescents and adults attempting and completing suicide. The notes contain certain recurring themes, an example being that the problems are not of the adolescent's making but are long-standing and insolvable so that death is the only solution. The authors of such notes also state that they know what they are doing, are sorry for their act, and beg indulgence. The motif of isolation and subsequent hopelessness is obvious.

Subsequent research has helped flesh out Jacobs' (1971) picture of the development of suicide. (Our presentation follows Hawton, 1986.)

BACKGROUND FACTORS   While suicide threats and thoughts are fairly commonplace in middle childhood in clinical populations, there are no data concerning whether these are related to subsequent suicidal behaviors. In regard to *family* variables, there is evidence that depression and suicidal behavior among relatives are found in families of children who threaten and actually commit suicide. Actual disruptions of the home by death or divorce and unhappy, dysphoric homes play a role in subsequent suicidal behavior. Child maltreatment is another important precursor to attempted suicide. These familial factors are greater in children who attempt suicide than in nonsuicidal, psychiatrically disturbed adolescents, and the loss of parents occurs earlier in the former group.

INTRAINDIVIDUAL FACTORS   There is a high prevalence of psychiatric disorders among adolescents who commit suicide. Interestingly, these include antisocial acting out as well as depressive disorders or a mixture of both, along with schizophrenia. The prevalence of disorders is less than in adults, probably because adolescents are still more environmentally reactive. Previous attempts at suicide and a high level of intelligence are also predisposing factors, while physical illness is not.

PRECIPITATING FACTORS   Information concerning precipitating factors in suicide is limited, probably because of the difficulty in obtaining detailed information. The first factor is a disciplining crisis, such as parents being told about truanting or about punishment by the school or the court. Other factors include fights with peers such as girlfriends or boyfriends and disputes with the family.

There is much more information concerning precipitating factors in attempted suicide. First, there is a complex relation with depression. Suicidal ideation increases around puberty and is correlated with severity of depression but *not* directly with attempted suicide. Rather it is hopelessness that is related both to depression on the one hand and to suicidal ideation and attempts on the other. As it is with adults, hopelessness is more consistently related to suicidal ideation and attempts than is depression; moreover, the correlation of suicide intent and depression is accounted for by their common association with hopelessness (Kazdin et al., 1983). Finally, attempted suicide is possible in the absence of depression, the majority of attempts being correlated with adjustment reactions or with crises.

Further information concerning attempted suicide comes from a study of 3,000 youths using free care at a medical clinic (Adolinks, 1987). Many of those who attempted suicide had been preoccupied with thoughts of death, and 40 percent had a two-year period of wanting to die. This might be called the preparation for the attempt. Also, not unexpectedly, drug use was common. Of thirty PCP users, for example, two-thirds had attempted suicide, as had 40 percent of those who used barbiturates, hallucinogens, and glue. The more unusual finding was that the combination of depression plus behavior problems significantly increased the risk of suicide attempts. Thus while 20 percent of the depressed adolescents attempted suicide, as did 9 percent of those with behaviors problems, the combination of both disturbances increased the percentage to 46. The finding is interesting in its own right and also underscores the fallacy of regarding depression and antisocial acting out as incompatible. Running away from home was another ominous sign; one-third of those who ran away three times attempted suicide. Finally, the attempt itself was often triggered by a traumatic event such as being assaulted, arrested, or incarcerated.

The feelings preceding the attempted suicide were, in order, anger, feeling lonely and unwanted, feeling worried about the future, being sorry or ashamed, along with the already mentioned hopelessness. Older adolescents were more worried about the future than were younger ones. The reasons adolescents gave for attempting suicide were, in order, relief from an intolerable state of mind or escape from an impossible situation, making people understand how desperate they feel, making people worry for the way they have been treated or getting back at someone, trying to influence someone to change his or her mind, showing how much they loved someone or finding out whether someone really loved them, and seeking help. Often several reasons were given rather than a single one. Experts who evaluated the adolescents generally agreed with these reasons, except they thought the adolescents were significantly more punitive and manipulative than they viewed themselves; that is, they used the attempt to get back at someone or to try to make someone change his or her mind. Experts also thought the adolescents were more frequently motivated by a bid for help than did the adolescents themselves. Only around half of the adolescents said they wanted to die, 40 percent saying they did not care if they lived or died. Typically the attempt was made with little premediation, although there may have been prior rehearsal either in general terms ("I hope I won't wake up in the morning") or in terms of a specific act. In many cases the act was done where it would be readily discovered, such as in the room next to one with people in it, although there were exceptions.

OUTCOME For the majority of adolescents who attempted suicide, adjustment improved within one month. However, about one-third experienced major difficulties in the form of increased psychological and physical disorders, poor marital adjustment, and increased crime. One in ten repeated the attempt, boys succeeding more often than girls. The risk for future disturbances was particularly strong in teenage males. The more disturbed the adolescent was before the attempt, the more apt he or she was to be disturbed subsequently. Family psychopathology was another less potent risk factor.

Management of the adolescent after the suicide attempt requires an expert assessment because the attempt can have different etiologies and therefore require different remedial techniques. It may also take a good deal of clinical skill to gain the confidence of the adolescent and the family so that they will cooperate with remedial measures. Family therapy is often recommended, especially for children and younger adolescents. For older adolescents, particularly those whose problems lie outside the family, an individual approach is required. Often treatment is organized around the principles of crisis intervention, in that it is brief, focused on clear goals, concerned with the immediate past and present, and directed toward improving the adolescent's problem-solving skills. When the suicide attempt is one manifestation of a deep psychopathology, long-term treatment might be required.

EVALUATION   While we know a fair amount about suicide and attempted suicide, the data lie like pieces of an unassembled jigsaw puzzle. There has been little attempt to relate or synthesize the findings. For example, one might expect that the different reasons for suicide attempts would be related to different etiologic variables so that an adolescent who attempts suicide to seek relief from an intolerable situation might do so as a result of perceived irrevocable loss of love, while retaliatory suicide attempts would be more likely in an aggressive, acting-out adolescent than in a depressed one. Even more important is the lack of a conceptual integration of the information, a relating of this integration to normal development and, above all, an understanding of why the etiologic factors eventuate in suicide rather than in other kinds of psychological disturbances. Most of the etiologic factors are not unique to adolescence; family dissolution and disharmony, loss of love, disciplinary crises, and so on happen at all ages and take their toll on children's adjustment. Yet it is only in adolescence that suicide becomes a relatively frequent response. Why is this so? What are the cognitive and affective characteristics of this period which allow suicide to become an actuality rather than a fantasy or a threat? Not only is there no answer, but the question itself often is not raised.

LOSS BY DIVORCE

One of the most significant changes during the past quarter century has been the rapid rise in divorces, which increased by 114 percent between 1970 and 1982. (Our presentation follows Hetherington and Camara, 1984, unless otherwise noted.) Demographers estimate that if the current rate continues, approximately half the marriages begun in the mid-1970s will end in divorce. Consequently, one out of every five children under the age of 18 lives with only one parent, and nearly half of them will live with one parent at some time between infancy and adulthood. While remarriage is common, approximately five out of every six men and three out of every four women remarrying, 40 percent of these remarriages end in divorce within a ten-year period.

Rather than being a discrete event, divorce is best conceptualized as a series of *transitional experiences*. The period immediately following the divorce is particularly stormy. During the first year more serious problems set in which gradually are mastered. By the end of the second year normal functioning is reestablished, except that boys may continue to be disturbed. As was true of loss by death, loss by divorce has an immediate impact on children, but its long-term effects are contingent on the amount of parental harmony and disharmony the children subsequently experience.

We will now examine the pattern of transitional experiences in detail.

Immediate Reactions

As might be expected, the period preceding and accompanying divorce is one of conflict and acrimony. What is unexpected, especially to the partners who look on divorce as a solution to their problems, is that the period following separation and divorce is one of continued or even escalated conflict. Contact with the legal system intensifies problems over custody and visitation because of the adversarial nature of the legal process. In fact, clinical child psychologists' concern over the distress that legal battles cause children prompted them to advocate *mediating* child custody disputes (Saposnek, 1983). Mediation occurs independent of the legal proceedings. It is conducted by a skilled professional who helps the couples set aside their personal vindictiveness and concentrate on working out an arrangement that is best for the children. While mediation is typically voluntary, it has been sufficiently successful to be mandated by law in certain states. (For an evaluation, see Saposnek et al., 1984.)

To return now to immediate reactions to divorce, the parents are apt to have wide mood swings from elation to depression and to feel anxious, inept, and stressed in heterosexual relations, with an increased rate of sexual dysfunction in divorced men. Other symptoms accompanying divorce include inability to work effectively, poor health, sleep disturbances, and increasing drinking, smoking, or drug use.

Most children respond negatively to the loss of the parent and, while reactions vary with age, anger, anxiety, depression, dependency, yearning for the lost parent, and fantasized reconciliation are common to most. Children are apt to become more aggressive, noncompliant, whining, nagging, and unaffectionate with parents, teachers, and peers, such responses being more intense and enduring for boys than girls.

Chronic Problems

There are numerous sources of stress, conflict, and disruption during the *first year*. Some of the most pervasive changes are associated with finances. Women who usually have custody of the children suffer a decrease in income at the same time that they become head of the household. This may force them to seek employment for which they might not be well trained or to move to a poorer neighborhood with a loss of accustomed social networks and support. Both consequences seriously disrupt their lives.

Both parents are beset by problems ranging from management of household routines to lowered self-esteem. Divorced men find it difficult to shop, cook, and do the laundry, their lives being further complicated by the economic stress of maintaining two households. Divorced women are less likely to eat with their children than are mothers of intact families, bedtimes are more erratic, and the children are apt to be late for school. Both parents feel they have been failures. Social life and the search for meaningful relations are difficult because socialization is generally organized around couples. Both men and women speak of intense loneliness, casual sexual encounters being an unsatisfactory substitute for fulfilling intimacy. Divorced adults are overrepresented in admission rates to psychiatric facilities and have increased risk for automobile accidents, illness, physical disability, alcoholism, suicide, and death from homicide. Paradoxically, the relation between marital disruption and psychopathology is stronger for men than for women, even though women are exposed to greater stress over child rearing and finances.

Both parents communicate less well with their children, are more erratic in enforcing discipline, are less affectionate, and make fewer maturity demands of them, this list being an exact mirror image of growth-promoting parental behavior. In the household without a father, mothers have less social and emotional support and less help in decision making and household tasks. The mothers, being unused to the authoritarian role, tend in their child rearing to be inept, becoming absolute, restrictive, and punitive. They are both inconsistent and ineffectual, particularly in relation to their sons, who become increasingly aggressive and noncompliant. For their part, fathers become more indulgent and permissive and less available after divorce, although they still have more success in controlling their children than do mothers. Visitations are apt to be stressful, having an artificial "fun and games" or "tour guide" quality that is unnatural for both parent and child. Again the boy suffers more than the girl because the father is more important to him in regard to sex typing and self-control.

Because children handle stress best when the environment is well structured and stable, predictable and secure, nurturing and supportive, it is not surprising that there is a significant increase in problem behavior after divorce, especially in boys. This gender difference may be partly because boys are more often exposed to parental battles and disagreements and get less support than girls, who tend to be protected. In addition, boys tend to become undercontrolled rather than overcontrolled, with their aggressive, oppositional, defiant behavior compounding and perpetuating the existing interpersonal stresses. Finally, children of divorce are deprived of what has been called the buffering effect of intact families. This means that in an intact family a good relation with one parent can attenuate the effects of a conflictual relation with the other parent. Such buffering is less likely when parents are divorced.

Period of Recovery

The *second year* usually marks a gradual recovery from the negative consequences of the divorce. The factors making for recovery are the expected ones. For parents, high self-esteem, low anxiety, feelings of being in control of the situation, tolerance for change, and freedom from economic concerns are associated with ease of adjustment to marital disruption. Within the family, low conflict, mutual support, and cohesiveness are related to coping with stress. Continued contact with a positively involved, supportive, non-

custodial father is the most effective support in child rearing that a divorced mother can have. Support from family and friends also facilitates achieving a healthy adjustment while forming a new intimate relation plays a particularly important role for both men and women.

As the divorced parents can lead a more satisfying life, the children follow suit. In addition, for boys, a good relation with an older brother or a stepfather is associated with improved social and personal functioning. An unexpected finding concerns the importance of grandparents, who frequently provide financial support to the mother and emotional support to both mother and child. Grandfathers help their grandsons by taking over skills training, educational, and recreational roles, while children in homes with both a mother and grandmother are better adjusted than those in which the mother is alone.

While schools and peers might be expected to play a positive role in helping children cope, they often do not. Even when boys' disruptive behavior begins to improve in the second year following divorce, teachers and peers continue to react negatively to them. Only if boys move to a new school where their reputation does not follow them are they treated well. In general, girls receive more support from teachers and peers than boys because they are more protected and because their internalizing behavior is more acceptable. In those rare instances in which schools do play a positive role, the teachers combine explictly defined rules and regulations with consistent, warm discipline and expectations for mature behavior. In short, they behave as a good parent would.

Good Divorce versus Bad Marriage

When the divorce rate began its climb, the idea of divorce as a creative experience enjoyed a certain vogue. Subsequent research has shown how unfounded and misleading the idea was. A more durable notion was that it was better for children to live with a single divorced parent than for them to be continually subjected to the noxious influence of an acrimonious family. This idea has proven too simplistic to be accurate. The dimension of harmony-disharmony must be added to the category of intact or divorced. An intact, harmonious family is best for children. A harmonious divorce is better than being part of a disharmonious family. However, a disharmonious divorce has the most detrimental consequences for children.

To view these findings in a slightly different way, "intactness" or "divorced" are not psychological variables. They may be considered descriptive or legal or sociological terms, but, in and of themselves, they define nothing psychological. Psychology enters when one begins to deal with the kinds of psychological variables that can be found in intact or divorced families. Either kind of family can have characteristics that promote or impede development, such as harmony and disharmony. It is these that affect children's lives. Thus divorce is detrimental to the extent that it contains features that incline children toward deviant development. By the same token, it can foster normal development to the extent that it contains growth-promoting features.

Developmental Considerations

One of the most interesting developmental studies is Wallerstein's (1984, 1985) ten-year follow-up of thirty children who were preschoolers and twenty-one children who were adolescents at the time of the divorce.

In the initial evaluation the preschoolers were significantly more disturbed than the adolescents. The general picture was one of severe distress: the children had extreme separation anxieties born of their fear that the custodial parent would leave them, as the noncustodial parent had left them, so that they would be totally bereft of caretakers. They were clinging, demanding of attention, and needful. There were a number of regressive behaviors such as enuresis and soiling, thumb sucking, and masturbation. Eighteen months later half the children looked even more disturbed than initially, boys more so than girls.

The adolescents were also disturbed by the divorce, but less so. They experienced a painful sense of betrayal, feelings of loss and anger, along with conflicting loyalties. They were concerned about their own future marriages and about financial security. However, they were able to distance themselves from the family by increasing social activities and avoiding home. The protective maneuvers were successful because subsequently almost all of them were able to be supportive of and empathetic with their parents. Part of their healthy adjustment was the adoption of a realistic orientation toward the future. The pathological reactions that did occur seemed to be due to deviant family patterns before the divorce, such as an openly seductive mother who became excessively overprotective, jealous, and preoccupied with her boy's health.

The reactions of the two groups make sense in terms of their different developmental status. Preschoolers are significantly more dependent on caretakers than are adolescents, who are beginning to think of becoming independent of the family. Preschoolers' reactions are also more intense than those of adolescents, who have learned to keep their feelings under control. Preschoolers have access neither to the adolescents' defense of distancing nor to their diversity of interests outside the home, which offer both relief and substitute gratifications. Thus not only is their psychological world falling apart, but also they do not have the defenses and coping mechanisms to master their distress.

The picture ten years later was unexpected. The preschoolers, who were now 12 to 18 years of age, were less disturbed than the adolescents, who now were young adults. To begin with, the preschool group had no predivorce memories, although half of them were over 5 years of age at the time, and they remembered only fragments of the conflicts during and after the divorce. And although their primary response to the divorce was fear, they had no memory of being frightened at that time. Even though they did not remember it well, the divorce had a significant impact on them. One-third to one-half had feelings of profound sadness, loneliness, and deprivation, speaking wistfully and longingly of the togetherness of intact families. They also missed parental help, which they imagined would come from the noncustodial father. Half had fleeting and tentative reconciliation fantasies.

Their relation with the custodial mother was close, open, and trusting. They were aware of her loneliness and financial difficulties, although a few were angry and complained of the mother's selfishness. The father remained psychologically important even when the mother remarried, regardless of how often he was seen. In some instances they knew of the father's failures and rejections, but still maintained a benign image, although they were angry if he failed to provide financial support. The importance of the father increased during adolescence, especially for girls. Significantly, the now-adolescents looked forward to the future with optimism. There was some moderate concern over repeating their parents' mistakes, but primarily they saw no relation of the divorce to their future lives. Their optimism as well as their general recovery from the initial trauma may have been due, in part, to

their remarkably consistent pattern of caretaking during the 10 years, 90 percent of them remaining with their mothers.

The picture of the adolescent group, who now were young adults, was different. The effects of the divorce were long lasting and continued exerting a major influence on their lives. These young adults continued to be burdened by vivid memories of marital rupture. Lacking the preschoolers' protective forgetting or repression, they retained images of violent quarrels or their distraught, tearful mother or their brutal father. Feelings of sadness, continued resentment, and a sense of deprivation were strong. The women especially were apprehensive about repeating their parents' unhappy marriage in their own adulthood and eager to avoid divorce for the sake of future children. Yet both men and women continued to be strongly committed to the ideals of a lasting marriage and to a conservative morality.

Wallerstein's (1984, 1985) findings are noteworthy for a number of reasons. First, they contradict the critical period hypothesis, which states that events happening early in life are more potent than later events in determining subsequent development. Next, they show how spurious it can be to extrapolate future development from data taken at one point in time while also illustrating the frustration of having to wait ten years to obtain evidence that such an extrapolation was faulty! Recall that in chapter 3 we discussed a research design called the longitudinal, cross-sectional approach, which is one solution to the problem of the inordinate amount of time required to collect longitudinal data. Finally, in regard to remediation, the data support the counterintuitive idea that it may be more important to help the seemingly well-adjusted adolescent than the obviously distressed preschooler if one had to make a choice.

Summary

From the beginning love and anguish are joined. One sign of infant attachment to the mother is an anxious protest as she leaves. Anaclitic depression is the pathologically extreme reaction when separation is prolonged and no adequate substitute care is provided. Certain infants are immune for some unknown reason, but others succumb. The behavioral hallmarks are agitation, anger, and anxiety followed by extreme withdrawal and despair.

The infant response to loss of the loved adult is global because infants are still relatively undifferentiated psychologically. Their needs are few—for pleasurable and interesting stimulation and for relief from distress—although such needs are consuming. Infants are also at the mercy of the environment because they are neither practiced nor versatile enough to satisfy their need for interesting activities, and they are totally incapable of relieving physiological distress. Cognitively, they are trapped in the present, knowing only, "I need my loved caretaker and she or he is not here." They cannot understand the multiple reasons for the absence or its temporal limits when such limits exist, such as "Mommy can see you in a week." One way they cope with despair is by denying the bond of love; the parent is treated as just another adult, so that the anguish of prolonged separation may be bypassed.

In middle childhood children still suffer from the loss of the beloved caretaker, but their reaction is no longer global, because they are more differentiated. The bond of love itself has been elaborated, the parent now being a source of approval and disapproval of good and bad behavior, an appreciative audience for acquired skills, a recipient of affectionate overtures, and a guide to managing interpersonal problems. Children also have a varied set of meaningful relationships with others, peers in particular, but also distant relatives and extrafamilial adults. They are more practiced and resourceful in pursuing their own activities and have a repertoire of coping devices and defense mechanisms at their disposal. Cognitively, they can grasp the nature of concrete reality. While the affective core of the response to loss remains constant, its expression becomes more moderate and age-appropriate: anguish and despair become sadness and crying; indiscriminate tantrums become disobedience and delinquency; agitation becomes restlessness and difficulty in concentrating on school work.

In middle childhood both the self and the affects associated with self-worth have developed to the point that they can serve as a new source of painful loss when normal development goes awry. Specifically, the self is conceptualized in terms of stable psychological characteristics rather than being defined physically in terms of actions, possessions, or the body. This development makes possible stable evaluations of the self as worthy or worthless, competent or helpless, while an increased ability to conceptualize time adds the possibility of being hopeful or hopeless about one's future. Concomitantly, children are more sophisticated in their understanding of affect and capable of sustaining affective states longer than was possible in the preschool period. When there is a devastating loss of self-esteem, therefore, the child is developmentally capable of experiencing depression marked by the cognitive triad of worthlessness, helplessness, and hopelessness. He or she is also capable of a sustained mood of sadness, which is at the core of depression, along with anger and anxiety, which often accompany it. In sum, children have developed to the point that loss of a feeling of basic self-worth can be as devastating as loss of the love of a parent through death or other separations. While the conditions producing loss of self-esteem are still somewhat speculative, they include derogatory labels by significant adults, an overinvestment in unrealistically high standards, too great a discrepancy between experienced success and perceived potential, a punitive conscience, and noncontingent reinforcement, which may produce learned helplessness.

The adolescent is sufficiently developed psychologically to experience depressed mood and the syndrome of depression as adults do. While pathological depression is relatively rare, it is still ominous as a possible prelude to suicide. Here the cumulative stress of multiple recent losses plus an exhaustion of coping mechanisms lead to progressive withdrawal and finally attempts at self-destruction.

While loss of love is painful throughout development, its total impact, as well as its effects on future development, are a function of context factors. It seems safe to assume that the same holds true for loss of self-esteem. It is clear that the formula, If children lose a parent through death or long separation, then they will subsequently be psychologically disturbed, is simplistic and inaccurate. A great deal depends on the quality of care children receive after the loss and, to a lesser degree, their feelings of helplessness, while the coping skills of the surviving par-

ent, the children's subsequent marital adjustment, and socioeconomic status all play a role.

Finally, our exploration of depression illustrates our thesis that psychopathology in childhood can best be understood within the framework of normal development. Moreover, the constant interplay between normal and deviant development enriches the understanding of both. Spitz's and Bowlby's research on anaclitic depression and maternal deprivation was a major force in stimulating the study of mothering and the development of attachment in normal infants, while the findings of researchers investigating the development of self and self-esteem in normal populations provided the crucial evidence for solving the mystery of the two sources of depression in disturbed children.

We will now shift our focus from loss to initiative and socialization. In the next chapter we shall see how the efforts of normal toddlers to establish their independence from socializing parents can go awry, as can the socializing parents' effort to teach toddlers to control their biological needs to eat and to urinate. The developmental model has alerted us to the fact that the shift from love to initiative and socialization is not an absolute one, since the two are interrelated, as the discussion of psychopathology will amply illustrate.

6

The Toddler/Preschool Period: Psychopathologies of Initiative and Early Socialization

The toddler and preschool period is a time of increased expansiveness on the child's part and increased restrictions on the part of the socializing adults. It is natural that these two should go hand in hand: toddlers who are now physically able to explore vast new regions of the environment inadvertently damage valued household items and personal possessions, leave chaos in their wake, and occasionally endanger themselves. Unfettered initiative must be limited by "No" and "Don't." Socializing parents want to teach their toddlers control of unacceptable behavior, while the enterprising toddlers brazenly assert their autonomy. The ensuing battles are fought over the issue, Who is going to control whom? If all goes well, the toddlers will emerge as socialized preschoolers who can both control themselves and be assured of their autonomy. In short, they are both self-controlled and self-reliant.

In this chapter we will discuss certain pathological deviations from this normal development. While healthy toddlers literally and psychologically turn their back on the mother, a few are terrified of autonomy and react with a disturbance of psychotic proportions. Its specific name is *symbiotic psychosis*. On the other hand, the healthy need for self-assertion evidenced in *negativism* can be carried to an extreme of *oppositional behavior*, which disrupts relations with caretaking adults, while blocking the child's own growth.

While the requirements for self-control affect many aspects of the

151

toddler's life, they are keenly felt when they intrude upon bodily functions. The young child lives close to his or her body, eating and elimination holding special pleasures and special fascinations. The socializing parents' demands can, therefore, trigger some of the most intense conflicts of early childhood. Such disturbances are sometimes referred to as habit disorders. We shall discuss two such disturbances—*eating disturbances* and *enuresis*—together with *obesity* and *anorexia nervosa*, which represent pathological indulgence in and avoidance of eating.

One final reminder: preschoolers are still in the process of learning and internalizing prohibitions. They are externally oriented, being cognitively and affectively bound to the immediate situation. Thus their conflicts, angers, and fears are directly reactive to parental behavior. It is not until middle childhood that prohibitions become sufficiently internalized that children can be at odds with themselves and can punish themselves with anxiety and guilt for behavior they themselves judge as bad. When this happens, neurotic disturbances make their appearance.

SYMBIOTIC PSYCHOSIS

Symbiotic psychosis was first described by Mahler (1952, 1965), who is still the principal authority on the subject. The term *symbiosis* comes from biology and means the mutual sustaining relation between two organisms. It aptly describes the healthy mother–infant relationship as the bond of love—or, to use the psychoanalytic terminology, as an object relation—is being formed. Recall that initially the infant is not capable of distinguishing "me" from "not-me," so there is a fusion between the self and the mother; only toward the end of the first year is the mother's independent existence grasped. True to her psychoanalytic orientation, Mahler regards

symbiosis, in which the mother sensitively cares for the infant and the infant utilizes the mother to structure his or her rapidly developing ego, as the bedrock foundation of healthy development. Consequently, when symbiosis fails to develop normally, the infant is vulnerable to severe psychological disturbances.

Mahler's thesis has its counterpart in objective studies of mother–infant interaction. Sensitively cared for infants are both emotionally secure and secure in their exploration of the environment. They also relinquish crying in favor of vocalizations that are the prelude to speech. Moreover the mother's responsiveness to their signals greatly enhances their feeling of controlling the environment through their behavior. Thus infants gain the confidence, the experience, and the techniques for mastering the challenges in the toddler period ahead. In Mahler's terms, their fragile ego is strengthened by the mother's sensitive care (see Ainsworth, 1973).

Failure of symbiosis may be due to the mother's being depressed, inconsistent, intrusive, and so on, various specific patterns of caretaking having the same adverse effect on the mother–infant relationship. But failure may also be due to the infant's intrinsically fragile ego. In this case, even good mothering cannot strengthen the ego to the point of coping successfully with the challenges of the toddler and preschooler period.

Maturation, particularly of the motor apparatus, propels the toddler into the stage of development Mahler calls the *separation-individuation phase*. While the healthy toddler eagerly turns away from the mother to explore the environment alone, the vulnerable toddler reacts with extreme panic over routine separations, such as sickness, going to nursery school, or the birth of a sibling. The child clings to the mother as if trying to "melt" into her body. There are also violent temper tantrums with shrieking, biting, and kicking, along with bizarre hallucinations and fragmented speech.

Mahler interprets the alternations between craving and resisting body contact as expressions of the symbiotic child's desire to reestablish the original fusion of the symbiotic period and the consequent fear of losing the self completely if this were to happen. This ambivalence is the core problem. Along with remnants of appropriate speech, it also distinguishes "pure" cases of symbiotic psychosis from autism, in which object relationships and appropriate speech patterns have never been established.

Symbiotic psychosis has not been sufficiently studied to trace its developmental course. Therapy is based on Mahler's etiologic theory, the therapist being a warm, supportive mother figure who gradually helps the child master the challenges of self-reliant living.

OPPOSITIONAL BEHAVIOR

Oppositional behavior, which also has been called negativism and noncompliance, is intentional noncompliance with adult requests, directives, and prohibitions (Wenar, 1982; for a review of oppositional behavior, see Gard and Berry, 1986.) The element of intentionality is essential because a child may not comply for reasons other than opposing authority, such as being absorbed in a game; therefore noncompliance is too broad a term to epitomize this behavior. Oppositional behavior and negativism are synonymous terms, the latter being found in the older, classical writings on the topic. In the following presentation, the term *negativism* will be used when dealing with normal behavior, *oppositional behavior* when dealing with a clinical entity. The decision to use the terms in this manner is an arbitrary, stylistic one.

In extensiveness, oppositional behavior can range from focal opposition expressed in a single symptom to a generalized oppositional character disorder. It also spans the developmental periods from toddlerhood through adolescence. Levy (1955), for example, writes about therapy with oppositional 2-year-olds, while other clinicians describe it in middle childhood and especially in adolescence.

The *Diagnostic and Statistical Manual of Mental Disorders* (American Psychiatric Association, 1987) helps flesh out the descriptive picture of disobedient, negativistic, and provocative opposition to authority figures. The manifestations typically involve violations of minor rules, temper tantrums, argumentativeness, provocative behavior, and stubbornness. However, unlike conduct disorders there are no violations of the basic rights of others or major societal norms and rules such as persistent lying, aggressiveness, and theft. Oppositional behavior is also one of the most frequently reported problems of children referred to clinics (Wicks-Nelson and Israel, 1984). Finally, oppositional behavior can accompany a number of other psychopathologies, particularly aggressive, antisocial conduct disorders, but learning disabilities and mental retardation as well.

Development

The precursors of negativism in normal development can be seen in the first few months of life when infants resist being fed before they are ready by clamping their jaws and lips together. Similar resistance to being weaned to a cup and, later, to being spoonfed have humorously been called the "battle of the cup" and the "battle of the spoon." Negativism flourishes in the toddler period, which is aptly described as the "terrible twos." Even at this tender age, toddlers show great versatility in their techniques, according to Levy (1955). Some are manifestly willful. "I *should* move my bowels, but I *won't*," as one toddler put it; or, from the exasperated mother's viewpoint, "I can't talk him out of anything; no matter what I do, he persists in having his own way." But direct confrontations can be alloyed with passive maneuvers; food refusals can become pickiness or dawdling. Finally, there are purely passive techniques, such as mutism or pretending not to hear or to understand parental directions.

In *middle childhood* school and friends play a special role in negativism, as would be expected from the developmental model. The toddler's "I won't" may become "I won't learn." If negativism is pushed to the extreme of oppositional behavior, the result may be underachievement and school failure. Often in such cases academic achievement is overly valued by parents who set high standards for the child; school failure represents the child's revenge. Levy (1955) observes that such parents need not be coldly intellectual; they can be quite warm and child-centered. Note that now a social institution—the school—has become the arena for acting out problems originating in the home. However, it is also possible that certain teachers or methods of teaching or even pervasive school atmospheres may provoke negativism independent of the home situation.

Adolescence is another period of heightened negativism because, as in the toddler period, the issue of autonomy comes to the fore. Opposition becomes part of the adolescent's angry reproach: "I'm not a baby anymore."

In adolescence, or even in middle childhood, the law becomes the coercive force and law enforcers become the coercive adults, especially for children of lower socioeconomic status. For those who are labeled juvenile delinquents the court is now the arena for acting out oppositional encounters. However, because the law becomes the new opponent, this does not mean that the old ones

fade away. A vivid picture of oppositional behavior from every developmental level is presented by D. C. Ross (1964) under the label of the "negatively organized child." A 15-year-old boy was brought to the clinic because he threatened to shoot his girlfriend's father after the father had forbidden her to see the boy. This was the climax of innumerable stormy oppositions to people in authority. At home no issue was too large or too small to become a battle of the wills—the tie he wore, the food he ate, the music he enjoyed, his disorderly clothes closet, his poor dental hygiene, his choice of friends and leisure-time activities. His parents relentlessly nagged, exhorted, pleaded, and scolded, which only succeeded in exasperating the boy. Despite superior intelligence, he was failing in school, probably in retaliation against his intellectually ambitious parents. Home life was unbearable, and he spent as little time at home as possible. Fortunately, he excelled in athletics and enjoyed working on a friend's farm where he could do as he pleased. Aside from this, his response to most of the demands placed on him was a defiant "I won't."

Research

Forehand (1977) and his colleagues have undertaken an extensive research program concerned with the nature and elimination of oppositional behavior, or what they call noncompliant behavior. (For a summary of their findings, see A. O. Ross, 1981.) Because they have used the behavioral model in their research, they have concentrated on the conditions that elicit and maintain noncompliance in a clinical population. They found that noncompliant behavior is maintained by parental attention, which serves as a reinforcer even though such attention often takes the form of anger and punitiveness. In addition, they discovered the types of parental commands which are apt to elicit noncompliance. The so-called alpha commands are specific and clear. They include commands that have a clearly designated, explicitly stated objective, questions that involve a motoric response, and instructions to stop an ongoing behavior or not to begin a behavior that is about to take place. The so-called beta commands are vague and interrupted. They are difficult or impossible to obey, either because of their ambiguity or because the parent issues a new command before the child has a chance to comply. Beta commands are more characteristic of parents of noncompliant children than are alpha commands.

Forehand's research has been primarily with preschool and early school-age children and has added significantly to our understanding of the parental role in eliciting and maintaining oppositional behavior. Furthermore, these insights have been used by Forehand as the basis of his therapeutic program, which is discussed later.

Negativism and Oppositional Behavior

Negativism is part of the normal development of the self-as-agent. Levy (1955) adds that it protects the child against submissiveness; for example, when he asked a negativistic boy, "What would happen if you gave in to your mother just once?" the boy replied that the mother would make him do everything her way and would never let him do anything on his own. Thus negativism can both enhance and protect the autonomy of the self.

While not originally aggressive, negativism can subsequently be used as a safer form of aggression than angry outbursts and direct attack either by children who are submissive and fearful or by children having to deal with strongly authoritarian adults. The passive forms of negativism, such as dawdling, pretending not to hear, mutism, and inattention, are favored by these children.

Finally, Levy (1955) and Anthony and Gilpin (1976) concur in regarding authoritarian demands as one of the principal causes of oppositional behavior. Such demands are multiform—for affection, achievement, neatness, self-control, cleanliness. It can also happen that certain parents consciously or unconsciously reward, condone, or identify with the child's oppositional behavior.

At a general level, mothers of oppositional children have been described as overcontrolling, aggressive, and depressed, while fathers have been described as passive, peripheral, and distant. Mothers are more negative toward their children and more critical of them than are mothers of normal children and engage in more threatening, angry, and nagging behaviors. Both parents give their children significantly more commands and instructions and do not allow enough time for the child to comply (Gard and Berry, 1986). As we have seen, the nature of the commands themselves may decrease the likelihood of compliance and increase the likelihood of opposition.

The literature lacks a full-dressed discussion of the difference between negativism and oppositional behavior. Levy (1955) distinguishes the two in terms of the excessiveness of the reaction—psychopathology is an exaggeration of normal behavior. Exaggeration, in turn, consists of intensity, pervasiveness, and persistence. Equally important, such exaggeration tends to block future development. Thus Levy writes of the rigidity of personality and of the social isolation resulting from oppositional behavior, both of which cut the child off from growth-promoting experiences with socializing adults and peers. Forehand's research also implies that a quantitative difference in the ratio of alpha to beta commands helps tip the scale in favor of normality or psychopathology.

Note that psychopathology as exaggeration is not the same as psychopathology as age-inappropriate behavior. While psychopathological negativism may be age-inappropriate (for example, when an 8-year-old "acts like a 2-year-old"), it is also found both in the toddler and adolescent period, where negativism is age-appropriate. Consequently, the clinical child psychologist's job of distinguishing normal from pathological negativism in these two periods is a particularly difficult one.

Treatment

Based on research findings, Haswell, Hock, and Wenar (1982) suggest the following techniques to prevent negativism from escalating into oppositional behavior. Because a rapid series of intrusive directives is the surest way to incite opposition, the caretaker should alert the toddler/preschooler that a transition is in the offing ("In a few minutes you will have to put your toys away"), wait until she has the child's attention or gently capture the child's attention before issuing a directive, and then give the child time to comply. In the face of noncompliance, a brief period of "time out" in which the parent does not attend to the child is better than continued pressure.

Treatment of oppositional behavior has been neglected. Predictably, psychodynamically oriented therapists prefer to explore the child's conscious and unconscious feelings toward family members, while atheoretical practitioners follow the commonsense advice of telling parents not to nag and coax and to avoid being dictatorial, overprotective, overcorrecting and putting the child into a "give in or lose" situation (Bakwin and Bakwin, 1972).

Recently, however, Forehand (1977) and other behaviorally oriented therapists (Ross, 1981) have begun a systematic exploration of techniques designed to reduce oppositional

behavior. In order to alter both the elicitors and reinforcers, parents are taught to replace their vague, interrupted beta commands with specific alpha ones, to shift from punishing noncompliant behavior to rewarding compliance with praise, approval, and positive physical attention, and to employ a "time-out" procedure of isolating the child for a brief period after noncompliance. It is also helpful to teach parents the general principles of operant learning rather than providing them solely with techniques for handling specific problems. While the successes in the home do not generalize to the school, they do affect other behaviors within the home; for example, one girl who was reinforced for picking up her toys spontaneously began to keep her clothes tidy. Successful treatment also reduces other undesirable behaviors such as tantrums, aggression, and crying. Moreover, there is evidence that the compliance of untreated siblings undergoes the same positive change, since the mother alters her behavior to them as well (Humphreys et al., 1978).

REVIEW

Let us review symbiotic psychosis and oppositional behavior in terms of the models of deviant development. Symbiotic psychosis is an example of age-inappropriate behavior. The toddler or preschooler who may have been developing with no signs of serious disturbance reexperiences separation anguish with the overwhelming intensity that marks its initial appearance in infancy. Oppositional behavior is an exaggeration of an age-appropriate behavior which blocks progress in important areas of development. While it may be inappropriate to a given age, it need not be. In symbiotic psychosis the toddler or preschooler regresses to the separation anguish of the infantile period; oppositional behavior represents a regression only when it is age-inappropriate. In symbiotic psychosis there is a failure of development (of normal symbiosis), and in oppositional behavior there is an exaggeration of normal development.

In regard to the deviant development of initiative, symbiotic psychosis represents an undermining of self-reliant expansion, as the toddler or preschooler is trapped between the double terrors of independence from and closeness to the mother. Just as in the case of autism and childhood schizophrenia, the child is devastated because the basic foundations of normal development have been destroyed. Negativism is quite different, since normal development takes place but in an exaggerated form. However, why the exaggeration occurs is unclear: such children may be normally autonomous but are forced to protect themselves against intrusive, demanding parents; or they may be protecting their fragile autonomy from further erosion; or they may have an inflated sense of autonomy because their parents have encouraged and condoned it. Or—as so often happens—all three explanations may be valid.

FEEDING PROBLEMS

YOU KNOW, I was 32 years old before it dawned on me that I didn't have to eat everything on my plate! I was alone in a restaurant, staring at a pile of turkey and dressing with gloppy brown gravy wondering how in heaven's name I was going to get all that food into my stomach. Then it hit me. This is just a lot of damned foolishness. I've been a good girl long enough. Now it's time to grow up.

On a more serious note, a young bachelor underwent psychoanalysis because of a number of fears, one being panic when eating out with a woman. He could tolerate business lunches but only felt really safe when cooking his meals and eating alone in his apartment. During therapy the following repressed material was uncovered:

MY MOTHER sat at the head of the table and served the family. (His father had died when he was 5 years old.) I remember that she would say to me, "Tell me when I've given you enough potatoes or peas," or something. But when I said, "That's fine," she would always take just a little more and plop it on my plate. It would make me furious, but I never could say anything to her.

He also reported the following dream:

MOTHER AND I were sitting on a pier overlooking a marina of some sort and she was sewing. Suddenly, she put the needle through my eyelid and pulled it closed with the thread. I didn't dare move because that would tear my eyelid off. When I woke up I still felt terrified.

We will return to this young man's memory and his dream after discussing early eating disorders.

As adults, most of us would not regard eating as the emotional high point of the day. It has its minor irritations and pleasures, which are quickly forgotten. Consequently, we tend to underestimate the significance of hunger and feeding in the life of the infant and toddler. We need the psychoanalysts to remind us of the importance of eating and of the interplay among somatic, psychic, and intimate interpersonal relations which it engenders. Physiological distress and relief from such distress are the most highly charged experiences of early infancy. The first ego, so the psychoanalysts maintain, is a body ego: the first dim notion of the self as good or bad depends on the ratio of bodily pleasures to bodily distress. Similarly, the first view of intimacy as pleasurable and trustworthy or noxious and untrustworthy depends on the sensitivity and reliability of relieving physiological distress and maximizing physiological pleasures.

The Infantile Period

Now let us focus specifically on eating, using Anna Freud (1965) as a guide to our conceptualization. One of the earliest conflicts between the infant and the socializing caretaker centers on feeding. In the 1920s and 1930s, C. M. Davis (1929, 1935) conducted a series of studies to determine what infants would do if given complete freedom to choose the kind and quantity of nourishment they wished. One-week-old infants could choose among four formulas and orange juice throughout the nursing period, while 6-month-olds were presented with a wide variety of foods for periods of six months to a year. The results were both enlightening and amusing. All the children were healthy and well-nourished at the end of the study, and there were no digestive disorders owing to the self-selection of food. However, there was a wide variation in the quantity eaten, including unpredictable food jags—three to four bananas at one meal, five to seven servings of potatoes, a full quart of milk in addition to a complete meal! Thus infants "naturally" have strong but shifting food preferences and vary widely in the amount needed to satisfy them at any given feeding. Such variability is a far cry from the adult caretaker's concern that the infant eat a given quantity of food and a balanced diet. The erratic nature of the infant's hunger also conflicts with the adult's need for regularity and intrudes on the adult's realistic commitments to activities other than feeding. A certain amount of disharmony between infant and caretaker is inevitable and, Anna Freud

notes, normal. If the mother is reasonably sensitive and flexible and the infant reasonably tractable and resilient, they manage to accommodate one another.

But many things can go wrong. The mother may be insensitive, depressed, inconsistent, neglectful, burdened by realistic problems; temperamentally the infant may be erratic, hypersensitive to distress, difficult to divert, or may transmit behavioral signals that are weak, undifferentiated, and difficult to read. Consequently, infants are frequently in a high state of distress. Note that, at this stage, infants react directly to the mother as her behavior impinges upon them, since they have not yet evolved a mental representation that can be sustained in her absence. Note also that their reactions to distress are primitive—crying, vomiting, unmodulated rage, refusal to eat, apathetic withdrawal—since the more sophisticated defenses and socially attuned coping devices have yet to develop.

The Toddler Period

In this period attachment to the mother has been established and initiative is running high. Again, Anna Freud points to normal conflicts, such as the battle of the spoon in which toddlers insist on feeding themselves and the battle of wills over the amount and kind of food they will eat, and the manner in which they will eat it. As in the infantile period, psychopathology consists of extreme versions of normal confrontations, this time between the willful toddler and the socializing caretaker. The following quotations from mothers who have brought their toddlers to a child guidance clinic illustrate just how intense these confrontations can become:

──────

I'VE TRIED EVERYTHING. I watch to see what he likes so I can give it to him next time, but next time he don't like it. I promise, "If you be good and eat, I'll get you a real puppydog all your own." But that don't work. Sometimes I get mad and say, "Damnit, you're gonna eat if I have to cram it down your throat." Then, sometimes I figure, "If he eats, he eats; if he don't, he starves. I can't be bothered no more." But nothing works. It's picky, picky here and picky, picky there until I think I'm going out of my mind.

She won't eat nothing but sweets all the time. You know and I know that's no good. It's going to rot her teeth for sure when she gets her full set and she's going to be fat all over. One day I forced her to eat her hamburger and potatoes and she just vomited it back up. I never saw a child that stubborn. Like a mule. ▬▬▬

Kanner (1977) estimates that a quarter of all toddlers and preschoolers have feeding difficulties. He believes the majority of problems are caused by parents who rigidly try to force the "correct diet" on the toddler or who are obsessively and coercively over-protective. Toddlers, in turn, may respond in a number of ways. At the most primitive level, they may gag and vomit or complain of stomachaches; at a more sophisticated level they may dawdle or become picky eaters; the more manipulative ones use eating to monopolize the parent's attention and dominate them, say by insisting on certain foods prepared in a given way, or by intentionally provoking and upsetting the parents.

Kanner maintains that, for therapy to be effective, the caretaker's attitude must change from one of concern with what the child is eating to concern for the child who is eating. Specific techniques such as rewarding desirable and ignoring undesirable behavior will not work because the toddler will perpetuate the battle. While the behavior therapists may well challenge his recommendations, Kanner's observation that toddlers will continue provocations on their own points to a significant advance over the infantile period.

Not only are toddlers differentiated from the mother but they are also aware of her vulnerabilities, and can intentionally set about to defy, subvert, and upset her. Such social sensitivity and intentional behavior is in striking contrast to the infant's primitive repertoire of reactions. The confrontation is still between caretaker and child; it is the technique for managing the confrontation which has changed.

However, the toddler has not developed to the point of internalizing the requirements of socialization so that the requirements become self-perpetuating, as in the case of the 32-year-old woman and the young bachelor, whose eating problems introduced our discussion. Let us take a second look at these vignettes in light of what we have learned.

In the first vignette, the mother's mandate, "Eat everything on your plate," created anxiety and guilt over disobedience so strong that the woman resisted critical evaluation of the mandate until adulthood. Yet the conflict between doing what she wanted or obeying her mother was readily available to the woman's consciousness, and the price paid for obedience was relatively minor. The young man faced a more serious dilemma. His rage is understandable. On the one hand, the mother implicitly said, "You are the decision maker; I will do what you say," but then she added, "What you decide does not matter; the ultimate power is mine." He felt betrayed. But why did he not protest? For fear of losing the mother's love, symbolized, so the psychoanalysts would claim, by food. As his dream indicated, any attempt to break away from the mother's control would be self-destructive. There is both a binding and a blinding—he could not face the mother's subversive control, and he could not break away and become independent of her. The impasse continued into adulthood, where the demands for independence reactivated it and its attendant anxiety. We also can see that the young man's anxiety involved both kinds of eating problems we have discussed—the conflict over autonomy in the toddler period and the infantile equating of being fed with being cared for and protected against the terror of isolation and helplessness.

The two examples also teach us something about the developmental model of psychopathology. Eating disturbances may represent exaggerations of developmentally normal disharmonies between caretaker and child, as Anna Freud claims. Subsequent experience may undo the damage they cause, they may persist but only cause minor discomforts, or they can serve as the nucleus of a crippling anxiety. What determines the difference between these outcomes will be discussed in chapter 8 on neurosis.

Developmental Consequences

Objective data on developmental consequences of feeding disturbances are meager. Heinstein (1963) found a relation between feeding practices and maternal warmth in infancy and problem behaviors such as disturbing dreams, finicky eating, and nail biting between 6 and 12 years of age; boys who were nursed for a long period by a cold mother were the most maladjusted children in the group. In general, personality damage seemed to occur when the intimacy of feeding was combined with coldness, oversolicitousness, or hostility.

In the realm of normal development, the Berkeley Growth Study (MacFarlane, Allen, and Honzik, 1954) uncovered two peak ages for food finickiness: between the first and sixth year of life, when 30 to 40 percent of the children evidenced the problem, and again around 12 years of age, when it was evidenced by approximately 20 percent of the children. In the early years, the finicky eaters came

from disharmonious homes in which conflict and tension between parents were high. However, it was not related to a variety of personality variables. In 12-year-old boys, by contrast, finicky eating was related to irritability, overdependence, attention demanding, temper tantrums, lying, and poor appetite; in girls finicky eating was only related to insufficient appetite. The authors speculate that the 12-year-old boys are highly conflicted over their dependency on the mother, wanting very much to break away and assert their masculinity but not being sufficiently secure to do so. Consequently, they vacillate between clinging and angry rejection. At a more general level, the study indicates significant sex differences in intrapersonal variables, and more important, it suggests that the same behavior problem might have different meanings depending on the developmental status of the child. The latter implication will be explored in greater detail as we discuss obesity.

OBESITY

Our understanding of obesity is neither as definitive nor as detailed as we might wish. Inconclusive research findings might be due to unresolved problems in assessing obesity (see Linscheid, Tarnowski, and Richmond, 1988) and to the complexity of obesity itself. While defined simplistically as an excess in weight, or more specifically as body weight greater than 20 percent of normal for height and weight, obesity varies in degree and chronicity. Thus a chronically and grossly obese child may be different in many respects from a child whose obesity is moderate and developing or remitting (Werry, 1986b). One difficulty in research on obese children, therefore, may be that generalizations are not warranted in light of the distinctions among the children themselves.

Obesity tends to persist rather than being "outgrown." The older the child, the stronger the relation to subsequent weight: there is a small but significant correlation between birth weight and weight-for-height ratios at 5 years of age, a highly significant correlation between 5 and 22 years of age, while 80 percent of 10- to 13-year-olds will still be overweight at 26 to 35 years of age (Wicks-Nelson and Israel, 1984).

Obesity puts the child at risk for a number of physical and psychological difficulties, although the evidence for the latter is somewhat contradictory. Among the physical difficulties are orthopedic problems, hypertension, and cardiovascular disease, which may shorten the life span. Obese children have also been described as having low self-esteem and poor self-image and as being depressed. There is some evidence that peers view obesity more negatively than physical handicaps, and it is reasonable to infer that ridicule and social isolation contribute significantly to the obese child's problems (Leon and Dinklage, 1983). One of the better studies of adjustment, in the sense that it used objective measurements, found that obese children had significantly more problems than children in the general population, but that such problems were not as severe as those of children being seen in a clinic for behavioral disorders (Wicks-Nelson and Israel, 1984).

However, findings concerning social stigma and psychological problems come almost exclusively from populations seeking medically supervised weight reduction. While there is evidence that children prefer a mesomorph (athletic) build and that this preference increases with age, there is no convincing evidence of a negative stereotype of an obese body build nor of discrimination against obese children (Jarvie et al., 1983). There is also no evidence for a decrease in self-esteem in the population as a whole (Wadden et al., 1984).

Such contradictory research findings suggest that clinical child psychologists should avoid stereotyping obese children as having low self-esteem and a poor self-image because of social stigma. Such problems are most likely to be found in a special group of children who are sufficiently dissatisfied with their weight to seek professional help in reducing it.

Obesity can be due to a number of factors. In the organic context, heredity accounts for around 10 percent of the variance in weight. One physiological theory claims that overfeeding in infancy may increase the number of fat cells (hyperplasia) and the size of these cells (hypertrophy), childhood onset of obesity being due to the former, adult onset of obesity being due to the latter. The set point theory, based on the observation that weight fluctuates within very small limits and that weight once lost is readily gained, postulates a kind of biological homeostasis regulating input and output to maintain a given individual at a given weight. Presumably, obese children have higher set points than nonobese ones. However, none of these organic theories has been satisfactorily validated. (See Linscheid, Tarnowski, and Richmond, 1988.)

In the interpersonal context, social learning theorists emphasize the crucial role obese parents play in reinforcing and serving as models of eating behavior. In the intrapersonal context, obesity is conceptualized as an imbalance whereby energy intake exceeds energy expenditure. On the intake side there is little evidence for the common belief that obese children eat more or different foods from their peers (Werry, 1986b), nor do they differ in eating styles, such as "wolfing" their food down (Israel, Weinstein, and Prince, 1985). However, there is evidence for increased inactivity and consequently decreased energy expenditure. Even when obese children engage in activities such as sports, they tend to be far less vigorous than their normal-weight peers.

The etiologic theory we will present in detail is Bruch's (1973) because, while speculative, it both expands and deepens our understanding of eating disturbances as a developmental deviation. Bruch delineates two psychogenic causes. The first is reactive obesity, in which the child eats excessively after experiencing a trauma such as the death of a parent. Such cases are rare in childhood and typically represent an attempt to ward off depression. Next, there is developmental obesity, which is intimately linked with the child's personality. This category is of greatest interest here.

Numerous specific problems are included within the category of developmental obesity. While Bruch does not do so, it is possible to order many of the problems developmentally. The symbolic meaning of food as love and autonomy in the infant and toddler period has already been discussed. In addition, food may symbolize the girl's wish to be a man and possess a penis, her wish to become pregnant, or her fear of pregnancy during the oedipal stage (if one holds to the psychosexual theory) or the preschooler's conflict over her sex-role identity (if one holds to the social-learning theory). Such problems may resurface in adolescence when eating may also serve as a substitute for sexual gratification and a way to avoid adult responsibilities. Other meanings of food seem to span the entire developmental age range: eating as an expression of rage and hatred or as a way of gaining a sense of power and self-aggrandizement.

We should also remember that while the meaning of eating is changing, the child is becoming more complex psychologically. The toddler's reactions to conflicts with the socializing adult are more socially sensitive, sustained, and intentional than the infant's. Continuing the trend, conflicts that could occur only in the context of a direct confrontation between socializer and toddler can eventually take place within the child; for example, the adolescent's fear of sex, which leads to overeating, may be of her own making rather than the result of a frightening sexual encounter.

We have here a concrete illustration of the point made earlier concerning deviant behavior. The same behavior—obesity—can have multiple causes: physiological, reactive, developmental. And, within the developmental category, the same behavior can have different meanings depending on when it occurs. Finally, the deviant behavior can vary in seriousness as a function of the age appropriateness of its underlying cause. A 6-year-old girl who becomes obese because she resents the power and status granted to boys is not as disturbed as a 6-year-old boy who becomes obese because he is terrified that his mother will leave him and he will be helpless. Now we begin to see why the clinical child psychologist's task of determining etiology is so difficult—and also why it is so important.

Why Obesity?

If a variety of developmental conflicts underlie obesity, why do certain children "choose" to overeat rather than evidencing other kinds of deviant behaviors? In attempting to answer this question, Bruch (1973) makes her most intriguing contribution to understanding deviant development.

To begin with, Bruch maintains that the infant is not born with a hunger drive that is experientially distinct from other states of physiological arousal. Consequently, hunger as a distinctive inner cue has to be learned. This is a novel hypothesis. By now Piaget has accustomed us to the idea that the infant must learn the nature of the physical and social environment. What we must consider seriously is the possibility that the infant must also learn to differentiate the internal environment of needs and affects.

How does such learning take place? In a way analogous to learning the external environment—more specifically, by feedback. The infant learns to differentiate a rattle from a string of beads because each responds differentially to exploratory behaviors such as shaking and mouthing. Analogously, the infant learns to differentiate inner drives and affects by the differential responses of the caretaker. The sensitive mother is constantly on the alert for specific cues from the infant so she can come to say, "That's his hungry cry," "She's just fussy and needs her nap," or "He's really mad." As she responds appropriately—now feeding, now soothing, now diverting—the infant comes to distinguish more clearly among inner states of arousal.

But suppose the mother interprets all distress as hunger. Perhaps she is overindulgent, perhaps she cannot tolerate negative affect, perhaps she is rejecting and pops a bottle into the baby's mouth in the hope that the infant will be quiet and quit bothering her. When verbal labeling enters the developmental picture, such mothers continue the pattern by responding to all signs of distress with, "Oh, he's just hungry." Consequently, the child will fail to differentiate inner states, so that a variety of needs and affects are regarded as hunger. Instead of being angry or bored or frightened or sexually aroused, the child feels hungry and eats. The self is similarly impoverished. Instead of learning, "I am a person who has a rich variety of sensations, needs, and affects," the infant learns, "I am a person who is hungry."

Bruch claims there is a further complication. As the self is impoverished, initiative suffers. By imposing her interpretations and insisting on them, the mother robs the child of the desire to explore and experiment independently. Bruch cites the case of a 14-year-old whose mother went down on her knees to tie his shoes during the interview, who answered all questions directed to him, and who hovered anxiously over him. While such children may well learn techniques for tyrannizing their mothers or the entire family, they feel helpless in meeting the developmental demands outside the family circle. Characteristically, they are sedentary, avoiding self-assertive, competitive, and aggressive activities which require motoric involvement. In fact, physical inactivity seems as important as food intake in contributing to obesity. The father also contributes to the child's difficulties, at times being passively subservient to his wife, at times demanding that the child look and act and achieve in accordance with the father's own standards. Thus both parents in their own ways try to impose their own needs and images on the child.

In sum, a diffuse body- and self-awareness plus a crippled sense of effectiveness are the psychological conditions underlying developmental obesity.

The Adolescent Picture

Adolescence plays into the vulnerabilities occurring during the first few years of life. The self is closely identified with the body, peers are intolerant of physical or behavioral deviations, the sexual drive must be managed, and independence from the family must begin. It is as if adolescence conspired to confront the obese child with developmental tasks he or she is least equipped to master. But Bruch insists that the adolescent can take all such difficulties in stride if self-image and self-confidence have not been damaged. It is the feeling of body- and self-diffuseness and helplessness in the face of impulses and demands for autonomy that may be devastating, both in terms of weight gain and emotional well-being.

Data on the developmental consequences of obesity which take into account both the physical and psychological components are meager. In a follow-up study, Bruch found that 40 percent of the children with severe adjustment problems continued to have them as adults; around one-third of the children were making a satisfactory adjustment as adults, some having lost weight, others remaining obese. The common element in this group was warm, accepting parents and absence of persecution for being fat.

As far as prognostic signs in middle childhood, Bruch lists severe inactivity associated with social isolation or withdrawal in the child and a family life marked by anxiety and discord with parents who are overpowering and pressuring.

Treatment

Because of the concern over fitness in our present-day society there is a plethora of diet and exercise programs available to the obese individual. Among psychological approaches, individual, family, and group therapies have been tried, behavior therapists being particularly ingenious in devising programs for children and parents. (See Linscheid, Tarnowski, and Richmond, 1988, for a detailed account of behavior therapies.) There is also evidence that behavioral treatment is more effective than no treatment or placebos (Epstein and Wing, 1987). While all approaches claim some success, none has the kind of documented superiority that would single it out as the therapy of choice. Initial weight loss is relatively easy to achieve no matter what the method; the problem of maintaining the loss over significant periods of time has not been solved (Werry, 1986b).

Expansion of the Developmental Model

Certain etiologic factors in obesity are familiar by now, particularly the overwhelming of initiative by intrusive parents. But Bruch adds a new perceptual-cognitive component. As a consequence, obesity becomes a developmental failure due to misinformation conveyed by the mother to the infant/toddler. It is a cognitive infantilization, so to speak, in that caretaking adults perpetuate the undifferentiated perception of drives and affects which characterize infancy.

ANOREXIA NERVOSA

Anorexia and Bulimia

As we have seen, child psychoses have been differentiated into a number of distinct categories, such as autism, schizophrenia, and symbiotic psychosis. On a smaller scale, a similar advance has taken place in regard to anorexia nervosa in that two clear subgroups have been distinguished. In brief, anorexia is a voluntary pursuit of thinness to the point of extreme emaciation or even death. It occurs primarily, but not exclusively, in adolescent females. However, anorectics use two different means of achieving thinness. The first group relies solely on strict dieting and are called *restricters*. The second group alternates between dieting and binge eating followed by self-induced vomiting or purging and are called *bulimics*. To further complicate matters, there is also a group of adolescents who have a pattern of frequent binge eating followed by vomiting or purging, but who have normal weight or may even be overweight. This kind of eating disorder, which is separate from anorexia nervosa, is also called *bulimia*. Thus there are restricters and bulimics within the population of anorectics, and there is a separate category for bulimia. The complex interrelations among these eating disorders is far from being untangled. We will review that literature after presenting each disturbance in detail.

Description

Anorexia means loss of appetite, and loss of appetite can occur in a number of normal and psychopathological conditions. It may be part of the transitory aestheticism of adolescence; it can result from a traumatic event (for example, a 10-year-old boy became disgusted by food after a man tried to force him to perform fellatio); the child may have a phobia about food or a compulsive food avoidance. Furthermore, as we have seen, loss of appetite is one of the marks of severe depression, and it can also stem from a schizophrenic delusion (for example, the food is being poisoned by germs released by secret Russian agents).

More important, "loss of appetite" fails to capture the essence of the psychopathology of anorexia nervosa, which is a voluntary restriction of food and an active pursuit of thinness, usually with pride in control over eating. As a result, there is at least a 15 percent loss of body weight without organic cause (DSM-III-R). Anorectics have a normal awareness of hunger but are terrified of giving in to the impulse to eat. There is also evidence that their perception of satiety may be distorted because they report feeling bloated or nauseous after eating small amounts of food (Garfinkel and Garner, 1986). The startling feature is that, unlike in ordinary dieting, the individual wastes away to a dangerous state of emaciation in pursuit of some ideal image of thinness. As the condition advances, diets become increasingly restrictive; one girl would eat only two chicken livers a day, another ate only celery sticks and chewing gum for a year before her death (Bruch, 1973). In fact, anorexia nervosa is one of the few psychopathologies that can lead to death; studies have reported a fatality rate of around 9 percent (Garfinkel and Garner, 1986).

Among the secondary symptoms of anorexia nervosa, excessive activity is one of the most common. At times the intensity of the activity is masked by its socially acceptable form, such as doing homework or participating in sports; but an activity such as running up and down the driveway until exhausted or literally walking around in circles may have a deviant quality. Amenorrhea is another common secondary symptom, menstruation often ceasing prior to weight loss.

Anorectics are reluctant to form close relationships outside the family, thereby isolating themselves from the important growth-promoting functions of peer relations in the adolescent period. Sexual relations, in particular, are avoided; Leon et al. (1985) found that both restricters and bulimics had a markedly negative evaluation of sex and lacked interest in sexual relations. While a decline in sexual interest is found in normal individuals who are starving, the negative evaluation is not typical. Even in treated anorectics, sexual aversions and fears remain in 20 percent of the population. Social problems also tend to persist in a number of recovered anorectics. Finally, there is a strong depressive element in both the adolescent and in the family members.

There is evidence that anorexia is increasing, especially in industrialized societies, and that the age of onset is moving upward. While it is most prevalent in white middle and upper class adolescents, it is found in all social classes and also among blacks and Hispanics (Silber, 1986).

Outcome is varied. For some, anorexia nervosa is a single, relatively mild disturbance, while for others, it is the beginning of a lifelong disorder. Follow-up studies show that 40 percent of anorectics totally recover, and 30 percent are considerably improved. However, 20 percent are unimproved or seriously impaired by depression, social phobias, or recurrent symptoms. Early onset (i.e., before 16 years of age) is associated with a favorable prognosis, while chronicity, pronounced family difficulties, and poor vocational adjustment are associated with a poor outcome (Leon and Phelan, 1985). While it was originally thought that bulimics had a poorer prognosis than restricters, it now seems there is no significant difference in the prognosis except that bulimics have more substance disorders (drug use and abuse) than restricters (Toner, Garfinkel, and Garner, 1986).

One final point: Research on anorectics is complicated by the fact that starvation per se significantly affects behavior, producing depression, irritability, social isolation, decreased sexual interest, and amenorrhea. Starvation can also significantly alter family interactions as members are helpless to alter eating patterns that produce striking emaciation and might eventuate in death. Thus the problem of distinguishing causes from consequences is a knotty one here, as it is in all severe disturbances.

Restricters and Bulimics

While both groups of anorectics are united by their pursuit of thinness, restricters tend to be conforming, reliable, insecure socially, obsessional, and both inflexible and nonpsychological in their thinking. Bulimics, who comprise about half the population of anorectics, are more extraverted and sociable but are more unstable and feel hunger more intensely. They tend to have problems with impulse control, such as stealing and substance abuse. While socially more skillful than restricters, their relations tend to be brief, superficial, and troubled. Their families also tend to be more unstable than those of restricters; there is more discord, maternal depression, paternal depression and impulsivity, and substance abuse. There may also be a prior history of obesity in the adolescent and the family. In fact, there is speculation that the bulimic's constitutional bias toward obesity makes weight loss difficult, the con-

stant vulnerability to breakthroughs of uncontrolled binge eating subjecting them to greater psychological distress than that experienced by the excessively controlled restricters. Whatever the reason, bulimics are more disturbed than restricters. (For a more detailed presentation, see Leon and Phelan, 1985.)

Etiology

Because anorexia nervosa is the result of voluntary actions, one would think it would be relatively easy to divert the adolescent from her health-endangering and even life-threatening course. If the adolescent "chooses" to become thin, why can she not "choose" to eat again? These typically bright, middle class girls seem strangely indifferent to their fate and stubbornly resist efforts to help them. To solve this puzzle, we must examine various etiologic accounts of this baffling behavior. Some accounts assume that the special stresses of adolescence are sufficient to produce anorexia nervosa, while others maintain that the special role eating plays harks back to a much earlier period when feeding oneself or being fed was a central issue in the parent–child relationship. Because a resolution of this disagreement is nowhere in sight, it is not possible to assign anorexia nervosa a definitive location along the developmental continuum.

Psychodynamic Approaches

One of the earliest hypotheses within the psychoanalytic framework regards anxiety about the sexual drive as a basic factor—a plausible notion in light of the absence or significant diminution of sexual activity both at the physiological and psychological levels. In this view, the specific symptom of food rejection is due to a reactivation of a misunderstanding of sexuality dating back to the oedipal period; namely, that women become pregnant by eating. The adolescent's avoidance of food, therefore, results from her unconscious fear of oral impregnation.

The hypothesis is developmentally sound and nicely accounts for food avoidance. As we have seen, curiosity about sex flourishes before the preschooler is capable of understanding its mature form. When told that a baby is growing inside a pregnant woman, the child assimilates this information in terms she can understand—the mother must have eaten something. (Similarly, birth is understood in terms of defecation since this is how something inside the body gets out.) This misunderstanding occurs even if the child is given correct and detailed information and even if the child can perfectly repeat the lesson she has learned. As is generally true of cognitive development, the child assimilates new information in terms that are most meaningful; things get inside the body by eating! "Impregnation," "uterus," "embryo," and "delivery" are concepts that will not be truly understood for years to come.

Despite its soundness, continued clinical study of anorectics revealed that the oral impregnation hypothesis applied only to a limited number of adolescents. Psychoanalysts began to theorize that the rejection of food stems from damage much earlier, at the *oral stage* of psychosexual development (see Sours, 1969, for a summary). The initial caretaking of the infant is marred by insensitivity usually taking the form of intrusive overprotectiveness or excessive control. The result is a hostile dependent relationship in which the exploited child cannot express her rage because of the fear that the mother will leave her alone and helpless. Other theorists, both within and outside the psychoanalytic tradition emphasize the devastating effect the mother's behavior has on the child's ego and identity, her self-assurance and self-respect.

The damage during the infant/toddler period is perpetuated by ingrained patterns of interaction which prevent the school-age child from correcting or compensating for it. The characteristic picture, surprisingly, is of attentive, concerned parents of a model child who is obedient, dependable, and considerate at home, and a popular high-achiever at school. When one examines the picture more closely, however, one sees that the child is living out a parental image of proper behavior which permeates every facet of her life—her physical appearance (thinness being especially valued), the food she eats, the clothes she wears, her friends, her activities. Any sign of resistance or self-assertion would result in painful self-recrimination. How could she go against the wishes of parents who are so obviously concerned about her welfare? Her own misery is either banished from consciousness or borne in silence.

Bruch (1973) adds that not only does the child feel that her life and her self are not her own, but even her body is not her own. Gaining or losing weight, sickness or health are viewed not in terms of bodily pleasures and pains but in terms of pleasing or displeasing parents. Eating, in particular, has nothing to do with personal enjoyment but has everything to do with parental preferences and values.

Adolescence, with its heightened sexual drive and its mandate to establish an independent identity, is shattering to the anorectic, as it is to the obese child. She becomes increasingly preoccupied with restricting food intake and pursuing the unattainable goal of thinness. However, theorists disagree about the meaning of this preoccupation. Some regard it as a primitive means of establishing control over submerged hostility, particularly toward the mother who is the original source of food. Others regard it as a desperate struggle to gain self-respect by achieving an idealized image. We now begin to understand why the anorectic cannot merely "choose" to eat again: her basic feeling of being loved and valued, her autonomy and initiative, her self-respect—all of which lie at the core of the human experience—are at stake.

But still a puzzle remains. The developmental drama just described is found in many severely disturbed adolescents. Why is its resolution acted out in terms of the body? Bruch (1973) again has the most provocative hypotheses, derived from her many years of studying the psychological meaning of the body. She claims that somatization is due to three factors, two of which have been discussed in relation to obesity: a feeling of helplessness and worthlessness, and an inability to discriminate hunger and satiety. The third factor, which involves the body image, is more variable and not as potent in obese children. Our body image is not an accurate representation of our features and physique but a composite made up of a multitude of experiences, among them being evaluations of our bodies by significant others (see Wenar, 1971). In the case of the anorectic, parental evaluations are so prepotent that the adolescent literally cannot see herself realistically. One patient had difficulty discriminating between two photographs of herself even though there was a seventy-pound difference in her weight. Another said she could see how emaciated her body was when looking in a mirror, but when she looked away she reverted to her belief that she was larger. Thus the image of the body, which is a reasonably accurate psychological construction in normal development, borders on a somatic delusion in the anorectic. Perception is determined not by reality but by deeply felt needs. According to Bruch, the anorectic's vain pursuit of self-respect through food refusal is expressed in the vain pursuit of a body which literally is never perceived as sufficiently thin.

As we have seen, the psychodynamic emphasis on the fear of sexuality in anorexia nervosa has been validated by objective studies. However, Bruch's hypothesis concerning a perceptual disturbance has not fared well. On the one hand, overestimation of body size is not consistently found among anorectics, and, on the other hand, such overestimations are found in a number of other populations, such as normal adolescents and pregnant women. Surely the feeling of being too fat is present but not the literal perceptual distortion of the body (Huon and Brown, 1986). However, Bruch is not totally off the mark because there is a correlation between body perception and prognosis, those who have the greatest overestimation having the poorest outcome both in regard to weight and psychological functioning (Leon and Phelan, 1985). Bruch also seems to be mistaken in saying that anorectics distort the sensation of hunger because the distortion is in terms of satiety, although it is not clear whether this is a cause or a by-product of the psychopathology (see Leon and Phelan, 1985).

Anorexia Nervosa and Deviant Development

At the beginning of the discussion, we described the normal battles for control between toddlers and parents which produce preschoolers who are both self-reliant and self-controlled. Anorexia nervosa shows this normal process going tragically awry. The parents assume total control of the child and often use love and concern as their technique for doing so. Because they seem to be acting for the child's good, her rebellion results in guilt and shame. Autonomy is surrendered. With the crisis of adolescence, the girl evolves a pitiful caricature of autonomy by asserting control over her food intake. However, it is control without self-confidence, nagging doubts leading to increasingly restricted food intake in pursuit of an unattainable ideal of thinness. Note that the girl tries to resolve her problem by involving her body rather than directly confronting the people responsible for producing it. Yet as she continues to fast, she may well produce a belated control over her parents through their worried concern, their catering to her culinary eccentricities, their helplessness to change her. While the victory may finally be hers, it is won at the price of impoverishing her life and endangering her health.

Finally, anorexia nervosa illustrates self-destructive negativism, in contrast to healthy self-assertiveness. The anorectic's rejection of parental attempts to help are understandable. But therapists often encounter the same stubborn refusal both to eat and to cooperate. The resistance may be passive, such as taking two hours to eat a bowl of corn flakes and trying the therapist's patience to the limit, but it is, nonetheless, a powerful impediment to treatment.

The Family Approach

Recently, anorexia nervosa has been conceptualized in terms of family interaction. When previous investigators studied the parent–child relationship, the focus was on the child and the effects of parental behavior on her development. In the family approach, each member is seen as affecting and being affected by the behavior of every other member in a dynamic interplay of influences. Thus the basic task is that of understanding patterns of interaction and the ways in which such patterns enhance or impede growth.

Minuchin and his coworkers (1975) describe four characteristic patterns of interaction in families of anorectic children.

1. *Enmeshment.* Members of the pathologically enmeshed family are highly involved and responsive to one another but in an intrusive way. They have no strong sense of individuality so that changes in one member or in the interaction of two members quickly reverberate throughout the entire family system. There is a lack of privacy, an exaggerated "togetherness." Minuchin and his group cite the example of a 15-year-old who complained that his mother always moved the furniture around when he was not at home—as if this were as much his business as hers. Enmeshed families have poorly differentiated perceptions of each other, and parents often speak of their children as a group. Roles and lines of authority are diffuse; children assume parental roles, or one parent enlists a child's support in struggles with the other parent.

2. *Overprotectiveness.* Family members of psychosomatically ill children are overly concerned for each other's welfare. A sneeze can set off "a flurry of handkerchief offers," criticism must be cushioned by pacifying behavior. The family's exaggerated concern for the ill child retards the development of autonomy, and the child, in turn, feels responsible for protecting the family from distress.

3. *Rigidity.* Pathological families resist change. Particularly in periods of normal growth, such as adolescence, they intensify their efforts to retain their customary patterns. One consequence is that the child's illness is used as an excuse for avoiding problems accompanying change. Since attending to the child's illness diverts the family from facing conflicts, the illness is constantly reinforced.

4. *Lack of conflict resolution.* This final characteristic is the result of the first three, although its manifest forms differ. Some families deny conflict; others bicker in a diffuse, scattered, ineffectual way; some have a parent who is an avoider, such as a father who leaves the house every time a confrontation threatens. An honest facing up to conflicts is often bypassed by adherence to a strong religious or ethical code that provides

a prefabricated answer to all interpersonal problems.

The picture of the family that emerges is congruent with the one presented by Bruch. However, Minuchin enlarges our understanding of how the child's illness supports the entire network of family relationships. He also expands our understanding of the various roles the child may play within the family pattern. *Triangulation* puts the child in the distressing position of siding with one parent against the other in a parental disagreement. In a parent-child *coalition*, the child does side with one parent; for example, a girl might staunchly defend her mother's being incapacitated by "sick headaches" while the father taunts her with pampering herself and "putting on an act." In *detouring*, the parents escape their conflicts by regarding the sick child as their only problem. Some require the child to reassure them that they are indeed concerned only with her welfare; others alternate between concern and exasperation over the child who is such a "burden" and "does not try to help herself."

Minuchin's ideas concerning etiology are also congruent with the ones already presented. The family of the future anorectic is overly concerned with diet, food fads, table manners. Their intrusiveness undermines the child's autonomy, and both her psychological and bodily functions are continually subject to their scrutiny. Adolescence is a particularly stressful time for the family. The child, sensing the stress, responds with a behavior such as dieting, which is subsequently used as a detouring mechanism and is subtly reinforced by the family. As the symptom becomes enmeshed in the family pathology, it gradually escalates into a full-blown anorexia.

Objective studies of families of anorectics, as we have seen, have revealed an increased incidence of instability, impulsivity, depression, and obesity which would support the general notion of the family's role in regard to genetic predispositions and to modeling disturbed behavior. However, Minuchin's hypotheses on specific patterns of family interaction have not been clearly verified. Moreover, Yager (1982) warns of prematurely stereotyping families both because of the diversity of personality characteristics among anorectics and because of the diversity of family patterns that have been described; for example, some initially disorganized families become integrated and resourceful as the adolescent recovers, while others begin to show serious signs of maladjustment as the adolescent improves. Thus it is not the validity of Minuchin's observations which is being questioned but their generalization to all families.

Other Approaches

The *sociocultural* approach emphasizes the fact that thinness has become the ideal of feminine beauty in our society, an ideal that body-conscious adolescent girls wholeheartedly embrace and that sets the stage for the anorectic's self-destructive pursuit of thinness. We will give a more detailed account of this approach when discussing bulimia, although many of the points made there could apply to anorexia nervosa as well. *Behavior theorists* speculate that food may become an aversive stimulus through conditioning or that a strong learned association develops between extremely negative thoughts and images about weight gains and food consumption (Leon, 1979). Such explanations account for the food avoidance aspect of anorexia nervosa, but do not address the positive goal of the pursuit of thinness. Finally, there are those who believe that a *physiological* dysfunction tips the balance between a dieting adolescent and one who becomes trapped in the excesses of anorexia. Various endocrine and physiological dysfunctions contribute to the view that anorexia nervosa is primarily a hypothalamic disturbance (Garfinkel and Garner, 1982). However, researchers have failed to find a dysfunction specific to anorexia nervosa, nor have they been able to determine whether the dysfunctions preceded or resulted from the disturbance. Finally, the fact that physiological functioning returns to normal when anorectics recover argues against an inherent physiological defect. The balance of opinion is that the majority of physiological correlates are secondary to starvation (Werry, 1986b).

A Multidimensional Model

Recognizing that anorexia nervosa is not due to a single cause but is the result of multiple factors, Garfinkel and Garner (1982) devised a multidimensional model of predisposing, precipitating, and sustaining factors. Intrapersonal predisposing factors include being female, lack of a sense of mastery and autonomy, maturational fears, conscientiousness and conformity, early feeding difficulties, rigid thinking, and physiological dysfunctions. Interpersonal factors include parents who emphasize achievement and fitness or who are conflicted, depressed, and impulsive. Superordinate factors include society's emphasis on thinness and the middle- and upper-class pressure for achievement. Precipitating factors include perceived loss of self-esteem and self-control (for example, through social or academic failure), new and unfamiliar situations, especially sexual intimacy, separation, or loss. (The sustaining factors are not relevant to the present discussion.)

Such a comprehensive framework bypasses the perplexities of single-cause thinking, such as, If X and Y come from the same family, why did X become anorectic and Y did not? However, it still leaves the issue of necessary and sufficient conditions unanswered: are the factors additive so that a certain critical number will result in anorexia nervosa; or are they differentially weighted so that, say, intrapersonal variables are more potent than others; or do different combinations result in different kinds of anorexia nervosa?

Treatment

Anorectics are difficult to treat successfully. While there may be an initial improvement in terms of eating and weight gain, less than half are making a satisfactory adjustment when follow-up studies are conducted. According to Bemis (1978), who has given us a detailed critique of treatment effectiveness, probing underlying motives by means of psychoanalysis is inappropriate because of the anorectic's hypersensitivity to intrusion. Bruch (1973) recommends a factual, noninterpretive approach to restore the patient's self-confidence. Behavioral therapies have achieved excellent initial results which often are not sustained over time. (See Garfinkel and Garner, 1982, and Linscheid, Tarnowski, and Richmond, 1988.) Minuchin et al. (1975) reports that family therapy has an impressive, sustained success rate, but the technique is too new to allow an evaluation of its efficacy in a large number of cases treated by a diversity of therapists.

Allowing for the unsatisfactory nature of the data, there is no evidence at this point for a treatment of choice. This may be due in part to the multiple goals of treatment itself. The first order of business is to increase food intake and weight. Studies indicate that there is no difference among behavioral, milieu, supportive, and medical treatments. Long-term goals involve a more permanent normalization of eating habits and attitudes as well as correcting the intrapersonal and interpersonal problems that accompany anorexia nervosa. Again, there is no evidence for the superiority of any one treatment modality, although there is some indication that psychoanalysis and prolonged psychotherapy are not helpful and may even be somewhat detrimental. (See Askevold, 1983, and Steinhausen and Glanville, 1983b.) It may be that the multidimensional nature of the disturbance itself requires the versatile use of different treatment modalities.

BULIMIA

Bulimia was classified as a separate eating disorder in 1980, and so the clinical and research literature is limited. Bulimia is characterized by recurrent episodes of binge eating or the rapid consumption of large quantities of food in a brief period of time, and repeated attempts to lose weight by severe dieting, self-induced vomiting, or the use of cathartics or diuretics. The typical bulimic is a white female who begins overeating at about 18 years of age and begins purging by vomiting a year later. Although she may be either under- or overweight, her weight is often within the normal range. Her family history usually includes obesity or alcoholism. (For a review of the literature on bulimia, see Schlesier-Stropp, 1984.)

The bulimic adolescent is preoccupied with thoughts of food, eating, and vomiting to the point that concentration on everyday matters is impaired. Johnson and Larson (1982), using an ingenious time sampling method, found that bulimics spent less time socializing and more time alone than normal controls. As one of them remarked, "Food has become my closest companion." Binges include foods not allowed at other times—frequently ice cream, bread, candy, doughnuts, and soft drinks (Gandour, 1984). Ironically, bulimics are terrified of losing control over eating. In their "all or none" way of thinking, even eating a small amount of a favorite food would result in a binge. In a less extreme form,

they also share the anorectic's fear of becoming obese and perceive themselves as fat even when their body weight is normal. Thus the bulimic's uncontrolled desire to gorge herself traps her between anxiety over anticipated loss of control or becoming obese on the one hand, and guilt, shame, and self-contempt following a binge on the other. In fact, Johnson and Larson (1982) speculate that originally bulimics are addicted to food and have moderate mood fluctuations and hit on purging as an ideal means of protecting themselves from their fear of becoming fat. However, the solution fails because the bulimic spends more and more time binging and purging and becomes increasingly terrified of uncontrolled hunger.

While there is no increase in family pathology, there is an increase in impulsivity, suicide attempts, stealing, drug use, and depression among bulimics (Weiss and Ebert, 1983). However, severe medical complications are not common, and while there are menstrual irregularities, amenorrhea is less frequent and of shorter duration than in anorexia nervosa. There is some evidence that sexual relations become less satisfactory after the onset of bulimia, although again there is no evidence of the negative attitude or loss of interest that is found in the anorectic (Schlesier-Stropp, 1984).

The Societal-Sexual Theory of Etiology

The role of societal pressures and sex differences are emphasized in etiologic accounts of bulimia and anorexia nervosa. Striegel-Moore, Silberstein, and Rodin (1986) turn two of the most obvious demographic features of bulimia (and of anorexia nervosa) into questions: Why women? Why Western and other industrialized societies?

In our society cultural norms dictate that fat is ugly and what is ugly is bad, while thin is beautiful and what is beautiful is good. Moreover, the message is more powerful among certain groups: women of higher socioeconomic status who are concerned with current trends in beauty and fashion, colleges and boarding schools where beauty and dating are emphasized, professions such as dancing and modeling which dictate certain body weights—all are fertile breeding grounds for producing bulimia. In addition, there is evidence that beauty is central in the female sex role stereotype while being peripheral to the masculine sex role stereotype. There is even some evidence that eating small meals is associated with being feminine while hearty eating is regarded as masculine.

However, the adolescent period is merely the culmination of lifelong acculturation since the family, the school, children's books, and the mass media all send the message that girls should be physically attractive. Two other sex-linked forces are at work. By middle childhood, a girl's self-concept is related more to what others think of her than a boy's and thus is more interpersonal. Next, a girl's body image of being thin is highly related to her self-concept of feeling attractive, popular, and academically successful. In adolescence, the pubertal increase in fat, coupled with the social sensitivity and intertwining of body image and self-esteem, is especially distressing and may well underlie adolescent girls' preoccupation with weight and dieting.

However, the above account of the adolescent's concern with thinness and dieting leaves unanswered the question why a selected few become bulimic (or anorectic). The most obvious answer is that bulimics have adopted the cultural stereotype of femininity to a greater degree than have other adolescent girls, but the evidence concerning this hypothesis is mixed. Consequently, Striegel-Moore, Silberstein, and Rodin (1986) state that there is not a single cause but a variety of risk factors. The girls may be genetically programmed to be heavier than the svelte ideal and, as has been suggested in the case of bulimic anorectics, also may feel hunger more intensely. These girls may begin puberty earlier, making them particularly unhappy with their weight. Personality characteristics may include an unusually strong need for social approval and immediate need gratification, poor impulse control, a tendency toward depression, and a fragile sense of self. As was the case with Garfinkel and Garner's (1982) multidimensional model, the present list of risk factors underscores the complexity of the etiologic issue while still leaving unanswered the critical question of the necessary and sufficient conditions for producing bulimia.

A COMPARISON OF EATING DISORDERS

At a purely descriptive level, one cannot help but be struck by the overlap among eating disorders. There are "pure" restricter anorectics, bulimic anorectics, and "pure" bulimics, who also may have a history of obesity. Is there some meaningful continuum here in terms of failures to regulate eating, and can this continuum be conceptualized in developmental terms? Neither question can be answered at present although there are some relevant empirical data.

What little evidence there is suggests that the two groups of bulimics have more in common than the restricter and bulimic anorectics. Garner, Garfinkel, and O'Shaughnessy (1985) found that normal-weight and anorectic bulimics resemble each other in frequency, duration, and quality of food eaten during a binge episode, in the increase in impulse-related behavior and perceived family pathology, and in a predisposition to obesity. However, the normal-weight bulimics were more trusting than both types of anorectics. Finally, the three groups had a good deal in common. They all shared eating and weight-related disturbances such as a drive for thinness and an ideal body size lower than their actual one, they all had accompanying psychological problems, particularly depression, anxiety, and obsessiveness, and they all were equally perfectionistic and fearful of maturity while viewing themselves as ineffectual. While such data tentatively suggest that it might be more meaningful psychologically to regard anorectic bulimics as a special subgroup of bulimics rather than as a special subgroup of anorectics, more comparative studies must be done before the issue of classification can be solved.

ENURESIS

YOU ARE a clinical child psychologist visiting an Israeli kibbutz. The client is a 5-year-old boy who wets his bed at night. In Berkeley, California, where you practice, only 20 percent of children continue to wet their beds, and at this age, bedwetting ceases to be part of normal development, becoming instead, the psychopathology of enuresis. But you also know a number of other facts. While toilet training is benign and child-centered on the kibbutz, bedwetting is twice as prevalent here as in Berkeley. Finally, the client, like other kibbutz children, is psychologically healthier than his Berkeley counterpart in that he rarely has tantrums or fears or eating and sleeping problems.

What do you decide? That the little fellow is generally coming along all right, that bedwetting at his age is not all that deviant in the kibbutz, and that paying undue attention might prolong it? Or is bed-wetting one way 5-year-olds have of saying "Something's troubling me!" and indeed, at this age, is deviant behavior the only way 5-year-olds can send such a message? If so,

you would want to investigate the situation further to find what has gone wrong.

Such decisions are never easy. Fortunately, you know one more fact that will help you decide. We will discuss it in time, but right now we will use the example to illustrate the child clinician's problem of shifting criteria of disturbance to fit different social contexts. As enuresis becomes more prevalent, does it lose its status as a symptom? Surely we would not say that of malnutrition, illiteracy, or gang violence, all of which are very prevalent in certain cultures and classes. But is bedwetting as serious as those conditions? At what point do we say, "This is just the way these children are brought up," and at what point do we say, "This is deviant development"? The problem of distinguishing differences from deviations is central for clinicians who choose to work with inner-city blacks or American Indians or Chicanos, as well as those who go to foreign countries.

The Nature of Enuresis

Nocturnal enuresis is the involuntary discharge of urine during sleep after 5 years of age. In primary enuresis the child has never been trained to be dry at night. In secondary enuresis there is a relapse after a period of dryness. The two types represent two kinds of developmental deviations, one in which development fails to take place (fixation) and another in which development occurs but the child returns to a previous stage (regression). There is a gradual decline in incidence from 20 percent of 4- to 5-year-olds to 2 to 3 percent of 14-year-olds (Lovibond and Coote, 1979).

Enuresis runs in families, so that some children are more prone to become enuretic than others, depending on whether their siblings are enuretic. There is also an organic factor since urinary infection, small functional bladder capacity, and low threshold of responsiveness of the bladder may be associated with bed-wetting.

Social disadvantage and low socioeconomic status are superordinate factors associated with a high incidence of enuresis. Familial factors include indifference to the child's physical and psychological well-being, family breakup through death or divorce, separation from the mother for at least one month, the birth of a sibling, and moving to a new home.

Enuresis can be associated with both personality characteristics and psychiatric symptoms. Enuretic 4-year-olds are more generally disturbed than are nonenuretic children, although no single kind of disturbance predominates (Kaffman and Elizur, 1977). Enuretics aged 5 to 7 and 11 show more problems at home and in school than nonenuretics (Essen and Peckham, 1976).

Specific nighttime training is not related to enuresis. The age at which toilet training is started may be. Recent evidence (Kaffman and Elizur, 1977) suggesting that "late" training (in other words, after 20 months) increases the incidence of enuresis is contrary to the view of many child-care experts who emphasize permissiveness. Coercion appears to be related to enuresis, but more definitive data are needed.

The treatment of choice is the "bell and pad" method, in which the child's urine activates a bell, which in turn causes the child to awaken and cease urinating. Then the child gets up to urinate or is helped by the parents. Repetition of the procedure night after night causes the stimulus of bladder distention preceding urination to elicit the response of awakening. This procedure arrests bed-wetting in 75 percent of the cases, although 41 percent relapse within six months of treatment. (For a more extensive review see Doleys, 1977. Shaffer, 1977, reviews the literature on enuresis while Hersov, 1977, does the same for fecal soiling, or encopresis.)

A Developmental Study

The kibbutz example that opened the discussion of enuresis is based on one of the few longitudinal studies of enuresis (Kaffman and Elizur, 1977). In the kibbutz, four to six infants are cared for by a trained caretaker, or metapelet (plural, metaplot) in a communal children's house. Each child spends four hours daily with his or her parents. Generally speaking, the children's development and the parent–child relationships are similar to those in traditional Western families. From the standpoint of research, the advantage of the kibbutz is that the metaplot rather than parents have the responsibility for toilet training, which, as has been noted, is generally benign and child-centered. In the study reported by Kaffman and Elizur, 153 children were assessed on a number of physiological, inter-, and intrapersonal variables from infancy to 8 years of age. They regard enuresis as beginning at 4 rather than 5 years of age, which DSM-III-R gives as the age of onset

While the investigators found the usual genetic and physiological predisposing factors in the 4-year-old enuretics (enuretic siblings, smaller functional bladder capacity, impaired motor coordination), the personality and interpersonal factors are of greater interest. The enuretic children had a significantly greater number of behavior symptoms than the nonenuretic ones, suggesting that they were generally more disturbed. Within this general context, two high-risk personality patterns could be distinguished. Around 30 percent of the children were "hyperactive," aggressive, and negativistic in response to discipline, had low frustration tolerance, and resisted adjusting to new situations. How difficult it must have been for these children to sit or stand still when being potty-trained! A smaller group of enuretics were dependent, unassertive, had low achievement and mastery motivation, and masturbated frequently, perhaps to compensate for their lack of realistic pleasures arising from the interpersonal and physical environment. In contrast, the nonenuretic children were self-reliant, independent, and adaptable, and they had a high level of achievement motivation. They also showed a negative response to wetness and urine contact, in contrast to their enuretic counterparts, who showed no such reaction. The authors note that the two sets of high-risk traits did not characterize all enuretics; like obesity, bed-wetting can be a single symptom, part of a personality pattern, or one element in a picture of severe emotional disturbance.

In the interpersonal sphere, the clearest relation was between parental disinterest and enuresis; while there was some correlation with both emotional coldness and indulgent infantalization, it was not statistically significant. In addition, temporary separation from the parents was the only stress related to increased bed-wetting, for the kibbutz children took in stride the stresses of a sibling's birth, hospitalization, and even war. Interestingly, absence of the metapelet produced no such reaction, suggesting that the parent–child relationship was central. While not statistically significant, a relationship between bed-wetting and the metapelet's behavior was suggested; permissiveness, low achievement demands, and insecurity on the part of the metapelet tended to be related to enuresis, whereas structured, directive, and goal-oriented toilet training in the context of a loving relationship enhanced early bladder control.

The authors draw some general conclusions from the data. For low-risk children the timing of toilet training does not matter. In the high-risk group, delayed training increases the likelihood of enuresis. The motorically active, resistive, and aggressive infant is difficult enough to socialize, but the difficulties are compounded during the "terrible twos and threes." In the interpersonal realm, a permissive attitude, combined with noninvolvement or uncertainty, tends to perpetuate bed-wetting since there is neither sufficient challenge nor sufficient support for the child to take this particular step toward maturity. Such a finding is congruent with studies of normal development that show that a child's competence is maximized when parental affection is combined with challenges and an expectation of achievement. Overall, the children's personality characteristics were more highly correlated with enuresis than were interpersonal variables.

The Problem of Prognosis

Let us now return to the decision concerning whether to recommend therapy for the 5-year-old Israeli boy. In their longitudinal study, Kaffman and Elizur found that 50 percent of enuretic children were identified as "problem children" when they were 6 to 8 years of age, in contrast to 12 percent of nonenuretics. Learning problems and scholastic underachievement were the most frequent symptoms, although some of the children also lacked self-confidence and felt ashamed, guilty, or depressed. While some children "outgrow" enuresis, the behavior problems of others increase (Essen and Peckham, 1976). The importance of the point cannot be overemphasized. Looking at a graph showing the progressive decline of enuresis, one would opt for the prediction that the child would "outgrow" his problem. But longitudinal studies that include intra- and interpersonal variables alert the clinician to the possibility that enuresis in some 4-year-olds may be the first sign of problems that will persist and perhaps escalate.

Unfortunately, Kaffman and Elizur did not analyze their data to discover why certain enuretic children are at risk. The kind of shaming which might well be responsible for their negative self-image in this country is minimal in the kibbutz, where the attitude is one of acceptance of bed-wetting. It may be that the child's aggressiveness or dependence and the uneasy permissiveness of caretakers continue to hamper the child in subsequent socialization and in achievement of the self-discipline necessary for making a successful school adjustment.

There is one final point to be made concerning the relation between psychopathology and development. The children who were not enuretic at 4 years of age evidenced a significant amount of fearfulness at 3 years of age. They showed diverse fears during the day and were especially frightened about going to sleep or would awaken crying for their caretakers. It is possible that such behaviors were a sign of the stress of toilet training, and that even in a benign setting the conflict between autonomy and losing parental love can take its toll on healthy children. The finding also underscores the limitations of using the symptom approach exclusively when defining psychopathology. A child clinician must decide when a disturbance is part of healthy growth (as in the fearful 3-year-old) and when it is the first sign of trouble to come (as in the enuretic 5-year-old). Longitudinal studies are all too rare in this regard. Until more data have accumulated, the clinician has no choice other than to evaluate the various etiological variables along with the child's general development and rely on the guidelines resulting from accumulated experience.

REFLECTIONS ON THE DEVELOPMENTAL MODEL AND ON INITIATIVE

We have learned a number of clinically useful lessons about the importance of contexts in understanding psychopathological behavior.

First there is the *organic* context, which includes the genetic and physiological factors in enuresis and obesity, as well as the vaguely defined biological vulnerability in symbiotic psychosis. Then there is the *intrapersonal* context. Symbiotic psychosis (like autism and childhood schizophrenia) engulfs the child; however, enuresis may be a reaction to a specific trauma, or the primary psychopathology, or one manifestation of another psychopathology such as antisocial acting out or depression. Failure to take the intrapersonal context into account can result in inappropriate recommendations for therapy and is responsible for a good deal of confusion in the research literature. In the *interpersonal* context, parental behavior has consistently emerged as a potent determinant of psychopathology; only in enuresis is there a suggestion that it may be less influential than the child's temperament. Pathogenic patterns of family interaction have been delineated for anorexia nervosa, and we suspect this approach could readily be extended to oppositional behavior and enuresis, where the roles of the mother and father in relation to the child have been tentatively explored. The *superordinate* context of socioeconomic status and culture holds some surprises: anorexia nervosa is found primarily in the well-fed middle class, while enuresis flourishes both in disadvantaged American slum children as well as well-cared for children in the kibbutz. The formula "poverty engenders psychopathology" proves far too simple to account for the psychopathology of toddlers—as it will again in the case of delinquents.

Then there is the all-important context of *time*. The same psychopathological behavior may have different meanings depending on when it occurs in the developmental sequence: witness the changing meanings of eating from infancy through the preschool period. Time poses the knottiest questions for the clinician: When is a disturbance temporary (as in the fearful 3-year-old who will be dry during the night a year later), and when is it the first sign of trouble to come (as in the enuretic 4-year-old)? Or again, when is disturbed behavior age-appropriate (such as the 5-year-old who gorges herself because of some unrealistic sexual anxiety), and when is it a regression to a previous developmental stage (such as the 5-year-old who gorges himself because of a sudden terror over being separated from his mother)? Research furnishes far too few guides to answering these questions; much of the time the clinician must rely on skill and experience.

We have also learned about different *models* of deviant development. One model involves failure to progress as expected: the mother–infant symbiosis does not develop; drives and affects are not differentiated as specific states of high arousal; control of bladder and bowels is not achieved. This, of course, is the *fixation* model of psychopathology. A variation of the fixation model involves an exaggeration of normal development—oppositional behavior and feeding problems being the prime examples—if such exaggerations are prolonged and block further growth. The second model is *regression*, the clearest examples being secondary enuresis, fear of oral impregnation, and the separation anxiety in symbiotic psychosis.

Finally, we have learned about the *deviant*

development of initiative and early socialization. Self-reliant enterprise can be totally undermined by a mother–infant interaction that traps the toddler between the terror of autonomy and the terror of a return to infantile dependence. In all the eating disorders the self-as-agent is usurped by parental *intrusiveness*, at times in the form of naked domination, at times in the form of solicitous concern for the child's welfare. While the enterprising component of initiative may suffer in the sedentary obese child, it may be accentuated in the anorectic. Even the child's perception of drives and affects can be distorted by parental usurption of the self-as-agent.

Our exploration of various psychopathologies now branches off in two directions. First, we will continue to explore initiative, but not the self-reliant expansiveness we have just discussed. Rather, the focus will shift to curiosity and exploration, which require the ability to pay attention and to work up to one's potential. Both can go awry, producing hyperactivity on the one hand, learning disabilities on the other. Then we will pick up the theme of socialization and follow it into middle childhood, a time when excessive socialization with its attendant anxieties may lead to neurotic behavior, while lax and punitive socialization becomes a precursor of conduct disorders.

7

Early Deviations in Curiosity and Task Orientation: Attention-Deficit Hyperactivity and Learning Disabilities

As we have just seen, initiative can go awry in the toddler period by becoming excessive and producing an oppositional disorder. However, initiative involves not only self-reliance and autonomy but curiosity and exploration as well. As Piaget has taught us, even infants are problem solvers, implicitly asking, What is that? and How does it work? until, by the end of the first year, they are actively experimenting with the physical and social environment. In a like manner, toddlers have a remarkable ability to give their undivided attention to the tasks involved in exploration. Subsequently, school adds an element of requiredness to intrinsic curiosity which, in turn, is transformed into the work of learning specific subjects.

Yet this ability to concentrate on the task at hand in the toddler and preschool periods can be seriously curtailed by an *attention deficit*, which prevents children from keeping their minds on a particular task and which also results in *hyperactivity*. In middle childhood a different deviation appears in intelligent, motivated children who are unable to achieve at an appropriate level in one or another academic subject such as reading or arithmetic. This deviation is called *learning disabilities*. In both instances that part of initiative responsible for enabling children to concentrate on and master increasingly complex tasks has been diverted from its normal course.

ATTENTION-DEFICIT HYPERACTIVITY DISORDER

Hyperactivity has been the problem child among child psychopathologies. No one is quite sure where it belongs, while some authorities claim it should not exist! For a while, hyperactivity was thought to result from a subtle form of brain malfunctioning called minimal brain dysfunction, or MBD (see chapter 12), which produced poorly controlled motor behavior. As the condition was better understood, emphasis shifted from motor behavior to cognition, and hyperactivity was considered to result from a basic defect in attention. Thus, DSM-III lists attention deficit with hyperactivity and attention deficit without hyperactivity. Subsequently, DSM-III-R simplified the dual diagnoses into the single Attention-Deficit Hyperactivity Disorder (ADHD). In the meantime, MBD withered away as an etiologic agent from lack of empirical support, although hyperactivity is still regarded as resulting from some yet to be discovered brain malfunctioning.

Whether this restless diagnosis has finally found its proper home remains to be seen. Meanwhile, we will take the characteristic behaviors at face value in order to locate hyperactivity among our basic variables. The most obvious feature of hyperactive children is their poor concentration and impulsivity. Beginning in the toddler/preschool period they lack the task orientation so characteristic of normal development. This weakened task orientation affects *initiative* in regard to their ability to work at a problem and get it done, and their venturing out confidently and mastering various social and academic challenges.

Before examining ADHD in greater detail, we shall first review the many assessment and diagnostic problems it has presented.

Problems in Assessment

Hyperactivity, in the form of fidgeting, impulsivity, and distractibility, is not only one of the most visible of behavioral constellations but also among the most frequent complaints parents and teachers make about supposedly normal children. It is ironic, then, that assessment has proved so difficult.

In part the problem is one that bedevils much of psychological assessment; namely, different measures of the same variable do not correlate very highly. Hyperactivity can be measured by mechanical devices that record the actual amount of body movement, by direct observation, or by interview ratings and questionnaire scores. In a way, a certain amount of disagreement among techniques is to be expected. The measurement of the sheer amount of bodily activity says nothing of how appropriate or inappropriate that activity is, while it is the quality of inappropriateness which lies at the heart of adults' evaluation of children's behavior as being hyperactive. Or again, behavioral observations in a given setting might be expected to differ from the kind of overall evaluations often tapped by interviews and questionnaires.

However, the problem in assessment goes deeper than variability among instruments. For various assessments to be highly correlated, the behavior itself must be reasonably consistent in different settings. There is evidence that this is not the case with hyperactivity, which increases in familiar, structured, task-oriented settings such as the classroom and decreases in informal or high-energy-expenditure settings such as the playground. Consequently, an inexperienced clinical child psychologist may brace himself or herself for assessing a hyperactive preschooler who is described as a "holy terror" at home only to find that the child is a model of cooperativeness in the unfamiliar, game-like testing situation.

Because the classroom is usually regarded as the acid test of hyperactivity, teachers' evaluations are often regarded as the most central in detecting hyperactivity. However, does it matter whether hyperactivity is situational or whether it exists in various situations? Apparently it does. A three-year follow-up study of preschoolers (Campbell, Endman, and Bernfeld, 1977) found that pervasively hyperactive children had a worse prognosis than did situational hyperactive children. Both groups showed more disruptive and inappropriate behavior (such as calling out or going to the teacher's desk) than did the control group but the pervasively hyperactive children had more inattention and were out of their seats and distracted from their tasks more often. Similar results were found in a five-year follow-up study of 10-year-olds. In fact, evidence on older groups suggests that children with situational hyperactivity often turn out to be no different from the control group (Rutter and Garmezy, 1983). Not only is pervasive hyperactivity predictive of future maladjustment, but it is also associated with the kinds of cognitive deficits presumed to lie at the core of this disorder.

Problems in Diagnosis

Because the behaviors comprising the hyperactive syndrome are commonly found in a number of other disturbances, the independence of the diagnosis has long been seriously questioned. Nor has the recent shift to an emphasis on attention deficit settled the issue. Prior and Sanson (1986) claim that ADHD has no unique diagnostic status because it is found in children with conduct disorders, learning disabilities, and other psychopathologies. Moreover, it has neither a specific, unique

etiology nor a specific response to treatment. They recommend either a return to the former diagnosis of Hyperactivity or that the syndrome be subsumed under Conduct Disorder.

There is also evidence for diagnostic independence, however. Many factor analytic studies show that hyperactivity emerges as a factor separate from *conduct disorders* both in the general population and in clinical samples. Other studies have shown that it is possible to separate purely hyperactive/inattentive children and purely aggressive/conduct-disordered children from those who have both disturbances provided that adequate measures are used. Children with ADHD have more cognitive and achievement deficits while aggressive/conduct-disordered children have more antisocial parents and family hostility and are more often from a low socioeconomic status. Moreover, ADHD children are frequently off task in classroom and playroom situations, which is not true of aggressive/conduct-disordered children. Not only does this latter group have better control of their behavior, but their social skills also may be better because the group may have some popular as well as some rejected children while ADHD children are rarely popular. Finally, the prognosis for aggressive/conduct-disordered children is ominous, while that of ADHD children is relatively benign, especially for situational hyperactivity. Children who have both ADHD and a conduct disorder tend to have the worst features of both disturbances, especially in regard to observed behavior, peer status, and outcome (Hinshaw, 1987).

The overlap of ADHD with *learning disabilities* is to be expected because inattention is apt to interfere with learning, while the stress of academic failure may result in restless, inattentive behavior. A sensitive clinician, however, can evaluate whether the hyperactivity/inattention antedated or followed the child's experience of school failure. Also the restless behavior of the LD child should be more confined to the classroom than is that of the hyperactive/inattentive child (Douglas, 1983).

Research evidence for a difference between ADHD and LD children comes from a study by Tarnowski, Prinz, and Nay (1986). They compared ADHD, LD, ADHD-LD children, and a normal control group on measures of sustained attention, selective attention, and span of apprehension. They found unique patterns of attentional deficits associated with each diagnostic group. The most important finding for our purposes was that the ADHD group evidenced deficits in sustaining attention, which, as we shall soon see, is one of the core features of this disorder. The LD group was characterized by difficulties with selective attention, while attentional deficits were most pervasive in the combined ADHD-LD group.

In sum, while overlap with conduct disorders and learning disabilities may be frequent, attention-deficit hyperactivity disorder can also be found "in pure culture" as a distinct category of psychopathology.

Implications for Research

This is not the first time we shall make this point nor will it be the last: unless researchers are able to study pure cases of a given diagnostic category, or unless they are able to control for possible confounds (as in the case of controlling for IQ when studying autism), there is no way of knowing whether the obtained results apply to this category. The point is nowhere more important than in the case of ADHD children. As we have seen, there is a good deal of overlap between this category and conduct disorders. Unless researchers are careful to eliminate conduct-disordered children from their ADHD population, or unless they have a comparison

group of conduct-disordered children, there is no way of knowing whether the results are specific to ADHD, to conduct disorders, or to children who have both disturbances. The same principle applies to learning disabilities and to situational versus generalized hyperactivity.

Unfortunately, past investigators have not been as scrupulous in selecting subjects and controls as they might have been. In part this is due to certain assessment instruments which include features of different diagnostic categories in a single instrument. In part it is due to the difficulty in locating pure cases because these are rarer than mixed ones. Whatever the reasons, research results often are confounded, and all too often one must rely on a few well-designed and executed studies. We should keep this caution in mind as we turn to examining the nature, etiology, and developmental causes of ADHD.

The Developmental Dimension

We begin with a descriptive overview of the development of ADHD children, relying on the work of Ross and Ross (1976). It is important to note at the outset that they present a composite description of the ADHD child, a compendium of the problems and difficulties encountered from infancy through adulthood. Thus their picture is an extreme one. In reality, there are individual differences among the children, as well as differences in degrees of hyperactivity.

INFANCY Irregularity characterizes the physiological and psychological functioning of ADHD infants. They may be calm one minute and then yell and appear almost apoplectic the next, their cry having a shrill, piercing quality "like a siren" or "like an animal in acute distress" rather than resembling the cry of normal infants. They do not fall asleep quickly or at regular times; there are only brief periods of quiet sleep, the infants being easily awakened with a startled reaction.

Infants usually show normal progress in growth and general development but exhibit advanced motor activity, often climbing out of their crib in the first year of life and sometimes wearing out the mattress with constant rocking. Thus their activity level is far above average. One important consequence is that the mother has difficulty nursing her squirming, wriggling, twisting child. The infant's personality is often described in negative terms, such as irritable, demanding, unsatisfied, and rarely smiling.

It is easy to understand how the above constellation of behaviors would be detrimental to a harmonious mother–infant interaction. Even an attentive mother might be bewildered by the infant's irregularity, frustrated by the difficulty in feeding, disappointed by the rarity of the social smile, and irritated by the negative personality traits. In turn, the infant is deprived of the security and growth-promoting stimulation which derive from a mutually satisfying interaction. However, Ross and Ross note that causation may run in the opposite direction, a rejecting, punitive or indifferent mother producing a fretful, restless, erratically functioning infant.

PRESCHOOL Preschoolers, more than infants, are a serious management problem for the parents because they are more mobile and fearless, and they do not learn from experience. One boy, for example, climbed out of a second-story window onto a tree, removed all the books from a large bookcase and threw them out of the window, and uprooted a number of new plants in the garden—all in the space of a week's time. The irregular mood and light sleep characteristic of infancy persist. These children have low frustration tolerance and a short attention span, and their temper tantrums are unusually intense. Their physical growth and development continue to be normal, although their running may have an unusual "driven" quality. Their adeptness at getting into and out of locked and closed rooms, emptying drawers, and opening bottles increases their vulnerability to accidents and accidental poisoning.

The hyperactivity of such preschoolers adversely affects the development of self-control and social relations. As they are relatively unresponsive to physical punishment, reasoning, and persuasion, the foundations of self-control cannot be firmly established. In structured social groups they tend to be aggressive and destructive, thereby alienating peers. Moreover, they seem unaware of others' feelings and of the fact that their behavior may be hurting or annoying them. Structured activities in a preschool setting also elicit restless, irrelevant behavior and poor conduct. It is not unusual for them to be shunted from one preschool to another in the hopes of finding one that will tolerate their behavior. In the process, their self-esteem begins to decline, especially if they have a successful sibling, and they may begin to develop techniques for gaining negative attention, such as teasing, name calling, or showing off.

Fortunately, hyperactive preschoolers get along well in relatively unstructured situations. (We have already noted the influence of situational variables on hyperactivity.) In free play, for example, their activity level and social behavior do not differ from that of normal children. They also can relate well in a one-to-one situation and a strange situation.

The hyperactive child's delay in language nicely illustrates how diverse variables interact to generate a network of psychopathological behaviors. The weary and exasperated mother may only infrequently engage in social talk with her hyperactive infant, thus setting the stage for a subsequent verbal deficiency. Words play a number of important functions.

They enhance cognitive development, since symbols for objects can be more readily and versatilely manipulated than objects themselves. Verbalization also serves as a check on action, since manipulating symbols can now take the place of manipulating objects. Because the hyperactive child is slow in making the transition to verbal symbols, touching continues to occupy a dominant place in transactions with the social and physical environment. Such behavior is apt to antagonize peers who dislike being held and grabbed, as well as increasing the likelihood that the child will handle and break valued household objects, thereby antagonizing parents. Thus the preschooler is not "merely" lagging in language; rather, the deficit reverberates to many other aspects of life.

MIDDLE CHILDHOOD   Hyperactive children are now less of a problem at home, primarily because they spend less time in the house. The Jekyll-and-Hyde quality of their behavior continues, normal periods alternating with periods of disruptive, distractible behavior. They have trouble sitting at the table throughout a meal, their attempts to help may end in disaster, and their actions may have a precipitous quality that dooms them to failure. Their low self-esteem and hopelessness, engendered by hostility and rejection from parents and peers, may result in feelings of unhappiness or depression.

Peer interactions continue to suffer. The hyperactive children's clumsiness and inability to sustain attention prevent them from playing games properly, while their tendency to be easily distracted and their poor emotional control result in their being labeled a quitter, a crybaby, or a poor sport. Even more unfortunate is the tendency for peers, like adults, to react negatively to children with high activity levels; thus, even when the children are friendly and helpful, they are likely to be rejected. Such punishment for socially acceptable behavior makes it difficult for the ADHD child to master the rules of social interaction.

In school, the teacher may complain that such children cannot stay in their seats, finish their work on time, keep their minds on their work, refrain from calling out, and inhibit aggression. These children seldom follow oral directions accurately and make errors because they do not stop to think. Since they may also settle down for a brief period and become obedient and industrious, the teacher believes they could control themselves all the time "if they really tried." The teacher's resentment is picked up by other children, so that the ADHD child's self-esteem continues its downward spiral, and school itself becomes a daily agony. It is not surprising that the combination of defects in attention and problem solving, on the one hand, and a sense of failure and lack of motivation, on the other, result in poor academic achievement; the ADHD child repeats grades and functions below potential in basic academic subjects. It is also not surprising that aggressiveness and antisocial behavior increase.

ADOLESCENCE   Although the high levels of activity associated with hyperkinesis decrease, adolescents do not outgrow their difficulties. On the contrary, they enter this period with problems arising from many sources: a poor self-image, rejection by parents and siblings, a lack of social skills, poor school performance despite adequate intelligence, and a strong tendency to be nonconforming and to engage in antisocial behavior. With these handicaps they must face the normal adolescent challenges of physiological changes and sexual adjustment, of peer acceptance, and of the choice of a vocation.

The ADHD adolescent is still more restless, distractible, and emotionally labile than are peers. Underachievement, poor self-esteem, and depression constitute major problems. Antisocial behavior now becomes a concern not only of parents and school, but also of society, leading to police contacts and court referrals for a significant number of hyperactive adolescents. Ross and Ross regard adolescence as a more difficult period for the hyperactive group than middle childhood.

ADULTHOOD   The majority of ADHD children will grow up without major psychopathology of either an antisocial or a psychotic nature. However, half or more of them will have lower educational achievement, poorer social skills, and lower self-esteem than normal controls, and they will show more impulsive/delinquent and immature/dependent personality traits. Thus even without formal psychiatric disturbances, they are far from "outgrowing" their problems as adults. Favorable prognostic signs are normal or above-average intelligence, well-functioning families, and the absence of aggressive conduct disorders. By the same token, a low IQ, family discord, punitive parenting, and a high level of aggression are poor prognostic signs (Campbell and Werry, 1986).

Core Characteristics

The core characteristics of ADHD are typically inattention, impulsivity, and hyperactivity.

INATTENTION   ADHD children have difficulty sustaining attention in tasks or play activities. This attention deficit affects a wide range of tasks from simple reaction time to complex problem solving requiring self-directed and self-sustained effort. In discussing ADHD children's attentional deficit, we shall rely heavily on the research of Douglas (1983) and her colleagues, who have conducted an extensive series of studies on this topic.

Attention is not a simple process. On the contrary, it is multifaceted, and so it is logical to ask what aspects have gone awry in the case of ADHD children. Douglas disagrees with the idea that such children are distractible, in the sense that their attention is readily "captured" by every extraneous stimulus in the environment. Studies that have introduced various kinds of distractions show that hyperactive children perform as well as normals. In one study, for example, the children were required to read with a telephone ringing, lights flashing, and the sound of a calculating machine. To express this idea in more formal terms, hyperactive children are not deficient in the *selective* aspect of attention, that is, in the ability to filter out irrelevant environmental stimuli in order to focus on stimuli specifically relevant to the task at hand.

The evidence in regard to distractibility is not totally consistent, however. Some studies have shown that highly interesting or salient stimuli embedded within the target stimuli will impair performance. Even though there may be some exceptions, the overall finding is that poor performance of ADHD children is not due to an inability to filter out or ignore irrelevant environmental events (Campbell and Werry, 1986).

The research showing that ADHD children have a basic deficit in *sustaining* attention is consistent and convincing. Two of the purest measures of sustained attention are: *reaction time tests,* in which a warning signal (such as a buzzer) is followed by a preparatory interval terminated by a stimulus (such as a light) to which the subject has been instructed to respond as quickly as possible (for example, by pressing a lever), and *continuous-perform-*

ance tests, in which letters appear on a screen one at a time, the child having been instructed to respond to a given letter (such as *X*) only when another letter (such as *A*) precedes it.

Not only are hyperactive children generally inferior to normal controls on these simple tasks, but their performance also deteriorates with time.

Douglas's studies illustrate the advantage of programmatic research in which a series of investigations successively tests interrelated hypotheses. A single study, rather than being isolated, provides salient leads as to which variable to control next or which one to alter during the actual conduct of a study. In the process, the investigator can develop a special astuteness by pursuing various facets of a complex psychological variable.

We shall focus on Douglas's program in its initial phase when she was concerned with the function of attention. Conceptually she noted that the selective aspect of attention could be differentiated from its sustaining aspect, even though some of the research literature had merged the two by maintaining that hyperactive children had difficulty sustaining selective attention (Douglas and Peters, 1980). The control inherent in the *laboratory* approach allowed her to study each aspect separately to see whether it was functioning in a normal or a deviant manner. The population of children she used was between 6 and 12 years of age, hyperactivity having been the major complaint for several years. Children were excluded whose behavior seemed to be due to emotional problems, who were neurotic, psychotic, or retarded, who had specific learning disabilities, who had been diagnosed as brain-damaged, or whose histories suggested brain injury.

To test the hypothesis concerning selectivity, researchers administered Color Distraction Tests to twenty hyperactive and twenty control children matched for age, sex, and IQ scores (Campbell, Douglas, and Morgenstern, 1971). (As we have seen, distractibility is used as a measure of selective attention.) The initial card contained pictures of red apples, green lettuce, blue grapes, and yellow bananas, and the subjects were instructed to name the colors. The first distractor consisted of the same pictures of fruit with a number of black and white pictures of familiar objects, which the subject was instructed to ignore while naming the color of the fruit. The second distractor consisted of the same fruit but with contradictory colors; for example, bananas were blue, red, or green, but not yellow, and the subject was instructed to name the color the fruit should be. In all three conditions, speed of color-naming was recorded. An interference score was derived from the difference between the speed of naming the colors in the initial condition and in the two distracting conditions. There was no significant difference between the scores of the hyperactive and normal children under either the initial condition or the two conditions of distraction. Therefore there was no evidence of increased distractibility in the hyperactivity group.

In testing the hypothesis concerning sustained attention (Sykes,

Douglas, and Morgenstern, 1973), twenty hyperactive and twenty control children were matched for age, sex, and IQ scores. A Choice Reaction Time Task was used to measure attention for brief periods. In this task subjects were required to press one of two buttons corresponding to one of two stimuli appearing on a screen; for example, either a circle or a triangle would appear, and the child had to press one of two buttons also marked with a circle or a triangle. In this task there was no difference between groups, indicating that attention for brief periods was intact in hyperactive children.

In the Continuous Performance Task (Visual Mode), twelve letters appeared one at a time at 1.5 second intervals on a screen, the child being instructed to press a button when the letter *X* was preceded by the letter *A*. While the letters were presented in random order, there were fifteen such *A-X* pairs in a run of 100 letters. In the Auditory Mode version of the procedure, the stimuli were presented by a recording of a female voice. In both versions of the tasks, the performance of the hyperactive group was significantly inferior to that of the control as measured by the number of errors, indicating a difficulty in sustaining attention for such children.

As was noted in the presentation of studies of autistic children, the laboratory not only allows for a refinement of differentiation (in this instance, selective versus sustained attention) but also for a systematic manipulation of variables (in this instance attention for auditory and visual material) which would be next to impossible with any other research methodology.

IMPULSIVITY   Another core characteristic of ADHD children is impulsivity. In ordinary terms, they "act before thinking." When confronted with a complex task, for example, they may accept the first solution that comes to mind, never challenging themselves to consider whether it is the best or most appropriate solution. They may blurt out incorrect answers in class or have difficulty taking turns in organized play, again because of a weakened ability to control the impulse to action. It is not by accident that we tell a child to *stop* and think; in fact, Douglas epitomizes this basic defect in ADHD children as an inability to stop, look, listen—and think.

A number of studies support the observation that ADHD children are impulsive (Douglas, 1983). On the Continuous Performance Task, for example, they respond to the preceding letter rather than to the target letter, or they respond to nonsignificant letters. On more complex tasks, ADHD children make not only very rapid responses but irrelevant and inappropriate ones as well, which suggests that they tend to respond carelessly and impulsively.

While ADHD children do not lack search strategies, they are deficient in them compared with normal children. This deficiency is evidenced in solving both perceptual and logical problems. In the Matching Familiar Figures Test, for example, the child is required to choose from a group of similar pictures the one that is identical to a standard picture, such as a man or a house. ADHD children perform in an impulsive manner, failing systematically to compare the standard with the entire array of pictures or failing to check back and forth between the standard and the array. Thus their basic weakness in attentional and inhibitional skills makes them respond prematurely and incorrectly.

Not only do ADHD children have inefficient strategies, but the advantage of having a strategy to begin with also does not occur to many of them. Tutors may complain that the children are unaware of their own role as problem solvers; they do not realize that they must make a deliberate effort instead of having the solution "just come" to them.

HYPERACTIVITY   While it seems counterintuitive, motor overactivity is a far less robust dimension of ADHD than is inattention (Campbell and Werry, 1986). There is some evidence that ADHD children are more active on a 24-hour basis (including sleep) than are normal control children and that they show greater restlessness in the form of task-irrelevant movements, squirming in their seats, and out-of-seat behavior than do normal controls. However, the differences are most marked with younger children and tend to decrease with age. Also, as we have seen, differences may depend on the situation. Even when group differences exist, they are not striking; many children diagnosed as ADHD do not have a higher than normal activity level. Finally, activity level does not clearly differentiate ADHD from other disturbances; for example, evidence of a significantly higher activity level than that found in conduct-disordered children is inconsistent.

Cognitive and Academic Correlates

Because the ability to sustain attention and inhibit disruptive impulses is basic to all cognitive processes, one would expect the deficiencies found in ADHD to have far-reaching effects. We will now examine the evidence concerning a number of these effects. (Our presentation follows Campbell and Werry, 1986.)

IQ AND ACADEMIC ACHIEVEMENT   While there is a good deal of disagreement among studies, the evidence suggests that ADHD children perform more poorly than normal controls on standard measures of intelligence. However, children vary widely in their functioning, and a number of them have average or above-average intelligence. Also, the research findings offer few clues as to what specific deficits might be responsible for the lower scores. In addition to such deficits there is always the possibility that inattention and impulsivity themselves might prevent children from doing their best, thereby spuriously lowering their score.

There is no doubt that ADHD children do poorly in school. They repeat more grades, receive lower marks in academic subjects, and score lower on standard measures of reading, spelling, vocabulary, and mathematics than normal children. Moreover, medication, which improves attention and impulse control, has little effect on improving academic achievement. Equally ominous is the fact that academic performance tends to deteriorate with time.

The reasons for poor academic achievement remain a matter of speculation. Some authorities favor a cognitive etiology, arguing that the core difficulties prevent the development of the problem-solving strategies and higher-level conceptualizations essential to academic success. Others stress motivational factors, school failures lowering self-esteem and progressively undermining the desire to achieve as the child grows older. Of course, there is no reason both processes cannot be taking place at the same time.

MEMORY   Evaluating memory in ADHD children is difficult because it is necessary to distinguish an inability to remember from a failure to attend to the material in the first place. However, it does seem that ADHD children's memory is intact as long as the list of stimuli is relatively short or as long as the stimuli can be grouped together in a meaningful way. However, memory deteriorates as the number of stimuli to be remembered increases. There is some evidence that this is so because ADHD children, instead of increasing their effort as the task becomes more difficult, actually expend less effort and use less efficient memory strategies.

HIGHER-ORDER PROCESSES The picture here is similar to that found in memory: adequate performance on simple tasks but deficient performance as the task increases in complexity. In a study of word knowledge, for example, ADHD children performed as well as controls when choosing between two alternatives, but more poorly when confronted with five. In general, ADHD children do poorly on concept formation tasks, which require careful attention to and effortful processing of relatively large amounts of information.

The ADHD children's poor performance on tasks requiring higher-order thinking seems to be due, in large part, to their general approach to the task and their choice of inefficient problem-solving strategies. In their approach they tend to be careless and casual, investing the minimal effort and readily engaging in task-irrelevant behaviors. In their strategies they tend to be rather haphazard and capricious rather than thoughtful and organized. In a task requiring the scanning of an array of stimuli they are apt to skip around, focusing on novel or striking ones instead of systematically examining them all, thereby failing to process all the relevant information. For example, when presented with pictures of flowers varying in two aspects of four dimensions (three or five petals, straight or curved stem, with or without leaves, and

set in a square or round background) and asked to find out which one the experimenter was thinking about by asking questions that could be answered either yes or no, the ADHD children's scattered attention prevented them from examining all the pictures in order to discover the basic dimensions and from solving the problem with the fewest questions.

The above findings raise an intriguing question. Suppose that, by some means such as medication or therapy or enticing rewards, one could get the ADHD child to become genuinely task-oriented: would the cognitive deficiencies remain? This question may be formulated in terms of *performance versus competence* and concerns whether a particular deficiency reflects a basic lack of ability (competence) or whether the ability is there but obscured by other factors such as indifference or fear or a reluctance to become deeply involved (performance). On this point of performance versus competence the evidence is mixed. Some data indicate that, even when told about a more effective strategy for solving a problem, the ADHD children did not recognize it as such, which suggests a competence deficit. However, other studies found that performance improved as the task became more interesting and that concept learning was equal to that of normal controls provided that every correct response was positively reinforced. Such findings suggest a performance deficit with intact cognitive abilities. In light of the limited data, answering the basic question of performance versus competence lies far in the future.

RESPONSE TO REINFORCEMENT ADHD children have their own special way of responding to reinforcement. As we have just seen, their performance will improve if every correct response is positively reinforced. What is unusual is that their performance actually deteriorates when reinforcement appears only after every second correct response or at regular intervals. The withdrawal of expected rewards can interfere with performance even on simple tasks. Such a pattern of response to reinforcement has led Douglas (1983) to hypothesize that ADHD children have an exceptionally strong need for immediate gratification. In fact, they tend to invest more energy and interest in obtaining a reward than in meeting the demands of solving a particular problem. Instead of being task-oriented, they work with one eye on the rewarding adult, as it were. Consequently, withdrawal of rewards is particularly upsetting. Douglas (1983) regards this need to have immediate gratification as being so important that she places it among the core characteristics of ADHD children.

The Organic Context

While minimal brain damage is no longer regarded as the primary cause of ADHD, the psychopathology is still considered organic rather than psychogenic in nature. A number of possible etiologies have been explored.

AROUSAL LEVEL Perhaps the most obvious inference about ADHD children is that their behavior results from a chronic state of hyperarousal. However, as was the case with activity level, the obvious inference turns out not to be the correct one. While many studies have produced conflicting results, the evidence points either to underarousal or to a combination of under- and overarousal.

Peripheral measures of arousal such as heart rate and skin conductance or Galvanic Skin Response indicate there is no difference between ADHD and normal control children in a resting state. However, ADHD children are somewhat less responsive than controls to specific stimuli or task demands. Central measures of arousal have typically employed the EEG. Here the results are less consistent

than with peripheral measures but they suggest that, at least in a subgroup of children, underarousal is the more common pattern (Campbell and Werry, 1986).

Douglas (1983) contends that arousal regulation is the principal problem that leaves ADHD children vulnerable to wide swings in either direction. In boring, repetitive situations the children are underaroused, which leads to erratic, stimulus-seeking behavior; in highly stimulating situations, such as being praised or frustrated, they become overaroused and engage in overexcited behavior. All too rarely are they in that state of moderate arousal which facilitates concentration and task orientation.

DRUG RESPONSE AND BIOCHEMICAL INFLUENCES One of the most frequently cited pieces of evidence for an organic etiology for ADHD is the response to *stimulant medication*, which has the paradoxical effect of increasing attention and task orientation. However, the case is far from being airtight (Rutter and Garmezy, 1983). While it is true that ADHD children respond favorably to medication in the short run, it is not clear whether the medication merely provides symptomatic relief or whether it corrects a basic biological dysfunction, especially because many children continue to progress after the medication has been discontinued. Finally, for the organic hypothesis to be convincing, the effects of the stimulant drugs should be specific to ADHD. However, these drugs have the same effect on normal and enuretic children and on normal adults. In sum, while the response of ADHD children to stimulant drugs is both interesting and important, it cannot be taken as proving the organic hypothesis in the case of this disturbance. A host of biochemical abnormalities have been implicated in the etiology of ADHD. While each has some support in research findings, none has proved specific to this disorder. Research may one day yield the biochemical disorder specific to ADHD; there is no such definitive evidence at this point.

NEUROLOGICAL AND PATHOLOGICAL FINDINGS There is no evidence of major neurological signs of damage or dysfunction in ADHD children. However, in certain children there is an increase in the so-called *soft signs* (see chapter 12) of central nervous system dysfunction. These consist of developmental delays in functions such as speech and motor coordination, nystagmus, and asymmetries of reflex. Not only is the concept of soft signs controversial, but there is also no evidence that they are specific to ADHD since they are found in other disturbances and in impaired intelligence. The same conclusion holds true for *minor physical anomalies.* These are subtle physical defects such as misshapen ears, widely spaced eyes, curved fifth finger, third toe larger than second, and very fine hair that cannot be combed, which initially were thought to be related to ADHD, but which subsequently turned out to be characteristic of a wide variety of disturbances including conduct disorders, autism, and retardation.

While there is an association between *pre- and postnatal events* and subsequent ADHD, such factors are weak and inefficient predictors. Various *toxic factors* have been implicated in the etiology of ADHD, but most have not withstood the test of replication and rigorously controlled research. The possible exception is a toxic amount of lead in the system due, for example, to a toddler eating paint chips containing lead. However, lead toxicity could account for only a small group of ADHD children. Food additives were popular culprits for a while, resulting in a number of children being placed on diets which reduce these additives. While a few children may have a special sensitivity to such additives, there is no evidence that it is characteristic of the population as a whole.

EVALUATION The search for the specific organic factors responsible for ADHD has been characterized more by false starts than by breakthroughs. In part, the search has been hampered by the intrinsic difficulty of building a bridge from physiology to behavior, especially deviant behavior. The search has also been needlessly hampered by poorly designed and controlled studies. However, in light of the impressive progress being made both on the psychological and physiological fronts, a solution to the etiologic riddle may come in the foreseeable future.

The Interpersonal Context

While the etiology of ADHD may lie in the organic context, the children develop in a social environment. The nature of their interactions with parents and peers can play a significant role in compounding or ameliorating the difficulties inherent in the disturbance itself. (For a detailed presentation of the evidence concerning social factors, see Campbell and Werry, 1986.)

PARENT–CHILD RELATIONS There is evidence that for ADHD children a negative, controlling mother–child interaction begins when the children are as young as 2 to 3 years of age, the children playing more aggressively, the mothers reprimanding them and redirecting their activities more than is the case for normal controls. The pattern persists into middle childhood, although it becomes less negative. It is also less negative in undemanding, unstructured situations such as free play, which minimize the children's deviant behavior. Interestingly, as the children's behavior improves with stimulant medication, so does the interaction, suggesting that the mother's controlling behavior may be a response to the intense, inappropriate, exasperating behavior of the children, to a certain extent.

Mothers report feeling drained by the stress of caring for their ADHD children, as well as socially isolated and distressed. There is also an increased amount of distress and disorganization in the families of ADHD children, although it is impossible to tell whether the children's behavior is a response to or a cause of the family picture.

PEER RELATIONS   As was true of the mother–child interaction, negative peer relations have been observed early in development, ADHD kindergartners being more disruptive of peers' play and engaging in more solitary play than normal controls (Campbell and Paulauskas, 1979). By middle childhood, ADHD children are talkative, aggressive, disruptive, and noncompliant and engage in more negative verbal interactions such as teasing and name calling.

ADHD children perceive themselves as unpopular and are, in turn, actually rejected and less likely to be regarded as popular or chosen as a friend. Moreover, ADHD children can be rejected after a single session in a play group. Somewhat paradoxically, ADHD children are able to see situations from the viewpoint of their peers in hypothetical situations, a cognitive ability called *perspective taking*, which is typically a facilitator of positive peer interaction. However, in actual interactions, their communication skills are markedly inferior so that they are apt to ignore peers or behave inappropriately. This social ineptness may be due to the children becoming overly aroused and excited by peer interaction, as Douglas hypothesizes. The discrepancy between inept behavior and sophisticated understanding is another example of the performance versus competence distinction.

In a way, it is easy to see how the ADHD children's impulsivity and lack of sustained attention to social cues would interfere with the mutuality, accommodations, and cooperativeness essential to positive peer relations. Unfortunately, many of the studies of peer interactions are confounded by the presence of aggression. So once again we are faced with the case of confounding ADHD with conduct disorders and being uncertain whether the core problems of the ADHD children make any unique contribution to faulty peer relations or whether such relations can be accounted for solely in terms of aggression.

The Developmental Model

Relating ADHD to normal development will be a primarily speculative exercise. As we have seen, parents and teachers frequently complain that normal preschoolers are inattentive, restless, and distractible. This suggests that ADHD may be an exaggeration of developmentally appropriate characteristics, just as oppositional behavior may be an exaggeration of the developmentally appropriate negativism of the toddler period. Evidence supporting this speculation comes from Barkley (1982), who found that while 40 to 97% of hyperactive children displayed hyperactive behavior in fourteen home settings (such as mealtime, bedtime, playing alone), between 0 and 33% of normal children evidenced the same behavior. The difference, then, is a quantitative one of frequency.

There are also some relevant developmental data on the core components of ADHD. Levy (1980) found that between 3 and 7 years of age, both the number of errors and the reaction time decreased on the Continuous Performance Task. He interprets these results as indicating a progressive increase in the ability to sustain attention and to inhibit irrelevant responses. The Draw a Line Slowly test, which measures motor inhibition, did not change between 3 and 4 years of age; however, there was a significant increase in time between 4 and 7 years of age, indicating an increasing ability consciously to inhibit motor behavior in normal children. Because both the capacity for sustained attention and motor inhibition increase during the preschool period, we can assume that this normal developmental trend failed to exert its full influence on ADHD preschoolers.

Turning to higher-order processes, there is evidence that 4- to 5-year-olds displayed no systematic pattern of scanning when trying to determine whether two objects are the same, with the result that their judgments may be inaccurate. In contrast, children over 6½ years of age proceeded slowly and systematically, looking back and forth at the corresponding features of each pair of stimuli. Thus they were able to detect both obvious and subtle differences which enabled them to make accurate judgments (Vurpillot, 1986). The ADHD children's unsystematic and partial scanning strategies, therefore, suggest a fixation or a developmental delay in this particular cognitive skill.

In the noncognitive realm, a study by Buss, Block, and Block (1980) found that not only was activity level fairly stable between 3 and 7 years of age, but that the personality characteristics that were correlated with it were also stable. As might be expected, the highly active children were described as more energetic, restless, and fidgety and less inhibited and physically cautious. The personality correlates are more interesting. The highly active children were more self-assertive, aggressive, competitive, and manipulative and less obedient, compliant, shy, and reserved. For our purposes the basic question is, do ADHD preschoolers have these same characteristics, only raised to the *n*th degree. If so, we could be sure we are dealing with an exaggeration of normal development.

Thus, most behavioral and personality characteristics of ADHD may represent an *exaggeration* of normal development, while problems with sustaining attention, motor inhibition, and problem-solving strategies may represent *fixations* or *developmental lags*.

If ADHD has an organic origin, then the exaggeration and fixations or lags must be due to some kind of physiological malfunctioning. However, punitive parenting, family discord, and low intelligence also serve to perpetuate the deviance.

Treatment

PHARMACOTHERAPY Stimulants are the treatment of choice for ADHD children. The three major groups are amphetamines, methylphenidate (Ritalin), and pemoline. A review of stimulant treatment shows that approximately 75 percent of the children improved (Barkley, 1977). However, it is important to note the kinds of behaviors that changed, as well as those that were not affected.

In line with the view that hyperactivity is the result of an attentional defect, many of the positive results concern a normalization of attention-concentration. In a laboratory setting, children were less impulsive and more planful on tasks requiring deliberation, made fewer errors of omission in tasks requiring sustained attention, evidenced fewer task-irrelevant behaviors, and in general were more goal-directed, more coordinated, and less impulsive when medicated. Their reaction time also decreased when rapid responses were required. Among cognitive functions, perception, memory, concept attainment, and cognitive style were also improved. In the classroom, teachers rated children as less noisy and disruptive, more task-oriented, and more appropriate in their social behavior. On the playground, there was an increase in appropriate activity. As we have already noted, the mother–child interaction also improves. Rather than either "speeding up" or "slowing down" behavior, therefore, the overall effect of the drugs is one of making behavior more appropriate to the situation. It is as if the child's self-regulating, adaptive mechanisms could come to the fore once he or she was no longer buffeted about by the reaction of the moment. Generally, an elevated positive mood accompanies medication, although negative affects such as depression, fearfulness, and withdrawal have also been observed.

A number of important variables are not affected by stimulants, however, the most important being academic achievement. Stimulants make hyperactive children more amenable to learning, but they obviously cannot provide the academic knowledge the children had failed to acquire, nor can they magically raise the overall level of their thinking. There is also no evidence that medication in and of itself significantly improves the long-term prognosis. Thus stimulants serve an important purpose by setting the stage for the therapeutic work that may still have to be done.

In sum, stimulants are remarkably effective in ameliorating many of the most troublesome behaviors of ADHD children, both in terms of task orientation and social adjustment. The most important single exception to this generally positive picture is academic achievement. However, stimulants cannot be regarded as a "cure" because, even with prolonged use, children will continue to have academic problems and might develop antisocial behavior patterns. Despite these limitations, the efficacy of stimulants is more firmly established than that of any other form of treatment (Gittelman, 1983a).

This summary of the advantages and limitations of medication also serves as a useful background for understanding the reservations certain professionals have voiced concerning the use of drugs with hyperactive children. Like any treatment, pharmacotherapy should be administered with a high degree of professional competence. The child's problems should be carefully evaluated, while the kind and dosage of medication should be constantly monitored. Similarly, the decision to discontinue medication should be made only after comprehensive assessment of the child's functioning at home, in the school, and with peers. Since there are few objective guides, all these decisions are a matter of clinical judgment. (See Kinsbourne and Caplan, 1979; hyperactivity is discussed under the heading Impulsive Extremes.) There is often a temptation to cut short this time-consuming procedure. At its worst, medication can be regarded as a quick cure-all or as a means of making the child more tractable and less burdensome to parents and teachers. Thus medication can be overprescribed or wrongly prescribed, while compliant behavior on the child's part can be equated with cure. The illusion that life's problems can be solved by taking a pill is a seductive one, and one that can operate to the disadvantage of the child who is its victim. (For a detailed discussion of medication, see Gittelman and Kanner, 1986.)

BEHAVIORAL APPROACHES   *Behavior therapists* have been the most versatile in applying their techniques to remedying many of the problems attendant upon hyperactivity and in documenting their successes. The techniques themselves have varied greatly: the traditional ones emphasize reinforcing desirable behavior while ignoring or punishing undesirable behavior, whereas the newer, cognitively based ones emphasize self-instruction in order to increase self-control (Douglas, 1980). Not only teachers but parents as well have been instructed in the use of behavioral techniques to increase the scope of the child's therapeutic environment. Behavior therapy has been successfully used to induce children to sit still and pay attention, to reduce their disruptive behaviors in class, and to improve performance on a variety of school tasks. They also have been employed to deal with behavior problems in the home.

While reports of success are impressive, most involve short-term management. The problems of generalizing success across settings and sustaining them over time remain to be solved. There are other "psychological" problems with behavioral therapy. Like patients who discontinue taking medicine as soon as they feel better, parents and teachers may discontinue their carefully worked out treatment program when the children become less hyperactive, but before they have sufficient self-control to do without environmental support. And as with medication, decreasing hyperactivity may be regarded as the sole therapeutic goal, while the child's learning and personality problems are ignored. Despite such limitations, behavioral therapy must be considered the psychotherapeutic treatment of choice.

MEDICATION VERSUS BEHAVIOR MODIFICATION A number of studies have addressed the issue of the relative effectiveness of medication and behavior modification. In general, the results indicate that there is no area of functioning, whether cognitive, academic, or social, which shows the superiority of behavior therapy over drug therapy. However, in certain instances, the addition of behavior therapy may be more effective than medication alone, say, in helping children with special social problems or in changing undesirable academic behavior (Gittelman, 1983a).

OTHER TREATMENT APPROACHES *Parent counseling* is employed to educate parents concerning the nature of hyperactivity, to relieve the guilt they often feel, as well as to deal with their frustrations and disappointment;

parental training instructs parents in the specific behavioral skills of observation, pinpointing behaviors to be changed, data taking, and devising strategies of reinforcement, punishment, and extinction. The advantages of parental training are that the therapeutic principles can be readily grasped, the parents can immediately become involved in changing specific behaviors, while the charting of these changes provides concrete evidence of change, thereby reinforcing the parent as well as the child. If behavioral techniques are also being used at school, parental training has the additional advantage of providing parent and teacher with a common language and a common base for coordinating their remedial efforts.

Family therapy has been used not directly to remedy the hyperactivity but to work through the problems that might have been generated by having a hyperactive child. Such children may have become a "scapegoat" on whom family members displace many of their own problems, or they may be used as a "negative bond" to hold a wavering marriage together. Helping families become aware of and change such patterns of interaction relieves the hyperactive member of the burden of rejection and discrimination.

MULTIPLE INTERVENTIONS Because ADHD has multiple etiologies and may involve disturbances in a number of intra- and interpersonal areas, multimodal treatment tailored to the needs of the individual child seems the most appropriate approach to remediation. Medication, behavioral treatment, remedial education, parental counseling, and family therapy all should be used as needed. Consequently, the proper treatment of the ADHD child requires a special cooperative effort on the part of the pediatrician, the school, and the mental health professional (Kenny and Burka, 1980).

YOU ARE a clinical child psychologist. A pediatrician has referred an ADHD 8-year-old, and you have completed your evaluation. You are now planning your treatment strategy. The mother has told you that the pediatrician has placed her child on a special diet rather than on medication to control his hyperactivity. You know that research shows this diet to be ineffective, but bringing this up with the mother would put her in a conflict between the two professionals responsible for helping her child. You might discuss the decision with the pediatrician at some later date when both of you have more time—if indeed such a day ever comes. Your immediate concern is with informing the pediatrician of your findings and of the treatment program you have in mind.

You next make an appointment to see the mother again in order to explain the findings and treatment plans to her. You also will start working on the family problems centering around having a hyperactive 8-year-old and three younger siblings. While well intentioned, the parents have become increasingly exasperated with the boy and have escalated their punitive behavior. Your initial conference will center around the two great principles of behavioral therapy—ignore the negative and reward the positive (thus reversing the present family pattern) and focus on specific behaviors (which will immediately involve the parents in the constructive task of observing and recording the child's behavior and its social consequences).

You know the psychologist at the boy's grammar school. She is young, unsure of herself, and overworked. While conscientious, she does not seem particularly resourceful. Since the mother took the boy to the pediatrician initially because the school had found him "unmanageable," you suspect that his teacher has also reached the end of her rope. Yet you will contact the school psychologist and see what can be done. The fact that other professionals are now involved might be a relief to the teacher and serve as an opening wedge to exploring other ways of dealing with the boy's management problems.

Because the boy is significantly below grade level in reading, he definitely will need more help in this area than is available in the schools. You know an excellent woman in remedial reading, but she is something of a prima donna who does not "believe in medication," regards special diets as "a hoax," and resents the "MDs who have no business making all the decisions and all the money off of children with educational problems." While she is infinitely patient with children, she is difficult and confronting with her colleagues. It would be easier on you to refer the child to a less talented but more cooperative reading specialist. For the moment you do not know which to choose.

You now have three names on your calendar and a question mark for the fourth. All will require a lengthy contact just to devise the remedial program. Implementing the program will require additional contacts in the future. All of this will take time, and time is always precious. Then there is the matter of billing. To charge the parents for all the time you will have to spend on the phone would confront them with a bill that would work a real hardship on their family budget. But you yourself cannot afford to charge them only for their direct contacts with you. You decide on a compromise—to charge for some of your time but not all, knowing the decision will mean a financial sacrifice on your part.

While the ideal of skilled specialists meeting the multiple needs of the ADHD child is an attractive one, its realization is exceedingly difficult. The sheer logistics of communication among specialists, as well as the added time involved, are problems in their own right. In addition, professionals differ in their degree of skill as well as in their willingness to cooperate with other professionals. They may be divided on the issue of medication and of behavioral therapy, each of which is apt to be strongly championed by some and equally strongly opposed by others. And the question of who has the ultimate responsibility for the child's welfare—which is the question of ultimate authority and power—can be a touchy one. Professionals are people with their own vested interests, vanities, personal and financial aspirations. To weld them into a cooperative team is a major undertaking.

LEARNING DISABILITIES

———

YOU ARE a clinical child psychologist. It has been a rough day. The climax was a phone call to the principal of Wyckwyre Junior High School. It is the kind of suburban school in which children from two-swimming-pool families do not speak to children from one-swimming-pool families. The call had been about Jon Hastings, a 16-year-old with a long history of school failures. The intelligence test showed him to be bright enough to do college work, and yet he is only in the eighth grade. He is articulate, has a talent for making miniature rockets and speedboats, and a real flair for drawing cartoons. Yet the written word is Jon's nemesis. He reads laboriously one word at the time, while his writing is even more painfully slow. Because of repeated failures and because he is now a social misfit with peers, he has begun cutting up in class and talking back to the teacher.

You had phoned the principal to suggest ways of bypassing Jon's reading disability. Since he is sufficiently bright to absorb most of the lecture material, could he be given oral examinations every now and then? If he were taught how to type, could he type instead of writing his examinations? Would the principal consider introducing special classes for all the learning-disabled children?

The principal was suave and ingratiating and a compendium of the resistances you have run up against in the past. He "understood your concern" but asked that you "look at the situation from my point of view." The school had "tried everything possible to no avail," "the boy is incorrigible," "you can't help a child unless the child wants help," and finally—you could feel this one coming, since you had heard it so often—"I can't give one student a favor without giving a favor to all of them. I'd have half the mothers in my office next day demanding something extra to pull their child's grades up." You had always doubted the validity of this "special-

favor" objection but had never found an effective way of countering it. Stalling for time you had asked if you could come and talk with the principal. He was most gracious. He would be happy to tell you about the school and have a student show you around—which was not at all what you had in mind.

A few years back an insightful but poorly educated mother had remarked, "When I get frustrations I come here and bring them to you. When you get frustrations, where do you put them?" The question comes back at times like these. ———

In chapter 2 on normal development, we saw how the inherently curious infant becomes the academically achieving student. While the drive to explore is potent, curiosity thrives on stimulation from the social and physical environment during infancy and the preschool period, verbal stimulation being particularly important in our present concern with learning disabilities. With school comes the requirement to learn and the beginning of the child-as-worker. Parental values concerning the importance of education and achievement will encourage maximization of the child's potential. Teachers wrestle with the problem of whether traditional or progressive education will best enhance the child's desire to master academic material. Peers serve to reinforce academic learning, although the study of their influences has been relatively neglected. Progress will also be affected by work habits and freedom from distracting anxieties and angers.

What can go wrong with this development? In the most extreme cases, biological and/or environmental factors render some children incapable of understanding the world in all its complexity, and they find academic subjects particularly perplexing. These children, the mentally retarded, do not learn at a normal rate because they lack the necessary intellectual endowment (see chapter 11). Other children suffer from being members of a social outgroup and from the physiological and psychological effects of poverty. Such children are not necessarily retarded but have spent their early years in an environment whose very fabric makes it difficult for them to adapt successfully to the requirements of middle-class education.

The third case is the *learning-disabled* (LD) child, who is intelligent enough to do better, whose family and cultural background are congruent with academic achievement, who has no gross physiological defect that would obviously impede learning, and who is reasonably free from crippling psychological problems arising from sources outside the learning situation. Yet the child does poorly, perhaps in reading or in spelling or in arithmetic or in all three. Why? The answer should be simple. Unlike autistic, hyperactive, or severely retarded children, learning-disabled children are both willing and able to cooperate with researchers, while their parents and teachers are eager to help find the source of their difficulties. Why, then, does the etiological question go unanswered, and why are the voluminous research findings fragmented, contradictory, and inconclusive?

At the heart of the mystery lies the fundamental question, How do children learn basic academic skills? Until the normal process is understood it is difficult to know what has gone awry.

One final point of a general nature: learning disabilities have a good deal in common with hyperactivity. Both affect that aspect of initiative that involves task orientation or the ability to set a goal and persist until it is realized. However, learning disabilities are a problem of middle childhood, whereas ADHD begins before formal schooling. Next, while the definitions of both conditions are deceptively simple, categorizing children has proven difficult. Learning disabilities also share with hyperactivity a history of shifting theories on etiology. While hyperactivity seems to have been attributed to a specific dysfunction—attention deficit—there is little agreement on the many causes that have been suggested for learning disabilities. In this unsettled state, the developmental dimension has received scant attention.

Before confronting the many problems raised by learning disabilities, it is best to get our bearings in terms of the descriptive characteristics of the psychopathology itself.

Definition

While the definitions of learning disabilities are legion, they all have as their central feature the idea of a *disparity* between the children's expected and actual academic achievement. The children are sufficiently intelligent and their instruction is sufficiently skillful to warrant a significantly higher level of achievement in one or more subjects than is actually obtained. In addition, definitions usually exclude certain conditions as primary sources of the disparity. The disability cannot be due primarily to sensory or motor handicaps, such as blindness or deafness, nor to mental retardation, emotional disturbances, or cultural disadvantage.

While these definitions seem clear-cut, they present a number of problems. There is no reason a child from a deprived background or a mildly retarded child or even a child with a sensory defect cannot also have a learning disability since the conditions are not mutually exclusive. As we have just seen, learning disabilities can also overlap with attention-deficit hyperactivity disorder, and as we shall discover, children with conduct disorders or juvenile delinquents may also have a reading disability. At a theoretical level, it is not clear what is cause and what is effect in these cases of overlap, and, at a practical level, assessment procedures are often not sufficiently sensitive to determine when LD is primary and when it is a secondary consequence of other deviations. As we have just seen with ADHD, overlapping disturbances present special research problems in regard to selecting "pure" cases or controlling for possible confounds in mixed cases.

Affective Aspects

While by definition learning disabilities should not be a consequence of a major psychopathological disturbance, there is reason to believe that LD children would experience special stresses which, in turn, might increase the incidence of emotional problems. Because they have at least average intelligence and do well in many academic subjects, unsympathetic or uninformed parents and teachers might assume they are merely lazy and could function adequately if they really tried. Consequently, the children may be continually pressured by increasingly irritated and exasperated adults to improve a situation they are helpless to change. Because effective learning requires reasonable freedom from intense affects (such as rage, anxiety, and depression) which interfere with the concentration essential to task orientation, emotional problems are seen as compounding the children's already existing learning disability (Goldstein and Dundon, 1987).

While affective variables are important, their importance should not be exaggerated. There are no emotional problems unique to LD children; on the contrary, such emotional problems are found in many other children who are educationally, intellectually, or emotionally handicapped, such as low achievers, the mentally retarded, or the neurologically impaired. While LD children may not be as well adjusted as nondisabled children, they are less disturbed than children seen in child guidance clinics and classified as emotionally disturbed. The presence of hyperactivity, rather than learning disabilities per se, is the single most important variable placing the

child at risk for emotional problems (Bruck, 1987).

THE CLASSROOM CONTEXT   The classroom plays an important role in aggravating or moderating the LD children's emotional problems. There is evidence that such children receive more criticism from teachers than do nondisabled children, that their initiations are more likely to be ignored, and that teachers are less likely to involve them in nonacademic interactions. This differential treatment may affect the LD children's self-perception and, equally important, may be communicated to other children in the class who model their behavior on the teacher's by expressing similar negative feelings (Bruck, 1987). The physical environment of the school, such as seating arrangement or lighting, does not influence the behaviors of the LD children as was once believed (Kasik, Sabatino, and Spoentgen, 1987).

Peer Relations

Just as the study of learning disabilities has expanded from cognitive to affective variables in the intrapersonal context, so it has expanded to include peer relations in the interpersonal context. The expansion is reasonable in light of the important role peers play in children's overall adjustment. In addition, early studies indicated that LD children's peer relations suffered especially in regard to acceptance and popularity. Such findings could be explained in two ways. One explanation is that the children were being treated in a prejudicial manner by their classmates; the other explanation is that the same cognitive deficiencies responsible for their academic disabilities negatively affected their social cognition as well. The two explanations obviously are not mutually exclusive.

Subsequently, a case was made that the social deficiencies were exaggerated by studies that had a number of methodological flaws (Bruck, 1986). There is no evidence that, as a group, LD children are held in low esteem by peers. In some instances, they may not be among the most popular children, in other instances they may be somewhat overly represented in the rejected category. However, most of them are making an adequate social adjustment (Dudley-Marling and Edmiaston, 1985).

Serafica and Walsh-Hurley (1987) argue persuasively that the failure to find a relation between popularity and learning disabilities is not sufficient grounds for rejecting the hypothesis that these children might be defective in social cognition. We know that popularity depends on a number of factors that have little to do with social cognition: physical appearance, athletic ability, academic achievement, and even one's name. Thus a peer nomination technique which asks, for example, who a child would like to sit next to in class, or play with, seems a weak measure of social cognition at best. What is needed are situations that require social skills such as decision making or conflict resolution, in which children cannot rely on clichés but need to understand different viewpoints in the process of arriving at a reasonable decision. Even in such situations one must make sure that the children are motivated to use their social cognitive skills and that failure to do so is not due to some extraneous factor such as sulkiness or selfishness. Only when such stringent conditions are met will we have a clear idea of whether LD children are deficient in social cognition.

A clue to a possible deficiency is provided by Perlmutter (1986), who found that LD children knew how to behave socially but could not distinguish when such social behaviors were appropriate. Thus they knew what to do but not when to do it. If they were accepted by the group and received positive messages from it, and if they had a

clearly defined role, their behavior resembled that of non–learning disabled classmates. One could infer from this finding that a large class that is socially complex and less socially structured would be likely to elicit inappropriate social behavior. It also follows that remedial programs that aim to provide LD children with social skills would be inappropriate, since this is not the area of deficiency.

Etiologic Hypotheses

Etiologic hypotheses regarding learning disabilities abound. As was the case with ADHD, the majority of these hypotheses fall within the organic context. While some have proved adequate in accounting for certain subgroups, none offers a satisfactory account for learning disabilities in general. (For a detailed presentation of etiology, see Schwartz and Johnson, 1985.)

Some learning disabilities are due to *central nervous system dysfunctions*. Children with cerebral palsy and epilepsy show an elevated rate of reading disability even when they are of normal intelligence. Children who have sustained a localized head injury, especially in the left cerebral hemisphere, are also likely to have difficulty reading (Yule and Rutter, 1985). Such cases are relatively rare, however,

A popular organic hypothesis states that *minimal brain dysfunction* (MBD) can cause learning disabilities. These minimal dysfunctions cannot be detected by the ordinary neurological examination but are evidenced by subtle behavioral indices, or "soft signs." The limitations of MBD will be presented in detail subsequently (see chapter 12); suffice it to say at this point that this hypothesis has had only limited usefulness in the understanding and treatment of learning disabilities. At one time MBD was thought to be the cause of learning disabilities and ADHD, with the unfortunate consequence that the two disorders became confused. In studies of MBD, for example, it was impossible to tell at times whether the population included hyperactive or learning disabled or both kinds of children.

A time-honored organic hypothesis concerns faulty cerebral dominance, or *cerebral laterality*. In its original form the hypothesis stated that LD children, particularly those with reading disabilities, failed to establish the normal dominance of one cerebral hemisphere over the other, the resulting competition producing the problems in learning. However, research has failed to provide convincing evidence that laterality problems underlie most learning disabilities. (The lateralization hypothesis will be discussed in greater detail in the section on reading disabilities later in this chapter.)

Finally, *genetic factors* may play a role in certain learning disabilities, although, as often happens, it is difficult to disentangle hereditary from environmental influences. In general, genetic factors should be considered as contributing to learning disabilities in certain instances rather than being the sole cause; for example, there is evidence that children with a severe reading disability have a genetic vulnerability which makes them prone to developing this disorder (Yule and Rutter, 1985).

In sum, the organic hypothesis in regard to learning disabilities is much like it is in regard to attention-deficit hyperactivity disorder—it is widely held, but the specific mechanisms responsible for the disabilities have eluded investigators to date. It is also important to note that organic hypotheses are not the only tenable ones. Learning theorists, psychodynamic theorists, and cognitive theorists all have their own etiologic hypotheses, each with sufficient evidence to lend it credibility. Some of these hypotheses will be explored when we discuss reading disabilities.

Prognosis

As we have seen, LD children may not be as well adjusted socially and emotionally as nondisabled children, but only a small portion have clinically significant problems. Difficulties in literacy skills persist into adulthood, low socioeconomic level significantly increasing the chances of persistence, high socioeconomic level significantly decreasing the chances. Despite this difficulty, the children tend to be successful occupationally as adults. Family relations and interactions with the opposite sex also do not suffer. However, the LD population is not without problems. As adults they have difficulty controlling their temper and have poor same-sex peer relations. But their problems do not tend to have clinical significance in the sense of requiring professional attention. In particular, learning disabilities are not a precursor of delinquency or drug abuse. While adult problems tend to have their roots in childhood difficulties, many problems do not persist beyond compulsory schooling (Bruck, 1987).

In sum, the adult picture resembles that of childhood. While having more than the expected number of problems, most of the adults function satisfactorily, and the problems they do have tend not to be sufficiently serious to be labeled psychopathological.

Remediation

Research has shown that LD children may have a number of behavioral problems that interfere with their meeting the demands of the traditional elementary school classroom. Specifically, LD children may be overactive, inattentive, impulsive, and distractible. Certain of these behaviors can be reduced by drugs and behavior modification. However, teaching the child to sit still is not tantamount to the child's being able to learn. On the contrary, the evidence indicates that academic performance is unaffected. Consequently, the therapist should regard hyperactivity and attentional deficits as secondary and concentrate on improving skills. Such direct remediation often has the effect of decreasing disruptive behavior.

Aggressiveness, on the other hand, is another matter, because it predicts future maladjustment, especially in combination with low academic achievement. Rather than being regarded as secondary, the behavior problem should be dealt with directly, along with the learning disability itself (Routh, 1979).

Up until now learning disability has been presented as a complex dysfunction requiring heroic remedial efforts. The picture is not wholly accurate. There is evidence that communication with children and parents about the meaning of the learning disability is associated with children having higher self-esteem than when they are told nothing. It seems reasonable that presenting a realistic picture of the dysfunction should reduce ambiguities and misunderstandings on the parents' part. It might also help check the dour anticipations that exceed those of the LD child himself. Moreover, teachers, especially those in regular classrooms who tend to have a negative attitude toward LD children, might also be helped to become more supportive through a discussion of the nature of the children's learning problem and some of its social and emotional concomitants (Serafica and Harway, 1979).

While seeking answers to the knottier issues concerning the nature, remedy, and prevention of learning disabilities, the clinician should not lose sight of simple remedial measures. There is much to learn, but there is also a good deal that is known. Sharing this knowledge with concerned parents and teachers may itself relieve some of the distress that places an added burden on the LD child.

Having obtained an overview of learning disabilities, we will now examine reading disability in detail since it plays a crucial role in academic success and since it has been more thoroughly studied than the other learning disabilities.

READING DISABILITY

A reading disability is usually defined as a failure to learn to read or make appropriate progress in reading despite at least normal intelligence and adequate instruction. The reading-disabled child has no gross neurological defect, although most definitions also include presumptive evidence of neurological involvement. The child's hearing, vision, and motivation to learn are adequate. The reading disability is not a secondary consequence of a severe emotional disturbance, such as autism, or a depressive reaction to a traumatic event, such as the death of a parent. The term *dyslexia* is frequently used instead of reading disability.

Overview

When the preschooler was a toddler, he or she caught on to the fact that the meaningless sounds people made could be used to convey meaningful ideas. Preschoolers must begin an analogous process in regard to reading. They must learn that those interesting squiggles on a piece of paper represent the verbal symbols they have mastered and that, if correctly interpreted, these visual stimuli, too, can convey meaningful ideas although in a somewhat altered form from speaking.

However, the preschooler's experience with learning to talk does not make learning to read an easy task. In reality, it is quite complex and involves a number of psychological processes. Fine *perceptual discriminations* must be made and *transformations* grasped, such as *E* is different from *F*, while *A* is the same as *a*. The *patterning* of letters within words and of words within sentences must be understood. There must be *cross-modal matching;* that is, symbols that were learned through audition must be transferred to the visual modality. Finally, and most important, these so-called mechanical aspects of learning to read must be used in the service of the principal goal of reading, which is to derive *meaning.* This scant and partial listing gives some initial idea of the complexity of reading and, by extension, of the many things that can go wrong and prevent mastery of the process. The listing also ignores important context factors—the child's general level of intelligence and personality, family and school environments, social class. For the time being, we will set such variables aside to concentrate on the process itself. As always, normal development will serve as the framework for understanding deviations in the form of reading disabilities.

Bottom Up or Top Down?

One approach to understanding the process of learning to read is to begin with the basic perceptual learning essential to recognizing letters and chart the progression until comprehension is finally reached. This is the bottom-up approach. Another view is that, from the very beginning, higher-order cognitive processes are involved and that the perceptual data are like an obscure code to be broken by the most sophisticated thinking at the child's disposal. This is the top-down approach.

Historically, the bottom-up approach was the more popular one, with an emphasis not only on vision but also on cross-modal matching and even motor behavior. Recently there has been a shift to a top-down approach as evidence has accumulated for the strong relation between reading and language. For example, verbal intelligence is a better predictor of later reading attainment than are

visual-motor tests, and one-third of preschoolers with delayed speech were backward in reading two years after beginning school (Yule and Rutter, 1985). Moreover, three-fourths of poor readers exhibit problems in nonreading tasks requiring processing of linguistic stimuli, such as oral vocabulary, listening comprehension, and the grammatical complexity of spoken language (Ceci and Baker, 1987), and reading-disabled children have a short-term memory deficit for verbal but not visual stimuli such as geometric designs or Hebrew letters (Vellutino, 1986). Remedial reading programs training visual-motor skills have not been successful. Finally, there is evidence of a significant relation between phonological awareness and coding (i.e., the awareness and coding of special sounds) and reading ability or disability (Maclean, Bryant, and Bradley, 1987, and Vellutino and Scanlon, 1987).

There is another issue more basic than whether perception or language holds the key to understanding learning to read and reading disabilities. This is whether an *analytic model* is appropriate not only for reading but for learning to talk or any other high-level cognitive achievement. The analytic model reduces complexity to its basic units, in this instance individual letters, and tries to reconstruct the process by which these units are combined into the next higher level, in this instance words, and these, in turn, are combined into even higher units, in this instance simple sentences, and so on. However, another viewpoint holds that such an atomistic model is too laborious and sluggish to account for the remarkable achievements of learning to speak or read. On the perceptual level, preschoolers are searching for relationships from the very beginning, relationships that could clue them in to recurrent patterns and sequences. They approach cognitive challenges with strategies rather than on a trial-and-error basis and are constantly on the lookout for rules that would organize large masses of discrete information at one fell swoop. Above all, their quest is for meaning. If they are forced into a painfully slow, letter-by-letter, atomistic approach, it is only because they must go through an initial tooling-up phase. As soon as their fund of information allows, their fleet minds will be searching for patterns, sequences, rules, and meanings.

The Top-Down Quandary

If the bottom-up approach suffers from having been too restricted and too atomistic to account for reading and its deficits, the top-down approach is currently suffering from a glut of undigested research findings. Even allowing for the complexity of reading, the number of deficits uncovered by investigators has become "punishingly complex to interpret and integrate" (Ceci and Baker, 1987, p. 103). Various studies have found RD children to have a deficit in speech perception, phonemic awareness, phonological coding in short-term memory, availability and use of memory strategies, syntactic knowledge, use of text comprehension strategies or metacognitive functioning (Stanovich, 1987)! How could such extensive deficits exist and RD still be regarded as a specific learning disability? And how could these intelligent children continue to do well in a number of academic subjects while so many cognitive processes are malfunctioning? There is no ready answer, and even the experts are divided as to how to deal with the problem.

Some experts claim the current situation is due, at least in part, to questionable data. The field of learning disabilities as a whole has recently entered a new phase in which controlled laboratory studies are replacing the previous, more descriptive data. It takes time for researchers to become sophisticated methodologists. A number of studies have been too liberal in including children whose intelligence is below average, have paid too little attention to low achievement in other academic areas such as arithmetic and spelling, and have not controlled for socioeconomic level and the possible presence of emotional disturbances and gross neurological impairment. (For a detailed critique, see Vellutino, 1987.) Thus many of the findings of this first wave of research may be discounted when more rigorous and definitive studies are done.

Even while recognizing the tentative nature of the data, some experts claim that the studies make a valid and crucial point about reading disability—namely, that it is not a uniform disability but may well be a common end product of a number of *cognitive deficits*. If studies fail to find the same results, therefore, it may be because the populations in the two studies were significantly different, the first being deficient in one cognitive process, the second in another. A solution to this problem of heterogeneity is to divide RD children into meaningful subgroups, perhaps by factor analytic studies or by focusing on a specific cognitive function and exploring the nature of the deficit; for example, a word-finding problem or difficulty in accessing words the child knows could be studied in terms of storage and retrieval in memory (Stanovich, 1987).

What holds for a reading disability must also hold for learning disabilities in general, which, according to this set of experts, no longer can be considered an entity with a well-defined symptom pattern but must be considered a collection of discrete problems having only a common domain (Vellutino, 1987). Research on such a diverse group of children runs the risk of being a futile endeavor. Predictably, such a conclusion is not acceptable to all experts in the field. While admitting that studying subgroups may be the best way to tease out deficient underlying processes, Worden (1986) maintains that there may also be common elements in all "learning inefficient" children, whether these children are generally retarded academically (underachievers), retarded in a specific academic area (LD), mentally retarded, or normally developing. The research strategy Worden recommends involves discovering the components of learning employed by successful learners, and using these components to locate the weaknesses of inefficient learners. These components include: (1) *memory strategies*, such as selective attention or rehearsal; (2) *monitoring practices*, such as identifying sources of difficulties or evaluating success in meeting goals; (3) *metastrategy information*, such as the knowledge of the benefits of having a strategy or employing strategies appropriate to time constraints and effort requirements; and (4) *motivation*, such as persistence, or attributing success and failure to oneself or to chance.

In sum, it may be premature to dismiss RD or other LD children as sources of information which can be generalized to all members of either group. Yet there may well be questions that can be adequately answered only in terms of meaningful subgroups. The decision as to when to treat the children as homogeneous and when to treat them as heterogeneous cannot be made on rational or theoretical grounds at this point. Rather, empirical studies will have to provide signposts as to which direction is more fruitful.

Developmental Considerations

The majority of studies have been done on children between 6 and 12 years of age, and the developmental dimension has rarely been explored in detail, either conceptually or empirically. However, there are some data and some provocative speculations that will be described briefly.

Stanovich (1987) outlines some broad developmental trends. There is evidence suggesting that specific cognitive processes are responsible for the earliest stages of reading disabilities, but that these become more generalized subsequently. In the first grade, for example, decoding speed, vocabulary, listening comprehension, and abstract problem solving are only weakly correlated but become highly correlated by the fifth grade. Or again, memory problems affect specific components of the reading process when children are learning to read, but become more pervasive as children grow older. There is also a possible reversal of direction of causation between cognition and reading disabilities: prolonged experience with reading failure may inhibit the growth of cognitive processes either by depriving children of the extensive reading that nourishes this growth or through negative motivational states that make children shy away from complex cognitive challenges.

There is also some evidence that poor decoders in the early stages of learning to read become poor comprehenders subsequently (Ceci and Baker, 1987). By adolescence most poor readers have cracked the rules for translating written symbols into sounds and no longer read in a halting manner. In a sense they have "outgrown" their decoding problem. However, they have difficulty drawing inferences from the text, such as inferring that the day was warm from the fact that people were wearing light clothes. This development corresponds to our model of psychopathology whereby the disturbance continues but its manifestation changes.

Evaluation

The inconclusive state of research on reading disability should not obscure one crucial point—the investigators now seem to be asking the right question. The previous emphasis on visual and motor processes to the neglect of cognitive processes and linguistic skills was far too atomistic and limited in scope to account for reading and its deviations. The fact that the right question is now being asked does not mean that the answers will soon be forthcoming, however, since the top-down approach is more complex than the bottom-up one. Generating a body of substantial empirical data and integrating concepts into a comprehensive framework that will encompass both normal and deviant development are major challenges that have yet to be successfully met.

Neurological Theories

While reading disability, by definition, is not caused by gross neurological damage, there have been repeated attempts to relate it to more subtle neurological dysfunctions. As early as 1925, Orton speculated that dyslexia resulted from a failure to establish hemispheric dominance between the two halves of the brain, a hypothesis that has been revived and revised in light of recent research on *laterality*. (This presentation follows Kinsbourne and Hiscock, 1978, and Naylor, 1980.)

Research on brain-damaged patients and on normal subjects has indicated that the left cerebral hemisphere is functionally specialized for certain kinds of language processing, such as letters, syllables, numbers, and words, while the right cerebral hemisphere is specialized for nonverbal, visual-spatial processing, such as face recognition, as well as for nonverbal stimuli such as music, emotional tone, and intonation patterns. The *progressive lateralization hypothesis* makes the reasonable assumption that, as the highly complex language of the adult develops from a nonlinguistic neonatal state, the cerebrum undergoes a similar development from functional symmetry to left hemisphere specialization. The failure to develop lateralization constitutes the neurological basis for dyslexia.

A traditional index of lateralization has

been hand preference in performing tasks, because each hand is controlled by the opposite cerebral hemisphere. In fact, a number of investigators reported a high incidence of left-handedness or ambidexterity in dyslexic children. Eye and foot preferences have also been used as indices of lateralization. A more recent technique called *dichotic listening* involves the simultaneous presentation of competing sounds in the two ears. Superiority in detecting right-ear sound is presumed to reflect left-hemisphere representation of language.

Despite the plausibility of and initial empirical support for the lateralization hypothesis, the bulk of the research shows that there are no important differences between normal and reading-disabled children in regard to handedness or eye preference. Dichotic listening studies have similarly failed to yield confirmatory data. In part, the contradictory findings have been due to methodological problems along with situational and experiential factors which can alter asymmetry of perception. (See Kinsbourne and Hiscock, 1978, for details.) Until the psychological processes involved in reading are more convincingly related to hemispheric functioning, there is no basis for regarding the lateralization hypothesis as tenable.

Nor has the developmental hypothesis fared any better. Far from being functionally equipotential, current research indicates that the infant's cerebral hemispheres are specialized. Anatomically, the neonate's temporal speech region is usually larger on the left side than on the right; patterns of electrical activity recorded off the infant's brain indicate asymmetries in response to speech and music; a right-handed preference has been shown in 3-month-old babies (infants retaining objects in the right hand significantly longer than in the left, for example); and there is right-ear advantage for speech and left-ear advantage for music in infants as young as 50 postnatal days. Thus, it appears that brain functions are lateralized from birth and that language does not become increasingly lateralized as the child matures.

More tenable hypotheses concerning lateralization have been proposed more recently (see Yule and Rutter, 1985). While each can explain certain empirical findings, none can marshal the kind of definitive data that would allow it to be preferred over the others, and each has its own difficulties.

Interpersonal Variables

As has been noted, reading disabilities and learning disabilities in general can originate in the interpersonal as well as in the organic context. The interpersonal literature tends to be clinical rather than being based on controlled studies, but it does describe the many ways in which difficulties originating in the family may spill over into the academic setting.

School is the prelude to the *adult world of work*, a setting in which esteem-worthiness matters more than love-worthiness and the child's productivity takes precedence over family evaluations. Under certain circumstances children may have a severe conflict over taking this step toward maturity. They may have a close, infantilizing relation with a mother, who—consciously or unconsciously—is threatened by their independence. Such a mother may assume responsibilities which rightfully should be the child's such as making sure they know their lessons. She may even usurp affective reactions, agonizing over a coming examination, loudly protesting a failing grade. The children fail both because their self-confidence is constantly being undermined and because closeness to the mother is still gratifying. For the boys the problem is further aggravated if the father does not provide a model of an achieving male in his work.

For certain children the competitive *achievement orientation* of school may be a source of anxiety. Psychoanalysts have been particularly sensitive to the competitive tensions between father and son and between mother and daughter, as well as to the trace of hostility implicit in any competitive situation. Handled correctly, these can prove a spur to achievement; however, they can be mismanaged so as to frighten the child unduly. A powerful, successful parent may inadvertently intimidate the child, who believes it is safer to fail than to compete with such a formidable rival. For children who are afraid of expressing anger, the destructive implications of competition become exaggerated. "For me to win you must lose" takes on the quality of a fight to the death.

Anger can block achievement in a subtle way. Recall that in the socializing bargain toddlers and preschoolers give up asocial pleasures and conform to parental standards of behavior because they receive love in return. In the school years certain pressuring parents can make achievement the sole basis for relating positively to their children who, in turn, come to feel manipulated and cheated. Their revenge, usually unconscious, is to fail in school, thereby keeping parents in a state of helpless exasperation while depriving them of realizing an ambition that obviously means more to the parents than to the children themselves. Adolescents may even jeopardize their own vocational future in a self-defeating effort to punish parents by being failures.

Treatment of Reading Disability

The number of reports claiming effective treatment of reading disability is mammoth. The number of well-designed, well-executed studies that could permit definitive conclusions concerning effectiveness is minuscule. In general, many methods can produce short-term gains which tend to diminish significantly or disappear over the following months (Yule and Rutter, 1985). Such an unimpressive record of success renders moot the issue of relative effectiveness of different approaches. (For a detailed presentation, see Gittelman, 1983b.)

TUTORING   On a commonsense basis, one might think that teaching reading skills would be the most effective way to help children with reading disabilities. Yet evidence supporting such a direct approach is unimpressive. Some studies show that very bright children might make gains, and an occasional well-designed study shows sufficient sus-

tained improvement to warrant a more prolonged treatment program.

UNDERLYING PROCESSES   Until recently, the most popular approach to treatment was to target and correct the perceptual and visual-motor deficiencies that presumably were responsible for the reading disability. For the most part, perceptual-motor training programs have been investigated in normal or disadvantaged preschool and kindergarten children, rather than in RD children. What controlled evidence there is fails to support the claim that these programs are effective in helping RD children.

8

Neuroses and Excessive
Self-Control

In the course of being psychoanalyzed, a middle-aged man recalls, "When I acted up as a kid my grandmother would scold me, saying, 'You're too young to have nerves!' For a long time after that I kept wondering, 'Am I old enough now?'—like having nerves was one of the signs of being grown up."

Grandmother, unknowingly, was a good Freudian. According to psychoanalytic theory, psychoneurosis or neurosis is a developmental achievement. Not that infants and preschoolers cannot suffer—as we have seen, they can; but they are not sufficiently sophisticated psychologically to have a classical neurosis until middle childhood.

However, Freud's concept of neurosis has always been a controversial one. His ideas concerning unconscious motivation, infantile sexuality, and the relation between adult psychopathology and childhood trauma were greeted with incredulity, shock, and derision by members of the professional community. While many of his concepts are now regarded as plausible or obvious, the psychoanalytic formulation of neurosis is currently under attack from two directions. As could be expected, behaviorally oriented psychologists regard the formulation as both incorrect and needlessly complex. Unexpectedly, DSM-III dropped the classification of neurosis completely, preferring diagnoses that are purely descriptive and have no etiologic connotations. Unfortunately, interest in childhood neuroses is currently in the doldrums and research is particularly sparse, so unverified claims and polemics flourish, while there is little substantive progress in understanding.

In light of the many controversies centering around neurosis, this chapter will proceed in the following manner. First, we shall look at behavioral descriptions of types of neurosis. These are noncontroversial and must be accounted for by any theory concerned with etiology. This descriptive introduction will be followed by a brief discussion of the reasons DSM-III abandoned the classification of neurosis. Then, because of our interest in diverse models of psychopathology, we shall examine and compare psychoanalytic theory and a conceptualization from within the behavioral camp. Finally, in a review of the research on the neuroses we shall focus on phobias in general and school phobias in particular. (For more detailed coverage of the topic, see Adams, 1979.)

THE DESCRIPTIVE PICTURE

Anxiety Neurosis

Anxiety neurosis is characterized by unvarnished fear, which erupts in repeated attacks of panicky feelings. In some cases the anxiety is described as free-floating, in that the children do not know what causes it, and they do not have any consistently effective means of alleviating it. In varying degrees children with an anxiety neurosis suffer from "nervousness," irritability, restlessness, insomnia, indecisiveness, and feelings of inadequacy. Inevitably there are autonomic concomitants, such as diarrhea, dilation of the pupils, dizziness, dryness of mouth, nausea, palpitations, sweating, and trembling.

Adams (1979) cites the case of a 9-year-old girl who was much closer to her alcoholic father than to her neurotic mother. The father described her as "nervous and high-

strung" like her mother. The child would become upset when the mother berated the father for his lack of business success, and since the mother claimed she was a better Christian than the father, the child also worried that her father would not go to heaven. On the other hand, she was fearful that the father might murder her mother when he came home drunk and belligerent. She also worried about the father's inability to provide her with candy, clothes, and material possessions, was afraid to go to sleep, and was concerned that nobody liked her. While she was initially a good student, her schoolwork declined as she became increasingly unable to concentrate in class. The girl's anxiety was not the free-floating kind but was constantly triggered by the reality of the family situation and by her own imaginings. In other instances, children's anxiety is far in excess of realistic provocations and is due more to intrapersonal factors.

Phobic Neurosis

Once called anxiety hysteria, phobic neurosis is marked by a persistent, intense, irrational fear of an animate or inanimate object or of a situation. The list of phobias is legion, including spiders, enclosed places, germs, heights, and even phobophobia, or a fear of phobias! Phobias should be distinguished from fears that may be developmentally appropriate (see chapter 2) or that represent a realistic reaction to a traumatic experience (such as being in an automobile accident). The hallmark of a phobia is that the fear is out of proportion to the reality of the situation. It cannot be explained or reasoned away. It is beyond voluntary control, unadaptive, and neither age- nor stage-specific. It persists over an extended period of time and leads to avoidance of the feared situations (Miller, Barrett, and Hampe, 1974).

The Hysterical Neuroses

Hysterical children often share three characteristics. First is an enchanted world view in which magical or primitive ideas are more potent than they are in age-mates. Religious beliefs or superstitions, for example, may be more vividly experienced and believed with more conviction. Next is an extreme expression of emotions. The children are overly dramatic, like ham actors, at the same time being self-centered rather than concerned with the feelings of others. Finally, there is an increased suggestibility. Hysterical children tend readily to pick up the symptoms of relatives and schoolmates, being copycats rather than empathizers (Adams, 1979). In all three characteristics runs the theme of immaturity and egocentrism, which becomes increasingly inappropriate as adolescence approaches. At the same time, the hysteric's self-dramatization tends to elicit responses such as, "Things can't be all that bad," or "Act your age," rather than reactions of sympathy and concern.

Conversion hysteria is marked by disturbed sensorimotor functions, such as paralyses or anesthesias of the arms or legs, functional blindness or deafness, and tics. It is crucial that all such symptoms be of psychological rather than physiological origin. One striking concomitant of these physical symptoms is a lack of anxiety concerning them; in fact, the child may seem quite comfortable with playing an acceptable sick role. This unconcern is called *la belle indifférence*. From the time of the Greeks to present-day Freudians, the "imaginary" physical symptoms of hysteria have been attributed to frustrated sexual needs.

Dissociative hysteria is marked by three characteristics: disturbances in consciousness, such as trances, stupor, or pseudodelirium; personality disorganization, as evidenced in depersonalization and multiple personalities; and odd motor expressions, such as sleepwalking, aimless running and pacing, or catalepsy (a condition in which the limbs keep any position they are placed in). There are two popular images of the dissociative hysteric. One is the individual with multiple personalities or with a split personality, which the media frequently mislabel as schizophrenia rather than hysteria. The other is the rural adolescent girl at a revival meeting, who suddenly has visions of religious figures, is unaware of her surroundings, writhes on the floor speaking in tongues and shouting she has been saved, while later having total amnesia for the episode.

Depressive Neurosis

This category has already been covered in our discussion of depression in middle childhood. In brief, the criteria are a dysphoric mood and loss of interest or pleasure in most of the usual activities and pastimes, together with poor appetite, insomnia, agitation, fatigue, diminution in concentration, and recurrent thoughts of worthlessness, helplessness, and hopelessness.

Obsessive-Compulsive Neurosis

The obsessive-compulsive neurosis is marked by intrusive ideas (obsessions) and impulses (compulsions) that seem to arise from sources over which the child has no control, are irresistible, and often recognized as irrational. Sometimes the neurosis appears to be an exaggeration of the usual ritualistic behavior of childhood; however, unlike ordinary rituals or routines, these engender intense anxiety or guilt when interfered with and consume an inordinate amount of time. The child recognizes the senseless nature of the behavior but is unable to change it. While hand washing is the most familiar example, other neurotic behaviors concern safety—such as continually checking the doors to make sure they are locked—or involve repeatedly counting to a particular number or touching objects a given number of times.

In certain children, obsessive-compulsive behavior has a more bizarre quality than those just depicted. Adams (1979) describes an 11-year-old who felt obliged to step on imaginary dots on the floor. He would not feel temporarily free of the compulsion until he had performed the ritual three times. He thought the dots might be fecal in nature, although he realized they were not really there, and was preoccupied with the idea that some of the toxin from the dots would enter his body through his anus. Subsequently his obsessive worries about germs, feces, and bodily harm nearly led him to a psychotic state.

Mixed Neuroses

While clinicians are constantly concerned with ordering psychopathologies into categories, children themselves fail to come in neatly packaged classifications. Most evidence a mixture of psychopathologies. The classification of mixed neuroses recognizes the fact that a variety of neurotic manifestations can be found in a given child.

CURRENT STATUS OF THE DIAGNOSIS

The controversy concerning the etiology of neuroses has affected the classification of the psychopathology itself. Because of the pervasive Freudian influence, neurosis had come to be identified not only with the behavioral manifestations of the psychopathology but also with the psychoanalytic interpretation. As this interpretation came to be increasingly questioned and as other etiologic accounts—particularly the behavioral—gained in popu-

larity, various attempts have been made to find a classification that would be strictly descriptive.

The solution of DSM-III was to discard the term *neurosis* altogether and substitute the more neutral term *disorder*. Thus a phobic neurosis becomes a phobic disorder, an obsessive-compulsive neurosis becomes an obsessive-compulsive disorder, and so on. The emphasis is on the purely descriptive characteristics of neurotic behavior: the presence of anxiety; the unacceptable, alien nature of the symptoms; the relative intactness of reality testing; the enduring nature of the disturbance; and the fact that the symptoms do not actively violate social norms. No longer united by an etiologic account, the traditional neurotic subtypes are no longer united in a single category but are dispersed among other categories; thus conversion hysteria is grouped with other conditions such as hypochondriasis and psychogenic pain disorders, in which the symptoms, while suggesting a physical disorder, have no demonstrable organic basis. Such disturbances are called Somatoform Disorders. Neurotic depression becomes absorbed into the general category of Affective Disorders, while phobias and obsessive-compulsive disturbances are considered two varieties of Anxiety Disorder.

As discussed in chapter 3, there is no agreement as to the optimal way of classifying childhood psychopathologies. Some of the current classifications are descriptive, others are tied closely to theories, while still others rely on statistical techniques to generate behavioral categories. In light of the uncertain etiology of all childhood psychopathologies, however, there is a clear advantage to having DSM-III confine itself to the descriptive approach. In this way a number of possible etiologies can be included, while there is no danger that its users will confuse the soundness of a clinical description with the validity of a particular etiologic theory. The descriptions themselves can also serve as a common behavioral base from which research—both theoretical and atheoretical—can emanate.

THE PSYCHOANALYTIC THEORY OF NEUROSIS

Psychoanalytic Theory and General Child Development

Conflict lies at the heart of the psychoanalytic theory of neurosis. (Our presentation in this section follows Nagera, 1966, and Shapiro, 1973.) In essence, the psychoanalysts conceptualize the development of self-control in terms of a conflict between what infants, toddlers, and preschoolers want to do and what socializing adults require them to do. Let us summarize the developmental picture.

In the *oral* period, the conflict is between infants' need for immediate physiological gratification—to eat, to sleep, and to be awake when biological rhythms dictate—and the caregivers' desire or ability to meet such needs. Note that in no sense is the conflict "in" the infants; it is strictly between infants and caregivers. In the *anal* period, the conflict is initially between the toddlers' wish to defecate whenever and wherever they please and the socializing adults' requirement for delay. By the end of toilet training the conflict has become internalized, toddlers now instructing themselves as to when and where they can defecate. The same paradigm holds for curiosity, where the conflict is between parental prohibitions and the desire to examine an attractive object. Eventually, children can selectively inhibit their exploratory behavior even when the parent is not present. Finally, in the *oedipal* stage, once again the conflict is initially external, the threatening

father opposing the boy's desire to possess the mother. By identification with the father the conflict becomes internal, with the boy now censuring his own erotic feelings.

The next component of neurosis is *anxiety.* Affect, like conflict, lies at the heart of psychoanalytic theory. Especially in early childhood, the purely intellectual comprehension of prohibitions would not be sufficiently potent to counteract children's desire to do what they want when they want to do it. It is the threat of parental punishment and withdrawal of parental love that provide an affect charge sufficiently strong to lead to the inhibition of socially unacceptable behavior. Returning to the conflict model, we now see that the conflict is between the desire to and the fear of gratifying strongly motivated behaviors.

With the introduction of anxiety the situation becomes more complicated. Anxiety is not only a deterrent; if sufficiently strong, it is exceedingly painful and can set into motion a whole array of maneuvers designed to protect the child from experiencing its distress. These maneuvers are called *defense mechanisms,* such as repression, projection, and reaction formation (see chapter 2).

These are the basic ingredients of a neurotic conflict. Yet according to Nagera (1966), preschool children reveal extreme versions of normal anxieties and defenses—an excessive fear of spiders, for example, or an intense disgust of messiness. What is more, such extreme reactions need not be the precursors of a subsequent neurosis. If this is so, if both the mechanisms and the behaviors characteristic of neurosis are present before middle childhood, why is neurosis considered a developmental achievement of that period? The answer must be in terms of a quantitative rather than a qualitative change. Only by middle childhood is that self-censoring faculty, the conscience, sufficiently strong and consistent to sustain deviant patterns of behavior which persist over time and are relatively impervious to environmental efforts to alter them.

The Nature of Neurotic Symptoms

Psychoanalytic theory states that neurotic symptoms have a symbolic meaning, which differs from the manifest content of the behavior. Freud was fascinated by the question of meaning: What does a dream mean? The peekaboo play of a 2-year-old? The delusion of a paranoid adult, who believes his guts are turning to stone? The slip of the tongue of a gracious hostess who says to a departing guest, "I'm so glad to see you go"? The simplest answer—and one many behaviorists prefer—is that behavior means what it says: a child who is terrified of spiders has probably been bitten by one or has been frightened by a picture of them or is imitating a parent who fears them. Undoubtedly this can happen, as the Freudians recognize. However, such a simple, realistic explanation cannot account for all of the bizarre, irrational features of psychopathological behavior. Freud thought that the meaning of a symptom had to be decoded, and, characteristically, he looked to development for the key, particularly the development of thinking.

In chapter 2 we saw that Freud and Piaget agree that an accurate grasp of reality is a developmental achievement. During the first half-dozen years of life much thinking does not conform to reality. Freud's special name for early ideation was *primary-process thinking*. "Primary process" is the primitive need to maximize pleasure and avoid pain. Once again we see Freud's emphasis on affects and motivation, this time in the realm of ideation. In normal life daydreams partake of this need-determined quality, in that we suddenly suspend realistic thinking and indulge ourselves

in sexual escapades or grandiose achievements or vengeful triumphs over enemies. Hallucinations are another form of need-determined ideation: just as the thirsty man in the desert can hallucinate an oasis, a psychotic adult with pent-up hostility can hallucinate a voice commanding him to kill the president of the United States.

One example of primitive thinking relevant to neurosis is what Freud called *symbolization* (Meissner, Mack, and Semrad, 1975, pp. 501–502). Here a concrete object is used to represent or substitute for another tabooed object or idea on the basis of a common element. A familiar example is the phallic symbol, in which an elongated object such as a knife or fountain pen symbolizes a penis; in a like manner, containers such as a vase or a box can symbolize the vagina. While there may be a few common symbols, symbolization is highly idiosyncratic: a car may mean masculine power to one boy, destructiveness to another.

ILLUSTRATION   The way the basic components combine to produce a specific neurosis can be illustrated by a phobia. The case in point is a 7-year-old girl who was terrified of spiders, which she feared would bite her. Psychoanalytically oriented play therapy revealed that the basic neurotic conflict was between a desire to express anger toward her mother and her primitive conscience's mandate that she be a good girl. Her self-condemnation as "bad" engendered anxiety, and—as is typical of phobias—a triple defense was set into play. First came repression, so that the girl could banish the angry thoughts and feelings from consciousness. Next came projection, in which the mother was seen as angry at the girl. Finally came displacement, in which a relatively innocuous object was invested with exaggerated destructive powers. Why a spider? Remember that there is never a pat answer to questions of symbolization, since the meaning can be highly idiosyncratic. In this instance the girl, having heard of the deadly bite of the black widow spider, equated both the quality of hostile attack and blackness with her mother, who made a great deal over the versatility of her "basic black" dress.

Neurosis and the Psychosexual Stages of Development

The Oedipus complex and the anal stage are the source of two prominent groups of symptoms—hysterical and obsessive-compulsive.

HYSTERICAL SYMPTOMS   Two varieties of hysterical symptoms will be dealt with. In *anxiety hysteria*, the child is unaware of the cause of anxiety because the forbidden sexual or hostile impulse has been repressed. However, repression is not successful and the impulse threatens to return to consciousness. Hence the recurrent waves of panic and the persistent "nervousness."

A *phobia* represents one method of mastering the helplessness evidenced in anxiety hysteria. As we have seen, projection and displacement focus the anxiety on an external source. The child now has something to be afraid of and ways of avoiding the frightening object or situation. The content of the phobia represents variations on the oedipal themes of sex and aggression, the variations being legion—biting animals, automobile accidents, and fires can be feared because of their violence, for instance, while "slimy" snakes, egg yolks, and the physical closeness of a confined space can be feared because of their erotic connotations.

OBSESSIVE AND COMPULSIVE SYMPTOMS   While obsessive and compulsive symptoms, like hysterical ones, may originate in an inability

to resolve the Oedipus complex successfully, in this neurosis the child regresses to the anal level. Recall that the conflict here is between conformity and rebellious self-assertion, and that in normal development the defense of reaction formation enables the child to make the transition from fascination with feces, dirt, and messiness to cleanliness, orderliness, and obedience. In the neurotic school-age child, the anal conflict returns in a highly charged repetitive manner. In a hand-washing compulsion, for example, the child can never dispel the nagging feeling that his or her hands are not absolutely and totally clean; rituals to insure safety, such as checking locks on doors at night, can never satisfy the child that the house is absolutely burglarproof.

Determinants of Normal versus Neurotic Development

While psychosexual theory may tell us what neurosis is likely to develop, it still does not answer the question of why a child becomes neurotic instead of continuing to develop normally. The classical answer proposed by Freud was in terms of *excessive* or *insufficient gratification* of libidinal and/or aggressive impulses at the various psychosexual stages. The infant who is indulged in oral gratification, for example, will have difficulty giving up these pleasures and will have a strong tendency to return to them when subsequent developments prove difficult; in a like manner, the infant who receives only meager gratification will continue to long for the missing pleasures, such longings becoming a regressive undertow in subsequent development.

However, subsequent observations of normal and disturbed children have introduced new elements, so that the current answer to our question, Why neuroses? is now in terms of the *balance of forces*, some making for psychopathology on the one hand, some for healthy development on the other (Nagera, 1966). Freud's classical formulation is still considered valid but incomplete.

What are the additional sources of vulnerability? Some are *constitutional* in that certain infants have more intense reactions of anxiety and rage than others and are persistently disrupted by their effects. Other vulnerabilities are *experiential,* failure to receive sensitive care in infancy being particularly important.

As for assets—constitution and maturation can be aligned on the side of health as well as on the side of vulnerabilities. Certain infants are innately rugged and resilient, either experiencing less intense anxiety or readily taking it in stride. Later on, they tend to grapple with and master difficulties and frustrations rather than having to retreat and protect themselves. Psychosexual development itself is maturationally determined, according to psychoanalytic theory, so there is always a strong force propelling the child on to the next stage and protecting him or her from becoming mired in the conflicts of the current one. In middle childhood, family entanglements become less intense, while concomitantly the development of friendships, achievement in school, positive relations with teachers, coaches, and other adult models all strengthen the child's ability to deal with conflicts constructively. Even a neurotic conflict can itself become a constructive force in the child's developing personality. Take, for example, the boy who handles his hostility toward a younger sibling by the reaction formation of being especially concerned with the plight of relatively weak and helpless youngsters; this, in turn, can lead to an interest in helping physically handicapped and mentally retarded children, and eventually to a successful vocation in one of the helping professions. As Anna Freud (1965) puts it, one can never be sure whether

a therapist is eliminating a neurosis or "nipping a future physicist in the bud."

THE FLUIDITY OF CHILDHOOD NEUROSIS Unlike their adult counterparts, which are remarkably fixed and persistent, childhood neuroses tend to be fluid. An adult may be terrified of riding in an elevator all of his or her mature years, but children are usually not similarly hamstrung by their disturbances. In part, this is because the child is changing more rapidly than the adult, and patterns of self-control and self-censoring are not as fixed. In part, this is because the child is more highly reactive to environmental events than is the adult, so that favorable or untoward happenings weigh more heavily in relieving or accentuating their neurotic disturbances.

This concept of fluidity has important implications concerning the *intrapsychic* aspects of the psychoanalytic theory. Those who misunderstand the theory describe it as claiming that all problems are due to internal conflicts between the id and the superego, leaving no room for realistic difficulties between the child and the environment. Now we see that this interpretation is wrong on two counts. First, it is not until middle childhood that a stable intrapsychic conflict is possible, and, second, all through middle childhood and adolescence, environmental influences continue to play a role in the fate of the neurosis. Only in adulthood is personality sufficiently formed to sustain a relatively self-perpetuating neurosis.

THE BEHAVIORAL APPROACH

One problem in presenting the behavioral theory of neurosis is that there is no single, agreed-upon behavioral theory; as was evident in chapter 1, there are extremists and moderates, purists and revisionists (see Mahoney, Kazdin, and Lesswing, 1974). Psychoanalysts are similarly divided among themselves. How large a gap there is between the psychoanalytic and behavioral theories, therefore, depends on which variation one chooses to present.

The two issues dividing behaviorists are: (1) whether the basic data of psychology must be palpable environment events and overt behaviors or whether "mentalistic" concepts, particularly cognitive ones, may be introduced, provided they are operationally defined and increase explanatory potency; and (2) whether the three principles of learning (i.e., classical conditioning, operant conditioning, and imitation) are adequate to account for all learned behavior or whether additional theories must be added.

"Private Events": The Controversial Area

Behaviorists are united in their objection to Freud's mentalism—the freedom with which he speculated about images, thoughts, and fantasies. Such a psychology runs counter to the behavioral emphasis on objectivity. References to mental events, if introduced at all, must be made cautiously, with great care to point to the behavior that necessitates their introduction. Recently, however, there has been a dissatisfaction with the gingerly treatment of images, thoughts, and fantasies, along with a vigorous attempt to give cognitive variables the status they deserve (Mahoney, 1974, 1977).

Bandura (1969) summarizes numerous studies showing the important role mediating symbols play in a variety of behaviors. Memory was improved by instructing subjects to associate two unrelated words with a distinctive image; for example, recalling "dog-bicycle" was facilitated if the subject imagined a dog riding a bicycle. Instructions to "Think *T*" aroused an autonomic response in subjects

who had previously received an electrical shock every time they were presented with and asked to pronounce the letter *T*. Instructions to imagine lifting different weights were followed by muscle contractions proportional to the imagined weights.

The explanation of private events also divides behaviorists. Purists such as Skinner insist that only the locus changes when one moves from overt to covert behavior; the conceptual framework and the learning principles remain unchanged. When a boy says, "That's good," to himself after receiving all A's on his report card, he is merely transferring reinforcement from the external to the internal environment; when a girl says, "I'm going to try harder next time," she is merely setting a standard of achievement for herself which had formerly been rewarded or modeled on others. Even complex thinking and planning can be accounted for by the chaining of prior, simpler symbolic activities just as, say, expert piano playing results from building up increasingly complex motor skills.

Other equally dedicated behaviorists claim the theoretical model must be expanded to accommodate the nature and complexity of symbolic behavior. Bandura (1969) inserts an "internal information-processing" system between stimulus and response which involves attending to stimuli, encoding the information, storing it either momentarily or permanently, and, ultimately, retrieving the stored information when it is needed to guide future behavior. (See also Mahoney, 1974.)

The Behavioral Theory of Neurosis

If the behavioral account of etiology is thin compared to the psychoanalytic, this is due to history more than to inherent inadequacies of the theory. The lion's share of interest and the greatest vitality and creativity have been in the realm of behavior therapy. Etiology has been treated something like a step-child.

In behaviorists' discussions of psychopathology, one may not find a heading labeled "neurosis"—or any other traditional diagnostic category, for that matter. They do not believe people "have" neuroses in the sense that they "have" physical illnesses. A disturbed person evidences certain behaviors which either society or the individual involved chooses to place in a special category. But such categorization in no way makes the behavior different, nor does it necessitate the introduction of any new psychological principles. On the contrary, all human behavior obeys the same principles of learning.

CONDITIONING OF INAPPROPRIATE RESPONSES
In discussing the behavioral viewpoint Bandura's (1968) presentation will be followed. (While Bandura's subsequent book, "Social Learning Theory," 1977, significantly expands the cognitive domain of the behavioral approach, the implications for a theory of neurosis has not been spelled out in detail. Therefore, the older work is more suited to this discussion.) Bandura would agree with the Freudians that the response that lies at the heart of neuroses is frequently anxiety. Anxiety-flight, just as anger-fight, can be adaptive when it is a reaction to realistic threat; when the response is inappropriate, however, when no real danger exists, the behaviorists regard it as psychopathological.

Traditional learning principles can account for the various ways in which innocuous and inappropriate stimuli come to elicit aversive emotional responses. The most familiar principle is aversive classical conditioning, in which a formerly neutral stimulus (the Conditioned Stimulus), occurring in conjunction with a stimulus (the Unconditioned Stimulus) which elicits an unpleasant affective response (the Unconditioned Response), itself comes to elicit that unpleasant response (the Con-

ditioned Response). The classical case is of 11-month-old Albert who, after being exposed to a number of pairings of a white rat (CS) with a loud, frightening noise (US), became frightened by the sight of the rat alone (CR). A variation in this same model is higher-order conditioning in which a stimulus, once conditioned, serves as the basis for further aversive conditioning when paired with neutral stimuli. In an experimental situation, names of persons or nations or even nonsense syllables that had been associated with words having negative connotations, such as "bitter" or "ugly," subsequently tended to be viewed as unpleasant. In realistic situations, a child who hears that sex is "dirty" may develop a disgust for sexual behavior even without engaging in it.

A negative affective response may also be acquired by vicarious classical conditioning. Here the mere observing of another person responding with pain or anxiety to a previously innocuous stimulus—say a buzzer that always preceded a shock—will subsequently produce an aversive response in the observer when the innocuous stimulus is presented. On this basis a girl whose parents are afraid of being burglarized can come to fear every creak of the stairs after bedtime, as her parents do.

In addition to such familiar mechanisms for learning a new response, Bandura notes that inappropriate behavior can result when irrelevant aspects of a complex social stimulus are attended to and generalizations made on the basis of what, in reality, are noncontingent relationships. He cites the example of a woman who wrote to "Dear Abby," warning other women that men who wear bow ties can never be trusted!

STIMULUS GENERALIZATION Once established, inappropriate behavior can spread by stimulus generalization. The classical example is, once again, little Albert, who after being conditioned to fear a white rat, subsequently was afraid of a number of white, furry objects. However, stimulus generalization in an 11-year-old is bound to be more complex than it is in an 11-month-old. Semantically related cues can take precedence over the sheer physical similarity of words; for example, subjects conditioned to "hare" will generalize to "rabbit" rather than to "hair." Generalization can also occur to categories of objects; for example, a subject who receives an electrical shock when a rural word such as "barn" is presented will also have an aversive reaction to other rural words.

REINFORCEMENT OF AVOIDANCE RESPONSES
The final component in the behavioral explanation of neurosis is the reinforcement of responses that enable the individual to avoid the conditioned aversive stimuli. Like psychoanalysts, behavioral theorists regard anxiety as an unusually potent motivator; any behavior that reduces or eliminates it will be reinforced. A wide array of such behaviors can be conceptualized as avoidance responses, one of the most important being "response inhibition." If an act is habitually punished, both the behavior itself and its cognitive representation come to elicit anxiety. In order to prevent such anxiety from occurring, not only the behavior but also its cognitive representation can be avoided. In other words, the child avoids both doing and thinking about doing a forbidden act. This, of course, is exactly the same process as repression. The difference is that behaviorists regard as superfluous the psychoanalytic assumption that the "ego" represses the forbidden idea into the "unconscious," where it continues to exist and press for expression. In fact, the entire gamut of defense mechanisms are congruent with learning theory as long as they are regarded as learned avoidance responses rather than protective devices initiated by the ego.

Specific Neurotic Behaviors

The behaviorist's etiologic account of *phobias* is the most convincing, the mechanisms of aversive and vicarious classical conditioning being well supported by laboratory studies on both animals and humans (Bandura, 1968). Behaviorists add that, once learned, the reaction of the social environment is a potent factor perpetuating the phobia. While a child might originally develop a fear of insects by modeling a parent, the subsequent attention received from the parent, either positive or negative, may further reinforce the phobic response.

Compulsive rituals can result from symbolic mediation. To illustrate: during toilet training, "dirty" may become a stimulus whose aversive consequences can be reduced by washing one's hands. On learning that sex is also "dirty," an adolescent may reduce the anxiety engendered by sexual thoughts and activities by taking a shower.

INTEGRATION AND EVALUATION

First let us look at areas of agreement. Both behavioral and psychoanalytically oriented psychologists agree that while anxiety holds the key to understanding much neurotic behavior, there is no qualitative difference between the anxiety which leads to appropriate, adaptive behavior and that which leads to inappropriate, maladaptive behavior—both kinds of behavior obey the same laws. Adherents of both schools agree that the child can adopt parental fears either by identification (psychoanalytic theory) or modeling (behavioral theory) and that, once initiated, such fears can be sustained by attention from significant figures in the environment. Both agree that the socialization process, with its inevitable conflicts generated by the desire to do the forbidden, is a source of anxiety. Both agree that anxiety, in turn, motivates various avoidance techniques, defense mechanisms being prominent ones. There also seems to be substantative agreement concerning the nature of anxiety neurosis, in that both the instigation to perform a forbidden act and the need to avoid conscious recognition of that act are strong, resulting in a high level of anxiety with no awareness of its source.

In their explanations of other neurotic symptoms the two approaches diverge widely. Principles of conditioning and imitation clearly apply to the formation of certain symptoms— a fact that psychoanalysts, for some unaccountable reason, have persisted in ignoring. On the other hand, the psychoanalytic theory is a thoroughgoing developmental one; the behaviorists only fitfully introduce a development component. The psychosexual theory provides specific hypotheses concerning the kinds of experiences, the timing of those experiences, and the interrelationship among those experiences that are crucial determinants of normal or pathological development. To reject this store of developmental hypotheses, while having little or nothing to offer in their place, would significantly impoverish our attempt to understand childhood neuroses.

GENERAL RESEARCH FINDINGS

Neurosis as Internalization

Behaviorally, the neuroses share a number of characteristics: a high level of anxiety (except in the case of *la belle indifférence*), which interferes with optimal functioning; less distortion of reality and grossly maladaptive behavior than is present in the psychoses; no major etiologic role played by organic factors; and suffering primarily turned inward on the self.

This last aspect of neuroses—turning suffering inward—has been amply demonstrated by factor-analytic studies of psychopathological behavior in children. Typical of such studies is Achenbach's factor analysis of a 91-item symptom checklist using 600 male and female psychiatric patients as subjects (Achenbach, 1966). The first principal factor was a bipolar one, which he labeled internalization–externalization. Among internalizing symptoms he included phobias, worrying, stomachaches, withdrawal, nausea, vomiting, compulsions, insomnia, seclusiveness, depression, crying—all indicating a distressed child. Externalizing symptoms included disobedience, stealing, lying, fighting, destructiveness, inadequate guilt feelings, swearing, temper tantrums, running away, and vandalism—all indicating a child in conflict with the environment. Indirectly the data support the thesis that neurosis is due, in part, to excessive self-control, the anxiety and guilt inherent in socialization becoming extreme. (For a detailed presentation of research, see Schwartz and Johnson, 1985.)

Constitutional Factors

Eysenck (1960) has been one of the most persistent champions of the hypothesis that there is a constitutional-genetic component in neurosis. This hypothesis was based on a statistical analysis of disturbed behavior that yielded a factor Eysenck labeled "neuroticism," which subsequently proved to be related to emotional reactions that were labile, intense, and easily aroused. Genetic studies also suggested that identical twins show a greater degree of similarity with regard to neuroticism than fraternal twins. Finally, there are clinical reports claiming that some infants are more prone to experiencing anxiety and have more difficulty in coping with it than others.

Eysenck's empirical data have not gone

unchallenged, while he himself recognizes and emphasizes the role of environmental factors in producing neuroses. A conservative conclusion would be that there might be a genetic or constitutional predisposition to becoming neurotic, but environmental influences are the major determinants.

The Family

The meager research on families has yielded reasonably good evidence that separation anxiety or school phobias occur with overinvolved parents and overdependent children. Overprotection can be manifested in several ways: restrictive control, intrusion into psychological and physical privacy, reinforcement of dependency, and exclusion of outside influence. Marital conflict, while related to aggressive, acting-out behavior, has not been found in anxiety–withdrawal disorders. Instead, there is a complex interaction whereby marital conflict accompanied by opposite-sex parent dominance puts the child at risk. Thus, for example, if a dominating father disparages a weak and whining mother, the son is not apt to develop anxiety or withdrawal disorders but the daughter is. (For details see Hetherington and Martin, 1986.)

FEARS AND PHOBIAS

Fear is usually defined as a normal reaction to an environmental threat. It is adaptive and even essential to survival because it warns the individual that a situation may be physically or psychologically harmful. Phobias are distinguished from fears on the basis of their intensity, which is out of proportion to the situation, their maladaptiveness, and their persistence. As we shall soon see, placing these definitions within a developmental context will make them less clear-cut than they now appear to be. But first we shall sum-

marize some relevant evidence. Unfortunately for our purposes, most of the literature concerns fears rather than phobias. (For a general discussion of fears and phobias, see Miller, 1983. For a detailed presentation of the following material, see Wenar, 1990.)

INCIDENCE AND PERSISTENCE   In a population of 7- to 12-year-olds incidence of phobias has been reported to be as low as 0.5 to 1 percent and as high as 10 to 20 percent. While most fears are transient, around half disappearing in three months, phobias are more tenacious; however, most of them improve in two to three years with or without psychotherapy, although psychotherapy can hasten the recovery. Adult phobias are more intractable, only 20 to 30 percent showing full recovery. A few childhood phobias, such as animal phobias, fear of physical injury, and psychic stress, may persist as adult problems. Childhood phobias may also lead to nonphobic adult disturbances. Phobic children have a variety of other problems, the association with depression being particularly close.

ETIOLOGY   The etiology of phobias remains a mystery. While it may be due to a terrifying experience or to imitation, in many instances it is not. For example, a frightening experience such as being in an automobile accident can fail to produce a lasting fear or a phobia, while an intense fear of spiders may develop in a child who has neither been bitten by one nor observed a phobic reaction in others.

STIMULUS CHARTING   With a few notable exceptions, research has consisted in charting the stimuli that elicit fear at different ages. Such a procedure does not meet our standards of a developmental approach because it fails to integrate the data with changes in other significant variables such as the self, cognition, social relations, and affect itself. To take one example: both a 5-year-old and a 15-

year-old may be afraid of robbers; however, there is no evidence that preschoolers are concerned over loss of property as adolescents are, so that a robber may well mean a strange, evil, intrusive individual more akin to a ghost than a real person. This point about development giving different meanings to similar behavior was made in earlier discussions of other psychopathologies.

Stimulus charting is also unsatisfactory because fear reactions and phobias both tend to be unstable in childhood, Miller (1972) citing the example of a child who was terrified of riding an escalator with his mother, but who readily rode it with a friendly researcher who was there to observe the phobic behavior. Moreover, fear is not an absolute response to a stimulus but a contingent one, especially in the early years; e.g., a 9-month-old may react to a stranger with interest while sitting on the mother's lap but react with terror if sitting a few feet away from the mother. Whether a stimulus will elicit fear depends on the child's general security, which often is affected by the familiarity or unfamiliarity of the social and physical setting, the level of cognitive development, which determines whether an event will be classified as familiar or strange, the child's immediate state of well-being, and more long-term temperamental characteristics, such as being tough and resilient or sensitive and easily frightened. (See Sroufe, Waters, and Matas, 1974.)

DEFINITIONS RECONSIDERED   By most definitions, fears have been considered adaptive, phobias maladaptive. The distinction may be appropriate for adults who, for example, recognize that their fear of sitting in the front row of a class is an irrational one. However, the distinction runs into difficulties when viewed developmentally. Many of the earliest fears, such as the fear of loud noises or sudden movement, are intense, persistent, and maladaptive in the sense that in the vast majority of instances there is nothing dangerous in the environment. Thus by adult criteria they should be regarded as phobias, whereas in reality they are part of normal development. Because of the importance of the developmental dimension a number of clinical child psychologists have added *age-inappropriate* to the list of criteria for phobias.

Developmental Reconstruction

Our presentation relies heavily on the research of Jersild and Holmes (1935), who, although working more than fifty years ago, are among the few who have explored the development of fears in its complexity.

THE INFANCY/PRESCHOOL PERIOD   In early infancy fear reactions might be regarded as innate because they appear early in development with no evidence of their being learned. Among stimuli that elicit such fear are loud noise, pain, falling, and sudden, unexpected movement. It is worth noting that such stimuli require little cognitive elaboration, the fear appearing and vanishing with the stimulus itself. Strangeness or unfamiliarity, whether in regard to people, objects, or situations, elicits fear in the latter half of the first year. The evaluation of a stimulus as "familiar" or "strange" requires a cognitive elaboration that is not necessary with innate stimuli. Moreover, such an elaboration is not possible in the earliest months of life. Neonates know little about the world into which they are born. They require time to become sufficiently acquainted with their new environment to begin regarding people, objects, and situations as familiar and recognizable or as unfamiliar and strange. In the early toddler period animals begin to elicit fear. In certain instances fear may be in response to the noise and sudden, unexpected movement chararcteristic of animals. However, even quiet animals may be effective stimuli, perhaps because of their unfamiliarity, although Jersild and Holmes (1935) speculate that there may be an innate fear of animals.

The change from the toddler to the preschool period is marked by a decline in the primitive fears of noise, falling, sudden movement, and strangeness, although fear of pain and of animals have an irregular upward trend. Memory makes fear less a situational response by strengthening anticipation so that children now respond to the threat or the danger of bodily injury and, subsequently, to warnings that are part of socialization. Thus children increasingly fear traffic accidents and fires in response to parental punishment and other fear-inducing techniques; subsequently, they come to fear doing things parents regard as "bad." Fear of imaginary animals and characters and fear of nightmares also become developmentally possible as the early preschooler comes to differentiate reality from fantasy and recognizes the latter as a special realm of cognitive activity.

Finally, the end of the preschool period witnesses the appearance of fear of personal inadequacy, failure, and ridicule, the examples cited by Jersild and Holmes (1935) involving learning the academic skills of numbers and writing, or fear of other school-related functions. Such fears indicate the development of the concept of an achieving self to the point that anticipation of failure is a source of concern.

MIDDLE CHILDHOOD By middle childhood, the cognitive distortions that characterize earlier periods have been corrected by and large, and the child's basic grasp of the social and physical environment resembles that of the adult. Fears follow this trend toward realism: fears of bodily injury, say, from traffic accidents or fires, increase; fears of ghosts and imaginary creatures decline. Fear of failure

increases, although it is never high in comparison with other fears. The old, primitive fear of sudden movement, falling, and strange people all vanish, although the fear of noise persists in response to thunder.

However, the tilt toward realism is not all-encompassing. While the fear of remote animals such as lions and tigers declines, fear of harmless animals such as rats and mice ranks high, while the fear of snakes far outstrips their actual danger. Fear of the dark and of nightmares also continues. A decline in fear of ghosts is compensated for by an increase in fear of fictional characters from stories, movies, and television. The finding is plausible. Imagination, by its very nature, is tangential to reality since it does not conform to the same rules as those governing the social and physical environment. Thus imaginary characters can retain their affective charge in the face of an increased cognitive realism.

In sum, middle childhood, like all other developmental periods throughout the life span, is marked by a mixture of realistic and unrealistic fear; only the proportions have changed.

ADOLESCENCE Adolescence brings with it new, age-appropriate fears. Sexual fears and concerns over money and work enter the developmental picture, as would be expected. Their increased cognitive ability enables adolescents to grasp and be concerned about a social context broader than home and school, as well as making it possible for them to project themselves into the future. Thus fears centering around war and peace make their appearance and dramatically increase between 14 and 18 years of age, along with more personal concerns about growing up and being able to cope with problems that lie ahead.

Adolescence also witnesses an increase in fears that are present only to a minor degree in middle childhood. The striking example is fear of failure or personal inadequacy, expressed primarily in the large number of school-related fears present throughout the entire period. Such fears may be due partly to the increased emphasis on achievement in high school, but they are also due to the adolescent's own increased ability to generate relatively stable standards and to be concerned over living up to them. As peer relations take on greater importance in adolescence, concerns over popularity and having friends begin to rise, especially for girls. And the increased self-consciousness of the adolescent is accompanied by an increased fear of looking foolish.

Finally, irrational fears, while infrequent, persist—for example, fear of the dark, of storms and noise, or mice and snakes. Fear of the supernatural is infrequent, but adolescence may bring with it new irrational fears, such as fear of cemeteries and of water (i.e., swimming alone, boating, deep water), which are rarely reported in middle childhood.

In sum, fears at this stage, as in previous ones, continue to reflect significant developments in the self, in social expectations and relationships, in cognition, and in physical maturation. Adolescence may also represent a further diminution of irrational fears, although they are not completely exorcised.

Overcoming Fears

The issue of mastery is particularly pertinent to clinical child psychology. Understanding what conditions lead to overcoming fears may furnish clues to understanding the conditions leading to failure to overcome them. Once again, the only researchers who have seriously explored the issue of mastering fears are Jersild and Holmes (1935).

Mothers used a variety of techniques aimed at helping their children overcome fears: explanation and reassurance, setting an example (such as walking into a dark room or petting a feared dog), providing the child with coping techniques (such as letting a fearful child turn off the lights himself at night), graduating the approach to a feared object, using distractions or counterstimuli (such as having a child ride horsey on a vacuum cleaner when the frightening motor is not running), and forewarning the child in preparation for a potentially frightening experience such as getting a shot from a doctor. Not only were the mothers ingenious, but their techniques have a surprisingly contemporary ring as well. However, they succeeded only fitfully. More typically, children overcame fears on their own; children's increased understanding of their environment and their increased ability to manipulate and explore were their greatest assets in achieving mastery. In fact, Jersild and Holmes (1935) concluded that if fears are mild, it is wise to let them run their course because they will be conquered more readily on the basis of children's growth and experience than on the basis of adult interventions. Using our own terminology, fears are overcome by *initiative*.

Why Phobias?

The literature is least satisfactory when it comes to determining the relation between fears and phobias, some authors stating that fears shade imperceptibly into phobias, others maintaining that we do not know whether they operate according to identical principles, or whether the principles governing the relationship change with age. Even if the former position were true, it would still leave unanswered the basic question, Why do fears become so intense and persistent that the factors responsible for openness to change, such as initiative, fail to serve their growth-promoting function? One might expect, for example, that animal phobias would be the most amenable to the corrective influence of increasing cognitive and emotional maturity, yet just the opposite is the case. One might also expect that the fluidity of personality in the second and third year of life would prevent the appearance of sustained phobias during these years, yet both animal and insect phobias have been observed. To compound the problems, what empirical data there are often blur the distinction between fears and phobias so that, for example, it is impossible to tell whether what is termed an intense or a clinical fear is the equivalent of a formally defined phobia. Consequently, any discussion of the relation between the two is bound to be tentative.

While disclaiming any intent of unraveling the etiologic mystery of phobias, Jersild and Holmes (1935) obtained data on sixteen preschoolers representing the extremes of a marked lack of fearfulness on the one hand and unusually high levels of fearfulness on the other. They found that both groups were in good physical condition, that there was no difference in the stability and security of the home atmosphere or in the mothers' understanding of the children's needs, and no difference in general friendliness and enjoyment of peer relations. However, there was a difference in certain personality traits: the fearful children were more frequently described as dependent on adults for help, easily upset emotionally, timid, shy, and insecure, and unable to stand up for their rights on the playground, while the least fearful children were described in the opposite terms. Such observations and inferences make sense in light of the previous hypothesis that self-confident exploration and the ability to test out the reality of fears is one of the major reasons they are mastered. Lack of confidence and a sense of personal ineffectuality or helplessness may exaggerate and perpet-

uate fears. Yet all of this is speculative and seems more relevant to disturbances in general rather than being specific to phobias. Jersild and Holmes (1935) concluded that "the elements which contribute to causing such individual differences in fear behavior . . . are quite intangible and not often expressed by the type of overt behavior which is easily observed and recognized" (p. 284).

Relative Effectiveness of Different Therapies

With diverse therapies claiming to cure phobias, the question that naturally arises is, Which is the most effective? In light of the dismal state of research on the neuroses, it is gratifying to report that one of the few model studies in all the therapeutic literature is addressed to this question. The study serves as a model for many reasons. The children were evaluated objectively by individuals other than the therapist, thus eliminating the unconscious biases which might creep in when therapists evaluate their own work. The groups of children receiving different treatment were carefully matched at the beginning to ensure that one was not better adjusted, more intelligent, and so forth than the other. Even more important, the therapists themselves were matched in terms of skill, so the outcomes would reflect the kind of therapy rather than the expertness with which it was implemented. The therapeutic goals were agreed upon, so that improvement in both groups conformed to the same behavioral criteria and was therefore comparable. Finally, the test of therapeutic effectiveness was made at the end of a follow-up period, since there is evidence that immediate improvement tends to wash out with time.

This study was conducted by Miller, Barrett, Hampe, and Noble (1972), who compared the relative effectiveness of a behavioral therapy (reciprocal inhibition), a psychoanalytically oriented play therapy, and a control group of children on a waiting list who received no therapy. All sixty-seven subjects were phobic, the ones in treatment receiving one-hour sessions three times a week for eight weeks. All children were evaluated at the end of a six-week follow-up period. There was no evidence that either therapy was more effective, which might have been, in part, because the actual behavior of the therapists from the two different schools was quite similar! There was a diminution of symptoms in all three groups. Whether the two therapy groups improved more than the nontreated control group depended on who evaluated them, parents of the treated groups reporting significantly greater improvement, a noninvolved clinician finding no differences among the three groups. Age proved to be a significant variable, 6- to 10-year-olds showing greater improvement with therapy than the controls, 11- to 15-year-olds failing to show such a difference. Similar results concerning the relative effectiveness of behavioral and psychoanalytically oriented psychotherapy have been found with adults (Sloane et al., 1975).

In light of the fact that poorly designed studies of therapeutic effectiveness have been so misleading in the past, our preference is to conclude that, at present, there is no treatment of choice for childhood neuroses. (For a detailed presentation of behavior therapy and its effectiveness, see Carlson, Figueroa, and Lahey, 1986. The psychoanalytic approach to treatment is described and evaluated by Lewis, 1986. The former authors state that it is impossible to draw any empirically based conclusions concerning the effectiveness of behavioral intervention or the superiority of one form of treatment over the other. The psychoanalytic tradition of reporting treatment of individual children also precludes statements concerning absolute and relative effectiveness.)

SCHOOL PHOBIA

A youngster with a school phobia is a pitiful sight. On a school morning, for example, a boy might sit at the breakfast table pale and silent, his eyes tearful, listlessly pushing a spoon around his bowl of oatmeal. If he forces himself to eat a spoonful and take a gulp of milk in response to parental coaxing, it is with great effort. Soon he says he has to go to the bathroom either to throw up or to have a bowel movement, which he might or might not do. As the time approaches for him to catch the school bus, he becomes increasingly agitated, pleading, crying, or shouting accusations at his mother. In no way can such distress be mistaken for malingering or attention getting; rather, it has all the behavioral and physiological characteristics of intense fear. However, if the child is allowed to stay at home, he is relieved and may resume his usual activities.

School phobia, also called *school refusal*, is defined as an irrational dread of some aspect of the school situation accompanied by physiological symptoms of anxiety or panic when attendance is imminent and resulting in a partial or total inability to go to school. It may be one of the most frequently diagnosed neuroses. (Our presentation follows Trueman, 1984.) School phobias occur in schoolchildren of all ages and may be found even at the college level. There is no difference in gender or socioeconomic status between phobic and nonphobic populations. The children have average intelligence, do satisfactory work academically, and do not dislike school. Some investigators have found physical illness to be a precipitating factor, but in many cases there is no obvious reason for the onset.

While there has been some effort to explore the difference between younger and older phobics (i.e., younger or older than 10 years of age) and between acute and chronic cases, the research has been limited and inconclusive.

The principal agreement among studies is that school-phobic children are more dependent, anxious, immature, and depressed than nonphobic children or than children who truant. They also have an increase in other behavior problems such as eating disorders, enuresis, and anxious and hysterical reactions, whereas truants have an increase in conduct disorders. There has been little interest in studying the disturbance within a developmental framework. (For a detailed presentation, see Herbert, 1974, and Graziano, DeGiovanni, and Garcia, 1979.)

ETIOLOGY School phobias can originate in diverse sources and can occur in different intra- and interpersonal contexts. Three frequently mentioned etiologies are fear of separation from the mother, lack of self-confidence, and an unrealistically high self-image which magnifies any threat of failure. In the self-reports of school-phobic children, for example, the most frequent fear is that harm will befall the mother in the child's absence, followed by a fear of being ridiculed and the fear of failure in school. However, reasons can overlap and change, while a number of children have no idea why they are afraid. Finally, a distinction has been made between a school phobia that occurs in a fairly sound personality and a healthy family setting and a school phobia that is part of a more pervasive disturbance within the child and his or her family (Herbert, 1974).

The diverse interpersonal relations have been organized into three patterns: (1) an overindulgent mother and an inadequate father, dominated by a willful, stubborn, demanding child at home who is timid and inhibited in social situations away from home; (2) a strict, controlling, demanding mother, a passive father, and a passive, obedient child at home who is often timid and fearful away from home but who may become stubborn and rebellious at puberty; and (3) a firm, controlling father and an overindulgent mother closely bound to and dominated by a willful, demanding child who is alert, friendly, and outgoing away from home (Hersov, 1960).

In one of the few studies comparing school-phobic with other neurotic children (Waldron et al., 1975), the former were found to have significantly more separation anxiety, to be more dependent and depressed, to have unrealistically high self-expectations, and to be preoccupied with mistreatment from adults outside the family. Their greater difficulties in adjusting to school antedated the appearance of the school phobia itself. The most frequent pattern of interaction was a hostile-dependent relationship between mother and child. Here, the child's hostility was disguised as a concern for the destruction that might befall the mother upon separation (for example, accidents, sickness, death), while the interaction itself was marked by intrusive overconcern, irritation, and/or badgering on the mother's part, passive defiance, babyish demanding, whining, and/or resistance on the child's. The next most frequent pattern involved the child's exaggerated fear of failure or teasing at school resulting from low self-esteem and lack of autonomy. There were overlaps between patterns, and both parents and children had more signs of disturbance than were found in the comparison group of neurotics. The fact that the child's fear may concern the parents rather than the school has led certain authorities to prefer the more general term *school refusal* to school phobia.

The above findings suggest that certain school phobias involve separation anxiety and a low degree of autonomy. In terms of our conceptual scheme, the basic problem is one of initiative which, in certain instances, is undermined by the mother but which, in other instances, is weakened by unknown factors.

As we have already noted, little attempt has been made to place school phobia within a *developmental context.* However, there is some evidence that separation anxiety predominates in younger children, while in older children the problem is specific to school and is characterized more by depression and withdrawal (Kelly, 1973). Such a progression would make sense developmentally in terms of the increasing autonomy and self-evaluation of the school-age period. One can speculate that the same parental overdependence underlying separation anxiety in the younger child might subsequently produce feelings of personal inadequacy in meeting the demands of school as school itself increasingly comes to resemble the adult world in terms of its work requirements and peer orientation. Older children may suffer either from a chronic sense of inadequacy or an overevaluation of their abilities, an unrealistically high standard of achievement rendering them vulnerable to overreacting to ordinary failures and setbacks.

While this speculation integrates a certain amount of the data, much more must be learned about school phobias before a comprehensive account will be possible.

PROGNOSIS   Most prognostic studies fail to relate age, intrapersonal, and interpersonal variables, or even severity and chronicity of disturbance to outcome. Among these studies short-term prognosis is generally reported as good, 83 percent of phobic children returning to full school attendance (Roberts, 1975). Many of these reports fail to consider subsequent relapses or the appearance of other school problems, however. The long-range outlook is not so bright; around half the population have significant adjustment problems. The results of Roberts's well-designed investigation are more optimistic than other studies, indicating that only 25 percent of school phobics had symptoms which created difficulties in attaining a reasonably stable and age-appropriate role; the remaining 75 percent, while not symptom-free, were making adequate adjustments. Because this investigation followed the children longer than many other more pessimistic studies, one might infer that children progressively "outgrow" their difficulties with age; however, Roberts could locate less than half her original group, so there is no way of knowing what kind of adjustment its members were making.

One of Roberts's most important findings was that age, sex, chronicity, acuteness of onset, and a wide range of intrapersonal and parental characteristics—with the exception of a psychotic illness in the mother—failed to predict adult outcome. The most potent prognostic sign was the successful and continued resolution of the symptom itself as evidenced by resuming school on a regular basis with a positive attitude and few subsequent difficulties in regard to school attendance. Such findings would delight those behaviorists who maintain that the symptom is the pathology.

Roberts's findings can not be generalized to all degrees of school phobias at all ages. In a follow-up study of thirty-four adolescents hospitalized for school phobias, Valles and Oddy (1984) found that their subsequent return to school did not significantly predict work adjustment as young adults and that there was no more than a slight tendency for the nonreturnees to have a less satisfactory social life. The major difference was that nonreturnees had more friction with their family, more anxiety, and more antisocial behavior than the returnees. However, the nonreturnees also had more friction with their families before being admitted to the hospital. The authors conclude that, in disturbed adolescents, returning or not returning to school does not make a crucial difference to future work and social adjustment; however, family problems persist and general adjustment suffers in nonreturnees.

THERAPY   School phobia is one of the psychopathologies that readily respond to therapeutic intervention; psychoanalysis and psychoanalytically oriented psychotherapy, behavior modification, cognitive therapy emphasizing the transitory nature of the symptom and the child's ability to overcome it, the ventilation of hostility—all have high rates of cure, as do medication and placebos (Kelly, 1973).   A controversial issue cutting across specific psychotherapies concerns the amount of pressure placed on the child to return to school, some therapists regarding an immediate return as essential even if some force must be applied, others recommending timing the return in keeping with therapeutic progress.   However, there is general agreement that the child should return as soon as possible, even if only for a brief period.

HYSTERIA

The societal context seems to play an important role in regard to the incidence of hysteria. Once prevalent among the middle class in Victorian times, it gradually declined, perhaps as attitudes toward sex became less repressive.   At present, childhood hysteria is rare but seems to occur most frequently among children from rural backgrounds or from those of lower educational and socioeconomic status, where, it is speculated, both repressive attitudes toward sex and superstition continue to contribute to its development (Proctor, 1958).

Hysteria occurs in both male and female children, even though it is most prevalent among adult females.   While of average or above-average intelligence, children with conversion reactions tend to be underachievers and to display other problems such as anxiety, depression, poor peer relations, and overdependence.   The psychopathology is often preceded by some precipitating event.   While mothers tend to be overprotective and fathers ineffectual, and while parents serve as models for or reinforce the child's somatic complaints, such a pattern of parental behaviors can in no sense be regarded as specific to hysteria. (For details, see Schwartz and Johnson, 1985.)

OBSESSIVE-COMPULSIVE NEUROSIS

Obsessive-compulsive neurosis is one of the least studied childhood disturbances.   (Our presentation follows Rapoport, 1986.) The child and adult forms are practically identical, one-third to one-half of adult cases having a childhood onset.   The most frequent symptom is cleaning rituals; the next most frequent are counting and checking rituals, along with repetitious thoughts of violent or sexual events. Obsessive-compulsive neurosis in children is not associated with depression as it is in adults, but is associated with anorexia nervosa, anorectic females having obsessive symptoms independent of their preoccupation with food.   It may also be associated with motor tics and conduct disorders.

The age of onset can be from 3 to 14 years of age.   An unexpected research finding is that the onset is sudden or over a few months with no evidence of prior obsessive or compulsive traits such as fastidiousness, superstitiousness, or ritualistic behavior.   For example, one teenager suddenly began getting up early in the morning and washing the walls of the room a few days each week.   In regard to general characteristics, children with obsessive-compulsive neurosis tend to be of above-average intelligence, to have a rigid moral code accompanied by marked guilt feelings, and to have an active fantasy life. Problems such as phobias and aggression toward parents are also present, along with an increased incidence of physical illness (Schwartz and Johnson, 1985).

The origins of obsessive-compulsive neurosis remain a mystery. At a speculative level, compulsions are viewed as exaggerations of ritualistic behavior that is part of normal development, such as avoiding lines and cracks on the sidewalk or making sure special toys are lined up in a prescribed order before bedtime. There is some evidence for a neurological link, since cases can follow encephalitis or seizures, particularly temporal lobe epilepsy. There is also some weak evidence that it is related to a variety of soft signs such as minor neuromotor disturbances and an abnormal EEG (Rapoport, 1986).

In regard to treatment, psychodynamic therapy has never been regarded as an appropriate technique. Psychopharmacological treatment has met with some limited success, as has behavior therapy when the family is cooperative.

9

Conduct Disorders— Inadequate Self-Control

YOU ARE a clinical child psychologist. You arrive at your office at eight in the morning. Mark Redfleish is already waiting. He says, "Hi, Doc! Dad dropped me off on his way to work." He is a lively, assured 11-year-old, nice looking, well built but small for his age. An all-American-type boy. Except that, for the past two years, he has been breaking into, ransacking, and robbing houses in the wealthy suburb where he lives. At first he threw the stolen silverware and hi-fi sets into a nearby lake. Then he established connections with a man who bought the loot with no questions asked. After a robbery was discovered, Mark would show up and offer to help put the house back in order. His manner was one of sincere concern, and he asked for no favors in return. He was finally caught because a careless remark revealed that he knew an item had been stolen before the owner had mentioned it to anyone outside the family.

Mark is bright, enterprising, and capable beyond his years. But he is also a daredevil and a loner. He loves to ride his motorbike at full speed over a downhill path through the woods, making it jump over small crevices and creeks, doing a "pop-a-wheely" by riding only on the back wheel, turning sharply at the end of the ride in a cloud of dust. At school he was the youngest boy to smoke marijuana and drink alcohol. He charmed his way into being taught how to drive a car and then bribed the caretaker's son into letting him use the jeep to ride on the back roads on the far side of the lake. Yet he is not a show-off or a braggart, nor is he responding to dares. Rather he is obeying an inner restlessness.

Other boys are sporadically attracted by Mark's daring and helpfulness, but friendships are short-lived. He enjoys luring younger boys into joining him in venturing into forbidden places—a beer-and-wine carryout, an adult bookstore, an abandoned quarry—because he likes being in command. In school he is restless and inattentive, except in shop, where his interests and skills make him the top student. He is a master of the sincere lie—looking the teacher straight in the face. One of them said, "I just can't reach him with anything. I could beat him or plead with him or take him on my lap and cuddle him, and it just wouldn't matter."

Mark's father, a successful surgeon, has little time for his family during the week but enjoys being with his son on weekends, going hunting and ice-skating in the winter, fishing and sailing in the summer. In his eyes, Mark could do no wrong. Even the robberies were extenuated: "Wild colts make good horses," was what he told you. Mark's mother is basically a kind and loving woman but lacking in resources. Early on she perceived Mark's disregard for her prohibitions concerning dangerous objects and activities, and she did not know what to do about his constant lying. But more than anything else, his sheer energy exhausted her patience. Affection and reasoning gave way to angry shouts and finally to whippings with a strap. Mark was determined not to cry; he sensed that if she could not hurt him, she would be powerless.

At ten o'clock you see Angelo Ruccio, another 11-year-old, for the second time. He will be brought by his parole officer, since the judge has said that either he gets psychological help or he will be confined in the juvenile correctional center. "That's like playing tennis with both hands tied behind your back," you think, but it is far better than having the boy sent to a punitive, ineptly run institution. The judge was lenient because Angie was the only member of his gang to get caught breaking into and robbing a corner grocery store. He was caught because he was obviously a not-too-bright follower who was doing what he was told.

Yet his loyalty to the gang far outweighs any sense of wrongdoing. And for good reason. School has been an endless series of humiliations and failures. He was passed primarily because he was not a troublemaker, and his teachers became tired of yelling at him for making mistakes and handing in sloppy homework. His family is large and poor,

and while they fight a good deal, they also have a sense of loyalty. The father is a laborer who is hired and fired according to the state of the economy. He is a bitter man who demands respect from his children but sees no reason for them to be good citizens in a society which has treated him so shabbily. To his mother—a meek, careworn woman—Angie is another mouth to feed, and while she prays to the Virgin every night to help her children, she wonders where she will get the strength to see her through another day.

So it is the gang that gives Angie a sense of belonging, of sharing, of being valued. While his slowness makes him the goat, the leader has taken a liking to him, and Angie's fondest dream is one day to become a leader himself. That will be a tough dream to shatter, and right now you do not know what you can put in its place.

You have been seeing Richard Hammer, a 10-year-old, for half a year, and he is making good progress. Rick's father owns a successful chain of hardware stores. He knows how to succeed and how to enjoy life. He has a large house with a swimming pool, a yacht, and a private plane. He also has a large family who shares in the pleasures success has brought. In this zestful, expansive atmosphere, Rick was out of place—"the runt of the lot," his father called him. He was a sensitive and shy youngster, more an onlooker than a participant. His vulnerability touched his mother's heart, and she hovered over him with a special mixture of protectiveness and good-hearted shaming, which alternately delighted and embarrassed Rick—and made him feel all the more inadequate. Rick was a serious student who did well in school and had a close friendship with a boy who, like himself, was a bright, quiet outsider.

All seemed to be going well until Rick's mother, while looking for an old lamp in the attic, came upon a box filled with various tools which her husband told her had been missing from one of his stores. When she confronted the family with her discovery, Rick began to cry and beg forgiveness. It was readily granted, and the matter seemed to be settled. A few weeks later, however, the mother found some money clips and three gold pen-and-pencil sets at the bottom of Rick's underwear drawer. They were poorly concealed, "as if he wanted me to find them," she said.   The parents decided that their son needed help.

In therapy Rick at first did not know why he had an irresistible urge to take things.   As it turned out, he had had the compulsion for four or five years but had always taken small items—a box of nails, a cheap pair of earrings.   The more serious thefts began around the time the oldest sibling became engaged.   The wedding became the center of everyone's attention, including the mother.   Gradually Rick began talking about feeling angry and cheated.   You begin to suspect that stealing was in part an expression of that anger, in part a bid for attention, in part a symbolic compensation for his feeling of being deprived of esteem.   ■■■■■■

CHILDREN WITH INADEQUATE SELF-CONTROL

The lesson is familiar—the same pathological behavior may have different origins.   In this case, the lesson is particularly important in light of the consequences of antisocial behavior, as we shall see.   Studies of groups of antisocial adolescents have yielded a number of subtypes.   We will be concerned primarily with the category of disorder which DSM-III calls *Undersocialized, Aggressive Conduct Disorder*, since it involves pathologically weak self-control.   This group has also been labeled *Psychopaths* or *Sociopaths*.   Two other categories will be described briefly, primarily for the sake of comparison: *Socialized, Aggressive Conduct Disorder* (DSM-III), sometimes called *Subcultural Delinquency*, and what we call *Neurotic Conduct Disorder*, characterized by the basically neurotic child who develops an antisocial rather than an intropunitive symptom. (For a more detailed presentation of categories, see Kazdin, 1987.)

One final word concerning nomenclature. *Conduct disorder* is the psychological term for antisocial acting out.   It should not be equated with *delinquency*, which is a legal term includ-

ing offenses that are criminal if committed by an adult, such as robbery or homicide, and behaviors regarded as illegal in children but not in adults, such as truancy from school, drinking alcoholic beverages, and driving a car.   These latter are called *status offenses*. While there is considerable overlap between conduct disorders and delinquency, they are distinct categories.   Much of the antisocial behavior of the preschool period and early childhood may be contained within the family or school and is not regarded as delinquent; by the same token, there are illegal acts, such as drug use, which may represent expected unconventional behavior in certain adolescents rather than psychopathology. (See chapter 10.)

Undersocialized, Aggressive Conduct Disorder

Traditionally regarded as the most severe disturbance of the conduct disorders, this pattern is marked by active, antisocial behavior.   Aggression may take such forms as temper tantrums, fighting, assault, or mugging.   Disregard for social values is evidenced in behaviors such as stealing, lying, robbery, vandalism, drinking, and rape.   Difficulty in accepting authority leads to conflict with parents, with the school, and with the law.   The undersocialized, aggressive child is impulsive, fails to learn from experience, and is deficient in guilt feelings and anxiety.   Relations with family and peers are shallow. Note that Mark is a special case.   He is more like an embryonic "con man" because he is more controlled and socially adroit than the usual child with a blatantly antisocial conduct disorder.   But the irresistible impulse to action, combined with a disregard for social and moral values, an unconcern for the feelings of others, an absence of guilt, and an inability to form a close relation with parents and peers, is sufficient to include him in the category.

Socialized, Aggressive Conduct Disorder

Children in this category, also called subcultural delinquents, have not developed in a deviant manner but have been socialized with a deviant set of values. Typically they come from a stable lower-class home in a deteriorated urban area. As was the case with Angie, they have little chance to learn the accepted values of society. The gang—with its emphasis on physical prowess and the ability to outwit others, its rebelliousness toward authority, and its desire for excitement—becomes central in their lives. Unlike their undersocialized counterparts, these children are fiercely loyal to peers; while they are relatively unconcerned over their antisocial acts, their failure to live up to the standards of the gang produces guilt. They are considered the least disturbed of the three types, because it is primarily the content of their socialization that is deviant.

Some sociologists have concluded that since children with a socialized, aggressive conduct disorder are reasonably sound psychologically, their problems are rooted in a faulty society, and social action is the remedy. Various theories have been proposed. The anomie theory states that lower-class people have the same values and goals as do middle-class individuals but are deprived of the means of achieving them. In their frustration they turn to deviant means. The term *anomie* refers to their state of being detached and dispirited. Other theorists have claimed that the lower class has a culture all its own whose values—such as being smart, tough, and daring—differ from those in the middle class. Neither theory is without its difficulties, and attempts at empirical validation have yielded equivocal results (see Achenbach, 1982).

Neurotic Conduct Disorder

The children here are no different from other neurotics, except that—like Rick—they engage in antisocial acts. In general, they are shy, self-conscious, hypersensitive, unhappy, guilty, worried—all the signs of excessive socialization. Why they go against the grain and act out rather than consistently internalizing their problems is an unsolved mystery.

INADEQUATE SELF-CONTROL AND ACTING-OUT BEHAVIOR

Self-control is essential to socialization. A 4-year-old may not attack a 2-year-old sibling in a rage, masturbate in the supermarket, or try out a new toy hammer on the hi-fi set. Honesty, truthfulness, respect for the rights and property of others, obedience to the authority first of parents, then of teachers, and finally of the law are required. The requirements are essential because toddlers and preschoolers have a strong desire for immediate gratification of their aggressive, sexual, and exploratory urges, and they tend to be greedy, egocentric, selfish, and self-seeking. The reasons why adequate self-control fails to develop or to function properly will be explored in this chapter.

Behaviors resulting from inadequate self-control are termed *acting out*, which includes aggression, temper tantrums, lying, stealing, truancy, vandalism, fire setting, disobedience, and bullying. Note that some of the behaviors, such as aggression and temper tantrums, have a high-intensity, impulsive quality; others, such as lying and stealing, may be of low intensity and premeditated. But they all involve a breach of socially accepted behavior.

For the first time in our discussions the *societal* context rivals the home and the school in importance: the 12-year-old who is caught cutting up all the clothes in her mother's closet or clogging the school toilets with sanitary napkins is in a different social situation from the one who is arrested for shoplifting. Getting into trouble with the law may involve the child in juvenile court and correctional institutions, both of which may have a special impact on the child's future.

The Development of Normal Control

At this point a review of the variables involved in the development of normal self-control is in order. First there are ones that give an *affective* charge to socializing directives—the bond of affection that makes the child educable, and later, sympathy and empathy, which counteract self-centeredness. Then there are a host of *intellectual* and *cognitive* variables. At the most basic level, the child must be able to remember the socializing message and recall it at appropriate times. Increased intellectual sophistication enables the child to progress from simple directives ("Don't touch that vase") to generalizations ("Everything in the living room is off limits") to conditional statements ("Don't take anything that belongs to somebody else unless you ask them first"). The development of *language* significantly facilitates the process of delaying and guiding action in accordance with socially accepted values. Concomitantly, the child becomes increasingly practiced in making decisions and taking responsibility for actions. A dependable, trustworthy *environment* also aids the child in postponing immediate gratification, as does the ability to find substitute gratifications or alternative means of achieving a goal.

The development of *conscience* and *ego ideals* plays a part in countering impulsivity and egocentrism. Cognitively, moral judgment progresses from a concern with immediate rewards and punishments for specific acts to the morality of shared standards, rights, and duties, while the ego ideal changes from superficial and exaggerated images of glamour and success to realistic, socially oriented images. The affects involved in the conscience and ego ideal are self-satisfaction and self-esteem on the one hand, guilt, shame, and inferiority on the other.

In the interpersonal sphere both *parents* and *peers* play an important role in the development of self-control. In general, the optimal family setting includes affection and consistency, age-appropriate requirements for self-control and autonomy, help in understanding consequences of one's actions, and explicitness as to values. Peers counter egocentrism by forcing accommodations and by valuing proven worth over pedigree.

Clearly, an impressive array of factors contributes to self-control. Now let us see what blocks and undermines its development. In this presentation a number of longitudinal studies will be explored, and then acting-out behavior in middle childhood will be examined in detail. The questions we shall be asking are: How well do the variables just enumerated account for the behavior of pathologically disturbed children? and What development model is most appropriate?

THE PRESCHOOL PERIOD

We will start with the hypothesis that many instances of acting out in the preschool period represent *developmental lags*. In the case of temper tantrums, we expect infants to react to frustrations with rage. During the "terrible twos," willful toddlers are also apt to strike out in anger when they do not have their way, but now they can intentionally try to hurt. By 5 to 6 years of age the incidence of severe explosions should be rare (MacFarlane, Allen, and Honzik, 1954). Their persistence suggests both that the child is not making appropriate progress in achieving self-control and that he or she will be ill equipped to adjust to the demands of school successfully.

The hypothesis of a developmental lag also holds for stealing and lying. Let us examine the former. For the toddler every attractive object is fair game for exploration; it is the socializing adult who divides the world into things that are "OK" and things that are "no-no's." Prohibitions based on property rights are particularly difficult for the toddler to grasp. There is nothing in an object itself which proclaims its status as "mine" or "yours," so other cues must be utilized such as location ("mine" comes out of the big box by the bed I sleep in) or frequency of use (the fire engine big brother plays with all the time is a "not-mine"). Concurrently the toddler must learn that it is wrong to take objects that do not belong to him or her. While taking property peaks at 3 years of age (MacFarlane et al., 1954), this should not be regarded as stealing, since the idea of property rights has not registered. Only after the meaning of prohibitions has been grasped and intentional transgression has occurred does "taking" become "stealing."

And so it goes for lying. A mark of early thinking is a failure to differentiate the physical world from the psychological world of thoughts, feelings, and wishes. The 3-year-old boy who believes there is a wolf under his bed at night may also honestly believe that his big sister started a fight, when he himself was to blame. Only after objective and subjective reality have been differentiated can the concept of lying become meaningful.

There is another cognitive problem arising from the preschoolers' tendency to be quite literal in their understanding of terms. To lie is not telling the truth—period. Thus people who communicate incorrect information which they were told are lying. For example, if a little girl was told by a mischievous older sister that a picture of a cat was a picture of a lion and the little girl subsequently told her younger brother that the pictured cat was a lion, the typical 4-year-old would say the little girl was lying! Many 4-year-olds and even some 6-year-olds reason in this way (Wimmer, Gruber, and Perner, 1984). The contingent nature of a lie, the fact that it is a deliberate deviation from a known truth, may be cognitively too difficult for the literal-minded preschooler to understand. By 6 years of age the child should have grasped the basic meaning of stealing and lying, although the understanding of both will continue to develop.

Now suppose a mother came to you as a clinician and said, "My 4-year-old is always lying to me." Suppose further that you found out these were mainly face-saving lies. Would you reassure the mother that "most children her age tell such lies, and there is nothing to worry about?" Not at all. The chance that there is nothing to worry about does not negate the importance of exploring context variables. In regard to the little girl, you would at least want to know if this is the only sign of disturbance. The clinician should look not only for other symptoms but also for evidence of a generalized developmental lag. For example, does the girl habitually shun peers and play alone? Is her play repetitive? Is she withdrawn whenever she goes outside the protection of the home? Does she prefer to be only with her mother? The context of the mother's complaint is equally important. Does it arise from a lack of information concerning normal development, or does the mother talk about the child with the kind of controlled exasperation which suggests that lying just provides an excuse for expressing an underlying resentment? You might also ask about the father and the general pattern of family interaction before deciding that information coupled with reassurance is all that is needed. While the developmental approach helps put behavior in perspective, it does not supply categorical answers.

One final clinical example. A 19-year-old mother is complaining about her 3-year-old.

▬▬▬▬▬

HE DON'T do nothing but bad [things]. If he don't like what I make him [to eat], he throw it on the floor. I tell him I'm going to take a strap to him, and he just yells back at me, "Shut up, you old mother fucker," and I whip him with all I got and he still don't cry until he have to. . . . He pees in the closet every time he takes a mind to, and he takes his BMs and rubs them in his hair right while I'm looking at him. . . . Now he's taken to getting up in the middle of the night and turning on the bathwater with the stopper in so there's water all over the place. . . . If somebody don't straighten him out soon, I'm going to kill him!   ▬▬▬▬

At first glance the boy's behavior would seem primitive and uncontrolled. However, note that he smears feces in front of his mother and gets up in the middle of the night to flood the bathroom, both of which suggest purposeful behavior. As it turns out, he knows quite well what he is doing. The mother is unmarried, childish, already worn down by poverty and lovelessness. Both emotionally and intellectually she was unprepared to be a mother at 16 years of age and felt burdened and resentful toward the baby. Fortunately for the boy, his grandmother was able to care for him, although only fitfully and grudgingly. The attention the boy received from his mother was primarily angry shouts and whippings. He was a resilient child, and in the toddler period he not only grasped the connection between doing "bad" things and exasperating his mother but also began to use it for all it was worth. The negative attention he gained from the mother

was better than neglect, while her distress was his revenge.

Is Acting-Out Behavior "Outgrown"?

Data to answer this question come from Kohn's (1977) five-year longitudinal study of 1,232 lower- and middle-class preschoolers. Kohn developed two scales, one entitled Interest-Participation versus Apathy-Withdrawal, the other entitled Cooperation-Compliance versus Anger-Defiance. It is the latter that interests us. Items at the Anger-Defiance extreme include "child expresses open defiance against teacher's rules and regulations," "child is hostile or aggressive with other children (teases, taunts, bullies, etc.)." The children's behavior was evaluated by their teachers.

High anger and apathy scores in the preschool period were more predictive of overall evaluations of disturbance and need for psychological treatment in the fourth grade than were social class, race, ethnicity, and broken homes. In fact, gender was the only demographic variable of any predictive potency; boys became more disturbed than girls. Incidentally, both sexes tended to become more disturbed and to achieve less as they progressed through school; boys showed the greatest change in the first and second grades, and girls became more apathetic during the first three grades but showed no consistent pattern of change in aggressiveness. Kohn notes that there is no evidence that the emphasis on "feminine" values of obedience and docility caused boys to become disturbed; rather, schooling accentuated the behavioral problems already present.

While aggressiveness was the most stable behavior over the five-year period, the significant correlation of 0.36 was sufficiently low to indicate that a good deal of change was also taking place. Analysis of the data revealed that 59 percent of the preschoolers scoring high in Aggressiveness were no longer disturbed in the fourth grade; moreover, 14 percent of the highest-scoring aggressive children were subsequently among the healthiest fourth graders, while 13 percent and 16 percent, respectively, of the preschoolers scoring highest on Interest and Cooperation were now rated either extremely aggressive or extremely apathetic.

The findings are both significant and sobering in light of the emphasis on early detection and remediation of psychological disturbances. Kohn rightfully points out that his scales are a giant step forward in detecting high-risk preschoolers. But he also admits that predictability becomes increasingly inaccurate with the passage of time. As they stand, his data mean that an intervention program at the preschool level would be wasted on 59 percent of the aggressive children, who would "spontaneously outgrow" their problem, while missing the 29 percent of extremely well-adjusted preschoolers who subsequently would become disturbed. Parenthetically, it is not clear how clinicians would go about telling the parents of a well-functioning preschooler that their child needs psychological help! Would a preventive program be worth the time and money involved? The question has no easy answer. In part, it depends on how readily the early difficulties could be remedied and how serious the consequences if they were not. If a year of psychological help would save 40 percent of the children from severe academic underachievement and eventual delinquency, a preventive program would clearly be called for. As the time-and-money cost of change goes up and the severity of the ultimate disturbance declines, the need for early intervention becomes less clear. While no one would quarrel with the idea of preventive mental health, some of the problems involved in its implementation are concretely illustrated by Kohn's data.

Etiologic Considerations

Both *temperament* and *parental behavior* have been frequently implicated as etiologic agents in acting-out behavior. In their well-known study of temperament, Thomas, Chess, and Birch (1968) documented an impression parents have long had that some infants are easy to care for, while others are difficult. The latter are irregular in physiological functions—such as the sleep-wake cycle, eating, and elimination—intense and negative in mood, and nonadaptable in that caretakers have difficulty in changing the infants' behavior in a desired direction. One suspects they have special problems in achieving self-control owing to their irregularity and the frequency with which they are engulfed by negative affect. Such characteristics certainly make the job of socialization particularly trying for the parent.

Longitudinal data indicate that, indeed, difficult infants have a significantly greater number of psychological disturbances in the preschool years than the rest of the population studied. However, the disturbances are primarily mild to moderate in degree and involve not only acting-out behaviors (temper tantrums, bossiness, protective lying, stealing) but also worry, anxiety when separated from the mother, and sensitivity to teasing. Thus, while a certain temperament may predispose an infant to mild or moderate psychological problems, it is not specifically related to acting-out behavior in the preschool period (Plomir, 1983).

There is also evidence that interpersonal variables affect self-control in the preschool years. In general, aggression increases if the parents are either severely punitive or permissive. Acting-out behavior also increases if discipline is inconsistent, one parent being restrictive, the other lax. Identification with a dominant, hostile parent is facilitated when there is disharmony between the parents and when both parents are cold; if disharmony decreases or the nondominant parent is warm, hostile identification also decreases. These findings apply to both normal and disturbed preschoolers and usually are more striking for boys than for girls. (For a more detailed account of the research, see Hetherington and Martin, 1986.) Peer interactions can also play an important role either in reinforcing the aggressive preschooler or in turning the passive, nonassertive child into an actively aggressive one (Patterson, Littman, and Bricker, 1967).

MIDDLE CHILDHOOD AND ADOLESCENCE

Early in our discussion we discovered that children evidencing neurotic behavior in middle childhood stood a good chance of achieving normal adjustment once they reached adulthood. Such fortunate malleability of behavior does not apply to acting out. Longitudinal studies of aggression, of disturbed children and of normal children who subsequently became disturbed, all document its fixed nature. It will be worthwhile to examine these studies in detail. (For a summary of studies of adolescence, see Gold and Petronio, 1980.)

Longitudinal Studies: Aggression

Olweus's (1979) review of sixteen longitudinal studies of aggression in males sets the stage. While not concerned with psychopathology, these studies do trace the course of a behavior that lies at the heart of self-control. Olweus concludes that there is a substantial degree of stability of aggression over time; indeed, it seems to be as stable as intelligence. Since there is a tendency for the most aggressive boys to drop out of longitudinal studies, the available data may even underestimate the degree of stability.

Olweus was able to summarize the findings with a simple formula: the younger the subject and the longer the interval of time between evaluations, the less the stability. Thus, for example, over the same interval of time, a 2-year-old's aggressive behavior will vary more than that of a 10-year-old; and at any given age, predictability decreases with the passage of time so that aggression is less predictable over a six-year interval than over a three-year interval. By the time the boy is 8 or 9, there is a substantial correlation with aggressive patterns ten to fourteen years later; by 12 to 13 years of age, the stability is even higher for the next 10 years and, as we shall see, has considerable predictive capacity for later antisocial aggression.

The stability of aggressive behavior in the face of environmental variation and influence designed to change it leads Olweus to conclude that it is a relatively consistent reaction tendency or motivational system within the individual. Far from reacting to environmental provocation, highly aggressive children may actively seek out situations in which to express their need. Learning theorists who prefer viewing aggression as environmentally elicited and sustained would challenge such an interpretation, and definitive tests of these discrepant viewpoints are lacking. Whatever the reason, the data themselves indicate that the control of aggression has a significant impact on future development.

Olweus offers two cautionary statements, however. Aggression should not be regarded as a simple trait that is expressed regardless of the situation, and its stability should not be interpreted as an inevitability. As always, we are talking in relative not absolute terms—of characteristics not caricatures, of probabilities not fate.

Longitudinal Studies: Psychopathological Development

In the 1950s, Robins (1966) compared 491 adults who had been seen at a child guidance center thirty years previously with a control group of 100 normal children matched for age, sex, IQ scores, race, and socioeconomic status. Children with IQs below 80 were eliminated. The population was predominantly male children of American-born Protestant parents of low socioeconomic status. Family disruption was high in the child guidance group, with only one-third of the children living with both parents. Approximately one-quarter to one-third of the fathers drank excessively and failed to provide financial support, while almost half of the mothers were severely nervous, mentally ill, or feebleminded.

The continuity of antisocial behavior was striking—45 percent of the clinic group having five or more antisocial symptoms as adults, compared with 4 percent of the control group. Conversely, the absence of antisocial behavior in childhood made the appearance of adult sociopathy extremely unlikely. Children referred for problems other than antisocial behavior—temper tantrums, irritability, fears, shyness, insomnia, tics—tended to be diagnosed as hysterics, alcoholics, or psychotics somewhat more frequently than the control group, but the differences were not as striking as with antisocial behavior; in fact, antisocial children were equally liable to become psychotic adults as were children referred for other behavior.

Antisocial—or what Robins calls sociopathic—behavior occurred solely in males, beginning early in the boy's schooling. However, age of onset did not predict adult status when severity of antisocial behavior was held constant; thus there is no evidence that early onset is particularly ominous. Theft, incorrigibility, running away, associating with bad companions, sexual activities, and staying out late were prominent reasons for referral. Most children were discipline problems in school—62 percent never graduated from grammar school—and were variously described as aggressive, reckless, impulsive, slovenly, enuretic, lacking guilt, and lying without cause. Almost four out of five appeared in juvenile court, and around half were sent to correctional institutions. Antisocial behavior was directed toward parents and teachers, businesses and strangers. Approximately half of the future sociopaths had fathers who were themselves sociopathic or alcoholic, while two-thirds came from broken homes.

As adults, almost every sociopath had marital problems and a poor work history and had been financially dependent on social agents or relatives. Three-fourths had multiple arrests and prison terms. They were impulsive, sexually promiscuous, vagrant, belligerent, and socially isolated.

Of greatest interest to us are Robins's findings concerning the predictive potential of childhood variables. The single best predictor was the *degree of antisocial behavior* as evidenced by the number of symptoms, the number of episodes, and the seriousness of the behaviors as measured by appearance in juvenile court and being sent to a correctional institution. Surprisingly, many variables frequently reported as childhood characteristics of adult sociopaths were not predictive when the level of the child's antisocial behavior was taken into account—parental deprivation and rejection, being a school dropout, poverty, foster home or orphanage placement, and antisocial behavior on the part of the mother.

Sex, age, class, and ethnic values determined the *kind* of deviancy, not the deviancy itself: for example, antisocial acts among women were confined to sexual and maternal areas and the Irish children were more likely to develop alcoholism than other ethnic groups. Nor does "bad company" predict future sociopathy. Rather than the good boy being led astray by the availability of delinquent gangs, the antisocial child seeks out other children on the basis of common interests—a point which Olweus made about normally aggressive children.

For boys who had fewer than six antisocial symptoms and therefore were not deeply enmeshed in antisocial behavior, it was the fathers who played the central role in determining their fate. More than two-thirds of such boys had fathers who were themselves sociopaths or alcoholics. These children were likely to live in lower-class neighborhoods, to receive little or inconsistent discipline, or to be sent to a correctional institution by a juvenile court wishing to remove them from the home environment. However, sociopathic behavior in middle-class fathers had the same detrimental effect upon predelinquent middle-class sons. For the boys with six or more antisocial symptoms, lack of discipline or inconsistent discipline was important in determining which ones would and would not become adult sociopaths.

One final point: in reviewing all the predictive variables, eleven involved characteristics of the child or the severity of his antisocial behavior; only two involved parental behavior, one involved family size, and two involved social institutions (juvenile court and correctional institutions). Thus, the child's current behavior predicts his future better than any context variable. This is too provocative a finding to let pass; we shall return to it after presenting the final longitudinal study.

Longitudinal Studies: Pathological Development in a Normal Population

In 1970, Lefkowitz, Eron, Walder, and Huesmann (1977) reevaluated 427 19-year-olds who had initially been studied in 1959 as third-graders. Unlike Robins's population, this one was predominantly middle class, all had finished twelve grades of school, there was an equal number of boys and girls, and the setting was a semirural county. Peer and parental ratings, personality tests, and self-report questionnaires were used to evaluate aggression that is "desirable neither for the individual nor society." The investigators were particularly interested in instigations to aggression—parental rejection, lack of parental nurturance, parental disharmony, and television violence—in parental punishment as a reinforcer of aggression, and in identification both with the parents and with the child's own sex role.

The intriguing overall finding was that while parental instigators were related to contemporary aggression, they were not predictive; identification variables, on the other hand, were. Specifically, when the children were third-graders, parental rejection was significantly related to aggression in both sexes, as were lack of nurturance and low school achievement in the case of boys, but none of these instigators was predictive. Punishment was related to neither present nor future aggression.

Identification with parents turned out to be the most potent predictor of aggression for both sexes. Boys who identified with their mothers and preferred girls' games were subsequently low on aggression; girls who identified with their fathers were also low, although their sex typing as revealed in game preference was not predictive. Parental religiosity was predictive of low aggression for girls but not for boys. Thus it seems that the boys' identification with culturally defined, nonaggressive, "feminine" values and the girls' identification with nonaggressive religious values mitigated their growing up to be violent.

Among sociocultural variables, the parents' upward mobility was strongly predictive of aggression for both sexes but particularly for boys. Upward mobility may well place special pressures on the child and involve special frustrations in the parent–child relationship. While violence in the suburbs may not be as prevalent as violence in the slums, it does exist as a serious problem, and the overly ambitious father may undermine self-control in his son, just as his psychopathic counterpart in families with low socioeconomic status does.

Lefkowitz's findings concerning the effect of television violence on aggression are of special interest in light of the controversial nature of the subject. It has been argued that viewing violent television has no lasting effects on actual behavior and that the correlation may well be due to the aggressive child's preference for such violent programs. Because Lefkowitz evaluated his subjects at different points in time, he was better able to resolve the dilemma regarding direction of effect inherent in correlational data obtained at one point in time. He found compelling evidence that watching violent television programs in the early years was a probable causative influence on a boy's later aggressiveness (Lefkowitz et al., 1977). Television violence was certainly not the only cause, but it was a potent one that operated independently of other influences on subsequent aggression, including IQ scores. The effect of television violence on girls was less pronounced and in the opposite direction, perhaps because girls are socialized to express aggression in fantasy rather than in action and because there are few aggressive female models on television. (The effects of television violence on aggression is still being hotly debated. See Freedman, 1986.)

Finally, like Robins, Lefkowitz found that the level of aggression in the third grade predicted subsequent aggression in both boys and girls better than any other variable.

Before leaving our presentation of longi-

tudinal data, there is one more finding which is worth noting: female delinquency seems to be increasing, and there is a shift from the traditional "feminine" crimes of sexual delinquency, running away, and incorrigibility to the more "masculine" crimes of auto theft, burglary, assault, and vandalism. Incidentally, here is another illustration of changing social attitudes—this time in regard to women—affecting the incidence and manifestation of psychopathological behavior. Such developments may also affect the generalizability of longitudinal data.

(For a general review of the literature on conduct disorders, see Kazdin, 1987.)

Longitudinal Studies: Evaluation

Rutter and Garmezy (1983) nicely summarize the findings concerning the persistence of antisocial behavior between childhood and adulthood. Generally speaking, antisocial adults were also antisocial children, although criminality may begin in adulthood in a minority of cases. While only about 50 percent of antisocial children become disturbed adults, they may not only be antisocial but also suffer from a variety of other adult disturbances such as social isolation and schizophrenia. By contrast, neurotic disorders in childhood rarely lead to antisocial disturbances in adults. The variety of antisocial behavior in childhood is a better predictor of continuance into adulthood than is any one particular behavior, while childhood behavior itself is a better predictor than is family background or child rearing. Social class makes little contribution to prediction.

The most intriguing and perplexing of these findings is that the child's current status in regard to aggression or antisocial behavior is more predictive of future acting out than any context variables. Many variables which have been regarded as crucial to deviant development—lack of parental love, neglect, cruel or inconsistent discipline, broken homes, gang membership, poverty—may be related to the child's current level of control but either have no effect on or do not play the determining role in his or her future status. Of course, context factors are not irrelevant. Parental identification seems particularly important, although it functions differently in different classes: for the lower-class boy not heavily involved in sociopathic behavior, having a sociopathic or alcoholic father is devastating, while for the middle-class boy, identifying with the mother (and, presumably, with nonaggressive "feminine" values) serves as a protection against subsequent violent acting out. Neglect or inconsistent parental discipline predicts continued difficulties for the lower-class boy already caught up in a pattern of serious antisocial acting out, while the religiosity of the middle-class family protects the girl from becoming an aggressive adult. Social mobility is positively related to future aggression in middle-class children, while being seen by the juvenile court and being in a correctional institution serve the same function for lower-class children. Yet we leave our discussion of longitudinal data with the feeling that a key element responsible for the self-perpetuating nature of aggression and antisocial acting out has eluded us. (For a detailed presentation of possible explanations, see Rutter and Garmezy, 1983.)

THE INTRAPERSONAL CONTEXT

Fritz Redl's writings will serve as our guide to understanding acting out (Redl and Wineman, 1951). Redl presents a detailed account of five 8- to 10-year-old boys who received milieu therapy in a residential home called Pioneer House for fifteen to nineteen months. Five other boys were also observed for one to three months. They all were healthy, had normal intelligence, and were of lower socio-economic status. Their behaviors included destructiveness, hyperaggressiveness, stealing, running away from home, truancy from school, temper tantrums, lying, "sassing" adults, and profanity; however, they were not so disturbed that they could not function in the community, since they attended public school and used neighborhood recreational facilities.

The boys had no positive, sustained relation with any adult. Their parents were brutal, neglectful, or self-absorbed; their homes were broken by divorce and desertion; and they had been shuttled between foster homes and institutions. They were in special classes at school or had been expelled. They ran with a delinquent gang or were lone wolves, committing impulsive delinquent acts. Thus there was a total absence of positive experiences in the home, the school, and with peers.

Some of Redl's vivid descriptions of the boys' behavior are primarily illustrative of low self-control; others offer clues as to etiology.

Poor Control of Inner Impulses

The boys at Pioneer House had little ability to modulate or contain high states of arousal. Even mild frustrations would produce strong, disruptive affective reactions: a door that accidentally jammed was immediately kicked and pounded and cursed with furious rage; a slight mishap during an enjoyable game would throw the group into wild outbursts of bickering, fighting, and griping. Neither anxiety nor guilt could be tolerated. The former would so quickly lead either to total flight or ferocious attack and diffuse destruction that the boys literally were only fleetingly aware of their fearfulness; for example, one boy reacted to his fear at bedtime by emitting high banshee wails, striking and cursing his pillow, and attacking other boys with a combination of vicious aggression and erotic teasing. While guilt feelings were infrequent, they had an equally disorganizing effect. Finally, the boys could manage neither the discouragement of failure nor the joy of success. Some were so sensitized to failure that they would not try even a potentially pleasurable activity; others reacted to their mistakes and limitations—no matter how tactfully handled by the staff—by sulking, tearful rage, or depressed fury. Success quickly spilled over into excited bravado and provocative depreciation of others.

Overreaction to External Stimuli

Weak control was also evidenced by low resistance to environmental lures. As might be expected, temptations to delinquent acts proved irresistible for the boys; a bit of loose change lying unnoticed on a desk was apt to be stolen, even if the boy had no prior intention of stealing. But the behavior did not have to be delinquent; it might just as well be mischievous or playful. One boy could not resist picking up and throwing a plastic knife on display in a store; the group could not resist wildly jumping up and down and breaking the springs on a mattress in a new bedroom where they were spending the night during Easter vacation. For these boys, it was as if to see was to act.

Of all environmental lures, excitement was the most irresistible. The mere sight of a boy throwing clothes or banging his fork ferociously against his plate or jumping back and forth on the furniture would trigger similar behavior in the onlooker. Redl calls this spread of excitement *contagion*. The exposure to even mildly excited group moods was apt to undermine control. Thus, when one boy escalated a game of sailing cards idly across the room to heaving several cards around, the other joined in until "the air was thick with checkers, cards, pieces of candy, all in

motion." Redl aptly describes the behavior as group psychological intoxication.

Developmental Implications

Throughout his discussion, Redl points to the normal counterparts of acting-out behavior. His theme is that all these signs of weak self-control would be developmentally appropriate for younger children. His point is well taken: one can readily imagine toddlers and preschoolers going into a rage when frustrated or sulking after failure or dashing heedlessly into the street at the sound of the ice-cream truck; and the phenomenon of contagion is well known to any preschool teacher desperately trying to bring her little savages back under control after a game of tag has escalated to the point of intoxication. Thus the model of poor self-control as a developmental delay is appropriate.

Etiological Factors

MEMORY   The prerequisite for socialization is that the toddler or preschooler remembers the situational behaviors that elicited positive or negative responses from the socializing adult. Having been punished for trying to poke a finger into the electric socket, the toddler is able to recall the punishment on the next exploration of electric sockets and inhibit the action. One of Redl's most provocative observations is that the boys at Pioneer House literally did not seem to remember past experiences; for example, the boys would insist on taking a favorite toy or gadget to school despite having such toys broken or destroyed time and time again in a playground battle. There was never a flicker of awareness of the relation between bringing the gadget to school and its certain destruction. Most puzzling of all was the boys' failure to remember pleasant experiences. When the staff tried to reexpose them to activities and games they had enjoyed, the boys would at first deny they had ever done anything like that before or, when they did remember, deny that it was fun.

When memory and recognition go, so does anticipation. There is nothing at the beginning of a sequence of behaviors to signal, "This will lead to punishment" or "This will lead to pleasure." The result is the common observation that antisocial, impulsive children fail to learn from experience. Redl notes that they do not learn from the experience of others, either; the fact that one boy was seriously injured by a car when skating in the street did nothing to deter the others, who merely said, "That dumb jerk don't know what's going on, anyway." If each behavior sequence is experienced anew, the child cannot evoke the increasingly complex and abstract guides essential to self-control. Naturally, this is an exaggeration in order to make a point: a child totally unable to learn from experience would be too dangerously impulsive to function in society. Here we are dealing with a deficiency in learning. Why such a deficiency exists is an unanswered question.

PERSPECTIVE   The boys in Pioneer House were pathologically weak in assessing social reality. They did not stop to consider the feelings and motives of others or to predict how others might react toward them. This same insensitivity was also evidenced in relation to the group code and social norms of proper behavior. One boy, for example, went around bragging that he was going to get a haircut, when he should have known that any evidence of special treatment would throw the group into a jealous rage—which it did; another boy took off his pants in a public park because he had gotten them wet and they itched.

This insensitivity to the thoughts, feelings, and actions of others was included in the discussion of *social perspective* (chapter 2). One of the pivotal developments between the preschool period and middle childhood is decentering, that is, shifting from cognitive egocentrism—in which the world is viewed primarily from the child's own vantage point—to cognitive perspectivism—in which a situation can be seen from the diverse views of the individuals involved. Objective studies tend to confirm Redl's clinical impression that impulsive, antisocial children are deficient in social-perspective taking. Chandler (1973) found chronically delinquent 11- to 13-year-old boys significantly deficient in perspective taking compared with a control group matched for socioeconomic status and ethnic background. In this instance, perspective taking involved the realization that a latecomer viewing the final cartoon in a sequence (for example, a father observing his son's alarm at a knock on the door) would have no basis for interpreting it in the same way as a person who had viewed the entire sequence (in this instance, pictures showing the boy accidentally breaking a window with a baseball). (See also Short and Simeonsson, 1986.)

However, more is involved here than mere insensitivity. Egocentrism also may include a tendency to attribute one's own thoughts and feelings to others. It is easy to understand how these two cognitive limitations would complement one another: If I am so self-centered that I cannot see you as an individual, my self-centeredness may well lead me to read my own intentions and feelings into your behavior. In fact, there is evidence that aggressive children do just that since they are more likely than their peers to interpret ambiguous gestures as hostile. Consequently, the aggressive child lives in a hostile world partly of his own making, which may be one reason his behavior is self-perpetuating. However, he is not totally misperceiving reality since other children are in fact more aggressive to him than to his peers.

Thus the cognitive picture is one that combines both realistic and unrealistic attributions (Dodge and Frame, 1982).

Let us return once more to Pioneer House using perspective taking as a concrete illustration of the "guiding and controlling function of thought" (chapter 2). If the boys immediately translate feeling into action, thinking can serve neither function (see Camp, 1977). On the other hand, the question, "How will others perceive and react to what I do?" of necessity serves to check action. The answer to the question changes as the child is progressively capable of grasping the values, motives, and intentions of others and, ultimately, of simultaneously being aware of his own perspective and the perspective of others. As this guiding function advances, behavior becomes more socially adaptive. The unfortunate braggart who was to have his hair cut should have been able to think, "I want to lord it over the others—but this is just the thing that will drive them wild, because they can't stand the idea of someone getting anything special." Once having decentered, he now would be in a position to act in a socially appropriate manner. However, as Redl cautions, knowing what is right is not equivalent to doing what is right. The boys at Pioneer House often were not able to decenter; other types of acting-out children—such as Mark, who was described early in this chapter—know but cannot resist the force of their impulses.

In normal development parental discipline, empathy, and peer interaction play central roles in the development of perspective taking (Gibbs, 1987). *Inductive discipline* in particular fosters perspective taking. Here the parent explains and reasons with the child and directs the child's attention to the effects of his or her behavior on the other person by saying, for example, "How do you think that made the other child feel?" or "How would you feel if someone did that to you?" Suc-

cessful *peer relations* require that, in order to accommodate to others, the individual child give up the egocentric need to do only what he wants to when he wants to do it. Through peer relations the child is also confronted with ideas, opinions, and values different from his own. Perspective taking is a purely cognitive achievement, however, which requires a strong motivational force to compete with the young child's egocentrism. According to Hoffman (1978) his affective charge is provided by *empathy*, which initially is an innate response but which is subsequently elaborated by conditioning and by cognitive development. Despite the plausibility of the rationale, research on the relation of perspective taking and empathy to prosocial behavior has produced mixed or marginally significant findings. (See Eisenberg and Miller, 1987, and Radke-Yarrow, Zahn-Waxler, and Chapman, 1983.)

It would be difficult to imagine the parents of the Pioneer House boys sensitizing them to the feelings of others; in addition, the boys' own failure to develop stable peer relations might have been particularly detrimental to the ability to decenter. Since peers, like any other group, cannot tolerate impulsivity and egocentrism, the boys might have been caught in a vicious circle: their inability to cooperate prevented them from having access to the very experiences that could have helped them advance in their social awareness. (See Carlson, Lahey, and Neeper, 1984.)

The Pioneer House boys not only lacked perspective on others, they lacked perspective on themselves. Redl describes it as "the evaporation of self-contributed links in the causal chain" (Redl and Wineman, 1951, p. 128). Children literally would not remember, even after a short time, their own share in provoking a fight or a chaotic scene. They forgot not only their feeling, motivations, and intentions but also their surface behavior, such as being the first one to throw a stone, thus beginning a free-for-all, or mishandling a favorite toy so that it eventually broke.

We are now in an area different from social perspective (which involves understanding how others perceive the self); we are in the realm of self-observation. The psychoanalysts write of the "observing ego" when dealing with the ability to be a spectator in relation to one's own thoughts and actions. Piaget (1967) sketches the development of the ability of children to reflect on their own thinking. Egocentric preschoolers believe that something is true, immediately comprehended, and universally accepted because they say or think it. It is only as this belief is challenged by social encounters that they can, in middle childhood, begin to challenge themselves as to what they mean and why they believe it to be true. This "inner social discussion" is the beginning of reflection or the ability to examine one's own thoughts. Why reflection fails to develop in acting-out boys is not known, although Minuchin et al. (1967) speculate that "fast and externally geared resolution of cognitive-affective stress that becomes the dominant coping style" inhibits cultivation of reflection (p. 198).

INITIATIVE Instead of being expansive and seeking new challenges, the boys at Pioneer House were frightened of newness. Perhaps because their environment had been both unpredictable and punitive, newness had become equated with danger. In place of normal exploration, their examination of a new object was characterized by "panicky haste, nervous incompleteness and a flustered jumpiness" or a "frenzy of aggressive handling and poking around" (Redl and Wineman, 1951, p. 119). Goal-directed behavior was well-nigh impossible. At times they denied newness, as when one boy insisted that, "This place ain't different; I been here lots of times before" when he was being taken on a trip, or when another boy claimed that

he saw his uncle driving a number of different trucks when he went for a ride. Such a fear of newness prevented the boys from diversifying their behavioral repertoire and further entrapped them in their repetitive patterns of acting out.

But initiative was lacking in an even more important way, namely, in the boys' inability to generate constructive activities or alternate coping devices. As Redl properly notes, normal school-age children, when left to their own devices, can call up memories of past interests or pleasures and proceed to pursue them. Normal children also have a variety of techniques to help them tolerate the tension of delayed gratification: they can take their minds off the unavailable goal by thinking of or actually doing other things, or they can use the "sour-grapes" technique of depreciating the desired goal, or they can reward themselves for having delayed so long or punish themselves for starting to yield to temptation, or they can transform the desired object into an abstract, less tempting image, or they can even go to sleep (Mischel, 1978). But all these devices must be generated, and it is just this generative ability which acting-out children lack. When they have nothing to do, they literally can think of nothing to do; when faced with frustration, they literally have no alternative to acting out their anger.

Twenty-five years after Redl stressed the importance of generating alternatives to boredom and frustration, psychologists began exploring the phenomenon under the label of *interpersonal problem solving*. While interpersonal problem solving can be simply defined as the analysis and resolution of problems involving other people, there is a certain amount of disagreement as to the specific functions involved. This discussion will follow the conceptualization of Spivack, Platt, and Shure (1976). They postulate the following components: an initial sensitivity to human problems, an ability to imagine alternative courses of action, an ability to conceptualize the means to solve the problem, sensitivity to consequences, and understanding cause and effects in human relations.

Of all the components, generating alternatives and means–end thinking proved the most important in this research. In the preschool period, generating alternative solutions to problems such as, What could you do if your sister were playing with a toy you wanted? was the single most significant predictor of interpersonal behavior in a classroom setting. Children who were deficient were rated by their teachers as being high on acting out or inhibition; for example, they were disruptive, disrespectful, and defiant; they could not wait or take turns; or they needed to be close to the teacher. In middle childhood, alternative thinking was still related to classroom adjustment, although not as strongly as it was previously, while means–end thinking emerged as an equally important correlate. For instance, when presented with the problem of a boy's feeling lonely after moving to a new neighborhood, the well-adjusted child could think not only of different solutions but also of ways to implement the solutions and overcome the obstacles involved, such as saying, "It would be easy if he found someone who liked to play soccer like he does, but he'd better not go to a kid's house at suppertime or his mother will be plenty mad!" Again, both impulsive and inhibited children were deficient in these two cognitive skills. It is interesting to note that the capacity to think in means–end terms was a developmental achievement, since it did not emerge until middle childhood. The data on adolescence were meager but suggested that means–end thinking and alternative thinking continued to be correlated with adjustment. The new component involved thinking of consequences or weighing the pros and cons of potential action: "If I do X, then someone else will do Y and that will be good (or bad)." Thus the developing child is able to utilize progressively advanced cognitive skills to solve interpersonal problems. Incidentally, such problem solving is not closely related to measured IQ.

Spivak and coworkers also have data on the kinds of parenting which facilitated interpersonal problem solving. An example of such parenting is the mother who focused on the child's own thinking ("Tell me what happened." "Why did it happen?" "What did you feel?" "How do you think the other child felt?" and so forth) and supported the child's attempts at solutions, though not always approving of the solution itself. In the process the parent served as a model of problem-evaluation, solution-attempting behavior. There was an interesting sex difference, however, the mother being effective only in relation to her daughter's problem-solving skills; wherever the son learned his, it was not at his mother's knee. Problem solving was discouraged by ignoring or disparaging the child ("Don't be a baby"), by absolutistic directives ("Stop crying and go outside and hit him back"), or by depreciating the child's alternatives ("That's the silliest thing I've ever heard of"). Under such conditions social problem-solving skills atrophied from sheer lack of use.

Other investigators have corroborated Spivak, Platt, and Shure's finding that aggressive children generate more aggressive and ineffectual solutions and fewer constructive ones than do nonaggressive children in their social problem solving. In addition, research has expanded to include situational variables that significantly affect the kind of solution an aggressive child will give. Lochman and Lampron (1986) found that 10-year-old aggressive boys were more likely to use aggressive solutions with peers than with parents and teachers. Also, aggressive solutions were more likely when there was hostile rather than ambiguous intent—for example, when a peer called the child an insulting name as contrasted with a peer who wanted to use the boy's baseball when the boy himself wanted to go home.

Returning once again to the Pioneer House boys, we can better appreciate how impoverished they were in terms of their repertoire of solutions to interpersonal problems. While Redl states that they were unable to utilize their past to provide alternative courses of action in the present, he might also agree that their past was barren soil for the cultivation of problem-solving skills.

CONSCIENCE   As could be predicted, the lack of love, of models, and of tutelage produced a defective conscience in the Pioneer House boys. While not completely absent, their conscience was fragmented and inefficient. There was a certain amount of acceptance of delinquent mores, along with pride in being tough, smart, and daring. (Note that conduct disorders often do not come in pure types, but may be a mixture of the socialized and unsocialized subtypes.) There were fragments of middle-class values, which were isolated vestiges from the past; for example, one boy would suddenly berate another for swearing. Inefficiency was evidenced by the lack of anticipatory guilt; when it appeared, guilt typically followed a transgression. Guilt also seemed specific to the individual making the original demands for good behavior; for example, after stealing, a boy might feel ashamed in his mother's presence, but only in that one setting and only in relation to that one incident. Such situationalism nicely illustrates our point concerning the importance of generalizing rules for proper behavior in the development of self-control.

Objective evidence of delayed moral development in children with an undersocialized, aggressive conduct disorder comes from Jurkovic and Prentice's study (1977), which showed them lagging behind neurotic and subcultural delinquents as well as normal controls on Kohlberg's scale of moral development. Compared to the other groups, they were more likely to think in terms of *preconventional morality* and less likely to think in terms of *conventional morality*. This means they were concerned primarily with avoiding punishment, with giving in order to get in return, and with deferring to the power of the maker of rules; they were less concerned with living up to family or group expectations regardless of the immediate consequences to themselves and with conforming to the "goodboy" image of being nice, conforming to rules, doing one's best, maintaining order, and respecting authority. An interesting aside is that the other three groups did not differ in their moral judgments despite different histories of delinquent behavior, proving that knowing what is right does not necessarily lead to doing what is right. (The complex relation between moral judgment and moral behavior is discussed in Jurkovic, 1980, and Gibbs, 1987.)

THE "DELINQUENT EGO"   The behaviors examined so far could fit into a model of developmental delays of various types and to varying degrees. However, the delay is not pervasive, since many functions are intact or even highly developed. The problem is that they are used to maintain and justify impulsive behavior rather than to enhance self-control. Redl cites many examples of what he calls "the delinquent ego." The boys were past masters of the "He did it first" and "Everyone else does it" technique for justifying their impulsivity. Other techniques included: "He had it coming to him," "I did it to save face with the others," "He's a no-good so-and-so himself," "But I made it up with him afterwards," and "Nobody likes me; they're always picking on me." Such defenses sound suspiciously like those that parents of healthy preadolescents have to deal with.

Initiative that was so lacking in many areas was fully deployed in supporting delinquent gratifications. A boy would seek out other children with similar impulses to gain support for his behavior, often abandoning the relationship after the deed was done. Or he would skillfully provoke another boy into starting some disruptive behavior so he could join in as a blameless participant. Or the group would readily champion the cause of one of its members not so much from genuine concern as from a desire to find an excuse to rebel.

In contrast to their usual imperviousness to adults, the children displayed a remarkable sensitivity when they were cornered. They knew precisely what modulation in the tone of voice meant that the adult would do nothing about their delinquent behavior and when it meant the adult had run out of patience. (Remember that the adults were therapeutic staff members who were trying to remain on an even keel with the boys.) They knew the staff's whims and weaknesses, sensing the kind of argument which would appease or divert them and knowing when cajoling or affection seeking would throw them off guard. They knew how to act cute in public, to wheedle things out of a suspicious storekeeper, to convince a guard that they were "good kids." As we have noted, they remembered all too well that people could not be trusted and were constantly on guard

against anticipated harm or against forming a positive attachment. To protect themselves from the latter, they provoked rejection (for example, by making impossible demands) or anger. Thus they avoided one more betrayal by "proving" that the staff was no different from all the other adults they had known.

Incidentally, this contrast between developmentally delayed and normal behavior has an interesting counterpart in the experimental literature. (For a more detailed presentation, see Achenbach, 1982). Initial evidence indicated that psychopaths might be different from normal individuals, since they did not learn from noxious experiences; for example, they showed smaller galvanic skin responses (GSR) than control subjects to a buzzer which had repeatedly been paired with an uncomfortable shock, and preferred frightening activities over onerous ones. Thus, they seemed to be deficient in normal anxiety. However, subsequent research revealed that their reaction depended on the kind of punishment involved: true, when learning a maze they were relatively unaffected by physical punishment or social censure such as being told they were wrong in a disapproving voice; but when deprived of money their maze performance was slightly better than that of normal subjects, while their GSR was the same! Instead of being incapable of experiencing anxiety, psychopaths have a different set of values. When these values are threatened, they, like the Pioneer House boys, react the same as normals.

Redl's *naturalistic* research is a prime example of the *clinical eye* nourishing a conceptualizing mind. Unlike the majority of clinicians, who are content with collecting vivid anecdotes, Redl was constantly asking, Why? In this, he differed from Kanner, who was primarily asking, What? That Redl was able to tease out so many variables involved in acting-out behavior and to place them in a developmental context is an achievement of the first order. His technique of observing children for prolonged periods in natural settings is also very much in keeping with the current emphasis on ecological validity, even though the research was conducted forty or so years ago.

Yet Redl's research also illustrates the limitations of naturalistic research utilizing the clinical eye. There is no concern for reliability, which would serve as a check for observer bias and increase the likelihood that the data are accessible to the scientific community. More important is the question of generalizability. Redl's observations were made on ten boys at most. What can one infer from such a small sample? Did Redl capture the essence of all such conduct disorders, or did he merely illuminate the psychological workings of a limited subpopulation? His ecological approach also prevented him from determining which of the many variables he delineated are essential and which are peripheral or even noncontributory to delinquency. More controlled studies, which could manipulate variables, would be required to answer such questions. Thus Redl's research is best regarded as hypothesis generating; while of great value, his findings need further testing either in the laboratory or through objective techniques in naturalistic settings.

INTELLIGENCE AND SCHOLASTIC ACHIEVEMENT
Redl paid scant attention to two intrapersonal variables that have consistently been shown to relate to conduct disorders, namely, low IQ scores and poor school achievement, particularly in reading. However, the reason for this relationship remains unclear. Research findings do not support the hypothesis that disturbance of conduct lowers the IQ, which, in turn, interferes with learning and scholastic achievement. Another possibility is that poor academic performance lowers self-esteem, which, in turn, leads to antagonism to the school and antisocial behavior. While there are some data supporting this hypothesis, IQ and behavior disturbances are also associated in 3- to 4-year-olds, and conduct disturbances may precede reading difficulties. These latter findings reduce the plausibility of this explanation (Rutter and Giller, 1983).

THE INTERPERSONAL CONTEXT—THE FAMILY

While family variables have been mentioned briefly in connection with other topics, they deserve to be discussed in their own right.

Criminal and psychopathological behavior in the parent puts the child at risk, often for similar behavior (Kazdin, 1987). As we have seen, alcoholism and criminal behavior on the part of the father are two of the strongest factors increasing the likelihood that his son will engage in similar behavior. Moreover, there is evidence that aggression is not only stable within a single generation but across generations as well. Huesmann, Eron, Lefkowitz, and Walder (1984), in their twenty-two-year follow-up study, compiled data on eighty-two subjects when they were 8 and 30 years of age and also on their 8-year-old children. The correlation between the parents when they were 8 years old and their 8-year-old children was higher than the correlation between the parents' behavior at age 8 and their behavior at age 30 (.65 versus .46). Similarly, truancy in the parents when they were children is related to truancy in their children, the risk increasing if both parents truanted. It is not clear what mechanisms are responsible for this continuity of behavior; neither genetic nor environmental explanations are totally satisfactory.

Family discord is fertile soil for producing

antisocial acting out, especially in boys. In fact, it has replaced the rather vague concept of the "broken home" as an etiologic agent. It is not the literal breaking up of the family—say, by divorce or death—but the turmoil surrounding the disruption which increases the likelihood of antisocial acting out. If, for example, a divorce produces a decrease in parental conflict, the child's conduct disorder also decreases; on the other hand, if parental conflicts persist, the likelihood of repeated antisocial behavior is increased (Rutter and Garmezy, 1983). Again, the mechanisms responsible for this relation and for the sex differences are not well understood.

Parental discipline has been studied by many investigators over a considerable period of time. As we have seen, an inconsistent mix of harshness and laxness either within or between parents is related to antisocial acting out. Youths with conduct disorders are more likely than other disturbed children to be victims of child abuse or to come from homes where spouse abuse exists. Laxness may be evidenced in a number of ways: lack of supervision in the form of parents being unconcerned with the children's whereabouts, absence of rules concerning where the children can go and when they must return home, or parents allowing the children to roam the streets and do what they will (Kazdin, 1987).

While inconsistent discipline increases the likelihood of antisocial acting out, consistently punitive discipline decreases it. However, there is evidence that the self-control achieved under such conditions is far from optimal. Unlike induction, which emphasizes understanding and empathy, harsh discipline is based on fear of punishment. The child's attention is not focused on the transgression and why it is wrong, but on the threatening, punitive parent. Socialization comes to be viewed as a matter of externally imposed demands, conflicts are resolved by violence,

and the purpose of conformity is to avoid getting caught (Gibbs, 1987).

In contrast to researchers who have studied general parental characteristics and discipline, Patterson (1982) has conducted a detailed analysis of the actual behavior sequences between parents of aggressive and nonaggressive children. His data indicate that parents, unknowingly, may systematically train their children to act in an aggressive, antisocial manner. One of Patterson's more ingenious discoveries is a pattern called the *reinforcement trap*. Here the child responds to a maternal directive, such as returning a toy to a sibling, with hitting, yelling, or other aversive behavior. To terminate such behavior, the mother retreats. On a short-term basis she is rewarded by relief from the child's obstreperousness, but she pays a heavy price. Not only is her socializing effort negated, but also she is reinforcing the child's tendency to use aversive techniques to get what he or she wants. Ahead lies further escalation on the child's part rewarded by maternal retreat. In addition, aggressive behavior, especially in boys, may be positively reinforced. While punishment is frequently used, it is often ineffective, perhaps because it is inconsistently applied or because coercive behavior has been rewarded. Patterson calls his account of the development of acting-out problem behavior the *coercion theory*.

THE SUPERORDINATE CONTEXT

Schools

The fact that, even within the same school district, there are very large differences in delinquency rates and psychiatric referrals for conduct disorders gives us our first chance to look at the school as a setting affecting the path of development. The contention that it does have a significant impact has been vigorously challenged by research that suggests it is merely a setting in which other variables—family influences, social class, genetic endowment, etc.—play out their roles in determining a child's fate (Rutter, 1983). Trying to answer the question concerning the impact of the school will give us an opportunity to follow the analytic reasoning of Michael Rutter, who brings the disciplined thinking of an experimentalist to the collection and evaluation of naturalistic data (Rutter and Giller, 1983).

The first deduction is the easiest: the fact that schools in the same area show different rates of disturbance means that we are dealing with something other than socioeconomic differences. But it does not follow that the "something else" necessarily has to be a school characteristic because, even in the same area, schools vary in intake of students. Thus, the fact that more disturbed children are located in a given school may mean only that the school admitted more of them to begin with. Citing evidence from his own and other investigators' research, Rutter and Giller (1983) concludes that intake cannot be the sole variable responsible.

Next, Rutter now reasons that it is not sufficient to show that intake was *not* solely responsible for conduct disorders; one must show that certain school variables *were* responsible as well. While he did find such variables, he adds that they are correlational for the most part and do not prove a causal relation. One can be sure of causation only if one varies a given condition and observes a comparable variation in the behavior of the disturbed children—for example, if a special classroom organization were instituted in a given school and the incidence of conduct disorders declined. Of course, this is exactly what a good experimentalist would say about correlational data.

Rutter now reasons that factors responsible for acting-out behavior in the school such as classroom disruption, damage to school property, and graffiti, might be different from factors responsible for acting-out behavior outside the school. This indeed turns out to be the case. Prominent among the within-school variables are the teacher's skill in classroom management and the model of behavior she provides, the amount of rewards and encouragement, the granting of responsibilities to the students, the degree of academic emphasis, and the general quality of school's physical plant. Thus classes that are poorly organized, where expectations for achievement are low, where there is a good deal of punishment and little praise, and where students are given little or no responsibility in planning activities are apt to foster acting-out behavior.

Antisocial acting out outside the school is related to two factors. First, such behaviors increase if there is a high proportion of students who are intellectually less able, this factor being more important than the race or socioeconomic status of the students. Rutter and Giller (1983) speculate that this means a child will have, as peers, a large number of children who do poorly on examinations and who therefore do not regard school achievement as a step to a rewarding future. Consequently, they will not identify with the school's goals and will develop a peer culture contrary to the school's educational objectives. Second, the overall climate of the school is important, a generally negative atmosphere and a rigid authoritarian control fostering antisocial acting out.

Socioeconomic Status

While there is some tendency for conduct disturbances to be most prevalent in the lowest socioeconomic groups and least prevalent in families with parents in professional or managerial jobs, the association is slight. It may well be that what association exists is due to the degree of family discord and disorganization found in the various classes since these are much more potent risk factors (Rutter and Garmezy, 1983).

THE ORGANIC CONTEXT

Genetic factors are of only minor importance in the broad spectrum of conduct disorders, although they might play a significant but not a predominant role in severe antisocial disorders that persist into adult life. Obviously, criminality per se cannot be inherited, and it is not known just what aspects of personality functioning are affected and how these, in conjunction with environmental factors, produce severe antisocial conduct disorders (Rutter and Giller, 1983). There is also a subgroup of delinquents characterized by diminished autonomic reactivity, which suggests an organic etiology, as does the association between conduct disorders and hyperactivity (Quay, 1986b). Magnusson (1988), for example, found that the combination of aggression and hyperactivity (i.e., motor restlessness and poor concentration) at 13 years of age was more predictive of adult criminality than either one alone. Moreover, adult criminality was also related to a lower mean level of adrenaline excretion at 13 years of age. Predictability was increased when this physiological variable was added to the psychological ones. Further analysis of the data revealed that low adrenaline excretion effected hyperactivity, not aggression, and that hyperactive boys had less adrenaline excretion in both nonstressful and stressful situations.

The reason for the relation between this constellation of psychological and physiological variables and criminality is a matter of speculation. One possibility is that a low level of arousal is akin to a painful state of boredom and that restlessness is an attempt to escape such boredom by increasing sensory stimulation. Another speculation is that low physiological reactivity results in an inefficient appraisal of environmental events as threatening which, in turn, produces an insensitivity to the social prohibitions and constraints that hold other children in check. Neither explanation is entirely satisfactory.

EVALUATION OF THE DEVELOPMENTAL MODEL

Our developmental model has served us well. The intrapersonal variables comprising self-control and the interpersonal variables responsible for its development have generally provided plausible explanations of the clinical data. In some instances, the clinical data have enriched our understanding. The study of interpersonal problem solving in particular has given us a much more detailed account of the process than we had when we merely referred to the ability to find alternative means of reaching a goal. While little new was added in regard to social cognition, we now have a better appreciation of it as a supplement to the usual material on conscience development. The one variable that was slighted, if not exactly omitted, was self-observation, which deserves to be more fully studied in its own right. Finally, most of the clinical and research data on antisocial behavior could be conceptualized in terms of a developmental lag or fixation.

TREATMENT

The continuity of conduct disorders from childhood to adulthood means that individuals and society pay a high price, in terms of personal suffering, and in dollars and cents, for the violence and antisocial behavior that characterize this disturbance. Thus there is an urgent need for prevention and treatment. Yet the multiple roots of conduct disorders— the cognitive and affective dysfunctions within the child, the psychopathology and discord within the family, the peer support by similarly disordered youths, the insensitivity and punitiveness in the schools and society at large—present major obstacles to success in both undertakings. While no program has clearly demonstrated its effectiveness in returning the conduct-disordered child to the path of normal development, there are a number of promising leads. (Our presentation follows Kazdin, 1987, and Rutter and Giller, 1983, who also have excellent discussions of the requirements for evaluating therapeutic programs.)

Family-Oriented Treatment

Since faulty child rearing practices and discord are closely related to conduct disorders, it is logical to assume that altering the pattern of family interaction in a positive direction would have a therapeutic effect on the child. One of the most successful and best documented techniques is called Parent Management Training (PMT) and is based on altering the interaction patterns described in Patterson's coercion theory (Kazdin, 1987). As the name implies, it is the parents who are trained by the therapist and who implement the recommended procedures in the home. First they must be taught to observe the sequencing of behaviors in order to arrive at a specific inventory of events leading up to aggressive and antisocial behavior and the consequences of such behavior. Then the therapist spends considerable time discussing social learning principles and the techniques derived from them. Reinforcement for prosocial behavior ("Try to catch the child doing something good") counteracts the image of the family as an armed camp. Establishing firm rules and adhering to them helps circumvent the

reinforcement trap. Negotiating compromises introduces an element of reasonableness and mutuality into the parent–child interactions. Punishments are mild, such as temporary loss of privileges. To give parents a concrete idea of how to implement these techniques, the therapist uses instructions, modeling, role playing (in which the therapist assumes the role of the parent and the parent assumes the role of the child, or vice versa), and rehearsal. The immediate goal is to develop specific parenting skills. Typically, the skills are first applied to relatively simple, easily observed behavioral sequences. As parents become more skilled, the focus shifts to more encompassing and problematic behaviors.

Parent Management Training has been extensively evaluated with behavior problem children and has been shown to bring problematic behaviors within the levels of adequately functioning peers. The gains are maintained from one to four years. In addition, sibling behaviors improve even though siblings are not the direct focus of treatment, while maternal depression tends to decrease. Thus PMT may alter many aspects of dysfunctional families.

Several factors contribute to treatment effectiveness. Families with multiple risk factors such as parental psychopathology and poverty show fewer gains than less pervasively disturbed families. Mothers who have social supports outside the home, such as friends or organizations, profit more from treatment than do socially isolated mothers. PMT also has limitations, the most obvious one being the need for parents who are willing and able to engage in the extensive training. A considerable number are too disturbed or too despairing to become involved or drop out during treatment. The high drop out rate during follow-up also suggests that the data on long-term effectiveness may be on the optimistic side. PMT has not been used extensively on adolescents so its effectiveness with this important group is uncertain. Finally, there is some evidence that PMT is more effective with aggressive than with non-aggressive behavior disorders such as stealing and truanting. While such limitations mean that PMT is not an all-purpose treatment, they do not detract from the impressive record of documented successes.

Institutional Treatment

There have been two approaches to evaluating the effectiveness of institutional care (Rutter and Giller, 1983). The first is to compare experimental with traditional care; for example, a liberal regime that encourages participation in the running of the institution and that allows frequent home visits is compared with a more traditional approach to discipline. There is no evidence that experimental programs are significantly more effective than traditional ones in lowering recidivism rates (i.e., subsequent criminal behavior). The second approach involves taking similar institutions and determining which factors make a difference in the delinquent's behavior and subsequent criminal activities. There is evidence that institutions do have a substantial effect on the delinquents during their stay. The characteristics of the successful institutions include firmness combined with warmth, harmony, high expectations of appropriate behavior, nonpunitive discipline, and a practical approach to training. Interestingly, many of these qualities are found in families associated with protecting the children from delinquency. The effects on recidivism after return to the community are less striking than the effects on behavior while in the institution, but some worthwhile, enduring effects have been documented.

Utah and Massachusetts have been leaders in devising effective institutional treatment. They closed their large training schools and replaced them with a network of a few small, secure units for violent and dangerous youths, who receive milieu and group therapy, are taught academic skills, and are given vocational training. Their progress is monitored when they return to the community. As a result, the number of new adult prisoners who are graduates of the juvenile system in Massachusetts has declined each year for the last eleven years (Schwartz and Levi, 1986).

Behavioral principles have been used to establish a *token economy*, in which delinquents earn tokens for acceptable behavior. These tokens can be exchanged for tangible rewards such as cigarettes or for privileges. Despite the initial enthusiasm for the token economy, there is little evidence that it is superior to other programs in well-run institutions. There is also no evidence of long-term benefits in regard to reducing recidivism rates when the delinquent returns to the community (Rutter and Giller, 1983).

Community-Based Treatments

The basic tenet here is that remedial measures should be applied in the child's everyday environment such as local recreational or youth centers. The general goal is to foster competence and prosocial behavior, especially in regard to peer relations, thus providing an alternative to the child's antisocial pattern. Among other things, this approach is seen as a solution to the problem of gains made in one setting, such as in well-run institutions, being lost when the delinquent returns to the community.

Community-based treatment are difficult to implement and to evaluate. However, there is some evidence that youths can benefit from such programs if they are run by experienced rather than inexperienced leaders, if the groups contain a mixture of youths with and without conduct disorders rather than containing only those with conduct disorders, and if the program is behaviorally oriented in that it reinforces prosocial behavior rather than dealing with group processes and social organizations (Kazdin, 1987).

A variation on the community approach is court or police-referred *juvenile diversion projects*, which, as the name implies, try to divert children and youths who have not yet been involved in serious offenses from further legal involvement (Peterson and Roberts, 1986). While there is great diversity among the programs, they typically rely on establishing an important personal relationship with the delinquent and providing recreational opportunities as well as "curbside counseling." Features of specific programs might include teaching interpersonal and academic skills, improving physical fitness, and vocational, personal, and social counseling. While special demonstration projects have shown gains in terms of decreased frequency of arrests and better school performance and positive responses to the family, serious questions have been raised about the quality and effectiveness of such demonstration programs when they are applied on a large scale.

Other Approaches

Cognitive therapies are aimed at remedying the many cognitive deficiencies found in children with conduct disorders. We have already discussed Spivack, Platt, and Shure's problem-solving skills training, which teaches children how to go about solving problems in a flexible, adaptive way rather than teaching them specific, socially approved solutions to specific problems. Studies of aggressive children and adolescents show that cognitive therapy results in significant changes in behavior at home, at school, and in the community and that gains are sustained up to a year. However, the efficacy of the treatment for children with a conduct disorder has not been demonstrated. There is even some

suggestive evidence that, among aggressive children, effectiveness decreases as level of aggression increases (Kazdin, 1987). Finally, we must ask whether a therapy that addresses itself to only one of many variables determining conduct disorders can be sufficiently potent, in and of itself, to bring about normal functioning; the gap between thinking and behavior is too great.

Group therapies try to use the power of peer pressure to support prosocial rather than antisocial behavior. Positive Peer Culture (Vorrath and Brendtro, 1985), for example, involves groups of eight to nine juvenile delinquents and represents an attempt to cultivate caring or helping behavior. First, the group identifies problems, such as "aggravates others" or "steals"; then an individual member is encouraged to accept responsibility for a problem. Finally, the group works on solving the problem. A skilled leader guides the interaction at every step. Despite the intuitive appeal of the rationale and the wide use of Positive Peer Culture, there is little well-documented evidence of its success.

Behavior therapies can alter specific aggressive and antisocial behavior, but durable changes among clinical populations have not been demonstrated. *Pharmacotherapy* has similarly been effective in altering aggressive behavior but not in changing everyday adjustment (Kazdin, 1987). *Individual psychotherapy* is generally ineffective except for those individuals who have a high level of anxiety, are introspective, and desire change (Rutter and Giller, 1983).

General Comments

The literature on remediation is frustrating because so many studies are poorly designed and describe populations, procedures, and outcomes in vague terms. Granted, well-designed and executed studies are difficult to do, but they remain the only means of evaluating the success or failure of a therapeutic procedure. However, two conclusions seem justified. First, there is no "cure" for conduct disorders, no therapy of choice with demonstrated effectiveness on the entire range of disturbances. However, there are a number of important leads as to how to increase the success rates of future endeavors. Next, in light of the multiple roots of the disturbance, it is unlikely that a single treatment of choice will be forthcoming. As we have seen, even successful procedure in a given setting may fail to generalize to or may be nullified by other settings. The implication is that a combination of procedures may be necessary to bring about significant and sustained change. Yet as Kazdin (1987) notes, the procedure should be not merely a jumble of well-intentioned efforts, but should be tailored to remedying the specific deficiencies and dysfunctions responsible for the conduct disorder at hand. While a prodigious undertaking, remedying or, ideally, preventing conduct disorders is the most important challenge facing clinical child psychologists today.

Whether recommendations to improve the lot of delinquents will be heeded is difficult to say. A number of groups made significant advances as the result of the social unrest of the 1960s and 1970s, blacks and women being the most prominent. Yet juvenile delinquents seem to have gained relatively little. To borrow a phrase from Redl, they are still "the children nobody wants."

Charting the developmental course of various psychopathologies has frequently taken us into the adolescent period. Now it is time to examine adolescence in its own right by discussing three of the disturbances specifically identified with it: schizophrenia, drug abuse, and homosexuality. As always, we shall be trying to understand these three conditions as normal development gone awry. In addition, we shall be concerned with evaluating their status as psychological disturbances. While schizophrenia is clearly a psychopathology, there is a question as to when recreational drug use becomes psychopathological drug abuse, while homosexuality is viewed by some solely as an alternate lifestyle to heterosexuality. Before confronting the issues concerning how and whether normal development has gone awry, it will be necessary to sketch the current view of the normal adolescent phase, where marked changes in its image have important implications for the clinician.

10
Psychopathologies of the Adolescent Transition

A dolescence marks the transition from childhood to adulthood. The body itself sets the stage with physical changes more rapid than those of any other developmental period except infancy, with hormonal changes during puberty, and with the advent of adult sexuality. (See Rutter, 1979a.) Society follows suit by requiring the adolescent to relinquish dependence on the family and assume responsibility for making decisions regarding those dual foci of adulthood, love and work. The transition is facilitated by the increasingly important role peer relations play and by the newfound cognitive sophistication that enables the adolescent both to envision future possibilities and to expand the situation-specific self-examination of middle childhood into the over-arching question, Who am I?

Until recently the image of adolescent transition has been one of turmoil, the inherent instability of the period being epitomized by G. Stanley Hall's phrase "storm and stress," coined in his classic turn-of-the-century study. Psychoanalysts, in a similar vein, characterize the period as marking the return of primitive impulses and unresolved conflicts from the early stages of psychosexual development while, according to Erikson, a weakened ego struggles to master an identity crisis and role diffusion. As if this were not enough, the more recent literature emphasizes the distress brought about by the generation gap and by alienation.

However, it is becoming increasingly clear that the image of adolescent turmoil is applicable primarily to the more visible and the more disturbed minority of adolescents. Most adolescents make the transition without significant emotional problems. While peer relations deepen and bickering with parents over everyday issues such as clothing and hair-style increases, the parent–adolescent relationship is generally harmonious, lines of communication remain open, and adolescents continue to share parental values and to turn to parents for guidance on matters of major concern. In a like manner, the search for identity goes on unaccompanied by crises, although there may be an increased anxiety about the future.

The revised picture should not be taken to mean that adolescence is uniformly serene. Moodiness, depression, and self-depreciation reach a peak in adolescence, even though such feelings characterize only a minority of this age group. Certain psychopathologies also show a sharp rise in adolescence: suicide and suicide attempts, alcoholism, drug abuse, schizophrenia, anorexia nervosa, and depression. Although the overall rate of psychopathology increases only slightly since other disturbances such as hyperactivity are on the decline, the new disturbances are far more serious than the ones they replace, making the overall picture an ominous one.

Adolescence also leaves its imprint on future development. In the Berkeley Growth Study the status of normal adolescents was predictive of their mental health at 30 years of age. As we have seen, a certain number of autistic children will develop epileptic seizures for the first time during adolescence, while others will begin their successful effort to lead a normal social life. As in middle childhood, neurotic disturbances tend to disappear with time, while psychotic disturbances tend to persist.

Erikson's concept of *identity* integrates many of the diverse strands of adolescent transition as well as providing specific leads as to assets and liabilities. (For a summary of research on identity, see Marcia, 1980.) Identity involves both inner continuity and interpersonal mutuality. It is a coming to terms with oneself and finding one's place in society. Adolescence is marked by an identity crisis because it is a "necessary turning point, a crucial moment" (Erikson, 1968, p. 16), in which the adolescent must master the tripartite challenge of finding a fulfilling vocation, sexual role, and ideology, or risk stagnation and regression. The adolescent faces the task of achieving an identity with the accumulated resources and vulnerabilities from the past— trust, autonomy, initiative, and industry on the positive side; mistrust, shame, doubt, guilt, and inferiority on the negative side. Cognitively the adolescent is capable of a more sophisticated level of self-exploration and a more realistic grasp of the options that society offers so that choices and decisions now have an air of commitment, of "playing for keeps," which was absent from middle childhood.

In light of the formidable nature of their undertaking, society grants adolescents a *moratorium,* a period for exploration and experimentation during which they are exempt from carrying the full responsibilities of adulthood. Adolescent exploration might include championing ideologies society abjures and engaging in behaviors society condemns or regards as delinquent, as exemplified by the activist movement and the "do your own thing" philosophy of the 1960s. Whether such behaviors are normal or deviant depends not so much on their manifest content as on whether they serve to advance the adolescent quest or whether they represent a kind of self-defeating defiance that is as detrimental to the individual as to society.

While the concept of identity will not integrate all the material we shall discuss, it will provide markers to orient us in our own search to answer the question, Why should particular psychopathologies flourish in adolescence?

SCHIZOPHRENIA

Description

DISORDERS OF THOUGHT   Certain disturbances involve the process of thinking itself rather than the content of thought: "It's like someone poured molasses into my thinking machinery. I've got to work and work to get from one idea to another, and sometimes the whole thing just stops running." "My mind keeps going in all directions at once. I don't know what's going to pop up next. That's why I'm so scared. My mind's going haywire."

These two adolescents are describing the collapse of directed attention, which is essential to orderly thinking. One result is *blocking*, which may be clinically manifested by long pauses before the adolescent can answer a question. Such sluggishness is different from the defiant silence or purposeful negativism of the psychopath or the frozen fearfulness of the neurotic. At the other extreme is *fragmentation*, in which tangentially related or even unrelated ideas constantly intrude and disrupt the adolescent's train of thought.

The content of thinking is disturbed in a number of ways. We shall describe only two. *Delusions* and *hallucinations* represent an extreme loss of reality contact. The former include delusions of grandeur (for example, an adolescent boy picked up a book he had never read, briefly flipped through the pages from beginning to end, and announced, "I know everything that's in this book.") and delusions of persecution (for example, a young girl was certain a neighborhood gang was planning to capture, rape, and torture her "like Patty Hearst"). Hallucinations are often auditory (for example, hearing voices), visual ones being infrequent. Perception of bodily sensations and functions can also be radically distorted (for example, the body is emitting a foul odor, there are roaches eating the brain, or feces will come out of the mouth if the adolescent speaks).

SOCIAL ISOLATION   The social withdrawal of schizophrenics can be evidenced in a variety of ways. They may be oblivious to others, puzzled or confused by things happening around them, excessively preoccupied with their own thoughts. Their affect might be blunted, or they might be touchy and hypersensitive, subject to inappropriate outbursts of anger or to silly laughter. Isolation from peers is particularly important.

DISORDERS OF MOTOR BEHAVIOR   Here one finds facial grimaces, odd postures and movements such as persistent rocking while standing or sitting, long periods of immobility, bizarre repetitive actions such as incessantly rubbing the forehead or angrily slapping the wrist or scratching the skin, even if it produces open, bleeding sores. (For a detailed account of adolescent schizophrenia, see Weiner, 1980.)

Theories of Schizophrenia

Etiologic theories of schizophrenia abound, the heredity-environment issue in particular being hotly debated. (For a comprehensive account of theories, see Garmezy, 1974.)

THE GENETIC THEORY   While the incidence of schizophrenia in the general population is less than 1 percent, the child of one schizophrenic parent has a 16.4 percent chance of becoming schizophrenic, the child of two schizophrenic parents a 39 percent chance—evidence strongly suggesting a genetic factor.

Suggesting, but certainly not proving, since environmental influences need to be controlled. More definitive data come from studies of children of schizophrenic parents who are adopted at birth and thus have the genetic endowment of one family while being reared by nonschizophrenic parents. Such studies have shown an elevated incidence of schizophrenia in the adopted children. While one might think that such data settle the issue of the inheritance of schizophrenia, we shall soon see that this is not the case.

But granting a genetic component still leaves the question of transmission unanswered. The *monogenetic-biochemical* theory holds that a single gene is responsible for the specific metabolic dysfunction that, in turn, produces the behavioral manifestations of schizophrenia. The *diathesis-stress* hypothesis states that only a predisposition to schizophrenia is inherited; its actual appearance is contingent upon the kind and amount of environmental stress the individual encounters.

INDIVIDUALLY ORIENTED THEORIES Learning theorists maintain that being raised by schizophrenic parents provides ample opportunity for the child to learn such behavior by imitation and reinforcement. It is also possible that disturbed parents do not reward responses to the usual social stimuli, so that the child responds increasingly to inappropriate, idiosyncratic cues. The resulting bizarre behavior may succeed in attracting attention, thereby being socially reinforced and personally reinforcing. The psychoanalytic theory emphasizes the schizophrenic's regression to the infantile period in which the ego and environment are not clearly differentiated and bizarre (primary-process) ideation abounds. Such regression is due to fixation at the early stages of psychosexual development, subsequent trauma, or a com-

bination of both. (For an elaboration of these theories, see Garmezy, 1974.)

FAMILY THEORIES We will concentrate on the family context, since some of the most important contributions to understanding psychopathology have resulted from the intensive scrutiny of schizophrenic families. The three major theories focus on three aspects of family interaction, which in turn are related to three characteristics of schizophrenia. (The presentation follows Mishler and Waxler, 1965.)

Gregory Bateson traces the origin of schizophrenia to a particularly vicious pattern of parental *communication* called the *double bind*, which traps the child between two negative injunctions. The often cited example is of a mother who stiffened when her schizophrenic son impulsively put his arm around her shoulder but, when he withdrew, reproached him with, "Don't you love me anymore?" This "damned if you do and damned if you don't" dilemma is compounded by a prohibition against escaping from the family and a further prohibition against calling the parent's attention to his or her incongruous messages.

The only way out of the intolerable dilemma of repeated exposure to the double bind is to shatter the bond of communication itself. Rather than trying to convey meaning, schizophrenics purposefully attempt to avoid conveying meaning. Making it impossible for the ordinary listener to understand them and their ideas is the schizophrenics' intent, escape, and protection.

Lyman Wynne locates the psychopathology not in communication but in the *structure* of the family as a whole. The drifting or scattered thinking of the schizophrenic represents the internalization of a diffuse or fragmented family structure. Amorphous patterns of interaction are marked by vague ideas, by blurring of meaning, and by irrelevancies. Note the following responses of a mother being interviewed for her schizophrenic child's developmental history.

▬▬▬▬

PSYCHOLOGIST: Was it a difficult delivery, or did everything go OK?

MOTHER: I know just what you mean. And I can say for certain that I'm not one of those women you read about where they are so brave and natural childbirth is just the greatest thing in their life. (Laughs) Believe me, when the time comes, I want the works when it comes to care.

PSYCHOLOGIST: But did everything go OK?

MOTHER: Well, there was this Dr. Wisekoff that I never liked, and he said all kinds of doom and gloom things, but I told my husband I was the one who had the baby and I was the one who ought to know, so my husband got into this big fight and didn't pay the bill for a whole year, and the doctor threatened to hire one of these collection agencies, and what that was all about, don't ask me—just don't ask me.

PSYCHOLOGIST: I see, but I'm still not sure . . .

MOTHER: (interrupting) But that's just what I mean.

▬▬▬▬

Later the psychologist, who was just beginning his clinical internship, told his supervisor that he wanted to shake the mother and yell at the top of his lungs: "But was the delivery difficult or easy!" One can only imagine how difficult it would be for a child to grow up surrounded by such diffuseness, accompanied by a total obliviousness to the diffuseness itself.

Like amorphous thinking, fragmented thinking can be traced to parental communication. In this case, parental communication is marked by digression from topic to topic, non sequitur reasoning and extraneous, illogical, or contradictory comments. In fragmented thinking itself, attention can be focused for brief moments but bits and pieces of memories become intermixed with current stimuli. The technical name for this abrupt shift from one topic to another is *overinclusive* thinking (Singer, Wynne, and Toohey, 1979).

Wynne delineates other faults in the family structure. The family members cannot maintain an appropriate psychological distance, detached impersonality unpredictably alternating with highly personal remarks and confrontations. However, there is a concerted effort to act as if there were a strong sense of unity, which results in what Wynne calls *pseudo-mutuality*. There are great pressures to maintain a facade of harmony, the child being allowed neither to deviate from nor to question a prescribed role. Beneath this facade lie pervasive feelings of futility and meaninglessness.

Our final theorist, Theodore Lidz, deals less in terms of total family structure than Wynne and more in terms of *roles and functions*. In the healthy family, maternal and paternal roles are clearly delineated as are generational or parent–child roles, while parents transmit to their children useful ways of adapting to the demands of society. There is also role reciprocity, which requires the acceptance of each member's role, values, and goals.

In the schizophrenic family, roles are blurred and parents use children to serve their own egocentric needs. Lidz delineated two kinds of distorted patterns. In the *skewed family*, more commonly found with schizophrenic boys than girls, the mother is overprotective, intrusive, dominating, and seductive, while the father is passive and weak. Because of her tenuous emotional equilibrium, the mother perceives events according to her own needs and insists that her son do likewise. The adolescent boy becomes increasingly fearful of being engulfed by his mother but moves toward autonomy produce unbearable guilt. In the *schismatic family*, more characteristic of schizophrenic girls than boys, there is continuing overt conflict between the parents, each depreciating the other to their children and often competing for the children's loyalty. The mother has little self-esteem or security and is constantly being undermined by her husband's contempt; the father is insecure in his masculinity, is in constant need of admiration, and uses domination as a substitute for strength of character. Disappointed in his wife, the father turns to his daughter to fill his emotional needs. His behavior may be highly inconsistent, alternating between tyrannical tempers and seductiveness or even maternal tenderness. The daughter is caught in a bind, since pleasing one parent alienates the other. The mother, who disparages herself, is a poor model of mature femininity, while the father, who disparages women, is an equally poor model of adult masculinity.

RESEARCH   Rodnick, Goldstein, Lewis, and Doane (1984) studied fifty-two intact families with either aggressive, antisocial adolescents or adolescents at risk for developing schizophrenia. The families were evaluated in terms of Lyman Wynne's concept of *communication deviance* (CD) and in terms of *affective style* (AS), which includes personal criticism, guilt induction, and excessive intrusiveness without strong positive support. A five-year follow-up study revealed that while adolescents in families with either a high level of CD or poor AS might become schizophrenic, they might also become neurotic or even normal. However, families with both a high level of CD and poor AS accounted for all the schizophrenic adults and none of the less disturbed or normal ones. Thus either high CD or low AS may produce a variety of outcomes aside from schizophrenia, but the combination of both places the adolescent at a high risk for becoming schizophrenic.

Studies have also shown that families of children at risk for developing schizophrenia have more marital discord expressed in dis-

agreements over demonstrations of affection, sexual relations, and proper conduct than families of children at risk for developing depression. Both kinds of families are less happy, accommodating, and confiding than families of normal children. Finally, fathers in the families of children at risk for schizophrenia are perceived by their children as more unaccepting and unconcerned than fathers in families of children at risk for depression (Watt, 1984). Excessive criticism and overinvolvement predict relapses, although they may also be involved in the initial development (Nuechterlein, 1986).

None of these studies validates the specific patterns of interaction that are claimed to produce schizophrenia, such as the double bind, psuedo-mutuality, or the skewed family. However, the evidence of a general connection between deviant family pattern and schizophrenia is sufficiently compelling to warrant the inclusion of family variables in studies taking a comprehensive approach to the etiology of schizophrenia.

THE HEREDITY–ENVIRONMENT CONTROVERSY While we are on the subject of research, let us return to the matter of obtaining definitive data on the heredity–environment controversy. One of the most sophisticated studies was conducted by Rosenthal and coworkers (1975), who examined 258 adults in four groups: adoptees who had a schizophrenic or manic-depressive biological parent; adoptees whose biological parents had no known psychiatric illness; adoptees whose biological parents had no known psychotic disturbance but were reared by persons with these disorders; and nonadoptees reared by a schizophrenic or manic-depressive parent. Subjects were given a 3- to 5-hour psychiatric interview, in which they were asked about their life with their adoptive or their natural parents. The information concerning the parent–child relationship was subsequently evaluated in terms of its positive or negative quality, and a correlation was done between this child-rearing variable and the degree of adult disturbance. The results showed that rearing patterns had only a modest effect on individuals with a genetic background for schizophrenia but an appreciable effect on persons without such a background. Thus the genetic background appreciably although not totally neutralizes the impact of child rearing with respect to psychopathological disorders; only when the genetic background is normal does child rearing have its maximum effect.

To which the family theorists might answer, "Not proven!" Recall of childhood events is notoriously unreliable in general, and one characteristic of schizophrenic families is the parents' efforts to blind the child to the reality of family life. In addition, parents who engender schizophrenia do not themselves have to be schizophrenic, although they are often described as disturbed. In fact, there is some evidence (Doane, 1978) that patterns of communication are more highly correlated with schizophrenia in the child than is the categorization of parents as schizophrenic or not. There is also evidence that family variables are distinct from parental psychopathology variables, and both are significant but independent predictors of the child's adjustment (Wynne, 1984). Until the genetic camp finds ways to control for the hypothesized pathogenic family interactions, its case will remain unproven.

And so the controversy goes on. While we might be sympathetic to the family theorist's objection, the evidence for a genetic component in schizophrenia is too impressive to be dismissed (Gottesman, 1978). For their part, many family theorists accept the concept of a genetic predisposition while maintaining that, in certain instances, familial variables are sufficiently potent to produce schizophrenia even when the genetic vulnerability is

absent. At present, the diathesis-stress hypothesis seems the most sensible resolution to the heredity–environment tug-of-war. The genetic component predisposes the child to schizophrenia, while various family patterns become one of many possible stresses leading to its actual appearance.

Developmental Studies

PROCESS VERSUS REACTIVE SCHIZOPHRENIA A critical developmental variable is the premorbid adjustment of the schizophrenic adolescent. In certain cases, labeled *process* schizophrenia, there is a long history of deviance, while in other cases, called *reactive* schizophrenia, the disturbance appears abruptly, often in reaction to a specific traumatic event. The distinction has important prognostic implications, process schizophrenics having longer hospitalizations and less favorable chances of recovery than reactive schizophrenics. It will be worthwhile examining the contrasting developmental pictures in some detail. (See Kantor, Wallner, and Winder, 1953. For a general discussion, see "Premorbid Adjustment and Schizophrenic Heterogeneity," *Schizophrenia Bulletin*, 1977.)

In process schizophrenia there is the likelihood of a severely disturbed parent in addition to chronic schizophrenia in relatives; in the reactive cases, parents tend to be neurotic, and psychosis in relatives tends to be acute. A higher percentage of process than reactive schizophrenics tend to be below average in intelligence. The first five years of the process schizophrenic's life are marked by psychological trauma, long and severe physical illness, and "odd" behavior, while the reactive schizophrenic enjoys good psychological and physical health. The middle years are characterized by difficulties at school, failure to get along well with peers, stubborn, quarrelsome, and antagonistic behavior for the process schizophrenic, with a personality change in adolescence involving withdrawal and retreat into fantasy. The reactive schizophrenic tends to be shy, quiet, and introverted, to be ignored rather than actively rejected by peers, and to make an adequate school adjustment. Adolescence merely exaggerates the tendency to withdraw under stress (J. D. Roff, 1974).

FOLLOW-UP AND FOLLOW-BACK STUDIES Both *follow-up* and *follow-back* research strategies have been used in an attempt to uncover the etiology of adolescent schizophrenia. In the former, children referred to a clinic are located when they are adults, and the clinical data on those who have and have not become schizophrenic are compared. The attrition rate is often high in such studies, and the sample may be biased in terms of acting-out boys, who are more likely to be referred to a clinic than either girls or children with internalizing disturbances. In the follow-back study, the childhood of adult schizophrenics is reconstructed from public records, such as school reports, child guidance clinic reports, or juvenile court records. Such data may be unsatisfactory because they depend on the conscientiousness and psychological sophistication of the reporters, but they also avoid the bias that may be introduced when an evaluator knows which children did and did not become schizophrenic.

The classic follow-up study was conducted by Robins (1966), who evaluated 436 adults who had been seen in a psychiatric clinic thirty years previously. The twenty-six adult schizophrenics were compared with those who had other psychiatric disturbances and with those who were making an adequate adjustment. No clear-cut preschizophrenic pattern emerged. However, as children, the adult schizophrenics displayed antisocial behavior that tended to be expressed within the family rather than in delinquent peer groups, and they tended to be depressed, worried,

and overly dependent. While their academic achievement was lower than that of normal adults, it was the same as that of alcoholics and sociopaths. Children who were shy and withdrawn or hypersensitive were not particularly at risk for becoming schizophrenic; rather, the high-risk children were actively disliked by peers, who regarded them as odd in some way.

Follow-back studies have comparable findings (Offord and Cross, 1969). To begin with, there is no one type of preschizophrenic personality. The usual stereotype of such children is that they are "shut in"—aloof, peculiar, friendless, keeping to and in themselves. The image is valid (although shyness alone is predictive neither of schizophrenia nor of any other adult disturbance), but is only one of many valid images. The preschizophrenic child is just as likely to be psychopathic as evidenced by stealing, lying, truanting, or running away from home. To complicate the picture even further, there can be a combination of psychopathic with neurotic behaviors, such as worrying, excessive dependence, nail biting, and depression. School retardation, an increased incidence of mental illness in the family, and early hospitalization for severe psychopathology are characteristic of these "stormy," preschizophrenic children.

LONGITUDINAL STUDIES An impressive number of longitudinal studies have been undertaken in the past few years. For an account of the major ones see Watt et al., 1984. A brief summary can be found in Nuechterlein, 1986. Before presenting a summary of their findings, it is worthwhile to examine some of the methodological problems the investigators encountered.

Methodological problems. Longitudinal studies are often regarded as the only means of disentangling cause-and-effect relationships (for example, is a child aggressive because he has punitive parents, or is punitiveness the only way parents have found to deal with a vigorous, willful child with a low frustration tolerance?), while avoiding the inevitable distortions of retrospective data. However, every solution creates its own problems. While the limitations of reconstructive data can be overcome to a degree by longitudinal studies, this strategy has its own difficulties, not least of which is *locating a population* (Garmezy and Streitman, 1974). Because schizophrenia occurs in less than 1 percent of the population, one would have to follow 1,000 randomly selected infants in the hope of obtaining only 10 schizophrenic adolescents. It would facilitate research considerably if one could locate a group of infants or children at risk for developing schizophrenia. The most popular solution is to study children of schizophrenic parents: regardless of whether one holds a genetic or environmental position, the chances of such children becoming schizophrenic are significantly increased.

Other problems arise from the *nature of schizophrenia* itself. Rather than being a single entity, it may well be a family of disturbances, possibly with a number of etiologies (Watt, 1984). Consequently, an investigator may account for only a subgroup of the entire population, or differentiating etiologic patterns may be lost when data are combined and represented only in terms of mean scores. Next, the etiologic variables involved may not be stable, trait-like ones that persist over time, but may wax and wane. We know, for example, that IQ, usually a highly stable measure from middle childhood on, is highly unstable in children of schizophrenics, the correlation over time being around .59 rather than in the .80s as it is with other groups, including children of psychotically depressed mothers (Lewine, 1984). Instability undermines long-range predictability, requiring instead periodic monitoring of variables to chart

their changing course. Added to this picture of instability is the fact that the definition of schizophrenia itself changed with DSM-III, requiring reclassification of original samples and reanalysis of data (Watt, 1984).

Next is the problem of *sample bias*. As we have seen, the design of choice has been to study children of schizophrenic mothers because there is an increased probability that the children will also become schizophrenic. However, since only 10 percent of adult schizophrenics have schizophrenic parents, the population followed longitudinally cannot be considered representative of schizophrenics in general. Schizophrenic women are also more apt to marry disturbed men, such as criminals, who in turn may bias the children's behavior by their own psychopathology (Rutter and Garmezy, 1983). Moreover, older, unmarried, anxious, socially incompetent, lower-class schizophrenic mothers who have had difficult pregnancies and deliveries are apt to give up their babies for adoption or foster parent placement (Watt, 1984). Far from being a random sample of infants, these would be at risk for a number of psychopathologies, even if their mothers were not schizophrenic. In short, investigators cannot control the situation to make sure that only variables intrinsic to schizophrenia are coming into play; instead, they confront a variety of potentially pathogenic variables that function as confounds in the developmental picture.

Finally, there is the problem of *attrition*, common to many longitudinal studies. The most severely disturbed subjects often are the most likely to drop out of the research with time, either because of uncooperativeness or because they have drifted on to other locations leaving no word behind.

Although there are problems, one methodological advance which the current crop of longitudinal studies shares is the inclusion of a severely disturbed but nonschizophrenic comparison group, typically psychotically depressed mothers and their offspring. This allows the investigators to make statements as to which variables are specific to schizophrenia and which are common to several disturbances in general. It also avoids the pitfall of designs that compare schizophrenic populations only with normal ones and then interpret findings as if they were specific to schizophrenia.

Findings. The picture of *pregnancy and birth,* in schizophrenic women is a grim one marked by an elevated incidence of prenatal complications, a long and difficult delivery, and low birth weight for the neonate. However, the picture does not differ significantly from that found in other psychotically disturbed but nonschizophrenic mothers. Some studies find a relation between prenatal events and socioeconomic status; others do not. (For a more detailed account of findings than will be presented here, see Watt et al., 1984.)

The *infants* of schizophrenic mothers are not extremely deviant in most respects, although they do show deficiencies in psychomotor development. There is suggestive evidence that they have little separation or stranger anxiety, indicating a possible disturbance in attachment; however, this does not distinguish the infants from those of other high-risk controls. There is some evidence that the psychomotor disturbance is no longer present by 30 months of age and that the *preschooler* might be socially unresponsive, possibly due to an earlier disturbance in attachment. While there is nothing that sets the preschoolers apart from other children exposed to extremely deviant environments, they are by no means healthy, having high levels of illness, fearfulness, negative mood, retardation, and social maladaptiveness.

The findings in regard to *middle childhood and adolescence* tend to be inconsistent across studies, and no clear picture emerges. The prepsychotic personality has been found to be "stormy" rather than shy or introverted, the children being aggressive and disruptive, less socially competent, concerned with achievement when rated by teachers, and both more aggressive and unhappy/withdrawn when rated by peers. However, often children are not significantly different from those of other severely disturbed parents, although there is some evidence that they are less shy and withdrawn than children of psychotically depressed mothers. Also, by adolescence, both scholastic motivation and emotional stability are lower for the schizophrenic group than for the comparison groups.

Only a modest subset of children of schizophrenic mothers stand out as being deviant in *attention* and *cognition*, the percents ranging from 11 to 44 (Watt, 1984). Children at risk for both schizophrenia and depression have significantly lower IQ scores than do normal controls, but, as we have seen, the schizophrenic-risk group shows the greatest variability in test scores over time. Also, in adolescence the decline in IQ scores is greater for the schizophrenic-risk than for the depression-risk group. While the two groups do not differ in regard to discrimination learning, censure for having made mistakes leads to significantly more errors in the group at risk for schizophrenia than in the group at risk for depression. There is also some suggestive evidence that the schizophrenic group's thinking is more primitive, but their fantasy life is less aggressive than that of children at risk for depression.

In the *organic context* Mednick, Schulsinger, and Schulsinger (1975) found that physiological reactivity was one of the most potent variables differentiating adolescents who would become severely disturbed from those who would not. Specifically, the latency of their galvanic skin response (GSR) was shorter, it did not habituate, it resisted extinction, and the rate of recovery was unusually rapid.

Mednick interpreted his data as indicating that the autonomic nervous system responded too quickly and persistently, causing the individual to be in a state of rapid, exaggerated, and untiring emotional reactivity. One way of escaping from this distressing state would be to think situationally irrelevant thoughts. Because of the GSR's rapid recovery rate, such thoughts would be immediately rewarded and would tend to become habitual. Unfortunately, Mednick's physiological data were not replicated, and currently the picture of psychobiological functioning is ambiguous at best (Nuechterlein, 1986).

Evaluation

The research on the precursors of adolescent schizophrenia is the most admirable in childhood psychopathology. Follow-up, followback, and especially longitudinal studies are the most time-consuming while devising and implementing multivariate studies is intellectually the most demanding. And yet, despite the heroic nature of the projects, the harvest of significant results has been meager. Much has been learned about the precursors of severe disturbances in general, but little about specific etiologic agents. Even the few differentiating variables are difficult to relate to the defining characteristics of schizophrenia itself. For example, clumsiness suggests neurodevelopmental immaturity, attention deficit suggests difficulties in processing information, and both the variability of IQ scores over time and the "stormy" personality characteristics suggest general instability, but it is not at all clear how these produce the cognitive and affective behaviors unique to schizophrenia.

Moreover, it is impossible to place the findings in a meaningful developmental context. Rather, the conceptualizations of various investigators present a picture that is fragmented—to borrow a term from the description of schizophrenia itself. Using Piaget's stages of egocentric thinking, Lidz proposes a regression model to account for certain thought disorders. On the other hand, data showing preschizophrenics to be emotionally immature in middle childhood suggest fixation rather than regression. Aspects of family theory, along with learning theory, however, suggest that bizarre patterns of thinking are modeled on parental behavior and need not represent fixations or regressions. Finally, conceptualizing schizophrenia as a solution to an intolerable situation suggests that it might be a new development unrelated to the past; for example, the decision to shatter communication and obscure one's self-definition may have no counterpart in normal or preschizophrenic development.

To conclude that many kinds of deviations are involved in a disturbance as severe as schizophrenia is probably correct, but far too general. The challenge is to come to grips with specifics and to narrow down possible etiologies to necessary and sufficient ones.

THE "CHOICE OF SYMPTOMS" One of the perennial questions confronting investigators of the etiology of psychopathology is, What determines the choice of a particular symptom? The question does not pertain to conscious choice, of course; rather, it involves the issue of accounting for the specific form a psychopathology takes. It is often clear why a child would be disturbed rather than normal, for example, or severely rather than moderately so, but what determines that he or she will become phobic rather than obsessive-compulsive, anorexic rather than suicidal, schizophrenic rather than manic-depressive? Looking over our past discussions, we can see how often the same etiologic agent is used to account for different disturbances; for example, domineering, intrusive parenting leads to negativism, anorexia, antisocial behavior, or adolescent schizophrenia. Even the current trend to conceptualize etiology in terms of the interaction of variables tells us little about the special patterning that eventuates in one kind of disturbance rather than another. Similarly, in the organic context physiological dysfunctions can distinguish normal from disturbed children but fail to differentiate among types of disturbances.

The question concerning choice of symptoms has not gone totally unanswered. In a number of instances, such as autism or antisocial acting out or depression, there is a reasonably close fit between etiology and clinical manifestations. Moreover, accounting only for the degree of disturbance, as in the case of adolescent schizophrenia, should not be dismissed as trivial. Certainly a formidable and plausible list of high-risk factors has been isolated: a genetic predisposition, obstetrical complications, psychopathological parenting and deviant family interactions, psychomotor and attentional defects, emotional instability, and poor adjustment to peers and to school. Such a list represents a mapping out of a territory that now must be explored more intensively if specific links to schizophrenia are to be established and these links placed in their proper developmental contexts.

Therapy

PSYCHOSOCIAL AND BEHAVIORAL THERAPIES First, some of the major therapies used with schizophrenics will be discussed briefly (Mosher and Keith, 1977).

In *individual psychotherapy* the emphasis is on establishing a positive relationship and interpreting reality in order to counteract the schizophrenic's isolation and faulty reality testing. Therapists must be versatile in finding ways of presenting themselves as warm and trustworthy, but they must also be able to understand and interpret the adolescent's mistrust, resistance, touchiness, and metaphorical communications. In interpreting reality, they must be careful not to antagonize the adolescent and jeopardize the positive relationship (I. B. Weiner, 1970). *Group psychotherapy* capitalizes on the individual's ability to receive support, understanding, and constructive advice from interacting with individuals who have similar problems, under the leadership of an experienced therapist. Some groups emphasize facilitation of insight into personal and interpersonal problems; most group work with schizophrenics, however, tends to be oriented toward providing support, offering an opportunity to form friendships, as well as developing social skills which enhance a positive adaptation to reality. *Family therapy* aims at correcting the deviations presumably responsible for engendering and maintaining the schizophrenia by promoting clear communication, developing constructive techniques for coping with stress, and substituting constructive for destructive role alignments.

The desire to help schizophrenics has produced heroic efforts to change the total environment. In *milieu therapy*, treatment becomes a twenty-four-hour affair, all individuals who interact with the schizophrenic being actively involved in implementing a therapeutic program. There is evidence that acute and chronic schizophrenics require somewhat different programs. The former respond best in an accepting, supportive, low-key environment oriented toward solving practical, down-to-earth problems. Chronic patients do better in a highly organized environment focused on changing specific behaviors (Mosher and Keith, 1977). *Rehabilitation* programs try to reintegrate the formerly hospitalized patient into the community by combining emotional support with vocational rehabilitation aimed at raising the level of independent functioning. The programs can be implemented in different settings, such as day-care centers or halfway houses, which provide a protective buffer from the stresses of living in the community. Such extrafamilial resources are particularly important for schizophrenics who are sufficiently recovered to leave the hospital but who cannot or should not return to their own families.

The picture in regard to relative effectiveness is far from clear owing to conflicting findings and methodological flaws in comparative studies (Mosher and Keith, 1977). In general, however, it seems that therapy becomes increasingly effective as it embraces more of the schizophrenic's social environment. Thus the effectiveness of individual and group therapy is controversial, while family, milieu, and rehabilitation therapies have a more positive record of success.

Behavior modification has been used extensively with adult schizophrenics (Redd, Porterfield, and Andersen, 1979). The basic techniques of modeling and contingent reinforcement have been applied with admirable versatility to change such behaviors as mutism, delusions and hallucinations, abstract reasoning, apathy, and withdrawal. Token economies, in which patients receive a token for appropriate behavior which can be redeemed for a reward such as cigarettes, candy, or a special privilege, have been particularly effective in hospital settings.

One of the most exhaustive and well-controlled studies of effectiveness was conducted by Paul and Lentz (1977). The patients were severely debilitated, chronic schizophrenics who had been hospitalized for an average of seventeen years. A token economy, in which progressively more complex, socially acceptable behavior was immediately rewarded, was compared with a milieu program in which patients were organized into self-governing decision-making groups, the staff serving a facilitating, supportive function. The behavioral program proved consistently superior over the four years of the study. When the programs were terminated, twenty-seven of the original twenty-eight schizophrenics in the behavioral program could be placed in a shelter-care facility in the community, while only nineteen of the twenty-eight patients from the milieu program could be so placed. Although the study is impressive, it was begun before it was known that chronic schizophrenics do best in a highly structured milieu; requiring that they function as autonomous decision makers may have put milieu therapy at a disadvantage.

PSYCHOPHARMACOTHERAPY The effectiveness of neuroleptics with adult schizophrenics has been well established. Neuroleptics are a family of drugs involving a blockage of postsynaptic receptor cells for dopamine, noradrenaline, and often acetylcholine, so that less is available to the brain. The drugs are effective with both withdrawn, retarded, uncommunicative schizophrenics and agitated, excited, overactive ones. Therefore they are not tranquilizers as was originally thought, but may affect an underlying defect common to both types of patients. Despite the success of neuroleptics with adults, well-controlled studies of their use with children are scarce. There is some clinical evidence that while schizophrenic children may respond less well than adults, adolescents respond equally well, making neuroleptics the treatment of choice. (For additional details, see Gittelman and Kanner, 1986.)

The Invulnerables

Bleuler (1974) followed 184 children of 206 schizophrenic parents and found that approximately 72 percent were functioning normally. The percentage is higher than is usually reported (which ranges between 35 and 50 percent), perhaps owing to the uncertainty of the definition of normality, perhaps because, as a family psychiatrist, Bleuler came to know his patients more thoroughly than most researchers know their subjects. But the mystery of normal functioning has deepened with the discovery of high-risk children who are making exceptionally good adjustments. Some have schizophrenic parents, some come from poverty backgrounds, and their home environment would seem inimical to normal development; for example, one 8-year-old girl's father was in jail, her mother was severely depressed and unable to see even to her children's basic needs for food, while her four siblings were either retarded or predelinquent school dropouts.

While the study of these invulnerable children has only recently begun, certain of their characteristics have been delineated. (Unless otherwise noted, our presentation follows Cohler, 1987.) Rather than being engulfed by their parents' psychopathology, the invulnerable children have the ability to distance themselves psychologically, showing a detached curiosity and understanding of what is troubling their parents while also being compassionate toward them. They have a high level of initiative. In the interpersonal realm this is evidenced by their taking advantage of the well parent's support or, lacking that, seeking out adults outside the family. Their capacity to make friends further enlarges their circle of growth-promoting social relationships. In the intrapersonal realm, the children's initiative is evidenced by their engaging in diverse activities outside of the home, holding down jobs, and having hobbies, all of which serve as buffers against the noxious influences of the home environment. While the invulnerable children are intelligent, more important is their ability to try to understand the events in their lives and figure out ways of coping with them. They also tend to be physically and personally attractive. A final research finding is that the ability to cope effectively is increased if the disturbed parent is hospitalized later in the children's lives rather than early, and if the parent has some ability to relate positively to the children.

Subsequently, however, invulnerable children pay a price for their remarkable ability to cope effectively with adversity. As adults they have a diminished capacity to form a sustained intimate relationship. They are concerned with their own needs and interests but reluctant to explore their feelings. They gravitate toward impersonal pursuits and vocations such as science and technology and are most comfortable in tasks requiring group cooperation rather than close relations. They gain support from participation in religious and social groups. Such a life pattern results from their defenses of distancing, suppression of affect, and intellectualizing. When they seek psychotherapy, it is because they have vague feelings of being unsatisfied despite being successful (Anthony, 1987).

Finally, the intensive study of these children and their lives suggests that "invulnerable" might not be the most appropriate adjective for describing them because it suggests they somehow have developed an immunity to all of life's stresses and distresses. On the contrary, they, like most other people, have their periods of setback marked by discouragement, uncertainty, and fear. However, they also have a basic strength that enables them to overcome such periods and to resume the positive course of their lives. Thus it is not their immunity that marks them but their resilience.

DRUG ABUSE

YOU ARE a clinical child psychologist. The time is 11:42 on a Saturday night. You get out of bed to answer the phone. It is Mitzi, the younger sister of your client Ada. She says Ada is high (on drugs) and has just hit her mother, knocking her down on the kitchen floor and bloodying her nose. You say you will be right over and hurriedly dress. Your husband grumbles about having "one hell of a family life, to say nothing of a sex life," adding, "I hope you charge them double for overtime." The last remark is ironic. Ada's mother has not paid you in two years. A widow, whose husband's jewelry business was going bankrupt at his death, she is a borderline psychotic barely able to keep herself together, much less manage her four children. As you are about to leave, your husband says, "How about me coming with you," but you refuse. The family lives in a deteriorating middle-class neighborhood, which is relatively safe.

When you arrive, the household is surprisingly quiet. Mitzi meets you at the door. She is a miracle—a mature, sensible, assured 14-year-old. She says her mother is upstairs resting. You will talk with her later. Ada is lying on the living room sofa. She is a strikingly beautiful 17-year-old, her voluptuous figure spilling over her tight, low-cut dress. "I'll sleep with anything," she had once told you, "man, woman, horse, dog, or pig." Then she had added with mock suffering, "But I'm really not bad; I'm just terribly, terribly lonely."

Ada has a brilliant, facile mind, and listening to her, you often cannot tell fact from fantasy, true feeling from mock sincerity. You are sure she frequently rode on a motorcycle with various gangs of delinquents, committed minor thefts, and then delighted in avoiding arrest either by crying or by being seductive with the police. "Pigs" is her favorite expression of contempt, which she applies to everyone—family, peers, teachers, the world in general. In spite of her obvious provocativeness, she constantly sees herself as unfairly victimized. Her one genuine desire is to graduate from high school (her father had been awed by education and "learning"), yet her uncontrollable restlessness in class has caused her to fail continually. Right now she is asleep on the sofa, snoring slightly—or perhaps she is pretending to sleep to avoid talking to you.

You try to decide what to do. Ada has a 22-year-old brother. (A second brother stays in his room much of the time, immobilized by fears and depression.) A high school dropout, he has already amassed a good deal of money by charming elderly people into buying expensive, unnecessary, defective hearing aids. Although Ada violently dislikes him, he is quite fond of her. Tomorrow you will phone to see if he will pay for a boarding school, so that Ada can realize her ambition of completing high school while receiving psychotherapy. If he agrees, you will have to talk Ada into accepting the idea. Mitzi will help, and Ada's mother would be glad to get her out of the house. If that fails, you will have to try to find some other resource, as you have been doing for over two years. While some would call this supportive psychotherapy, you think of it more in terms of "rolling with the punches."

Clearly Ada is not a normal, well-adjusted adolescent. But many cases of adolescent drug use are considerably less clear-cut. Often the clinician must decide whether to regard drug use as part of a pattern of normal development or as a symptom of maladjustment. Making this determination necessitates evaluating all of the contexts, which are even more numerous than those of conduct disorders: to the intrapersonal, interpersonal, and societal we must add the physiological and historical contexts as well. The last is particularly important, since history offers scant support for equating drug use with deviant behavior.

Historical Context

Most cultures have used alcohol: mead was possibly used around 8000 B.C. in the Paleolithic era, the biblical Noah became drunk, and the Indians who met Columbus had their own "home brew." Drugs have been used in religious ceremonies, to medicate, to counteract fatigue, to increase fierceness in battle, as well as for recreation. Cultures have applied different sanctions to drugs, one drug having multiple uses, for example, while another is strongly prohibited.

In modern times, there were more opiate

addicts in the United States at the turn of the century than there are now, many being women using opiate-based patent medicines to treat various physical complaints. Some physicians considered opium as a cure for alcoholism, while heroin was regarded as less harmful still, medical journals stressing its nonaddictive properties. It was after the Harrison Narcotics Act of 1914, banning opiates, that the number of women addicts decreased, while male addicts turned increasingly to crime in order to obtain the now illegal drugs. The current drug scene is as much a patchwork as its historical context. By far the most lethal forms of drug abuse are alcoholism and smoking, yet legal sanctions against them are relatively benign.

In recent years, both drug use and its study have had their own developmental trends. (Our presentation follows Johnston, 1985, except when otherwise noted.) In the late 1960s and 1970s use of illicit drugs burgeoned into what some described as a drug epidemic, as marijuana along with other stimulants, sedatives, and analgesics joined the traditional drugs of nicotine, alcohol, and caffeine. Since the early 1970s the majority of adolescents have experimented with one or more of these illicit drugs by the end of high school. The fact that the so-called epidemic spreads primarily among adolescents and young adults suggests that the teens and early twenties are particularly important developmental stages for drug behavior to become established or fail to do so.

Since the 1970s, age of onset has changed from high school to junior high school, as an increasing number of eighth and ninth graders become involved in drug use. The period of highest risk for initiation of legal and illegal drugs peaks at eighteen and declines sharply after that. Stabilization of use of both kinds of drugs appears within one year after high school graduation and declines around 22 years of age, perhaps as a result of psycho-

social maturity and the assumption of an adult role (Kandel and Yamaguchi, 1985).

Overall use peaked in 1979 and has steadily declined through 1985. Within this overall pattern there are fluctuations in the use of specific drugs; for example, the use of cocaine or crack increased sharply from the middle of 1975 to 1985, while daily cigarette smoking declined rapidly between 1975 and 1980, when it leveled off. Alcohol use has long been stable at progressively higher levels for children in higher grades, going from 10 percent of sixth graders to over 90 percent of twelfth graders (Johnston, O'Malley, and Jerald, 1987). *Multiple use* has also increased so that it is possible that regular use of a variety of psychoactive substances is the norm among users of any drug. For the most part, multiple drug use can be grouped into five categories: (1) predominantly alcohol, (2) predominantly depressant drugs, (3) predominantly recreational drugs such as cannabis, hallucinogens, and stimulants, (4) high use of solvents, and (5) a category that includes high use of alcohol, depressants, and recreational drugs (Wilkinson et al., 1987).

What forces determine this long-range waxing and waning of drug use is a matter of speculation. Certainly the original epidemic was part of the massive rebellion of youth against the political, social, and moral values of the adult world which swept the country during the decade between 1960 and 1970. However, its very prevalence gradually may have eroded the shock value of drug use as a symbol of rebellion while youth, along with the entire country, turned to a generally more conservative set of values and toward an emphasis on health and fitness inconsistent with drug use.

The nature of the *study of drug use* has also changed (Shore, 1985). The initial surveys were limited to the most general questions, such as whether the individual ever used drugs and if so what kind. Subsequently, more specific and meaningful issues began to be explored. The distinction between experimental or recreational use of drugs and drug abuse was drawn, and there was more concern for understanding the etiology of each. Developmental considerations were introduced in regard to the age and precursors of use and the transition from legal to illegal drugs, while the roots of drug use itself were sought in earlier childhood or even in the preschool period. Finally, the scope of inquiry expanded so that drug use could be viewed in the context of various intra- and interpersonal variables as well as within the context of the adolescent transition itself.

For our purposes the basic question is, To what extent is drug use part of the adolescent transition, and to what extent is it a significant deviation from normal development? We are also interested in any guidelines that would enable us to distinguish normal use from pathological abuse, and we would like to know the conditions that produce one or the other. Before attempting to answer these questions we must become acquainted with the nature of drug abuse and the findings in regard to context variables. First, a description of the diverse types of drugs and the reasons for taking them will be presented.

Classification of Drugs

Our coverage of drugs will be selective. Caffeine (coffee, Coca-Cola, NoDoz), nicotine (cigarettes and cigars), tranquilizers (Valium, Miltown), antidepressants (Elavil), and miscellaneous drugs such as nonprescription sedatives, antihistamines, and glue will be omitted. Selectivity within categories will also be maintained, the concern being with the physiological and psychological effects of the drug under scrutiny. (For a comprehensive drug chart, see Calhoun et al., 1977.) All the drugs are *psychoactive* in that they affect the central nervous system in such a way as to produce alterations in subjective feeling states.

CANNABIS   This classification includes marijuana ("grass," "pot") and hashish ("hash"), small doses of which produce relaxation and euphoria. With intermediate doses there is the illusion of thinking more clearly, although judgment and memory become impaired, while heavy doses induce hallucinations, delusions, and thought disorders. Cannabis is used to get high, to escape, to relax.

HALLUCINOGENS   This category includes PCP—phencyclidine ("angel dust")—lysergic acid diethylamide—LSD ("acid")—and mescaline (peyote), which produce visual imagery and increased sensory awareness, as well as anxiety and nausea. They may also cause panic in unprepared individuals and sometimes precipitate or intensify an already existing psychosis. Curiosity, consciousness expansion, and seeking for meaning are typical reasons for use.

NARCOTICS   Opium, heroin ("horse," "H"), methadone, morphine, and even cough syrups belong in this category. All are central nervous system depressants that produce relief from pain, euphoria, and impaired intellectual functioning and motor coordination. They are usually taken to get high and as an escape.

STIMULANTS   There are two principle stimulants: amphetamines ("speed," "uppers," "pep pills"), which include Benzedrine ("bennies") and Dexedrine ("dexies"), and cocaine ("coke," "crack," "snow"). Both are central nervous system stimulants that increase alertness and produce euphoria, along with insomnia and loss of appetite. They are taken for stimulation, to get high, and to relieve fatigue.

BARBITURATES   This category includes Nembutal ("yellow jackets"), Seconal ("red devils"), Quaalude ("ludes"), and Doriden ("goofers"). All these are central nervous system depressants inducing relaxation and sleep, slowing down reaction time, impairing judgment and coordination, weakening emotional control; sometimes they also produce euphoria. They are taken to relax and sleep or to get high.

ALCOHOL   Whiskey, gin, beer, and wine ("booze," "hooch") are all central nervous system depressants inducing relaxation and drowsiness, while interfering with reaction time, coordination, judgment, and emotional control. Alcohol is drunk to relax, to escape tensions and inhibitions, and to get high.

Complexities of Drug Abuse

Drugs vary in psychological and physical dependence potential, narcotics, barbiturates, and alcohol being high on both, cannibis and hallucinogens being moderate to low on psychological dependence while entailing no physical dependence. In addition, physical tolerance affects the course of drug taking; the body seems to become sensitized to marijuana so that the individual requires less of the drug to achieve a high with time, while opiates produce high tolerance resulting in an ever-increasing need for larger quantities. Note that tolerance and dependence (or addiction) may vary independently; tolerance develops rapidly for most hallucinogens, although they are not physically addictive. Both factors affect the lengths to which the adolescent must go to maintain a habit, as well as the degree of difficulty in breaking it.

In addition to the differential legal risks involved in maintaining various drug habits, there are differential risks in regard to physical consequences. The long-term effects of marijuana use have been disputed by scientists:

for example, prolonged, heavy use lowers the male sex hormone, testosterone, but there is no clear evidence of impaired sexual functioning; or again, chronic use impairs one part of the body's immune system, but there is no clearly established clinical effect of such impairment. However, its acute effects in impairing both classroom learning and driving skill remove marijuana use from the category of a harmless pastime (Peterson, 1980). The long-term effects of LSD are similarly in doubt. By contrast, chronic heroin use may be devastating. Loss of appetite leads to malnutrition and susceptibility to disease; carelessness concerning injection techniques and the sterility of needles may result in tetanus, blood poisoning, and hepatitis; too large a dose may result in a coma and death. Overdoses of barbiturates cause accidental deaths as well as suicides, while withdrawal from both barbiturates and alcohol is harrowing, dangerous, and potentially fatal. In most instances, adverse effects come about by habitual use of high dosages, both of which indicate drug abuse rather than casual or recreational use.

As we have already noted, many individuals are multiple drug users. At times drugs are combined to heighten their effect, such as the "speedball," which is a vicious combination of cocaine and heroin. Sometimes one drug will be used to offset the negative features of another; for example, a depressant such as a barbiturate can be used to counteract the "crash" that comes when the effect of amphetamines wears off.

ESCALATION   A final complication is the risk of escalation. While marijuana may be a relatively benign drug, for example, it may also be the first step along the path leading to more potent and dangerous ones. On the other hand, drug use peaks around 22 years of age and then declines to a relatively low level afterwards. Thus a simple escalation model, which assumes that a process once set in motion has a built-in propensity to accelerate, receives little empirical support.

When escalation does take place, it follows a predictable pattern: for males, the progression is from alcohol to marijuana to illicit drugs; females follow the same pattern except that cigarettes are part of the initial step along with alcohol. Thus legal drugs are a necessary intermediate between nonuse and marijuana, and there is a low probability that those who never use marijuana will progress to other illegal drugs (Kandel and Yamaguchi, 1985).

There is also evidence that different determinants may be involved at each stage of escalation (Kandel, Kessler, and Margulies, 1978). Adolescents who begin to drink have engaged in a number of minor delinquent activities, enjoy high levels of sociability with peers, and are exposed to peers and parents who drink. The transition to marijuana use is preceded by involvement with peers who use marijuana, by a belief and value system that favors or condones marijuana use, and by participation in the same minor forms of deviant behaviors which precede involvement with hard liquor. While parental and peer models of illicit drug use also precede the transition to the use of hard drugs, depression and lack of closeness to parents are equally important.

Thus the influence of peers, while the most potent determiner of drug use, changes in nature: in the early stages a general sociability or group membership makes the adolescent susceptible to using drugs, while in the final stage a single best friend plays an important role. Parental behavior is also influential in leading the adolescent to experiment with hard liquor, the model they present being more important than their beliefs and values. In the final stage, it is the quality of the parent–child relationship that matters, warmth and closeness shielding the adolescent from involvement in more serious drugs. The intrapersonal variables change from values and beliefs condoning drug use to feelings of despair as the adolescent moves into involvement with hard drugs.

The developmental progression is of more than academic interest; locating individuals within the sequence furnishes important leads as to the focus of psychotherapy, since peers are particularly influential in the early stages, while the transition to hard drugs adds the element of negative self-esteem and alienation from the family.

Escalation can also refer to an increase in drug-engendered criminal activity and/or negative motivational syndromes, such as a profound indifference to one's personal fate and the requirements of constructive social living. While the data are not conclusive, longitudinal studies suggest that such deviant behavior tends to precede drug use. In regard to criminality, one study showed that delinquency, particularly crimes against property, anteceded the use of drugs (Johnston, Bachman, and O'Malley, 1977). While there was a relation between the seriousness of the crime and the seriousness of the drug used, changes in the latter were not paralleled by changes in the former. The authors speculate that the association between drugs and crime might be due to the adolescent's social environment or personality characteristics; for example, delinquents tend to become part of a deviant peer group that approves of drug use, while both delinquency and drug use appeal to adolescents who are already "deviance prone." The authors are also careful to state that their conclusions do not apply to addicts, nor do they deny that criminal behavior might increase in order to support the habit. Other data indicate clearly that narcotic addiction increases the frequency of income-generating crime (McGlothlin, 1979).

In a like manner, negative motivational states are likely to precede drug use, or both kinds of deviant behavior may result from other factors (Kandel, 1978). To cite one example: among high school students, a reduction in aspiration for college tended to precede rather than follow the initiation into illicit drugs other than marijuana. However, as with criminal behavior, such findings do not preclude an increase in deviant behavior following addiction, since regular use of heroin, amphetamines, and barbiturates has been shown to lead to adjustment problems such as alcoholism, violence, unemployment, and marital breakup (Robins, 1979).

In one instance the fear that drug use will cause severe psychopathology is justified: the "speed freak" who injects amphetamine into his veins for three to four days readily engages in paranoid and violent behavior. The psychosis seems to be drug-induced rather than the drug triggering a latent paranoia. In fact, this is the only drug-induced psychosis which is behaviorally identical to a "functional" psychosis (Bootzin and Acocella, 1988). Aside from this instance, the evidence linking drugs to psychopathology is not clear.

INTRAPERSONAL VARIABLES   Personality variables have been studied primarily in relation to marijuana use (R. Jessor, 1979). One of the most consistent findings is that prospective users rate higher on expectation for independence and lower on academic aspirations and motivations than do prospective nonusers. They tend to be nonconformists, unconventional, and rebellious, although not necessarily aggressive, while placing a low value on achievement and having low expectations of being able to gain achievement satisfaction. Another characteristic is that users, as compared with nonusers, tend to be more open to experience, more aesthetically oriented, more interested in creativity, play, novelty, and spontaneity. On the negative side there is some tendency for future users to have depressive moods.

CONTEXT VARIABLES   The influence of parents and peers has already been discussed, the latter being the most potent predictor of drug involvement. Low grades and high frequency of school absences have consistently been found to precede involvement in marijuana use in high school. Poor performance seems to be a matter of motivation, since, in terms of both intelligence and aptitude, future users are as gifted intellectually as nonusers. A study of servicemen in Vietnam documents the impact of the sociocultural context on older adolescents and young adults (Kandel, 1978). The easy availability and superior quality of drugs, especially heroin, both accelerated the timing of initiation and increased the number of users of marijuana and narcotics. However, it was the soldier who was already predisposed to use drugs who was most strongly affected by the situational lures rather than the drug's availability equalizing use among men from different social and behavioral backgrounds.

We are now in a position to answer the first question raised at the beginning of the discussion. It is easy to understand why drug abuse can be regarded both as one aspect of adolescent rebellion and as a serious disturbance. It can be both. It can reflect nothing more than the desire to be independent and a chafing at being shackled with schoolwork; but a persistent use of hard drugs may be motivated by despair and a regressive longing for parental love, and it may increase criminal and other maladaptive behavior, as well as being a threat to health or to life itself.

Why Adolescence?

In order to answer the second question concerning the appearance of drug use in adolescence, a study by Jessor and Jessor (1977) will be discussed in detail. The study has a developmental conceptual framework which places drug use in the context of a number of important intrapersonal and interpersonal variables.

CONCEPTUAL FRAMEWORK   According to the Jessors, highly prized roles and rewards vary with age in our society. The adolescent, especially the early adolescent, has limited access to the valued goals of adulthood, such as autonomy, prestige, sex, and mobility. In addition, age norms ignore individual differences in the desire and readiness to pursue adult goals. Consequently, certain adolescents who are ready to make the transition are constantly frustrated and tantalized by the perceived attractiveness of mature status.

Furthermore, the Jessors state, the transition from a less mature to a more mature adult status is marked by problem behavior, which they define as behavior that is undesirable by the norms of conventional society. It should in no way be regarded as deviant or psychopathological. Many problem behaviors, such as drinking and sexual intercourse, will be regarded as acceptable and will be encouraged when the adolescent is old enough to be considered an adult. In essence, the Jessors regard adolescence as a period in which departure from accepted norms is not only to be expected but also may be a sign of healthy development. Their particular term for an adolescent's readiness to engage in problem behavior is *transition proneness*.

VARIABLES STUDIED   Jessor and Jessor regard behavior as a result of interactions between the individual's personality and the perceived environment. All variables were studied by means of an annual questionnaire submitted to 432 high school and 205 college students every year for a four-year period. This longitudinal design enabled the authors to investigate the factors related to beginning drug use at different ages. The population was drawn from a small, university-dominated city known for its attractive natural setting and comfortable standard of living. The authors claim that, while the population is hardly typical, the findings are generally congruent with those from studies with more representative populations.

CORRELATES OF DRUG USE   In the personality realm, drug use in both high school and college was positively correlated with tolerance of deviance, and with a perception of drug use as being more positive than negative, while drug use was negatively correlated with religiosity. Among high school students, academic achievement and the need for peer affection (both of which were negatively related to drug use) and the valuing of independence over achievement were second in importance, while a critical attitude toward society was third. For the college population, only a critical attitude toward society, along with alienation (for females), were significant correlates. It may be that where drug use is relatively low, as in high school, a wide variety of personality variables must be engaged in order to tip the balance in its favor; where it is prevalent, as in college, drug use may become more a matter of going along with what others are doing.

Jessor and Jessor epitomize the personality dimension underlying their findings in terms of conventionality–unconventionality. The adolescent who does not use drugs is likely to value academic achievement; to be unconcerned with independence from the family, accepting of the social status quo, and involved in a religion; and to regard transgressions as having more negative than positive consequences. The individual with high proneness to problem behavior in general and drug use in particular has the opposite characteristics.

Among environmental variables, friends'

approval and modeling of problem behavior, along with parental approval (or lack of disapproval), were all significant correlates for both high school and college students. For high school students, parental support and control were negatively related to drug use, while these variables were no longer important for college students.

The Jessors also analyzed their data in terms of the relative contribution of each variable to problem behavior and drug use. In general, both personality and environmental variables always appeared as major contributors, underlying the authors' thesis that behavior is a product of both intrapersonal and context variables. The specific variables contributing most to marijuana use were having friends who serve as models for problem behavior, a critical attitude toward society, and a tolerance of deviant behavior. The social-criticism variable distinguished marijuana use from the other problem behaviors studied.

Summarizing the results of the study of all problem behaviors, the authors present a complex but coherent picture. The transition-prone high school adolescent values independence more than academic achievement, is critical of society and its institutions, is tolerant toward transgressions, and views the use of drugs and sex positively. Parents are perceived as not disapproving of problem behavior; their influence is less than that of friends, while friends and peers serve as models for problem behavior. The reverse of this cluster is characteristic of conventional high school adolescents. Finally, this cluster of variables can be used to predict the onset of drug use, especially for females. The results for college marijuana users are similar although less clear.

General developmental trends are congruent with the above picture. Among personality variables, valuing of independence increases from high school through college

while religiosity and alienation decrease; valuing of academic achievement declines in high school but levels off in college, while criticism of society and tolerance of deviation increase in high school but similarly level off in college. Predictably, high school is, in general, a time of more pervasive personality change than is college.

One final note: self-esteem, alienation, and internal locus of control had little to do with problem behavior. Thus marijuana users felt no more inferior or alone or helpless than nonusers. Despite the importance of peers, popularity was unrelated to problem behavior. Actual grade-point averages were independent of problem behavior, perhaps because they are closely tied to intellectual ability rather than to attitudes. And, finally, socieconomic status was unrelated to problem behavior.

Magnusson's (1988) study of early and late maturing girls (defined in terms of age of menarche) complements Jessor and Jessor's study. He found that early maturers engaged in more norm-violating behavior—or what the Jessors would call problem behavior—such as staying out late without parental permission, cheating on exams, truanting, smoking hashish, and getting drunk. Peer relations proved to be the link between physiological maturation and norm violation, early maturers seeking out older peers. These older peers actually engaged in or were perceived as engaging in norm-violating behaviors. Late maturers evidenced similar problem behaviors after they had biologically "caught up" with their early maturing peers. Age of physiological maturity did not affect antisocial behavior or alcohol consumption when the girls became adults, although it did significantly affect marriage and vocation. In sum, Magnusson's data indicate that, with girls, the organic variable of age of menarche is an important determinant of what the Jessors call transition proneness.

Magnusson (1988) is conducting a landmark longitudinal study that may well have a major impact on our understanding of developmental psychopathology. By now we are familiar with his general thesis: psychopathology is the result of the interaction among intrapersonal, interpersonal, and organic contexts as well as the interaction among variables within each of these contexts. In fact, his project is an implementation of the interactive model introduced in the first chapter. This in itself is noteworthy. As we have seen in discussing various psychopathologies, a multivariable, interactive model of etiology has replaced the single-variables ones. All too often, however, investigators have gone no further than this or have acted as if the complex model were a solution to the problem rather than being a restatement. Only a few, such as Jessor and Jessor (1977), have been bold enough to tackle the challenge of multivariable, interactive research head on.

Magnusson's design is impressive. His sample consisted of 3,244 children drawn from a Swedish community of about 100,000 inhabitants. He conducted two longitudinal studies—one from 10 to 23 years of age, the other from 15 to 27 years of age. Follow-up data were available on 1,393 subjects. Smaller groups of children were studied more intensively than was possible with the entire population. The data were obtained from the children, their parents, teachers, and peers, from medical examinations, and from official records, which are usually thorough in Sweden. The principal adult psychopathologies Magnusson is investigating are criminality, alcohol abuse, and mental illness. However, he is as interested in the protective factors that prevent children at risk from becoming disturbed adults as in the factors that produce such disturbances.

A distinguishing feature of Magnusson's approach is its emphasis on variables within individuals rather than on variables within populations. To illustrate, Magnusson obtained measures of six problem behaviors of 13-year-old males: aggression, motor restlessness, lack of concentration, poor peer relations, underachievement, and low motivation for school. A cluster analysis yielded groups of boys who had no problems, who had single problems (poor peer relations or underachievement), two problems (aggression and motor restlessness), three problems (motor restlessness, lack of concentration, and low school motivation—a pattern suggesting a learning disability), and four to five problems. There were three groups in this last category, which Magnusson called multiproblem boys. In general, no cluster predicted mental illness at age 23, so we shall concentrate on criminality and alcohol abuse. Some of the findings were to be expected: boys with no problems at 13 years of age had few problems as adults, while aggression and hyperactivity predicted both criminality and alcohol abuse. However, other findings were unexpected. It was the multiple problem boys who became disturbed adults, about half those with four to five problems becoming criminals, for example. Even more unexpected was that single variables alone were unrelated to adult criminality or alcohol abuse. This finding applied to peer relations and, more surprisingly, to aggression. It was only when aggression was accompanied by hyperactivity that it predicted criminality, and only as poor peer relations were accompanied by four other problem behaviors that it also became predictive.

Magnusson's point is that if one looks at only a single variable within a population and studies its relation to adult psychopathology, one might reach an erroneous conclusion concerning its importance. In reality, it is the limited number of multiple-problem children—only around a quarter of the population in this instance—who are responsible for the significant predictions. Not that Magnusson is against studying "pure" cases or single variables in a population. His concern is that researchers have been neglecting the group of multiple-problem children who, ironically, are the most liable to grow up to become criminals and alcoholics.

DRUG USE AND ADOLESCENCE   The Jessors have taught us a good deal about marijuana use in adolescence. Especially in high school it may well be only one in a constellation of behaviors which might include drinking, sexual intercourse, and delinquency. Concomitantly, there is a developmental pattern in which the valuing of independence progressively increases while the valuing of academic achievement declines; tolerance of unconventional behavior increases while acceptance of the conventional ideology in regard to society and religion declines; the influence of the family declines while a peer orientation and a utilization of peers as models increases. Within this developmental pattern there are individual differences in transition proneness or the adolescent's readiness to change.

The Jessors also supply an explicit answer to the question, Why does drug use enter the developmental picture during adolescence? They view the changes described above as part of the normal transition from the status of being a child to the status of being an adult. "Problem behavior may be viewed, at least in part, as an aspect of growing up" (p. 238). We are reminded of the terrible twos—which have humorously been referred to as the first adolescence—in which behavior that is difficult to manage and socially disruptive is part of normal development.

Yet the Jessors' interpretation of their data cannot be accepted without reservations. First, they studied only marijuana users and not addicts and serious drug users who, as we have just learned, might well be psychologically disturbed. And they present no evidence that the delinquent behaviors correlated with drug use represented the kinds of minor transgressions many adolescents engage in rather than being a manifestation of serious lapses in self-control. Their most reassuring finding is that, although marijuana use increased in college, delinquent behavior leveled off; there is also no evidence that marijuana use, as distinct from marijuana abuse, is associated with maladjustment or psychopathology (R. Jessor, 1979).

These reservations are not criticisms of the Jessors, who do not share our interest in psychopathology and who also recognize that certain transition-prone adolescents may well be disturbed. Rather, the reservations serve as a reminder that their study only partially answers the clinician's concern with separating normal from disturbed adolescents. In searching for an appropriate developmental model to guide us in making this distinction, reference to the terrible twos and the discussion of negativism may be helpful. In chapter 6 we saw that an exaggeration of normal problem behavior which threatens to jeopardize future growth could be regarded as psychopathological. The same principle could be applied here. When rebellion, defiance, and antisocial behaviors become ends in themselves rather than means for promoting autonomy, adolescents may be in a state not of transition but of stagnation. Or again, if problem behaviors seem primarily directed against the parents—if adolescents seem to be going out of their way to defy and upset parents, if unconsciously they are behaving like "bad children" in order to prolong their status as children—then we begin to suspect that fixation rather than transition is calling the tune.

Erikson's writings on identity are useful at this point. In keeping with the Jessors he states that youths often go to extremes during the moratorium in order to test the "rock bottom of some truth" before committing themselves to a particular way of life (1968, p. 236). These extremes may include not only rebelliousness but also deviant, delinquent, and self-destructive behaviors. It is only when such tendencies defeat the purpose of the moratorium by fixating the adolescent or necessitating a permanent retreat to primitive behavior that they become psychopathological. Take for example a *negative identity*, which in many ways is the adolescent counterpart of the toddler's negativism. Here the adolescent perversely identifies with all the roles that have been presented as undesirable or dangerous in the past; in despair of realizing the unattainable positive roles, the adolescents become "the last thing in the world" the parent would want them to be. If, in addition, authorities such as judges or mental health workers also label them as "delinquents" or "addicts" or "psychopaths" or "alcoholics," adolescents will make sure they become what the community has called them, thus abandoning the freedom of choice essential to a constructive outcome to the moratorium. (For a conceptualization of adolescent delinquency in terms of negative identity, see Gold and Petronio, 1980.) In a

like manner, the depression and moodiness of the normal adolescent is different from the *despair* evidenced in the abandonment of the desire to grow, expand, and find new meanings in life. The devaluing of academic achievement also differs from a *work paralysis*, which suffocates even recreational and avocational activities in a pall of futility, just as an antireligious stance differs from an immobilizing *confusion of values*. Thus the difference between normality and deviance is a quantitative one, psychopathology not only being more extreme but (and this is the essence) representing a retreat from the struggle to establish an identity rather than a progression—no matter how painful to the adolescent and to society—along the way to reaching that goal.

In addition to Erikson's conceptualization, DSM-III-R furnishes three criteria that are helpful for determining when drug abuse exists. First, there is a *pattern of pathological use* which, depending on the substance, may be marked by an inability to cut down or stop use, a need for daily use in order to function adequately, or continued use despite a serious physical disorder which the substance will exacerbate. The second criterion is *impaired social or occupational functioning*. Impaired social functioning includes failure to meet important obligations to family and friends, display of erratic and impulsive behavior, inappropriate aggressiveness, and legal or criminal behavior due to drug abuse, such as a car accident due to intoxication. Occupational impairment includes missing work or school or being unable to function effectively in such settings because of the effects of drugs. The final criterion is a *duration* of one month.

The simplest *empirical* answer to the question, What makes an individual become a drug abuser rather than a drug user? is early onset of drug use. One-half of the males and two-fifths of the females who use drugs before age 15 will become drug abusers. There is also a chance they will have other psychiatric symptoms such as antisocial behavior, depression, alcoholism, and phobias (Robins and Przybeck, 1985). Why should early onset be predictive of future abuse, or why should late onset protect the adolescent against abuse? Is it that the later initiators are more mature, or that they have evaded to some extent involvement with a problem-prone peer group, or that they are more conventional? The answers to such questions await future research (Jessor, 1985).

Precursors of Drug Use in Early Childhood

With drug use beginning in junior high school, its precursors are being sought during the grammar school period. (Our presentation follows Hawkins, Lishner, and Catalano, 1985, unless otherwise noted.) Among *intraindividual variables,* aggressiveness and rebelliousness are related to subsequent drug use. One study, for example, showed that aggression in first-grade boys predicted drug use ten years later. Conversely, a strong investment in prosocial behavior prevents both antisocial behavior and drug use. Other intraindividual variables, including self-esteem, locus of control, sensation seeking, and psychopathology, are only weak predictors of drug use. In the cognitive realm, nearly all fourth to sixth graders are knowledgeable about marijuana and one-quarter of kindergarten children at least know what it is (Bush and Iannotti, 1985).

Among *family* variables, parental modeling of drug use and a direct role in regard to parental drug use are particularly important in the grammar school years. Thus the more family members use alcohol or marijuana, the more likely it is that the children will use them. Children's serving alcohol or buying cigarettes for their parents is also related to future drug use. By contrast, parental beliefs have little effect (Bush and Iannotti, 1985). This finding that modeling is more potent in determining children's behavior than are expressed beliefs is a common one in normal development. Generally positive family relations discourage initiation into drug use, even if parents themselves are users, while disharmonious family interactions increase the likelihood of both imitating drug-using parents and of becoming a user. While parental variables are important, their relative strength as an etiologic variable is disputed.

The data concerning *school* are mixed. While low performance in grammar school is related to subsequent drug use, it is not clear whether the relation is a direct one or whether it is due to antisocial acting out in school, which results in low performance as well as being a precursor of drug use in its own right.

Early *peer relations* have not been sufficiently investigated to cast any light on how they influence future drug users who are still in grammar school. Research on this most important variable is clearly needed. Among *superordinate* variables, socioeconomic status, race, and ethnicity have not been conclusively shown to be related to drug use.

Treatment

Drug abuse comprises such heterogeneous behaviors that we cannot expect a single treatment modality to be appropriate to them all. The goal is to decrease dependence on the drug while developing attitudes and a life-style that will minimize the likelihood of future drug involvement (Schwartz and Johnson, 1985). Unfortunately, no specific treatment or combination of treatments has been successful in eliminating drug abuse, much less proving itself to be the treatment of choice.

Drugs that produce a physical dependency, such as alcohol and heroin, require a detoxification program under medical management. The physiological and psychological withdrawal reactions may be treated with tranquilizers, while vitamins and a high-carbohydrate diet combat the effects of poor nourishment. In the case of heroin addiction, methadone—a synthetic opiatelike drug—can be substituted. It blocks the craving for heroin, can be taken orally rather than intravenously, and has a longer-lasting effect. Moreover, since it is legally available, it eliminates the necessity of engaging in criminal activities to support the habit. However, methadone maintenance involves substituting one drug for another and does not alter a life-style that may include criminal activities and the use of other drugs such as alcohol and barbiturates.

Individual treatment of drug abuse has been unsuccessful, whether it is psychotherapeutically or behaviorally oriented. The former often requires a willingness to change and the formation of a positive relationship between client and therapist, both of which may be lacking in the drug abuser. The latter often involves pairing of a noxious stimulus, such as a nausea-inducing chemical or a painful electric shock, with the drug, and its effectiveness has not been clearly established (Callner, 1975). Psychotherapy combined with medical treatment fails to help the majority of addicts, although those who are older and are in the upper socioeconomic group relapse less frequently.

Outpatient counseling programs represent another approach to treatment and are useful when the drug abuser is unwilling to become involved in residential treatment. Here the individual is provided support in developing a drug-free life-style, is given opportunities for acquiring vocational skills, and is offered help in dealing with personal problems through individual or group therapy (Schwartz and Johnson, 1985).

Group approaches to treatment have met with some success, although satisfactory evaluative data are often lacking. Alcoholics Anonymous capitalizes on group support. Each new member is assigned an exalcoholic who is available at any time to give advice and to help the member resist the temptation to drink. During regularly held meetings, members confess, and recovered alcoholics give inspirational speeches. There is a strong religious element, members being encouraged to rely on the healing power of God.

Various total living environments have also been tried. Some are modeled after Synanon and are run by exaddicts. The structure is that of an autocratic family, the new members first being given menial household chores but gradually being allowed to do more responsible work as they can abstain from taking drugs. Group therapy sessions allow emotional catharsis, while the staff constantly tries to instill spiritual values which will lead to self-reliance. The Synanon approach strives to create new social roles for its members who remain within the organization. Other approaches also utilize the principles of the therapeutic living arrangement but eventually try to help its members make the transition back to the community.

The difficulty in judging treatment *effectiveness* is that many of the programs have not been adequately evaluated, and well-controlled studies with objective data are extremely rare. One of the more ambitious studies was conducted by Sells and Simpson (1980), who evaluated 3,131 individuals in fifty-two treatment units representing four kinds of treatment. The definition of success was drug abstinence along with absence of criminal and other severely deviant behaviors. A four-year follow-up study revealed that success rates ranged from 20 percent to 37 percent, which might suggest modest success were it not for the fact that individuals seen for drug-related intake evaluations but not treated showed a 21 percent success rate. The most successful programs involved methadone maintenance and a therapeutic community approach for heroin and other opiate addicts, and an outpatient drug-free program for polydrug (excluding marijuana) and nonaddicted opiate users. Outpatient detoxification programs were not successful. Other than this unsuccessful program, the programs had a lower rate of highly unfavorable outcomes than the untreated controls, ranging from 14 to 16 percent compared with 24.5 percent. Thus while certain forms of treatment may be better than no treatment at all, the success rate is low. One reason for this poor showing is that drug use and abuse may be deeply embedded in the individual's social network or may be related to other personality disturbances.

The only ray of hope in this dark picture comes from Robins's study of Vietnam veterans (Robins, Davis, and Nurco, 1974). She found a 95 percent remission rate for narcotics addicts after their discharge in the United States. While it is reassuring to learn that heroin addiction is not necessarily permanent, we are also left wondering how the dramatic change in living involved in shifting from a wartime to a peacetime existence could be replicated or even simulated in any known therapeutic setting.

Prevention

The recognition of the complexity of drug use and the importance of developmental factors has important implications for prevention. For one thing, it means that prevention cannot be regarded as a single measure applicable to individuals of all ages and stages of involvement. (Our presentation follows Hawkins, Lishner, and Catalano, 1985, except when otherwise noted.) Prevention can have a number of distinct *goals.* One goal might be the prevention of drug abuse, because abuse

takes the heaviest toll in terms of personal and interpersonal suffering, and because drug use tends to have run its course after early adulthood. A second goal might target specific drugs, such as tobacco because of its health hazard, or alcohol and marijuana because they serve as stepping stones to the use of illegal drugs. A third goal might involve delaying the age of first use because of the ominous relation between early use and subsequent abuse. The goal of preventing use of any and all drugs is the most controversial because the danger of experimental or recreational use of drugs is not a clear and present one. The issue of total prevention is, in turn, part of a broader one of how much conventional and unconventional behavior is desirable during the adolescent transition. Do wild colts make good horses, or does "wildness" prepare the way for antisocial acting out in adulthood? Will the conventional adolescents be imprisoned in conventionality all their adult life, or are they being prepared for the demands of mature, responsible behavior? Such questions concerning normal development need to be answered before the goal of total prevention can be properly evaluated.

Different goals require different *preventive measures.* Such measures in the grammar school period should concentrate on the home, on familial disharmony and parental drug use, and on other factors responsible for aggressive, rebellious behaviors in the child. Schools should also play a role in preventing feelings of failure, alienation, and rebelliousness. In the adolescent period, the focus should shift to peers. There has been some disillusionment with a purely informational approach and "scare techniques" because information has typically been provided by representatives of the very adult society against which the adolescents are rebelling. Murray and Perry (1985) describe a program that addresses itself and offers alternatives to the needs that drug use serves, such as social acceptance, stress reduction, recreation, and relief from boredom and loneliness. They claim that merely trying to teach adolescents to "Say no to drugs" is insufficient because it does nothing about the needs drug use serves. While the rationale of the program is plausible, its actual effectiveness remains to be seen.

HOMOSEXUALITY

The classification of psychopathologies has its own developmental history. The same social ferment in the 1960s that forced the recognition of poverty as a mental health problem (as well as an economic one) was instrumental in eliminating homosexuality from the American Psychiatric Association's list of psychopathologies in 1974. It was replaced by "sexual-orientation disturbances" in people who are "disturbed by, in conflict with, or wish to change" their homosexual orientation. However, the issue concerning homosexuality as psychopathology was hotly debated, and there were strong objections to the final decision. For our purposes, the controversy serves to organize the discussion around the question, Is there any basis from a developmental point of view for regarding homosexuality as deviant behavior, or is it better regarded as an alternate style of sexual behavior on a par with heterosexuality? To phrase the question in terms of our developmental variables (chapter 2), Does homosexuality divert the child from the path leading to a mature love relation?

Before starting, we need to repeat a lesson already learned: a given psychopathology can occur in conjunction with other psychopathologies while not being causally related to them. A homosexual adult might be neurotic or psychopathic or schizophrenic simply because he or she has multiple problems; there

is no reason to assume that a deviant choice of a sexual partner is the core problem. Moreover, intrapersonal factors determine how disruptive homosexuality itself might be. In certain instances a strong urge to engage in homosexual behavior may precipitate a terrifying panic; in other cases, a homosexual relation may be regarded as acceptable and fulfilling; in still other cases, for an exceptionally withdrawn, isolated individual, a homosexual attachment may be the one human contact preventing a general personality deterioration.

Definition

The simplest definition of homosexuality is sexual behavior between people of the same sex. More differentiated definitions add the elements of frequency of sexual behavior and number of partners in a given time span. At a more covert level, homosexuality has been defined as a desire for same-sex contact and/or conscious sexual arousal from thinking about or seeing persons of the same sex. In such instances, the individuals may or may not engage in homosexual behavior because fear or moral scruples prevent them. Some definitions locate homosexuality in the self-image and require that individuals consider themselves homosexual regardless of their actual behavior. Finally, there are latent homosexuals, whose desires are either unconscious or who will turn to homosexual behavior only when heterosexual outlets are unavailable, such as in prison. When diverse behaviors are subsumed under a common label, one can expect a contradictory and confused literature.

In spite of varying definitions, there is general agreement concerning certain characteristics of homosexuality. The landmark research of Kinsey, Pomeroy, and Martin (1948) showed that, rather than being dichotomous, there is a continuum of behavior from heterosexual to homosexual. The Kinsey study found, for example, that 37 percent of adult males had one homosexual experience to orgasm since adolescence, 18 percent had as much homosexual as heterosexual experience, and 13 percent had homosexual impulses, which they did not act on. The incidence of homosexuality in women was lower, being only 13 percent. The estimate of individuals who are exclusively homosexual in terms of persistent and exclusive behavior ranges between 2 and 5 percent (West, 1967). Homosexuals vary as widely as heterosexuals in behavior and personality, the effeminate male and the tough female representing only a small minority. Nor can homosexuals be classified in terms of their assuming an "active" or a "passive" role in their sexual relations; both males and females alternate between the roles. Homosexuality is distinct from *transvestism*, which involves obtaining sexual gratification through dressing in the clothes of the opposite sex. While some transvestites may be homosexuals they typically masturbate in private. Homosexuality should also be distinguished from *transsexualism*, which is a gender identification with the opposite sex; for example, from early childhood a boy may be convinced that he really is a girl and has been assigned the wrong body. It is the transsexual who typically seeks sex reassignment through surgery and sex hormones. Most transvestites and transsexuals are male. (For further discussion, see Bootzin and Acocella, 1988.)

MULTIPLE DIMENSIONS OF SEX   A number of dimensions of sexuality will be relevant to our discussion. There is variability within and there are complex relations among these dimensions.

First, there is *anatomic sex differentiation*. Variability ranges from distinct differentiation into male or female at one extreme to her-

maphroditism (in which a single individual has both male and female reproductive organs) at the other extreme and includes instances in which the external genitalia appear to be at variance with the internal reproductive system owing to a physiological anomaly; for example, a malformation of the infant's penis may result in his being called a girl (Money and Ehrhardt, 1972). Then there is *gender identity* or the self-classification as male or female which develops in the toddler and preschool period. It is not unusual for children during this period to believe they can change their gender identity merely by changing their appearance. And while cultures may prescribe distinct *sex roles*, individuals combine all degrees of masculinity and femininity in their behavior, as we shall soon see. Then there is *erotic preference*, which involves the ideal choice of a sexual object. Finally, there is the capacity to enjoy and sustain a *love relationship* over time. Erotic preferences are numerous—they can involve not only the same or the opposite sex but also children, animals, and inanimate objects such as clothes—while a love relationship can last from a year to a lifetime.

Just to give a sample of the complex interrelations that exist among these varying dimensions, an infant who is physiologically a girl can be raised as a boy because of an anomaly of external genitals, while a preschool boy with no anomalies can become convinced that he is really a girl—a conviction that might last into his adult years and eventuate in his seeking a sex change. A woman may submit to intercourse with her husband as required by her sex role while ideally preferring a homosexual partner, while prisoners or sailors might engage in homosexual behavior not from preference but because only males are available.

CONCEPTUALIZATIONS   In chapter 2 we learned that there were two quite different conceptions of sexual development. The first is in terms of sex role and involves the learning of behaviors and feelings society regards as appropriate for the male and the female. This conceptualization is favored by social-learning theorists, who account for sexual development in terms of reinforcement by and imitation of socializing agents. The psychoanalytic theory views sexual development in terms of eroticized intimacy, which begins in infancy and goes through the special transformations that comprise the psychosexual stages. Psychoanalysts are concerned with understanding the love relations that exist between and among individuals. Their term for this relation is *object choice*.

Sex role and object choice are not only conceptually distinct but behaviorally distinct as well. In adults, for example, transvestism can accompany all degrees of heterosexual and homosexual preferences. Or again, certain heterosexual men are aroused by the sight and touch of female clothing, especially underwear, which they put on in order to increase the pleasure of their heterosexual foreplay and intercourse. Thus, feminine sex-role behavior can serve a masculine sexual preference.

In reviewing the literature on homosexuality, consequently, the distinction between sex role and object choice must be kept in mind, so we do not assume that findings concerning one automatically apply to the other. Incidentally, the literature often implies that the difference is a theoretical one involving the psychoanalytic and social-learning theories, rather than an actual distinction between two aspects of sexuality.

The Organic Context

As with many psychopathologies, homosexuality has multiple roots. We will now examine the most important of these etiologic factors in detail, beginning with the organic context.

Until recently, the case for an organic etiology of homosexuality was weak. Certain studies suggested a *genetic* component in that they found a higher concordance rate for homosexuality among identical twins than among fraternal twins and a higher rate of homosexuality among brothers than among males in general. However, some findings failed to replicate, while others could not satisfactorily eliminate a determining role for the environment. Studies of *circulating sex hormones* have also failed to find convincing evidence of differences between adult homosexuals and heterosexuals. However, a number of experimental studies of animals and a smaller group of studies of humans suggest that the key to understanding both homosexuality and heterosexuality lies in the *prenatal brain differentiation*. (Our presentation follows Ellis and Ames, 1987.)

Sexual orientation is determined primarily by the degree to which the nervous system is exposed to testosterone and certain other sex hormones while neuro-organization is taking place in the fetus. According to Ellis and Ames's (1987) hypothesis, there are two stages to this brain organization, the first of which determines sexual orientation, or what we call erotic preference. If the level of the sex hormones is in the typical female range, the individual will prefer males on sexual maturity; if the level in the brain is in the typical male range, the postpubertal preference will be for female sexual partners. Sexually typical behavior, or what we have called sex role behavior, is determined in the second stage, again due to the biochemical processes determining masculinization and feminization of the brain. The crucial timing seems to be between the middle of the second month and the middle of the fifth month of gestation. Sexual inversions, such as homosexuality, occur either because of unusual features in the genetic programs that control these biochemical processes or because of external agents that interfere with such processes.

Ellis and Ames (1987) cite a number of studies in which such inversion has taken place in humans. Certain *drugs* taken by the pregnant mother can be one cause of sexual inversion. Mothers who took various types of progestins during pregnancy had genetic females with ambiguous external genitals which were surgically feminized. The infants were reared as females, but their sex-type behavior was highly masculine although, at puberty, they did not become homosexual. Thus the drug affected sexually typical behavior, which is determined in the second stage of fetal development, but not sexual orientation, which is determined in the first.

Ellis and Ames (1987) assign only a minor role to environmental factors. Stress on the mother during pregnancy is one such factor. For example, the significant increase in the proportion of homosexuals born in Germany during and immediately after the Second World War has been attributed to the unusual stress on German citizens (Dorner et al., 1980). Admittedly, the causal explanation is speculative. The only postnatal influence Ellis and Ames consider is lack of social experience with peers, a condition that has been studied only in animals. Other evidence against an environmental position is the failure of therapy to alter sexual orientation when it is purely homosexual; the most favorable prognostic sign is the amount of heterosexual experience the client has had, which, in turn, suggests a bisexual orientation.

Ellis and Ames's (1987) case for an organic etiology for homosexuality is a strong one, but has not gone unchallenged. Moore (1985) argues that the evidence fails to support the notion that early hormones affect behavior directly through brain differentiation. Rather, she believes there is a constant interplay between hormonal and external, social factors, each influencing the other to a significant degree. Either homosexuality or heterosexuality can result from this interplay.

While we can conclude that Ellis and Ames's (1987) case might not be proven, we also must recognize that there is now evidence for an organic factor in homosexuality and that an extreme environmental position is not tenable. While it is best to think in terms of an interaction, little is known of the relative weight to assign to organic and environmental influences.

There is one final complication, and this concerns the nature of human sexuality itself. While we are dealing with the choice of the same sex or the opposite sex, such a choice does not exhaust the sources of erotic gratification. The range is impressive and includes children and animals, inflicting and receiving pain, viewing or exhibiting sexual organs, and inanimate objects such as shoes and dolls. It is highly unlikely that a physiological explanation alone could account for the many manifestations of sexual behavior in adults.

Intrapersonal Variables

THE EROTIC DIMENSION One of the most comprehensive studies of homosexuals and heterosexuals—and one to which we will refer frequently—was conducted by Bell, Weinberg, and Hammersmith (1981), who interviewed 979 adult homosexuals and 477 adult heterosexual men and women in the San Francisco area. In analyzing their data, they used a technique called a path analysis, which enabled them to distinguish variables directly related to adult sexual preference, those with an indirect effect, and those with no effect.

One of Bell, Weinberg, and Hammersmith's most provocative findings was the important role that children's *homosexual feelings*, as distinguished from homosexual behavior, played in determining the ultimate adult sexual preference. This does not mean that all future homosexuals had such early feelings; only 59 percent of the adult population did, in contrast to only 1 percent of adult heterosexuals. However, the relation was so strong that homosexual feelings should not be considered an independent childhood variable that predicts adult sexual preference, but part and parcel of the same homosexual variable that runs from childhood to adulthood.

Homosexual arousal occurred somewhat earlier for future homosexuals than heterosexual arousal did for future heterosexuals (11.6 years versus 12.9 years). It is these feelings more than homosexual activities which appear to be crucial to the development of adult homosexuality, since they occurred typically three years or so before the first homosexual activities, such as mutual masturbation or oral-genital contact. However, the data suggested that, for black homosexuals, homosexual activities were important precursors of adult homosexuality for unknown reasons. Finally, homosexual men and women did not particularly lack heterosexual experience during childhood and adolescence; however, they found such experiences ungratifying. The same was true of the heterosexual adults in that those who had homosexual experiences found those experiences ungratifying.

PERSONALITY CHARACTERISTICS The strongest predictor of adult sexual preference in the Bell, Weinberg, and Hammersmith (1981) study was *gender conformity,* or what we would call sex role behavior. As children, half of the future homosexuals preferred the activities typical of the opposite sex and disliked sex-appropriate activities; e.g., boys did not like sports and rough-and-tumble play, preferring music, playing house, drawing, cross-sex dressing, and pretending to be a girl. Again,

this finding should not be taken to mean that all future homosexuals had atypical gender traits or interests while they were growing up; about half the homosexual men had typical masculine interests while nearly a quarter of the heterosexual men had feminine interests.

Interpersonal Variables

PARENTAL RELATIONS In seeming agreement with other studies, Bell, Weinberg, and Hammersmith (1981) found that homosexuals, more than heterosexuals, felt close to their mothers, whom they also viewed as strong and dominant. However, there was no evidence that they identified with their mothers. Homosexuals more than heterosexuals had a negative relation with their father marked by anger, dislike, and lack of closeness, admiration, and respect. This negative relationship went along with a weak identification with the father, who was perceived as ineffectual. The unexpected finding and the unique contribution of Bell, Weinberg, and Hammersmith's path analysis is that these early parental relations had either no effect on adult gender preference or a very weak one at best. What influence they had was primarily an indirect one in that, taken together, they played a role, although not a major role, in determining the child's gender conformity.

There is one more finding relevant to the issue of the role of parents. The special subgroup of adults who sought psychotherapy were different from the population as a whole in that having a cold, distant, hostile father did play an important role in the etiology of their sexual preference. This means, for one thing, that therapists wrongly generalized from their clients to the population of homosexuals as a whole, a common pitfall in clinical research. But it also suggests that the quality of the father–son relation may be important not to the development of homosexuality but to the degree of distress that accompanies that sexual preference in adulthood.

Capitalizing on the general finding that cross-gender behavior (or what Bell, Weinberg, and Hammersmith call gender nonconformity) is one of the best predictors of adult homosexuality, Green (1987) studied sixty-six boys between 4 and 12 years of age (average age 7.1 years), whose parents had contacted a clinic because of their concern over their sons' effeminate behavior. Specifically, the boys preferred clothes, toys, and companionship of girls, evaded such traditional sex-typed activities as sports and rough-and-tumble play, and more than once expressed a wish to be a girl. The comparison group consisted of fifty-six nonclinic families matched for demographic variables including age, sibling position, parents' marital status, educational level, and ethnic background. Of the forty-four boys available for a follow-up evaluation at adolescence and young manhood, three-fourths were homosexuals or bisexuals, while only one of the boys in the control group had become homosexual. Green's (1987) retrospective data from parents has the advantage over those of Bell, Weinberg, and Hammersmith (1981) in that they were collected during childhood and might have been less subject to the distortions of recall; however, the fact that he selected a clinical sample might have introduced a certain amount of bias.

Green's (in Roberts, Green, Williams, and Goodman, 1987) data permitted him to raise an intriguing question: Are the factors responsible for cross-gender behavior in a group of feminine boys the same or different from those responsible for cross-gender behavior in boys considered masculine (since even masculine boys display some feminine behaviors)? Interestingly, he found only one common element, which was absence of the father. Other than that, the pattern of variables was different. In the feminine group, the mother's low level of premarital sexual experience, the father's desire for a daughter when the mother was pregnant, and the mother's approval of her son's early cross-gender behavior were significantly related to the boy's feminine behavior. In the comparison group, the father's masculinity was negatively related while parental dislike for household nudity, masturbation, and social sex play (a general measure of conservative sexual standards) was positively related to the boy's femininity, along with the serendipitous factors of the son's perceived beauty as an infant and his small size.

The authors rightly conclude that the findings do not readily fit into any model of sexual identity formation. One might say that, in the feminine group, the father's desire for a girl and the mother's approval of feminine behavior might fit a social learning or reinforcement model. However, the overall results are more impressive for the variables that did not turn out to be significant as for those that did. Among the former category were the mother's desire for a girl, her domination and masculinity, the unavailability of the father in intact homes, and his initial approval of feminine behavior. According to a social learning or reinforcement model, these should have contributed to feminine behavior as well. One might also think that having a small beautiful infant would set the stage for parental feminization of the boy, but this variable was not significant in the feminine group.

Where do these studies leave us? First, Bell, Weinberg, and Hammersmith (1981) and Roberts, Green, Williams, and Goodman (1987) agree that biological factors play an important role in the etiology of homosexuality. The question now is, How much of a role? Moreover, both studies conclude that there is no simple relation between parental behavior and eventual sexual preference. Rather, the adult outcome is probably due to a complex sequencing of events functioning as "choice points" which can be decided in a number of ways, each choice inclining the child toward a homosexual or a bisexual or a heterosexual adult orientation. In the psychoanalytic camp the same image of sexual development was expressed by Anna Freud (1965), who wrote, "the balance between heterosexuality and homosexuality during the whole period of childhood is . . . precarious, and the scales are . . . readily tipped in one direction or the other by a multitude of influences" (p. 197). She concludes that a person's final sexual orientation is not decided until after puberty.

ADULT RELATIONSHIPS While interesting in its own right, the new model of the development of sexual preference and erotic choice fails to answer our basic question: Does homosexuality jeopardize the chance for establishing a *mature love relationship*? The most relevant study in this regard was done by Bell and Weinberg (1978), who studied 979 homosexual adults and 425 matched heterosexuals in the San Francisco Bay area. Unlike other studies, which treat homosexuals as a group, these investigators divided their population into five empirically derived subgroups.
(1) The Close-Coupled homosexuals would correspond to the "happily married" heterosexuals. They were living with a same-sex partner, had few sexual problems, engaged in relatively little cruising (that is, seeking contacts for the sole purpose of a temporary sexual outlet) but were not worried when they did, had few difficulties in finding and maintaining affection from their partners, were sexually active, and had few regrets about being homosexual. (2) The Open-Coupled, while also living with a special sexual partner, were not happy in the arrangement. They tended to seek sexual satisfactions outside

the relationship through cruising but were worried about this activity. While they were quite active sexually they were concerned about their partner's or their own responsiveness to sexual requests. They also tended to regret their homosexuality. (3) The Functionals come closest to the image of the "swinging single": they scored high on the number of sexual partners and level of sexual activity, low on concern over their homosexuality. (4) Like the Functionals, the Dysfunctionals also had a high level of sexual activity and many partners but had a number of sexual problems in regard to their adequacy and regretted being homosexual. They most closely conform to the stereotype of the tormented homosexual, being poorly adjusted not only sexually but socially and psychologically as well. (5) Finally, the Asexuals were not "coupled" and rated low on sexual activity, number of partners, and amount of cruising. They had more sexual problems than the group as a whole, more regrets over their homosexuality, and were less exclusively homosexual than the group as a whole. They lead lonely, solitary, withdrawn lives.

Since Bell and Weinberg did not similarly classify their heterosexual group, no comparison of categories is possible. However, as they stand, the categories clearly refute any stereotype of "the homosexual" as well as the idea that homosexuals somehow have different kinds of relationships with their sexual partners. Certainly, heterosexuals also are happily or unhappily married, happy or unhappy swinging singles, or isolates.

While the categories were applicable to men and women, interesting differences were found. The lesbian was more apt to be involved in a quasi-marriage requiring a high degree of fidelity (that is, there were many Close-Couples); lacking this, they tended to find their homosexuality problematical, since they did not enjoy brief, varied sexual relations (that is, there were few Functionals).

Males were less satisfied with quasi-marriages (there were more Open- than Close-Couples) but could enjoy the pleasures of being "swinging singles" (or Functionals).

The homosexual's psychological adjustment was related to sex and category. Generally speaking, lesbians were as well adjusted as their heterosexual counterparts while the homosexual male was less well adjusted. On the positive side, the homosexual male and, to a less extent, the lesbian experienced more happiness and exuberance than the heterosexuals. Among categories, the Dysfunctionals, Asexuals, and to a less extent, the Open-Coupled males accounted largely for the greater degree of maladjustment in homosexuals. Signs of lowered adjustment included psychosomatic symptoms, lowered self-acceptance, loneliness, increased worry, depression, tension, paranoia, and suicidal feelings. The Close-Couple and Functional males were generally as well adjusted as their heterosexual counterparts except, interestingly, for heightened loneliness and tension in the latter.

About half the males and two-thirds of the females had no regret concerning being homosexual. Those who were unhappy listed as reasons social rejection, restrictive opportunities for social participation, not being able to have children, and loneliness.

The work histories of male homosexuals were no different from those of male heterosexuals in terms of number of jobs held and job satisfaction. Approximately one-quarter felt restricted, but 11 percent found their homosexuality to be an advantage in obtaining a job. Lesbians had more job changes than female heterosexuals, but there was no difference in job satisfaction. There were no differences between homosexuals and heterosexuals in regard to having close friends, but the pattern of friendships differed, homosexuals being less favorably impressed with the

opposite sex than heterosexuals and having fewer opposite-sex friends.

In sum, Bell and Weinberg's data clearly show that adult homosexuality per se should not be equated with psychopathology, although it increases the likelihood that specific categories of males will be less well-adjusted than heterosexual males in general. These findings are illuminating, but they are not totally satisfying for our purposes. One of our major concerns has been the development of love, and in this area the psychosexual theory has proven the best guide. Freud recognized that homosexuality has no necessary connection with mental illness (Bootzin and Acocella, 1988), but he did maintain that it necessarily limits the ability to establish and maintain a relationship that is mutually satisfying both psychologically and sexually. And it is on just this critical issue of the ability to love maturely that data are incomplete.

Bell and Weinberg's study suggests that Freud was wrong in assuming a necessary limitation in the ability to love maturely. The impression of some Close-Couples is that they had achieved a stable, mature, mutually satisfactory relationship. But does homosexuality decrease the likelihood that such a relationship can be established? We do not know. Approximately 10 percent of males and 30 percent of females in Bell and Weinberg's report could be classified as Close-Couples, but comparable data on their heterosexual controls are lacking.

Before leaving the topic of adult adjustment, it is worth noting that the variables related to the development of homosexuality in the Bell, Weinberg, and Hammersmith (1981) study did not differentiate the five patterns of adult adjustment. Thus, while that study helped us understand the development of homosexuality, it tells us nothing about developmental precursors that make homosexuality either a sustained, fulfilling love relationship or an unstable relationship fraught with bitterness and dissatisfaction. Aside from the finding that homosexuals who sought psychotherapy had cold, distant, hostile fathers, the critical question concerning precursors remains to be answered.

Finally, there is the issue of parenthood. Certain homosexuals were unhappy because they were unable to have children, which suggests an important limitation, a lack of fulfillment in their lives. It should not be inferred that homosexuals cannot be good parents since there is evidence that the children of lesbian mothers do not differ from those raised by single heterosexual mothers or from the population of children in general in regard to their psychosexual development and their general adjustment (Golombok, Spencer, and Rutter, 1983). Nor should it be inferred that all heterosexual couples who choose not to have children are necessarily unfulfilled. But in the overall evaluation of homosexuality, we should know its implications in regard to the desire to become parents and the ability to be good parents. From our perspective, the fate of the abilities to love and to parent lie more at the heart of the "homosexual issue" than any concern about mental illness or general adjustment.

IS SOCIETY TO BLAME   A strong case has been made that the homosexual's psychological disturbance is the result of the prejudice and discrimination built into the religious and legal fabric of our society, as well as the ridicule and contempt homosexuals encounter in their daily lives. If homosexuals were treated as human beings who differ only in their sexual preferences, the argument goes, then they would be as well adjusted as heterosexuals.

Certainly, prejudice and discrimination could well be primary roots of the homosexual's disturbance. In this respect he or she is much like the juvenile delinquent, the mentally retarded, the psychotic, and a host of other individuals who have suffered from being labeled mentally ill or emotionally disturbed. Our society has been unjustifiably punitive and shamefully remiss in its attitude toward and treatment of those members who are regarded as deviant.

Yet recognizing the role of society is not the same as regarding it as the sole etiologic agent. With children, this single-cause hypothesis seems particularly unconvincing. The literature contains hints that other than social forces are at work. True, some effeminate boys report that being teased was a source of bitter unhappiness, but their effeminacy was not. However, there are also reports (West, 1967) of adults feeling angry at being tied close to their mothers, at being babied and restricted, at being forced into feminine activities and hindered in making dates. Here homosexuality seems definitely to have gone against the grain and to have resulted from pressure on the child to fulfill parental needs. Such a pattern of family dynamics is familiar to the clinician and may well exist independent of social forces.

Although we cannot fail to recognize the importance of the social context, there is inadequate evidence that it is the sole etiologic agent in producing increased maladjustment in certain homosexual adults. Unless such evidence is forthcoming, the multideterminant model is preferred.

Summary

The question whether homosexuality is a psychopathology cannot be answered categorically. There is evidence that homosexuality does not preclude the development of a mature love relationship and that it may not be incompatible with good parenting, although evidence for the latter is preliminary. There is also evidence that, throughout childhood and into adulthood, society's punitive treatment causes needless suffering. Yet there are other instances in which future homosexuals grow up in an exploiting and neglectful family to become adults who are resentful of their treatment, unfulfilled sexually, and dissatisfied with their lot. In such instances, homosexuality can be considered as deviant development. The challenge is to determine the forces that make the difference between the groups, so that the former can be given the social acceptance it deserves while the latter can be given the psychotherapeutic help it needs.

Thus far, these discussions have implicitly assumed that the developing child is not significantly deviant either intellectually or physiologically. The assumption has not always proved correct; in certain instance of autism, for example, both mental retardation and organic brain pathology have been shown to be present. However, the etiologic import of intellectual and organic deviations has had to be demonstrated. The procedure will now be reversed, and mental retardation or a lack of organic intactness will be assumed, so that we may ask, What developmental deviations—if any—ensue?

11

The Developmental
Consequences
of Mental Retardation

W̲e shall use the American Association on Mental Deficiency's definition of mental retardation, which is: significantly sub-average general intellectual functioning existing concurrently with deficits in adaptive behavior and manifested during the developmental period. It is an interesting definition that deserves to be examined in detail. But first we shall sample a few of the conditions that may result in mental retardation (MR).

ETIOLOGY

A number of *genetic anomalies* can be accompanied by MR, the best known being Down's syndrome (mongolism). Children with this anomaly have three number 21 chromosomes instead of the normal two. Hence, the condition is also called "trisomy 21." However, Down's syndrome can also be caused by a number of other chromosome abnormalities. These children have distinctive physical features: almond-shaped eyes that slant upward; a flat nasal bridge; a relatively small mouth with a furrowed tongue that tends to protrude intermittently in infancy; small, abnormally shaped and positioned teeth; small, square hands with a short first finger and a single crease running across the palm. Their IQs vary widely from profound to mild retardation, although the modal mental age of school-age children is approximately that of a $3\frac{1}{2}$- to 5-year-old.

Phenylketonuria (PKU) is caused by a specific recessive gene. The affected infant lacks certain liver enzymes necessary for metabolizing the amino acid phenylalanine. Instead, phenylalanine accumulates and is converted to phenylpyruvic acid, a toxic substance that damages the brain. Although not totally satisfactory, screening methods based on the newborn's blood plasma can detect PKU, and a special phenylalanine-restricted diet can prevent retardation. The successfully treated child's intelligence is within the average range but somewhat lower than the intellectual level of the family.

A host of *pre- and postnatal* factors can damage the central nervous system and result in MR. Rubella (German measles) contracted by the mother during the first trimester of pregnancy can cause a number of impairments, MR being one. Syphilis is another cause of MR as well as of fetal death. Exposure to massive doses of radiation in the first few months of pregnancy, chronic alcoholism, age (35 years or older), and severe emotional stress throughout pregnancy are among the numerous maternal factors that increase the risk of MR in the infant. Prematurity and prenatal asphyxia (oxygen deprivation during or immediately after delivery) are hazards at birth. Postnatal sources of mental subnormality are head injuries (most commonly resulting from automobile accidents and child abuse), encephalitis, and meningitis (inflammations of the brain resulting from infections by bacteria, viruses, or tuberculosis organisms), particularly if they occur during infancy.

Clinical disorders associated with MR include cerebral palsy, seizure disorders (epilepsy), and lead and mercury poisoning from chemical pollutants ingested by the child (for example, by eating lead-based paint or shell-fish that have absorbed methyl mercury from industrial waste).

The foregoing list is intended solely to provide a quick overview of genetic and physical etiologies. In each instance the relation to MR, the degree of retardation, and the percent of affected children vary widely; it would be erroneous to conclude, for example, that all children with cerebral palsy or with seizures are also retarded, since a considerable portion are not. (A detailed account of the complex relation between etiology and mental retardation can be found in Wicks-Nelson and Israel, 1984.)

Social factors play an important role in mental subnormality. Children's IQ scores tend to be positively correlated with the socioeconomic status of their families, the effect becoming progressively more manifest as the child grows older. Social class even affects the long-range prognosis of some of the pre- and postnatal sources of MR listed above. Sameroff and Chandler (1975) conclude that social status tends to reduce or amplify intellectual deficits in high-risk infants. In advantaged families infants who suffer perinatal complications generally show no or small residual effects in follow-up studies, while infants from lower-class homes with identical medical histories show significant retardation subsequently. They conclude: "Social and economic status appear to have much stronger influence on the course of development than perinatal history" (p. 209).

Children with MR caused by *psychosocial disadvantage* function typically, but not necessarily, at a mildly retarded level, but have no clear cerebral pathology. The family is impoverished, MR always occurring in its immediate members and often in the larger family circle. Another label is "cultural-familial MR," reflecting the assumption that both genetic and environmental factors play a role in its production (Achenbach, 1982). There are many reasons for the connection between poverty and retardation. All the pre- and postnatal risk factors previously discussed are more prevalent among the poor, while health care is grossly inadequate. Families tend to be large, the home may be disorganized and lacking in the kind of personal attention and physical objects such as books and "readiness" games that promote intellectual growth and prepare the young child for school. Parents may feel overwhelmed by problems of everyday living, lonely, and discouraged, preferring the child to be passive and conforming.

It is important to avoid stereotypes of "the poor," since there is a great diversity of behaviors among them; nor should we infer that brutality, neglect, disorganization, and other conditions inimical to intellectual growth are unknown in middle- and upper-class families. It is just that among the poor, such conditions can be found with greater frequency.

Finally, MR can be due to *severe emotional disturbances*. Whether it is possible or desirable to differentiate conditions in which the emotional problem underlies retardation from conditions in which retardation underlies emotional problems is a controversial issue still being debated by experts. The chicken-and-egg etiologic puzzle remains to be solved not only by researchers but by the clinician faced with the problem of evaluating and diagnosing an individual child. In both instances, the solution has yet to be found.

THE INTELLECTUAL DEFICIT

Returning now to the definition of mental retardation, we see that the first criterion involves "significantly subaverage general intellectual functioning," typically as measured by a standardized intelligence test, such as the Stanford-Binet or the Wechsler Intelligence Scale for Children. Numerically, an IQ score that is more than two standard deviations below the mean is regarded as a significant deviation from average intelligence. Depending on the test, such a score is between 67 and 69. IQ scores are also used to make finer classifications within the retarded range, although the nomenclature varies. For purposes of this discussion, IQ scores in the range of 52 to 69 would classify a child as mildly retarded, 36 to 51 as moderately retarded, 20 to 35 as severely retarded, and below 20 as profoundly retarded. For educational purposes, children with IQs between 55 and 80 are classified as educable, those with IQs between 25 and 55 are classified as trainable, while those with IQs below 25 are classified as custodial.

Far more important than the classification of retardation is the attempt to understand the nature of the underlying intellectual deficit. The research on learning and memory is particularly rich.

Two Cognitive Theories

Two theories have been used by investigators trying to discover the differences in thinking between normal and retarded children. The *Piagetian* model has been used to test the hypothesis that retarded children go through the same stages of cognitive development (namely, sensorimotor, preoperational, concrete operations, and formal operations), but at a significantly slower rate than do normal children. The more popular model, however, has been *information processing*, which analyzes thinking into a series of processes that bridge the gap between incoming information and an individual's response. A simplified version of this model will be presented here. First, there is the *sensory register*, which receives information from the environment. While its capacity is relatively large, it can hold impressions only briefly. Consequently, some information is lost while the remainder is passed on to *short-term memory*, *attention* playing a role in determining what information is transmitted. Short-term memory can hold information only 30 seconds or so and is therefore a temporary working memory. Information is passed on to *long-term memory*, again with a certain loss. Long-term memory has a large capacity and can hold information more or less permanently. These are the structural features of the model which operate automatically. Other processes involve techniques that facilitate memory and are under the volitional control of the individual. These processes or *strategies*, such as *rehearsal*, *mediation*, and *clustering*, are particularly important because they increase the chances that information will be held longer in short-term memory and will fit with information already stored in long-term memory. They will be discussed in detail later. In order to be useful, information has to be not only stored in memory but *retrieved* as well, although relatively little research has been done on retrieval in mentally retarded children. The challenge for investigators using the information processing model, therefore, is to atomize the learning process into its basic components to determine which are and which are not functioning as they do in children with normal intelligence.

ATTENTION TO RELEVANT CUES   In the basic research paradigm, which is called *discrimination learning*, the child is presented with a succession of stimuli, two or three at a time—say, objects differing in color, shape, and size—and on the basis of being told that a choice is either right or wrong, the child must learn to choose the correct stimulus—say, the red object. To illustrate: A girl is presented with a red circle and a blue square; guessing that "circle" is the correct response, she chooses the first figure and is told she made a correct choice. Next time a green circle and a blue triangle are presented and she is told her

choice of the circle is incorrect. She must now change her hypothesis. If she remembers the original circle was also red, she strongly suspects "red" to be the solution, which she verifies when another red object is shown. If she does not remember, she must adopt another hypothesis such as "triangle" or "green."

The learning curve for children of normal intelligence rises quickly at first and then levels off. For retarded children, choices are no better than chance for a number of trials, followed by rapid improvement.

Further investigation reveals that MR children often do not attend to relevant aspects of the situation; they are not asking themselves, Is it color? or shape? or size? On the contrary, they have a strong initial preference for position which they persist in using despite being told that their choice is frequently incorrect. Once they can break this irrelevant set, they learn rapidly. By the same token, if given a task in which position is the relevant cue—for example, the correct object is the first one—they learn as fast as or faster than normal children. In a special sense they are not slow learners but slow to catch on.

The retardate's preference for position responses has its counterpart in normal development, since position habits have been observed to interfere with discrimination learning in 1-year-olds. Such habits no longer seem to affect discrimination learning in the toddler and preschooler, although the evidence is not conclusive on this point. If the retardate's preference does in fact represent a fixation, it is one that goes back to earliest childhood and may significantly interfere with subsequent learning. (For a review of the studies see Reese and Lipsitt, 1970.)

However, investigators have not been satisfied with the general explanation of failure to attend to relevant cues and, using the information processing model, have set out to pinpoint the source or sources of malfunctioning. Most of the studies have been done on mild to moderately retarded children who are organically intact. (Unless otherwise specified, our presentation follows Borkowski, Peck, and Damberg, 1983.)

ATTENTION Mentally retarded children may have a basic attentional deficit. For example, they have slower reaction times in simple reaction time experiments involving a preparatory signal, such as a buzzer, followed by a stimulus, such as a light, to which the subject must respond as quickly as possible, by pressing a button, for example. Another kind of evidence of a decreased ability to maintain adequate attentional levels is the increase in off-task glancing both in simple and complex tasks. In regard to more complex functioning, there is evidence that mentally retarded children are deficient in the general attentional skills involved in the efficient accumulation of perceptual information, the detection of appropriate stimuli, and the translation of such stimuli into an appropriate response. Retarded children need more time to recognize the material than do normal children. They compound this inefficiency by reacting on the basis of less information and thereby making errors rather than taking more time to increase the chances of being correct.

MEMORY There is no evidence that retarded children have a deficit in *short-term memory*. The situation in regard to *long-term memory* is more complicated because long-term memory depends on the use of a number of strategies designed to aid retention and organize the incoming information. Such strategies include rehearsal, mediation, and clustering, and, as has already been stated, are under volitional control.

Rehearsal, which is clearly evident by the third grade in nonretardates, typically consists of repeating each new item along with all the prior ones; for example, in remembering a series of numbers a child may think, "six, six-three, six-three-eight," and so forth. Research indicates that MR children are deficient in rehearsal. If they are trained, their performance improves, but frequently they will not spontaneously use such aids. As with learning, they fail to do what they are capable of doing. And again, as with learning, this failure has its counterpart in normal development, since first-graders also make no use of their ability to rehearse (Flavell, 1977).

Remembering improves if incoming information is organized in a meaningful manner, a strategy called *clustering*. Present the average child with, say, a list comprised of three categories of words arranged in random order, and the child will tend to recall them by categories; for example, the words following "dog" will tend to be other animal words in the list, those following "apple" will be the other food words, etc. Both retarded and young children of normal intelligence show little evidence of using the strategy of clustering. While retardates can be taught to do so, once again they fail to use this aid spontaneously.

Memory is also facilitated by *mediation strategies*. The research paradigm here is paired-associate learning. Initially two stimuli are presented and subsequently, only the first is shown, with the child being asked to recall the second. Paired-associate learning can be facilitated if the child ties the two stimuli together in a meaningful manner; for example, *sun* and *bird* are more readily associated if related by, "the sun shines on the bird." While 5- to 6-year-olds can produce and use mediational strategies, younger children and retardates do not use them. If retarded children are provided with mediators or even instructed to generate them, their learning is significantly improved. However, if the experimenter no longer instructs the children, they may fail to continue using mediators on their own. Training them to "get into the habit" has met with only limited success, being effective primarily with the mildly retarded. Thus it is not that MR children are deficient in and cannot use higher-level strategies; for some unknown reason, they fail spontaneously to use the abilities they possess (Robinson and Robinson, 1976).

The findings concerning a possible deficit in long-term memory are contradictory and inconclusive because it is exceedingly difficult to control all the prior processes in order to obtain an unconfounded evaluation of this one alone.

The retardate's deficit in *retrieval* of information has not been extensively studied. However, there is evidence that the same deficiency in categorization which hampers memory also adversely affects retrieval. It makes sense to assume that items stored singly in memory would be more difficult to retrieve than ones stored by categories that represent superordinate organizations of such individual items. As was the case in short-term memory, the deficit seems to be one of lack of use of category knowledge rather than lack of category knowledge itself.

More recently, two higher-order processes that affects memory strategies have been added to the information processing model. The first is called *metacognition*, which is an understanding or awareness of when, where, and how to employ a strategy. In short, it is information about one's own cognitive processing. Metamemory refers specifically to information about memory, such as knowing it takes more time and effort to memorize a long list of words than a short one. While metamemory improves dramatically with age in normal children, the rate of improvement is much slower in retardates; for example, they lag behind normals in estimating their memory span and in apportioning study time appropriately (Haywood, Meyers, and

Switzky, 1982). *Executive function* refers to the child's ability to select, monitor, evaluate, and revise strategies depending on the situation. Preliminary evidence indicates large individual differences among retardates, some being capable of sizing up task demands and inventing strategies that lead to good performance, others being deficient. The reasons for this variability remain to be discovered. However, executive functioning may be one of the most important keys to understanding mental deficiency. Much of the evidence so far suggests that retardates do not uniformly suffer from a cognitive deficit but that they may fail to use the abilities they possess. They do not grasp the principle that, regardless of the task, it is better to have a plan than to proceed haphazardly by trial and error, or that plans must be appropriate to the task at hand and must be monitored and changed as they are evaluated as being inefficient or inappropriate. This use of resources may be one cognitive component of what we have called initiative.

PROBLEM SOLVING   While problem solving was not in our simplified model of information processing, it has been a topic of interest among investigators. Problem solving typically requires attention, abstraction, planning, and logical thinking. The same failure to generate relevant hypotheses that mars discrimination learning in retardates also affects the more complex task of solving problems. The classic twenty-questions task has been modified so that, in the simplest case, only one question is sufficient to supply the information necessary to make a correct choice. Even here, retarded children ask noncritical questions as frequently as critical ones. Once the information is supplied, they can use it effectively, however.

GENERALIZATION   While MR children can be trained to do a specific problem successfully, they characteristically do not generalize to similar problems. It is as if each task is a new one that must be mastered in its own right. The impediment to learning is obvious.

Reviewing all of these findings concerning intellectual deficits we are struck by the complementary interplay between normal and deviant development. The question, Why do retardates fail to advance? is countered by the question, Why do nonretardates succeed? If retardates continue to use position as a strategy in discrimination learning, why do preschoolers gradually abandon it in favor of strategies that take note of objects' characteristics? If retardates fail to use rehearsal to improve memory, how do nonretardates come to use it? We do not know the answers.

Certainly, in studying retardates we have arrived at new insights into normal children. We tend to take learning in such children for granted—to assume they will "naturally" go about learning in the right way, that they will automatically see the relevant cues and search for the relevant information. We also assume that once having hit upon a successful problem-solving strategy, they will "naturally" continue using it. Now we realize that what we have assumed requires an explanation. Nothing happens "naturally." How children learn is as much a puzzle as how they fail to learn.

ADAPTIVE BEHAVIOR

Recall that the definition of mental retardation specifically includes adaptive behavior as well as measured intelligence. Intellectual level and adaptation are undoubtedly related; however, the correlation is not so high that the latter can accurately be inferred from the former. In certain instances the correlation may be quite low. Inner-city or rural-poverty children can make perfectly adequate adjustments to their environments while failing in school. The so-called six-hour retarded child (i.e., the child who is regarded as retarded in school but adjusts well outside of school) should not be stereotyped on the basis of an IQ score as being capable of making only a marginal adjustment in all situations. To stereotype children in this way runs the risk both of underestimating and of failing to develop the potential in a significant number of them.

In order for adaptive behavior to be a useful concept, however, it first had to be defined in terms of specific behaviors, and then instruments had to be developed to assess it. (For a detailed discussion of both issues, see Coulter and Morrow, 1978.)

In the majority of instances, adaptive behavior is defined in terms of two skills: independent functioning and responsible social relationships. The former includes the ability to meet basic physical needs such as eating, toileting, and dressing, and the ability to function as an integral member of the community in terms of communicating adequately, handling money, traveling, etc. The latter includes participating in group activities, helping others, etc. The conceptualization also includes both a developmental and a cultural component, in recognition of the fact that adaptive behavior changes with age and varies with the social context.

The AAMD Adaptive Behavior Scale (Nihira et al., 1974), which operationalizes the concept of adaptive behavior, is constructed along developmental lines. The items selected evaluate functioning in ten areas: self-care, sensory and motor development, handling money and shopping, language development, understanding danger, domestic activity, vocational activity, self-direction, responsibility, and socialization.

A number of factor-analytic studies of the Adaptive Behavior Scale have been done. (For a review of the findings see Nihira, 1978.)

In general, they show that it contains three factors—personal self-sufficiency, community self-sufficiency, and personal-social responsibility. Nihira's study of 3,354 institutionalized subjects between 4 and 69 years of age adds a developmental perspective to these factors (Nihira, 1976).

Personal self-sufficiency is found at all ages and involves the ability to satisfy immediate personal needs such as eating, toileting, and dressing. Community self-sufficiency involves independence beyond immediate needs, along with self-sufficiency in relation to others; for example, using money, traveling, shopping, and communicating adequately. Personal-social responsibility involves initiative and perseverance, the ability to undertake a task on one's own and see it through to completion. These last two factors emerge around 10 years of age and are either weak or nonexistent in younger children. They also represent higher-level behavior than the mere satisfaction of immediate needs.

Developmental trends differ according to the degree of retardation. In general, the greater the retardation, the less rapid the development during childhood and the lower the final level of adaptation. For personal self-sufficiency, for example, 90 percent of total growth is achieved by 10 to 12 years of age in the mildly retarded groups, while the severely retarded groups achieve the same percent of growth between 16 and 18 years of age. Only the profoundly retarded continue to grow throughout the life cycle, although their rate is the slowest and their level the lowest of all the groups.

For the mildly retarded children there is a rapid increase in personal self-sufficiency during childhood, which is gradually replaced by an accelerated growth in community self-sufficiency during adolescence, a trend that seems congruent with development in non-retardates. In moderately retarded children, community self-sufficiency grows more slowly,

equaling personal self-sufficiency by adolescence but never rising above it subsequently. In the severely retarded, community self-sufficiency is consistently lower than personal self-sufficiency throughout the life span, indicating that in an institutionalized population competence in caring for immediate physical needs is the area of highest achievement.

PERSONALITY DEVIANCE

Not only intellectual limitations but emotional problems may also interfere with adaptation. While there is no such thing as a typically retarded child, since variability of personality is the rule, having to cope with the demands of a complex society generally increases the likelihood of maladaptive behavior, so that behavior problems are more frequent in the retarded than among normal children (Rutter, 1971). Most of the information that follows comes from studies of mildly retarded school-age children and adolescents. (For a detailed presentation, see Robinson and Robinson, 1976.)

MR children and adolescents usually show higher levels of *anxiety* than do nonretarded individuals of the same age. Such anxiety plays a dual role in regard to academic performance. Its energizing properties can facilitate the performance of simple tasks, enabling retarded children to do well on simple arithmetical computations, for example. It is on complex tasks, such as concept formation, that anxiety disrupts effective intellectual functioning. And it is just such complex thinking that is increasingly required in school. Thus from both an intellectual and an emotional point of view, the retarded child tends to be increasingly handicapped in regard to having a successful experience in school.

Repeated experiences of failure, in turn, take their toll on *initiative*. MR children are less curious and venturesome, less prone to accept challenges and enjoy mastery for its own sake, than are children with normal intelligence. Thus the failure spontaneously to utilize what they have been taught, which characterizes their intellectual functioning, has its counterpart in a pervasive passivity in the personality realm. In addition, MR children tend to develop a generalized expectation of failure, unlike other children who can take failure in stride and try to do better next time.

A related consequence of repeated failure is a distrust of one's own resources and a turning to the environment for cues on how to proceed. This special kind of dependency is called *outer directedness*. In and of itself, outer directedness is not deviant; in fact, it is adaptive when one has reached the limits of one's abilities, as well as being the basis of learning by imitation. It is just that in the retarded, outer directedness may be carried to the extreme of excessive reliance on others for direction. A related pattern of behavior is the retarded child's tendency to be conforming and cooperative rather than competitive and self-assertive. Again it is not the behavior but its excessive use that is maladaptive.

We now see that the MR child has a dual handicap, one intellectual, the other motivational. The problem may further be compounded in institutional settings where docility and conformity to a drab routine are rewarded, while assertiveness and initiative are punished. The challenge to researchers is to disentangle basic intellectual handicaps from those that result from motivational and environment influences. The therapeutic challenge is to find ways our society can accommodate the realistic limitations while maximizing the assets of the retarded child, which in turn will result in a more balanced mixture of successes and failures than presently exists. It is helpful to remind ourselves that in certain societies MR is not stigmatized or even viewed as a problem that needs correcting. Our achievement-oriented society might profit from such examples of acceptance.

PEER RELATIONS

Guralnick (1986) is a prime example of an investigator who utilizes the framework of normal development to understand the *peer relations* of retarded children. His short-term longitudinal study of fifty-two mildly delayed 4½-year-olds suggested, at first glance, that changes over a year's time were similar to those of normal children; for example, associative play increased while solitary play decreased, verbal interaction supplanted motor and gestural communications, and interactions became more positive and reciprocal. Yet closer inspection revealed marked deficits in retarded preschoolers. Not only did solitary and parallel play remain the dominant form of social interaction (despite the decrease in the former), but the majority of delayed children also rarely engaged in sustained back-and-forth exchanges with peers; on the contrary, their characteristic pattern of interaction was a two-unit initiation-response sequence (i.e., A responds to B's social overture and B responds to A's). Moreover, social interaction lagged substantially behind the children's cognitive development; for example, at a developmental age of 3 to 3½ years, 25 percent of interactions should involve playing with other children or cooperative group play, whereas the delayed children at this developmental age engaged in associative play only 10 percent of the time while cooperative play was totally lacking. More ominous was the finding that progress during the year was so fragile that, at the beginning of the next school year, the children reverted to the level of social behavior that was characteristic of them at the beginning of the previous year.

One possible factor contributing to the developmental lag in social interaction is that retarded children are often grouped together in an educational setting and therefore cannot learn from or model themselves on children progressing at a normal rate. Since social interaction is facilitated when normal children of different chronological age are grouped together, one might expect a similar facilitation when retardates are *mainstreamed*, or placed in educational settings with normally developing children. However, the limited data available suggest that involvement with normal children produces only modest improvement in social and play interactions among preschoolers, perhaps because the tendency to form socially separate subgroups in a powerful one during this period (Guralnick, 1986). Thus while midly retarded and normal children interact frequently and in similar ways, moderately and severely retarded children receive only infrequent attention from normal classmates. Interestingly, the interactions that do occur are not aversive, nor is there a failure in communication; on the contrary, the speech of normal children is simpler and more repetitive when they address cognitively less advanced children, and they are extremely persistent, creative, and successful in achieving their interpersonal goals. Even with mildly retarded children, the pattern of communication shows subtle differences, the normal children justifying and mitigating their requests less often than they do with peers at the same cognitive level. In sum, when interacting with severely retarded peers, normal children initiate, control, and assume an instructional mode, thereby being more "adultlike" than "peerlike" in their communication style. As the intellectual discrepancy between participants decreases, peer relations become more balanced and reciprocal, although in subtle ways the retardate is still not treated as a co-equal.

DOWN'S SYNDROME CHILDREN

While impressive advances have been made in understanding the intellectual deficits and the adaptive behavior of retardates, developmental studies that relate these intrapersonal variables to the context variables of family and class are quite rare. Instead of summarizing the general literature, therefore, we have chosen to present in detail a single study that has a developmental orientation.

Overview

Until recently, Down's syndrome (DS) seemed to be an ideal form of retardation to study because of its simple, clear-cut etiology—a chromosome anomaly—and a predictable constellation of personality traits, the typical child being affable, docile, affectionate, mischievous, stubborn, and having a talent for mimicry. However, the current picture is far from simple. Down's syndrome can result from a number of chromosome abnormalities (Robinson and Robinson, 1976), each of which might or might not have a differential effect on development. At the same time numerous exceptions have been discovered to the "typical" behaviors. (Our discussion will follow D. Gibson, 1978.)

INTELLIGENCE   A generally accepted view is that in infancy there is only a very mild developmental lag, although laboratory studies suggest that standard tests might be too gross to detect more subtle defects in functioning that may be present. The favorable early developmental picture is followed by a precipitous but phasic decline in intellectual functioning. While mental age never keeps pace with chronological age as it does with children of normal intelligence, there is a growth spurt to approximately 18 months between the first and fourth year of life, followed by a plateau in mental growth for approximately one year; between approximately 5 and 9 years of age there is another spurt, bringing the child's mental age to 31 months; again there is a plateau until a final spurt between 11 and 13 years of age, which increases the mental age to 40 months, although many children do not evidence this third spurt. Measured intelligence for DS children ranges from the mild to the profound levels of retardation, the average IQ being around 44. Hartley (1986) concludes that, while there are delays in many areas in DS infants, given a stimulating environment it is not until school age that problems are sufficiently severe to warrant intensive and specialized training. Lack of ability to handle more advanced cognitive strategies and processes along with a limited ability to comprehend instructions, to plan alternative approaches to problems, to attend to several variables at once, and to express ideas clearly are all major handicaps to a normal life.

SOCIAL SKILLS Social skills have a good deal in common with adaptive behavior. Unlike intelligence, social age (SA) continues to grow throughout childhood and early adolescence in DS children. Thus a 15-year-old might have a mental age (MA) of 4 years and an SA of 7 years. However, SA declines to approximate MA in adolescence and adulthood. The most favorable developmental picture is found in children with an affable personality, relatively good intelligence, and few secondary physical complications such as organic brain pathology, who also receive good physical and psychological care. At their worst, the older DS individuals become restless, aggressive, stubborn, and destructive, as do other severely retarded adults.

PERSONALITY One reason the positive stereotype of the DS child as being affable and affectionate lasted so long is that contradictory behaviors were dismissed as exceptions to the rule! Gibson concludes that, "the empirical research has provided no firm grounds either for accepting or rejecting the classical personality stereotype for DS" (1978, p. 123). There is some evidence that positive prognostic signs include a relatively high intelligence with only a modest decline with age, good physical and psychological care, and being female.

PSYCHOPATHOLOGY Estimates of frank psychopathology have ranged from none to 60 percent depending on the degree of the defect, the child's general health and care received, the length of time in an institution, the presence of organic brain damage, and the general developmental history. Generally speaking, however, psychopathology is less common and acute in younger DS children than in other moderately to seriously retarded children, the frequency perhaps increasing as adulthood approaches.

The Developmental Study

Carr (1975) periodically evaluated thirty-nine home-reared and six boarded-out DS children from the time they were 1.5 months until they were 48 months of age. A control group of forty-two normal children was matched for age, sex, and social class. In keeping with the summary just presented, the DS childrens' initial IQ was somewhat lower than that of the normal controls (that is, a score of 80 compared with a score of 100) but declined in the subsequent months until it was around

40 for the home-reared and 20 for the boarded-out children at 24 months of age. The mean score of the boarded-out children was significantly below that of home-reared children, and the mean score of DS girls was significantly above that of boys.

EVERYDAY PROBLEMS   Carr's data contain many instances in which the specific nature of the infant's and toddler's retardation affected development. In regard to *feeding*, the infants were less alert and eager for food, had weaker sucking reflexes, and were sleepier than the normal controls. The mothers did not feed on demand simply because the infants were so undemanding—rarely crying and having to be awakened in certain instances—and fewer infants were breast-fed because of the difficulty involved in getting them to suck. Understandably, the mothers were more anxious over feeding than were mothers of normal infants.

Not only was bottle-feeding the rule, but DS children also remained dependent on the bottle owing to their lag in motor development. At 12 months they were like 8-month-olds, lacking the control of grasping necessary for self-feeding. More mothers of DS than normal children reacted with concern over feeding, forcing or encouraging the toddler or saving the food until later. However, the majority of DS mothers, like their normal counterparts, were unconcerned about the toddler's eating habits. While the 4-year-old DS preschoolers lagged behind the controls in self-feeding, two-thirds were capable of eating ordinary family meals, and feeding was no longer a problem to most of the mothers. Here, we see the infant "outgrowing" a problem and maternal concern diminishing.

As could be predicted from their lag in motor development, DS children were less adept at *dressing* themselves at 15 months and at 4 years of age and were less helpful to their mothers during dressing.

Toilet training showed the opposite development from feeding, in that the DS children "grew into" deviant behavior. At 15 months there was no difference between groups in terms of the age at which training was started and in terms of maternal attitudes; by 4 years of age the DS children were significantly retarded in all aspects of toileting—they wet their beds and wet or dirtied their pants more and were less adept at self-care. Unlike early feeding, differences in toilet training did not differentially affect the mother's attitudes even though the DS children had many more accidents.

Combining walking, eating, dressing, and toileting at 4 years of age into a single measure of independence, Carr found that between one-half and one-third of DS children needed little more looking after than the normal controls. This relatively advanced adaptive behavior compared with their measured IQ is in keeping with the findings presented in the previous section. Furthermore, there was evidence that interpersonal factors played an important role in determining the independence of the brighter DS children, but had little effect on the most retarded.

Crying in 15-month-old DS children also showed the imprint of their developmental delay. While there was no difference between groups in frequency, the DS children were more likely to cry because of physical upset such as hunger, tiredness, or pain, while normal children were more likely to cry for "psychological" reasons such as boredom, being teased, or not getting what they wanted. The difference is understandable, since mentally the DS children were more like 9-month-olds.

In an interview, over half of the mothers in both groups spoke of difficulties they had encountered in the first 15 months of their children's lives. The control mothers mentioned sleeping problems, while mothers of DS children emphasized feeding problems. Most striking, however, was the distress of the latter over the condition of their retarded children, their disappointment, resentment, and worry. Some spoke of being unable to adjust to the shock of having a DS child or were concerned about the child's future social acceptance or anticipated increasing difficulties.

BEHAVIOR PROBLEMS AND DISCIPLINE The DS children's placid infancy extended into the toddler period, during which time they had significantly fewer *temper tantrums* than did normal children. By 4 years of age, however, the difference had disappeared.

Getting into mischief—taking things out of the cupboard, knocking objects over, fiddling with light switches and plugs, putting things down the toilet—again showed a trend heavily influenced by the DS children's delayed development. While they were less mischievous at 15 months than the controls, this may have been because they were less mobile, none of them being able to walk. By 4 years of age, DS children had surpassed the controls in "naughtiness," as if they were belatedly going through the phase their normal counterparts had left behind. They were also more housebound, so that their mothers were more aware of their behavior than that of normal children who, for example, might be playing in a mud puddle in the garden. At 4 years of age there were few significant differences between DS and control children in regard to *aggressiveness*.

Ninety percent of children in both groups were said to be happy, so the incidence of *distress and upset* was low. While the DS children did not live up to their stereotype of being unusually happy children, retarded development did not result in an increase in unhappiness at 4 years of age. Half of all the children were described as easy children

with only five DS and six controls being regarded as problems. The types of problems were similar in both groups, namely, oppositional behavior, rudeness, attention seeking, and mischievousness.

Maternal discipline of DS children changed from being more permissive and child-centered, more comforting, and less punitive when the child was 15 months old to being comparable to the control mothers in terms of the amount of smacking and the handling of tempers at age 4. This increased toughness might have been due to the children's increased tantrums and naughtiness, as well as their being perceived as less fragile than they were at 15 months. Carr notes in passing that other studies suggest that this trend continues until mothers of DS children become stricter than those of normal children. On the other hand, mothers of DS children bribed and rewarded less on the theory that the children would not understand what the rewards were for, especially if they were promised rather than immediately administered. In a like manner, mothers preferred to smack the children rather than sending them to bed, because they believed the children could not remember the reason for the punishment for any length of time and would begin playing or wrecking the room. In sum, the mother's evaluation of her child's mental abilities biased her toward the immediately effective approach of smacking.

OTHER CONTEXT VARIABLES The DS child did not seriously disrupt *family life*, at least in the early years. Contacts with friends, relatives, and casual acquaintances continued as before. Only 21 percent of the mothers described themselves as lonely, especially if they did not receive psychological support from relatives and friends, although there is no way to tell how much their own behavior contributed to their isolation.

The majority of children in both groups

enjoyed *school*. Both groups of mothers regarded peer contacts as the main benefit, followed by learning self-help skills for the DS group, handicrafts for the control group. Since the DS group was in school for a full rather than half day, they had more *peer contact* than did the controls. At home both groups participated equally in the play of their siblings and their siblings' friends, the DS children often taking the part of pupil or patient in games of school and hospital. The one significant difference was that the DS children had far fewer friends of their own who came to play.

While *social class* impacted upon many maternal behaviors, it affected both groups in similar ways.

LONGITUDINAL COMPARISONS   In what ways did behaviors when the children were 15 months of age affect behaviors at 4 years of age? No significant relations were found for feeding in the DS group; for both groups, children who helped with dressing at 15 months were more likely to dress themselves completely at 4 years; and in both groups the tendency to have temper tantrums was stable over time. A good deal of consistency was found in parental life: the same mothers were working, the same fathers were participating in child care, parents were going out or staying at home as frequently and expressing the same degrees of contentment with their lot. The overall picture, then, is of parents continuing to behave "in character," of family styles being preserved, and of children being influenced in the same manner by early experiences.

The principal difference between groups was in regard to toilet training. Both groups conformed to the familiar pattern—children who were started early and whose mothers were concerned about progress were more reliably trained than those who started late and whose mothers were unconcerned.

However, the difference was that the controls showed no evidence of adverse effects from early training while, for the DS children, such training was associated with temper tantrums. Thus the DS mother had to choose between having either a clean child or an easily manageable one.

Comments

Carr's study provides us with a number of insights into the complexity of the early development of DS children. There were many areas of overlap with a nonretarded population, and in regard to sleeping and tantrums, the DS families were at a slight advantage. If clinicians focus on differences, it is only because differences are their special concern, both in terms of understanding and remedying them. And, undoubtedly, the DS children did evidence special problems—feeding problems in infancy and, later, problems in regard to toileting, dressing, and getting into mischief. We saw how they could grow out of their feeding difficulties and grow into trouble making and learned that their mothers were in a no-win situation in regard to toilet training, having to choose between cleanliness and manageability. As for the DS mothers, they took all the developmental deviations in stride with the exception of early feeding. However, they were markedly worried over the future, anticipating—probably realistically—that the most difficult problems were yet to come.

DEVELOPMENTAL MODELS

The exploration of intellectual and adaptive deviations of the MR child has revealed a variety of models of deviant development. In certain instances retardates seem to be hampered by a slow *rate* of growth; for example, the growth of community self-sufficiency in moderately retarded children, or the DS child's mischievousness at 4 years of age when normal counterparts have passed through this stage. The *pattern* of growth may also be different; recall the spurts and plateaus in the DS children's mental age, which contrasts with the relatively continuous change in the normal population. There may be growth failures or *fixations*, such as the utilization of position in discrimination learning or the failure to rehearse as an aid to remembering. There is the *exaggeration* of normal behavior as evidenced in the retardate's outer-directedness and reliance on external cues.

Finally, we come to a possibility that has not been raised since the discussion of autism, namely that the children evidence behaviors that have very little counterpart in normal development. In the intellectual sphere there is a controversy as to whether certain kinds of thinking in retarded children are *qualitatively* different from those found in normal children. There is evidence favoring both the quantitative and qualitative points of view (Weiss, Weisz, and Bromfield, 1986). When cognitive development is conceptualized in Piagetian terms, the data support a quantitative interpretation. Retarded children go through the same stages of cognitive development that normal children do but at a slower rate. For example, profoundly retarded children advance no further than the sensorimotor stage, moderately retarded no further than the preoperational stage, mildly retarded no further than concrete operations, while formal operations are beyond the reach of all retarded children. However, the information processing model presents a mixed picture, often with no clear-cut pattern in regard to the various components of the model. In memory, for example, the overall finding is that mentally retarded children's performance is inferior to that of normal children at similar developmental levels; thus 10-year-old retardates with a mental age of 6 years are inferior to normal 6-year-olds with a mental age of 6 years. However, in certain kinds of memory, such as verbal paired-associate learning, retardates are as good as children at similar developmental levels. Or again, retardates are inferior to developmentally matched children in regard to explaining strategies but equal them in concept usage and hypothesis testing. Only in the area of discrimination—of words, pictures, and three-dimensional objects—as well as discrimination learning do retardates evidence an overall inferiority to their developmentally matched counterparts. There is always the possibility that the kinds of motivational factors we have discussed may be responsible for the retarded children's performance rather than a genuine intellectual deficit and, until this potential confound is eliminated, no definite conclusions about a basic deficit can be drawn. Even allowing for motivational factors, however, it is difficult to understand how they could selectively affect only certain aspects of intellectual functioning and not others, such as one kind of memory and not another. As things now stand, the evidence suggests that retarded children may be deficient in a number of fundamental cognitive processes, although further research is needed to pinpoint which processes these are. The model of retardation as a slow rate of normal development seems too simple to account for many research findings, and the data suggest that the retardate's thinking may be qualitatively as well as quantitatively different from that of normal children.

REMEDIAL AND PREVENTIVE PROGRAMS

One aspect of programs for the mentally retarded that is of special interest is the involvement of the federal government. (For an extended discussion of remedial and preventive programs, see Robinson and Robinson, 1976.) Legislative activity was climaxed by Public Law 94-142, known as the *Education for All Handicapped Children Act of 1975*. Its purpose was to assure that all handicapped children have a free public education tailored to their unique needs, to assure the rights of handicapped children and their parents or guardians, to assist states in providing education, and to assess and assure the effectiveness of efforts toward education. Two specific requirements have had far-reaching effects. The first is that an *individualized education program* (IEP) be devised for each child. Implementing an IEP involves assessment of the child's present level of functioning, setting goals, and providing educational services and procedures for evaluating educational progress. Parents as well as various professionals participate in the decision-making process. The second requirement is that handicapped children be educated in the *least restrictive environment*. This requirement reversed the seventy-five-year-old trend of placing handicapped children in self-contained special settings, such as special classrooms for the educably mentally retarded (EMR). The contention was that such classes were ineffective in helping many EMR children learn basic academic and occupational skills, that minorities were overrepresented and that advances in education have made individualized instruction in regular classes feasible.

MAINSTREAMING   One unanswered question is whether MR children are best educated in special classes or in regular classrooms where teachers are trained to meet their particular educational needs. Educating retardates in regular classrooms is called "mainstreaming." In keeping with the social fervor of the times, special classes have been labeled another form of "discrimination" and "segregation." The claim has been buttressed by poorly designed studies showing that MR children in special classes fare worse than those in regular classes. Such studies ignored the fact that children were often placed in special classes because they were doing poorly or were so disruptive that it was impossible for the teacher to handle them in the regular classroom.

In reality, we know little about the relative merits of special classes compared with mainstreaming. As we might have expected, the few good studies that have been done indicate that there are advantages and disadvantages to each (Robinson and Robinson, 1976). Keeping in mind the tentativeness of the data, the evidence suggests that children with IQ scores above 75 to 80 do better academically in a regular class, while EMRs do better in a special class. Specifically, EMR children tend to have a more positive self-image than if they are in regular classes, perhaps because they use other MR children as the reference group rather than comparing themselves with normal children. Their social adjustment also tends to be better, since they are apt to be social isolates in regular classrooms. However, the picture is not a simple one: in urban settings, retarded children in regular classes are rated high in peer acceptance, while they are rated low in suburban areas where, presumably, more status is given to academic achievement. In regard to academic achievement, retardates in integrated programs at times make higher scores than those not in such programs, but this finding does not apply to all retardates in integrated classes (Haywood, Meyers, and Switzky, 1982).

Let us turn for a moment to the theme of the clinician in the political arena. The studies of mainstreaming indicate how important it is for clinicians to keep their critical (as well as their clinical) wits about them. It is difficult to argue another viewpoint when words such as "segregation" and "discrimination" are being bandied about. However, the clinician's main concern is insuring that the retardate receives the best of care and the most expert attention. A child who is deprived of these is indeed being discriminated against. Whether such goals can best be achieved through mainstreaming or special classes or some combination of the two should be decided on the basis of well-conducted evaluations of the two settings. The clinician does little service to the retarded child, or to society, by echoing slogans or failing to call attention to evidence that runs counter to current opinion.

The Developmental Picture

Because severe and profound levels of retardation tend to persist into adulthood rather than being "outgrown," it is clear that special preventive and remedial measures need to be taken. However, the situation is somewhat deceptive in regard to children at less retarded levels who comprise the vast majority of the MR population. Most of them live in the homes of parents or other relatives or with foster parents. And most of them function well, going to school during middle childhood, moving reasonably freely about the community, and participating in family life. Many of them subsequently hold jobs. Thus one may have the impression that these mildly to moderately retarded adults are absorbed into society and that their difficulties are solely in connection with having to attend school. However, the impression is misleading, because they turn up in a disproportionate number both on the welfare rolls and on police blotters (Haywood, Meyers and Switzky, 1982). While they do not need the kind of extensive care that severely retarded children do, they are clearly at risk in regard to making an adequate adjustment to society.

Special Education

Children with IQ scores between 55 and 80 are classified by most school systems as educably mentally retarded and are expected to perform at least at a third-grade level and occasionally as high as a sixth-grade level by the time they finish school. The trainably mentally retarded (TMR) with IQ scores between 25 and 55 are taught to function in a restricted environment because they are not expected to master traditional academic skills.

In special education classes, EMR pupils are taught academic subjects as tools to enhance social competence and occupational skills. Small classes with individualized attention are recommended. Between 6 and 10 years of age the EMR child, whose MA is between 3 and 6 years, is given the kind of readiness programs usually found in kindergarten; the emphasis is on language enrichment and self-confidence, along with good health, work, and play habits. EMR children between 9 and 13 years of age, whose MA is about 6 to 9 years, can master the basic academic skills involved in the three R's. At the junior and senior levels the applied emphasis continues; for example, the children are trained to read the newspaper and job application forms and to make correct change. Occupational education stresses appropriate work habits such as punctuality and following directives, since most vocational failures are due to poor adjustment rather than low mental ability. After formal schooling, sheltered workshops and vocational rehabilitation centers help the mildly retarded adjust to our complex society.

The curriculum for TMRs emphasizes self-care and communication skills, work habits, following directions, and rudimentary social participation. Reading instruction, for example, is likely to include recognizing signs such as "Stop," "Men," and "Women," while arithmetic is limited to making change. The majority of these children do not achieve social or economic independence as adults, although they can engage in useful work and adjust well in the protective setting of the family.

Psychotherapy

Until recently, MR children were deemed unsuited for psychotherapy because of their limited comprehension and verbal ability, poor impulse control, and passivity in problem-solving situations (LaVietes, 1978). Typically, "environmental manipulation" was recommended in terms of consulting with parents and teachers and exploring resources in the community. While such counseling still plays a prominent role in remediation, a number of therapeutic techniques have been adapted to the special needs of the MR child. Nonverbal techniques such as play and art therapy can serve the dual function of tension release and self-expression. Verbal techniques can be used for reassurance, support, discussion, and advice, as well as for clarifying and interpreting feelings. Group therapies have become the most popular variant of psychotherapy; some take the form of discussions, others revolve around activities such as play, handicrafts, movies, or trips, while still others focus on the reflection and interpretation of feelings. Parent groups offer the opportunity for discussion in a setting of shared problems and mutual concern.

By far the most successful and widely used therapeutic technique is behavior modification, employing the operant principles of changing undesirable behaviors by altering the specific consequences which reinforce them and by reinforcing new, more socially acceptable responses. This technique has been used to encourage a wide array of behaviors: self-help behaviors (toileting, feeding, dressing), work-oriented behaviors (pro-ductivity, task completion), social behaviors (cooperation, group activities), nonacademic classroom behaviors (attending, taking turns, talking at appropriate times), academic learning (arithmetic, sight vocabulary), as well as decreasing undesirable behaviors such as attention getting and aggressive or self-injurious behaviors. An important fringe benefit is that parents can actively participate in the therapeutic program in the home setting. Equally important, behavior modification, more than any other single therapeutic technique, has been responsible for changing the prevailing attitude of helplessness among professional and nonprofessional caretakers. While data on relative effectiveness of various psychotherapies are meager, behavior modification has provided the clearest evidence that the behavior of MR children can be changed.

In the realm of *cognitive* remediation, there are programs that represent a frontal attack on the deficits revealed by the information processing model. As we have seen, structural features of memory are unmodifiable, but the control processes or strategies are under voluntary control and therefore may be amenable to training. Even when mnemonic devices such as rehearsal and mediation are taught and maintained over a period of weeks or even months, however, they remain specific rather than becoming general principles of remembering. Thus the basic challenge is to find a way for retarded children to learn and retain generalized modes of thought that can be applied to new situations. Remedial educational methods, called "instrumental enrichment," have had some preliminary success in teaching EMR adolescents effective processes of thinking and problem solving, such as systematic search, problem analysis, accurate data gathering, and inhibition of impulsive responses. There has even been some initial success with these methods in teaching the retarded adolescents how to generate new strategies for attacking problems they have not encountered before (Haywood, Meyers and Switzky, 1982).

Prevention

The diversity of preventive programs reflects the diverse etiologies of MR itself. A number are medically oriented—such as genetic counseling, therapeutic abortions, elimination of defect-producing illnesses, and compulsory tests for phenylketonuria—and as such lie beyond the province of this discussion. More relevant are the compensatory educational programs, especially those involving preschool children. Project Head Start is perhaps the best known, but there are also specialized programs for stimulating premature and blind infants (Robinson and Robinson, 1976). Some programs concentrate on enhancing specific skills such as speaking or reading; others try to increase readiness for formal schooling, while still others are concerned with the child's social and emotional development. Prevention in general will be examined in more detail in chapter 16.

While there have been literally hundreds of compensatory education programs designed to prevent the decline of IQ often found in lower-class children, only a handful meet the minimal criteria for adequate evaluation of effectiveness: i.e., more than thirty clearly disadvantaged children, cognitive benefits measured by reliable, valid instruments, and statistically significant gains that are also educationally meaningful. *Infant stimulation* programs have been particularly popular. Typically they were based on the "sensitive period" hypothesis that early experiences play a particularly important role in determining subsequent development, and the observation that a number of lower-class mothers, perhaps from ignorance or immaturity or realistic burdens or different value systems, were not providing infants with the kind of stimulation that enhances cognitive development. While such programs played an important role in finding ways to involve mothers who were disinterested or suspicious or uncooperative, they were often so poorly designed and unsatisfactorally evaluated that it was impossible to judge their effectiveness.

One of the few programs that meets the criteria for evaluation of effectiveness and is closely linked with developmental data and theory was conducted by Slaughter (1983). She studied eighty-three black mother–child dyads randomly recruited from low-income housing projects. The two-year short-term longitudinal design began when the infants were 18 months of age and ended when they were 44 months. The choice of age was based on developmental studies showing that the difference in average IQ performance between children of higher status and children of lower status backgrounds emerges between 18 and 42 months of age. The purpose of the study was to prevent the decline in IQ in nonretarded toddlers.

Next, Slaughter (1983) turned to the literature on normal development, which showed a correlation between maternal behavior and intellectual growth. Mothers who facilitated cognitive growth tended to be warm, sensitive to the child's developmental needs, consistent and firm but flexible in socialization demands. They provided appropriate play material and both guided and expanded their child's play. Finally, they talked a good deal to their child, sometimes in response to the child's vocalizations and speech, but not necessarily so. Mothers who did not facilitate cognitive growth had the opposite characteristics, being authoritarian, restrictive, and lacking in warmth.

Implicit in Slaughter's procedure is a point that is often overlooked, namely, that maternal behavior is a psychological variable, but race and class are not since neither is defined in psychological terms. Class, for example, is typically measured in terms of income, years of education, and profession, none of which is a psychological variable. Race and class become meaningful when they are translated into psychological terms, such as patterns of maternal behavior that might be more frequently found in lower-class than in middle-class mothers.

Slaughter also relied on reviews of early prevention studies which showed that home-based, moderately structured programs produced the most striking short- and long-term gains in intelligence and achievement. Neither curriculum content per se nor degree of specificity of parental tutoring was related to such gains, the inference being that the gains were due more to positive effects of home-based programs on parental attitudes and parent–child interaction. Some parents, for example, seemed to have developed a greater sense of control over their lives and a more flexible attitude toward their child's development while becoming more involved and responsive in their interactions and using a more elaborate language style with their child. Thus the findings from these longitudinal intervention studies complemented the previously described correlational studies.

On the basis of the above findings from previous studies, Slaughter (1983) devised two kinds of interventions. Because of the importance of play as a facilitator of cognitive development, her first intervention was a demonstration program stressing the role of the adult in stimulating play through the use of toys. A primary goal of the program was to encourage verbal interaction between mother and child using play as a vehicle. The toys were selected for their cognitive stimulus value and were demonstrated by a specially trained "toy demonstrator" who modeled the play with a new item while the mother observed. The demonstrator then invited the mother to imitate this approach and encouraged her to use it in subsequent play. The

second intervention was called the "mothers discussion group program" and consisted of weekly 1½-hour meetings of ten to fifteen mothers, initially to share concerns about child rearing and, later, to discuss more general problems. Under the guidance of a trained group leader, the mothers were expected to learn from each other as well as to receive psychological support. The goal was to provide educational experiences that would promote independent thinking and decision making in regard to child rearing and family life in general. Finally, there was a control group that did not receive any intervention.

In the final evaluation, children in the intervention groups were intellectually superior to those in the control group. While the intervention did not significantly raise IQ scores, it prevented the 13-point decline found in the control group. Mothers in the discussion group were significantly higher than the control group in a measure of ego development involving the perception of the self and relations to significant people in the social environment. These mothers also interacted more with their child and were more likely to expand on the child's ongoing play. The children of mothers in the discussion group also verbalized more during play. Finally, mothers in the discussion group were more open to outsiders (i.e., persons other than relatives and friends) in that they were willing to use social institutions as resources and perceived them as beneficial.

Thus, while both interventions were effective in regard to maintaining the children's level of IQ, the discussion group had more wide ranging effects, involving the mother's personality, her interaction with her child, and her attitude toward community resources. The finding was unexpected since it was thought that the toy demonstration program, being more specific, would be the greater facilitator of constructive maternal behavior and of children's verbalization. In

accounting for the change, Slaughter speculated that the discussion group developed an
interaction akin to that of an extended family
in that the mothers felt close and comfortable
enough to share problems and to give and
receive help. Equally important, the problems and solutions were congruent with their
own experiences rather than having the aura
of being imposed upon them by well-meaning
professionals. Thus the group effected a
change in the mothers' social reality which,
in turn, changed their personality and parenting styles.

While Slaughter did not do a follow-up
study, a number of such studies have been
conducted. Their history is instructive in
itself. When Head Start and the various
infant stimulation programs began, it was
believed they would produce permanent
changes, more or less inoculating the children
from subsequent intellectual decline. Such a
belief was naive and contrary to what is
known about development. Disadvantaged
children, like middle-class children—or perhaps even more than middle-class children—
need growth-promoting stimulation throughout childhood. If, after a preventive program, they attend inadequate schools and
come home to indifferent parents, there is no
reason to assume they will be sufficiently
motivated to maintain their gains on their
own.

Subsequent programs specifically involved parents and, whenever possible, school
systems. As a result of this more comprehensive approach, a number of early education programs for children from low-income
families have had long-lasting effects in the
areas of school competence (i.e., fewer children placed in special classes or failing to be
promoted), standardized intelligence and
achievement tests, children's attitudes and
values such as being proud of themselves for
their accomplishments, and positive maternal
attitudes toward school performance (Lazar
and Darlington, 1982). Despite such encouraging findings, there is also some evidence
that the children, while doing better than
those from low-income families who have not
had special educational programs, still lag
behind the school population at large. Thus
the challenge to close the achievement gap
still exists.

12

Deviations from Physiological Intactness: Brain Damage and Physical Illness

---

Throughout life, but particularly during childhood, the body is the stage on which some of the most significant developmental dramas are enacted. We have already explored the importance of eating and elimination in the normal and psychopathological development of children who are physically healthy. If children are brain damaged or chronically ill, we might rightly suspect that they must contend with special stresses and problems. They may be able to take such stresses in stride and even be stronger because of them. But they may also be taxed beyond their ability to cope successfully. For example, there is evidence that among 10- to 12-year-old children with chronic handicapping physical conditions, such as asthma, diabetes, heart disease, polio, and orthopedic deformities, twice as many (11.5 percent) have psychopathological disturbances as children in the general population (Rutter, 1977).

BRAIN DAMAGE

A visitor to a remote Bohemian town was impressed by the fact that, at the stroke of five every evening, the artillery sergeant lowered the flag and ordered his squad to fire a cannon. His curiosity impelled him to inquire how the sergeant knew when it was precisely five o'clock. The sergeant informed him that this particular town boasted of one of the best clockmakers in all of Europe, so each morning when he passed the clockmaker's shop he reset his watch. In this manner he was sure the cannon was fired exactly on time. Still not satisfied, the visitor went to the clockmaker and inquired how his clocks could be so precise in a town with almost no communication with the outside world. "I have a special advantage," the clockmaker replied. "There is a most remarkable artillery sergeant living here. Every evening at precisely five o'clock the garrison gun goes off, so I reset all my clocks when I hear its sound." (For further details of this charming anecdote, as well as a critique of the concept of brain damage, see Birch, 1964, pp. 3–12.)

The Problem

In order to determine whether dysfunctions of the brain are related to deviant behavior, it is essential to have independent and reliable assessments of both brain and behavior. This essential condition is rarely met. As in the anecdote of the sergeant and the clockmaker, psychologists, impressed by the precision of certain diagnostic procedures in medical science, assume that evidence of a damaged or malfunctioning brain can be clearly established, while physicians, impressed by the reliability of certain psychological tests, assume that the behavioral disturbances are objectively documented. Neither is correct. The resulting confusion is predictable.

In order to place the literature on brain damage in proper perspective it will be necessary first to understand some of the complex problems inherent in trying to build a bridge between brain and behavior. Next, we will examine some of the literature on manifest brain dysfunctions before turning to the more controversial concept of minimal brain damage.

THE PROBLEM OF DEFINITION "Brain damage" can be defined in a number of different ways.

A strictly neurological definition concerns itself with the nature, site, and size of damage to the brain. A behavioral definition is concerned with the functions impaired by the damage: motor and communication disorders, sensory and perceptual deficits, intellectual impairment, convulsive disorders, and so on. Brain damage can also be conceptualized in terms of a wide array of etiologic factors, such as traumatic injury, anoxia, encephalitis, epilepsy, cerebral palsy, and lead poisoning, to name a few. Each approach is valid, but the complex interrelations among them have yet to be worked out. Therefore, it is important for us to realize at the outset that "the brain-damaged child" is an abstraction that glosses over crucial distinctions among children. The diagnosis "brain damage" is meaningless without reference to etiology and, more important, to the specific psychological functions that have been impaired and the nature of the impairment itself.

Moreover, there is a *quantitative versus qualitative* controversy among experts. Those championing the former claim that behavioral deviations are a function of the sheer amount of brain damage. At one extreme of the quantitative continuum lies massive damage which can result in death; at the other extreme lies minimal brain dysfunction and its presumed psychological correlates, including hyperactivity. The qualitative viewpoint, by contrast, argues that in light of the well-known localization of brain functions, the effects of damage depend on the site and size of the damage as well as the age at which it occurs. The controversy is far from settled. (For a more detailed account of the points presented in this and subsequent sections, see Werry, 1986a.)

THE PROBLEM WITH ASSESSMENT Because of the delicacy, inaccessibility, and complexity of the brain, most assessments are indirect and inferential. For example, there are "silent" sections of the brain which have no externally measurable functions; consequently, diagnostic techniques may fail to detect substantial brain damage. Conversely, positive diagnostic signs can occur in the absence of brain damage. (Our presentation follows Schwartz and Johnson, 1985.)

While *autopsy* is the surest technique for establishing brain damage, it is, of course, no help in diagnosing a living child. Diagnosis of brain damage frequently relies on the child's *history*, covering factors such as pregnancy and delivery complications, developmental milestones such as sitting up, walking, and speaking, and illnesses. Not only is there evidence that such information is often unreliable, but there is also no direct relation between the information and brain damage. Paradoxically, developmental histories are the least useful yet most frequently used of all diagnostic procedures. The *neurological examination* covers such classic signs as failure of the patellar (knee-jerk) reflex and presence of a Babinski reflex, restriction of the visual field, and loss of sensation and function in any part of the body. The examination is most accurate when there are lesions in non-silent areas of the brain. In other kinds of brain damage the findings may be ambiguous, or they may even be normal in children with head injuries and encephalitis. While *psychological tests* are invaluable in assessing specific cognitive deficiencies in the brain-damaged child, in and of themselves they are insufficient for making a diagnosis of brain damage.

Remarkable progress has recently been made in techniques for visualizing brain structure and functioning. The traditional *electroencephalogram* (EEG), which measures electrical activity of the brain, can detect gross damage, but most of the records fall in a no-man's-land between normality and pathology (Werry, 1986a). In fact, 10 to 20 percent of normal children also display abnormal records. However, there have been two ad-

vances in electroencephalographic techniques which hold promise of increased sensitivity to brain damage. The first is the *event-related potential*, or ERP. When a stimulus such as a light or sound is presented, the brain produces a characteristic response or ERP. Knowing the ERP in the intact brain allows diagnosticians to detect malfunctions such as visual disorders and deafness in very young or mentally retarded children who cannot be tested by the usual techniques. Next, developments in computer analysis and computer graphics have made it possible to use many recording leads simultaneously rather than the few recording leads of traditional EEGs. Consequently, a computer-drawn, detailed picture of the brain is now available.

There have also been advances in *imaging* techniques for visualizing brain structure. The traditional *x-ray* could detect only gross abnormalities. However, *computerized axial tomography*, or CAT scans (also called computer-assisted tomography and abbreviated CT scans), using computer-driven x-ray machines, produces exceptionally detailed images both of the brain's surface and of the levels below, making it possible to localize lesions at any level of the brain. A newer imaging method called *nuclear magnetic resonance* (NMR) produces even clearer images. *Positron emission tomography* (PET scans), unlike imaging techniques which produce static pictures of the brain and reveal only structural or anatomical deficits, can detect abnormal functioning in brains that might look structurally intact. Because brain cells metabolize glucose, radioactive glucose is introduced into the cerebral artery and the rate at which it is metabolized in various parts of the brain is recorded. The resulting PET images are compared with those of a normally functioning brain.

While all of these technical advances hold promise for significantly improving the ability to detect brain damage, they have not been used extensively with children, and the results tend to be disappointing (Werry, 1986a).

One might hope the various assessment techniques described above might complement one another, so that ambiguity in one would be clarified by certainty in another. While multiple assessment is desirable and can pay off in terms of increased certainty of diagnosis, such an outcome is by no means guaranteed. All too often a battery of tests contains little more than redundant ambiguities. As Werry (1986a) concludes, "the diagnosis of brain damage, unless gross, depends on a group of medical, historical, and psychological measures, most of which are of low or untested reliability, discriminate poorly between normal and *mildly* brain damaged populations, and apparently measure a variety of unrelated functions instead of some homogeneous variable 'brain damage' " (p. 303).

THE PROBLEM WITH TIMING The Kennard principle states that it is better to have your brain lesion early—if you can arrange it. Indeed, there is evidence of greater "sparing" of psychological functions if the damage occurs early in development rather than late. Recently, however, the principle has been challenged as being overly simple (Schneider, 1979). An unusually thorough study of children who had localized head injuries found no relation between age and the presence or absence of psychopathology. The age range was from the preschool period through adolescence (Rutter and Garmezy, 1983).

Whether early lesions are more or less disruptive of subsequent behavior than similar lesions sustained at maturity depends on a number of factors. (Our discussion follows Teuber, 1975.) Most obviously, the effects on behavior depend on the site and size of the lesion, some parts of the brain showing resilience after early lesion, other parts showing less or none at all. Next, the effects of lesions depend on the nature of the particular psychological function being studied. Finally, time itself is the most important variable, since some deficits take time to recede after early lesions, whereas others take time to appear. Thus no conclusions can be drawn from assessments made at only one point in time.

Teuber speculates that different regions of the brain have different "commitments" to specialized functioning early in development and therefore have different degrees of ability to take over the function of a damaged region. Moreover, in taking over such a function, a price may be paid: the "adopted" function may not be quite as highly developed as it would have been in the original region, while functions appropriate to the undamaged region may suffer. To illustrate, Teuber cites a study of fifty children who had brain damage in infancy either to the right or to the left cerebral hemisphere. The children were examined between 8 and 18 years of age, their normal siblings serving as controls. Language development, which is usually the province of the left hemisphere, can "escape" and be assumed by a potential language zone in the right hemisphere; that is, the right hemisphere is not totally "committed" to its specialties and can assume another function. However, a price is paid, in that the usual functions of the right hemisphere—dealing with visuospatial problems such as copying a design with blocks or fitting jigsaw-type pieces together—suffer. Moreover, there is suggestive evidence that the "right-hemisphere" language is subtly impaired in terms of higher functions such as comprehension. By contrast, the left hemisphere cannot as readily assume the visuospatial functions of a damaged right hemisphere because it is early "committed" to language and language-related activities.

This complex pattern of commitment or adaptability is, in turn, affected by the context of time. Certain right-hemisphere functions are severely affected whether the damage occurs early or late, since the left hemisphere cannot take them over; with certain language functions, however, later damage to the left hemisphere is more deleterious, since the right hemisphere becomes progressively inefficient in assuming the language function.

Incidentally, we might draw a parallel between the Kennard principle and the concept of a critical period in development. In chapter 1 we noted that while there was some supportive evidence, there was also sufficient contradictory data to question the concept as a general guide to the relation between time and development. A single formula seems far too simple to capture the complexity of normal and psychopathological development.

THE PROBLEM OF CAUSALITY　Correlation does not prove causation, as we all know. Yet, when a study shows a correlation between psychopathological behavior and brain damage, we tend to assume that the latter is the cause. The assumption is naive and may be misleading. Brain damage occurs within the same intrapersonal and interpersonal contexts as all the psychopathologies discussed so far. Such context factors may significantly affect the child's reaction to brain damage or in certain instances be more potent in determining future behavior than brain damage itself.

Let us take two examples. Suppose we find a correlation between brain damage and the now-familiar pattern of acting out in school, evidenced by inattention, disobedience, truanting, and underachievement. In all probability a sizable number of the children will also come from homes characterized by parental disharmony, emotionally disturbed or irresponsible parents, and a large number of siblings—conditions that increase the likelihood of acting-out behavior in organically

intact children. Thus, the onus would be on the organicist to show that the presence of brain damage significantly affected our understanding of etiology, our prognosis, and our therapeutic interventions. Next, let us return to the study of children with head injuries (Shaffer et al., 1975). The authors reconstruct the etiology of deviant behavior in terms of an interaction between organic and psychological factors. Children from unhappy or uncaring homes are especially likely to be accident-prone, so that the brain injury itself may have been psychologically determined. Once it occurs, the injury may then increase the child's vulnerability to the noxious influences in the environment, while having a further negative effect on family cohesiveness and happiness. In such a complex interweaving of factors, it might be practically impossible to isolate the contribution of brain injury to the child's disturbance; however, to assume that the organic brain pathology was solely responsible for the child's emotional disturbance would be naive. In reality, few causal links between brain damage and psychopathological behavior have been clearly established.

Summary of Findings

As we have just seen, "brain damage" or "the brain-damaged child" covers such a variety of pathological conditions that they are more a convenient fiction than a specific, clearly delineated entity. We have also seen that the constant interweaving of physiological and psychological variables makes it difficult to establish what is cause and what is effect. However, the age-old challenge of relating the functioning and malfunctioning of the brain to normal and deviant behavior has yielded a number of reasonably established relationships. (Unless otherwise noted, our summary follows Rutter and Garmezy, 1983, and Werry, 1986a.)

There is evidence that brain damage increases the risk for subsequent psychopathology. Rutter (1977) compared 99 children between 5 and 14 years of age with cerebral palsy, epilepsy, or other clearly established brain disorders, with 189 children from the general population of 10- and 11-year-olds, and with 139 10- to 12-year-olds with physical disorders not involving the brain, such as asthma, diabetes, and heart disease. The rate of psychological disturbance in the brain-damaged group was 34.3 percent of the population, while the rate of psychological disturbance in the group with other physical handicaps was 11.5 percent (which still was almost twice that of the normal population). A subsequent study (Rutter, 1981) showed the risk of psychopathology in brain-damaged children was increased threefold over that in children suffering orthopedic injuries. This does not mean that all brain-damaged children are at risk, however; on the contrary, only when biological factors result in *major brain disorders* is the risk of psychopathology significantly increased, although, even here, it is not inevitable. Aside from this special group, the risk of psychopathology is minimal and difficult to detect. Nor is there clear evidence of a direct relation between increased severity of damage and increased risk for psychopathology in this more moderately damaged group. Finally, the functions most powerfully affected by brain damage are cognition, sensory and motor functions, and seizure thresholds. It is when these are impaired that psychopathology is most likely to appear.

In light of the importance of the brain, the above findings may seem unexpectedly benign. However, it is important to remember the remarkable recuperative powers of the brain—for example, from injuries, strokes, or infections. While the brain may not be able to replace dead neurons, it has reserve capacity, duplication of functions, and the impetus of growth itself to aid its recovery. Also, as we shall soon see, the ameliorating potential of the social environment has been underestimated until relatively recently.

Generally speaking, there is no evidence that brain damage leads to a characteristic clinical picture that can be labeled "the brain-damaged child." Effects tend to be nonspecific, with behavior the same as that found in other disturbed populations. However, there are possible exceptions in that brain damage might lead to social isolation or acting-out behavior, at least in a certain group of children.

The situation in regard to *pre- and postnatal* factors mirrors that of brain damage itself. In certain extreme instances the risk is high; for example, fetal immaturity or true prematurity increases the risk of anoxia and deep brain damage, which, in turn, can result in death or in mental retardation, cerebral palsy, or epilepsy. But in the majority of cases, so-called high-risk babies fail to show subsequent abnormalities of behavior. To be more precise, the immediate effects of the insult to the brain become less important with time, while the effects of the social environment become increasingly important. As Sameroff and Chandler (1975) have shown, the long-term effects on most infants depend on their social class and on the caretaking they receive. With sensitive and appropriate caretaking and a generally growth-promoting environment, at-risk infants will become well-functioning children. If the caretaking is poor and the environment is punitive or barren or stressful, they will become children with diverse intellectual and psychological problems, as they would even with no insult to the brain. What the pre- and postnatal insults do is increase the probability that such problems will appear.

Werry (1986a) neatly sums up the empirical findings. "The child's behavior is a complex, ever-changing distillate of past and present forces—biological, psychological, and social. In this mélange of influences, unless accompanied by gross distortions such as physical or mental handicap or active epilepsy, most brain insults or disorders appear as only an 'inefficient predictor' of later behavior" (p. 316).

An Illustrative Developmental Study

A longitudinal study evaluated anoxic infants when they were 3 and 7 years of age (Corah et al., 1965; Graham et al., 1962). In the first phase, 116 anoxic and 159 normal 3-year-olds were assessed in terms of their cognitive and personality development. Anoxic children did significantly poorer than the controls on all tests of cognitive functioning, including the Stanford-Binet, a vocabulary test, and a concept test. There was significantly greater impairment in conceptual ability than in vocabulary skill, while perceptual-motor functioning (such as is needed to copy simple designs correctly) was unimpaired. While the anoxic group was evaluated less favorably than the control group in terms of overall personality development, the only specific variable differentiating the groups was distractibility. Characteristics such as impulsivity, demandingness, infantilism, negativism, and fearfulness, while somewhat more prominent in the anoxic group, were not statistically significant. In general, the differences in personality were not as striking as those in cognitive development.

By 7 years of age, when 134 normal and 101 anoxic infants were located, the pattern was reversed. The overall difference in intelligence was no longer significant, although the anoxics evidenced a significant deficit in vocabulary (which the authors interpreted as a continuation of the children's difficulty with conceptual and abstract thinking) and perceptual-motor ability. However, the most striking differences between groups was in the area of social competence. The most discriminating technique was the Vineland Social Maturity Scale, which indicated that the anoxics were more dependent than the controls. Evaluations by psychologists, psychiatrists, and parents indicated that anoxic children were more impulsive and distractible (recall they were also more distractible as 3-year-olds), had difficulty communicating their ideas despite adequate verbal ability, were less socially sensitive, and had less emotional control. In their communication, for example, they would use words and gestures excessively and inappropriately, while in their social interaction they were obtuse to the demands of others and ignored the effects of their behavior on others. Interestingly, there were no significant differences between groups in terms of teachers' ratings, indicating that the children's behavior in school was different from their behavior at home and with professionals.

In light of our concern with prognosis it is worth noting that there was no predictability from infant behavior to behavior at 7 years of age. The finding is not surprising because, except in cases of extreme damage, predictions from infancy are notoriously inexact. While there were a number of significant correlations between behaviors at 3 and 7 years of age, the order of the relations was fairly low and subject to error. Thus, some consistency of behavior was uncovered, but it was not striking.

One final point: the differences between groups, even when significant, were minimal. In some of the discriminating measures, the differences were smaller than sex or socioeconomic status differences. There was no evidence for an all-or-none effect with the anoxic children having one cluster of personality characteristics not to be found in the control children. On the contrary, there was a great deal of overlap between groups, indicating that for most measures the children's behavior could not be distinguished.

We learn two important lessons from this study. The first is a variation on a theme we have encountered before: behavioral correlates of brain damage are a function of when one evaluates the children, since they are apt to "grow out of" certain deficits (such as a lower IQ score) and "grow into" others (such as a deficit in social competence). The second lesson is that, while anoxia increases the risk for subsequent deviant behavior, most such infants will be developing normally when they enter school.

Unfortunately, the study does not provide us with those nice insights into the reasons for the changing developmental picture that we found in Carr's study of Down's syndrome children. (See also Fraiberg's 1977 model study of the effects of blindness on attachment and initiative in infancy.) Did the distractibility and lowered conceptual ability seen at 3 years of age progressively interfere with the preschoolers' ability to become self-sufficient, to control their behavior and speech, to monitor and accommodate to the behavior of others? Did parents become increasingly irritated with or overprotective of their children? Were the children increasingly rejected by peers? All such questions concerning the processes underlying the documented change can only be answered by future research.

MINIMAL BRAIN DYSFUNCTION

Definition

Minimal brain damage or minimal brain dysfunction (MBD) syndrome refers to children of near average or higher intelligence in whom deviations of central nervous system functioning are manifested by various symptoms, the most characteristic being hyperactivity, perceptual-motor impairment, emotional lability, coordination deficits, disorders of attention, memory, thinking, and speech, impulsivity, and specific learning disabilities (H. E. Rie, 1980). Since the child may have average or above-average intelligence and since the signs of disturbed functioning are subtle, he or she may be regarded as merely "lazy" or "nervous." Etiologic factors implicated in MBD include genetic influences, temperament, brain damage, perinatal stress, lead poisoning, food additives, and early sensory deprivation, among others, but none of the evidence is definitive.

The definition has an appealing plausibility. It makes sense to postulate that (1) there are degrees of brain dysfunction; (2) minimal CNS dysfunction is difficult to detect; and (3) such dysfunctions selectively affect specific psychological functions. Furthermore, it seems reasonable to assume that organically caused psychological dysfunctions should be responsive to medication. Undoubtedly there are children in whom this constellation of events occurs. However, whether it occurs frequently is open to serious question and there is concern that it might not occur in the majority of children diagnosed as MBD and treated with drugs. As we shall now see, the evidence supporting the definition of an MBD syndrome is often flimsy or controversial.

The Assessment of MBD

If clear-cut instances of brain damage are difficult to detect, how much more problematic are instances of presumed MBD, which elude the traditional neurological assessment techniques. Since the majority of MBD children have no evidence of gross, demonstrable neurological impairment, the diagnosis must depend on the so-called soft signs of CNS dysfunction. Rutter (1977) lists three groups of such signs. The first group involves developmental delays in functions, such as speech, motor coordination, or perception. Being developmental in nature, lack of skill in the various functions is normal in young children, and their clinical significance depends on the degree of impairment in relation to the child's mental and chronological age. Unfortunately, there is no way to determine whether such signs are indicative of brain damage rather than a maturational delay or intellectual retardation not related to CNS damage. The second group of soft signs involve nystagmus and strabismus, which also may be due to either neurological or nonneurological causes. The third group consists of slight abnormalities that are often minor examples of classical neurological signs, such as slight asymmetries of tone or reflex. The difficulty in detecting these abnormalities adversely affects the reliability of the assessment.

Minor congenital physical anomalies have also been used as evidence of MBD. Such anomalies include malformed or asymmetrical ears, a curved fifth finger, a furrowed tongue, and a third toe longer than the second. While the detection of these anomalies is reliable and stable over time, and while they may well represent some type of atypical physical development, their relation to organic brain dysfunction is obscure (Rutter and Garmezy, 1983).

Neeper and Greenwood (1987) sum up the status of soft signs as follows. Their origin is uncertain, but they most likely have multiple origins. There may well be a genetic component and a relation to brain damage, especially in children with clear postnatal insult. The uniform assumption of brain damage, however, is unwarranted. While soft signs are not a useful diagnostic tool at present, there is sufficient evidence of their relation to important psychological variables to warrant continued research. There is reasonably convincing data indicating that they

increase as IQ declines and decrease with age and that they are more frequent in boys than in girls. There is some evidence that soft signs differentiate children with attention-deficit disorders, learning disabilities, anxiety, depression, conduct disorders, risk for schizophrenia, enuresis, encopresis, and neurological impairment from normal children, although they do not differentiate one disturbance from another.

One constant criticism of the research on soft signs has been its poor quality. Therefore, Shaffer and coworkers' (1985) exemplary study is particularly impressive. While it is often the case that as well-conducted studies replace poorly conducted ones, initial findings tend to be weakened or vanish altogether, in this instance the opposite occurred. In this study the investigators reevaluated sixty-three male and twenty-seven female adolescents who had soft signs when they were 7 years old. The sample was drawn from a normal rather than a disturbed population. The most frequent soft signs involved motor coordination, such as awkwardness in finger-nose touching and the inability to perform alternating movements of hands and feet in a smooth, rhythmical fashion. The investigators found that adolescent males with two or more soft signs had significantly lower IQ scores and significantly more psychological disturbances than males with zero to one soft signs. These findings did not hold for females, however. For both male and female adolescents two or more soft signs were related to a significant increase in anxiety-withdrawal and, for males only, a significant increase in affective disorders. For both groups, soft signs were more potent predictors of subsequent anxious-withdrawn behavior than a host of other variables such as socioeconomic status, family disharmony, and anxiety-dependency at 7 years of age. However, the combination of soft signs and anxiety-dependency in early childhood was the most potent predictor of subsequent anxiety-withdrawal. Of equal interest was the failure to find any relation between soft signs and the subsequent appearance of attention-deficit disorders or conduct disorders, both of which have been regarded as being due to minimal brain damage. Finally, unlike other studies, this one did not find a decline in the number of soft signs with age, perhaps because it was longitudinal rather than cross-sectional, or because it evaluated a nonclinical population, or because of other differences. However, the quality of the study is sufficiently high for this single result to raise questions about previous findings.

Shaffer and coworkers' research nicely solves many of the problems of using naturally occurring behavior in a longitudinal design while introducing the kind of rigorous analysis of data typically associated with the controlled laboratory study.

Subjects were children of every fifth woman registered in one year at a large pediatric clinic. Children with obvious neurological damage and mental retardation were eliminated. The decision to use a *nonclinical sample* was an important one. We have seen the danger of generalizing to all children on the basis of data from a clinical population, such as generalizing to all obese children on the basis of ones who were sufficiently distressed to seek out special weight reduction clinics. This all too frequent error in clinical research results in exaggerating the degree of disturbance in the population as a whole. In addition, an unselected population provides a base rate for the occurrence of a given behavior (such as soft signs) and furnishes a guide to how frequently the behavior must appear in order to place the child at risk for developing a psychopathology (this frequency is two or more in the case of soft signs). The selection of every fifth woman eliminated *sample bias*, which might result in spurious generalization to populations significantly different from the one studied, say in education or socioeconomic status. The *control* group was drawn from the same population and matched with the experimental group in terms of age, income, anomalous family situations, welfare dependency, and maternal education. This strategy solved the difficult problem of locating children comparable to the experimental ones in all important respects except the variable being studied which, in this case, was soft signs. Finally, the *attrition rate* was around 10 percent, which is remarkably low for a longitudinal study.

The investigators used either standardized instruments or ones that achieved satisfactory reliability with this particular research group. *Instrumentation* is particularly important in doing research with soft signs, which are often unreliable because of the high degree of subjectivity involved in the criteria, such as "awkward" or "lack of rhythmical alternation."

However, high reliability did not solve the problem of prevalence since the number of soft signs diagnosed here was higher than in populations from other settings. This means that the threshold for calling a behavior evidence for a soft sign was lower than in other settings, even though this lower threshold was uniformly shared by all the members of the research team. To insure that soft signs would be similarly diagnosed in all settings would require further objectification of the criteria.

Data on behavior variables were gathered from the adolescents, parents, and teachers, insuring that assessment of disturbances was based on information from a *variety of sources*. The behavioral ratings and the soft sign evaluation were made by different investigators and were therefore done *blind*. This means that the ones making the behavioral evaluations would not be biased by knowing whether the adolescents had soft signs. Such independence of evaluation is not routinely done in clinical research; for example, it is not unusual for therapists to evaluate the results of therapy. The danger of this procedure is obvious.

The researchers evaluated a broad range of psychological disturbances rather than focusing on attention-deficit hyperactivity disorders and conduct disorders, the two most frequently linked with soft signs. The choice of a broad-gauged approach was particularly apt in light of the uncertain relation between soft signs and specific psychopathologies. Next, variables other than soft signs were studied for their possible relation to psychological disturbances. Specifically, the variables of being a single parent, of having four or more children, of having psychiatric treatment or a police record, of low income and education, and of marital dissatisfaction were combined into a category called social disadvantage. By means of a statistical technique called regression analysis, the investigators were able to ascertain that social disadvantage made no significant contribution to their findings. In sum, the investigators' *broad-gauged approach* to both the dependent and independent variables allowed them to capture significant relations and eliminate nonsignificant but plausible ones.

Finally, the investigators analyzed the data for possible *confounding* of variables. Because soft signs at 7 years were correlated both with low IQ and anxiety-withdrawal in adolescence, it was possible that low intelligence, rather than soft signs, might have led to anxious-withdrawn behavior. However, statistical analysis indicated that the relation between soft signs and anxiety-withdrawal was independent of IQ. Next, anxiety might have confounded the results in that high anxiety in the initial testing situation might have caused the kind of motor incoordination judged to be indicative of soft signs. However, this possibility was eliminated by the finding that the 7-year-olds who were high in anxiety but did not have at least two soft signs did not become anxious-withdrawn adolescents.

Like all skilled researchers, the investigators not only made a good case for their interpretation of the data but systematically eliminated other plausible interpretations as well. In general, this process of entertaining and testing alternate hypotheses either results in a strengthening of the hypothesis under investigation or points to the need for further research. In either case it is the mark of a sophisticated investigation.

Returning now to MBD, there is no evidence that the behaviors that define the syndrome are in fact related (Weiss, 1980). Typically, there is a low degree of interrelatedness among organic measures (such as neurological and EEG findings) and behavioral ones (such as cognitive deficits and emotional lability), while strictly psychological variables such as hyperactivity, distractibility, and emotional lability also fail to show the predicted cohesiveness. Generally speaking, factor-analytic studies produce a number of unrelated dysfunctions.

Note that, unlike the situation with autism, subsequent research is disconfirming rather than confirming the existence of a clinical entity of MBD. Yet the children so diagnosed are undoubtedly disturbed and require a comprehensive assessment, including a careful history, an evaluation of intrapersonal factors (such as specific cognitive functions and personality variables) and of context variables (such as family and school), along with a neurological examination (Weiss, 1980; Wohl, 1980). Instead of the global diagnosis of MBD, however, specific areas of dysfunction should be delineated, such as "poor visual-motor coordination and short attention span when dealing with numerical problems"; and, instead of assuming an organic substratum, the entire gamut of etiologic possibilities from neurological to intrapersonal to interpersonal should be explored.

PEDIATRIC PSYCHOLOGY

Just as the relation between brain and behavior has long intrigued researchers, so has the relation between psychological adjustment and physical health. In lay terms, does the mind influence the body as well as the body influencing the mind? If so, does this influence extend to the point of causing physical illness or significantly affecting recovery once an illness exists?

In the 1950s the general theme of the mind–body relation was couched within a *psychosomatic* framework. Psychological factors were viewed as causing certain illnesses, most commonly ulcers, asthma, ulcerative colitis, rheumatoid arthritis, and hypertension. The psychosomatic formulation did not deny that such illnesses might be due to organic causes, but these illnesses also could exist when no such causes could be identified.

Within the psychosomatic camp there were those who championed the idea that each illness was caused by a *specific* and characteristic unconscious psychological conflict. Ulcers, for example, were caused by unacceptable dependency needs in driven overachievers; hypertension was due to repressed hostility in overcontrolled individuals, while asthma resulted from an unconscious, infantile cry for the nurturant mother. (See Alexander, 1950.) There was also the idea that each illness had a characteristic constellation of personality traits so that one could speak of an ulcer or asthmatic personality, for example. While popular for a decade or so, the specificity approach has languished for lack of validating data.

A more *general* approach to etiology was proposed by Selye (1956) whose central concept was that of *stress* or the wear and tear on the body. While the body's heightened state of mobilization during stress can be adaptive, its emergency measures can become excessive if stress is unduly prolonged, resulting in damage to vulnerable body parts and functions. The stress model has proved more durable than the concept of specificity and continues to generate psychophysiological research. There is some evidence, for example, that adolescents who experience a greater number of life stresses, such as parental disharmony, failing a class, or being caught in a theft, visit the doctor more frequently and have higher rates of diagnosed illnesses. Or again, life stress has been related to respiratory tract illness and to the frequency of accidents in children (Wicks-Nelson and Israel, 1984). However, the links between stress as a psychophysiological variable and specific diseases have not been forged in most instances.

Gradually it became apparent that the psychosomatic framework was too narrow to encompass the complex interweaving of psychological and physical variables. The resulting attempt at a comprehensive definition of the field has been variously called holistic or behavioral medicine, health psychology, or, when applied to children, *behavioral pediatrics* or *pediatric psychology*. The DSM-III-R classification is Psychological Factors Affecting Physical Conditions. We prefer the term "pediatric psychology" because our sole interest is in children, while "behavioral pediatrics" limits the field to the behavioral model. The fact that the label "developmental pediatrics" does not exist is significant; most of the conceptualizations and research deal with "the child" and make no concerted attempt to integrate ideas and findings into a developmental framework.

In regard to *etiology* the current model recognizes that all disorders result from an interplay of psychological and biological factors, now one and now the other being more prominent in given instances. The same holds true for the *course* of the disease. In addition, the model has expanded to include not only interpersonal variables such as the parent–child interaction but also superordinate ones such as the family or the child's social class. Thus the model used to represent the complexity of etiological variables is now the comprehensive, interactive one presented in chapter 1.

The concern with illness per se has been expanded to include a host of health-related issues. One involves the psychological aspects of *treatment* of physical disorders. This would include various facets of the hospitalization experience, some of which are social, such as separation from parents and relating to other hospitalized children, some of which involve medical treatments that may be painful or frightening, some of which involve academic and recreational activities. In regard to *health maintenance*, noncompliance with medication and treatment regimens is surprisingly frequent, even when the child's health or life is at stake. Obviously, there are significant personal and interpersonal problems involved with the *dying child*. Finally, a recent phenomenon in the area of *prevention* involves psychologists being consultants to well-baby clinics or to pediatricians in the community.

The following presentation will sample some of the research in the various facets of pediatric psychology. (For a more detailed presentation, see Wicks-Nelson and Israel, 1984.)

Physical Illnesses

Whether there is a significant increase in psychological disturbances in physically ill children is uncertain. While we have already cited one study showing that the incidence of disturbances was twice that found in the normal population but not as great as in neurologically damaged children (Rutter, 1977), other studies have failed to find any significant differences. A reasonable conclusion at this point is that most children do not have an increase in psychological disturbances, although certain subgroups may. To take two examples: only in a small group of children with severe asthma was there evidence of disturbed behavior (Wicks-Nelson and Israel, 1984), and, while 36 percent of recently diagnosed diabetic children had depression and other psychological problems, almost all had recovered at the end of a nine-month period (Kovacs et al., 1985). There is general agreement that psychopathology, where it exists, tends to be of the internalizing type, such as anxiety and withdrawal, although oppositional behavior has also been noted. There is tentative evidence that the degree of threat to life, the severity and visibility of the handicap, the nature of the medical procedures, and parental reactions to illness are significant factors in determining the degree of disturbance in the child. However, the majority of chronically ill children seem to adjust well to the stresses involved, and many of those with psychopathology are affected only to a minor degree (Werry, 1986b).

Asthma

Asthma illustrates the complex interaction between physiological and psychological factors characteristic of the current approach to pediatric psychology. (Our presentation follows Wicks-Nelson and Israel, 1984.) Asthma is a disorder of the respiratory system manifested by intermittent episodes of wheezing and shortness of breath called dyspnea, or severe, life-threatening attacks, known as status asthmaticus, which require emergency medical treatment. The basic cause of asthma is unknown, but, for whatever reasons, the children have hypersensitive air passages which make them more responsive to a variety of irritants than are nonasthmatic children. Such irritants are regarded as *trigger mechanisms* rather than causes of asthma. Typically they involve a number of agents: respiratory infection can trigger an attack, as can allergies to inhaled substances such as dust or pollen and ingested substances such as milk or chocolate. A variety of physical factors—such as cold temperature, tobacco smoke, exercise, or rapid breathing—can also set off attacks. Psychological factors, particularly anxiety in anticipation of or during attacks, are also considered trigger mecha-

nisms, although the exact role of such factors is a matter of controversy.

Previous *psychosomatic* conceptualizations assigned etiological roles to various psychological factors. The credibility of these conceptualizations rested partly on an apparent increase in psychological problems, partly on the observation that when certain children were removed from the home, say, to be sent to a special hospital, their asthma disappeared. However, none of the conceptualizations has been validated by objective testing. There is no "asthmatic personality" as has been proposed; nor is there an increased incidence of psychopathology in such children except in severely ill ones. Even here the psychological problems may be due to the severity of the illness rather than being the cause of asthma, since children with severe physical handicaps (which clearly are not due to psychological factors) show a similar increase. The *psychoanalytic* hypothesis that asthma is a suppressed cry for the mother also failed to be supported. Specifically, there is no evidence of a special relation between the mother–child interaction and severity of asthma, nor does awareness of imminent separation from parents increase symptoms in chronic asthmatic children. The *learning theorist's* speculation that asthmatic attacks are classic conditioned responses to initially allergic reactions—say, to pollen—has not been demonstrated in the laboratory. Nor is it consistent with the fact that a conditioned response extinguishes readily if not repeatedly paired with the unconditioned stimulus which, in our example, would be pollen. Operant explanations that emphasize the role of parental attention as reinforcing asthmatic attacks have received only modest support by laboratory studies and, at best, can account for the persistence of such attacks, not for their etiology.

Research designed to implicate psychological factors in the *precipitation* of asthmatic attacks has been more successful. When asthmatic children were instructed to visualize their most frightening and angry experiences, or when stress was experimentally induced, or when the children were told that the aerosolized saline solution they were inhaling was an allergen or irritant, there was a significant reduction in air respiratory flow, which is what happens in an asthmatic attack. There is also some evidence that negative affect, especially anger, may trigger an attack in a few children (Werry, 1986b). In a clever reversal of roles in one study, the parents left home temporarily rather than the children, thereby controlling for the possibility that some physical feature of the home, such as dust, was responsible for the attacks, rather than the parents. In one special subgroup of children who were rated as emotionally reactive, the asthma improved during separation; the rest of the group was not affected.

Thus, as the expanded pediatric psychology model would predict, asthma is the result of a complex interaction of physiological, intraindividual, and interpersonal variables, research suggesting that the last two serve as triggering mechanisms rather than etiologic agents.

The findings with children have been paralleled by those with their *families*. As with the children, initial evidence of increased disturbance was largely due to sample bias in that only families needing and seeking professional help were studied. The failure to include a comparison group of physically handicapped children also made it impossible to determine whether disturbances were specific to asthma or whether they could be found in any deviant physical condition. As was true with children, there is no evidence of an overall increase in disturbed relations among family members, although there may be under special conditions, such as severe asthma (Werry, 1986b).

In regard to *treatment* the effectiveness of

psychotherapy is difficult to evaluate because of the poor quality of the studies. Behavior therapy is only minimally effective in changing respiratory function but is more effective in teaching compliance with treatment and in managing the emotional problems secondary to the asthma (Werry, 1986b).

Juvenile Diabetes Mellitus

Juvenile diabetes will serve to introduce the variable of compliance with medical regimens. (Our presentation again follows Wicks-Nelson and Israel, 1984.) The most common endocrine disorder in children, juvenile diabetes is a chronic, lifelong disorder of energy utilization caused by the pancreas producing insufficient insulin. Its more benign symptoms include excessive thirst, weight loss, and fatigue, but, if not controlled, the child lapses into a coma. The illness is also referred to as "insulin-dependent" diabetes. The treatment regimen is unusually demanding. It includes two injections of insulin per day, testing urine two to four times a day, weekly 24-hour collections of urine, and dietary restrictions. The procedures are necessary because the dosage of insulin must be adjusted on the basis of daily tests for levels of sugar in the urine and considerations of factors such as diet, exercise, general physical health, and emotional state. If the regimen is daunting, the stakes are high; "insulin reactions" can result in irritability, headaches, and shaking, or, in extreme cases, unconsciousness and seizures.

The typical sequence in *management* is as follows. The first task for the professional team involves gaining and maintaining control of the diabetic condition. Control may be followed by partial remission. Ironically, this "honeymoon period" may lead to overoptimism on the part of parents and children and undue casualness in regard to implementing the therapeutic regimen. Once control is achieved, responsibility must be shifted to the parents and ultimately to the child. The shift involves an educational program for the family concerning the disorder and its management. Very often formal classes are conducted for both parents and children. Research indicates that the average 12-year-old is sufficiently sophisticated to assume responsibility for self-care. Despite education, both parents and children often have misconceptions or insufficient knowledge concerning the disorder.

Psychological factors play various roles in the disease process and its management. (For a detailed presentation, see Delamater, 1986.) In the intrapersonal realm, the findings parallel those concerning asthma; i.e., there is no "diabetic personality," nor is there a significant increase in psychological problems in the group as a whole. In children with severe diabetes there may be an increase in anxiety and depression along with a decrease in general life satisfaction and a negative self-concept. However, the evidence even here is not conclusive.

A number of studies have examined the critical variable of *compliance* with the treatment regimen. In the superordinate context of the *family*, there is no evidence of a "diabetic family" having a distinctive pattern of interacting; however, there is evidence that supportiveness, competence, clear communication, and positive family interaction facilitate control of the illness. On the negative side, clinical studies suggest that poor control is related to chronic family conflict, inadequate parenting, noninvolvement in treatment, and financial difficulties. More recently, however, attention has shifted away from studying broad family characteristics and focused on the family's response to the treatment regimen itself. The situation-specific reaction of supporting or not supporting the regimen has proven more predictive of compliance than have broad family characteristics, with

the exception of conflict, which is an equally potent predictor at both the general and the situation-specific levels.

Surprisingly, there is no evidence that knowledge of the disease facilitates compliance to the therapeutic regimen; in fact, some studies suggest that a higher level of knowledge is found in patients who are in poor metabolic control than in patients in good metabolic control. However, there is tentative evidence that programs that concentrate on disease management skills rather than knowledge of the disease may meet with some success. There is also a suggestion of an interesting developmental trend in regard to assuming responsibility for controlling the illness. With adults, belief that self-care would decrease chances of long-term complications is apt to enhance compliance at least in around one-quarter of the population. In children, a similar belief that they are in control of events is ineffective; instead, self-blame is related to effective management. Thus it appears that children are motivated by the more primitive and even unrealistic notion of guilt, while adults have a more mature notion of responsibility. Even with adults, however, noncompliance remains a baffling problem.

Because of our interactional approach, psychopathology can never be viewed as exclusively "in" the child. The balance among interpersonal, intrapersonal, and organic factors is constantly shifting as we go from one psychopathology to another with no one context ever being the exclusive etiologic agent. However, there is a group of conditions in which the deviation lies primarily in the social environment, with the children playing only a minor role in the fate that befalls them. The two categories of deviations we will be concerned with are neglect and abuse, the latter being divided into physical and sexual abuse.

13

Deviations within the Interpersonal Context: Neglect and Abuse

---

Neglect is currently considered a form a child abuse. However, the literature is meager compared with that concerned with infants reared in bleak or substandard institutions. Studies of institutionally reared infants are also developmentally oriented, and so are more suited to our goal of viewing psychopathology as normal development gone awry. While the literature is typically conceptualized in terms of maternal deprivation, our preferred designation is *privation* because the infants have not been deprived of adequate maternal care but never have received it. In DSM-III-R, privation is subsumed under Reactive Attachment Disorders of Infancy or Early Childhood.

PRIVATION

The pioneering investigation of privation was done by Spitz (1945), who opened the door to numerous subsequent studies. As is well known, Spitz was a consultant to a foundling home whose infants were wasting away and dying, a condition called *marasmus*. He found that while the institution was hygienic and the infants were given a nourishing diet, they received only minimal stimulation from the social and physical environment, as well as from the gross motor activities of their own bodies. The caretaker–infant ratio was 1:8, and feeding and toileting were done in a routine, impersonal manner. There were no toys, while sheets hanging over the railing screened out the environment. Finally, a hollow worn in their mattresses prevented the infants from turning in any direction. A more isolated, sterile environment would be difficult to imagine. Spitz's famous prescription was "tender loving care in a one-to-one relation." Once the infants received adequate mothering, marasmus disappeared.

Spitz showed that, far from being a sentimental luxury, mothering is essential to healthy psychological development and, in certain instances, to life itself. However, neither Spitz nor subsequent research proved that institutions per se hamper normal development. It is privation—the absence of nurturance and appropriate stimulation—which is inimical to psychological growth, whether in institutions or in the home. Indeed, Russia and Israel have shown that institutions can embody the best of care, and infants seem to thrive in these settings. Nor did Spitz show that caretaking must be done by the mother or a mother substitute. The effects of a single caretaker compared with multiple caretakers are being vigorously investigated, and while the findings are not conclusive, it is clear that the number of caretakers does not tip the balance in favor of normality or severe psychopathology.

The Effects of Privation

Privation, or the lack of growth-promoting nurturance and stimulation from the social and physical environment, differs from deprivation, which is concerned with the loss of a loved one once the bond of love has been established. Loss was our concern in chapter 5; lack is our concern here.

One of the most detailed accounts of the effects of privation is presented by Provence and Lipton (1962), who studied seventy-five infants intensively during the first year of life. While the institution was orderly and clean, as was the one Spitz studied, it was not as psychologically sterile. The cribs were not shielded, there were age-appropriate toys, a radio played music softly. Yet it was clearly impoverished. The caretaker-to-infant ratio was 1:8 for eight hours of the day, 1:25 for the remaining sixteen. While most of the caretakers liked the infants and some even had favorites, the institutional policies and schedules limited caretaking to the bare essentials of feeding, bathing, and diapering. Motor activity was also limited, since the infants spent only four hours at most outside the crib, while visual and auditory stimulation was monotonously the same day after day.

In regard to the effects on development, there was a two- to five-month period of grace in which development proceeded normally. Then it began to deviate, primarily in the direction of retardation or failure of age-appropriate behavior to appear, although there were also some behaviors not typical of normal infants. As could be predicted, language and social ties, the functions most dependent on interpersonal interaction, were most adversely affected; motor development, with its strong maturational thrust, was least affected. But the effects were significant in all areas.

In the second half of the first year, the infants' behavior was characterized by an affective blandness and a lack of initiative. In relating to adults they were generally amiable and responded with mild pleasure. But there was no attachment to a single adult, no intense pleasure when one approached or distress at separation. Nor did the infants turn to adults for play and pleasure or for relief from distress. They were even deficient in techniques for warding off unpleasant stimuli; if they did not like an adult touching them, they would cry helplessly rather than trying to push the hand away. Precursors of this bland and impoverished responsiveness were observed as early as the second month of life when the infants failed to make the normal postural adjustment to being held and carried. The social smile appeared on schedule at age 3 to 4 months, but at times there was an intense and preoccupied looking at adults, which was striking and unusual. However, this preoccupation did not facilitate visual discrimination, since the infants did not respond differentially to a stranger and a familiar attendant or, indeed, to a face versus a mask.

We can readily understand the institutionalized infant's blandness in light of what we know about normal attachment. Why should the infant look to anyone to maximize pleasure and minimize pain when no one has provided the appropriate sensory stimulation and prompt relief from distress? Infrequent experience with caretakers hampers both discrimination and the pleasure of recognition. "People" are just that—an undifferentiated mass in which anyone can be substituted for anyone else. Similarly, the pervasive language delay—seen from the second month as a diminution in vocalization and, by the end of the first year, as a failure to use language to communicate and to develop simple words such as "mama"—is understandable in terms of the lack of verbal stimulation.

Reaction to toys had the same quality as reaction to people—blandness. Spontaneous play was meager, and there was little of the enterprising, experimental behavior seen in normal children. There was no toy preference, no distress at the loss of a toy or effort to regain it. The development of the object concept in Piaget's sense was markedly delayed. The infants were best in activities requiring imitation of adults and poorest in those requiring them to figure out a solution on their own.

Recall that the infants were not deprived of toys as they were of human contact. Why, then, did they not explore, especially if there is an intrinsic drive to do so? Provence and Lipton (1962) speculate that exploration languished because it lacked the generally vitalizing effect of sensitive caretaking. Here we have an instance of deviant development highlighting a relationship between variables which might be overlooked in normal development. It may be that the exploratory urge in normal infants is less autonomous than it has been pictured; instead, it must be reinforced by the caretaker, who mediates exploratory activity through the introduction of interesting objects, or by the generally vitalizing effect of affective ties to the caretaker.

As has been noted, motor development was less affected than other functions by lack of stimulation, although sitting, pulling to stand, and walking were all delayed. There were also unusual motor behaviors in the second six months—prolonged, affectless rocking on all fours, hand waving, or posturing. In addition, movement lacked the smoothness of performance seen in the normal infant; instead, it went by fits and starts, inactivity followed by sudden, jerky, poorly controlled activity.

Provence and Lipton frequently observed that the infants did not function in keeping with their capabilities. Motorically, they were able to approach, grasp, and manipulate objects, but from 6 months on they reached for toys less frequently than did normal infants. Their repertoire of sounds at 6 months was average for their age, but they did not communicate vocally or vocalize for their own entertainment. Maturationally, they were capable of stimulating and exploring their body and thereby defining their body image, but grasping their feet, sucking their thumb, poking their belly button, and all other normal body-oriented activities were strikingly absent. The lack of initiative in relation to people has already been described. Thus neither the social environment nor the physical environment nor their own body was utilized as a source of stimulation and play or as comfort from distress.

What a striking contrast between the pervasive blandness of these infants and the imperviousness, repetitiousness, and resistance of the autistic child, or the disjointed, erratic behavior of the schizophrenic child—and incidentally, what a contrast to the mentally retarded child, who makes maximum use of his or her limited potential! These institutionalized infants seem to be basically normal individuals in whom the vitality of growth has been sapped. True, some of their behavior is strange—the staring at adults, the mannerisms with the hands, the fitful outbursts of motor activity—but it generally does not puzzle the viewer. The lack of the vitalizing influence of sensitive caretaking seems to hold the key to understanding the infants' lack of initiative, their superficial, indiscriminate social responsiveness, and the retarded development of specific psychological functions.

Developmental Picture

Because they seem less disturbed than psychotic children, we would expect institutionalized children's development to be less deviant and the chances of reversing the damage to be greater. Such is the case. However, the total impact of privation depends on its duration and the kind of environment the child subsequently lives in; the child who goes from a bleak institution to a series of cold, rejecting foster homes will be more damaged than one who experiences consistent love and care in a single foster home.

Institutionally reared preschoolers tend to be lacking in deep attachments, clinging, overly friendly with strangers, and attention-seeking. Such behaviors continue into middle childhood. Institutional children also tend to be more attention-seeking, restless, disobedient, and unpopular in school than normal controls. They approach the teacher and other children more but tend to relate in socially unacceptable ways, such as calling out in class and disregarding the teacher's directions. In addition, they have greater difficulty in concentrating on the task at hand (Rutter, 1979b). In terms of our developmental model, their work orientation has been undermined.

Reversibility

That institutionalized children are not fated to deviant development is shown by the pioneering research of Skeels (1966). Again, there were two groups of infants being reared in an impoverished institutional environment, in this instance an orphanage. However, at 19 months of age, a group of thirteen toddlers was sent to an institution for the retarded, where each one was cared for by an adult who became particularly fond of him or her. In addition, this one-to-one relation was supplemented by frequent interactions with other adults in the environment.

Initially, the toddlers' average IQ score was 64, while the control group of twelve toddlers who remained in the orphanage had an average IQ score of 86. However, about eighteen months after the transfer, the "mentally retarded" experimental group now had an average IQ score of 92, while the control group's IQ score had declined to 61—a dramatic reversal of positions. Subsequently eleven of the toddlers were adopted and maintained their gains, while the two who were institutionalized suffered a decline. Most impressive of all were the results of a follow-up study when the experimental children were between 25 and 35 years of age. In general, their adult status was equivalent to that of children reared by natural parents in terms of education, occupation, and income.

By contrast, the control group continued to function at a retarded level.

While the Skeels study proved that the adverse effects of a bleak environment are reversible, it also suggests that such dramatic results are not easily achieved. No less than a totally rehabilitative environment was required. Thus the cost of reversing initial damage is high, although the cost of doing nothing is even higher, not only in terms of wasted human potential but in monetary terms as well: the control group cost the state five times as much as the experimental group!

Children adopted after infancy can also escape some of the damaging effects of privation. Although those adopted after 4 years of age can develop a deep relationship with their adoptive parents, they still tend to show attentional problems in the classroom and to have poor peer relations in middle childhood (Rutter, 1979b). Even without adoption, the picture is not totally gloomy. Rutter and Quinton (1984) studied the adult adjustment of eighty-one women whose institutional rearing was punctuated by episodes of living with their disharmonious family. The women clearly had been damaged: twenty-five had personality disorders and criminal records compared with none in a control group, and only one-fifth of them were making a good adjustment compared with three-fifths of the control group. The unique feature of the study is its exploration of the factors that protected one-fifth of the group from the fate of the majority. The first was a positive school experience. This experience was not necessarily academic—the women did not have a higher IQ than the rest of the group— but it might have involved peer relations or sports or participation in the arts. Incidentally, such experiences had little effect on the women in the control group who were making a good adjustment and who presumably had other sources of feelings of self-worth. The next protective factor was a good marriage.

While others in the group tended impulsively to marry inadequate, disturbed, or criminal men, the women who were doing well planned their marriage and had spouses who were making a good psychosocial adjustment. In fact, the characteristics of the spouse were by far the most powerful ameliorating factor. The results are interesting in themselves and also offer us a rare glimpse into the conditions under which children "outgrow" their deviant behavior.

PHYSICAL CHILD ABUSE

Physical child abuse is a major cause of death of children in the United States (Alexander, 1976). If not killed, the abused child may sustain traumatic injuries to any part of the body: bruises, lacerations, burns, internal hemorrhages, or fractured or broken bones, including the skull. The facts are shocking. Equally startling, the very existence of child abuse was hushed up until early in the 1960s. Since then attention has understandably been focused on protecting the child from further abuse, on remedial measures for parent and child alike, and on a search for causes in the hope of eventual prevention.

The search has proved difficult. The naive assumption that the abusing parent must be manifestly psychotic has not been borne out. Gradually the focus of research has shifted from the intrapersonal context of the abusing parent to the interpersonal context of the parent–child interaction and the superordinate context of socioeconomic status and society. Concomitantly, the causal model has shifted from a simple linear one ("If the parent has a given personality disturbance, then he or she will be apt to abuse the child") to an interactional one in which child abuse is the end product of the interplay among a number of variables and contexts. Instead of an absolute relation between two variables, therefore, causation now becomes a contingent affair, a complex network of relationships whose patterning may change as the component variables themselves increase or decrease in strength or even appear or disappear over time. We have already met this interactional model in chapter 1 (see Figure 1.1) and have seen it used in accounting for a number of psychopathologies.

Recently, D. A. Wolfe (1987) has conceptualized the research findings in terms of deviations from normal development, a conceptualization particularly congenial to our own orientation. Physical child abuse is regarded as a pathological extreme of the normal *authoritarian* pattern of child rearing. Similarly, physically brutal acts are viewed not as inexplicable outbursts but as the result of forces that tip the omnipresent tension between anger and control in favor of the former. We will follow Wolfe's (1987) elaborations of both these themes after presenting a general orientation to child abuse.

Definition

Child abuse includes acts of commission and omission. The most frequent type of behavior in the former category is *physical abuse*, defined as nonaccidental physical injuries resulting from acts on the part of adults responsible for the child's care. Major injuries include brain damage, internal injuries, burns, severe cuts, bruises, and lacerations, while minor injuries include less serious cuts and bruises. Acts of omission involve extreme *neglect* on the part of responsible caretakers so that a child's life, health, or safety is endangered. Despite the general equating of child abuse with severe physical injury, two-thirds of maltreated children experience neglect, and of physical abuse cases 88 percent involve only minor physical injuries (Wolfe, 1987). Also, about one-half of maltreated children experience both physical abuse and neglect. Finally, the vast majority of physical abuse occurs within the context of disciplining, suggesting that it should be considered an extreme deviation from normal child-rearing practices.

Causes

Studies of child abuse nicely illustrate the point that deviant behavior is often the result of complex interactions among intrapersonal, interpersonal, and superordinate contexts.

THE SUPERORDINATE CONTEXT This country has the highest level of violence of any Western society as evidenced by statistics on crime and murder. The right of schools to use corporal punishment on disobedient children has been upheld by the highest court in the land, the U.S. Supreme Court, in *Ingraham v. Wright*. Thus there are those who claim that child abuse is tacitly encouraged by an American society that is complacent about aggression in general and condones punitiveness toward children in particular (Belsky, 1980). Moreover, the rate of violence is higher among family members than it is among any other social group. As shocking as physical abuse of children is, it is even more disturbing to realize that it is just one manifestation of family violence in a society marked by violence.

While there is no difference in *race* in regard to maltreatment of children, there tends to be more neglect and slightly less physical abuse among blacks, while there is more physical abuse or a combination of abuse and neglect among whites. Socioeconomic status and, more specifically, *poverty* are strongly related to child maltreatment, which increases significantly in the lower class and with poverty. Neglect in particular is related to such indices of poverty as inadequate housing and substandard living conditions. In addition, the rate of child maltreatment has increased over the past decade as the economic hardships of the poor have increased and the economic status of minority children has deteriorated. While more frequent, child maltreatment is not confined to the lower classes, however, since it is found at all socioeconomic levels. (For further details, see Wolfe, 1987.)

The *families* in which maltreatment occurs have special characteristics. The mothers tend to be younger than in other families in the general population; they may be in their teens when they have their first child. Abusive families also tend to have an above-average number of children. As can be inferred from the role of poverty in maltreatment, unemployment and job dissatisfaction run high, these two factors being responsible for an increase in other forms of intrafamily violence, such as wife beating, as well as for physical abuse of children. Finally, abusive families tend to be socially isolated. Friendships are brief, ending in quarrels and bitterness. When mothers do relate it is to women as distressed and beset by problems as themselves. We shall soon see how important this pattern of stress and isolation is in physical child abuse.

INTERPERSONAL CONTEXT   Almost all (97 percent) of maltreatment is by parents. Taking maltreatment as a whole, females exceed males in regard to frequency; however, males are responsible for more major and minor physical injuries, while females are more neglecting. Unfortunately, most of the research has been done on females, and there is no way of knowing at this point whether the findings are equally applicable to males.

Until recently, it was thought that abusing parents were themselves abused as children, the violence being passed on from one generation to another. Subsequent studies, however, showed that less than 15 percent of adults who report being abused were subse-quently abusive toward their own children. Thus the intergenerational effect is far less potent than was once believed, although it still should be regarded as one of many factors predisposing the parent to abusive behavior (Wolfe, 1987).

THE INTRAPERSONAL CONTEXT   When the magnitude of child abuse became evident, an initial reaction was that the *parents* must be severely disturbed psychologically. This belief turned out to be erroneous; only about 10 percent of such parents have a psychiatric disturbance. Next, a host of personality traits were attributed to the parents, who were described as less intelligent and more hostile, impulsive, immature, self-centered, rigid, domineering, dependent, narcissistic, child-like, and passive than nonabusing parents. The very length of the list made the idea of there being an "abusive personality" sink under its own weight. In addition, the traits themselves often proved to be nondiscriminating between abusing and nonabusing parents. Clearly, a new approach to the role of the parent was needed.

In regard to abused *children*, there is no evidence of a gender difference. Neglect is most frequent in the infant and toddler periods and declines with age. Despite the public image of its coming early in development, physical abuse increases in middle childhood, the highest rate being found between 12 and 17 years of age, perhaps due to the increase in parent–child conflict in early adolescence.

Finally, there is evidence that children are not solely the victim of abuse but that they play a role in eliciting it. Prematurity, mental retardation, physical handicaps, and congenital malformations are overrepresented among abused children, suggesting that these children place more demands on the caretakers than do their physically normal siblings. There are even reports that certain infants have a particularly irritating and grating cry which nurses or even foster parents find intolerable.

While the data concerning the role of the child in producing abuse needs further documenting, they were instrumental in the shift away from thinking of parents as sole causal agents to thinking in terms of an interaction between parent and child as well as an interaction among variables. It is this newer viewpoint that we will now explore.

An Interactional Model

DISCIPLINE As we have already noted, physical abuse most frequently occurs in the context of discipline. Among the types of discipline we have described (see chapter 2) the one most akin to physical abuse is *authoritarian* discipline. Here parents control children's behavior according to an absolute set of standards, discourage verbal give-and-take, and value obedience and respect for authority, work, and tradition. Such an "old-fashioned" approach to discipline ("children should be seen and not heard") can be used with respect for children and concern for their welfare. As with all discipline, as much depends on how the practices are implemented as on the nature of the practices themselves.

With physically abusive parents, however, there is an overemphasis on physical punitiveness and an insensitivity to the children's needs (LaRose and Wolfe, 1987). Ironically, such an authoritarian approach, while extreme, tends also to be ineffective. Because parents are locked into one kind of discipline, they cannot deal with different situations in a versatile, appropriate manner; neither can they serve as models for or help their children develop a flexible repertoire of ways to deal with interpersonal problems. If, for any number of reasons, escalation occurs, punitiveness may become brutality.

If physical abuse represents an extreme deviation from the normal pattern of punitive, authoritarian discipline, the question becomes, What factors tip the scale in favor of brutality? (Our presentation, unless otherwise noted, will follow Wolfe, 1987.) Note that the question is phrased in terms of factors, meaning that we will be dealing with a number of variables rather than with a single cause. These variables are derived not only from the inter- and intrapersonal contexts but also from the context of time since both past and contemporary events play a prominent role in producing physical abuse. To take one example of this multivariate approach, a stressful pregnancy puts the mother at risk for subsequently becoming physically abusive if she is also anxious, ill prepared for motherhood, and lacking knowledge about children. What is more, these variables will include not only vulnerabilities and deficiencies but, equally important, resources and capabilities as well. One lesson clinicians have learned is that psychopathology typically is not the result of pathogenic forces alone but of the balance between such forces and those favoring healthy adaptation and growth.

Also note that the question uses the image of tipping a scale. The implication is that a number of parents with different personalities may be living in a "zone of vulnerability," but will not physically abuse their children unless there are changes that undermine restraint and provoke a violent outburst. Thus physically abusive parents are not a breed set apart from all other parents. As we shall see, it is the ill-equipped parent who must deal with a difficult child in a highly stressful situation which sets the stage for physical abuse; but this triad of forces characterizes nonabusive parents as well as abusive ones.

PATTERNS OF INTERACTION Research on parent–child interactions allows us to view the family at closer range than does the description of disciplinary techniques. The data indicate that members of abusive families interact less frequently than do those of non-abusive controls, but, when they do, there is proportionately more negative than positive behavior. The latter finding is particularly important. Members of physically abusive families often engage in antagonistic behaviors such as criticism, threats, and shouting. However, such behaviors can be found in carefully matched control families as well. What sets the physically abusive family apart is the lack of positive exchanges that would offer relief from the atmosphere of imminent and overt hostility while allowing the family to develop constructive ways of relating to and supporting one another. In sum, the overall picture is of family members trapped between avoidance and anger.

THE ROLE OF STRESS   Stress is the catalyst turning a difficult family situation into an abusive one. There is no one type of stress that leads to physical abuse, just as there is no one type of abusive parent. Rather, stress arises from multiple sources such as poverty, marital disharmony, or lack of preparation for parenting. Moreover, the impact of stress is not absolute but relative to the characteristics of the individual who must cope with it; for example, a child's school failure may infuriate one parent while being a matter of indifference to another. Moreover, here as elsewhere, there are certain buffers, such as an experienced, stable grandparent in the home or a convivial work setting, that may serve as moderating factors. Thus one cannot expect a one-to-one relation between the amount of stress and the degree of violence.

TRANSITIONAL STAGES   It is possible to conceptualize physical abuse as developing in a series of stages if one keeps in mind that the transitions are not inevitable and that parents can move back and forth among them. (We continue to follow Wolfe, 1987.)

The *first stage* is marked by a reduced tolerance for stress and a disinhibition of aggression. There are three destabilizing factors contributing to this state of affairs. The first is *poor preparation for parenting*. This may be due to the mother's own family, which relied upon punitive authoritarian discipline and was deficient in empathy, reasoning, and the cultivation of problem-solving and social skills. Thus the mother has learned that the principal way to cope with frustration is attack. The next component is *low control*, which may be viewed as another untoward consequence of punitive, authoritarian rearing. In general, people who have a variety of resources to deal with life's varied difficulties feel they are in control of situations and of themselves. An impoverished repertoire of coping mechanisms is accompanied by a feeling of vulnerability to losing control: If attack does not work, what can I do then? The final component is *stressful life events*, which tend to be common, everyday problems of parenting, marriage, and work, rather than major crises such as severe illness. Such contemporary events further tax an already burdened system.

Counterbalancing the three destabilizing factors are *compensatory* ones: a supportive spouse, friends or organizations, socioeconomic stability, success at work or school, or people who can serve as models of effective coping. Parental behavior is the result of the relative strength of both destabilizing and compensating factors.

The *second stage* is characterized by poor management of acute crises and provocations. The punitive, authoritarian parent uses short-term and possibly self-defeating solutions to problems, such as excessive alcohol or drug use, relocation to escape from debtors, or, in the case of children, harsh punishment. With time, some increasingly feel they are losing control. The principal means of counteracting this feeling is redoubling the intensity of power assertiveness and punishment.

There are three destabilizing factors that turn punishment into abuse. The first is *conditioned emotional arousal*. The potentially abusive parent has had many experiences of being angry with the child. By a process of classical conditioning, specific aspects of the child's behavior or appearance, such as a facial expression or whining, can come to be associated with irritation or rage. In the future, similar behaviors or appearances on the child's part will serve as stimuli to arouse similar affects in the parent. Thus parents are increasingly likely to be in a mood that would result in aggression toward the child. The second destabilizing factor involves *attribution*. In this case a person who is unaware of the source of anger misattributes it to a current event, which provokes him to aggression. A common example is a man who feels irritable when he comes home from work and spanks his son for leaving the tricycle in the driveway. This has been called transfer of arousal and is akin to the defense mechanism of displacement. In any case, the child becomes the victim of the parent's anger. The third destabilizing factor is an intensification of aggression by the attribution of *intentionality*. Research has shown that aggression is more likely when an act is viewed as deliberate rather than accidental. In the second stage, the parent views the child's acts as purposely defiant or provocative, thereby justifying excessive punishment.

Compensatory factors in the second stage include improvements in the child's behavior, say, through maturation or a positive experience in school or with peers. There may be community resources that can offer relief from the home situation, such as day care facilities. Finally, parental coping resources can be increased through the intervention of concerned individuals or professionals, so that stress is perceived as less overwhelming.

The *third stage* is characterized by habitual patterns of arousal and aggression. Here the preceding pattern of increased stress, arousal, and overgeneralized response to the child becomes habitual. In part the change comes about because some children easily *habituate* to existing levels of intensity of punishment so that harsher measures are required to maintain a given level of compliance. In part, parents are immediately *reinforced* by venting their anger and making the child comply. However, in the long run they are paving the way for further escalation of punishment while concomitantly failing to help the child find alternative modes of behaving that would decrease or eliminate the necessity of punishment. Thus the parents' complaint, "No matter what I do he won't listen" and "He only listens if I get really mad" are justified to a certain extent. What the parents have failed to grasp is their own role in this impasse. Finally, as we have seen in chapter 9, the combination of punitiveness and neglect is the breeding ground for *behavior problems* which, in turn, exasperate the parents.

Compensatory factors in this final stage, unfortunately, are minimal. Parents, either on their own or through help from others, may come to realize the self-defeating nature of their behavior. The child in turn may respond positively to noncoercive measures. Finally, community services such as crisis intervention centers may become involved and help change the pattern of parental behavior.

PROCESSES Many of the processes involved in the above developmental stages can be explained in terms of *learning principles*. The fact that incidental features of the child's behavior present during an angry exchange come to elicit parental anger can be due to classical conditioning. Such conditioning can account for the escalation of parental anger even if the child's behavior does not change significantly. Many behaviors can be strengthened by reinforcement, such as the temporary effectiveness of harsh punishment in forcing the child to obey. Imitation also figures prominently in the model; for example, parents imitate the authoritarian discipline they observed in their own parents while their children develop behavior problems by imitating parental aggressiveness. However, these learning principles have to be supplemented by a cognitive one of *attribution*. An attribution is an inference about the causes of behavior or about a person's characteristics; for example, a child may attribute his poor grade in math to being poorly taught (cause) by a crabby teacher (characteristic), while the teacher may attribute the same failure to careless mistakes (cause) by a spoiled child (characteristic). (For further information concerning the theory and its application to psychopathology, see Harvey and Weary, 1981.) Examples of attribution are the aroused parent, who is unaware of the source of his feelings, attributing them to some current provocative behavior on the child's part or the parent attributing intentionality to the child's behavior and thereby justifying parental anger. In both instances minor provocations or transgressions become major ones, thereby increasing the likelihood of punitiveness.

ABUSIVE PARENTS   While we have referred to many parental characteristics, it would be worthwhile to flesh out the picture, always keeping in mind that most of the research has involved abusive mothers. Such mothers tend to be socially isolated from family and friends, to have a disproportionate rate of negative to positive interactions, to be angry, and to have a low frustration tolerance and a high level of emotional reactivity to prov-

ocations. They tend to communicate and stimulate their children less than do control parents, to be intrusive and inconsistent rather than varying their discipline to make it appropriate to the seriousness of the child's transgressions. Not only are they inept in parenting but they are ineffective as well, their children complying less frequently than those in a control group. While they are intellectually aware of normative behavior for children of different ages, they are peculiarly insensitive to their own child's needs and abilities. This insensitivity leads them to forcing a child to behave in a manner beyond his or her abilities and to be exasperated when the child fails. The number of stressful life events does not differ from that of control populations, but the mothers perceive their lives as more stressful and themselves as unhappy, distressed, depressed, guilty, and having low self-esteem.

ABUSE AND NEGLECT   Because abuse and neglect can coexist, we might expect similar parental characteristics. However, there are also some significant differences. (Our presentation follows LaRose and Wolfe, 1987.) Neglect is not as influenced by contemporaneous events; while physical abuse can be triggered by opposition, fighting, accidental occurrences, or dangerous or sexual behavior on the child's part, neglect results from more chronic adult inadequacies and failures. Neglectful parents have more life stresses than do abusive ones and more unmet needs, resulting in loneliness and discontentment, and they are less well adjusted. They interact less with their families than do physically abusive parents, who, in turn, show more verbal and physical aggression. However, neglectful parents have an even greater imbalance between negative and positive interactions than do physically abusive ones. The overall picture, then, is of neglect as being a more chronic condition than abuse and of the parents being more disturbed, more stressed, and more dissatisfied.

The Abused Child

There is a well-nigh insolvable *methodological problem* involved in studying the effects of physical abuse on children. As we have seen, many of the characteristics of their environment are inimical to healthy development: poverty, isolation, violence, insensitive caretaking, just to name a few. Such an environment alone is sufficient to produce deviant development. How then can one determine the effects of physical abuse per se as one more noxious experience? While theoretically it would be possible to find a control group matched for all significant factors except physical abuse, the practical problems involved in doing so are nearly insurmountable. Most studies have settled for matching for demographic criteria such as socioeconomic status, income, and education. While the hope is that these criteria will capture the crucial psychological variables, there is no guarantee that they do.

With this methodological caution in mind, we shall attempt a developmental reconstruction of the effects of physical abuse, relying on Martin and Kempe (1976) and Wolfe (1987) unless otherwise noted in our presentation. As much as the literature allows, we shall view physical abuse in terms of deviations from the path of normal development. (A more detailed account of normal development than will be presented here is found in chapter 2.)

PREGNANCY   Pregnancy is stressful; not only are there physical complications, but a number of mothers also report being beaten by their mate. There is twice the risk of prematurity and ten times the risk of a cesarean section as in the normal population; mothers from lower socioeconomic status have to con-

tend with inadequate nutrition and medical care as well as the tensions in the home. Yet the mother may look forward to the baby with an idealized expectation that somehow all of her problems will be solved and all of her needs will be met. Understandably, her deepest longing is that she will be given to, since she is too beset with problems to feel she has much to give. As we have already noted, a stressful pregnancy in an anxious, ill-prepared mother is also linked with subsequent abuse and related problems.

ATTACHMENT   From normal development we know that infants who are sensitively cared for become securely attached to their caretaker and that a secure attachment facilitates the subsequent development of competence in regard to both the social and physical environment. In the case of physical abuse, the picture deviates significantly from the norm. Mothers who have idealized expectations of their own needs being met are disappointed and resentful at having to care for the infant. In general, abusive and neglecting mothers fail to provide sensitive caretaking and consequently have insecurely attached infants who either cling to them or react with anger. The abused infant also may fail to initiate or respond to social contact, and affect may be shallow when it appears. Social signals may be ambiguous, and parents do not know how to interpret, say, an ambivalent mixture of bidding for physical contact and anger. The abused 1- to 3-year-old may approach adult caretakers less frequently than the nonabused child, and the approaches themselves may be oblique, such as taking small backward steps in the direction of the target person or coming toward such a person from behind. The growth-promoting effect that a secure attachment has on subsequent development of competencies is also jeopardized (Egeland, Sroufe, and Erickson, 1984).

Empathy, which is akin to attachment,

suffers along with it. Abused toddlers, unlike their nonabused counterparts, show no concern when witnessing distress in other toddlers, such as crying. When they do respond, it is often in terms of fear, anger, or attack. Even at this early age, then, they resemble their parents, who either isolate themselves from interpersonal tensions or respond aggressively to them.

Clinical observations furnish some information concerning the subsequent nature of attachment in the preschool period. Abused preschoolers are described as joyless and hypervigilant, both of which seem natural consequences of joyless, unpredictable caretaking. Because they have been punished according to parental mood, the children become adept at reading mood changes in adults. They seem constantly on guard, as if asking, "Where is the danger? What are the telltale signs that the adult is about to strike out at me?" When brought to the hospital after being abused, such behavior can become "frozen watchfulness," as the child sits quiet and immobile, surveying every move the staff makes. In order to cope with this fear of unpredictable violence, the child seems further to be asking, "What can I do in order to divert or distract or placate or please the threatening adult?" Consequently, the children are described as "chameleons in their adaptation to various people" (Martin and Kempe, 1976, p. 107).

INITIATIVE   Initiative suffers in a special way. The constant concern over doing what the parents want the child to do overwhelms self-reliance. Toddlers dare not turn their backs on parents or venture out independently but must always keep a wary eye on them. In addition, parents' unrealistic expectations concerning socialization subject the child to continual failure. As a result, low self-esteem is one of the abused child's prominent characteristics by the preschool period.

The intellectual expansiveness that is part of initiative also suffers. The incidence of mental retardation and learning disorders is high in abused children. In part, this is the result of prematurity and organic brain damage resulting from physical abuse. But the deficiencies may also be psychogenic. "Learning, competency, exploration, initiative, autonomy are not valued in most abusive homes; indeed, they may be the basis for physical assault by the parents" (Martin and Kempe, 1976, p. 193). Gross motor development and language seem particularly vulnerable in the preschool period. Recall that the normal toddler is all over the place and into everything; it may be just this natural expression of curiosity which the abusive parents find intolerable. In a like manner, language may suffer both because of inadequate verbal exchanges with parents and because the child may be hit for questioning, complaining, expressing feelings, or "sassing." The preschooler's talking, like the infant's crying, is regarded as an irritating intrusion. The above-mentioned sense of failure also undermines the child's motivation to learn and achieve. Consequently, preschoolers can lag as much as twenty points behind their nonabused peers while both physically abused and neglected children lag significantly in verbal and mathematical abilities in middle childhood.

SELF-CONTROL   Requirements for self-control typically begin in the toddler period and are most effective when parents are consistent, sensitive, warm, and communicative. Because such qualities tend to be lacking in the authoritarian, abusive parent, it is not surprising that the onset of socialization is a vulnerable period for their children. Parents tend to be inconsistently punitive, to punish in anger, to offer no reason for punishment except that the child should obey. Such an indiscriminate, inconsistent use of parental power hampers the development of stable self-control and inclines the toddler and preschooler toward various psychological disturbances.

Predictably, abused children have an elevated level of aggression that comes to be used as the legitimate or predominant means of solving problems. By middle childhood behaviors such as hitting, yelling, destroying, pushing, and grabbing are widely reported at home and at school. Poor self-control is also evidenced by distractibility and resisting directions in school. There is also suggestive evidence that, in adolescence, abused delinquents commit more violent crimes than do nonabused delinquents.

SOCIABILITY It is not surprising that peer relations suffer in abused children. In the preschool years these children are as wary of peers as of adults; for example, they may avoid friendly overtures with a mixture of approach and avoidance, such as walking toward a playmate with their head turned to the side. In middle childhood abused children tend to be rejected or neglected. In part this is due to their poorly controlled aggression, in part to the fact that their socially isolated parents do little to foster outside contacts and cultivate social skills.

GENERAL ADJUSTMENT By middle childhood abused children are evidencing an increase in psychological disturbances. Not only do they have conduct disorders, but they are depressed, hopeless, and lacking in self-esteem as well. A history of chronic abuse is particularly ominous.

The "Breed Apart" Fallacy

In discussing a given psychopathology the emphasis of necessity is on the ways it deviates from normal development. The danger of such an emphasis is that individuals evidencing a particular disturbance will come to be viewed as a breed apart. Moreover, there is a tendency to emphasize and magnify deviations when a disturbance is first being described and studied; only after studies using representative samples and proper control groups are done do the differences between normal and disturbed populations tend to moderate or even disappear. Such has been the case with child abuse. While there are distinctive features, many of the so-called deviations can be found in nonabusive families who are similarly beset by poverty, unemployment, and marital disharmony.

A case in point is Starr's (1982) study of ninety-seven abusive families matched with ninety-two nonabusive families for social class, race, age, income, family type (such as single parent or nuclear family), and family composition, among other demographic variables. Of the 190 variables studied, only ten showed a statistically significant difference between abusive and nonabusive families. A number of these could be anticipated from our review: violent disagreements between parents leading to hitting and throwing, fewer visits with people and meetings with relatives, insensitivity to the emotional complexity of the child, increased amount of neglect. However, many of the findings were unexpected. While there was some evidence of social isolation, there was also no difference between the two groups in the number of telephone contacts or the number of good friends and helpful neighbors. Thus the picture is one of partial but not total social isolation. There was no difference in the way the mothers were reared by their own parents, in their current feelings of being overwhelmed, in the amount of affection they displayed and spanking they administered, and in the children's temperament. Clearly, the similarities outweighed the differences by far.

What are some possible interpretations of

finding such as Starr's (1982)? One is that a number of crucial differences have not been investigated in the research to date but might be uncovered subsequently. Another possibility is that there is a thin line between abuse and nonabuse so that relatively minor shifts in the total constellation of psychological factors can tip the balance in one direction or the other. Regardless of how one views them, the finding of significant overlap between abusive and nonabusive families has an important practical implication. The palpable brutality of severe physical abuse has galvanized the nation into taking legal measure and funding programs aimed at protecting children and helping their families. However, for every abused child there is one being reared in a similar, only slightly less damaging environment of punitiveness, indifference, insensitivity, and violence. What is more, the plight of such children has worsened in the 1980s. Lacking the shock value of physical injury, these children are largely ignored by the public. The idea that maltreated children are a breed apart thus serves to divert attention from the magnitude of the problem of children with blighted childhoods.

Remediation and Prevention

Remediation has followed the trend in etiology in that it initially emphasized the role of the parents and then shifted to the interpersonal context. From the beginning there also have been those concerned with the superordinate variables of socioeconomic status and society and more specifically with the effects of poverty and societal violence. (For a detailed presentation of remedial and preventive programs, see Belsky, 1978, and Wolfe, 1987.)

Individual psychotherapy was offered to parents in an effort to supply the nurturant and caring relationship they might have missed in their own childhood and to help relieve the parents' emotional burdens. However, this approach to remediation met with little success, studies showing that around one-third of the parents reabused their children during treatment while two-thirds relapsed after treatment (Wolfe, 1987). Subsequent efforts have been *behaviorally* oriented and are concerned with altering specific patterns of parent–child interaction, this interpersonal orientation being more in line with advances in understanding the nature of child abuse. Many of the programs resemble the ones used with parents of conduct-disordered children since the patterns of family interaction are similar. These behaviorally oriented programs have already been described in chapter 9 so they will not be presented again here. (See Azar and Wolfe, in press.)

Preventive measures have as their goals the development of positive child-rearing practices, especially in the early stages of development, along with increasing the parents' and children's abilities to cope with stress and adapt flexibly to problem situations. Measures promoting skills for both parent and child go hand in hand with reducing stress on the family, whether interpersonal or economic. (For a detailed account of primary prevention, see Rosenberg and Reppucci, 1985.)

Some preventive programs are broad-scale efforts to enhance parental competence by disseminating knowledge about child rearing. The media can be used to provide information about child development, parenting skills, and coping strategies, or about the nature of child abuse and ways of seeking help. Other programs target high-risk groups such as single, teenage parents or isolated families and ones undergoing crises. Hospital staff in perinatal and well-baby clinics along with social workers and nurses in the community can provide information about child rearing and coping skills. The effectiveness of the many kinds of preventive programs is largely unknown. Some programs changed the attitudes of high-risk parents toward child rearing, for example, but their effect on actual behavior was not assessed. There is suggestive evidence, however, that home visits by nurses or parent aides who provide parent education, enhance social support, and link families with health and human services, are the most effective means of decreasing child abuse in high-risk populations (Rosenberg and Reppucci, 1985). Apparently, consistent personal involvement has a greater impact than the more impersonal media programs or the more limited contact characteristic of lectures, demonstrations, and discussions.

While *early intervention* does not protect children from abuse, it has the advantage of being specifically targeted to the needs of individual families rather than being broadgauged as preventive programs tend to be. The goals are often the same—change destructive patterns of interaction, increase knowledge and competence, and decrease stress. A variety of approaches are available to achieve such goals, such as child management training, parent education and support groups, anger and stress management, and methods for treating the conditions that precipitate abusive episodes. Some of the skills parents are taught involve the use of positive reinforcement and nonviolent discipline, so they can correct their faulty notion that if punishment does not work, increasing its severity will. Training in relaxation and positive imagery may be offered to help parents control their anger.

For the children, medical care, play therapy, remedial classes to compensate for developmental delay, and temporary or permanent institutional or foster-home placement, are available. Behaviorally oriented therapy helps the child respond to parental anger in ways other than defiance, which only serves to escalate anger.

Those who view child abuse as a social problem advocate a number of programs of social action. Because there is evidence that lack of day-care facilities may be related to child abuse, increasing the number and availability of such facilities might reduce the caretaking pressures on the parent and lessen child abuse. Crisis nurseries have been established where parents can bring the child for a few hours when they have reached the limits of their endurance. There are also advocates of heroic social action to eliminate the poverty and the widespread acceptance of violence—as evidenced by corporal punishment and television programming—which are assumed to foster child abuse.

While all intervention programs claim a measure of success, it is too early to determine their relative effectiveness or their effectiveness over time. The ideal goal of preventing the abuse before it occurs is even further from realization.

SEXUAL ABUSE

Recognition of the prevalence of childhood sexual abuse followed recognition of childhood physical abuse and produced even greater shock waves throughout the professional community. The fact that the majority of instances occurred within the family or with familiar adults rather than being committed by sexually perverted strangers, was even more disturbing. As was the case with physical abuse, the pressure to understand and to do something about sexual abuse outstripped researchers' ability to produce data from well-designed studies which could serve as the basis for understanding and action. Consequently there was a good deal of misinformation or only partially correct information. Only now are we beginning to understand certain aspects of sexual abuse and its consequences, while many crucial questions remain to be answered. (For a summary of the current situation, see Finkelhor, 1986a.) The paucity of solid data in no way mitigates the stark conclusion that physical and sexual abuse are not rare acts performed by psychologically deviant outsiders; rather, they are part of the lives of a significant number of children and are typically perpetrated by those entrusted with these children's care.

Prevalence

Prevalence estimates from various studies range from 3 to 62 percent of all children. (Our presentation follows Peters, Wyatt, and Finkelhor, 1986). Even the lower percentage would mean the sexual abuse is far from uncommon while the higher percentage would mean that it is of epidemic proportions. However, the obvious conclusion is that definitive information concerning prevalence is not available. It will be instructive to examine the many reasons why this is the case.

DEFINITIONS One reason reported prevalence rates vary so widely is that studies use different definitions of child sexual abuse. There is general agreement as to *age*, the upper limits varying between 15 and 17 years in most studies. However, there is no agreement about whether abuse should include *noncontact* experiences such as exhibitionism and sexual propositions along with contact experiences. Some conservative investigators exclude such noncontact experiences, while other investigators choose to report incidence with both kinds of experiences. Studies differ in the extent to which they include *subjective* and *interpersonal* elements such as whether the experience was considered abusive, unwanted, coercive, or the result of pressure or force. Other studies disregard such elements and tally only frequency of acts.

Peers present another unsolved problem. Some investigators exclude them because a certain amount of sexual experimentation is considered normal. Others argue that, especially among adolescent girls, sexual acts can be violent and intrusive and could well be justified as abusive. A final area of disagreement involves the *age difference* between abuser and child. In general, a five-year difference in age is the usual criterion, although some investigators prefer a ten-year difference as the criterion in the case of adolescents while others exclude all voluntary experiences in adolescence no matter what the age difference.

However, even after reanalyzing the data from various studies using the same definition for all of them, discrepancies in incidence continue to be present. Therefore, factors other than definitional differences must be at work.

SAMPLE CHARACTERISTICS Since none of the studies involved a representative or a random sampling of the population as a whole, it may be that differences in prevalence rates represent true differences among subsamples. However, there is no evidence that rates of sexual abuse vary significantly by *social class* or *education*. In this regard, it is different from physical abuse and neglect. Nor is there evidence that sexual abuse varies with *ethnicity* in that the prevalence is no higher among blacks than among Caucasians. In general, there do not seem to be *regional* differences in sexual abuse except in the case of California, where the prevalence rates tend to be higher than elsewhere. Whether this represents a true difference in prevalence or a greater willingness to be candid in responding to questions is a moot point.

METHODOLOGICAL FACTORS Since neither differences in definitions nor differences in samples can account for discrepant findings, it is possible that such findings are due to the ways in which the data were collected.

Sampling techniques significantly affect prevalence rates. For studies using a stratified or a random sample of a heterogeneous population, such as a particular city, the variation in prevalence is quite wide, ranging from 6 to 62 percent. For studies using a homogeneous population on a nonselective basis, such as undergraduate students in a psychology course, the results are highly consistent and fall between 11 and 22 percent. Thus there is a trade-off between representativeness of the population and consistency of results. However, some of the variability in the studies using heterogeneous populations may be due to other factors.

It would seem reasonable to suppose that differences in prevalence might be due to differences in *response rate*, especially considering the sensitive nature of the topic. Thus a sample in which a large number of people were willing to answer a questionnaire would also have a large number of people willing to admit to being sexually abused as children. There is no evidence that this is so since there is no consistent relation between low response rate and prevalence. However, *mode of administration* does significantly affect reported prevalence rates, face-to-face interviews yielding rates of 22 percent or above, self-administered questionnaires and telephone interviews yielding rates of 22 percent or lower. While one might think that the anonymity of a self-administered questionnaire would encourage frank disclosure, the skillfully conducted interview is much more effective in this regard.

Finally, prevalence rates are positively correlated with the *number* and *specificity* of questions. For example, asking a single general question such as, "Were you sexually abused as a child?" will result in a lower reported rate of prevalance than asking a series of specific questions in regard to different kinds of abuse and different perpetrators. Specific questions give the embarrassed respondent

less chance to avoid the topic than a single general question and also provide more detailed information as to what behaviors are included within the general category and more clues to help jog the respondent's memory.

In sum, sensitive interviewing of samples from the general population employing a number of specific questions seems the preferred way of obtaining prevalence data if one can assume that the higher percentages are more representative of the true prevalence than the lower ones. There is still one problem, and it is an important one. Prevalence studies typically rely on adults' *memory*, and memory can be notoriously unreliable, especially in regard to early childhood when events may have been misunderstood or misinterpreted. One might think that a way to check on distortions in recall would be to collect data on the actual number of proven sexual abuse cases with children. However, such a survey would include only cases that were reported and had become a matter of public record. There is no way of knowing how many unreported cases there might be, although, in light of the sensitivity of the topic and the moral and legal consequences of child sexual abuse, one can assume that the number would be considerable. Thus recall is preferred even though its limitations should be kept in mind.

GENERAL COMMENTS   One reason for giving a detailed critique of the prevalence data is to counter the impression that we know how widespread child sexual abuse is. Even the lowest rates indicate that the problem is serious; however, more definitive studies that take advantage of what has been learned to date should be conducted.

Moreover, the points made about sexual abuse can be generalized to prevalence studies of other psychopathologies. The issues of definition of terms, sample characteristics, and sampling techniques, mode of administration, and types of questions are relevant to any attempt to gather data on prevalence. It follows that percentages should not be viewed as absolute indices of cases in the population since they result from choices made in regard to definition and procedures. The most credible studies are those that make the most defensible choices in terms of what is known about the particular psychopathology and about methods for obtaining information.

The Sexually Abused Child

While much of what is known concerning characteristics of the sexually abused child is preliminary, and while many of the studies are not as well designed as one would wish, there is a fair amount of information available. The best data come from samples of the adult population which have a built-in comparison group so that the characteristics of the abused subjects can be compared with those of nonabused subjects. (Our presentation follows Finkelhor and Baron, 1986.)

In regard to *sex differences* almost all studies find that females outnumber males, the ratios ranging from 1.5 to 1, to 4 to 1. However, there is suggestive evidence that abuse of boys is underreported perhaps because victimization is at odds with the masculine role, perhaps because of the homosexual character of most abuse. Thus the tendency to study girls and neglect boys is an unfortunate one. The mean *age* of sexual abuse is between 8 and 12 years, although this average conceals the fact that some ages represent greater degrees of vulnerability than others. Specifically, there is a dramatic increase in sexual abuse between 6 and 7 years of age and again between 10 and 12 years, when children are victimized at more than double the average rate. It is not clear why there should be this age differential.

As we have already noted, there is no relation to social class and no difference between blacks and Caucasians. For example, the proportion of sexually abused blacks corresponds to the proportion of blacks in the population as a whole. However, there is suggestive evidence that there may be an increased incidence of sexual abuse among Hispanic girls and lower than average incidence among Asian and Jewish girls. The idea that there is more sexual abuse in isolated *rural* as compared with *urban* areas is not borne out by the data in that the findings are contradictory and inconclusive. *Social isolation* does appear to be an important variable, sexually abused children having fewer friends and lacking closeness to peers and siblings. Unfortunately, the data cannot answer the question whether the social isolation preceded the sexual abuse and therefore could be considered a risk factor, or whether it followed it and was the result of shame or parental prohibitions against playing with other children.

The strongest association is between sexual abuse and *parental* and *familial* variables. Parental absence in the sense of living without a natural mother or father for a lengthy period of time during childhood significantly increases the vulnerability to sexual abuse among girls. The relation is particularly strong in the case of living without the natural father. There is also a tendency for mothers' employment outside of the home to be associated with increased risk of sexual abuse in their daughters. The findings on mothers' unavailability due to physical illness or disability are inconclusive but are suggestive of a risk factor.

Along with parental absence, poor relations with the parents is another high-risk factor, abused women, for example, recalling their mothers as being cold and distant as well as harsh and punitive. However, as was the case with social isolation, it is not clear whether parental alienation preceded or was a consequence of sexual abuse. In addition, the women pictured parental relations in a negative light in that the marriage was an unhappy one and there was little affection between parents. Finally, there is evidence of a strong relation between having a stepfather in the family and increased risk for sexual abuse in the girl.

There are two problems with the above findings. The first is that they are descriptive rather than being psychologically meaningful. Thus the bridge between the risk factors and sexual abuse becomes a matter of speculation. Do absent or distant parents supervise and protect their daughters less and thus increase the chances of victimization? Do unhappy parents have unhappy, needful daughters who are vulnerable to the seductive promises of closeness and material rewards which may be a prelude to abuse? Are stepfathers more often perpetrators than natural fathers because they have not formed an attachment through infant caretaking, an attachment that serves to counter subsequent incestuous feelings? Or is it that the taboo against stepfather–stepdaughter sex is less strict than it is in the natural father–daughter relation? It will take much more information than is now available to relate the current descriptive findings to sexual abuse in a meaningful way.

The second problem with the findings is that they pay scant attention to characteristics of the child other than demographic ones. The developmental dimension in particular is all but ignored, as if it did not matter whether the victim were a 4-year-old or a 14-year-old. Obvious physical characteristics such as attractiveness and obvious cognitive factors such as knowledge concerning sexual abuse have received little attention. Then there are a host of psychological variables such as the child's intelligence, overall psychological adjustment, temperament, and competence which need to be investigated.

For such studies, the recall of adults may not be valid, and abused children themselves probably will have to be evaluated. Using children as subjects will also help clarify whether certain correlates of sexual abuse preceded or were the result of the abuse.

Initial and Long-Term Effects

Finkelhor and Browne (1986) have conceptualized the initial and long-term effects of sexual abuse in terms of four trauma-causing or *traumagenic dynamics*.

1. *Traumatic sexualization*. Sexual abuse may result in shaping the child's sexuality in a developmentally inappropriate and interpersonally dysfunctional manner. This can come about in a variety of ways. The child may be repeatedly rewarded by affection, privileges, and gifts for developmentally inappropriate behavior and may also learn sexual behavior is a means of manipulating others into meeting developmentally inappropriate needs. Traumatic sexualization may occur when certain parts of the child's body are given distorted importance or become a fetish and when the offender transmits misconceptions and confusions about sexual behavior and sexual morality to the child.

The psychological impact of traumatic sexualization is an increased salience of sexual issues, a confusion of sex with caregiving or caregetting, and negative associations or aversion to sex or intimacy. The behavioral consequences of this impact might be sexual preoccupations, precocious or aggressive sexual behavior, promiscuity, and prostitution on the one hand, and sexual dysfunctions and avoidance of or phobic reactions to sexual intimacy on the other.

2. *Betrayal*. Betrayal is the children's discovery that a trusted person on whom they depend has done them harm. During or after abuse, for example, children can come to realize that they have been manipulated

through lies or misrepresentations about proper standards of behavior, or they can realize that a loved adult treated them with callous disregard. Children can also feel betrayed by family members not involved in the abuse but who are unwilling to protect or believe them or who change their attitude after disclosure. In all probability, the intensity of the feeling of betrayal depends on how loving and trusting the child was of the abuser and of the family.

Betrayal can lead to a number of affective reactions: depression and grief on the one hand, anger and hostility on the other. Young children in particular can become clinging because of an intense need to regain a sense of trust and security. Betrayal can produce a mistrust of others and subsequently can impair the adult's ability to judge the trustworthiness of others. This impaired judgment may in turn lead to a continued vulnerability to physical and sexual abuse and even to a failure to recognize that their partners are sexually abusing their own children.

3. *Powerlessness.* When a child's will, desires, and initiative are constantly opposed, disregarded, and undermined, the result is a feeling of powerlessness. In sexual abuse, this can result when a child's body is repeatedly invaded against the child's will and when the process of abuse involves coercion and manipulation on the part of the offender. Powerlessness is strongly reinforced when the child's attempts to halt the abuse are frustrated and when efforts to make adults understand what is happening are ignored. Finally, a child's inevitable dependence on the very adults who abuse and ignore produces a feeling of being trapped.

Powerlessness can have two opposite effects. The children may feel anxious or helpless and perceive themselves as victims. As a protection against such terrifying feelings they may go to the opposite extreme of identifying with the aggressive abuser or, less

dramatically, have an exaggerated need to dominate and be in control of every situation. The behavioral manifestations of powerlessness may be a number of neurotic symptoms such as nightmares, phobias, eating disorders, along with running away from home and truancy. There may also be learning and employment difficulties as victims feel unable to cope with the usual demands of life. At the other extreme, the children may become aggressive and antisocial or subsequently engage in child abuse themselves.

4. *Stigmatization.* Stigmatization refers to the negative connotations such as badness, shame, and guilt that are communicated to the child and then become incorporated into the child's self-image. Such negative meanings can come directly from the abuser, who may blame or denigrate the victim, or they may be implicit in the pressure for secrecy with its implication of having done something shameful. Stigmatization may result from the child's prior knowledge that the sexual activity is deviant and taboo, and it may result from the reaction of others who blame the child or regard her as "damaged goods" because of the molestation.

The psychological impact on the child consists of guilt, shame, and lowered self-esteem. Behaviorally, it may be manifested by isolation, and, in extreme cases, suicide. The child may gravitate to various stigmatized levels of society and become involved in drug abuse, criminal activity, or prostitution. Stigmatization may result in a sense of being different from everyone else and a constant concern over being rejected if the truth were discovered.

EMPIRICAL EVIDENCE   The above conceptualization represents an attempt to integrate the research findings from studies of child sexual abuse. The findings themselves will now be summarized, again with the caveats that the data are often inconclusive and that a number of studies are poorly designed. (Our presentation follows Browne and Finkelhor, 1986).

The empirical literature on *immediate effects*—defined as the period two years after the initial abuse—is particularly sketchy. There may be a significant increase in psychopathology over that found in a normal population although not as great as that found in a clinically referred population. One of the most common effects is fear, along with anger and hostility. Guilt and depression have also been frequently observed. Unexpectedly, there is no evidence of a significantly lower self-esteem when compared with a normal population. Sexual problems such as open masturbation, excessive sexual curiosity, and exhibition of the genitals, increase. School problems, truancy, running away from home, and early marriages have also been found.

The evidence concerning *long-term effects* is more substantial than that on short-term effects. Adults demonstrate more psychological impairment than do their nonvictimized counterparts, but less than one-fifth suffer serious psychopathology. While it is reassuring to know that extreme disturbances are relatively rare, the victims of child abuse do suffer from a wide range of problems. Adult women victimized as children are more likely than nonvictimized women to experience depression, anxiety, mistrustfulness, poor relations with parents, children, and peers, feelings of isolation and stigma, self-destructive behavior, low self-esteem, substance abuse, and a tendency toward revictimization. Sexual maladjustment such as sexual dysfunction, promiscuity, and avoidance of sexual activity have also been reported, although studies have yielded conflicting findings.

In regard to *prognosis*, a number of studies have found that many experiences of abuse over a long period of time are more traumatizing than a single incident. Also, a pre-ponderance of studies indicate that abuse by fathers or stepfathers has a greater negative impact than abuse by other perpetrators. Abuse by males is more disturbing than that by females, and adults are more traumatizing than teenagers. Presence of force also seems to result in more trauma for the victim. The prognosis is worse when the families are unsupportive of the victims or when the victims are removed from the home, although the last finding is tentative.

Age at the onset of abuse has produced contradictory or negative findings, and the data are also ambiguous in regard to the prognosis with different types of sex acts. There is no simple relation between revealing or keeping abuse a secret and the child's subsequent adjustment. Finally, abuse by relatives, apart from fathers and stepfathers, has not been consistently shown to be more traumatizing than abuse by nonrelatives.

The Abuser

As was true of physial abuse, there is no type of person who sexually abuses children, nor is there a simple cause. To begin with, child sexual abuse is just one manifestation of a more general state of being sexually aroused by children, or *pedophilia*. Pedophilia can be manifested in manifold ways: masturbating to advertisements of children in their underwear, a lifelong pattern of being sexually aroused by fondling children, or a sudden incestuous impulse toward a daughter in a man who had heretofore engaged only in adult heterosexual relations. Since the diversity of the behavior has its counterpart in the diversity of theories and since the research data tend to be somewhat scattered, it will be helpful to present Araji and Finkelhor's (1986) summary of empirical findings.

Limiting this summary only to better established findings, the child sexual abuser can be characterized as follows. He is sexually aroused by children, is immature and socially inadequate, has difficulty relating to adult females, commits abuse while under the influence of alcohol, and was sexually abused himself. The picture, while sketchy, is at least a coherent one of early childhood vulnerability, a general social ineptness, blocking of adult heterosexual gratification along with being sexually aroused by children and disinhibition of prohibitions through drinking.

The picture is quite different from the one characterizing the physical abuser. There the punitiveness that may play a predominant role in authoritarian discipline is exaggerated by a number of factors—stress, impoverished parenting skills, and social isolation, among others—so that it becomes violence. The transition from normality to psychopathology can be traced with reasonable ease. Not so with sexual abuse. Normal parental love involves many sensual pleasures for the child—snuggling, kissing, bathing, and "riding horsey," to name only a few. While these may be erotically arousing to the child on occasion, such arousal is not their intent since both tenderness and playfulness are part of non-erotic parental love. What then goes wrong with the normal process? There has been a plethora of speculation but a paucity of empirical evidence. Only as more definitive data accumulate will we be able to decide which normal processes have gone awry and in what ways.

Assessment, Prevention, and Treatment

Sexual abuse is by far the most difficult deviation to detect and to prevent.

ASSESSMENT   The obstacles to obtaining accurate information as to whether sexual abuse actually occurred are numerous. Especially in the preschool period there are *cognitive* impediments since preschoolers' thinking tends to be concrete and their attention span short, and they can mouth ideas they do not really understand. Moreover, they do not have a firmly established understanding of chronological time, causality, or logical sequencing. Consequently, responses to questions might be rambling, full of irrelevances, inaccuracies, and idiosyncratic meanings. Equally important, preschoolers are mindful of pleasing or displeasing adults and might agree or disagree with statements on that basis alone rather than trying to decide whether a statement were true or not. (For details, see Waterman, 1986.)

Yet at any age obtaining accurate information is difficult. The subject matter itself is taboo so that the child does not have a readily available *vocabulary* to describe events that happened. Abuse often takes place with a familiar adult or family member in the context of seductive promises and flattery along with intimidations and threats. Thus the event is embedded in a highly charged *affective context* which can lead to various defensive maneuvers on the child's part such as denial or avoidance.

There is yet another complication in that the accusation of being a sexual abuser is part of a more general pattern of *parental relations*. In divorce proceedings, for example, the accusation may be motivated by vindictiveness rather than reality or by a misperception of reality born of vindictiveness. (For a detailed examination of this issue, see MacFarlane, 1986.) While it is important to protect the child from further sexual abuse, it is equally important to protect adults falsely accused. A different kind of complication arises from the fact that sexual abusers tend to be stepfathers or, to a lesser degree, natural fathers. Consequently, the mother may be forced to choose between believing either her child or her mate, who denies any wrongdoing. She may well side with her mate, dismissing the child's report as foolish, imaginary, naughty, and so on. The child, in turn, feels betrayed, powerless, and entrapped, as we have seen.

It follows that interviewing a child concerning sexual abuse requires a number of skills. Foremost is the ability to establish and maintain the kind of relationship that will make the child feel sufficiently secure to talk about affectively charged experiences. With younger children, puppets and toys may lessen anxiety by transferring frightening events into the world of pretend. However, the child must understand that the purpose of such props is to make it easier to talk about an event that really happened. In this sense, the situation is basically different from pretend play, which allows the child unlimited freedom to fantasy. There are other techniques for overcoming initial resistance such as a stepwise procedure whereby the child first denies but then successively agrees that sexual abuse "may have happened," then that it "sometimes happens," until the child finally admits that it "did happen."

There are a number of more specific interviewing skills. The interviewer must learn the child's names for body parts, sexual activities, and people. Especially with toddlers and preschoolers genitals are almost never known by their correct anatomic labels but are given a variety of nicknames such as "pee-pee" or "Suzie" or "pottie." Again at this age different people can be called by the same name such as "Uncle," or a person may be given a fabricated name such as "Mr. Tickle." Another source of confusion is that a general word like "hurt" may be the only one the child has to describe a sexual encounter, although it equally well might refer to a physical injury. Anatomically correct drawings and dolls and, whenever possible, photographs of implicated adults are helpful in decoding the child's terminology.

Finally, the interviewer must avoid the mistake of asking questions so general that their true intent is lost (for example, "Did anything upsetting happen when your mommy was in the hospital?") and must avoid asking a series of leading questions to be answered by yes or no since, as we have just noted, the need to please adults by agreeing with them may outweight the desire to tell the truth. Because children are often frightened into silence by doing something they do not comprehend and may not even have a language to describe, leading questions may be unavoidable. However, the most convincing evidence of sexual abuse is that which comes from the child and describes in the child's own terms what transpired. (For further details, see MacFarlane and Krebs, 1986.)

Because interviewing children concerning sexual abuse requires skill and knowledge of child development, the number of professionals qualified to do such interviewing is still limited. The magnitude of the problem itself caught professionals by surprise, so that training individuals to deal with it at a high level of professional competence will again take time. The stakes are high. If assessment is ineptly done, an innocent child may be subjected to continual sexual abuse or an innocent adult will be subjected to the ignominy and penalties of being labeled a child sexual abuser.

PREVENTION   Effective preventive programs are urgently needed since most children do not reveal their victimization and, when they do, families are unlikely to seek help. Therefore some broader approach than treatment is required. The challenge of preventive programs is to make their message concerning sexual abuse comprehensible to children and palatable to adults. (Our presentation follows Finkelhor, 1986a.)

The goals of prevention are to educate *children* concerning the nature of sexual abuse, who potential abusers are apt to be (i.e., familiar individuals rather than strangers), and ways of coping with sexual abuse such as saying no, running away, or telling a trusted adult. In certain cities trained staff conduct workshops for children of all grades in the school; there are also films, educational coloring books, and television ads teaching children to identify possible molesters.

There are many problems in designing preventive programs, one of the more obvious being the wide age range covered by sexual abuse. Moreover, the material concerning the nature of sexual abuse itself has to be simplified and sanitized because descriptions or depictions of explicit sexual activities would be unacceptable to the public. "Uncle Harry forces you to kiss him," for example, may fail fully to convey the idea of a sexual imposition. Most material is even more indirect, dealing, for example, with touches that make the child feel good and touches that make him or her feel bad or confused. Yet limitations are inevitable considering the sensitivity of the issue itself and the constraints that public opinion places on content. By contrast, programs designed to prevent physical abuse can vividly portray the message by pictures of bruised and battered preschoolers.

As with all preventive programs, the critical issue is *effectiveness*. On the positive side there is evidence indicating that children learn from such programs; however, some of the learning is lost with time, and former misconceptions reappear. It may be unrealistic to expect a program permanently to inoculate children against all future misunderstandings and counterpressures, such as a parent's adamant belief that "Nobody in our family would do anything like that." Finally, there are little data concerning how effectively knowledge translates into action, enabling children actually to avoid or report sexual abuse. To assume that information alone can protect the child is to ignore the power differential between child and adult and the potency of the latter's seductions, threats, and rationalizations.

Preventive programs with *parents* would be more palatable if sexual abuse were primarily committed by strangers and "perverts." That this is not true magnifies the already difficult task of explaining the various kinds of sexual overtures to children. Ironically, parents readily inform their children concerning the dangers of being kidnapped, but are reluctant to talk about someone touching their genitals, even though the latter is far more likely to happen than the former. There is some evidence that this abdication of responsibility to inform is uniform over all socioeconomic levels and over all ethnic backgrounds. In their defense, it can be said that parents are concerned about alarming their children unduly or making them mistrustful of closeness and affection.

Parents' avoidance of the admittedly difficult topic of sexual abuse is unfortunate because their close and continual contact puts them in a unique position to be effective educators. Their reluctance should be countered by information concerning the nature and extent of the problem, while their embarrassment over dealing with sexuality should be countered by guides concerning how to describe abuse in terms that children can understand and that are acceptable to the parents themselves. While promising preventive programs for achieving these goals have been devised, there are little data concerning how extensively they are used and how effective they are.

TREATMENT　As has already been noted, only a small fraction of sexual abusers receive treatment. While a number of approaches claim positive effects, the results are not uniformly positive nor are the measures the most critical ones; for example, success is often evaluated in terms of attitude change, short-term reports of behavioral change, and physiological measures. What remains to be demonstrated is whether treatment significantly reduces the recidivism rate of the offenders (Finkelhor, 1986b).

14

Differences within the Interpersonal Context: Ethnic Minority Children

W e have now finished our presentation of deviant development. However, we have not addressed the large group of children who have been reared in significantly *different* environments. These are the ethnic minority children who are of concern to the clinical child psychologist for a number of reasons.

First, it is estimated that 20 percent of the population of the United States are members of ethnic minority groups and, by the turn of the century, it is projected that ethnic groups will constitute 25 percent of the population (M.E. Bernal, 1989). Therefore there is a high probability that practicing clinicians will encounter these children and their families. As with all clients, accurate assessment and effective treatment depend on the clinical child psychologist's ability to establish rapport and to understand the client's point of view. This is not a major problem for an Anglo-American clinician with Anglo-American clients, who are in the majority in the United States; both literally and figuratively the clinician can speak their language. Speaking the language of minority children both literally and figuratively becomes a major problem for Anglo-American clinicians since such children may have a significantly different way of life.

In addition to establishing rapport and understanding, the clinical child psychologist must decide whether a child is disturbed. This is difficult to do unless the clinician knows the culture of the child. Many ethnic minority groups are family-oriented and authoritarian. The adolescent transition to independence, which plays such an important role in Anglo-American society, is not expected in cultures in which adolescents continue to be part of the family and subject to parental authority. Thus interpreting behavior as a "failure to resolve adolescent dependency needs" may be in error because such needs are not resolved in terms of independence. Similarly, the feminist's image of the liberated woman is at odds with the view of woman as wife and mother which prevails in many cultures. Consequently, behavior that might be regarded as docile and subservient by Anglo-American standards might be fulfilling and adaptive in other cultures.

Aside from its importance to effective clinical practice, the study of ethnic minorities helps dispel the ethnocentric belief that "our way" is both the only way and the best. In reality, there are many ways of rearing children, many sets of values, each having its assets and liabilities. Clinical child psychologists have learned this lesson in regard to individuals. Children differ and, because of this, there are innumerable fulfilling lifestyles. Both the sensitive scholar and the popular extravert can be developing normally although each has a different mix of the variables we regard as essential such as attachment, initiative, and self-control. The same is true of cultures. The Anglo-American culture is only one of many, and perspective on it can best be gained by a knowledge of diversity. In this way an ethnocentric view of what is good for children can be replaced by an understanding that our society, like all others, involves its special combination of factors that tend to promote and impede development. The United States has the highest rate of crime of any industrialized country, for example, while the crime rate in mainland China is low. Among the many variables contributing to the low crime rate is the closeness of the Chinese family, the constant surveillance of the child, and the deep sense of shame if the child commits an antisocial act. On the other hand, the Anglo-American emphasis on autonomy and independence opens up avenues of individual initiative that would not readily be available to the traditional Chinese adolescent.

One final point: Discussing characteristics of ethnic minorities is bound to run roughshod over variations within groups. A middle-class black family may have little in common with a black family from the slums, just as a third-generation Japanese family may have little in common with a first-generation one. In the category of Pacific Asian Americans there are an estimated twenty-nine distinct cultural groups ranging from preliterate to technologically advanced societies. Yet simplification is necessary in the initial stages of becoming acquainted with various cultural minorities and should not be considered caricaturing. Still, the limitations of such simplification must be kept in mind.

Since it would be impossible to do justice to the richness of the field of ethnic minority children we have decided to concentrate on three themes, using a single minority group as an exemplar of each. While this strategy prevents comparisons among minority groups the loss is unavoidable. (For a detailed presentation, see Powell, 1983. For a discussion of ethnic families, see Harrison, Serafica, and McAdoo, 1982.) The themes are the *ethnic socialization* in black children, *cultural diversity* among Japanese-American children, and *clinical practice* with Mexican-American children. But first we will need some definitions and general observations to serve as a background for discussing the three specific themes.

A note about nomenclature: There are no agreed-upon labels for various cultural groups. Some authors prefer the precision of Anglo-American or Afro-American to more general terms such as black, white, or American. Certainly not all blacks or whites are Americans just as not all Americans are members of the white majority that defines the culture. At times terms are used to differentiate a minority from a majority status; for example, Mexican-Americans are differentiated from Mexicans who still live in Mexico. However, in other instances, no such distinction is made since it is clear from the context; for example, one can read about the Japanese and know from what is written whether the reference is to the people in Japan or in the United States. Our presentation, like the literature in general, will not use a standard nomenclature throughout. Labels will be used interchangeably, and no differentiations are intended. The groups referred to should be clear from the context.

DEFINITIONS AND GENERAL ISSUES

Both "ethnic" and "minority" belong in the superordinate context and take us into the province of sociology and anthropology rather than psychology. In fact, this is the first time that the superordinate context serves as a point of departure. Because the realm is alien to psychology, we will not try to master its concepts and methodologies; rather, we will stay only long enough to become acquainted with some basic definitions and with some essential background data. (See Atkinson, Morten, and Sue, 1983.) Then we shall return to the intra- and interpersonal contexts and concentrate our presentations there.

Definitions

There is no general agreement on the definition of *ethnic groups*. We shall use a slightly amended version of Rotheram and Phinney's (1987) broad-gauged conceptualization, which

is most suited to our purposes. Ethnicity is a common ancestry, race, and national origin on the one hand and shared values, social customs, language usage, roles, and rules of social interactions on the other. For the purpose of federal surveys, the Office of Management and Budget has established five ethnic groups in the United States: American Indian or Native Alaskan, Asian or Pacific Islander, black, Hispanic, and white. In the literature, blacks may be referred to as Afro-Americans and whites as Anglo-Americans. While there are 26.5 million blacks in the United States, which represents 11 percent of the population, the Hispanic population of 15 million is the fastest growing one and may be the largest within the next two decades. As of 1980 there were in the United States 3.5 million people of Asian or a Pacific island origin and almost 1.5 million American Indians and Alaskan natives, which represents a 57 percent increase over the 1970 census (U.S. Department of Commerce, 1980).

The simplest definition of a *minority group* is one having fewer members than the majority group. Obviously, not all ethnic groups are minorities, such as whites in the United States (although whites are a minority group worldwide), and not all minority groups are ethnic, such as the physically handicapped or the Quakers. M. E. Bernal (1989) adds two more characteristics which, while not generally agreed upon, are relevant to our concern with psychological adjustment. She regards an ethnic minority as being powerless or subordinate and the object of discrimination. Native Americans and blacks, for example, experience powerlessness and discrimination along with conflict with the dominant group; Polish or Irish Americans by contrast have never been relegated to a subordinate role and are not in conflict with the dominant group.

Ethnic socialization refers to "the developmental processes by which children acquire the behaviors, perceptions, values, and attitudes of an ethnic group, and come to see themselves and others as members of such groups" (Rotheram and Phinney, 1987, p. 11). *Ethnic identity* is "one's sense of belonging to an ethnic group and the part of one's thinking, perceptions, feelings, and behavior that is due to ethnic group membership" (Rotheram and Phinney, 1987, p. 13). Ethnic identity is an important part of an individual's total identity but should not be equated with it.

General Issues

In this section we shall begin with the superordinate context and then proceed to the inter- and intrapersonal ones. As always, we shall be concerned with the context of time.

Changing Societies

As we saw in chapter 1, societies, like individuals, change over time; being black or female or homosexual in 1950 was quite different from being black, female, or homosexual in 1980 because of the social revolution that took place in the interim. Other societies undergo their own changes; Mexico, for example, has seen increased industrialization, while Japan has seen increased democratization. Thus it is important to know the cultural history of minority groups; one wave of immigrants, for example, may be predominantly illiterate farmers or factory workers, while another wave from the same country may represent a predominance of well-educated technicians and professionals. Even describing the "traditional" culture of a country involves an arbitrary stopping of the clock at one era in that country's continually evolving culture.

Ethnicity and Socioeconomic Status

The relation between ethnicity and mental health is difficult to determine because of the presence of confounding factors, particularly socioeconomic status. To take one example: the evidence indicates that blacks are far more likely to become official delinquents than whites. For the sake of argument, let us assume this difference is not due to spurious factors such as a bias on the part of police to report blacks rather than whites. However, there is evidence that economic disadvantage, as measured by low income, slum housing, and parental unemployment, is also related to delinquency. Since blacks are overly represented among the economically disadvantaged, how can one tell whether the delinquent behavior results from ethnicity or poverty? In fact, there is some evidence that the black-white difference does not hold independent of lower-status jobs and poor-quality housing, along with other variables such as intelligence and poor school achievement. Moreover, it is extremely difficult to design and implement studies in which all of the variables are controlled except ethnicity. Currently, it is not clear whether ethnicity per se has a direct effect on childhood disturbances independent of other factors (Farrington, 1986).

Ethnic Patterns

After reviewing the literature, Rotheram and Phinney (1987) were able to delineate four dimensions that are central to differentiating the social behavior of ethnic groups. These dimensions are: "(1) an orientation toward group affiliation and interdependence versus competition; (2) an active, achievement-oriented style versus a passive, accepting style; (3) authoritarianism and the acceptance of hierarchical relationships versus egalitarianism; and (4) an expressive, overt, personal style of communication versus a restrained, impersonal, and formal style" (p. 22). The Anglo-American pattern values independence and competition, achievement, egalitarianism, and an expressive style of communication. This picture contrasts with many other patterns which emphasize the primacy of the family and the group, deference to and respect for the father and other authority figures, and valuing the good of the group over individual assertiveness and advancement.

Minority-Majority Relationships

Since many minority groups have ethnic patterns that are at variance with the Anglo-American pattern, what are the possible relationships that can result? One possibility is *assimilation*, in which the minority group loses its distinctiveness and becomes part of the majority group. This is the basis for the image of America as a "melting pot" in which diversity is homogenized into a uniform cultural pattern. At the other extreme is *pluralism*, in which the customs, values, and possibly even the language of different groups are maintained within a culture, resulting in a heterogeneous society made up of distinct groups. A middle position is *acculturation* or *accommodation*, in which elements of various groups are included in the culture. An analogy would be our government, which represents all the people but still accommodates to local interests of our geographic regions which are part of the country while retaining their distinctive local flavors (Rotheram and Phinney, 1987).

There is a difference of opinion concerning the result of the above relations between the minority and majority cultures. One view emphasizes the conflicts and dilemmas confronting children who must either identify with the dominant group and thereby alienate themselves from the family, or retain the minority group patterns and suffer various degrees of discrimination, ridicule, and rejection for being an outsider. The resulting stresses can place children at risk for developing psychopathological disturbances. Other authorities, while recognizing the stresses inherent in the situation, claim that the conflicts can be growth promoting. Just as bilingual children have advantages over children knowing only one language, so children who are knowledgeable about and can adapt to different cultures while maintaining their own identity have a richness of experience and a versatility in adapting which children knowing only one cultural pattern lack (Rosenthal, 1987). In all probability both outcomes are possible, but little is known about what determines whether children will go one way or the other. It may be that minority groups who share values with the dominant culture, such as the Asian-Americans' valuing of education and industriousness, would have a less problematic relationship than, say, blacks, who have the same values but who for centuries have been demeaned and disparaged.

Ethnic Identity

Ethnic identity, which will figure prominently in subsequent discussions, has a number of components. (Our presentation follows Rotheram and Phinney, 1987). First there is ethnic *awareness*, or the understanding of one's own and other groups. This entails the acquisition of knowledge concerning the critical attributes of one's own ethnic group and how it differs from the ethnic groups of others. Next, there is *ethnic self-identification*, or the labels used for one's group. This includes both formal and informal labels, the latter often having pejorative connotations, such as dago, spic, or coon. Then, there are ethnic *attitudes*, or the feelings about one's own and other groups. Such feelings may be the result of experience but may be based on stereotypes or prejudice. Finally, there are ethnic *behaviors*, or the behavior patterns specific to a given ethnic group. These may be specific, such as bowing versus shaking hands, or general, such as expressing feelings versus being self-contained.

Developmental Considerations

Ethnic self-identification may seem simple to adults but, in reality, it involves high-level cognitive processes. In many ways it is akin to gender identity. Preschoolers very early learn that certain labels are given them, such as "girl" or "Chinese," and they can parrot these labels. But then they are left on their own to figure out what the labels mean. This involves three basic processes. First, they must determine what are the essential elements in the label so that, if the elements were not present, the label would not be applicable. Next, they must discover what characteristics distinguish this particular label from labels given other groups, such as "boy" or "American." If there were no such differentiating features, then labels would not be necessary. Finally, they must learn that the label is consistent across situations and over time, that one is always a girl or Chinese wherever one is throughout one's lifetime (Aboud, 1987).

While children eventually master these three cognitive challenges, the process takes a number of years and may involve many errors along the way. In our discussion of the development of the self (in chapter 5) and of gender identity (in chapter 10), we found that the preschooler thinks in concrete terms, such as, "A girl is a person who is small and wears dresses," or "The self is someone who plays ball"; only in middle childhood does thinking become abstract and accurate. A similar progression takes place with ethnic identification.

Some general trends in understanding ethnic identity will be summarized as a background for the more detailed examination of the process in black children. Simple perceptual recognition of different ethnic groups seems to be a function of the salience of perceptual cues, skin color and hair type being particularly important. Thus children can recognize blacks and whites by 3 to 4 years of age but not Chinese, Hispanics, or American Indians until around 8 years. Adults show a similar lack of differentiation within ethnic groups when they say, for example, that all Orientals look alike. In both instances, perception has not become sufficiently detailed to permit fine discriminations.

Self-identification is typically measured by presenting the child with dolls or pictures of children from different ethnic groups and asking, Which one looks most like you? Black and white children can perform the task by 5 years of age, although there is improvement in accuracy until 9 years of age. A similar technique can be used to determine which groups are different from the child, a task that children from various ethnic groups perform correctly more than 80 percent of the time by 4 or 5 years of age. Research also shows that children from different ethnic groups use different criteria for recognizing their own group and differentiating it from others. French Canadians use language, Chinese use eyes, food, and language, and American Indians use possessions and activities. Blacks rely on skin color and hair type as criteria (Aboud, 1987). Incidentally, this diversity of criteria shows the limitations of research techniques using appearance alone, such as dolls or drawings of different ethnic groups.

A more difficult challenge involves conceptualizing the essential features of ethnic groups and the self as a member of a group. One technique for measuring this conceptual ability involves presenting children with pictures of a number of people belonging to different ethnic groups and asking them to put all the members of the same group in separate piles. Next, the child is asked to place a stick figure representing himself in one of the piles to determine the accuracy of self-identification with the group. The categorization task becomes accurate only around 7 years of age.

Ethnic constancy can be measured by asking a child if he would be the same if dressed like another ethnic group—for example, asking a white child, "If you dressed like an Eskimo, would you be white or an Eskimo?" Temporal constancy can also be measured. For example, an American Indian child can be asked, "How long have you been an Indian?" and "Will you be an Indian 10 years from now?" While achievement of constancy is not well documented, the evidence indicates that it happens around 8 years of age. (For more details concerning the research along with a critique of the limitations of the techniques used, see Aboud, 1987.)

THE ETHNIC SOCIALIZATION OF BLACK CHILDREN

As we have seen, ethnic socialization refers to the developmental process by which children acquire the behavior, perceptions, values, and attitudes of an ethnic group and come to see themselves and others as members of that group. Before tracing this development, it will be helpful to have some general background information from the *superordinate context*.

Blacks, or Afro-Americans, as an ethnic group, have some special characteristics of their own. Primary among these is the fact that blacks were involuntarily incorporated into the existing society and permanently assigned an inferior status by legal, economic, and social forces (Spencer, 1987). It was not until the civil rights movement of the 1960s that they began to gain full status as citizens and began to take pride in themselves, their past, and their achievements—a reorientation epitomized by the change from being called Negro to being called black (Cross, 1987). For our purposes this shift means that for the first time black children could identify with their own ethnic group and feel proud rather than inferior.

However, the process of change has been hampered by lingering prejudice and particularly by poverty. Black infants have a 50 percent chance of being born into poverty and a 75 percent chance of living in poverty if the family is headed by a female. In 1982 47.3 percent of all black children lived in families with income below the poverty level, compared with 16.5 percent of white children. Along with poverty go inadequate prenatal care, high infant mortality, poor health, low school achievement, high dropout rates, and inadequate vocational preparation, the last three serving to perpetuate the poverty cycle (Spencer, 1987). The relation between poverty and increased risk of various kinds of psychopathology has long been established. While there has been an increase in the number of middle-class black families in recent years, the plight of the poor has worsened. Moreover, affluent blacks tend to identify with middle-class values and are as segregated from poor blacks as wealthy whites are segregated from poor whites (Norton, 1983).

A few more findings from the superordinate context will help flesh out the picture. The majority of black children are raised in families living in urban areas in predominantly black communities. The extended family is a common pattern serving many support functions. Black families of all income levels, for example, rely on relatives to care for children while they work and, in 1975, 40 percent of black children were living in households composed of the mother and other relatives (Norton, 1983). A more ominous trend is for black children to become increasingly dependent on peers rather than on parents which, in turn, increases the likelihood that they will become juvenile delinquents (Myers and King, 1983).

Ethnic Awareness

As we have seen, the basic cognitive tasks in ethnic awareness are grasping the essential features of one's own ethnic group and identifying with that group, learning to differentiate one's own group from other groups, and coming to understand that ethnicity persists over situations and over time. This process lasts from the preschool period into early middle childhood. Black children conform to the progression just described, although there is one baffling variation called *misidentification*, in which black children say they are most similar to a white doll or photograph rather than to a black one. This misidentification should not be confused with self-labeling because such children do not claim they actually are white. When the results were initially reported, they were interpreted as evidence of black self-hatred, an idea that has largely been discredited. A simpler explanation is that, while the home life of white children is exclusively oriented toward white activities and values, black homes contain a mixture of black and white cultural elements, thereby encouraging the development of a bicultural orientation (Cross, 1987). Another explanation is that preschoolers who say they are similar to whites also prefer whites over blacks so that they are merely expressing a desire to be identified with a preferred group (Vaughan, 1987). Recall that preschoolers believe they can readily change from one ethnic group to another by looking or dressing like that group. Thus identification is more labile and subject to wish fulfillment than it will be from middle childhood on.

Studies of black children have revealed the complexity of the cognitive progression from ethnic self-identification through ethnic immutability. We will deal with the issues of categorization, salience, overgeneralization, inconsistency, and lack of conservation. (Our presentation will follow Ramsey, 1987.)

CATEGORIZATION Generally speaking, categorization is possible as early as 3 to 4 years; for example, children this age can distinguish cats from toys even though they are not able to generate appropriate verbal labels for the groups. In a like manner, children this age can classify people as black or white using visible characteristics such as skin color, hair type, and clothing. However, when questioned about reasons for groups, they often mention details unrelated to race. This may be an example of preschoolers' verbal reasoning lagging behind their perceptual cognition, which is not unusual in early development. As we have seen, categorizing a number of different ethnic groups and giving the correct reasons take a longer time to develop.

SALIENCE Despite their ability to categorize, the importance or salience of race varies across tasks. For example, preschoolers and elementary school children were presented with photographs of classmates and unknown peers. When asked to describe the photographs, the children often listed details of the photographs such as clothing and hair styles and, in the case of familiar children, activities a particular child did rather than gender or race. When asked to say who was different from them, however, they often used race as the defining factor. Thus the salience of race varies as the child is concerned with similarities or differences.

OVERGENERALIZATION Preschoolers tend to overgeneralize because they have difficulty categorizing in terms of a superordinate and a subordinate variable simultaneously. A preschooler may say "Chinese always eat in restaurants" or "Black children always fight" after observing such behavior. It is difficult for them to grasp the fact that particular behaviors such as eating and fighting may vary even while the more general ethnic category remains the same. Affect-laden experiences are particularly likely to be overgeneralized.

There is an important inference from this finding. A preschooler's saying "All blacks are bad" may sound like a prejudice when, in reality, it is the result of a cognitive limitation. It therefore differs significantly from an adult's saying, for example, that blacks are lazy or shiftless or violent because adults are cognitively capable of simultaneous categorizing but may systematically ignore evidence contradicting their evaluations. This is a true prejudice.

INCONSISTENCY Preschoolers are often inconsistent in their ethnic beliefs. A white child can make a negative generalization about all blacks being bad one minute and then proceed to play with blacks the next. Piaget made the same observation about preschoolers' understanding of rules; after saying rules could never be broken, preschoolers will proceed to improvise whatever rules they feel like when actually playing a game of marbles. Thus perception of an ethnic group should not be equated with actual behavior.

CONSERVATION Finally, preschoolers do not conserve ethnic characteristics, which means in Piagetian terms that they do not grasp the idea that such characteristics are immutable. Rather, they believe ethnicity can be changed by changing appearances. Skin color, for example, may be seen as a temporary condition, black children regarding their pink palms as proof that they were once lighter and can "get pink" at some future time.

In sum, for all their adeptness in categorizing ethnic groups, preschoolers think in ways that are more dissimilar than similar to the ways of adults. Therefore one should avoid reading adult meanings into preschoolers' adultlike statements. Due to their cognitive limitations, preschoolers' categories are often unstable, concrete, overgeneralized, and idiosyncratic. Viewed in their developmental context they become precursors of the more accurate and stable understanding to come, but they are still far removed from this understanding. Thus, instead of trying to eliminate "prejudice" in the earliest years, one might do better to eliminate the racist experiences that subsequently will turn the unstable cognitions of the preschoolers into fixed beliefs.

Ethnic Attitudes

Ethnic socialization involves not only cognition but affect as well. As preschoolers learn what ethnicity is, they also learn to attach positive and negative connotations to their own ethnic group and the ethnic groups of others. Such affect-laden evaluations are called ethnic attitudes. It would be incorrect to assume a close relation between cognition and affect such that the more information children have, the more positive their attitude becomes. There is evidence, for example, that 6- to 11-years-olds' preference for ethnic groups does not correspond to their information concerning these groups (Vaughan, 1987).

OWN GROUP ATTITUDES The development of attitudes in black children differs from that in white. (Our presentation follows Aboud, 1987.) Children under 4 do not express consistent preferences. Beginning at 4 years of age, white children consistently express favorable attitudes toward their own group and continue to do so for the next three years. While many studies find similar results in 7- and 8-years-old, some report a decline in group preference. It is impossible to tell whether this decline represents a genuine change or an increased awareness that it is not socially desirable to express a preference for one's own ethnic group over those of others.

Studies of black children find a more variable picture of attitudes between 3 and 8 years of age, 27 percent showing own group preference, 16 percent showing white preference, and 57 percent showing no preference. An analysis of the effect of age indicates an increase in black preference or no change up to 8 years of age. Between 8 and 11 there is a trend toward a decrease in preference, perhaps because of the same social desirability factor mentioned in connection with the data on white children. Incidentally, American Indian, Hispanic, and Chinese minority children express even less own group preference than do blacks.

The explanation of the data is somewhat speculative. One possibilty is that children value their ethnic group as this group values itself. There is some evidence that minority groups' preference for whites reflects the high value whites place upon themselves. As black adults place a similar positive value on their own group by actually promoting black causes, their children hold more pro-black attitudes. In fact, the same increase in own group preferences happens to black children who are adopted by white parents with pro-black values. The preference of black children for whites has also been likened to the desire of girls at certain ages to be boys, the former being the result of racist elements in society, the latter the result of sexist elements in society. As these features of society change, so might the valuing of other groups (Katz, 1987).

OTHER GROUP ATTITUDES Here again blacks and whites differ. Whites hold moderately negative attitudes toward different groups as early as 4 years of age. Some studies report similar findings through 12 years of age; others report a decline. The decline may represent a genuine decrease in prejudice due to increased familiarity with other groups, although school integration per se does not reduce the prejudice of white children. A second possibility is the now familiar one of increased sensitivity to socially desirable ways of responding to assessment instruments.

A much smaller percentage of blacks expresses negative attitudes to whites than whites to blacks, and such attitudes are consistent from 4 to 12 years of age. Pro-white attitudes often become neutral or anti-white in older children, although the reasons for such age trends are unknown.

ATTITUDE TRANSMISSION There is little information concerning how attitudes are transmitted in the preschool period. The most obvious hypothesis is that children's statements reflect parental attitudes. However, the data in this regard are contradictory. Some studies show little correlation between the attitudes of parents and those of children (Katz, 1987). However, there does seem to be a link with socioeconomic status, members of low-income groups making more cross-racial pejorative remarks than members of middle-income groups. While preschoolers may merely parrot adults' statements, there are instances in which anti-black feelings become intense and personally meaningful (see Ramsey, 1987). How frequently this happens is unclear.

Another possible explanation is in terms of deviations from normative behavior. Preschoolers are still in the process of being socialized as to acceptable ways to dress, eat, talk, and play. To see children who differ in regard to such social norms may be perplexing or upsetting or may lead to name calling, teasing, and anger (Ramsey, 1987). Even in middle childhood the line between in-group and out-group may be firmly drawn and the boundaries protected by disparagement of children having an out-group status.

While the above speculations have a certain plausibility, they are no substitute for solid empirical data, especially because the issue of reducing prejudice is such a pressing one.

Personal and Ethnic Identity

The developmental picture grows dim during middle childhood and adolescence, although there are some noteworthy findings. One of the most important is the lack of relation between personal identity and ethnic identity. Remember that we are now in a period during which we can expect ethnic awareness and ethnic attitudes to have a stability and a consistency they lacked during the preschool years. Yet a number of studies have shown that, although black children as young as 7 years of age are aware of the social devaluation of their ethnic group, their self-esteem does not suffer; on the contrary it is comparable to that of white children. The shift from the word "Negro" to "black" following the civil rights movement, for example, also shifted children's evaluation of their ethnicity in a positive direction but had no effect on their self-esteem, which remained average or above (Cross, 1987).

There are a number of reasons self-esteem may develop independent of children's knowledge of society's view of their racial group. To begin with, children react most intensely to significant others in their immediate environment, particularly parents but also other adults, siblings, and peers. Despite racism in the economic, political, and social structure, black families have interacted with their children in ways that foster a positive sense of self. And while it is easier for blacks without overwhelming economic and social pressures to interact in such a manner, positive self-esteem in the children is found in all socioeconomic levels (Norton, 1983).

An interesting insight into how self-esteem is preserved is provided by research on child-rearing practices. As we noted in our discussions of discipline, it is not only what parents do but how they do it that determines children's behavior. Judged by white standards, black families are authoritarian, but, unlike their white counterparts, mothers do not produce rebellious daughters (who were the subjects of the research), but assertive and independent ones. The reason is that the authoritarian pattern was not accompanied by rejection, repressed hostility, and dogmatism, but by spontaneity and warmth. Moreover, mothers viewed the development of toughness and self-sufficiency as the best preparation for black women to deal effectively with the racism and sexism they might encounter in the white society. In the best sense of the phrase, then, the discipline was for the child's own future good (Norton, 1983).

Black Identity and Adjustment

In adolescence, ethnic identity follows the same developmental trends characteristic of this period. It now involves an appreciation for psychological characteristics and values rather than emphasizing physical appearance and manifest behaviors as it previously did. Adolescents are now able to view the past and the future and struggle with the issue of finding a fulfilling place in society as a black. Such generalities apply to most adolescents; the special issues involved in being black and adolescent have not been sufficiently explored empirically (see Rosenthal, 1987).

However, there is some information on the issue of general adjustment. In the past the emphasis has been on the insoluble nature of the identity problem. If adolescents choose to identify with whites, they run the risk of becoming alienated from their own group and of being at odds with their family. If they try to live in both worlds, they may suffer from marginality, oscillating between the two groups while being a member of neither. Recently, other alternatives have been viewed as possibilities. As a result of the civil rights movement, black adolescents identify with their own group with a sense of pride. It is also possible to become bicultural, selecting appropriate features of the black and white cultures and flexibly adapting to both.

While not conclusive, research suggests that, whatever difficulties adolescents face, they do not result in pathologically low levels of self-esteem. In this respect adolescents resemble school-age children. In regard to general adjustment, studies of diverse minority groups indicate that conflict and maladjustment are not inevitable and adolescents from minority groups are not fated to suffer intense psychological distress because of conflicting cultural norms. Unfortunately, there is little information concerning the extent to which blacks in particular conform to this pattern. Data on middle-class blacks are especially meager. Knowing that the process of achieving identity is not inevitably pathogenic tells us little about the kinds of risks involved, the price paid, and the resources and coping devices used in successful transitions. Much remains to be learned.

CULTURAL DIVERSITY AND THE JAPANESE CHILD

As we have already noted, an appreciation of ethnic diversity helps dispel the ethnocentric bias that there is a single or best way to rear children. Just as the proverbial fish was the last animal to discover water, we may be totally unaware of the most obvious features of our society until we confront diverse cul-

tures. Once aware of what we do and what kind of children we produce, we can begin to ask the questions, What are our strengths and weaknesses? and How can we do better?

Ideally, we should discuss all the major ethnic groups in our society, but practical considerations limit us to one. The choice of the Japanese is arbitrary; many other groups would do as well. We shall begin with the superordinate context and describe traditional Japanese values and how these determine family characteristics. Then we shall briefly describe the impact of values on child-rearing practices. Finally, we shall see how the traditional values have been modified with successive generations of Japanese-Americans.

Characteristics of Japanese Culture

We begin with a reminder: while it is possible to describe general characteristics of the Japanese culture, the culture itself is undergoing change. After World War II both Western and democratic ideas began to play an increasingly important role in Japanese society, while national goals were changed from warlike conquest to industrial productivity. While such changes are not our direct concern, they do affect the characteristics of immigrants to this country at different points in time.

At the most general level American and Japanese cultures can be contrasted in the following manner. In America the emphasis is on change, individuality, self-assertion, and equality. The Japanese culture emphasizes tradition, vertical relationships, interdependence, and self-denial. Both cultures value diligence, education, and postponement of immediate pleasures for future gratifications. (Our presentation will follow Yamamoto and Iga, 1983, unless otherwise noted.)

VERTICAL ORGANIZATION The culture in the United States values equality and upward mobility; even rail splitters, peanut farmers, and actors can become president. The Japanese culture, by contrast, is highly stratified. It has been compared to a pyramid with a few people at the highest level and an increasing number at successively lower levels. The hierarchy is rigidly stratified, making for keen status consciousness. Even language varies according to whether the person is of higher or lower rank, and a person of higher rank does not bow as deeply as one of lower rank (Yamamoto and Kubota, 1983). While the lower strata are required to serve the people in the higher strata, the emphasis is on mutual obligation and loyalty. Thus the relation between classes is not like that of master and servant but one of interlocking responsibilities, individuals in the higher strata being as bound by prescribed duties and behaviors as those in the lower.

INTERDEPENDENCE   Instead of Anglo-American individualism, epitomized by the lone cowboy riding off into the sunset, the Japanese culture's pervasive emphasis is on interdependence. A person identifies himself or herself within a social group rather than as an independent individual. The group may be the family, the school, or the workplace. Group cooperation and participation are taken for granted in everyday activities. This cooperation in turn fosters a sense of togetherness and results in long-lasting relationships. The emphasis on physical togetherness even reduces the need for verbal communication, and Japanese distrust verbal skills, which they feel may indicate glibness or possibly dishonesty. Finally, not only subordinates but authority figures as well must conform to group objectives. Thus a corporation must be as totally committed to the employee as the employee is to the corporation. In fact, executives and production line workers may dress alike and eat in the same cafeteria, a custom that symbolizes interde-

pendence and subordination of all individuals to group objectives.

Another aspect of interdependence is an emphasis on *empathy*, which is a highly valued virtue as well as being a far cry from "looking out for number one." The cultivation of the ability to feel what another person is feeling goes along with the motivation to help others achieve their wishes and goals. Part of this emphasis on empathy is an attempt to maintain consensus or positive feelings of agreement between people. Confrontations are avoided; accommodations are essential. Self-restraint is another means by which problems are avoided.

Finally, at the national level, the strong sense of group membership is related to an equally strong sense of being different from others. The traditional Japanese tend to see themselves as a separate, unique people, their interdependence not extending to a belief that all men are brothers and all are members of one world.

Family Patterns

The vertical organization of Japanese culture is found in the family as well. (Our presentation follows Yamamoto and Kubota, 1983, unless otherwise noted.) Primogeniture and lineage are an integral part of Japanese culture. The eldest son becomes head of the household and is responsible for both his parents in their old age and for his brothers and sisters. Consequently, males are preferred above females, the first-born male being of special importance.

In the family, rankings are related to seniority and gender, the father having the most authority, followed by the mother in an unofficial capacity, the eldest and then the next eldest sons. In fact, the Japanese language contains no words for brother and sister per se, but designates whether they are older or younger. First-born sons and daughters also have their special words. "From the time a Japanese infant awakens until the time he or she goes to sleep, education focuses on the importance of behavior toward elders and awareness of position in the vertical hierarchy" (Yamamoto and Kubota, 1983, p. 238). The American family, by contrast, is more egalitarian both in regard to the children and the parent–child relationship. Discipline tends to be child-centered rather than authoritarian, the parent respecting the child's point of view and being sensitive to the child's feelings. The goal of child-centeredness, of course, is the enhancement of autonomy rather than the perpetuation of vertical relationships.

Interdependence is expressed in a high degree of family togetherness. Families do everything together, including eating, bathing, sleeping, and participating in recreational activities. Characteristically, hierarchical relationships are preserved, the members with the highest status being served or bathed first, for example. Children sleep with parents in a common sleeping room, but the status hierarchy is reversed since the youngest sleeps closest to the mother.

Family members are dependent and restrained rather than autonomous and spontaneous as in the American culture. Other-directedness and externality are further consequences of interdependence, children not only being concerned for the welfare of other family members but also feeling that their behavior is constantly monitored by them. Anglo-American culture, by contrast, values inner-directedness and internal control. For the Japanese, the success of the family as a group, rather than individual achievement, is highly prized. Finally, interdependence characterizes not only present relationships but past and future ones as well. Ancestors are worshiped and family members are accountable to them. Good behavior

and high performance are demanded to honor ancestors and the family name. Future orientation is shown in two ways. First, parents are frugal in order to provide their children with the best educational advantages. Children, in turn, are expected to show filial piety and take care of their parents in old age. Consequently, there is no need for social security.

Parental relations are somewhat paradoxical. As we have seen, the father is the respected head of the household. Yet because he is hardworking he spends relatively little time at home and regards it primarily as a place to relax. Consequently, it is the mother who is with the children most of the day. Although she defers to and is dominated by her husband, she plays the pivotal role in actual child rearing. Moreover, the husband gives his paycheck to her and receives an allowance to take care of expenses involved in his work. While the influence of the woman is very strong in practical, day-to-day family life, she is also expected to devote herself to the betterment of her children and to be patient, self-sacrificing, and long-suffering. The contrast with the contemporary image of the Anglo-American father and mother is obvious.

Child Rearing

The goal of Japanese ethnic socialization is the same as with all ethnic groups—namely, to produce an adult whose values and behaviors are congruent with those of the group itself. The responsibility for socialization is the Japanese mother's, unlike American society in which both mother and father share in the process.

The attachment of the Japanese child to the mother is particularly strong because of the mother's attention and indulgences. The child is looked upon as the center of the universe and is the object of lavish affection.

Japanese mothers are always with their babies, rocking them, lulling them, trying to keep them quiet and contented. In this way the infant is protected from experiencing intense affects such as distress or rage. The American mother, by contrast, leaves the infants alone more but also talks to and stimulates them to a greater degree. Already we see the beginnings of a pattern of behavior emphasizing closeness, dependence, and moderate affect as contrasted with autonomy, companionability, and achievement. Weaning is characteristically prolonged, usually occurring long after infants can understand what is being said to them. Toilet training is not severe, and masturbation is not condemned. The Japanese mother bathes with her baby, again unlike the American mother, who typically is outside the tub. In the first year or two of life the baby is carried on the mother's back in a strap. When she goes out in winter, the mother wears a coat covering both of them. The child sleeps with parents until about age 10.

Because of the strong dependency of the child on the mother, separation is a source of anxiety. When being seriously disciplined, the Japanese child will be locked outside of the home, unlike the American counterpart, who will be locked in the room. Disciplining also relies more on shame, ridicule, and teasing than is the case with American children. The appeal to duty and responsibility is also greater, along with the guilt engendered when the child fails to live up to expectations. Physical punishment does occur within the home. Outside, disciplinary measures are usually a discrete pinch or a comment that will make other children laugh at the misbehaving child. Finally, children are disciplined by threats of harm from devils, ghosts, and malevolent strangers and are rewarded with sweets for good behavior (Yamamoto and Kubota, 1983).

Generational Changes

While it is essential to have a picture of traditional Japanese culture as a reference point, it is equally important to know how succeeding generations modified the pattern through adopting elements of the American culture. The point is valid for a number of minority groups although the Japanese seem particularly eager to assimilate, while their congruent values of education, hard work, and respect for superiors facilitate the process of assimilation into the American middle class (Yamamoto and Kubota, 1983).

THE ISSEI GENERATION   The Issei, or first-generation Japanese, arrived shortly after the turn of the century when Japan was only beginning to be industrialized and the tradition of caste and class was strong. The majority of immigrants were poorly educated, tended to be from rural areas, were disadvantaged educationally and culturally, and had been without employment in their native country. Most spoke only Japanese and were preoccupied with the problem of survival.

First regarded as a source of cheap labor in this country, they were subsequently subjected to blatant racism, violence, restrictive legislation, and anti-miscegenational statutes. They coped with their strange and hostile environment by trying to be inconspicuous, adopting Western dress, and being polite, stoic, nonemotional, and self-effacing, as well as hardworking and conscientious. While adaptive, such mechanisms also perpetuated both a physical and psychological "ghettoization." Issei rarely ventured out into their new environment and so had no experiences to counteract their suspicion and fear of it. This image was communicated to their children along with the need to be hypervigilant, stoic, and nonoffensive in the larger community.

THE NISEI The Nisei are American-born children of the Issei immigrants and are considered second-generation Japanese-Americans. They were raised before World War II and were bilingual, with Japanese as their primary language. They came to be known as the model minority, the Quiet American, and the most educated and successful ethnic group in the United States, but the process by which they achieved this status was a painful one.

While their parents, the Issei, were plagued by physical hardships and marginal living standards, they were relatively free of psychological stress. Their insulated, self-contained communities provided the kind of group support inherent in the traditional Japanese culture. Their children experienced more conflict since they had greater contact with American culture, particularly in school. The American way of life to which they were exposed and the American friendships they formed set them apart from their parents' generation, while the customs and behaviors they learned at home, such as martial arts for the boys and playing Japanese instruments for the girls, made them different from their peers. Thus they were incompletely and superficially immersed in two cultures without feeling totally Japanese or American. The severely autocratic role of the Issei fathers, the prohibition against dating until early adulthood, and the insistence on maintaining social distance with non-Japanese created ongoing generational conflicts as well as psychopathological reactions. How prevalent such reactions were is impossible to know since mental illness is reacted to with great shame by the family and is kept secret until the behavior is too blatant to conceal.

The hysteria following the bombing of Pearl Harbor was a turning point for Japanese-Americans. The majority of their community leaders were arrested, separated from their families, and placed in a segregated facility in Crystal City, Texas, with the designation of dangerous aliens. West Coast families were uprooted and placed in concentration camps in the spring of 1942. The few Nisei who questioned the constitutionality of incarceration without due process were labeled traitors and imprisoned. Thus the Japanese communities were destroyed as sociocultural entities. The people found they had to live in cramped quarters and use centralized eating, bathroom, and laundry facilities. The lack of privacy and the communal facilities disrupted traditional family life, depriving the Nisei of its stabilizing influence. But it emancipated them as well. The necessity of communicating in English with federal representatives escalated Nisei into roles of prominence overnight, while it simultaneously contributed to the erosion of established roles and functions within the family unit. Peer groups, organized around athletic competition between blocks, became primary socialization units. Older Nisei were selected as coaches and parent surrogates, while parental supervision itself gradually dissipated over time.

Educational facilities were grossly inadequate, and absenteeism was common along with restlessness and a desire for increased control over one's destiny. Because it was possible to leave the camps under special dispensation between 1942 and 1946, Nisei attended colleges and universities in unprecedented numbers, making them the most educated ethnic subgroup within the United States. They also formed an all-Nisei combat unit, which became the most decorated battle unit in World War II.

The post–World War II era had an air of starting over. Compared with the Issei, the Nisei were better educated and more worldly and were sufficiently flexible to abandon ghetto life and its attitude of coexistence in exchange for an assimilated form of living in mainstream America. Their diligence and education enhanced employment opportunities and facilitated acceptance by the majority culture.

THE SANSEI   The Sansei, or grandchidren of Issei immigrants, resemble middle-class white American children in attitudes, belief, and life-style. Most no longer speak Japanese. Sansei, like Nisei, tend to identify themselves not with Japan but with the camp in which the Nisei spent the four impressionable years between 1942 and 1946. They continue to show some of their parents' characteristics in that they are less aggressive socially than Anglo-Americans and overachieve in school. But the majority do well and have the reputation of being model children.

The well-educated Sansei appear to be seeking an identity that is neither wholly Japanese nor wholly American but an amalgamation of elements in both cultures. On the one hand, more and more Japanese women are college graduates and young adults are increasingly using entitled services such as economic aid to students and legal, social, and human services. On the other hand, there is still a reliance on the family as a primary resource for solving potential problems along with an involvement in Asian community-based projects in health and community development. However, there are certain academic and vocational problems. Because Japanese students have the reputation of being high achievers, teachers may not realize that there are individual differences in ability and may expect too much of those who do not perform at a superior level. Vocational choices are another potential source of stress because the culture values careers in the sciences, engineering, and medicine over those in the arts and humanities. Thus individuals with interests and talents in these latter areas may not be supported by their cultural group or may face pressures to change.

The picture is much less positive if the Sansei's education stops with high school or earlier. The blue-collar class tends to discriminate against them more openly than the middle class, the options for work are more limited, and these Sansei become progressively alienated from their college-bound peers. Consequently, they are at risk for drug abuse and narcotic addiction as well as for conflicts with family, peers, and police (Santa, 1983).

Evaluation. The American emphasis on equality and autonomy might give Japanese-American children opportunities for maximizing their potential which otherwise might not be available to Japanese children locked into specified roles and stratified classes. One thinks particularly of the traditional role for Japanese girls in this regard. Yet the very emphasis on individuality may not provide sufficient protection against isolation on the one hand and social irresponsibility on the other. Such vulnerabilities may not exist in traditional Japanese child rearing with its emphasis on interdependence, group identity, and group monitoring. In sum, we are dealing with a balancing of assets and vulnerabilities between cultural patterns just as we do among individual children.

HELPING MEXICAN-AMERICAN FAMILIES AND CHILDREN

While understanding ethnic socialization and diverse ethnic values is important, the pragmatic reason for learning about ethnic groups is to enable clinical child psychologists to evaluate and help families and children who are having problems. Our thesis is that these clinical goals of accurate evaluation and effective help can be achieved only by understanding ethnic backgrounds and modifying clinical procedures accordingly. We have chosen the Mexican-American culture to illustrate this thesis. As with the Japanese-

American culture in the previous section, the choice of ethnic group is arbitrary. Before proceeding to clinical considerations, it will be necessary to describe the traditional Mexican values and how they have been modified over successive generations of immigrants.

Traditional Values

In place of the Anglo-American values of individualism and egalitarianism, traditional Mexican values emphasize interdependence and hierarchical status. Thus their world view stresses harmony, communality, cooperation, and obedience (Trankina, 1983). Research comparing Mexican and American families and children has enriched this overall picture in regard to these characteristics. (Our presentation follows Diaz-Guerrero, 1987.)

CONTROL   American children tend to struggle for mastery of problems and challenges in their environment, while Mexican children are more passively obedient and try to adapt to environmental stress. Thus, in a test called *Filosofia de Vita*, or Views of Life, Mexican children tended not to endorse statements such as "Man can change the world to suit his own needs." Or again, when Mexican children were told a story of a girl who disagreed with her friend as to how a game should be played, the children tended to acquiesce rather than to imagine the heroine trying to get her own way. Such fatalism may help Mexican children cope with inevitable or unchangeable events such as death or chronic illness, but it is poorly suited to adapting to rapidly changing or achievement-oriented environments.

OBEDIENCE   Mexican children are more obedient than Anglo-American children; for example, in the *Filosofia de Vita* test they were more apt than American children to endorse statements concerning absolute obedience to the father, mother, and teacher. They are also more apt to seek help in solving problems from authority figures such as parents, siblings, or police officers. However, as Mexico has become more industrialized over time, there is a concomitant trend toward self-assertion and away from obedience, since assertiveness correlates with high achievement scores in school, with higher social class, and with an autonomous, dominant, aggressive personality.

INTERDEPENDENCE   Interdependence is expressed in numerous ways. The Mexicans are family-centered rather than being individually centered as are the Anglo-Americans. When approaching an examination in school, for example, the Mexican child is fearful not so much of individual failure as of a failure to support the family system. In games or other activities, Mexican children tend to be cooperative, while Anglo-American chidren are highly competitive even when such competiton is dysfunctional. Finally, at a more general level, Mexican children would not endorse statements such as "Work first, friendship second" or "I do not need the approval of others" on the *Filosofia de Vita* test while Anglo-American children would.

In sum, Mexican children tend to be fatalistic, family-centered, and cooperative in contrast with Anglo-American children, who cope actively with challenges and are individualistic and competitive.

ADDITIONAL VALUES   Diaz-Guerrero (1987) devised an instrument to reveal additional distinctive and common values, administering it to sixty Mexican and sixty Mexican-American mothers and children. Note that we might expect more overlap between the groups than if we were contrasting Mexicans and Anglo-Americans. *Machismo,* or the superiority of men over women, was endorsed by both groups but to a significantly greater extent by the Mexican mothers. Statements included "Men are more intelligent than women" and "Submissive women are best." Mexican mothers endorsed the importance of virginity ("To be a virgin is of much importance for single women") more than did Mexican-American mothers. Both groups equally endorsed the Abnegation scale, which is the belief that women suffer more than men, the Fear of Authority scale, which concerns children's fear of their parents, and the Family Status Quo scale, which deals with faithfulness and loyalty of the wife to her husband. However, the Mexican mothers, in contrast with the Mexican-American ones, thought it was more important for children to respect and obey than to love their parents and that family reputation should be defended even by extreme measures. Although both groups of mothers rejected the idea that women should not be independent in regard to work and dating, the Mexican women were less rejecting than were the Mexican-Americans.

Mexican-American Characteristics

Mexican-American culture shows both continuities and change in regard to its Mexican roots and is heavily influenced by generational and economic factors.

FAMILY STRUCTURE   The interdependence of Mexican-Americans is nicely illustrated by the structure of the family, which is neither nuclear nor extended but a combination of the two. As in Mexico, the family unit is of prime importance to its members and is organized in terms of status hierarchies. The father is dominant and his authority must be respected. While formally having less status, the mother is the one who actually unites the members into a family as well as creating a strong bond of love with the children. Grandparents also play an important part in family life. Sex roles are clearly demarcated; males are granted independence at an earlier age than females and are expected to achieve in the outside world.

Family members also have ancillary relationships that serve as a support system as well as transmitting information and providing access to resources such as jobs. There is a fictive kin system called *compadrazgo*, or godparents, whose members are usually selected from close friends or relatives. They are responsible for the well-being of the child, thereby serving as a source of security for the child and support for the parents. There are neighborhood helpers (*servidores*) who further extend the social network in terms of assisting with chores and providing companionship. Natural healers bring relief from various health, mental health, and life crisis problems through a variety of healing modalities such as massage, herbs, and spiritual treatment. Religious counselors also play a role in helping Mexican-American families cope with problems (Vega, Hough, and Romero, 1983).

The prime *values* of Mexican-American families are religion, interdependence, honor, machismo, self-respect, and self-sufficiency. All members are expected to protect the family image, honor, and well-being. Respect within the family is hierarchically organized by age and sex, with older males being given the most respect. Family members are expected to do assigned chores and other family-related physical tasks and to contribute to the family's economic well-being (Mejia, 1983).

CHILD REARING   Mexican-American parents value a close, warm relationship within the family. Their family-centeredness is expressed not only with their children but also in their close relation with their own parents and the frequency of visiting relatives. Parents encourage their children to be more dependent on the family than do Anglo-American parents, for example, believing that their child's best friend should be a sibling. They allow fewer small decisions such as what to wear, encourage the children to play near home, worry when a child is not at home, and do not encourage children to bring their friends home as much as do Anglo-American parents. As we have seen, obedience to authority and loyalty to the family are essential.

The model child is not viewed as one who is achievement-oriented and successful in the academic and economic spheres. Rather, such children are skilled in human understanding and interpersonal relationships. They are polite, socially adept, courteous, respectful of elders, and deserving of respect as well as being mindful of the dignity and individuality of others. Such values, along with their noncompetitiveness, place Mexican-American children at a disadvantage in achievement-oriented *schools*. There is evidence, for example, that teachers praise, encourage, and direct questions to Anglo-American children more frequently than to Mexican-American children. Teachers also view Mexican-American children as lower in confidence and eagerness to learn (Mejia, 1983). Mexican-American children who start school close to Anglo-Americans in measured achievement will fall behind them at each grade level. They may be subjected to discrimination and cultural exclusion, being regarded stereotypically as lazy, dirty, satisfied with a subordinate role, or products of a rural folk culture. The children may react with confusion and may look to their peers for support. Such groups, in turn, may be viewed as a threat to the stability and safety of the school by administrators and school personnel (Trankina, 1983).

Generational Changes and Socioeconomic Influences

The Mexican immigrants who came after the Mexican Revolution of 1910 were laborers with little if any formal education. (Our presentation follows Vega, Hough, and Romero, 1983.) Today, immigrants come from mid-sized cities and reflect changes in Mexico itself in regard to urbanization and technological advances. They are in better health, have more education, may be acquainted with current production processes, and have more of a middle-class ideology. In addition to different characteristics, immigrants have different degrees of acculturation. The less acculturated ones have low educational and occupational status and high family solidarity and ethnic identification, while the highly acculturated ones have the opposite characteristics.

The *immigration experience* is a stressful one often involving a temporary disruption of the family as the father is away seeking employment in the United States. Once here, immigrants must come to grips with a new and alien culture. An essential source of support is the *barrio*, or community, whose families provide temporary housing for the immigrants as well as advice about jobs and techniques for getting along in the new environment. Most immigrants will always identify themselves as Mexicans even though they will gradually acquire new habits and values.

The immigrant is usually a victim of poverty and cultural marginality. Repeated absence of the father may disrupt the marital relationship and lead to divorce, which is more frequent than it is among Anglo-Americans. The mothers, only a third of whom have completed high school, stand little chance of improving the economic lot of the family. In addition, the high birth rate among Mexican-American women means that mothers are further burdened with the care of large families.

The *second generation* has developed a culture that is neither Mexican nor middle-class Anglo-American, but a unique blend of Mexican traditions and elements from other cultures. In many cities black expressions, music, and dance styles are highly influential; in other cities the influence of Latin cultural groups is strong. Having a synthetic culture not only sets Mexican-Americans apart from the dominant American culture but also is a potential source of stress within the family. Often immigrant parents regard the innovations as harmless idiosyncracies, but they also can be viewed as degrading or showing a lack of respect for oneself and for others. While many potential conflicts are avoided by discretion, when problems do surface, the resulting stress can be severe.

In contrast to the immigrants who speak only Spanish, the second generation is bilingual, being taught Spanish at home and English in school. The typical result is a child who understands Spanish and speaks it haltingly but relies primarily on English.

As to *socioeconomic status*, a disproportionate number of Mexican-Americans live in poverty. There is the *underclass*, consisting of poor, uneducated transients who migrate in search of employment and a stable support system to tide them over until they can cope using their own resources. The families are large, Spanish-speaking households living in chronically overcrowded conditions. The *low-income* families resemble the underclass except for employment and residential stability. They have limited education, work at semi-skilled or service jobs, and have large, unacculturated families. The children are unlikely to be high achievers or to do well in school, thereby continuing the cycle of poverty.

The immigrant *working-class* family tends to be better educated than the previous two classes, some having completed high school.

They have stable employment in skilled or semi-skilled occupations, their homes are ample if overcrowded, and they have the resources to save money and take an occasional vacation. Their involvement in the community facilitates the social mobility of their children, who are aggressive, mobile, articulate, and independent, some eventually acquiring a good deal of wealth.

The *middle class* is similar to the Anglo-American middle class. The parents are rarely immigrants unless they were also from the middle class in Mexico, the household is English-speaking, and education is stressed. However, adolescents, because they stand out as a distinct minority, may have a particularly difficult time with their ethnic identity, not knowing whether to renounce their cultural origins or to be proud of their Mexican-American heritage and participate in networks that provide ethnic support.

Helping the Children and Their Families.

Like all children, Mexican-American children may be seen by a clinical child psychologist because of one of the psychopathologies we have discussed. Like all impoverished children, their chances of becoming psychologically disturbed are significantly increased (the connection between poverty and mental illness has long been established). In addition, the children may have problems unique to being a minority such as experiencing racial discrimination or cultural conflict. At this point there are few studies of the independent effects of poverty and ethnicity on the development of psychological disturbances (Farrington, 1986).

Undoubtedly, Mexican-American children are at risk for developing mental health problems. The ones living in poverty are in poor health and receive inadequate pediatric care. A high incidence of unemployment, substandard housing, alcoholism, and drug abuse are indicative of family disruption, which, in turn, is related to an increased incidence of juvenile delinquency. In regard to school, Mexican-Americans have the highest dropout rate after the sixth grade of all groups in the southwestern United States. (For details, see Trankina, 1983.)

Regardless of the nature of the problem or the source of risk, Mexican-American children and their families must be treated in a manner congruent with their ethnic values and customs if psychological services are to be maximally effective or, indeed, if they are even to be accepted. We shall now examine a number of implications of this theme.

MENTAL HEALTH SERVICES Despite the increased risk for psychopathology, mental health services are underused by Mexican-Americans and, incidentally, by other minorities as well. A number of factors contribute to underuse. Mental health facilities located in middle-class neighborhoods are apt to be perceived as foreign, unfriendly, and not really there to serve Mexican-Americans. Poor people in general are unaccustomed to forms and paperwork, while Mexican-Americans may be especially suspicious if they have relatives or friends who are illegal aliens. The initial personal questioning may arouse feelings of vulnerability or being intruded upon. Moreover, many families view mental health care as similar to medical care, expecting expedient appointments and prescriptive courses of action. And, finally, there is the communication problem: an English-speaking staff can do little for families who speak only Spanish or whose understanding of English is limited.

Ideally, then, facilities should be near the *barrio* and have bilingual staff members. Bilingualism is important not only for communication and rapport but for diagnosis as well, since there is evidence that Spanish-speaking schizophrenic patients interviewed in English were judged significantly more pathological than when they were interviewed in Spanish. Forms should be in Spanish and reduced to a bare minimum. Long waiting periods should be avoided, crisis intervention should be available to the more pressing cases, along with casual contacts with the family during a waiting period. Clinic hours should be extended to accommodate working parents. (See Trankina, 1983.)

Although more controversial, it is also possible that forces within the culture itself serve as impediments to using mental health facilities. Family pride may lead to an attempt to conceal disturbances, and fatalism may produce a tendency to accept rather than remedy them. Natural healers may be consulted initially since they are familiar and their methods are congruent with cultural traditions. The extended social network as a resource may be preferred to professional advice.

RAPPORT Equally important as the administrative features of a mental health facility are the techniques used to establish rapport. The friendly impersonality and task orientation of the professional dealing with Anglo-Americans is not suited to the Mexican-Americans. Rather, the quality Mexican-Americans value is *personalismo*, which is a combination of warmth, empathy, and equality between clinician and client. Since touching is more frequent than in Anglo-American society, a clinician might extend her hand upon meeting a new client, introduce herself by including her first name rather than a formal title, and engage in small talk in order to establish an atmosphere of friendly give-and-take. The clinician may talk about her own past as she inquires into the past of the parent. *Personalismo* also includes an attitude of respect and tactfulness. Thus sensitive clinical topics should be approached slowly and cautiously, and confrontations should be avoided (Trankina, 1983).

Because many clients view the clinician as they would a medical doctor, they tend to expect advice and direction. Thus they expect an active approach from the clinician such as questions focused on the presenting problem followed by concrete solutions. The nondirective approach, a probing into details of childhood history, or requests for introspection should be used sparingly (Ruiz and Padilla, 1983).

ASSESSMENT   Our general thesis is that clinicians cannot accurately evaluate minority groups without a knowledge of their ethnic background. By the same token assessment instruments such as psychological tests which have been standardized on Anglo-Americans cannot be used uncritically with minorities as was frequently done in the past, not only in clinical practice but in research as well. Typically minority groups were found to be inferior not necessarily because of a basic inferiority but because of biases in the tests themselves. The language or the content of test items may have been unfamiliar to minority children, for example, or such children may have tried to avoid any answer that could remotely be interpreted as criticism of the family.

E. M. Bernal (1989) lists a number of biases that might spuriously lower the scores of Mexican-American children on intelligence and achievement tests. Many of these tests require a degree of proficiency in English which Mexican-American children may not have. Clinicians may mistakenly assume that the ability to engage in a conversation is a sufficiently sensitive measure of mastery of English when it is not. Specifically designed tests of proficiency should be used instead. If proficiency is low, test results may reflect a limited ability to understand the task itself rather than an inability to do it well. To take just one example: a number of words in a vocabulary test may have no exact equivalent in Spanish; consequently, a child's vague definition may represent his lack of familiarity with the word or his attempt to define it in terms of its nearest Spanish equivalent.

Various extraneous interpersonal and intrapersonal variables may adversely affect test scores. While acculturated chidren score highest with English-speaking examiners, less acculturated ones score highest with Spanish-speaking ones. Some children lack test-taking skills, hurrying through as quickly as possible to escape an unpleasant situation. Merely having taken tests over the years does not necessarily remedy the situation. Personality factors, particularly high anxiety and self-deprecation, may lower scores. Both of these personality variables may increase with age rather than dissipating, while children in transition from a lower to a higher socioeconomic status are particularly prone to having them.

Knowing the sources of bias suggests remedies: devising special tests for Mexican-American children or using English proficiency measures in interpreting standard test results; having the test administered by a Spanish-speaking psychologist for certain groups of children; helping children develop useful test-taking attitudes and skills as well as reassuring them and relieving their anxiety. (For further details, see Bernal, 1989.)

Even standardized test results can be useful to the clinicians if properly interpreted, however. Achievement tests, for example, may be important measures of the level of a child's current functioning as compared with Anglo-American peers. However, saying "Juan is two years behind in reading and arithmetic" is different from saying "Juan is a slow learner." The first statement leaves open the issues of etiology and ability; the second does not. In a like manner, it is proper to conclude that "Maria looks to her family for advice and support concerning dating and friends. While this is to be expected, it might be a source of difficulty when she is with her adolescent peers, most of whom are American." Such a statement is quite different from "Maria's problem is that she has unresolved dependency needs in relation to her family."

FAMILY VARIABLES   The family variables described in the preceding section have some important clinical implications. (For additional details and information, see Trankina, 1983.)

Because of the interdependence of family members, the strength of family ties, and the importance of the *compadrazgo*, some form of family therapy would generally be more appropriate than individual therapy. When not specifically doing family therapy, the clinician should constantly be mindful of the reverberations of remedial measures throughout the network of familial relations. In one case intrusive grandparents were causing marital problems, and the therapist made the mistake of recommending that the grandparents stay out of the picture. This recommendation only intensified the problems. The therapist then changed tactics so as to increase the couple's self-confidence, only gradually focusing on the grandparents' involvement at a level the parents themselves determined. This tactful approach, in which change took place within the context of respect for traditional relationships, succeeded where the confrontational approach had failed.

By knowing familial values, the clinician can interpret behavior differently than with Anglo-Americans. A mother walking her children to and from school, for example, may be a natural expression of family closeness rather than suggesting overprotection. A respectful, cooperative school-age child should not be suspected of having difficulty

expressing aggression toward parents or competitiveness toward peers; in fact, anger toward parents is often indicative of a significant rupture in the parent–child relationship. While rebelliousness is considered part of normal development for Anglo-American teenagers, the same is not true for Mexican-Americans. For a clinician to encourage rebellion on the assumption that it is essential to the development of adult autonomy might only create overwhelming guilt in the teenager. Mexican-American adolescents may also be more mature than Anglo-Americans since the older sons are encouraged to contribute to the family's finances while the older daughters care for the younger siblings. To treat them as typical teenagers, rather than as young adults, would be demeaning. Finally, values can be more rigid in certain areas than they are in Anglo-American families: pregnancy can result in the teenager being disowned, perhaps having to live with relatives or friends, while homosexuality is impossible for many parents to accept no matter how much effort is made to change their attitudes.

FAMILIAL ROLES   At the heart of the *male role* is machismo. However, the term means more than masculine superiority and forcefulness. Masculine self-esteem depends primarily on raising a successful family and, second, on having a high standing in the community. Thus it encompasses a strong sense of personal honor, family loyalty, love of children, and respect for the aged. However, the more narrowly defined aspects of machismo are clearly present, especially in the *palomillos* or social groups, in which young males display their prowess through drinking and feats of daring. In addition, the groups offer social support, giving help and advice to members who are having marital, familial, or work problems.

One risk of machismo is that the young boy will identify only with its aggressive aspects or even that he will be encouraged by his father to be too aggressive. If acting-out behavior brings such boy to a clinical child psychologist, the relation with the father must be handled with the utmost tact. The clinician might accommodate the father in scheduling visits after hours or meeting the father at home, rather than assuming the stance of the expert who knows best what the father should do. It also might be a good strategy to appeal to paternal values incompatible with aggressiveness, such as pride in the family whose reputation is being threatened by the boy's antisocial acting out. Whatever is done, the father cannot feel that his authority is being threatened by the clinician, but rather that the clinician needs his help in making important decisions about the family.

The *female role* is a family-centered and subservient one. The mother is expected to be nurturant and self-sacrificing while the daughter's socialization stresses caring for the children and the home. The daughter is allowed to spend less time away from the house than the son, and her social activities are more limited and carefully monitored. This situation is undergoing rapid change both in Mexico and in this country, since women want more education and vocational opportunities and more freedom in their social and sexual life. The change may be particularly difficult for Mexican-American adolescents who have such strong ties to the family and who might encounter resistance from all the more conservative members of the familial network. Group therapy may be helpful in such cases, individuals sharing experiences and receiving support from peers, all of whom want more independence.

In our society, the macho male and the dependent female are no longer the accepted images of sex roles. Rather, there is overlap and sharing of qualities between males and females. Because we are in a state of transition, feelings may run high concerning how faulty traditional sex roles were and how much better the current situation is. However, the clinical child psychologist cannot let such personal feelings interfere with the desire to do what is best for the child. In certain instances the clinician may decide that machismo or dependence should be supported because a change in roles would engender unbearable family conflict and individual guilt and because the child would be more fulfilled in the traditional rather than in the contemporary model. Respect for ethnic culture entails this kind of respect for ethnic diversity. To decide that minorities must conform to the culture of the majority is to devalue diversity and to make decisions that may be detrimental to the children and their families.

In the concluding section of our discussions of differences within the interpersonal context, we have introduced the concepts of assessment and remediation. Because these are the activities that concern practicing clinical psychologists the most, they deserve a full-dress presentation of their own.

15

Psychological Assessment

We have repeatedly seen that in order to be understood, behavior must be evaluated in context. The context of time is crucial and includes not only the child's current age but past history as well. Within this temporal framework both intra- and interpersonal factors must be considered: a severely retarded 8-year-old who steals because she has not fully grasped the principle of property rights is different from an 8-year-old of average intelligence who steals in order to be accepted by her friends; schizophrenic behavior in a child whose parents are also schizophrenic may not represent as severe a disturbance as the same behavior in a child with psychologically intact parents. Our goal has been a scientific one, namely, to understand all variables relevant to the production of psychopathological behavior.

Clinicians, however, vary in their need to evaluate psychopathological behavior in terms of all relevant contexts. In part, this variability is a function of different theoretical allegiances. Psychoanalytically oriented clinicians strive for a comprehensive understanding not only of present and past but also of conscious and unconscious determinants of behavior. Trait psychologists are satisfied with assessing the relatively permanent predisposition of individuals to behave in a certain way, such as aggressively, anxiously, or dependently. Clinicians with a systems orientation concentrate on current patterns of interpersonal interactions, particularly in the family. Behaviorally oriented clinicians focus on specific patterns of behavior in specific settings, while nondirective clinicians reduce assessment to a bare minimum.

Another kind of constraint on comprehensive assessment arises from the clinician's primary role as a help giver. Characteristically, he or she wants to understand a problem in terms that are congruent with a particular school of therapy and to devise and implement remedial plans as quickly as possible. One might think there would be a complementary relation between understanding and helping: the more we understand, the better we are able to help. However, such is not the case. Our increased understanding of conduct disorders and of autism has outstripped our ability to remedy these conditions, while the flowering of behavior therapies has not been paralleled by comparable advances in understanding the etiology of the psychopathologies that are successfully treated.

The present discussion will begin with the clinician who seeks a comprehensive understanding of the child's psychopathology, noting how those with different goals, particularly behavioral clinicians, would abbreviate and alter the procedure. This strategy allows the widest scope in presenting assessment techniques, as well as affording a glimpse into the assessment process at its most complex. Coverage of specific techniques will be selective, and knowledge of the construction, reliability, and validity of major psychological tests, commensurate with that gained in an introductory course in psychology, is assumed. (For a detailed coverage of assessment, see Schwartz and Johnson, 1985.)

THE ASSESSMENT PROCESS

Clinicians never assume that within the space of a few hours they will be able to understand the nature and origin of the problems that bring a particular child to their attention. They realize they are viewing parents and child under special circumstances that both limit and bias the data they will obtain: the child who is frightened by a clinic waiting room may not be a generally fearful child, just as one who is hyperactive in school may be a model of cooperation when taking an intelligence test; parents may have their own misperceptions and blind spots in regard to their child's behavior, along with varying degrees of willingness to reveal information about themselves and their child. Thus, an initial session is only the first step toward understanding.

In attempting to assimilate and integrate the massive amount of data they collect, clinicians implicitly proceed like hypothesis-testing scientists. No single bit of behavior is definitive, but each is suggestive. As these bits accumulate, certain initial hunches tend to be confirmed and others discarded. By the end of the assessment process, the clinician can make some statements concerning the child's problem with a reasonable degree of assurance; other statements will be tentative and qualified; and a number of questions will remain unanswered.

To illustrate this hypothesis-testing process briefly: Tom is a 10-year-old boy referred for a learning problem; specifically, he is lazy, failing reading and arithmetic, and beginning to be disruptive in class. Upon being introduced to the psychologist in the waiting room, Tom is unusually friendly and communicative. Most children are cautious initially, and rightly so. The psychologist mentally notes Tom's behavior and wonders what it might represent. Perhaps this is a basically healthy boy whose problems have been exaggerated; perhaps he has been too close to adults at the expense of becoming alienated from peers; perhaps he is a charming sociopath; perhaps his social skills are a defense against some unknown fear. During the interview the boy continues to impress the psychologist as a bright, alert, open youngster.

However, Tom's behavior begins to change on the intelligence tests: he tends to say "I don't know" too readily when items become difficult; he quickly destroys a puzzle he had put together incorrectly as if trying to cover up his mistake; and he uses his conversational skills to divert attention away from the test material. When encouraged to respond to difficult items, it is clear that he does not know the correct answer.

At this point he seems neither a sociopath nor fearful nor prematurely adult; both his enjoyment of people and his openness seem genuine. Yet, the test adds a significant bit of data: he has only average intelligence. The psychologist then speculates, "If his sociability misled me into thinking he was intellectually bright, his parents and teachers might have also been misled into setting unrealistically high goals and pressuring him to achieve them." This hypothesis naturally would have to be checked by interviewing the parents and a telephone call to the teacher. It also raises further questions, such as the effects of being regarded as lazy on the boy's self-image, which could be explored by further assessment. In regard to diagnosis, the clinician is tentatively thinking in terms of a specific developmental disorder, in that the boy's problem seems to result from a significant discrepancy between his social and intellectual development. Another possibility is that Tom has a learning disability which undermined his confidence on a variety of intellectual tasks.

Hypotheses are never generated out of the blue; rather, clinicians use a variety of sources: their preferred theoretical framework, the clinical and research literature relevant to the problem at hand, accumulated knowledge passed on from seasoned clinicians to novitiates, as well as their own experience. In this instance, the hypothesis generated by the discrepancy between Tom's social and intellectual development derived from a discussion of a similar case with his supervisor during the clinician's student days; the question concerning Tom's self-image came from the clinician's interest in the self-concept. Equally valid questions could be raised concerning the effects of Tom's failure on the family dynamics or on his status with teachers and peers at school. As we shall subsequently see, the very openness of the clinical process is a source of concern to certain psychologists, who would like to see assessment become less of an art and more of a science.

INITIAL SOURCES OF DATA

Referrals

The first data concerning the child come from the referral, which usually contains information about the problem as perceived by concerned adults, its duration and onset, its effects on the child and on others, and what measures, if any, have been taken to remedy it. Parents and teachers are the major sources of referrals.

The fact that children are not self-referred, as are most adults, has an important psychological implication. There is a great deal of difference between seeking help and being told one needs help. Children may or may not feel the need, may or may not understand why they are being brought to the clinic. Parents may either fail to tell them why or give them reasons they do not understand or agree with. After establishing some rapport, the clinician should clarify why the child is there, what the assessment procedures are, and why they are being done.

Observation

The clinician's assessment begins on first seeing the parents and child. Their appearance and interactions provide clues as to family characteristics and the relationships among its members. First impressions furnish information concerning the family's social class and general level of harmony or disharmony, as well as its stylistic characteristics—reserved, demonstrative, authoritarian, intellectual, and so on.

Once with the child, the clinician systematically gathers certain kinds of information. The *overall impression* of the child's personality is always important: "an all-American boy"; "he already has the worried look of an old man, as if he does not know what it is like to be a child"; "a perfect little lady, a real showpiece for her mother"; "he has that sullen look, like he is constantly spoiling for a fight"; "a direct, honest, no-nonsense preadolescent girl, somewhat on the tomboy side." Such impressions help define the child's social-stimulus value, which may be a potent elicitor of positive or negative reactions from others.

The child's *body* and *body language* provide important clues to physiological intactness as well as to personality variables. Significant departures from the norms of height and weight may indicate a medical problem or, more important, may cause the child to be teased and rejected by peers. The body can be read for more subtle signs of disturbance: bruises and scars suggest accident proneness or abuse; needle marks on the arm suggest drug abuse; squinting or putting the face close to the paper when drawing or writing suggests a visual defect.

Body language includes a wide array of expressive behaviors. Psychological tension is often embodied in physical tension: a strained facial expression, a forced laugh, a tense posture when sitting, pressured speech or stuttering, "nervous gestures" such as nail biting. A monotonous voice, slouched posture, masklike face, and slow movements suggest depression or withdrawal.

Finally, the child's *relationship* to the clinician furnishes an important clue as to his or her perception of adults. It is natural for children to be reserved initially, since in reality the clinician is a stranger. However, as they discover that the clinician is interested, friendly, and benign, they should become relaxed, cooperative, and communicative, although still reluctant to talk about sensitive topics. Certain children never warm up; they sit as far back in their chair as possible, speak in an almost inaudible monotone, rarely look at the examiner or else watch intently, as if he or she were a kind of monster who might strike out at any minute. Some children turn the examination into a power struggle: when the examiner asks questions they cannot answer, such children ask the examiner questions or try to find a topic such as television or movies or sports which they know more about than the examiner. Provocative children begin to "test the limits," mischievously peeking when told to close their eyes or destroying a puzzle when told to leave it intact.

But a relationship involves two people, the clinician as well as the child. Clinicians are not standard stimuli; they have their own styles of behaving, as well as their own talents and vulnerabilities. It is essential, therefore, that clinicians understand their own individual characteristics and include this understanding in their evaluation of the child. They may naturally be effusive or confronting or self-contained or intellectual, and such characteristics may naturally turn some children off or appeal to others. Knowing their own vulnerabilities, clinicians can see that they are becoming impatient with a whining child or angry with a provocative one or frightened by a hyperactive one and can then make sure that such reactions do not further undermine the child's self-control. While professionals can be expected to be objective about themselves as well as knowledgeable and resourceful in relating to children, they cannot be expected to transcend their own personalities.

Generally speaking, observation as used by many clinicians may be nearer an art than a science because the procedures are unstandardized and the target behaviors so wide ranging. However, observation per se is not unscientific. Behavioral clinicians, for example, bring to assessment the structure and reliability that the more open-ended approach lacks.

The Interview

Information concerning the child and the family comes primarily from interviewing the parents. Typically, the interview begins with an account of the present problem. Next, a detailed history, technically known as a *case history*, is obtained in order to explore the antecedent conditions that might have contributed to the present difficulties. Among the topics covered are the child's prenatal history, birth history, and early development. The subsequent adjustment of the child within the family and with peers is explored, along with social and academic adjustment at school. For teenagers, information is obtained concerning sexual development and work history, as well as possible drug and alcohol use and delinquent behavior. The clinician also inquires about major illnesses and injuries. To complete the picture, the parents may be asked about their own marital and occupational adjustment, their specific goals, satisfactions, and dissatisfactions, and their relation to their own parents.

But what about the studies showing the unreliability of parental histories? While disqualifying parents as sources of accurate information concerning many aspects of development, the studies do not render their histories useless, because it is still important

for the clinician to know the parents' perception of the facts. Whether the child was a "difficult" infant and a "bad" toddler may not be as important as the parents' perception or memory of the child as difficult and bad. However, the argument that it is the parents' perceptions that matter has its limitations. If a mother says, "My boy was doing all right in school until he had that bad accident on his bike," it would be important to know that the trouble actually started a year before the accident when she and her husband were on the verge of getting a divorce because of his extramarital affair. The mother's account suggests an organic etiology, while the actual sequence suggests a psychogenic one. Incidentally, the mother may not be trying to deceive the clinician and may firmly believe the accuracy of her account. The clinician must realize that in cases where accuracy matters, interview data should be verified, say, by medical or school records. In many instances, however, accuracy is impossible to establish.

There is one final aspect to the interview. In the process of interviewing, the clinician is beginning to know the parents, while the parents are also beginning to know the clinician. Since there is no hard and fast line between assessment and therapy, skilled interviewers can use this initial contact to lay the groundwork for the trust and respect that will be so crucial in future contacts with the parents.

Children are also interviewed concerning their view of themselves, their problems, and their relations with family and peers. It is not unusual for children to give rather limited responses to inquiries, however, partly because they do not understand the nature and purpose of a psychological evaluation (even after the clinician has explained it), partly because they are reluctant to talk about personal problems with a strange adult, and partly because most children are untutored in the skill of conceptualizing and communicating feelings and problems.

In an effort to bypass such obstacles, a *play interview* may be conducted with preschoolers and those in the early years of middle childhood. Children may be presented with a dollhouse and a doll family and encouraged to do anything they like. Theoretically, as the children play, they begin to express the problems they are having within the family. However, it takes a great deal of skill to decode such fantasies and to differentiate typical and age-appropriate themes from personalized, deeply felt ones; for example, a baby falling out of the crib may or may not be an expression of a hostile wish toward a younger sibling; but if the baby falls out of the crib, lands on the street, and is run over twice by an automobile, the clinician can be more confident of the interpretation! (For a detailed discussion of interviewing skills with children, see Kanfer, Eyberg, and Krahn, 1983.)

PSYCHOLOGICAL TESTS

Of all professionals dealing with psychopathologically disturbed children, psychologists have been most concerned with developing assessment techniques that can be objectively administered and scored, that have norms based on clearly defined populations, and that have established reliability and validity.

Intelligence Tests

The two most widely used intelligence tests for children are the Stanford-Binet and the Wechsler Intelligence Scale for Children or WISC. Until its most recent revision, the format of the Stanford-Binet had remained the same. It consisted of six items located at mental age levels 2 through 14, with subsequent items going from average adult to superior adult. The content of the items varied widely, from building a tower of blocks, to copying a circle, to defining words, to repeating digits, to explaining why certain statements are absurd. No effort was made to have comparable items at the various mental age levels. The scoring allowed for the computation of a child's mental age and intelligence quotient.

The fourth edition of the Stanford-Binet (1986) represents a major revision of the format. To begin with, the concept of mental age has been abandoned. Instead of different kinds of items located at different mental age levels, items of the same type are grouped into fifteen tests, each test requiring a somewhat different cognitive skill and fund of information. Moreover, these fifteen tests have been organized into four broad areas of cognitive abilities. In the *Verbal Reasoning* category are tests on Vocabulary and Comprehension (e.g., questions such as, What does envelop mean? and Why are there traffic signs?). *Quantitative Reasoning* includes tests on Quantitative Ability (e.g., counting and knowledge of fractions) and on Number Series (e.g., figuring out the next two numbers in a series of numbers which increases by 4). *Abstract/Visual Reasoning* includes tests on Copying Figures (e.g., copying a diamond or two intersecting circles) and on Pattern Analysis (e.g., putting blocks together to make a pattern depicted on a card). *Short-Term Memory* tests include remembering a series of digits and remembering sentences. At a higher level of abstraction, Verbal Reasoning and Quantitative Reasoning are regarded as *crystallized-abilities*, which are greatly influenced by schooling although they also develop by general experiences outside school. Abstract/Visual Reasoning is regarded as a *fluid-analytic ability*. It requires the invention of new cognitive strategies and is more dependent on general experiences than on schooling.

The items in each test are arranged according to difficulty; thus the more items children successfully complete, the higher their intelligence compared with children their own age. However, instead of an IQ, the results are expressed in terms of Standard Age Scores (SASs). For the total scale, the mean score is 100 and the standard deviation is 16. For example, a child with a total score of 116 will be one standard deviation above the mean or in approximately the 84th percentile. Since the same formula was used for IQs, the SAS and the IQ scores are comparable. The test can be used from 2 to 23 years of age.

The trend away from tests comprised of disparate items and toward items based on categories of cognitive abilities is illustrated by the Kaufman Assessment Battery for Children (K-ABC) (1983). Here intelligence is defined in terms of two styles of functioning called sequential processing and simultaneous processing. The former involves temporal ordering of stimuli when solving problems; for example, repeating numbers spoken by the examiner or reproducing a series of hand movements made by the examiner. The latter requires simultaneous integration of stimuli that are spatial or pictorial in nature; for example, assembling several identical triangles into an abstract pattern to match a model, or naming an object in a partially completed drawing. The K-ABC also includes an achievement scale that measures knowledge of facts or crystallized abilities; e.g., vocabulary, arithmetic, and reading comprehension. The test is for children from 2½ to 12½ years of age.

The most recent revision of the WISC is the WISC-R (Wechsler, 1974), which—like its predecessors—consists of twelve subtests, the items in each arranged according to increasing difficulty. Six of the tests—Information, Similarities, Arithmetic, Vocabulary, Comprehension, and Digit Span—comprise the Verbal Scale, because they require facility in using verbal symbols. The remaining six—Picture Completion, Picture Arrangement, Block Design, Object Assembly, Coding, and Mazes—comprise the Performance Scale, because they involve concrete material such as pictures, blocks, and jigsaw puzzles. Note that "verbal" and "performance" refer to the form in which the task is presented, not the level of thinking required; certain performance subtests require higher-level thinking than certain verbal subtests. Scoring yields a Verbal IQ and Performance IQ, as well as a Full-Scale IQ. (For a detailed discussion, see Kaufman, 1974.)

While the IQ score is important, it is only one of many pieces of information gained from an intelligence test. The discrepancy between the Verbal and Performance IQs on the WISC-R furnishes clues as to the child's differential ability to handle the two kinds of tasks: the child who has a Full-Scale IQ of 100, a Verbal IQ of 120 and a Performance IQ of 80 is quite different from a child with the same overall IQ but with a Verbal IQ of 80 and a Performance IQ of 120. The second child may be particularly penalized in school, where the manipulation of verbal symbols becomes increasingly important. Analysis of successes and failures on individual items may provide further clues to intellectual strengths and weaknesses. A child may do well on problems involving rote learning and the accumulation of facts, but poorly on ones requiring reasoning and judgment; an otherwise bright child may be weak in visual-motor coordination, which, in turn, might make learning to write difficult.

An intelligence test furnishes important clues as to the child's *style of thinking*, regardless of IQ. Note the responses of two equally bright 8-year-olds to the question, "What should you do when you lose a ball that belongs to someone else?" One child answered, "I'd get him another one." The other said, "I'd pay money for it. I'd look for it. I'd give him another ball." (The examiner asks her to choose one of the possibilities.) "I'd try to find it. If I couldn't, I'd give him money for it because I might not have the kind of ball he wants." Both answers receive the same high score, but one is clear, simple, and to the point, while the other is needlessly cluttered with alternatives.

Styles of thinking are closely related to psychological health or disturbance. Intelligence is not some kind of disembodied skill existing apart from the rest of the child's personality. On the contrary, a psychologically sound child tends to think clearly, an impulse-ridden child tends to think impulsively, an obsessive child (like the one just quoted) tends to think in terms of a series of alternatives which, in turn, may hamstring the ability to act. And, surely, a schizophrenic child tends to think bizarrely, as is revealed in this rambling, fantasy-saturated answer to the simple question, "Why should a promise be kept?" "If you don't keep a promise you get into trouble; you go to court; like teenagers give up promises; they're usually armed, guys who run around the forest and woods, the woods near the house. We go there to catch frogs, and we always have to have older people go with us because of the teenagers with guns and knives. A child drowned there not long ago. If you don't keep a promise they start a gang and drown you."

For clinicians, an intelligence test has a rich yield of *observational data*. To begin with, they can see how a given child copes with the challenge of solving intellectual problems. For some children, intellectual challenges are their "thing," and they work for the sheer pleasure of working. Others do what they are told in a joyless, dutiful manner; solving the problems is a burden, a chore. For still others, the tests are a chance to show off or just one more in a long series of humiliating failures.

The intelligence test also allows the clinician to evaluate the child's *work habits*. Some children are task-oriented and self-motivated; they need almost no encouragement or help from the examiner. Others are uncertain and insecure, giving up readily unless encouraged or prodded, constantly seeking reassurance that they are doing well, or asking to know whether their response was right or wrong. Finally, the tests yield information concerning the child's capacity for self-monitoring, which is the ability to evaluate the quality of the responses. Some children seem to be implicitly asking, "Is that really correct?" or "Is that the best I can do?" while others seem to have little ability to judge when they are right or wrong, an incorrect response being given with the same air of uncritical assurance as a correct one. Earlier, this same deficiency in the ability to stand apart from themselves, as it were, and observe what they were doing was noted in certain impulse-ridden, mentally retarded, and hyperactive children.

In sum, it is for good reason that intelligence tests are so frequently administered as part of the assessment procedures. The IQ score itself is related to many aspects of the child's life—success in school, vocational choice, peer relations; and IQ is a better predictor of future adjustment than any score on a personality test. In addition, the test provides data concerning general areas of strength and weakness, the kind and degree of impairment of specific intellectual functions such as immediate recall or abstract reasoning, the child's coping techniques, work habits, and motivation, stylistic characteristics of thinking that may well be related to personality variables, and the presence of distorted thinking, which might indicate either organic brain pathology or psychosis (see Kaufman, 1979).

Yet, care must be taken that an intelligence test is used appropriately and that results are properly understood. As *IQ* became a household term, so did the misconception that the score represents an unalterable intellectual potential existing independent of background and experience. In order to counteract this belief that IQ is destiny, many clinicians do not report the score to parents. Rather, they talk in terms of categories of intelligence, such as average, below average, superior. Then, taking into account the child's background and experience so as to correct for their possible biasing effects on the test score, they go on to describe strengths and weaknesses, which in turn may lead to a discussion of remedial plans.

Infant intelligence testing requires special skill in accommodation so as to elicit an optimal performance. The examiner must know how to intrigue the infant with the test material, allow for distractions, temporarily become a comforting caretaker in response to fretting, postpone testing when distress becomes too great—in short, the good examiner must have the sensitivity, flexibility, and warmth of a good parent.

One of the best constructed standardized infant tests is the Bayley Scales of Infant Development, which evaluates development between 2 and 30 months of age (Bayley, 1969). The Mental Scale evaluates the infant's vocal and verbal behavior, memory, generalization, classification, and simple problem-solving ability, among other things; the Motor Scale evaluates gross-motor and fine-motor coordination and skills; and the Infant Behavior Record assesses the infant's social relations, responsiveness to objects, activity level, interests, emotions, and tendency to approach or withdraw from stimulation.

Younger infants may be examined by means of the Brazelton Neonatal Behavioral Assessment Scale (Brazelton, 1963), which was designed to measure the infant's available responses to the environment. Of particular interest are measures of self-regulatory behavior, such as infants' ability to modulate their state of arousal in order to be receptive to incoming stimulation, along with the activities infants use to quiet themselves. Thus, among other things, the scale measures infants' ability to maintain an optimal alertness without becoming distressed and disorganized by physiological stimuli from within or by stimuli from the social and physical environment. (For a review of infant assessment, see Self and Horowitz, 1979.)

Brief intelligence tests have been devised to estimate the child's intelligence in less time than it takes to administer and score the Stanford-Binet and the WISC. The Peabody Picture Vocabulary Test (PPVT) requires the child to identify which of four pictures corresponds to a given word (Dunn, 1965). The words themselves are graded in difficulty. The test takes approximately 15 minutes and is designed for children between $2\frac{1}{2}$ and 18 years of age. Brief tests are useful as screening devices and are helpful in ascertaining the child's general level of intellectual functioning. However, they should not be used as a substitute for the more comprehensive intelligence test when a precise and detailed evaluation of intelligence is required.

Group intelligence tests such as the Otis-Lennon Mental Ability Test (Otis and Lennon, 1967) are especially suited for administration in school settings. (For a comprehensive discussion of intelligence testing, see Sattler, 1982.)

Personality Tests

PERSONALITY INVENTORIES Personality inventories consist of a series of statements to be judged as characteristic or not characteristic of an individual. The judgment is usually in terms of true-false. While adults most often fill out their own inventories, children's inventories are usually filled out by an adult who knows the child well, typically the mother.

The Personality Inventory for Children (PIC) is one of the most comprehensive (Wirt et al., 1977). Its purpose is to provide a "comprehensive and clinically relevant personality description of individuals primarily in the range from six to sixteen years of age" (p. 1). The inventory consists of 600 true-false items which are organized into twelve scales. Some of these scales evaluate intrapersonal variables—specifically, Somatic Concerns, Depression, Delinquency, Withdrawal, Anxiety, Psychosis, Hyperactivity, Social Skills, Achievement, and Intellectual Screening (intelligence); others evaluate interpersonal and historical variables—specifically, Family Relations and Development.

The 600 items comprising the scales were culled from files of child guidance clinics and the authors' clinical experience. The items were administered to populations of disturbed children. The control group of 2,390 normal children between 6 and 16 years of age enabled the authors to establish cutoff scores, above which a given child's score could no longer be considered in the normal range. Finally, the authors devised three additional scales to determine if the informant was being unusually defensive or untruthful.

On the whole, the PIC shows how useful and fruitful an empirical, atheoretical approach to assessment can be. The authors regard it as an objective intake or screening device, leaving it to the clinician to decide how much additional information is needed before formulating a diagnosis and treatment plan. Despite its objective format, the authors also state that the PIC should not be used by untrained, nonprofessional personnel. [The Children's Behavior Check List (CBCL) has been discussed in Chapter 3.]

PROJECTIVE TECHNIQUES In all the assessment instruments discussed so far the stimulus material is as clear and unambiguous as possible. Intelligence tests ask questions such as, "Why should a promise be kept?" and "Who discovered America?" Items on personality inventories cannot always be so straightforward, but the goal of clarity is the same. Projective techniques take the opposite tack by using ambiguous or unstructured material; either the stimulus has no meaning, such as an inkblot, or it has a number of different meanings, such as a picture that is to be used as the basis of a story. Theoretically, the particular meaning attributed to the unstructured material is a reflection of the individual's particular personality. The term *projection* does not carry the connotation of a defense mechanism designed to protect the individual from facing frightening and unacceptable impulses; rather, it is a more general term that connotes a reading of personally meaningful material into an unstructured situation, the material itself being both positive and negative, conscious and unconscious. However, the disguised nature of the responses allows the individual to express ideas that would be too threatening to talk about directly; for example, a girl who is too frightened to talk about her anger toward her mother may feel free to tell a story about a daughter being angry with and defying her mother.

The *Rorschach test* is a series of ten inkblots, which the child views one at a time after being instructed to tell the examiner everything the blots look like. The child's responses are recorded and subsequently scored and interpreted in terms of a number of personality variables. We shall briefly mention only three: intellectual characteristics, personality structure, and specific perceptions and affects.

Rorschach responses reflect three kinds of thinking: abstract, global thinking—the need to "get it all together" and achieve a comprehensive overview or understanding; concrete, down-to-earth involvement with practical issues in the here-and-now; and concern with minutiae and a need for preciseness in the smallest detail. No one kind of thinking is ideal since healthy adaptation requires all three; a successful Girl Scout camping trip entails an overall plan, a realistic grasp of what food and equipment will be needed, and maps that are accurate to the last detail. However, individuals differ in the kind of thinking most characteristic of them. Psychopathological conditions produce exaggerations of the three types of thinking: a psychotic adolescent boy in a manic phase may have grandiose ideas of his intellectual prowess, such as believing that he knows everything in the world there is to know; an anxious individual may cling desperately to the mundane requirements of a day-to-day existence, any slight deviation from a routine being viewed as a potential danger; while a compulsive girl may waste her energies on trivia such as making sure that her shoes are arranged in a perfectly straight line, that there is not a speck of dust on any of the furniture, that her clothes are immaculately clean.

The Rorschach also reveals the kind and degree of emotional responsiveness (roughly translated as extraversion), inner resources and fantasy life (roughly translated as introversion), and rational self-control an individual has. As with the intellectual characteristics, all three elements are present in healthy individuals, but different ones predominate; some individuals have outgoing, expressive, convivial, and colorful personalities; others are reflective, intellectual, and "deep"; while still others are unemotional, self-controlled, and straight-laced. The Rorschach furnishes valuable information as to when such normal personality characteristics become extreme to a pathological degree: the reactive individual may become an impulse-ridden or violently acting-out one; inwardness may become pathological isolation and paranoid suspiciousness; while the self-contained individual may become so massively inhibited that any affect is perceived as a terrifying threat.

The content of the individual's responses provides clues to specific affects and perceptions of human relationships. The exuberance of the response, "the Eiffel Tower with fireworks going off all around" contrasts with the dysphoric affect in the response to the same card, "the inside of a mouth with food that is in varying stages of decay." In a like manner, "two waiters ready to serve dinner" puts men in a subservient but positive role, which contrasts with the destructiveness implicit in the response to the same card, "two cannibals getting ready to boil a missionary in a pot."

Exner (1974–1978; Exner and Weiner, 1982) has made two important contributions to Rorschach analysis. First, he took the numerous scoring systems and integrated them into a single comprehensive one. Next, he provided norms for children between 5 and 16 years of age so that clinicians can now evaluate the deviancy of a given child's responses in terms of a normative population his or her age.

The question of the validity of the Rorschach has bedeviled psychologists since it gained popularity some fifty years ago. Psychometricians have been dismayed by its poor performance, some recommending it be banished altogether, while some practicing clinicians regard it as indispensable in revealing information no other technique can match. A review of research (Klopfer and Taulbee, 1976) suggests that there have been a sufficient number of positive findings to reassure the clinician and a sufficient number of negative ones to gladden the hearts of nihilistic psychometricians. The decision to use the Rorschach, therefore, becomes one of personal preference.

The *Thematic Apperception Test* (TAT) consists of thirty pictures, although only around ten are used for a given individual. The instructions are to tell a story identifying the people in the picture, explaining their thoughts and feelings, and describing their past, present, and future. The examiner records the story and asks questions concerning elements that may have been omitted. Some pictures are for males, others for females, and still others are for both sexes, but all are purposefully ambiguous; for example, a figure sitting on the floor leaning against a couch may be male or female, may be exhausted or depressed or suicidal or merely resting. Some cards contain single figures. Others suggest interpersonal situations, such as the nuclear family, same- and opposite-sex parent–child interactions, and same- and opposite-sex adult relations.

Unlike the Rorschach, the TAT has no standard scoring procedure. However, most systems assume that the heroes of the stories represent various aspects of the individual's self-concept, although not necessarily the conscious view of the self. Thus special attention is paid to the hero's needs, interests, traits, and competence. In the interpersonal sphere, themes concerning parents and the family unit are of special interest, stories being analyzed for the way parents are viewed and the hero's interaction with parental figures. Stories also reveal the nature and strength of the affect accompanying the various themes, along with the effectiveness of coping devices in dealing with the problems generated in the stories.

Let us return to Tom, the 10-year-old boy with the learning problem. The clinician was wondering whether the pressure to meet impossible academic goals had affected Tom's self-image and relations with his parents. Here one of Tom's TAT stories will be used to illustrate the process of analysis. However, a word of caution before starting: no one story—just like no one bit of behavior—is significant in itself; it is merely suggestive. Only as themes occur repeatedly and can be

fitted together into some cohesive entity does the clinician have confidence in the interpretation of the data. A single story is being presented only because of limitations of space. The inferences drawn are repeated in other stories as well.

The card depicts a boy looking at a violin, which is on a table in front of him. His expression is ambiguous. The following is Tom's story.

WELL, THERE is a little boy, and his mother told him to practice the violin, and he don't want to practice the violin, so he just sits there staring at it. After a while he fell asleep, and he has a dream and—now I have to think up a dream. He dreamed he was the greatest violinist in the world, and fame and success brought him riches and happiness. He bought his mother beautiful things, and his father—he bought him nice things and everything he wanted. He enjoyed living in such luxury. I don't want to end it yet. These are hard to figure out. He had a special violin, and no other violin could he play because this was the only one that ever worked for him, because there was only one that could play the right tunes. It seemed like magic that it played all right. He kept it by his bedside because if he lost the violin he would lose his wealth and everything. It was almost like magic. Finally, there came a time when his rival realized he could only play that one violin, and he sent some bandits to break up his violin and ruin his career. Just as the bandits were going to break the violin in half, he woke up.

This particular picture often elicits stories concerning responsibility and achievement; in terms of our conceptual scheme, the stories concern work. Tom's opening sentence contains the familiar theme of a child having to do something he does not want to do because his mother says he must. However, Tom's method of coping with this conflict is quite unusual—he escapes into a dream. It is as if telling a story about being pressured to work was not sufficiently safe, and Tom needs the twice-removed protection of a fantasy within a fantasy. The dream itself is richly imaginative, suggesting a creative potential in Tom. And what a contrast between the initial picture of the boy who is incapable of resolving the conflict of imposed duty, and the grandiose, world-famous, supremely rich, and happy achiever. The achievement is not solely egocentric, since it also enables the boy to give the parents everything they wanted. But, interestingly, Tom is not able to end on this theme of magical, compensatory fulfillment. Instead of bringing security, grandiose achievement is accompanied by a state of heightened vulnerability, since a competitive rival sets out to destroy him. And once again Tom cannot cope with the situation he creates, this time the anxiety over the competitive aspects of achievement. The boy in the story wakes up as one might from a nightmare in which anxiety has reached an intolerable level.

We can infer that Tom's situation of trying to meet unrealistic expectations has affected his view of himself in relation to his parents. Out of his impotence he has generated a compensatory image of grandiose success, which both allows him to fulfill parental expectations and to be on the giving end in regard to his parents. In its own right, this exaggerated image and reversal of parent–child roles could not be considered a healthy resolution. In addition, the wishful image cannot be sustained because of the destructive competitiveness Tom perceives to be an integral part of achievement. Thus there is an impasse at both the reality and the fantasy levels. In sum, the pressures of unattainable goals has engendered a feeling of helplessness and a concern over loveworthiness on the one hand and a fear of competitiveness and achievement on the other. However, Tom has the great assets of a lively imagination and an openness in expressing ideas in a disguised form when they are too painful to face directly. One would expect that he would be a good risk for psychotherapy and that he would make significant progress.

In general, the TAT has fared better in reliability and validity studies than has the Rorschach. Not only does it differentiate various psychopathological groups, such as psychotics and delinquents, but it has also stimulated interest in studying a number of the needs which it taps, the achievement need being the outstanding example. (For further information concerning validity studies, see Klopfer and Taulbee, 1976.)

OTHER PROJECTIVE TECHNIQUES The Children's Apperception Test (CAT) was designed on the premise that children will more readily identify with and therefore tell more meaningful stories about animal than about human figures (Bellak, 1954). The scenes depicted derive from Freud's psychosexual theory of development, such as a lion king sitting on a throne and a little mouse peeking out of a hole in the wall. The fact that the original premise has not been confirmed has relegated the CAT to the status of an ancillary technique: a child who tells meager stories on the TAT may possibly respond more freely to the CAT.

The Roberts Apperception Test for Children (RATC) (McArthur and Roberts, 1984) represents a more successful effort to adapt the thematic approach to children. There are twenty-seven stimulus cards (of which only sixteen are administered to a given child) depicting common situations, conflicts, and stresses in children's lives—for example, parental support and conflict, sibling rivalry, peer interaction, dependency, school attitudes, fear, and aggression. The RATC provides criteria and examples for scoring the stories in terms of adaptive and maladaptive functioning; for example, a constructive resolution to a problem is healthier than an unrealistic, wishful, or magical solution. Interrater agreement on scores is high. Finally, there are norms on well-adjusted children ages 6 to 15 which aid the clinician in evaluating an individual child's disturbance.

Of the many *drawing techniques,* the Draw-A-Person Test (DAP) is one of the most widely used. According to Machover's (1949) procedure, the child is first asked to draw a person, then to draw a person of the opposite sex. Next, a series of questions follows, such as "What is the person doing?" "How old is he(she)?" "What does the person like and dislike?"—although such questions have not become part of a standard procedure. Theoretically, the child's drawing is a projection of both the self-image and the body image. Various characteristics of the drawing are interpreted in terms of psychological variables—a small figure indicating inferiority, faint lines suggesting anxiety or an amorphous identity, an overly large head indicating excessive intellectualization—while the answers to the questions are interpreted thematically, so that a figure who is "just standing there" suggests passivity, while one who is a cheerleader suggests activity and exhibitionism. The figure may represent either the self or the idealized self; Tom, for example, may have drawn either a very small or a very large male figure. While its popularity attests to its clinical utility, the DAP only rarely has met the test of validation (see Klopfer and Taulbee, 1976).

Other Psychological Tests

ACHIEVEMENT TESTS　An assessment of academic achievement is important in deciding whether a child has a learning disability and in evaluating the effectiveness of a remedial program; low academic achievement may also contribute to the development of a behavior problem. As with intelligence tests, there are individual, group, and short forms of achievement tests. Again, as with intelligence tests, individually administered achievement tests allow the clinician to make behavioral observations of the child and to analyze the nature of the child's failures, both of which may provide helpful clues as to motivational and academic problems; for example, a boy who gives up without trying is different from one who fails after trying his best, just as a girl who fails multiplication problems because of careless mistakes is different from another who fails because she has not grasped the basic process of multiplying. Typically, achievement tests are of the pencil-and-paper variety and cover reading, spelling, arithmetic, social studies, and science.

In many instances, a global measure of achievement in the principal school subjects suffices to answer the clinician's questions and the Wide-Range Achievement Test (WRAT) may be used (Jastak and Jastak, 1978). The WRAT provides tests for reading, spelling, and arithmetic, covers an age range from 5 years to adulthood, and can be administered in twenty to thirty minutes. Its reliability is high, as are correlations between WRAT scores and those on other tests measuring achievement in the same school subjects. The Woodcock-Johnson Psycho-Educational Battery (1977) is another achievement test which evaluates reading, math, written language (including grammar, punctuation, and spelling) and knowledge of social studies, science, and the humanities. The Gray Oral Reading Tests, Revised (1986) and the Woodcock Reading Mastery Tests, Revised (1987) may be used when the clinician is particularly interested in evaluating a child's reading.

Among group-administered achievement tests, both the Iowa Test of Basic Skills (Lindquist and Hieronymus, 1955–1956), designed to assess vocabulary, reading comprehension, work-study skills, and arithmetic in children in grades three through nine, and the Stanford Achievement Test (Kelley et al., 1964), which has five batteries of tests for children from first through ninth grades covering word and paragraph meaning, science and social studies concepts, spelling, language, and arithmetic concepts, have satisfactory reliability and validity and are widely used.

ABILITIES TESTS   A different approach to assessing learning disabilities is that of evaluating the abilities directly related to academic achievement rather than achievement per se. An example of such an approach is the Illinois Test of Psycholinguistic Ability (ITPA) (Kirk, McCarthy, and Kirk, 1968). The scale is made up of twelve subtests sampling variables theoretically involved in language communication. Only a portion of the test will be described.

Certain subtests evaluate simple abilities, such as auditory and visual reception or auditory sequential memory as measured by the ability to repeat an increasingly long series of digits. Vocal association uses analogy statements, such as "A dog has hair; a fish has ———," to tap the ability to relate concepts presented orally; the ability to express concepts readily, or verbal expression, is evaluated by showing a child familiar objects and instructing him or her to "Tell me all about this." The ITPA can be administered to children from 2 to 10 years of age. Research on its ability to diagnose reading disorders has yielded both positive and negative findings, and, like many other assessment instruments, its clinical utility has outstripped its proven validity.

TESTS FOR ORGANIC BRAIN DAMAGE   A neurological assessment usually begins with an intelligence and an achievement test. These tests not only provide information as to the children's intellectual level and academic progress but, more important, they also provide clues as to what psychological functions might be affected by organic brain damage. As we have seen, the manifestations of brain damage may range from a slight deficit in sensorimotor abilities to a pervasive disruption of every aspect of a child's intellectual and personality functioning. It follows that there can be no single diagnostic test for organicity. (For an overview of assessing special populations of children, see Magrab and Lehr, 1982; neurological assessment in particular is treated by Chadwick and Rutter, 1983.)

If brain damage potentially affects a variety of functions, then a battery of tests casting a wide psychological net would seem to provide a reasonable strategy for capturing the elusive diagnosis. Two of the most widely used are the Reitan-Indiana Neuropsychological Test Battery (1969) for children 5 to 8 years of age and the Halstead Neuropsychological Test Battery for Children (1969), which is applicable to children 9 through 14 years of age. The diversity of the tests may be seen in the following sampling. The Category Test requires the child to abstract principles based on variables such as size, color, number, and position from visually presented material. In the Tactual Performance Test, the blindfolded child is required to fit variously shaped blocks into a form board with the preferred, nonpreferred, and both hands and then, with blindfold, blocks, and form board removed, to draw a diagram of the board. This test evaluates memory and spatial location, both of which may be adversely affected by organicity. In Trailmaking B, the child is given a piece of paper on which twenty-five circles are scattered about; the circles are randomly numbered from 1 to 13 and randomly lettered from A through L. The child's task is to connect alternate numbers and letters, that is, to go from A to 1 to B to 2 and so on. The score is the time taken and the child is penalized for errors. Among other things, Trailmaking B is a test of flexibility of thinking, a facility that may be impaired in certain kinds of organic brain damage.

Tests of individual functions are more widely used than time-consuming batteries, but their popularity is rarely buttressed by solid evidence of diagnostic accuracy. A frequently used means of evaluating *perceptual motor coordination* is the Bender Gestalt Test for Young Children (Koppitz, 1973), consisting of nine figures which are presented one at a time for the child to copy; for example, a row of dots, a juxtaposed circle and diamond, two wavy lines intersecting. As a test of *memory* the Benton Visual Retention Test (1974) may be used for visual material, and the Wechsler Memory Scale (1987) may be used for verbal memory in adolescents.

Currently, specialized techniques are being developed on the basis of research concerning the effects of various kinds of brain damage on children of different ages. These techniques have two advantages. First, they are specific to children of different ages rather than representing downward extensions of adult techniques. Next, they are specific to the various kinds of brain damage such as seizures or head injuries. Thus they promise to increase the power of psychological tests to reveal psychological dysfunctions at various ages.

BEHAVIORAL ASSESSMENT

As we have noted, the scientist's quest for comprehensive understanding of psychopathology differs from the clinician's pragmatic goal of obtaining information relevant to implementing a particular kind of remediation. The most recent example of tailoring inquiry to a therapeutic procedure is behavioral assessment. Since behavior therapy focuses on the current situation, assessment aims at obtaining a specific account of a child's problem behaviors along with their immediate antecedents and consequences. (See Ross, 1980, chap. 6. For a more extended discussion, see Evans and Nelson, 1977.)

Behavioral assessment utilizes many traditional diagnostic procedures but the emphasis differs. In obtaining *referral information* the clinician focuses on the question of who has seen what behaviors in which situations. The answers provide initial clues as to the behaviors considered troublesome, the settings in which they are manifested, and the individuals who observe them.

The *behavioral interview* aims primarily at obtaining behavior-specific accounts of the problem and the environmental factors that may be maintaining it. The behavioral clinician also inquires into attempts to change the troublesome behavior and the results obtained. Adults directly involved with the child's problem, such as parents, teachers, and relatives, are interviewed. Generally speaking, obtaining historical information is minimized, since the clinician is only incidentally interested in reconstructing etiology. However, such information is sought to the extent to which it may throw light on the current situation.

Some of the main features of the behavioral interview deserve to be presented in detail. To begin with, general descriptions of the child, such as "nervous," "bad," or "lazy," must be translated into specific behaviors. Because of their generality, the exact behavioral referents of such descriptions are obscure; in addition, the same behavior may be interpreted differently—one parent labeling it "restless," another "active"—just as different behaviors may carry identical labels—"nervous" meaning hyperactive to one parent, fearful to another. Next, the interviewer inquires concerning *antecedents* or a description of the situations in which the problem behavior occurs. Again, specificity is of the essence: "Sue-Anne starts yelling when we're eating" is not as helpful as, "Sue-Anne starts yelling when her dad and me are at supper, and he tells her 'Eat all your corn' or 'Help clear the table' or 'Do the dishes' or some other (dinner) chore." Next, the clinician inquires as to events that occur immediately following the problem behavior, namely, its *consequences.* Here, as in every aspect of the interview, behavioral specificity is sought in terms of exactly who is present and what is done: "After Sue-Anne starts yelling, her dad smacks her, and she just keeps on until sometime he can't stand the noise and leaves the house and I don't see him the rest of the evening."

Certain ancillary information is helpful. The clinician may obtain an initial inventory of potential reinforcers to be used in therapy by asking what the child enjoys, such as favorite foods, recreational activities, or pastimes. The parents may be asked what behavior they would wish to have as a replacement for the present objectionable ones. The clinician may assess the amount of time the parent has to participate in a therapeutic program if one were deemed desirable and evaluate the parent's ability and willingness to do so. Finally, the child may be interviewed to obtain his or her perception of the problems as well as a list of likes and dislikes.

The interviewer's emphasis on specific behavior in no way eliminates the problems inherent in conducting any clinical interview. Parents are personally involved rather than objective reporters; for example, in the preceding illustration, the mother may have cited only the father's behavior as an antecedent and omitted her own out of defensiveness or vindictiveness toward her husband or dislike of the clinician—or out of honest obliviousness. Thus the behavioral clinician must be as skilled as any other in establishing rapport, constructively handling negative feelings, judging the accuracy of the information, and when it is suspect, finding ways of eliciting

a more realistic account without antagonizing or alienating the parent.

Psychological tests are used sparingly; personality tests which reveal underlying attitudes, motivations, and perceptions of self and others are regarded as useless. Preference is for *behavior checklists,* which are typically composed of a listing of behavior problems, such as disobedience, attention seeking, social withdrawal, or truancy from school. The adult who knows the child best checks the characteristic items. Some checklists also include positive items, while others are environmentally oriented, requiring the parent to designate the setting and social consequences for each of the problem behaviors.

BEHAVIORAL OBSERVATION The behavioral approach has made a unique contribution by adapting the technique of naturalistic observation—previously used primarily for research purposes—to assessment goals and placing it at the heart of the process. It is easy to understand this emphasis on direct observation, since abnormal behavior is assumed to develop and to be maintained by environmental stimuli, while behavior modification corrects problem behaviors by altering the environmental conditions maintaining them.

On the basis of information obtained from the referral, checklist, and interview, the clinician identifies the target behaviors to be observed. These behaviors are, in effect, the operational definition of the child's problem, "bad" becoming translated into "yelling at her father during supper" in our example. While behavioral clinicians are always sensitive to the individuality of the child, they have found sufficient commonality among certain problems to have developed standard *behavior codes* for particular settings. Disruptive behaviors in the classroom, for instance, frequently fall within categories such as the child being out of his or her chair without permission, touching, grabbing, or destroying another child's property, vocalizing, speaking or noisemaking without permission, aggressiveness, and failure to do the assignment.

The behavioral clinician's next task is to determine the frequency of the target behavior in order to establish a *baseline* for its natural occurrence against which to evaluate the effectiveness of the therapeutic intervention. Observations are scheduled for the specific periods in which the problem behavior is most likely to happen. Depending on the natural occurrence of the target behavior, the period may last half an hour to an entire day, while observations may be made daily or only on particular days. Our obstreperous little girl, for example, needs to be observed for only about thirty minutes every day at suppertime, provided both parents are present.

There are a number of different methods for quantifying behavior observations. *Frequency* involves counting the number of times the target behavior occurs within a specific period. Frequency divided by time yields a measure called *response rate;* for example, a disruptive boy may leave his seat without permission five times in a fifty-minute class period so his response rate would be 5/50 or .10. In *interval recording* an observer has a data sheet divided into small time units, such as twenty seconds; aided by a timing device such as a stopwatch attached to a clipboard, the observer indicates whether the target behavior occurred in a given unit. Frequently, a *time-sampling* method is used in which the observer observes the child's behavior for twenty seconds and spends the next ten seconds recording the target behaviors which occurred in that twenty-second interval. This sequence is repeated for the duration of the observational period. Typically, only the presence or absence of target behavior is recorded. Some data are lost if

a behavior occurs more than once during an interval, but such losses are often unimportant. Interval recording is usually more practicable than the frequency method when the observer wishes to record a number of behaviors. Finally, *duration* consists of measuring the interval of time between the onset and termination of the target behavior. This method is appropriate when decreasing the time spent in a particular behavior, such as head-banging, is a therapeutic goal.

In addition to being used to determine the frequency or duration of target behavior, observation provides information concerning antecedent and consequence events. However, this aspect of data gathering has not been formalized into specific procedures. Often the data are in descriptive or narrative form rather than being quantified. As always, the observer is aware of the setting-specific nature of the relationships observed and is alert to the possibility that the setting may significantly alter the functional meaning of behavior; for example, a mother's reprimand may tend to decrease provocative behavior when mother and child are alone, but it may increase such behavior when the father comes home, especially if he sides with the child.

Theoretically the baseline phase should continue until the target behavior has become stable. Because of the variability of human behavior, such an ideal is often difficult to achieve. The general consensus is that there should be a minimal baseline period of one week of data collection. (For a comparison of traditional and behavioral assessment, see Ciminero, 1977.)

THE RELIABILITY OF OBSERVATIONAL DATA Everyone would agree that Sue-Anne's "badness" is nearer the behavioral level than is Tom's concept of himself as helpless. As personality characteristics become increasingly inferential, they become increasingly difficult to evaluate in terms of reliability and validity. This is one reason why achievement tests, which can be correlated with school grades in similar subjects, are more readily validated than projective tests, whose behavioral referents may be obscure. How would you go about determining whether Tom "really" felt helpless, for example? Note, however, that we are dealing with *levels* of inferences from behavior, not with inferential versus noninferential personality characteristics. Behavioral checklists contain primarily inferential descriptions rather than being composed of behaviors that are "out there" for everyone to see. Even experts can disagree as to whether a child is "hyperactive" or merely "lively," "withdrawn" or merely "self-contained," "aggressive" or merely "attention seeking." Thus behavior assessment reduces but does not eliminate the problem of the reliability of behavioral observation.

But what about reliability after personality characteristics have been operationalized? Certainly Sue-Anne's yelling is "out there" for anyone to see—and hear! In this particular instance the issue of reliability may be irrelevant. But for most problems the target behavior is not so clear; on the contrary, naturally occurring behavior may well be equivocal, while its variability makes interpretation and inference inevitable.

Researchers using naturalistic observation have found it necessary to train observers in order to insure reliability. Typically, two or more trainees observe, record, and score the behavior of the same child. Disagreements are discussed and reconciled. Additional observations are made and scored until agreement between observers is at least 80 to 85 percent. Even after training is completed, it is highly desirable to "recalibrate" the observers periodically by repeating the training procedures. Such intensive training further

attests to the fact that problem behavior is not "out there"; the emperor's new clothes notwithstanding, the untrained eye is an inaccurate observational instrument.

Behavioral clinicians rarely have the time or the personnel to train for accurate observation. Consequently, they must rely on untrained adults, such as parents and teachers. The expected decline in reliability has been documented (Achenbach and Edelbrock, 1978). In general, a given individual is consistent with himself over a period of one week to one month; even after six months, consistency is marginal but adequate. Reliability between similar observers such as parents or teachers is satisfactory but not so high as to prevent disagreements between mother and father or teachers. Reliability plunges precipitously between adults who view the same child in different situations, such as parents and teachers, teachers and mental health workers, or even teachers who see the child in different settings. This last finding suggests that many problem behaviors are situation-specific. Thus reliability is affected both by the implicit definitions and biases of the observers, and by the different information input they have in terms of the situations in which they have observed the child.

The question of reliability is not as crucial to behavioral clinicians as it is to researchers. Up to a point they can say that the objective existence of the problem behavior is not as important as the fact that parents or teachers perceive the behavior as the problem. But they cannot always say this. In certain instances they may judge that the behavior falls within normal limits or that the parent is too disturbed to give an accurate account of the child. In such cases focus shifts from child to parent. Once again, the relative objectivity of the behavioral assessment does not exempt the clinician from acquiring highly developed clinical skills. (For a comprehensive discussion of naturalistic observation, see Kent and Foster, 1977.)

CLINICAL ASSESSMENT: ART AND SCIENCE

While differences in assessment procedures can best be understood in terms of clinicians' different theoretical and therapeutic allegiances, there is another, related source of disagreement. As scientists, psychologists strive for objectivity and precision, which require, among other things, clearly delineated procedures that are available to the scientific community. It is no accident that psychologists in the past championed intelligence tests in particular and the mental measurement movement in general over impressionistic evaluations. Nor is it by chance that behavioral assessment, with its explicit procedures for observation, its relative disinterest in historical antecedents, and its dismissal of inferred personality characteristics and motivations, is exercising a similar appeal. Concomitantly, there is a mistrust of the hypothesis-testing clinician initially described in this discussion. While utilizing theoretical and experiential guides, the process by which this clinician generates, tests, accepts, and discards ideas is nearer to an art than a science. He or she may indeed come up with impressive insights but also may be seriously in error; more important—and this is what concerns the critical psychologist— there is no clearly established procedure for deciding in favor of one outcome over the other.

This tug-of-war between the art and science of assessment took the form of clinical versus actuarial prediction forty years ago; today it may well take the form of clinical versus computerized prediction. Suppose, for example, that the PIC were perfected and information concerning all possible profiles fed into a computer. Could not the computer print out a personality evaluation as valid as that of the clinician utilizing any other assessment technique? Forty years ago a strong case was made in favor of the actuarial-computer approach and documented by research findings, although the issue was never settled. (For a rebuttal and reevaluation of the issue, see Janis, 1969, pp. 778–801. See also Wiggins, 1981.)

Certain clinicians might answer that scores are only one kind of information to be gained from a test, as we have seen in discussing intelligence tests. To limit assessment to such scores would be to eliminate the added behavioral data so vital to understanding an individual child. If such data have yet to be standardized and are of unknown reliability, their clinical utility justifies their use for the present.

These clinicians rightly claim that there are a number of important areas for which no standardized, clinically useful instrument exists, family interaction being the most prominent example. Thus they can do no more than put the pieces of assessment data together as best they can. Moreover, it is just such efforts to understand complex, heretofore unsystematized data that can ultimately serve as the basis for objective assessment techniques. Recall that the PIC relied heavily on the accumulated clinical experience of its authors for its categories and items. Instead of polarizing the clinician and actuarially inclined psychologist (or the computer) the two should complement one another, the clinician exploring the territory that one day will be formally structured into objective assessment techniques whose reliability and validity can be tested.

One final point: While techniques and goals may vary, all clinical assessment requires a high degree of professional competence. Clinicians must be skillful and sensitive in handling the many interpersonal problems inherent in dealing with troubled parents and children; they must be knowledgeable concerning the procedures they use and the problems they are called upon to evaluate; they must be well acquainted with and abide by the ethical principles of their profession; and they must have received adequate academic and professional preparation, which for a clinical child psychologist typically involves a PhD or PsyD from an accredited university and at least two years of supervised experience (American Psychological Association, 1979).

The dovetailing of assessment and psychotherapy which has been emphasized will become clearer after we learn more about the major schools of psychotherapies themselves. This topic is covered in our final discussion.

16

Remediation and Prevention

Our discussion will now turn to some of the ways in which psychopathological behavior can be changed and ways to prevent it. In the realm of remediation, three of the major psychotherapies—psychoanalytic, client-centered, and behavioral—will be presented, with emphasis on the conceptualization of development that provides the basic rationale for the therapeutic techniques each employs. Next, the effectiveness of individual therapy with children will be discussed, followed by a brief survey of group and family psychotherapy. Prevention will take us into the realm of the community mental health movement. The origins and nature of this movement and some of the many efforts at prevention and remediation it has generated will be described and evaluated.

THE PSYCHOANALYTIC APPROACH

Classical psychoanalysis is a highly specialized technique appropriate for only a limited range of psychopathologies. Here, as in the remainder of this section, the presentation will be based on Anna Freud's writings (A. Freud, 1965; Scharfman, 1978. Another influential figure in this field is Melanie Kline, who disagreed with Anna Freud on many points concerning child psychoanalysis [see Segal, 1973].)

The Developmental Model

Since classical psychoanalysis grows directly out of the psychoanalytic theory of neurosis, we need to review briefly what we have learned about this theory. Recall that psychopathology originates in the psychosexual stages, when the possessiveness, rivalry, death wish, and castration anxiety of the Oedipus complex act as particularly fertile breeding grounds for neurosis. Not only is the preschooler overwhelmed, but also the forces for growth are not sufficiently strong to overcome the traumatic impact.

Unable to master the psychosexual anxieties, preschoolers are tempted to regress. Returning to more babyish behaviors, however, is unacceptable to the mature elements in their personality. Thus they are trapped, being able neither to progress nor to regress. If they cannot master the anxiety, at least they can defend themselves against it, using repression and other defenses, such as displacement and projection. In certain instances the defenses work in the sense of providing developmental pathways that will be serviceable throughout life. But there is always the vulnerability attendant upon an unmastered phase of development, and subsequent experiences may exacerbate the underlying disturbance, the special combination of fixation point and defenses producing the specific neurotic symptoms of hysteria, phobias, obsessions, or compulsions.

The essence of psychoanalysis consists of reversing the defensive process, reconfronting the individual with the original trauma so that it can be mastered belatedly. Successful psychoanalysis is epitomized by Freud's aphorism, "Where id was, there shall ego be." The once-overwhelming hates, jealousies, and fears can now be revived and viewed from a more mature perspective. The ensuing insight into the root of the problem exorcises it. The result is a "widening of consciousness" in two senses: the individual can face previously unacceptable aspects of his or her personality, and the energy used for defensive maneuvers can now be employed in growth-promoting activities.

The Therapeutic Process

Psychoanalysis depends on the establishment of a *therapeutic alliance* between therapist and patient—a bond sufficiently strong to sustain the patient through the many stormy sessions that lie ahead. The sessions themselves are held four to five times a week for a period of three years or more. Another general feature of psychoanalysis is the maximizing of free expression during the psychoanalytic hour. Adult patients are initially instructed to lie down on the couch, facing away from the analyst, and say everything that comes into their mind—a technique called *free association*. It is from the basic data of free association that the analyst tries to understand the patient's life as the patient perceives it. Suggestions, advice, directions as to how to handle problems, and medication are minimized and ideally avoided altogether.

There are two major techniques for undoing the work of defenses. The first is called analyzing the *resistance*. Since defenses protect the patient from anxiety, he or she will find numerous ways to retain them. This accounts for the paradox that despite great suffering the adult neurotic will resist attempts at cure. The maneuvers used to resist bringing painful ideas and feelings into consciousness are numerous. A patient may lie on the couch and say that nothing comes to mind, for example, or he may bring up a personal feeling and quickly change the subject or impersonalize it by talking about the current state of society, or he may steep himself in psychoanalytic theory so that he "knows the answer" to his problem before the analyst, or he may even engage in a "flight into health," claiming that all his problems have been solved and that he never felt better in his life! The analyst's task is constantly to call attention to such evasive maneuvers and help the patient to focus on the threatening material which prompted them, the therapeutic alliance giving the client courage to explore such material.

Next, classical psychoanalysis involves analysis of the *transference.* The intense, prolonged one-to-one relationship stimulates the revival of previous intense relationships to the parents. Thus, feelings once directed toward parents are transferred to the therapist. Again it is the analyst's function to call attention to transferences, so that in exploring them, patients can begin to gain access to the distressing relationships that played a decisive role in their neurosis.

The patient's verbal productions form the leading edge of psychoanalysis. After a period of time, the analyst begins to make *interpretations* as to the meaning of these productions once the meaning seems reasonably clear. Such interpretations are often very simple: "You must have been angry at your older brother for always being so much better than you were." "Wasn't it frustrating to have such a 'perfect' mother?" "You seem always to run away from this idea that you are as sexy as any other girl." Correctly timed, such interpretations produce insights; prematurely timed they are rejected and fuel the patient's resistance. Nor does a therapeutic cure come in one blinding flash of insight. Instead, the same material has to be approached again and again from many different directions and through many different experiences in order for the insight to be firmly established—a process called *working through.* The defense of being a sweet little girl or a nonentity or a hellion, for example, is expressed in countless ways, so the patient must confront and reevaluate these variations on the theme of his or her core conflicts before

insights can become stable and generally serviceable.

Child Psychoanalysis

Applying classical psychoanalysis to children has required certain major changes in procedures and techniques but not in the basic goal. For a number of reasons the therapeutic alliance is different with children than with adults. Children do not voluntarily seek therapy, nor do they necessarily suffer intensely from their neurotic problems. They live more in the present than do adults, so they cannot be expected to endure the pain of psychoanalysis for the sake of some future good. In attributing causes for their behavior, they tend to externalize and place the responsibility on others rather than examining their own actions. By the same token, they look to the therapist as someone who will change the environment, so that they will not have to go to school or obey their father, for example. Children often lack the capacity for self-observation or self-monitoring that enables adults to participate in an intense emotional experience while at the same time observing themselves reacting. One can readily understand how such an ability facilitates the gaining of insight. Finally, during times of developmental stress such as adolescence, children are reluctant to add to their emotional burdens by confronting their anxieties.

Children's personalities are also not as firmly structured as those of adults, who can maintain an intrapsychic conflict relatively independent of environmental events. A child is always more responsive to environmental influences even when neurotic; for example, the resolution of a phobia may come about by some growth-promoting forces within the environment and not represent a "flight into health." Thus the child analyst must keep track of reality to a much greater extent than is necessary with adults. Children's transferences, unlike those of adults, do not involve feelings toward parental ghosts dating back to the distant past. Because children are still living with and dependent upon parents, their transference tends to be more dilute and obscure; for example, the irrational anger a girl brings to a therapy session may be due to the fact that her parents have entered a stormy phase in their relationship or that a parent, envious of the therapist's influence, has begun catering to the child in order to win her over.

A radical change in technique is necessitated by the fact that children cannot free-associate, and *play* has to be substituted. However, play is not the equivalent of free association. Through associations, adults provide the key to the idiosyncratic meaning of events or dreams; since children provide no such key, the analyst must actively try to decode the meaning of their fantasies. In addition, adults are encouraged to say anything that comes into their mind, while children cannot be similarly encouraged to do anything they like; such a lure too often leads to aggressive acting out, such as damaging property, endangering their safety, or attacking the analyst, all of which overwhelms their already weakened ability to reflect upon their own behavior.

The play material itself is the kind which taps fantasies rather than skills—a doll family, crayons, clay, etc. The analyst watches for signs that a theme is of special importance: repetition, excessive affect, an abrupt termination (which suggests anxiety), regression in the form of more infantile play or speech, loss of control, such as scattering the toys around, or a "they lived happily ever after" dismissal of a conflict situation (Peller, 1964). Interpretations are simple and closely attuned to the play: "I bet that family was really scared when the hurricane started coming toward their house." "I wonder why the

little girl always wanted to look at the monkeys in the zoo." "Being locked in a closet for two years after being bad does seem a long time." After obtaining clues as to the meaning of the child's fantasy, both from play material and conversations, the analyst can begin building a bridge from the safe disguise of make-believe to the child's own feelings; for example, "That hurricane sounds like what you told me about your mother and father having all those fights." Through such interpretations the child, like the adult, is led back to the original traumatic situation and helped to recognize, reevaluate, and master it. And as with adults, the roadblocks of resistance must be overcome, while the transference is used for clues concerning feelings toward parents.

The analyst recognizes that age itself significantly affects the manner in which a psychoanalysis can be conducted; the play material that delights the preschooler becomes increasingly inappropriate toward the end of middle childhood and would be considered demeaning to the adolescent. In fact, adolescents are particularly difficult to help, since they eschew fantasy play, while their tenuous self-control makes them reluctant to explore their feelings via free association. Finally, psychoanalysis stresses the importance of analysts being aware of and learning to manage their own *countertransference*—the many difficult feelings, such as irritation, impatience, or sexual attraction, that children arouse in them during the long, intensive involvement.

Psychoanalytically Oriented Psychotherapies

Since the conditions necessary for a classical psychoanalysis are difficult to meet in childhood, numerous adaptations have been made in order to help a wider variety of disturbed children. At times these variations serve the basic goal of enabling the child to deal with and master traumatic, unconscious material; more often the goal itself is changed to a general one of helping the child adapt, even though the core problem may go unresolved.

A number of the modifications involve the use of techniques which, in classical psychoanalysis, play only a minor role or are regarded as obstacles to achieving the basic goal. One of the most important modifications is that of providing a *corrective emotional experience*, typically by encouraging inhibited children to express forbidden feelings so they can discover that they are neither rejected nor punished for doing so. A too proper girl, for example, may find that there are no disastrous consequences to getting angry first with the therapist and then with significant people in her environment. Closely related to the corrective emotional experience is *reassurance*, in which the omnipotence the child invests in the therapist is used to counteract disabling fears and bolster crippled self-confidence and self-esteem. The implicit message often is: "There is nothing to be afraid of; you can do it if you really try; you are worthy of love and respect."

The therapist can perform an *educational* function that has nothing to do with academic instruction despite its label, but which is more akin to good parenting. Educational measures may involve ways of dealing more effectively with id impulses, such as telling an overly sensitive boy that it is all right to become angry when the situation warrants or discussing sexual techniques with a shy adolescent. At times the measures are directed toward the ego, the therapist supplying adaptive techniques to substitute for maladaptive ones; for example, telling a socially isolated child that if she shared her toys rather than acting superior and keeping them to herself, she would have more friends. Finally, the measures may be directed to the superego, such as telling a child that stealing is wrong for a number of reasons and that he should not give in to his impulses.

The above techniques are differentially emphasized depending on the child's problems. Emotionally deprived children, say, from bleak institutions or bleak homes, need large supplies of love more than anything else; preschizophrenic children with a tenuous hold on reality need a therapist who will serve as an "auxiliary ego," helping them to define and cope with reality while distinguishing it from their own primitive fantasies; for certain delinquents, the therapist must first establish a positive transference and then build up a serviceable set of moral guides. Typically, however, disturbed children have a variety of problems rather than representing "pure" cases, so that the psychoanalytically oriented psychotherapists must use a variety of skills.

The common denominator in this diversity of techniques is the therapist's allegiance to the genetic theory of psychosexual development and to the structural theory of id-ego-superego. Yet the psychoanalytic approach does champion certain other concepts. The approach is comprehensive or *holistic* in that it assumes that psychopathology can be understood only in terms of intrapersonal factors (the balance between id, ego, and superego), interpersonal factors (the relation between the child and significant figures, particularly parents), and time, or the historical dimension. It offers a variety of therapeutic techniques aimed at *meeting the child's needs* as these are revealed by the comprehensive evaluation. Next there is an emphasis on the affect generated by intense interpersonal relationships. Freud's belief that the passions of love, hate, fear, and guilt hold the key to pathology clearly implies that such feelings and their interpersonal contexts should be central in correcting psychopathology—hence the emphasis not only on children's *relationship* to parents and sibs but also on their relationship to the therapist and the therapist's feelings toward them. There is the belief that broadly based *motivational systems* underlie specific behaviors and that, as much as possible, those systems should be changed. Castration anxiety, for example, has manifold expressions in terms of fear of authority and competition, as well as being expressed in maneuvers to circumvent such fears; as the anxiety is allayed, many maladaptive behaviors will lose their reason for being.

THE CLIENT-CENTERED APPROACH

15-YEAR-OLD GIRL: When dad starts that same old lecture (in a singsong voice) "No nice girl *I* ever knew went around in dirty jeans, and no nice girl *I* ever knew let a boy touch her body on the first date," I could just explode on the inside.

THERAPIST: You feel all angry on the inside then.

GIRL: Yeah. But then (glumly) sometimes I look at him and he looks so worn out and there's this cancer thing he's got . . .

THERAPIST: It sounds like you feel sad about your father's condition—getting old and sick, I mean.

GIRL: Or just mixed up so I don't know where I'm going at times, except maybe crazy (with a little laugh).

THERAPIST: So it's as if the mad feeling and the sad feeling make you feel all mixed up?

The therapist is doing the two things that epitomize the client-centered approach—*reflecting* and *accepting* the client's feelings. The therapist's manner is sincere, interested, warm. This type of therapist will never interpret, unlike the analyst, or tell clients how to solve their problems, unlike the be-

havior therapist. Primarily the therapist will accept and reflect feelings.

On the face of it, the client-centered approach makes little sense, and its practice seems too simple to be regarded as a skill. In reality, the therapy is based on an explicit developmental model of psychopathology, is one of the most demanding of its practitioners, and has exerted a powerful influence on the professional community.

The Developmental Model

Our discussion will be based on the ideas of Carl Rogers (1959), founder of client-centered therapy. Rogers stresses the primacy of the individual's experience and of the individual's self. Maturity is the ability to *experience a feeling fully* so that there is congruence between experiencing the feeling, awareness of the feeling, and expressing the feeling. If the three elements are not present, the individual is apt to be disturbed; a repressed individual cannot allow certain feelings into consciousness, an overintellectualized individual talks about feelings in an impersonal manner, while an inhibited individual is afraid to act upon feelings. The *self* is the concept of who one is and of one's relations with others. While it may not be totally conscious, it is available to consciousness.

Rogers is explicit about the conditions that facilitate or block the attainment of maturity. First he postulates an *actualizing tendency,* which is an inherent tendency in each organism to develop all of its capacities in ways that serve to maintain or enhance it. This is the growth principle—an innate push toward expansion, differentiation, and maximization. It includes the tendency to be creative, to learn new things painfully rather than to settle for the complacency of acquired learning, to develop toward autonomy rather than to be controlled by external forces. Moreover, each organism has an *organismic valuing process,* which leads it to value positively those experiences that maintain and enhance it, while valuing negatively those that have the opposite effect. Thus each individual has a built-in guide to what is best for personal growth, innately seeking enhancing experiences and avoiding those that are detrimental.

The *self* begins to emerge as a portion of the toddler's experience becomes differentiated and symbolized in an awareness of being and an awareness of functioning. Thus both "I" and what the "I" can do become part of conscious awareness. As awareness of the self emerges, the individual develops the *need for positive regard*, which is a universal need for warmth, respect, sympathy, and acceptance. With time, the need can become more potent than the organismic valuing process.

An essential requirement for healthy growth is that the need for positive regard continues to serve the organismic valuing process; in other words, it is essential that the people the child loves and values continue to foster the child's need to experience and decide for himself. In our terminology, affection must enhance initiative. This can be done only if the child receives *unconditional positive regard*. Here, no experience of the child is perceived by others as more or less worthy of positive regard. Children are intrinsically valued, and their experiences are not viewed judgmentally as being "good" or "bad" by adult standards.

But Rogers does not advocate total permissiveness. He recognizes that children cannot be allowed to do everything they like. However, discipline should take place in the context of an explicit and sympathetic recognition of the children's feelings: "I know you are mad at your baby brother, and I understand why, but I just can't let you hurt him because he has his feelings too." When this is done children never have to view themselves as "bad" and never have to disown their feelings. Consequently, their openness to experience and feelings is preserved.

Normal development goes awry because of what Rogers calls *conditions of worth*. Instead of unconditional positive regard, significant adults, particularly parents, say, in essence, "I will love you on the condition that you behave as I want you to." If children do what parents consider to be good, they are loved; if they do what parents consider to be bad, they are not loved. Because of the strong need for positive regard, children eventually make parental values into self values. At this point children are no longer in touch with their organismic valuing process, no longer open to experience and capable of deciding for themselves whether an experience is growth-promoting. By incorporating alien values they become alienated from themselves. Because of alienation, children begin to distort experiences in order to fit the imposed model of a "good boy" or a "good girl": the aesthetic boy believes he has to be a competitive go-getter because this is his father's ideal, the bright girl is hounded by feelings of inadequacy because her mother disparages intellectual achievement. Self-alienation is also a state of vulnerability to anxiety as the organismic values continue to press for their rightful place in the self. Children do not recognize such values but can only try to defend themselves against them. When distress becomes too intense, anxiety runs rampant and therapy is required.

How different the Rogerian model is from the Freudian. Freud sees humanity as endowed with primitive drives that must be socialized or else society itself could no longer exist. Rogers follows Rousseau's idea that the child, like the primitive "noble savage," is innately good, and it is socialization that has the potential for destroying the natural tendencies to growth and self-actualization. Understandably, Rogers has had a strong appeal for those who turn their backs on convention in order to "find themselves" and search for a way of life that would express "the real me." He is also in harmony with the existential emphasis on the primacy of the individual's experience and the importance of individual choice. One hears echoes of Shakespeare's "To thine own self be true" along with the "me" generation's "If it feels right, it is right."

The Therapeutic Process

In light of what we have learned, we can understand how the client-centered therapist, by offering the child unconditional positive regard, will help undo the damage of conditional love. The focus is continually on feelings because these hold the key to maturity. And because of the growth principle, the therapist has complete confidence in the client's ability to solve his or her own problems with the minimum of direction—hence the general name *nondirective therapy.*

A number of therapists have adapted Rogers's principles for children; Axeline's (1964, 1969) approach is presented here. The major change in procedure is the introduction of play material for children below the preadolescent age range. The material is simple and conducive to self-expression—dolls, animals, clay, sand, building materials. Construction toys and games of skill are avoided as being too structured to produce varied and individualized behavior. While the formal arrangement resembles that of psychoanalysis, the purpose is quite different. Rather than using play as the basis for interpretation, therapists limit their activity to reflecting the themes and affects the child introduces.

Some of the basic features of nondirective therapy deserve to be elaborated. Therapists are, quite literally, nondirective. After discussing the ground rules for the therapeutic hour and describing the procedure in general terms they leave the direction of the sessions up to the child. As we have seen, therapists do not interpret the meaning of the child's behavior, nor do they introduce any material from the child's past, from the reality of the child's present situation, or from previous sessions. If, for example, they learn that the child has started setting fires, they wait until the child is ready to make such behavior part of the therapeutic session. Thus responsibility is always on the child's shoulders. What therapists communicate implicitly is a faith in the child's ability to decide what is best for his or her own growth.

We can now understand both why the past has little intrinsic value and why diagnosis plays only a minor role in nondirective therapy. Therapists have no need to "know the answer" ahead of time; in fact, such a need might well interfere with the therapeutic process. Not only do they want to learn about the child only through the child, but as much as possible they also want to experience life as the child experiences it. Their reflection of feeling is not a mechanical technique; with it goes a genuine effort to feel their way into the child's experience. Therapists are not onlookers; they are empathetic participants.

We can also understand why it is so demanding to be a nondirective therapist. First it means relinquishing the role of authoritative adult. Moreover, the therapist's acceptance of and respect for the child must be genuine. As we have already learned from Anna Freud, when children are given freedom to do what they like, many of them begin to gravitate toward destructive acting out. Not only that, but they also have a genius for finding ways of teasing, testing, and provoking adults. For the therapist to maintain an attitude of acceptance and understanding rather than self-defense and retaliation requires a forebearing disposition and self-discipline.

However, not everything children do is

accepted; certain limits are essential. There is the limit of time, since the children must leave at the end of the session whether they want to or not. Children are not permitted to do things that deviate significantly from the world of reality; specifically, they are not allowed to attack the therapist or themselves physically or to destroy the playroom and its contents. However, the therapist, like the good parent, is understanding of the motive, even while preventing the behavior, thus avoiding judging the children as "bad."

One final word about the technique of reflecting feelings. Its *structuring* properties are obvious, since the therapist is implicitly sending the message, "While we are together, feelings are what we will be dealing with." But there is more than that. In the permissive atmosphere of the therapeutic session, the child begins to explore feelings that formerly had to be banished from conscious awareness. In fact, some of these feelings may never have been clearly recognized for what they were. Thus, reflection also serves a *defining* function rather than being a mere echo of what the child already knows. What is more, as feelings are explicitly defined, they come under conscious control. As the boy realizes his resentment for being pushed into the alien role of a go-getter, as the girl can face her fear of being rejected by a nonintellectual mother, such feelings become part of the self. The once-divided self is whole again.

THE BEHAVIOR THERAPIES

Behavior therapy is the most vigorous psychotherapy on the current scene. The past thirty years have witnessed an exuberant expansion of therapeutic techniques that has been somewhat disconcerting to those concerned with conceptual clarity. And if behavior therapy represents the marriage of the clinic and the laboratory, there are signs that the honeymoon is drawing to a close; little irritations are surfacing, and the two partners are searching for a more sober and mature basis for their relationship.

First, a conceptual framework sufficiently broad to embrace all the behavior therapies will be presented. Then the therapies themselves willl be sampled in terms of their underlying rationales. Finally, we shall turn to some of the practical and theoretical problems that have accompanied the field's rapid growth.

Note that a special discussion of the *developmental model* will not be presented. Because of their origin in learning theory, behavior therapies have inherited an emphasis on universal laws of behavior acquisition and elimination. The ways in which such laws are translated into action depend on the particular culture into which the infant is born. Instead of a universal sequence of behaviors, as found in Freud's and Piaget's theories, progression is determined by the particular behaviors a given society values at different ages. While allowing for physiological maturation, behaviorists ever since Watson have favored an environmentalist position.

However, a developmental dimension is implicit in the laws of learning which behavior therapists use. A reinforcer is neither an object (such as candy) nor a behavior (such as praise) but anything that is likely to increase the probability that a behavior will occur. What a reinforcer will be, therefore, clearly is a function of the child's developmental level. In a like manner, implementation of cognitive behavior therapy obviously depends on the level of the child's cognitive development, even though behavior therapists eschew the notion of universal stages.

Conceptual Framework

Behavior therapies are characterized by attention to specific, currently *observable behaviors* of the client, by a concern with *objective measures* of the outcomes of their interventions, and by a reliance on the *research laboratory* to provide general principles of behavior change that can be used as the basis of therapeutic intervention and as a place to put clinical findings to rigorous experimental tests. Rather than being a special set of techniques, behavior therapies are "an *approach* to abnormal behavior . . . characterized by (an) empirical methodology" (A.O. Ross and Nelson, 1979, p. 303. Our presentation follows Ross and Nelson, pp. 303–335. For a more detailed presentation, see Ross, 1981.).

To elaborate: pragmatic considerations have dictated the emphasis on specific behaviors, since these are most amenable to change. Behavior therapists would not deny that such behaviors may be rooted in the past, but the past cannot be altered, the present and the future can. Among ongoing behaviors, the therapists deal with three response systems—overt-motor, physiological-emotional, and cognitive-verbal. All must be considered in a comprehensive treatment program, since they are not necessarily correlated; a boy who is constantly fighting in school may tell the therapist that "everything is OK" and he only fights "a little every now and then." Incidentally, this concentration on the present has resulted in a relative neglect of etiology; thus the behaviorists' contributions to the field of developmental psychopathology do not match their contributions to remediation.

In the constant interplay between the clinic and the laboratory, principles of learning have been extensively used to generate therapeutic procedures, while both social and developmental psychology have provided conceptual underpinnings for therapeutic techniques, although to a lesser degree. Perhaps even more significant than the application of laboratory findings is the incorporation of experimental procedures into psychotherapeutic practice. Behavioral assessment (as described in chapter 15) sets the stage for the objective, reliable measurement of target behavior, as well as providing leads to the specific antecedents and consequent events that elicit and maintain these behaviors. The behavior therapist then proceeds to reason very much like his or her experimental counterpart: If behavior X is due to antecedent Y and consequent Z, then as Y and Z are changed, so should X. The therapeutic intervention, like an experiment, consists of testing out the hypothesis, the crucial measure being a change in the base rate of the target behavior X in the desired direction.

The simplest design in evaluating therapeutic effectiveness is the *A-B* design, in which the dependent measure is evaluated both before intervention (baseline or A) and during intervention (B). If, for example, a therapist hypothesized that temper tantrums in a 3-year-old were being sustained by maternal attention, he might advise the mother to ignore them. If the base rate went down, the therapist would have evidence that the hypothesis was correct. Such a design is adequate for clinical work because it demonstrates whether change occurs. However, for a more stringent test of the hypothesis that change was caused by the intervention rather than by other variables, the reversal or *A-B-A-B* design is used, in which the therapeutic procedure is repeatedly applied and withdrawn. If change in the target behavior occurs only in the presence of the intervention, then a causal relationship can be more readily assumed.

While the behavior therapist's procedure is akin to the experimentalist's, therapy cannot be equated with experimentation. Uncontrolled variables (such as a boy improving because his father obtained a better job), ethical considerations, and the inevitable complexity of dealing with ongoing problems of living prevent therapy from having the required purity. However, questions raised by therapeutic efficacy can be referred back to the laboratory to be examined under properly controlled conditions. If, for example, a child with a snake phobia begins to handle snakes after watching movies of other children doing so, is it because the anxiety has diminished or because the incentives and techniques for handling snakes are now enhanced, even though the anxiety level itself remains unchanged? The question whether it is better to diminish anxiety or enhance coping skills, along with a number of other questions raised in the context of behavior therapies, has provided grist for the experimental mill. In sum, the interaction between the clinic and the laboratory and the objective documentation of the efficacy of various intervention techniques are the hallmarks that clearly distinguish behavior therapies from other approaches to remediation.

Behavior Therapies Derived from Learning Theory

In the prototypical instances of behavior therapy, principles of learning—specifically, classical conditioning, operant learning, and imitation—have formed the bases of intervention procedures. Exemplars of the application of each principle will be examined. (For an account of how behavior therapies are applied to various psychopathologies, see Morris and Kratochwill, 1983.)

CLASSICAL CONDITIONING *Systematic desensitization,* as developed by Wolpe (1973), is a procedure for eliminating anxiety-mediated problems. In such problems, initially neutral stimuli come to elicit powerful anxiety responses as a result of classical conditioning. The bond between the conditioned stimulus and the anxiety response can be broken, however, by *reciprocal inhibition,* in which the stronger of two incompatible responses tends to inhibit the weaker. The therapist's task, therefore, becomes one of pairing anxiety-

eliciting stimuli with a more powerful, incompatible response. The response Wolpe uses is deep muscle relaxation, since obviously an individual cannot be simultaneously anxious and relaxed.

Two preliminary steps are needed to implement the therapy. First, the child must be instructed in the technique of relaxing various muscle groups throughout the body. The child is also required to make up a graduated sequence of anxiety-eliciting stimuli, going from the least to the most intense. A girl with a school phobia, for example, may feel no anxiety when she awakens and dresses, mild anxiety at breakfast, increasingly strong anxiety while waiting for the bus and approaching school, while the most intense anxiety comes in the free period before classes start.

In the therapy proper, the children imagine each of the steps, pairing them with the relaxation response. If the anxiety is too strong at any particular step and they cannot relax, they return to the preceding step. Over a series of sessions the children gradually are able to relax in response to even the most intense anxiety-producing stimuli. For adults, around sixteen to twenty-three treatment sessions are required to reach this goal. It is interesting that the therapeutic gains, which relate solely to imagined representations of reality, transfer to reality itself. While Wolpe's rationale has been questioned and the specific variables responsible for improvement have not been satisfactorily isolated, the therapy itself has been successful in treating a host of problems, including school and hospital phobias, examination anxiety, fear of authority, maternal separation anxiety, and asthma.

OPERANT LEARNING Behavior therapists have made extensive use of the operant principle that behavior is controlled by specific antecedent and consequent stimulus events. *Contingent management,* or the manipulation of rewards and punishments that follow or are contingent upon the response, has been particularly potent in decreasing the strength of undesirable behaviors or increasing the strength of adaptive ones. There are two kinds of positive consequences: reward or positive reinforcement, and removal of an aversive stimulus or negative reinforcement. There are also two kinds of negative consequences: positive punishment or administering an aversive stimulus, and negative punishment or the removal of a pleasant stimulus. Two procedures are used if the behavior one wishes to strengthen is not present in the child's repertoire or is infrequently emitted: *chaining* or *shaping*, in which components or successive approximations of the desired behavior are differentially reinforced, and *prompting*, in which instruction, modeling, or physical guidance is used to elicit the desired response. Behavior therapists frequently combine these various ingredients to increase the effectiveness of their therapeutic program. To teach a very retarded child how to feed herself, for example, the therapist might use shaping by first reinforcing her hand movements toward a spoon, then her grasping the spoon, then her lifting it up, and finally her bringing it to her mouth. The therapist might use prompting by demonstrating feeding himself or by actually guiding the girl's hand through feeding movements.

Examples of the application of operant principles are legion, some involving a therapist, others involving parents who not only can be taught how to implement a therapeutic program with relative ease but who also are in a position to control a wider range of behaviors than can be elicited in a therapeutic setting. (The examples are from Ross and Nelson, 1979.) We shall begin with instances of simple reward or punishment and proceed to programs combining both. The language skills of 2- and 3-year-old children were enhanced when their mothers reinforced naming of objects with praise or bits of food, while the tantrums of a 21-month-old were extinguished when the mother ignored them, thereby withdrawing the attention that had been sustaining them. In programs combining extinction with reinforcement, aggressive dependent behavior was ignored while cooperative independent behavior received parental attention; the mother of an effeminate boy ignored his feminine behavior while praising his masculine behavior; self-stimulation and self-injurious behavior in severely disturbed children was punished by a brief electric shock or a slap, while adaptive behavior was rewarded.

Instead of direct reinforcement, a child can be a given a *token*, which subsequently can be redeemed for rewards such as prizes or privileges. In one therapeutic program children were given tokens for cooperative behavior and doing chores while losing them for undesirable social behavior. In *time out*, the child is isolated for a brief period, thereby being punished by the withdrawal of reinforcers. In one complex program an acting-out boy was isolated for two minutes when he was aggressive and disobedient, while less severe misbehavior was ignored and cooperative behavior was rewarded by special attention and treats. In another complex program, the tantrums of a 3½-year-old autistic boy were treated by time out. A shaping technique was used to teach him to wear glasses, since he was in danger of losing his vision. First he was rewarded for holding the empty frames, then for bringing the frames to his eyes, and finally for wearing the prescriptive lenses. To treat his echolalic speech, he was first rewarded for saying the label for a picture the therapist held and then rewarded for saying the label without the therapist's prompting. His eating problems were decreased by temporarily removing his plate when he ate with his fingers and by temporarily removing him from the dining room when he threw food or took it from someone else's plate.

Training parents to be behavior therapists is not without its problems. The parent must be motivated to learn the techniques and sufficiently conscientious to use them over long periods of time. While parents typically want their children to change, they are not uniformly agreeable to the idea that they must also change. The problem of parental involvement may be compounded when the complaint originates in the school or in the court, as it often does. Thus parents themselves may need special reinforcement from the therapist.

OBSERVATIONAL LEARNING Observational learning or modeling has not been extensively employed as a primary (rather than an auxiliary) therapeutic technique. However, observing fearless children interacting with a phobic stimulus, such as a snake or a dog, has successfully eliminated phobias. The model may be presented either in real life or on film. Modeling is often combined with reinforcement of the desired behavior; for example, in teaching verbal behavior to autistic children, the child is immediately rewarded with food upon each successful imitation of the therapist's vocalization.

Cognitive Behavior Therapies

Cognitive behavior therapies are the newest and most controversial additions to the family of behavioral techniques. Not that there is a strict dichotomy between traditional and cognitive behavior therapy. Traditional procedures employ cognitive elements as a means of achieving behavioral change: in desensitization, for example, children imagine various situations and instruct themselves to relax, both of which are cognitive activities. For their part, cognitive therapies are concerned with changing specific overt behaviors, are

ahistoric, systematically monitor the relation between intervention and behavioral change, and retain allegiance to the clinic-laboratory symbiosis. However, cognition now becomes the primary object of the therapeutic thrust, since the basic goal is to change the way the child thinks. When this has been accomplished, behavior will also change. Of the varieties of cognitive therapies, only those concerned with self-control, cognitive restructuring, and social skills training will be discussed. (For a comprehensive discussion, see Mahoney, 1974.)

SELF-CONTROL There is an Achilles heel to traditional behavioral techniques: the very design that proves their effectiveness—the A-B-A-B paradigm—leaves the child forever dependent on external agents for maintenance of the new, more adaptive behavior. Such a situation presents practical problems, since therapists cannot see children indefinitely, while the enthusiasm of parents and teachers may wane. The situation is also ethically unacceptable to a society that values self-determination so highly. Therefore behavior therapists have set about finding ways by which external control can become internalized. One technique, within the traditional model, is called *fading* and involves the gradual removal of contingencies. Delinquents, for example, were first given tokens for every acceptable specific behavior but, after reaching a level of consistently high performance, were placed on a merit system, where privileges were freely available as long as the delinquents continued to behave appropriately.

Other behavior therapists have attacked the problem of self-control directly (Kazdin, 1980). Rather than equating self-control with some vaguely defined trait, such as will power, these therapists conceptualize it as a deliberate undertaking by the individual to achieve a self-selected outcome. This involves, among other things, forgoing immediate rewards for future ones (for example, doing homework instead of looking at television), selecting cues congruent with eliciting the desired behavior (leaving the recreation room and finding a quiet place to study), monitoring one's behavior, and rewarding or punishing oneself as the goal is or is not realized. Each component can be subjected to study in a laboratory setting and, individually or in combination, can serve as the basis for intervention techniques.

One cognitive technique involves increasing self-control in impulsive or hyperactive children by means of *self-instruction* (Meichenbaum and Goodman, 1971). The rationale is the familiar one that verbal symbols (words) serve both to delay and to guide behavior. Impulsive children, who are presumably deficient in "self-talk," should perform better on specific tasks if they learn how to instruct themselves properly. The procedure relies on modeling, reinforcement, and a graduated performance task. For the purpose of illustration, the task of copying a rectangle has been chosen. First the adult performs the task, talking aloud in order to delineate each step in the procedure: defining the task ("Let's see, what do I have to do? I have to copy this picture"), focusing attention ("I'm going real slow and careful"), self-monitoring and self-reinforcement ("I did that corner really well"), and self-evaluation ("That's pretty good, except next time I could get that line straighter if I went slower"). Next the children perform the same task with the therapist giving explicit instructions. Then the children perform the task, first instructing themselves aloud, then whispering the instructions, and finally guiding their performance via private speech. In short, the children's haphazard, impulsive self-instructions are replaced by planful and critical ones.

Understandably, self-control procedures are not without shortcomings. While de-signed partly to alleviate the problem of maintaining gains in traditional behavior therapies, the procedures themselves can begin to deteriorate over time in the absence of external reinforcement. For example, schoolchildren who have been taught to reward themselves for acceptable behavior in the classroom might gradually begin rewarding themselves for disruptive behavior. Once again we see how tenuous self-control is in middle childhood and the concomitant dependence on adult guidance.

COGNITIVE RESTRUCTURING Long a therapy in its own right, Ellis's (1970) Rational Emotive Therapy (RET) has been included under the behavior-therapies umbrella. Ellis assumes that psychopathology results from misperceptions and mistaken cognitions. He lists twelve such irrational ideas, such as "Everyone must love me for everything I do," "I need someone stronger than myself to rely on," "It is easier to avoid than to face life's difficulties." The therapist, through a kind of Socratic dialogue and logical examination of the clients' ideas, helps them achieve emotional insight into erroneous beliefs while assigning specific tasks that enable them to put their newfound understanding into practice.

Like all behavior therapies, cognitive restructuring emphasizes specific behavioral change. With self-instruction, it shares an emphasis on the importance of private monologues and provides reinforcement for systematic observation and alteration of dysfunctional thought. While its technique of rational self-examination makes it poorly suited for young children, it has been presented in order to highlight some of the problems with cognitive behavior which will soon be discussed.

SOCIAL SKILLS TRAINING Social skills training derives from studies showing a positive correlation between social relations and adustment.   Children who are successful in their peer relations, or what we call *sociability*, are apt to have a positive self-image, to perform well in school, and to be socially adjusted as adults; on the other hand, unsuccessful children are subject to academic and behavioral difficulties and are at risk for a variety of adult maladjustments including alcoholism, antisocial behavior, and psychiatric disturbances (Michelson and Mannarino, 1986).   Thus improving children's sociability should positively affect present and future adjustment.

Unfortunately, little is known concerning the specific behaviors that predict children's level of peer acceptance or ratings of social competence by parents, teachers, and other experts.   Nor do we know how these behaviors are affected by age, as they surely are, or by sex, race, or setting.   Lacking such information, social skills trainers are ''flying blind,'' either using idiosyncratic definitions or regarding almost any behavior as a social skill (see Gresham, 1986).   Such conceptual, definitional, and empirical difficulties have not prevented social skills trainers from developing a rich repertoire of techniques, a few of which will be briefly described.   (For a more comprehensive account, see Michelson and Mannarino, 1986.)

Some techniques involve *modeling* in which the child observes live or film exemplars performing the desired prosocial behaviors. Modeling in and of itself is not sufficiently potent to bring about significant change, but modeling followed by immediate rehearsal of the observed behavior is.   Multiple models who are similar to the child and who display a wide range of behavior are more effective than single, dissimilar ones displaying a narrow range of behavior.   *Reinforcement* such as attention and approval has also been used to increase desirable and decrease undesirable social behavior.

In *coaching and practice* the trainer specifically instructs the child how to behave, such as how to speak to parents or teachers, and provides feedback concerning how well the child performed.   Coaching requires clear and detailed guidelines for socially desirable behavior while practice underscores the importance of actually performing the requisite behaviors.   Like modeling, however, coaching and practice are most effective when used in conjunction with other techniques.   *Interpersonal problem solving*, in which children are taught to identify interpersonal problems, generate alternative solutions, and evaluate consequences of behavior, has already been discussed in relation to conduct disorders (see chapter 9).   In regard to overall effectiveness, interpersonal problem solving may have some impact on the adjustment of normal and high-risk children but may not be effective with severe behavioral and social problems.

Social skills *training packages* assume that multifaceted treatments will have greater impact, durability, and generality than single treatments.   A package might cover a number of specific social skills such as complimenting others, standing up for one's rights, initiating, maintaining, and terminating conversations, and dealing with authority figures and with mixed-sex interactions.   The program itself might be implemented by lectures from the trainer, by modeling, by rehearsal with feedback from the trainer and peers, and by homework assignments.

While social skills training represents a vigorous movement within the behavioral tradition, it is still in the experimental phase. Diverse approaches are being used, some of which work while others do not.   Thus evaluation of overall effectiveness would be premature.

Practical and Theoretical Problems

The principle *practical* problem with behavior therapies is not with producing but with maintaining change (Ross and Nelson, 1979). In learning-theory terms, the problem is one of generalization over situations and over time. Generalization over situations, or stimulus generalization, cannot be assumed; behaviors changed in the home, for example, may remain at their pretreatment level in the school situation. This is congruent with the behaviorist's view that behavior is situation-specific rather than the result of underlying traits. Generalization over time is another problem. In our discussion of various psychopathologies we have seen many instances in which initial gains fail to be maintained, while even self-control techniques may deteriorate.

In order to increase the likelihood of generalization, a number of procedures are recommended. Among them are the transfer of behavior control from the artificial therapeutic setting to contingencies in the natural environment, training the behavior in multiple situations or training multiple behaviors for the same response class (the former being stimulus generalization, the latter response generalization), and training for generalization by making the appropriate response class deliberately broad (Ross and Nelson, 1979).

The principle *theoretical* issue is whether cognitive behavior therapy should be regarded as behavior therapy at all. (See Ledwidge, 1978. For a lively exchange of ideas, see Mahoney and Kazdin, 1979, and Ledwidge, 1979.) In the discussion of neurosis we saw that some conservative behaviorists are reluctant to deal with "mental" events because the major thrust of behaviorism historically involved a rebellion against mentalism and a defining of psychology as the study of objective behavior. In their defense, cognitive behaviorists maintain that inner events such as thoughts or feelings are perfectly admissable as long as they can be operationally defined in behavioral terms and their inclusion increases the predictability and con-

trol of behavior. Those who admit private events, however, disagree as to whether such events conform to the classical laws of learning or whether some new theory is required. While there is some preference for an information-processing model among the revisionists, there is no generally accepted cognitive theory. Mahoney (1974), for example, presented his own theory which he regards as more attuned to psychopathological behavior than information processing.

Furthermore, conservatives object that cognitive restructuring, in particular, lacks all the hallmarks of the behavioral approach: Ellis's twelve irrational ideas are nearer to the broad motivational systems of Freud and the self-systems of Rogers than they are to target behaviors, while the theory is not buttressed by a convincing body of research findings.

Evaluation

With a movement as vigorous and controversial as cognitive behavior therapy it is possible to give only a provisional evaluation of its status within the behavioral camp and its effectiveness. (Our presentation follows Beidel and Turner, 1986.) There is little evidence supporting the claim that cognition is a new kind of variable requiring new laws; the established principles of cognitive learning seem adequate to account for the data. Ironically, cognitive behavior therapists have ignored the rich laboratory findings concerning basic cognitive processes in constructing their theories and devising their procedures. Thus they have not been true to the claim that behavior therapies represent a marriage of the clinic and the laboratory.

Next there is no convincing evidence that therapeutic results are due to changes in cognitions, which in turn produce behavioral changes. Since most therapies include behavioral as well as cognitive components, the two variables are confounded and it is impossible to say which is the effective agent. In fact, in techniques aimed at eliminating phobias there is evidence that only after children are helped to practice new, nonfearful behaviors in connection with the phobic object do they begin to change their cognitions about themselves and their ability to master the situation. Thus one can make a case that cognitive changes are contingent on behavioral ones rather than vice versa.

Finally, there is evidence that, while cognitive behavior therapy is superior to no therapy at all, it is not superior to the more traditional behavioral techniques such as progressive desensitization. While Beidel and Turner (1986) do not deny that cognitive behavior therapy has the potential for expanding the theoretical basis of behavioral therapies, their critique implies that the therapists have sold their behavioral birthright for a mess of cognitive porridge.

RESEARCH ON EFFECTIVENESS OF THERAPY

Outcome Studies

After reading the literature on psychotherapy one comes to two conclusions: everything works, and nothing works.

The impression that everything works is partly due to the policy of professional journals of accepting only articles that show positive results. Thus it is never clear how often a given therapy was tried and failed. There is also a common element to psychotherapies, compounded of the therapist's humanness interacting with the client's desire to change, which guarantees a modicum of success to anyone attempting to help children, no matter how strange or exotic the technique might be. Finally, everything may seem to work because standards of research design and objectivity of evaluation have been lax in

regard to evaluating therapeutic outcomes. Whatever the reasons, the literature on outcome of psychotherapy is almost an unbroken series of success stories.

On the other hand, Eysenck (1952) rocked the therapeutic community with a survey showing that a variety of psychotherapies with neurotic adults were no more effective than the improvement that could be expected from spontaneous recovery. After conducting a similar study with children, Levitt (1957) reached a similar conclusion.

A critique of Eysenck's research will not be attempted; since the problems with his study are common to all research on therapeutic *outcome,* it would be more fruitful to present these. Then we will present two newer studies with a more positive picture of therapeutic effectiveness.

The first problem in studying therapeutic effectiveness is one of *matching* groups. Since psychopathologies differ in amenability to change, the groups should at least be equated in terms of the nature and severity of disturbance. But other variables might also affect outcome—not only demographic ones such as age, intelligence, and socioeconomic status, but also therapy-specific ones such as motivation for treatment and expectation of being helped. The problem of matching is particularly difficult in the therapy, no-therapy study, since it is unethical to withhold treatment from a group of needy clients solely for research purposes. Other strategies must be adopted, none of which is totally satisfactory. Some studies have used matched clients on the waiting list, although there is no guarantee that such clients will not receive help from other sources during the waiting period. Another possibility is to use the client as his or her own control, as in the behavior therapists' *A-B-A-B* design.

The therapy or therapies being investigated must be competently conducted, and therapeutic *competence* is difficult to measure, although the number of years of experience has served as a practical guide. *Criteria of outcome* differ radically among psychotherapies; the specific changes a behavior therapist would accept as defining successful completion might well be rejected by a Freudian or Rogerian. *Follow-up* evaluations are important to insure that initial differences in effectiveness do not wash out in time or even reverse themselves. Finally, research on psychotherapy, like all psychological research, is hampered by lack of adequate *measuring instruments*. It is chancy to accept either the therapist's or the client's judgment concerning outcome because both are subject to bias; for example, parents report their children have continued to improve after therapy when objective measures indicate that they have not or that their behavior has actually worsened. To avoid bias, individuals not involved in the therapy should evaluate the client by means of objective instruments before and after treatment. Standardized tests may be used, but they may not be sensitive to crucial therapeutic variables, while specialized assessment techniques run the risk of being inadequately standardized.

To return to the question of effectiveness, there have been heartening signs that psychotherapy with children is indeed effective. The reversal of previous findings was due to the use of a statistical technique called meta-analysis, which is particularly suited to aggregated data. The basic analyses were conducted by Casey and Berman (1985) on seventy-five studies of therapy outcome, and by Weisz, Weiss, Alicke, and Klotz (1987) on 108 studies. Both sets of investigators found that around 80 percent of the treated children were functioning at a higher level than untreated children, an impressive showing indeed. Weisz and coworkers (1987) also found that children between 4 and 12 years of age improved significantly more than adolescents between 13 and 18 years of age. In addition,

gains were sustained in follow-up studies conducted five to six months later. Both studies agreed that whether children received individual, group, or play therapy or whether parents were also in therapy did not affect outcome significantly.

The studies differed somewhat in other results. While both reported that behavior therapy was superior to nonbehavior therapy, Casey and Berman (1985) did not accept this finding as conclusive because the two classes of therapies involved children with different problems and used different measures of treatment efficacy. Thus behavioral techniques might have seemed superior because the children treated were less disturbed and because efficacy was measured in terms of simpler behaviors. Also, these investigators found that the greatest improvement was observed in cases of phobias, impulsivity, and somatic problems while Weisz et al. (1987) did not find differences in effectiveness among disorders.

The results of both studies have limitations as well as perplexities. Neither the full range of childhood disturbances nor the full range of psychotherapies has been studied. The internalizing disorders such as phobias and withdrawn behavior along with the externalizing disorders such as conduct disorders, aggression, and hyperactivity are adequately sampled, but not the severe disturbances such as autism and schizophrenia, somatic disturbances such as anorexia, or learning disabilities. The behavior therapies are well represented as is client-centered therapy but not the psychodynamic therapies since these typically do not employ the kind of research design and methodology that would lend itself to statistical analysis (Kovacs and Paulauskas, 1986). A perplexing result is that therapeutic efficacy depends on who is evaluating it. Casey and Berman (1985), for example, found that while therapists, observers involved in the research, and parents

reported improvement, the children themselves and their teachers and peers did not.
There is no easy resolution to this problem
of disagreement among evaluators. One might
argue that therapists, observers, and parents
are more skilled and knowledgeable observers, or that therapy is situation-specific, affecting home but not school and peer relations. But if significant change has taken
place, why are the children themselves unaware of it?

One final result is important. Therapeutic
effectiveness is enhanced when outcome is
measured in terms of activities similar to those
occurring during treatment. For example, if
modeling has been used to help a child
overcome a dog phobia, the effectiveness of
treatment would be measured in terms of the
child's subsequent reaction to dogs. The
implication is that effectiveness is facilitated
when children have specific problems that
can be specifically targeted in treatment. The
obverse of this implication is that children
with diffuse or multiple problems may be
more difficult to treat successfully.

In sum, meta-analysis has shown for the
first time that a positive answer can be given
to the question, Does psychotherapy with
children work? Yet the answer is still a
qualified one. It would be more accurate to
say that there is now evidence that many
types of behavioral therapy are effective, particularly with young children who have a
specific behavior that can be targeted for
change. However, it may not be as effective
with adolescents and with children who have
diffuse and multiple problems. Moreover,
effectiveness in treating a number of disturbances has not been evaluated. Finally, there
is little evidence concerning psychodynamic
therapies, even though these, along with
client-centered therapies, are the most commonly used methods of treating children. In
fact, child psychotherapists have lagged behind those working with adults in translating
their psychodynamic techniques into specifically described procedures and then designing studies in which there are objective measures of the population and outcome along
with appropriate control or comparison groups
(Kovacs and Paulauskas, 1986). Until there
is a willingness to undertake such studies,
the effectiveness of psychodynamic therapies
will remain unknown.

Process Studies

Instead of studying outcome, some researchers are asking the process question: "What
combinations of therapist, client, and technique produce what kinds of change?" In
the summary that follows, the findings are
derived primarily from research with adults
unless otherwise specified. (For comprehensive coverage, see Garfield and Bergin, 1978.)
We will first discuss nonbehavioral psychotherapies, which have been interested primarily
in the effects of patient and therapist characteristics, of patient–therapist match, and of
specific therapeutic techniques on improvement.

For adults and children alike, the general
rule is that the more disturbed the client, the
less likely is improvement, and that children
with conduct disorders and psychotics are
less amenable to psychotherapy than are neurotics. Younger children improve more than
older ones, while sex is not systematically
related to improvement. The long-standing
belief that individuals from the lower socioeconomic status do not respond to psychotherapy has been successfully challenged;
evidence suggests that a good deal depends
on how competent and comfortable the therapist is in dealing with racial and class differences between the client and himself or
herself. The client's motivation to change is
positively related to outcome; the role of
expectations is more ambiguous, but the evidence suggests that if these are realistic and

if the client is willing to work to fulfill them, they are facilitative. The client's willingness to collaborate actively in the therapy and to assume responsibility for change are also facilitative, while readiness to reveal intimate information and feelings is not clearly related to outcome.

In regard to the therapist, a good personal adjustment facilitates positive change, perhaps because the client identifies with the healthy aspects of the therapist's personality. On the other hand, the importance of warmth, empathy, and genuineness has been recently challenged, while there is no evidence that the therapist's value systems or biases per se have a direct impact on therapeutic outcome. In the realm of the therapeutic alliance, it is important that therapist and client like one another, that there is relaxed rapport and open communication, that the therapist conveys a capacity to understand, and the client feels understood. Anger, boredom, or detachment on the part of the therapist hamper therapy or lead to termination. Therapy can be enhanced if both parties either share similar values or have complementary ones, such as a submissive client matched with an authoritative therapist.

Client variables such as motivation to change carry the most weight in determining outcome, with therapists' personal characteristics coming next and techniques running a weak third (Bergin and Lambert, 1978). Thus research findings contradict the widely held and strongly defended position that the choice of therapy is the most important determinant of outcome. The evidence suggests that in training therapists, the cultivation of interpersonal skills may be more advantageous to future clients than the teaching of a particular technique.

Behavioral therapists have also become interested in nonspecific variables that might influence therapeutic outcome, such as the client's expectancies and the therapist–client relationship. There is evidence, for example, that the relationship variable together with behavioral techniques can affect the outcome, either enhancing or hindering goal attachment. This should not be surprising because clients have been shown to improve under the so-called attention placebo condition in which they receive attention from a therapist, such as playing games or reading stories, but receive no formal kind of psychotherapy (Sweet, 1984). The finding concerning the importance of the relationship opens up two avenues of investigation. The first is the development of a behavioral assessment instrument that would objectively measure the relationship variable. The second is the inclusion of this measure in the design of studies so that it will be possible to tell how much therapeutic effectiveness is due to the specific behavioral technique and how much is due to the general factor of the relationship.

Other research findings contain some surprises; for example, behavior therapists tend to be warmer, more natural, and more involved than psychoanalytically oriented psychotherapists, who place the relationship at the heart of the therapeutic process (Sloane et al., 1975).

As behavioral and nonbehavioral therapists have begun dealing with the same variables, they have started talking to each other more than in the past. Instead of "my therapy" versus "your therapy," there is recognition of overlap, of sharing common techniques and problems. Such a development is all to the good in terms of advancing understanding of the therapeutic process and using a variety of techniques in helping children.

THE FAMILY APPROACH

While various schools of psychotherapy have adapted their techniques to treating families rather than individuals, it will be more fruitful to examine those conceptualizations that have broken new ground by regarding family interaction as an entity to be studied and understood in its own right. (Our presentation follows Whiteside, 1979.) Through the discussion of anorexia nervosa and schizophrenia, we are already familiar with the basic premise and some of the concepts generated by the family approach. Now we need to examine both in greater detail.

The basic premise is that the family is a superordinate unit, an entity over and above the interaction of its individual members. In searching for a congenial theoretical framework, family therapists have gravitated toward viewing the family as an *open system.* It is a system because it is the product of the dynamic interaction among a set of mutually interdependent components. It is open because it interacts with other systems. Expressed concretely, family members are in continual interaction with one another and each family interacts with other families as well as with other social institutions. As an open system, the family has certain characteristics:

WHOLENESS   Families, like individuals, have their own defining characteristics, which cannot be derived from the personalities of its members. At times, families are characterized by psychological terms, such as *hostile*, *inhibited*, or *inadequate*; at other times, therapists use colloquial expressions, such as *tough* or *slippery*. Thus family therapists subscribe to the principle that the whole is greater than the sum of its parts.

INTERDEPENDENCE   The family is formed by highly complex interlocking relationships, so that a change in any one member will affect the remaining members. The nature of relatedness ranges from trivial to profound, from routine functions such as putting out the garbage to meeting the deepest needs for love or for respect.

FEEDBACK   Family therapists reject linear causality, in which *A* causes change in *B*, for a circular conceptualization in which *A* both affects and is affected by *B*. Since the family is a system, this feedback may well involve multiple reverberating influences among family members.

HOMEOSTASIS   A family limits the variations in behavior which each member is allowed, thereby bringing stability to the system. When the limits are exceeded, feedback functions to bring the system back in balance. Some states of equilibrium are maintained at the cost of curtailing individuality; for example, all the family members may be required to behave as if there were never any disharmony. Other states of equilibrium can allow for both individuality and adaptation to changing circumstances.

RULES   These are the persistent and observable regularities in family relationships. Rules may govern trivial behavior such as, "Brush your teeth before bedtime," or they may define broad areas of relationships such as, "Female family members are inferior to male members." While some rules are conscious and explicit, others are implemented without awareness.

COMMUNICATION   Communication, the warp and woof of the fabric of family interaction, is the means by which interactions are established and negotiated. Indeed, a family member cannot avoid communicating, since silence itself can send potent messages such as "I will not do what you want me to do" or "I do not consider myself part of this group." A communication has a given content, an expressive component, and an implied relationship. "Go upstairs to bed," spoken in an angry voice, conveys both the literal message, the anger of the speaker, and the fact that he or she is in command. The same content could be conveyed in a way that indicates meekness and uncertainty as to authority.

CHANGE   In first-order change, variation occurs within the rules of the system. Therapists have noted that if the system requires a disturbed member in order to maintain homeostasis and if one member of the family improves, another may become disturbed. In second-order change, the system itself is altered; instead of using a disturbed child as an excuse for not facing its basic conflicts, the family is helped by a therapist to confront such problems. Naturally, both first- and second-order change can occur outside of therapy, and the latter can be in the direction of greater or less adaptability.

A well-functioning family system is characterized by explicit rules, clarity of communication, flexibility, openness to change, and respect for individuality. Such qualities enable it to successfully perform its functions of socializing the child while enhancing autonomy. A malfunctioning system is characterized by covertness, manipulation, and rigid, ambiguous, or amorphous rules; individuation is sacrificed to a false image of togetherness. The child feels bewildered or imprisoned or betrayed but, in the most insidious cases, is prevented by family maneuvers from realizing what is happening. We have seen many exemplars of such faulty systems. In Minuchin's concept of *enmeshment* and *overprotection,* family members are highly involved with one another in an intrusive, overconcerned manner that robs each member of a sense of individuality (Minuchin et al., 1975). In Bateson's concept of the *double bind,* the individual is confronted with an insolvable dilemma of being condemned regardless of what he or she does, while

being prevented from calling attention to the trap that has been laid. Wynne et al. (1979) describes the *diffuse* and *fragmented* family structure, along with the inability of family members to maintain an appropriate *psychological distance.* Lidz (1973) delineates the *skewed* family with its dominating mother and passive father, and the *schismatic* family in which conflicted parents compete for the child's loyalties.

The systems approach redefines the nature of psychopathology. The disturbed child becomes merely the "identified patient," the symptom, as it were, that something has gone wrong. The pathology itself is in the system. The child may be a *scapegoat,* protecting parents from facing their own unresolved problems; concern over antisocial acting out, for example, may divert parents from facing their own chronic conflicts in regard to who makes decisions in the family. In fact, confronting parents with the fact that the entire network of familial relationships must be examined and changed may be the jolt that initiates the process of change.

Family Therapy

At the beginning of therapy families are trapped in defensive maneuvers that block growth and distort reality. Therapists initially try to cut through defenses, to facilitate openness, and to uncover sources of pain. They are especially skilled in sensitizing families to mixed, contradictory, obscure, and vague communications, often pointing to the expressive as well as to the manifest content. They help family members face conflicting needs and the self-defeating results of their defensive protection. At times they support the system in order to convey a message of understanding and trustworthiness; at times they upset the system's equilibrium so that the underlying issues may be brought to light. One such technique involves confronting parents with an alternate interpretation of the child's behavior, such as pointing out that an immature adolescent boy wants to spare the parents the pain of his growing up and becoming independent of them. While catharsis or release of pent-up emotions might well take place in the process of therapy, this is not the goal. The goal is restructuring the family system. Only then can experiences that have been avoided or denied be mastered.

While there are many kinds of family therapy, we have chosen to discuss Satir's, since she pays greater attention than most therapists to the role of the child. (See Satir, 1967. For a comprehensive presentation of family therapies, see Goldenberg and Goldenberg, 1980). Satir regards self-esteem as the basic human drive and defines the mature individual as one who is in touch with his or her own feelings, can communicate clearly, and can accept the individuality of others. Separating from the family and becoming a clearly delineated self represent the key to maturity or pathology.

There are a number of ways in which self-differentiation can be blocked. If either or both of the parents have a poor self-image they will tend to view the child as a means of achieving self-esteem. Consequently the child is not viewed as an individual and is saddled with the burden of fulfilling parental needs. Any difference in the child's outlook is translated as a lack of love for the parents. Since the parents themselves may well be in conflict, the child who turns to one for help risks losing the other. (One catches glimpses of Rogers in Satir's theorizing.)

Satir, like many other family therapists, emphasizes the role of communication in enhancing or blocking development. The parent who has low self-esteem does not communicate clearly. The messages are vague or uncertain or contradictory, or there is a disjuncture between the content and the expressive component. Since the child's self is formed partially by interactions with the parent, such communications prevent the child from achieving a clearly defined self-image.

Finally, there is the matter of family rules. Ideally the rules should give children the freedom to disagree, to ask questions when they do not understand, and to acknowledge their own feelings. However, family rules may be rigid and unrealistic such as, "Only good feelings may be expressed," or "You must not feel angry or jealous of your sibling." Family rules can also be uncertain or contradictory, leaving children baffled as to where they stand and what they should do.

It follows that one goal of therapy is to help the family discover the rules regarding emotional interchange in order to ascertain which are still valid and which no longer apply. This emphasis on rules has the advantage of relieving the child of the role of "the sick one," while relieving parents of guilt over having done something "wrong." In the good sense of the word, the situation is depersonalized as all members of the family set out to understand the causes of the pain they are feeling. As the rules causing pain are exposed, the family has a chance to change them, which, in turn, enhances the family's feeling of being in control of its destiny. Families must also learn to communicate and to individuate so that each member can report completely and congruently what he or she feels and thinks, while uniqueness is valued and differentness is openly acknowledged and used for growth.

Being both an experienced professional and an outsider, the therapist is in a favored position to detect incongruent, covert, and confused messages and to articulate implicit rules. But even more important, the therapist must model open communication by being warm, empathetic, and involved while sending messages that are clear, congruent, and reality-based. Thus, while the family is examining the faults in its system that produce pain, they have constantly before them a model of what communication and a mature relationship should be like.

Effectiveness

In regard to effectiveness, Hazelrigg, Cooper, and Borduin (1987) found that family therapy had positive effects when compared with no treatment and with alternative treatment controls. Positive changes were found in terms of specific effects on presenting problems and general effects on the family system as a whole. Follow-up studies showed that positive effects continued over time, but the effects were weaker and more variable than at the end of treatment. Recidivism as a follow-up measure showed family therapy to be more effective than alternative treatments, however.

The above findings have a number of important qualifications. To begin with, only twenty studies were found which were sufficiently sophisticated methodologically and sufficiently objective in assessment techniques to be included in the statistical analysis. Thus the sampling of family therapy in general and of specific family therapies was limited. The same is true of the kind of problem treated; most of the studies involved children with conduct disorders. The effectiveness of family therapy in treating other kinds of disturbances is unknown. Only eleven studies had alternative treatments such as group therapy or medication, and, even within this meager sampling, there was great variability; for example, family therapy was clearly more effective than bibliotherapy (i.e., informative and self-help literature) but not more effective than hospitalization. Consequently, much needs to be learned about the effectiveness of family therapy relative to a variety of other treatment approaches. As with the effectiveness of child psychotherapy

in general, the present findings are encouraging but tentative and incomplete.

GROUP THERAPIES

Group therapies are difficult if not impossible to epitomize. They involve diverse ages (from preschoolers to adolescents), psychopathologies (the entire gamut has been treated on a group basis), special-interest groups (father-absent boys, teenage pregnant girls), techniques (structured tasks, games, discussions ranging from dreams to current happenings, fantasy play, role playing, dance, body movement, and art), goals (release of inhibitions, relief of anxiety and guilt, increased controls and coping skills, modification of the self-concept, insight), and conceptual models (psychoanalytic, nondirective, behavioral, gestalt, and transactional analysis). They are performed in a variety of settings (child guidance clinics, private practice, schools, hospitals, detention homes), with the therapist's role varying from passive observer to active director. Adequate coverage would take us far afield (see Kraft, 1979). Unlike family therapy, group therapies have a catch-as-catch-can quality resulting from the lack of an overall integrating framework. Therefore our discussion will be limited to a presentation of some of their general characteristics.

The rationale of group therapy derives from the inherently social nature of human beings that is clearly evident from infancy on. The general goal is to enable children, isolated from healthy peer contact by withdrawal or hostility, to establish growth-promoting social interactions. A number of curative factors are at work in a group setting (Yalom, 1975). One is *universality*, or the reassuring discovery that many others share the child's feelings and experiences. There are various sources of *interpersonal learning experiences*, some coming from direct interaction among the group members, others from imitation of peers and modeling of the therapist's behavior, and still others from group cohesiveness and the sense of "we-ness" that develops with time; for example, groups may form clubs which serve to check the impulsive behavior of its members, bolster self-esteem, deepen the sense of loyalty, and serve as a forum for reality-testing discussions. The therapist is also a source of information concerning ways children can get along together constructively. The group experience may involve *catharsis,* or the release of pent-up feelings in an accepting and sympathetic setting, as well as providing a chance to relive and correct *distortions originating in the family;* for example, the manipulatively helpless child finds no support from the group or the therapist, the disconfirmation of expectations serving as the opening wedge to change. There is the opportunity for children to see themselves as others see them, thus gaining *perspective* and ultimately a sense of responsibility for their actions; for example, if aggression starts getting out of hand, the therapist can call a halt, either challenging the group to examine the cause and suggest remedies or taking the lead in discussing the value of self-control. There are positive feelings that accompany *altruistic* behavior on the child's part, as well as the *hopefulness* that comes from the knowledge that previously insoluble problems can be resolved. (For a detailed account of group therapy, see Slavson and Schiffer, 1975.)

PREVENTION

The Community Mental Health Movement

In the 1960s, community mental health was heralded as the third mental health revolution. If Pinel had unshackled the insane in 1792, thereby proclaiming their right to be treated as human beings, if Freud had shown that neurosis conformed to the same principles that accounted for normal behavior, then community mental health would prevent psychopathology through social interventions. (Our presentation follows Korchin, 1976.)

Mental health problems were viewed as intimately connected with social problems—primarily poverty, along with racism, crime, inadequate housing and education, job discrimination, and unemployment. Concern shifted from the individual to the social institution, from therapy to prevention, from clinic to community. The mental health worker's place should be in the community rather than in an office, both to make services readily accessible to populations most in need of them and to mobilize human resources within the community itself. Social action and advocacy were added to the mental health worker's functions. As if that were not enough, the movement aimed at maximizing human potential as well as ameliorating psychological suffering.

A number of factors were responsible for such a radical departure from traditional clinical thought and practice. The connection between poverty and psychopathology had been convincingly demonstrated prior to the 1960s, but largely ignored. Ironically, the greater need of the poor was accompanied by an equally great inequity in the delivery of services to them. The largely middle-class clinician preferred to treat the middle-class client, while the poor tended to be shunted into custodial hospitals where they received grossly inadequate care. It was the *social ferment* of the 1960s—the riots, the protests, the demands of impoverished blacks for equality—which opened the eyes and seared the conscience of mental health workers. That there was both ideological and financial support at the national level assured the translation of community mental health goals into actual programs.

The second factor contributing to the momentum of the community mental health movement was a *dissatisfaction with psychotherapy*, which was viewed as both ineffectual and inefficient. Eysenck's outcome study with adults and Levitt's similar study with children have already been discussed. While the claim of ineffectualness subsequently proved to be exaggerated, the verdict is still a qualifed one: psychotherapy may be superior to no psychotherapy for certain psychopathologies, but it is least effective for populations that are most troublesome to society—children with conduct disorders and psychotics. But even if it were completely effective, psychotherapy is costly in terms of time, effort, and money. Moreover, the task of providing sufficient numbers of therapists to conduct it is a hopeless one. To take only one example: it has been estimated that of the 12 million disturbed children and adolescents, 90 percent are not receiving appropriate services (Cummings, 1979). To offer services would therefore require a vast expansion of training and clinical facilities. This estimate does not even include adults and the aged, whose needs are equally great.

Finally, the deplorable condition of *mental hospitals* at the end of World War II was a factor underlying the shift in concern from changing individuals to changing institutions. Not only were many of these hospitals grossly understaffed, but the requirement that patients be submissive and accept a role of being inadequate and incompetent also fostered regression rather than recovery. Nor was brutality and inhumane treatment unknown; children were beaten, deprived of clothing and toilet facilities, placed in solitary confinement, and sexually abused. Mental institutions were a major disgrace in the affluent American society, just as prisons continue to be to this day.

The shift to *prevention* took its cue from the history of medicine, which shows that no major disease has been eliminated by therapeutic measures alone, but only through preventive ones. In addition, prevention captured the spirit of the mental health movement in that it required professionals to reach out to the most needy populations and to show members of these populations how to assume responsibility for helping themselves. Along with its high-minded ideology, the outreach approach had the potentiality for solving the practical problem of understaffing.

In sum, the community mental health movement can be characterized as follows. It is more likely to be concerned with *social groups* than with individuals in regard to prevention or intervention. It *interprets mental health broadly* to encompass social and physical as well as emotional well-being in the belief that all these factors are interrelated. It is concerned with enhancing competencies and adaptive responses rather than being oriented toward psychopathology alone. And, finally, it tends to be proactive, seeking out the children who might profit from its various programs rather than waiting for the disturbed child to be brought to a professional. Thus *prevention* rather than remediation is the movement's special goal. (Peterson and Roberts, 1986, contains a more detailed account of community prevention and intervention than will be given here.)

Preventive and Remedial Programs

BIOLOGICAL APPROACHES Since the physiologically damaged or defective neonate is at risk in regard to subsequent psychopathologies, among them mental retardation, hyperactivity, and schizophrenia, a number of programs have been instituted to prevent such damage from occurring. Sterilization, birth control, and therapeutic abortions are highly controversial issues in American society, while involuntary sterilization is generally unacceptable. *Family planning*, in which the adults discuss voluntary sterilization, contraception, and abortion with a qualified professional, is more palatable.   As the number of pediatric disorders found to have a genetic base is increasing, *genetic counseling* is becoming increasingly important as a preventive technique.   The degree of genetic risk, the severity of the abnormal condition, and the effectiveness of existing therapies are presented, along with the psychological and social consequences of the abnormal condition.   As with family planning, the purpose of counseling is to enable parents to arrive at an informed decision concerning the present fetus and future pregnancies.

PRENATAL AND HEALTH CARE   A number of prenatal factors can increase the risk of neurological impairment with concomitant intellectual and behavioral deficits in the newborn—infectious diseases such as rubella, malnutrition, obesity, radiation, drugs, and possibly emotional stress.   In order to reduce the chance of prematurity and congenital anomalies, the mother should receive adequate medical, dietary, and emotional care during pregnancy.   There has been a special concern for the pregnant teenager of lower socioeconomic status, whose age alone places the fetus at risk and whose class membership increases the likelihood that her diet ("Coke and junk food") is deficient, that she has received inadequate medical care, and that emotional support from the father and family is lacking.   Providing adequate prenatal care to the poor has involved increasing the facilities and devising ways to make such facilities more accessible than they have been in the past.

The Maternal and Infant Care (MIC) outreach program decentralizes services into neighborhood settings and provides prenatal and postnatal care and family planning in areas where there are few private physicians. The multidisciplinary staff, aided by community members, carries out case findings in churches, stores, schools, laundromats, and other gathering places.   In addition to medical attention, dental care and counseling for emotional and vocational problems is available.   The clinic is open in the evening and on weekends, and staff members make home visits.   The program has been effective in reducing infant mortality among the high-risk population it serves (Millar, 1979).

Because of the relation between physical and mental health, a number of *health-related* programs are relevant to the goal of preventing psychopathology.   The Supplemental Food Program for Women, Infants and Children, known as WIC, is concerned with nutrition and provides food supplements to low-income pregnant and lactating women and to infants and young children up to the age of four.   The program is federally funded but implemented by state and local social service agencies.   Studies of effectiveness, while being criticized on methodological grounds, suggest that WIC has positive effects on cognitive development and adjustment.   In middle childhood the emphasis of health-related programs is on positive health habits such as exercise and dental hygiene.   In the preadolescent and adolescent periods programs have taken on the more serious challenge of preventing smoking, drinking, and other forms of drug use.   These have already been described in chapter 10.

Intellectual Development and School Adjustment

It is for good reason that so much attention has been paid to intellectual development and school adjustment: both play an important role in determining the difference between normality and psychopathology.

Some programs, especially those concerned with intellectual stimulation in the first few years of life, involve parent education. They may have any of a number of goals:

1. To impart information about normal development to mothers, many of whom (particularly teenagers) literally do not know what behavior to expect.

2. To instruct mothers in ways to stimulate cognitive growth. Some mothers do not understand why they should talk to their infants, for example, since infants "don't answer back and don't know what I'm saying anyway," as one mother put it. They are also taught how to use simple household materials, such as string, plastic cups, cereal boxes, and aluminum foil, to make mobiles and other objects that will pique the infant's curiosity.

3. To encourage mothers to express warmth and pride in their infants so as to foster the bond of affection.

4. To enhance the mother's own feelings of competence. This may involve not only increasing her caregiving skills but also helping her with realistic problems in regard to her future and her family.

Some programs are conducted on a group basis which allows the mothers to compare notes on their infants' development, share problems, and learn from one another as well as from the leader. It is often helpful to conduct the groups in the hospital where the mother delivered the infant, since she knows both setting and staff. However, many mothers cannot or are unwilling to manage the demands of scheduled meetings. Programs are therefore conducted in the home at their convenience.

One of the best known early intervention programs is Project Head Start, which is national in scope and provides positive educational and social experiences for disadvantaged preschoolers. Head Start centers may differ, some emphasizing training in specific skills such as reading or arithmetic, others stressing enriching cultural experiences. Head Start and other preschool programs have been subject to intense scrutiny in regard to effectiveness. One of the most impressive findings is that children who participated in these preschool programs were less likely to be referred to special education classes in high school than were comparison children. Some projects showed affective gains as well, ranging from children's more positive attitude toward school to parents' increased aspirations for their children (Peterson and Roberts, 1986).

Undoubtedly the most familiar early intervention program is *Sesame Street*, which was designed to enhance the recognition of letters and numbers, conceptual thinking, and the understanding of the physical and social environment, such as relationships in the family and social roles. Evaluation of this and similar television programs indicates that they positively influence cognitive variables along with prosocial attitudes and behaviors, although some findings have been equivocal.

School-based programs may be aimed not only at academic achievement but also at helping children with adjustment problems. One of the oldest of such programs is Cowen's Primary Mental Health Project (PMHP) (Weissberg et al., 1983). Elementary schoolchildren who were less well accepted by peers, judged as more maladjusted by teachers, in poor health, and achieving lower test scores and grades than their contemporaries were first seen by school psychologists and social workers, who established a positive relationship, provided educational assistance, and helped devise constructive goals. Later paraprofessionals also assisted in the program. Results suggested that children receiving this intervention had fewer nurse referrals, higher grades and achievement test scores, better teacher-rated adjustment, and lower self-rated anxiety than children not receiving the intervention.

Social Approaches

Recall that the community mental health movement aims at changing the social context in which psychopathology is apt to develop. This involves establishing new community resources and changing existing ones.

One community resource is the *crisis center* for individuals or families experiencing a sudden traumatic change such as the death of a parent, an eruption of violence by an alcoholic father, or a suicide attempt by an adolescent. Crisis intervention is immediately available, brief, and focused on a specific problem. It may take place in drop-in centers, on hot lines, in pastoral counseling, or with police officers trained in family intervention. Depending on how the crisis is resolved, the client may or may not be referred for more extended help. There are *halfway houses* to help adolescents who were previously institutionalized for various psychopathologies make the transition to independent community living. *Day-care centers* enabling mothers to work without depriving their children of stimulation and attention have become a permanent fixture on the social scene.

By far the most ambitious addition to community resources, however, has been the *Community Mental Health Center* (CMHC), established by the Community Mental Health Act of 1963. Mandated services include inpatient and outpatient care, partial hospitalization such as night hospitals for patients able to work during the day, 24-hour emergency services, and consultation to community agencies and professional personnel. CMHCs frequently foster self-help groups consisting of individuals who are at risk for or are showing early signs of psychological difficulties, such as single parents, children of divorced parents, or parents of children with chronic illnesses. As much as possible, the groups are encouraged to develop their own problem-solving and social skills after an initial period of guidance from the professional staff. CMHCs also have programs to enhance social networks, a term designating the people to whom distressed individuals can turn for support, such as relatives, friends, and neighbors. Such people provide opportunities for ventilating feelings and obtaining information while serving as role models of successful coping.

Despite its initial lofty ideals in regard to prevention, this function of CMHCs has all but vanished with time. Federal support has declined and in order to survive CMHCs have had to rely increasingly on money from other sources such as insurance reimbursement, which pays only for treatment of existing disorders. (Preventive and remedial programs for child physical and sexual abuse have been discussed in chapter 13.)

Among *institutions*, the community mental health movement has had the greatest impact on mental hospitals. In part, the decline in population there has been due to the discovery of more effective psychopharmacological agents; but it also has been due to professional and public concern over the detrimental effect many large state hospitals were having on their patients. There has been a vigorous movement protecting the rights of psychologically disturbed and mentally retarded children in regard to the decision to institutionalize them, as well as their right to humane treatment, appropriate therapy, and periodical evaluation once institutionalized. While programs to capitalize on the therapeutic potential of mental institutions have been inaugurated, they cannot be said to have had a major impact. The same is true of programs for improving the juvenile justice system. One program which has been successfully implemented has been federal and state mandated *deinstitutionalization* which returned a large number of patients to the community. Unfortunately, the community did not always have adequate facilities to absorb and care for them so that they joined the ranks of the homeless.

Another important feature of the current scene is *legislation* that has countered society's tendency to insulate itself from the fate of the deviant. Notable are the Education for All Handicapped Children Act of 1975, Public Law 94-142, which prescribes free appropriate public education for children who are mentally retarded, deaf, orthopedically and visually impaired, seriously emotionally disturbed, and learning disabled; legislation in regard to the mentally retarded; and the Child Abuse and Treatment Act, Public Law 93-274, which serves as a legal deterrent to child abuse by encouraging the reporting of such abuse and requiring that the abused child receive appropriate treatment.

Problems and Reevaluation

Because the mental health needs of the poor had been ignored, community mental health programs were formulated largely on the basis of ignorance rather than experience. Predictably, the high idealism, optimism, and enthusiasm that marked their birth were subsequently tempered by innumerable problems that surfaced during their implementation. While some mental health workers have been disillusioned, most are now more cautious, sober, and realistic concerning the potential of the movement. Some of the difficulties it has encountered will be touched on briefly.

There are two *ideological* problems. When a parent figuratively knocks on a clinician's door and says, "My child needs help," the clinician is being requested to intervene in the lives of parent and child. But when a mental health worker figuratively knocks on a parent's door and says, "You and your child

need help," the situation is different. On what basis does the worker have the right to make this statement; at what point does help become intrusiveness and a violation of privacy? The question is a particularly sensitive one in these days of heightened concern for the rights of minorities, and there have been court rulings that the community worker has no right to change a family's life-style in the name of mental health (Korchin, 1976).

The second ideological problem concerns the "different versus deficient" issue. The initial conceptualization of the poor was in terms of deficit—they were culturally deprived. Closer acquaintance revealed that this deficit model was not accurate, since the poor may have their own culture, which is different from that of mainstream America. But if the poor were merely different, would this not undermine the basis for trying to change them? Our democracy was founded on respect for diversity. Why then should not American society accommodate to the culture of lower-class blacks, for example, rather than trying to homogenize them? The question has no easy answer. All concerned parents might agree on certain issues: a child should not suffer from sickness or malnutrition or brutality or neglect. But regardless of a certain fundamental agreement, the line between "disadvantage" and "stylistic difference" in child rearing is not clear. At what point does openness in expressing feeling become bewildering parental inconsistency? At what point does an extended family shade into inadequate love and care from adults?

The community mental health movement has met *resistances* at both the individual and the social levels. The assumption that the poor were thirsting to become middle class proved naive; there were many who saw no reason to exchange lower-class "soul" for middle-class "success." The well-intentioned mental health worker also has had to contend with the poor's suspicions born of many years of being treated with indifference, disrespect, and contempt. In the volatile 1960s it was not unknown for the community worker to become the target of the pent-up rage of the poor. Finally, the poor are often preoccupied with immediate problems of living—how to pay the rent, how to buy food and clothes—from which they rightfully want relief. And immediate relief of needs is at variance with prevention. It is difficult to convince a sorely beset mother that she should play games with her toddler because three years from now the child will do better in school.

Nor were institutions ripe for reform. While the ills of mental institutions might have originated in inadequate budgets and staff along with a depreciated social status, institutional organization and operation had been codified into rules and regulations which, for one reason or another, had been accepted as the way things were going to remain. Change was upsetting and intrusive. Other social institutions—the schools, the police, the hospitals, the courts—were also uncertain how much they wanted to go along with the new movement, and few wholeheartedly agreed to be the vehicle for realizing the mental health ideology.

In response to the urgent social needs in the 1960s, community mental health programs proliferated. As the crisis subsided, proven merit and *accountability* entered the picture. What was the evidence that the intended population was really being helped and, since federal money was often involved, that taxpayers were getting their money's worth? Many programs either lacked evaluation or were unsatisfactorily evaluated; still others failed to demonstrate significant improvement in the population served. Primary prevention of childhood psychopathologies has been particularly disappointing. In medicine, primary prevention works best when the etiologic factors are known and methods

of prevention are available. Neither of these conditions is met in a number of childhood psychopathologies, especially the severe ones such as schizophrenia and conduct disorders (Schwartz and Johnson, 1985). The situation in regard to proven effectiveness is better with early intervention, especially in the areas of preschool and school-based programs. While there are other programs with proven effectiveness, they tend to remain at the level of demonstration projects rather than having widespread use (Peterson and Roberts, 1986).

Aside from the urgent need for evaluation, intervention faces a number of obstacles. One is inherent in development itself. The fact that, over time, a certain percent of children will "grow out of" a disturbance and another percent will "grow into" the same disturbance means that there will be a degree of inefficiency in any intervention since it will be "wasted" on the former group and miss the latter. Even in the case of a relatively stable behavior such as aggression, the inefficiency might be appreciable. Inefficiency, in turn, is related to cost-effectiveness. If a condition were easy to remedy so that, for example, a series of television programs or school demonstrations would be sufficient, then remediation would be worthwhile. Yet, in most cases, more basic and costly remedial efforts are required. By what criteria and at what point could one decide that the effort was, or was not, worth the price in terms of both money and manpower? The question has no easy answer.

Next, there is a practical problem that affects the entire mental health venture. Both ideological and financial support at the federal and local levels has waxed and waned. In times of massive social unrest, as in the 1960s, programs are amply funded. Otherwise funding varies with economic conditions and the social philosophy of the political party in power. While certain features of community mental health have become part of the national scene, the movement is far from playing its envisioned role as the third revolution, a number of programs barely surviving much less expanding. Thus lobbying for government resources, the use of volunteer agencies, and perhaps enlisting assistance from private industry may be necessary to insure interventions for all children who could benefit from programs of proven effectiveness (Peterson and Roberts, 1986).

Children's Rights, Advocacy, and Political Action

The concern for *children's rights* arose from the recognition of children's helplessness when adults failed to discharge their responsibilities—in the brutally abusing home, in the court, in mental institutions. In 1970 the Joint Commission on the Mental Health of Children listed a set of rights that apply to all children: the right to be wanted, to be born healthy and live in a healthy environment, to obtain satisfaction of basic needs, to receive continuous loving care, to acquire the intellectual skills necessary to cope effectively with society, to receive appropriate care and treatment, and to be as close as possible to their normal setting. What had formerly been regarded as "needs" were thereby transformed into "rights."

In the case of child abuse, adjudication, and in some states, institutionalization, children's rights are enforced by laws. Whether more rights should have legal backing is a matter of debate. The rights of children must be weighed against those of parents and siblings, and the legal profession has traditionally been reluctant to intrude in family life except under the special conditions of divorce and custody litigation. The developmental dimension further complicates the picture, 13- to 18-year-olds being able to make decisions, such as receiving therapy, which would be meaningless for a child under 6

years of age. It may be that children's rights are too complex and individualized to be codified and implemented by lawyers and judges whose training includes little or nothing of child development. (For a more extended discussion, see Hayes, 1979.)

Another response to the "child as victim" has been *advocacy*. An advocate is a person who tries to insure that programs and services based on sound developmental knowledge are available to all children. Advocates perform diverse functions. Case advocacy is concerned that the individual child is appropriately treated by an agency: for example, an advocate might hear individual grievances, investigate, and render a judgment in a state training school for delinquents. Class action litigation is undertaken on behalf of a class of children who have been deprived of their constitutional rights, such as the case of handicapped children being excluded from public school or students suspended without due process. Monitoring involves watching the conduct of those serving children in order to hold the systems accountable for what happens; for example, seeing that judicial decisions are complied with and that funded agencies are implementing legislation. Legislative advocacy attempts to insure that statutory provisions serve the needs of children as well as protecting their rights (Knitzer, 1976).

It is clear that the community mental health movement has placed the clinical child psychologist and other mental health professionals in the *political arena*. One cannot strive to alter public policies and institutions, change laws, and accept federal, state, and local funds while avoiding politics. However, political activism has another root. Our actual record of achievements has for years belied our stance that we are a nation deeply concerned with the welfare of our children. The infant mortality rate, for example, is higher here than in thirteen other industrialized countries. The need for psychological care has been repeatedly documented and largely ignored. The 1978 President's Commission on Mental Health explicitly stated that mental health care for children and adolescents was inadequate or nonexistent, and that an alarming number of children suffer from indifference, neglect, and abuse. Drug and alcohol abuse and suicide rates among adolescents constitute major problems. Troubled children and adolescents, especially of racial minorities, are often shunted from one service to another, increasing their confusion and despair. While an estimated 90 percent of the 12 million disturbed children and adolescents do not receive appropriate services, federal funds were proposed (not appropriated) to serve only 15 percent, these being the psychotic, autistic, chronic, or "grossly maladaptive" children whose problems are most intractable. The children for whom intervention would probably be most fruitful were ignored. (For further details, see Cummings, 1979, and Tuma, 1989.) It is argued that one reason for national apathy is that children have no political constituencies; consequently, professionals along with concerned members of the community must spearhead the adoption of political measures on their behalf.

The nature and extent of political involvement remains a controversial issue. Clinicians who publicly opposed the Vietnam War as "bad for the mental health of children" or who advocate adopting a national guaranteed minimal income might be said to be dabbling in political and economic matters which lie beyond the realm of their expertise, while at the same time undermining their credibility in regard to psychological issues which fall within their province. At the other extreme conservative psychologists claim that we know far too little about developmental psychopathology even to attempt to shape national and local policy. Yet it can be argued that, whenever such policies are to be made, input from an experienced clinical child psychologist would probably be more valuable than input from most lawmakers.

Traditionally, clinical child psychologists have not been political activists. In the political arena, as in other aspects of community involvement, they are learning a new role without a clear mandate from colleagues as to what this role should be and with little or no formal training for it. Since there is every evidence that political involvement will become increasingly important, the clinical child psychologist, of necessity, will become more seasoned and skillful, as well as better trained for political encounters.

Summing Up

If the community mental health movement represents a third revolution, it is a revolution that will take decades to accomplish its goals. While not changing the direction of mental health care, it has had a significant impact on the etiologic theories of psychopathology, on attitudes toward and programs for the needy, as well as on prevention and remediation. It has added the essential and neglected ingredient of the societal context.

Child clinicians have much knowledge and skill to offer society and should be included as shapers of appropriate social policies; in turn, they have learned a great deal from their efforts to reach out and help the poor and racial minorities. There is every reason to believe that this mutual enhancement of the profession and of society will continue to characterize the community mental health movement.

Glossary

Abilities tests. Tests designed to evaluate abilities directly related to academic achievement.

Achievement tests. Tests designed to assess academic achievement.

Actualizing tendency. In Carl Rogers's theory, the inherent tendency for an organism to develop all of its capacities in ways that serve to maintain and enhance it.

Adjustment disorder. Deviant behavior that is a reaction to a specific event or events, such as parental death or divorce.

Advocacy. See *Child advocacy.*

Aggression. Behavior for which the goal is physical or psychological injury or destruction; anger or hatred may be the accompanying affect.

Anaclitic depression. The infant's reaction of despair following the loss of a loved and needed caretaker.

Anal stage. In Freud's psychosexual theory, the second stage of development, in which pleasure is derived from retaining and evacuating feces and the toddler confronts the issue of autonomy versus compliance.

Anorexia nervosa. A prolonged refusal to eat, often due to a fear of being obese and resulting in at least a 20 percent loss of body weight. *Restricters* rely on dieting; *bulimics* alternate between binge eating and dieting and rely on vomiting and purging.

Anoxia. Deprivation of oxygen during or immediately following birth; may cause damage to or destroy brain cells.

Anxiety. As used here, anxiety refers to the anticipation of a painful experience.

Anxiety disorders. See *Psychoneurotic disorders.*

Anxiety hysteria. See *Phobia.*

Anxiety neurosis. A state characterized by intense, diffuse anxiety, which may be "free floating." Also called anxiety type and overanxious disorder.

Anxiety type. See *Anxiety neurosis.*

Attachment. The bond of love that develops between infant and caretaker.

Attention-deficit hyperactivity disorder. Developmentally inappropriate inattention accompanied by motor restlessness and impulsivity.

Authoritarian discipline. Discipline requiring strict, unquestioning obedience.

Authoritative discipline. Discipline requiring compliance with standards for mature behavior, accompanied by love, communication, and respect for the child.

439

Autism. See *Early infantile autism.*

Avoidance learning. A form of learning in which an organism, having experienced an aversive stimulus, behaves so as to prevent future encounters with that stimulus.

Baseline. In behavioral assessment, the frequency of the natural occurrence of behavior targeted for change by behavioral techniques.

Behavior therapies. A group of therapies characterized by attention to specific, current behaviors; objective measurement; and reliance on principles of behavior change derived from the laboratory.

Behavioral assessment. Procedures designed to locate specific behaviors—along with their antecedents and consequences—that subsequently can serve as targets for modification through behavioral techniques.

Behaviorism. A theory inaugurated by John B. Watson according to which the study of overt behavior is the sole basis for a scientific psychology.

Brain syndrome (or *organic brain syndrome*). A group of disorders caused by impairment of brain tissue, particularly the cerebral cortex. They may be characterized by impairment of cognitive functions, lability of affect, and personality disturbances.

Bulimia. Recurring episodes of binge eating followed by vomiting and purging.

Castration anxiety. In Freud's psychosexual theory, the universal fear among preschool boys in the oedipal stage that the rivalrous father will emasculate them for wanting to possess the mother.

Central nervous system (CNS). The part of the nervous system that includes the spinal cord and the brain.

Chaining. See *Shaping.*

Child abuse. See *Physical abuse* and *Neglect.*

Child advocacy. The attempt to insure that programs and services based on sound developmental knowledge are available to all children.

Childhood schizophrenia. A psychosis appearing in middle childhood; characterized by marked withdrawal, bizarre thinking and behavior, loss of reality contact, and inappropriate affect. Also called schizophreniform psychotic disorder.

Client-centered therapy. See *Nondirective therapy.*

Coalition. Salvador Minuchin's term for a family pattern in which a child sides with one parent against the other.

Community mental health movement. The effort to eliminate the social conditions responsible for the production and perpetuation of mental health problems.

Compulsion. An irrational act that an individual is compelled to do.

Conditions of worth. Carl Rogers's term for conditions set by parents under which they will grant their love and respect for the child.

Conduct disorders. Behaviors in which children act out their feelings or impulses toward others in an antisocial or destructive fashion. Also called *undersocialized, aggressive type*, and *sociopath* or *psychopath*.

Conversion hysteria. See *Conversion type* (*of psychoneurotic disorder*).

Conversion type (*of psychoneurotic disorder*). Primarily, the loss or alteration of bodily function attributable to an internalized psychological conflict.

Corrective emotional experience. In psychoanalytic therapy, the discovery that expression of anxiety-laden feelings does not lead to punishment or rejection.

Critical period. The assumption that early experiences have disproportionately potent influence on later development.

Defense mechanisms. Stratagems for reducing anxiety. (See also *Repression, Reaction formation, Projection,* and *Displacement.*)

Delinquency. A legal term for offenses that are criminal if committed by an adult.

Delusion. A firmly held, irrational belief that runs counter to reality and to the individual's culture or subculture.

Depression. In its psychopathological form, depression is marked by a depressed mood, loss of self-esteem, intense self-deprecation, and guilt. Eating and sleeping disturbances as well as agitation may also occur.

Deprivation. See *Privation.*

Detachment. The final phase of an infant's reaction to the loss of a loved caretaker when socially acceptable but superficial contact is established when caretaker returns. Also called restitution.

Detouring. Salvador Minuchin's term for parents'

avoidance of their own conflicts by regarding their child as their sole problem.

Developmental crises. Crises inherent in normal development.

Diathesis-stress hypothesis. The hypothesis that abnormal behavior results from a genetic predisposition combined with environmental stress.

Displacement. A mechanism of defense in which an impulse is directed toward a target that is safer than the original one.

Dissociative hysteria. A psychopathology characterized by disturbances in consciousness, such as trances, personality disorganization (including multiple personalities), and odd motor expressions (including sleepwalking).

Double bind. A communication pattern that traps the recipient between two negative and inescapable injunctions. There is also a prohibition against drawing attention to the bind itself.

Down's syndrome. A form of mental retardation caused by a chromosomal abnormality and accompanied by distinctive physical features. (Once called mongolism.)

Drug abuse. A pattern of pathological use of a chemical substance causing significant impairment of functioning.

DSM-III. The third edition of the *Diagnostic and Statistical Manual,* a diagnostic classification system adopted by the American Psychiatric Association.

DSM-III-R. Revision of *DSM-III.*

Dysthymia. See *Depression.*

Early infantile autism (or *infantile autism*). A psychosis of infancy marked by extreme aloneness, a pathological need for sameness, and mutism or noncommunicative speech.

Ego. In Freud's structural theory, the psychic component responsible for learning the nature of reality in order to gratify the id's demands for maximal pleasure, on the one hand, and avoid the painful censure of the superego, on the other hand.

Egocentrism. In Jean Piaget's theory, the tendency to view the physical and social world exclusively from one's own point of view.

Ego ideal. In Freudian theory, the individual's idealized self-image.

Electra complex. The female counterpart of the Oedipus complex in the preschool girl; characterized by the desire to take possession of the father and eliminate the rivalrous mother.

Electroencephalogram (EEG). An instrument used to record electrical activity in the brain by means of electrodes attached to the scalp.

Encopresis. In children 3 years of age and older, withholding of feces and involuntary defecation not directly caused by physical disease.

Enmeshment. Salvador Minuchin's term for excessive involvement by individual members of a family with one another so that there is no strong sense of individuality.

Enuresis. Involuntary urination during the day or night in children 5 years of age or older.

Ethnic socialization. The process of acquiring the behavior, perceptions, values, and attitudes of an ethnic group and seeing the self and others as members of such groups.

Externalization. See *Internalization-externalization.*

Extinction. The gradual disappearance of a learned behavior through the removal of reinforcements.

Fading. In behavior therapy, the gradual removal of reinforcements so that the desired behavior may become autonomous.

Family therapies. A group of specific techniques based on the assumption that it is necessary to treat the entire family to correct the faulty pattern responsible for producing a disturbance in single members.

Fixation. The persistence of normal behavior beyond the point where it is developmentally appropriate. This arrest of development may be psychopathological, depending on the degree or intensity.

Fragmentation. A thought disorder in which tangentially related or unrelated ideas disrupt the chain of thought.

Free association. The basic psychoanalytic technique for uncovering unconscious material by encouraging the patient to say whatever comes to mind.

Functional disorder. A designation given to disturbances that are primarily psychological rather than primarily organic in origin.

GAP report. A diagnostic classification system devised especially for children by the Group for the Advancement of Psychiatry.

Gender identity. Self-classification as male or female.

Group therapies. Therapeutic techniques in which individuals work together to solve their problems through social interaction guided by a trained leader.

Guilt. The painful affect accompanying judgment of oneself as bad.

Habit disorders. Psychological disturbances centering on the social regulation of bodily functions, particularly eating and elimination.

Hallucination. A sensory perception occurring in the absence of any appropriate external stimulus.

Homosexuality. A preferential erotic attraction to members of the same sex.

Hyperactivity (or *hyperkinetic syndrome*). See *Attention-deficit hyperactivity disorder.*

Hysterical neurosis. A condition characterized by overly dramatic emotional expression, suggestibility, and a magical view of the world.

Id. In Freud's structural theory, the biologically based source of all psychic energy.

Identity. In Erik Erikson's theory, the search for inner continuity and interpersonal mutuality that begins in adolescence and is evidenced by a vocational choice.

Imitation (modeling). Learning by observing the behavior of others (models).

Induction discipline. Discipline based on reasoning and appeals to the child's pride and concern for others.

Information processing. The step-by-step conversion of sensory input into knowledge by means of operations such as attention, memory, organization, and retrieval.

Initiative. Self-reliant expansiveness.

Intelligence quotient (IQ). A measurement of intelligence derived from the relation between the child's mental age and chronological age.

Intelligence tests. Standardized techniques for measuring intellectual functioning.

Interactional psychotic disorder. See *Symbiotic psychosis.*

Internalization. The process by which behavior that was once dependent on environmental factors for its maintenance comes to be maintained by intraindividual factors.

Internalization-externalization. A classification of psychopathologies based on whether the child suffers (internalization) or the environment suffers (externalization).

Interpretation. In psychoanalytic therapy, interpretations consist of the therapist pointing out the meaning of material the patient is not aware of.

Intrasensory integration. The process of perceiving the equivalence of stimuli presented in different sense modalities.

La belle indifférence. A lack of concern for the physical symptoms resulting from a conversion hysteria.

Lateralization hypothesis. The hypothesis that the cerebrum undergoes progressive left-hemisphere specialization as language develops.

Learned helplessness. Nonresponsiveness to a noxious stimulus that has occurred independently of the organism's efforts to avoid it.

Learning disabilities. Learning problems due to a disorder in one or more of the basic psychological processes involved in understanding or in using spoken or written language and not due to mental retardation, emotional disturbance, environmental disadvantage, or specific perceptual or motor handicaps.

Lesbianism. Female homosexuality.

Libido. Freud's term for the biologically based drive to obtain erotic bodily sensations; also equated with sexual drive.

Mainstreaming. The term given to placing retardates in regular classes.

Marasmus. René Spitz's term for infants who waste away and sometimes die due to a lack of adequate mothering.

Masked depression. Underlying depression in children in middle childhood which is masked by a wide variety of deviant but nondepressive behaviors.

Medical model. A model of psychopathology emphasizing the role of organic dysfunction in the etiology of psychopathologies as well as classification and interpretation of psychopathological behaviors in terms of diagnostic entities.

Mental retardation. Significantly subaverage general intelligence and deficits in adaptive behavior; manifested during the developmental period.

Milieu therapy. A mode of treatment in which the daily environment is ordered so as to be therapeutic.

Minimal brain damage (or *minimal brain dysfunction*).

Term applied to children of average or above-average intelligence in whom deviations of function of the central nervous system are manifested by hyperactivity; perceptual-motor impairment; emotional lability; coordination deficits; disorders of attention, memory, thinking, and speech; and specific learning disabilities.

Modeling. See *Imitation.*

Multiaxial classification. Diagnostic system whereby individuals are assessed in terms of a number of dimensions rather than in terms of a single classification.

Mutism. Refusal to speak despite an ability to do so.

Negative reinforcement. Increasing the probability that behavior will occur by removing unpleasant or aversive consequences.

Negativism. A heightened state of opposition to adults which flourishes in the toddler and early preschool period.

Neglect. Acts of omission on the part of caretakers which endanger the child's health or safety.

Neurotic delinquent (or *neurotic personality disorder*). Behavior characterized by antisocial acts which are limited and repetitive, suggestive of a specific underlying conflict.

Nondirective therapy. Carl Rogers's therapeutic procedure, which utilizes warmth, acceptance, and reflection of the client's ideas and feelings to remove the obstacles to self-actualization. Also called client-centered therapy.

Object concept. In Jean Piaget's cognitive theory, the infant's separation of self from the physical world and the realization that objects have independent existence.

Object relation. In Freudian theory, the term used for an emotional attachment to another person.

Obsession. An irrational thought, the repeated occurrence of which is beyond the individual's conscious control.

Oedipus complex. In Freud's psychosexual theory, the universal desire of the preschool boy to take possession of the mother and eliminate the rivalrous father.

Omnipotent thinking. Belief that one can control events that, in reality, lie beyond one's power.

Operant conditioning (instrumental conditioning). A form of conditioning in which the persistence of a response depends on its effects on the environment.

Oppositional disorder. Purposeful defiance of adults' requests resulting in violation of minor rules. (See *Negativism.*)

Oral stage. In Freud's psychosexual theory, the first stage of development, in which pleasure is derived from sucking and biting and attachment to the caretaker is formed.

Organismic valuing process. In Carl Rogers's theory, the innate tendency for an organism to value experiences so as to optimize its development.

Overanxious disorder. See *Anxiety neurosis.*

Overinclusiveness. A thought disorder in which ideas flit from one tangential association to another.

Overprotection. Excessive and unrealistic concern over another's welfare.

Pediatric psychology. The study of the role of psychological factors in the origins, treatment, and prevention of physical disorders and the effects of such disorders on future development. Also called *behavioral medicine, behavioral pediatrics,* and *health psychology.*

Pedophilia. A state of being sexually aroused by children.

Permissive discipline. Indulgent or neglectful discipline.

Perseveration. A thought disorder in which the individual dwells on a single idea.

Personality disorders. Deeply ingrained, maladaptive behaviors that, while more pervasive than the psychoneuroses, still do not significantly diminish the individual's reality contact.

Personality inventories. Personality assessment technique in which a series of statements is judged as characteristic or not characteristic of the individual.

Phallic stage. In Freud's psychosexual theory, the third stage of development, in which the preschooler is expansive and assertive and derives pleasure from stimulating the genitals.

Phobia (or *phobic neurosis*). An intense, persistent, irrational fear of an animate or inanimate object or of a situation.

Physical abuse. Nonaccidental physical injury resulting from acts on the part of the child's caretakers.

Pica. The ingestion of substances not ordinarily considered edible.

Play therapy. Using play to encourage the child to express important ideas, conflicts, and feelings symbolically rather than through direct verbal communication. The procedure depends on the kind of psychotherapy being used, such as psychoanalytic or nondirective.

Positive reinforcement. Use of rewards to increase the probability that behavior will occur.

Precausal thinking. In Jean Piaget's theory, the tendency to view the physical world in animistic terms, as having life and purpose, for example.

Preconscious. In Freudian theory, the region of the mind that contains material that is not conscious but can be brought into consciousness.

Prevention. The emphasis in the community mental health movement on forestalling the development of mental health problems rather than on treating them after they have appeared. *Primary prevention* averts the appearance of psychopathology; *secondary prevention* involves early diagnosis and prompt treatment to shorten its duration; and *tertiary prevention* maximizes the psychological functioning of those with irreversible psychopathologies.

Primary-process thinking. In Freudian theory, unrealistic thinking based on immediate need gratification rather than on reality.

Privation. A lack of growth-promoting stimulation from the social and physical environment. Privation refers to infants who never had such stimulation; *deprivation* implies that such stimulation was available but was withdrawn.

Process schizophrenia. Schizophrenia characterized by a long, gradual onset.

Projection. A mechanism of defense in which anxiety-provoking impulses are denied in oneself and attributed to others.

Projective techniques. Personality assessment methods using ambiguous or unstructured stimuli. The most popular are the Rorschach, consisting of a series of ink blots; the Thematic Apperception Test (TAT), consisting of a series of ambiguous pictures; and human figure drawing.

Prompting. In operant conditioning, the use of instructions, modeling, or guidance to elicit a desired response.

Pseudo-mutuality. L. C. Wynne's term for a facade of harmony used by families to cover pervasive feelings of futility.

Pseudoneurotic. According to Lauretta Bender, a basically schizophrenic school-age child who presents a number of neurotic symptoms.

Pseudopsychopathic. According to Lauretta Bender, a basically schizophrenic school-age child who presents a number of acting-out symptoms.

Psychoactive drugs. Drugs that affect the central nervous system so as to alter subjective states of feeling.

Psychoanalysis. A psychotherapeutic technique relying upon free association, dream interpretation, play, and the analysis of resistance and transference to provide insights into the unconscious roots of disturbed behavior.

Psychodynamic theory. The Freudian and neo-Freudian theories that aim to understand the basic motivations of human behavior. Both emotions and unconscious motivations play a major role.

Psychoneurotic disorders (anxiety disorders). A group of disturbances characterized by intense, chronic anxiety.

Psychopathology. Abnormal behavior that may have psychological and/or biological causes. As used here, psychopathology is synonymous with abnormality, deviance, and psychological disturbance.

Psychophysiological disorders. Physical symptoms arising from the dysfunction of and structural damage to an organ caused primarily by prolonged psychological and social stress.

Psychosexual theory. Freud's developmental theory in which each stage—the oral, anal, and phallic—is marked by a change in the source of erotic bodily sensations and a distinct personality development.

Psychosis. A disorder so severe and pervasive as to interfere with the individual's capacity to meet the ordinary demands of life.

Psychosomatic disorders. Physical disorders presumed to be caused in part by psychological factors.

Punishment. Presentation of an aversive stimulus which decreases the probability that the response leading to it will occur.

Rational emotive therapy. Albert Ellis's cognitive restructuring therapy, in which the client is helped to identify and correct irrational ideas responsible for disturbed behavior.

Reaction formation. A mechanism of defense in which a child's thoughts and feelings are diametrically opposed to an anxiety-provoking impulse.

Reactive schizophrenia. Schizophrenia that appears suddenly, often in reaction to a specific traumatic event.

Reading disability. Failure to learn to read or to make appropriate progress despite normal intelligence and adequate instruction.

Reciprocal inhibition. The inhibition of the weaker of two incompatible responses by the stronger one. Utilized in systematic desensitization.

Regression. The return of behaviors that once were developmentally appropriate but no longer are. Whether or not the behaviors are psychopathological depends on the degree or intensity of regression.

Reinforcer. Any stimulus that increases the probability of a response.

Reliability. The consistency with which an assessment instrument performs.

Repression. The basic mechanism of defense in which anxiety-provoking impulses and ideas are banished from consciousness.

Resistance. In psychoanalytic therapy, devices used by patients to avoid bringing painful material to consciousness.

Restitution. See *Detachment.*

Rigidity. Excessive and unrealistic resistance to change.

Rorschach. See *Projective techniques.*

Schismatic family. Theodore Lidz's term for families which are characterized by overt conflict between parents, mutual depreciation, and competition for the child's loyalty.

School phobia. An irrational dread of school. Also called school refusal.

Self-actualization. See *Actualizing tendency.*

Self-control. The ability of the child to behave in a socially acceptable rather than a socially unacceptable manner when the two are in conflict.

Self-instruction. A behavioral therapy designed to increase self-control by teaching impulsive children how to guide their behavior by first talking out loud and then to themselves.

Separation anxiety. The anxiety engendered by the caretaker's departure after an attachment has been formed in infancy.

Separation-individuation. Margaret Mahler's term for the toddler's healthy assertion of autonomy in relation to the mother.

Sex role. Culturally approved behaviors and attitudes for males and females.

Sexual abuse. Sexual activities between a child under 17 years of age and an individual at least 5 years his or her senior.

Shaping. An operant-conditioning technique in which responses that successively approximate the desired one are reinforced.

Situational crises. Crises that, while not inherent in normal development, are frequently encountered and are typically weathered.

Skewed family. Theodore Lidz's term for families in which the mother is dominating and overprotective and the father is weak and passive.

Socialized, aggressive conduct disorder. See *Subcultural delinquency.*

Soft neurological signs. A group of behavioral criteria from which, in the absence of demonstrable impairment, minimal CNS dysfunction is inferred.

Stage theories. Theories that assume that development proceeds by qualitatively distinct reorganizations of behavior and that the sequence of such reorganizations is invariant.

Status offense. Behavior regarded as illegal in children but not in adults, such as drinking alcoholic beverages.

Stimulus generalization. The tendency of an organism, conditioned to a particular stimulus, subsequently to respond to similar stimuli.

Subcultural delinquency. Antisocial behavior resulting from conformity to familial or group standards that deviate from society's standard. Also called socialized, aggressive conduct disorder.

Substance abuse. See *Drug abuse.*

Superego. The moral component, or conscience, in Freud's structural theory. Initially, it is perfectionistic, requiring absolute obedience and punishing transgressions with guilt feelings.

Symbiosis. The interdependence and mutual enhancement of mother and infant.

Symbiotic psychosis. An early psychosis evidenced by intense separation anxiety, extreme ambivalence toward the mother, and fragmented speech. Also called interactional psychotic disorder.

Symptom. A psychological, behavioral, or biological manifestation of a disorder or illness.

Syndrome. A group of behaviors or symptoms which tend to occur together in a particular disorder.

Systematic desensitization. A behavior therapy for extinguishing anxiety by pairing a graded series of anxiety stimuli with the incompatible response of relaxation.

Thematic Apperception Test (TAT). See *Projective techniques.*

Therapeutic alliance. In psychoanalytic therapy, the positive bond between patient and therapist.

Time out. In behavior therapy, isolating the child for brief periods in order to extinguish undesirable behaviors.

Token economy. A behavioral therapy in which socially desirable behavior is rewarded by tokens that can subsequently be exchanged for rewards of the client's choosing.

Transference. In psychoanalytic therapy, the projection onto the therapist of intense feelings once directed toward significant figures, typically the parents.

Transsexualism. Gender identity with the opposite sex.

Transvestism. Obtaining sexual gratification by dressing in the clothes of the opposite sex.

Triangulation. Salvador Minuchin's term for a family pattern in which the child is forced to side with one parent against the other.

Unconditional positive regard. In Carl Rogers's theory, the parents' intrinsic valuing and acceptance of the child.

Unconscious. In Freudian theory, the region of the mind that contains material that has been repressed or has never been conscious.

Validity. The degree to which an instrument evaluates what it intends to evaluate.

Work. The ability to do what is required to be done; task orientation.

Working through. In psychoanalytic therapy, the process by which the patient gains insight into the many ways in which a single conflict is expressed.

Bibliography

Aboud, F. E. 1987. The development of ethnic self-identification and attitudes. In J. S. Phinney and M. J. Rotheram (eds.), *Children's ethnic socialization: Pluralism and development*, pp. 32–55. Newbury Park, Calif.: Sage Publications.

Abramowitz, R. 1976. Parenthood in America. *Journal of Clinical Child Psychology* **5,** 43–46.

Abramson, L. Y., and Sackeim, H. A. 1977. A paradox in depression: Uncontrollability and self-blame. *Psychological Bulletin* **84,** 838–851.

Abramson, L. Y., Seligman, M. E. P., and Teasdale, J. D. 1978. Learned helplessness in humans: Critique and reformulation. *Journal of Abnormal Psychology* **87,** 49–74.

Achenbach, T. M. 1966. The classification of children's psychiatric symptoms: A factor-analytic study. *Psychological Monographs* **80** (7, whole no. 609).

Achenbach, T. M. 1978. Psychopathology of childhood: Research problems and issues. *Journal of Consulting and Clinical Psychology* **46,** 759–776.

Achenbach, T. M. 1979. The child behavior profile: An empirically-based system for assessing children's behavior problems and competencies. *International Journal of Mental Health* **7,** 24–42.

Achenbach, T. M. 1980. DSM-III in light of empirical research in the classification of child psychopathology. *Journal of the American Academy of Child Psychiatry* **19,** 395–412.

Achenbach, T. M. 1982. *Developmental psychopathology.* 2d ed. New York: Ronald Press.

Achenbach, T. M., and Edelbrock, C. S. 1978. The classification of child psychopathology: A review and analysis of empirical efforts. *Psychological Bulletin* **85,** 1275–1301.

Achenbach, T. M., and Edelbrock, C. S. 1981. Behavioral problems and competencies reported by parents of normal and disturbed children aged four through sixteen. *Monographs of the Society for Research in Child Development* **1** (46, series no. 188).

Achenbach, T. M., and Lewis, M. 1971. A proposed model for clinical research and its application to encopresis and enuresis. *Journal of the American Academy of Child Psychiatry* **10,** 535–554.

Achenbach, T. M., and McConaughy, S. H. 1987. Empirically based assessment of child and adolescent psychopathology. Practical applications. *Developmental Clinical Psychology and psychiatry* **13**. Newbury Park: Sage Publications.

Achenbach, T. M., McConaughy, S. H., and Howell, C. T. 1987. Child/adolescent behavioral and emotional problems: Implications of cross-informant correlations for situational specificity. *Psychological Bulletin* **101,** 213–232.

Adams, P. K. 1979. Psychoneuroses. In J. D. Noshpitz (ed.), *Basic handbook of child psychiatry.* Vol. 2, *Disturbances in development.* New York: Basic Books.

Adolinks. 1987. Risk factors for suicide attempts. **4,** No. 2.

Ainsworth, M. D. S. 1969. Object relations, dependency and attachment: A theoretical review of the mother-infant relationship. *Child Development* **40,** 969–1025.

Ainsworth, M. D. S. 1973. The development of the infant-mother attachment. In B. M. Caldwell and H. N. Ricciuti (eds.), *Review of child development research,* vol. 3. Chicago: University of Chicago Press.

Alexander F. 1950. *Psychosomatic medicine.* New York: W. W. Norton.

Alexander, J. 1976. How psychologists can help stop child abuse. *Journal of Clinical Child Psychology* **5,** 13–14.

American Psychiatric Association. 1980. *Diagnostic and statistical manual of mental disorders.* 3d ed. Washington, D.C.

American Psychiatric Association. 1987. *Diagnostic and statistical manual of mental disorders.* 3d ed., revised. Washington, D.C.

American Psychological Association. 1979. *Revised ethical standards of psychologists.* Washington, D.C.

Ansbacher, H. L., and Ansbacher, R. R. (eds.). 1956. *The individual psychology of Alfred Adler. A systematic presentation in selections from his writings.* New York: Harper & Row.

Anthony, E. J. 1987. Children at risk for psychosis growing up successfully. In E. J. Anthony and B. J. Cohler (eds.), *The invulnerable child,* pp. 147–184. New York: Guilford Press.

Anthony, E. J., and Gilpin, D. C. (eds.). 1976. *Three clinical faces of childhood.* New York: Spectrum.

Appleton, T., Clifton, R., and Goldberg, S. 1975. The development of behavioral competence in infancy. In F. D. Horowitz (ed.), *Review of child development research,* vol. 4. Chicago: University of Chicago Press.

Araji, S., and Finkelhor, D. 1986. Abusers: A review of the research. In D. Finkelhor (ed.), *A sourcebook of child sexual abuse,* pp. 89–118. Beverly Hills: Sage Publications.

Ariès, P. 1962. *Centuries of childhood.* R. Baldick, trans. New York: Vintage.

Askevold, F. 1983. What are the helpful factors in psychotherapy for anorexia nervosa? *International Journal of Eating Disorders* **2,** 193–198.

Atkinson, D. R., Morten, G., and Sue, D. W. (eds.). 1983. *Counseling American minorities: A cross-cultural perspective.* 2d ed. Dubuque, Iowa: William C. Brown.

Axeline, V. 1964. *Dibbs in search of self.* New York: Ballantine.

Axeline, V. 1969. *Play therapy.* New York: Ballantine.

Azar, S. T., and Wolfe, D. A. In press. Behavioral intervention with abusive families. In E. J. Mash and R. A. Barkley (eds.), *Behavioral treatment of childhood disorders.* New York: Guilford Press.

Bakwin, H., and Bakwin, R. M. 1972. *Behavior disorders in children.* 4th ed. Philadelphia: Saunders.

Baltaxe, C. A. M., and Simmons, J. Q. III. 1985. Prosodic development in normal and autistic children. In E. Schopler and G. B. Mesibov (eds.), *Communication problems in autism,* pp. 95–125. New York: Plenum.

Bandura, A. 1968. A social learning interpretation of psychological dysfunctions. In P. London and D. Rosenhan (eds.), *Foundation of abnormal psychology.* New York: Holt, Rinehart & Winston.

Bandura, A. 1969. *Principles of behavior modification.* New York: Holt, Rinehart & Winston.

Bandura, A. 1977. *Social learning theory.* Englewood Cliffs, N.J.: Prentice-Hall.

Bandura, A., and Walters, R. H. 1963. *Social learning and personality development.* New York: Holt, Rinehart & Winston.

Barkley, R. A. 1977. A review of stimulant drug research with hyperactive children. *Journal of Child Psychology and Psychiatry* 18, 137–165.

Barkley R. A. 1982. Guidelines for defining hyperactivity in children: Attention deficit disorder with hyperactivity. In B. B. Lahey and A. E. Kazdin (eds.), *Advances in clinical child psychology,* vol. 5, pp. 137–180. New York: Plenum.

Battle, E. S., and Lacey, B. 1972. A context for hyperactivity in children over time. *Child Development* 43, 757–773.

Bayley, N. 1969. *Bayley Scales of Infant Development manual.* New York: Psychological Corporation.

Beadle, K. R. 1979. Clinical interaction of verbal language, learning and behavior. *Journal of Clinical Child Psychology* 8, 201–205.

Beck, A. T., Sethi, B. B., and Tuthill, R. W. 1963. Childhood bereavement and adult depression. *Archives of General Psychiatry* 9, 295–302.

Beidel, D. C., and Turner, S. M. 1986. A critique of the theoretical bases of cognitive-behavioral theories and therapy. *Clinical Psychology Review* 6, 177–197.

Bell, A. P., and Weinberg, M. S. 1978. *Homosexualities. A study of diversity among men and women.* New York: Simon & Schuster.

Bell, A. P., Weinberg, M. S., and Hammersmith, S. K. 1981. *Sexual preference: Its development in men and women.* Bloomington: Indiana University Press.

Bellak, L. 1954. *The Thematic Apperception Test and the Children's Apperception Test in clinical use.* New York: Grune & Stratton.

Belmont, L. 1980. Epidemiology. In H. E. Rie and E. D. Rie (eds.), *Handbook of minimal brain dysfunctions: A critical view.* New York: Wiley.

Belsky, J. 1978. A theoretical analysis of child abuse remediation strategies. *Journal of Clinical Child Psychology* 7, 117–121.

Belsky, J. 1980. Child maltreatment: An ecological integration. *American Psychologist* 35, 320–335.

Bemis, K. M. 1978. Current approaches to the treatment and etiology of anorexia nervosa. *Psychological Bulletin* 85, 593–617.

Bender, L. 1947. Childhood schizophrenia: Clinical studies of 100 schizophrenic children. *American Journal of Orthopsychiatry* 17, 40–56.

Bender, L. 1957. Specific reading disability as a maturational lag. *Bulletin of the Orton Society* 7, 9–18.

Bender, L. 1962. *The Bender Visual Motor Gestalt Test for Children.* Los Angeles: Western Psychological Services.

Bender, L., and Faretra, G. 1972. The relationship between childhood schizophrenia and adult schizophrenia. In A. Kaplan (ed.), *Genetic factors in schizophrenia.* Springfield, Ill.: Charles C Thomas.

Benton Revised Visual Retention Test. 1974. San Antonio, Tex.: Psychological Corporation.

Bergin, A. E., and Lambert, M. J. 1978. The evaluation of therapeutic outcomes. In S. L. Garfield and A. E. Bergin (eds.), *Handbook of psychotherapy and behavioral change: An empirical analysis.* 2d ed. New York: Wiley.

Berkowitz, L. 1973. Control of aggression. In B. M. Caldwell and H. N. R. Ricciuti (eds.), *Review of child development research,* vol. 3. Chicago: University of Chicago Press.

Bernal, E. M. 1989. Increasing the interpretative validity and diagnostic utility of Hispanic children's scores on tests of achievement and intelligence. In F. C. Serafica, A. I. Schwebel, R. K. Russell, P. D. Isaac, and L. B. Myers (eds.), *Mental health of ethnic minorities.* New York: Praeger.

Bernal, M. E. 1989. Minority mental health curricula: Trends and issues. In F. C. Serafica, A. I. Schwebel, R. K. Russell, P. D. Isaac, and L. B. Myers (eds.), *Mental health of ethnic minorities.* New York: Praeger.

Berry, K., and Cook, V. J. 1980. Personality and behavior. In H. E. Rie and E. D. Rie (eds.), *Handbook of minimal brain dysfunctions: A critical view.* New York: Wiley.

Bibring, E. 1953. The mechanism of depression.

In P. Greenacre (ed.), *Affective disorders,* pp. 13–48. New York: Hallmark-Hubner.

Biller, H. B., and Davids, A. 1973. Parent–child relations, personality development and psychopathology. In A. Davids (ed.), *Issues in abnormal child psychology.* Monterey, Calif.: Brooks/Cole.

Binet, A., and Simon, T. 1916. *The development of intelligence in children.* Baltimore: Williams & Wilkins.

Birch, H. G. 1964. The problem of "brain damage" in children. In H. G. Birch (ed.), *Brain damage in children: The biological and social aspects.* Baltimore: Williams & Wilkins.

Blank, M., Weider, S., and Bridger, W. H. 1968. Verbal deficiencies in abstract thinking in early reading retardation. *American Journal of Orthopsychiatry* **38,** 823–834.

Bleuler, M. 1974. The offsprings of schizophrenics. *Schizophrenia Bulletin* **8,** 93–107.

Block, J., and Haan, N. 1971. *Lives through time.* Berkeley, Calif.: Bancroft.

Bootzin, R. R., and Acocella, J. R. 1988. *Abnormal psychology: Current perspectives.* 5th ed. New York: Random House.

Borkowski, J. G., Peck, V. A., and Damberg, P. R. 1983. Attention, memory, and cognition. In J. L. Matson, and J. A. Mulick (eds.), *Handbook of mental retardation,* pp. 479–498. New York: Pergamon Press.

Bowlby, J. 1960. *The psychoanalytic study of the child.* Vol. 15, *Grief and mourning in infancy and early childhood.* New York: International Universities Press.

Bowlby, J. 1973. *Attachment and loss.* Vol. 2, *Separation: Anxiety and anger.* New York: Basic Books.

Bowlby J. 1980. *Attachment and loss.* Vol. 3, *Loss, sadness and depression.* New York: Basic Books.

Brackbill, Y. 1958. Extinction of the smiling response in infants as a function of reinforcement schedule. *Child Development* **29,** 115–124.

Brazelton, T. B. 1963. *Neonatal Behavioral Assessment Scale.* Philadelphia: Lippincott.

Breslow L., and Cowan, A. 1984. Structural and functional perspectives in classification and ser-iation in psychotic and normal children. *Child Development* **55,** 226–235.

Bretherton I. 1985. Attachment theory: Retrospect and prospect. In I. Bretherton, and E. Waters (eds.), Growing points in attachment theory and research, pp. 3–38. *Monographs of the Society for Research in Child Development* **50** (1–2, series no. 209).

Bretherton, I., and Waters, E. (eds.). 1985. Growing points in attachment theory and research. *Monographs of the Society for Research in Child Development* **50** (1–2, series no. 209).

Bronfenbrenner, U. 1977. Toward an experimental ecology of human development. *American Psychologist* **32,** 513–531.

Brown, G. W., Harris, T.O., and Bifulco, A. 1986. Long-term effects of early loss of parent. In M. Rutter, C. E. Izard, and P. B. Read (eds.), *Depression in young people: Developmental and clinical perspectives,* pp. 251–296. New York: Guilford Press.

Brown, R. T., and Borden, K. A. 1986. Hyperactivity at adolescence: Some misconceptions and new directions. *Journal of Clinical Child Psychology* **15,** 194–209.

Browne, A., and Finkelhor, D. 1986. Initial and long-term effects: A review of the research. In D. Finkelhor (ed.), *A sourcebook of child sexual abuse,* pp. 143–179. Beverly Hills: Sage Publications.

Bruch, H. 1973. *Eating disorders: Obesity, anorexia nervosa, and the person within.* New York: Basic Books.

Bruck, M. 1987. Social and emotional adjustments of learning-disabled children: A review of the issues. In S. J. Ceci (ed.), *Handbook of cognitive, social and neuropsychological aspects of learning disabilities,* vol. 1, pp. 361–380. Hillsdale, N.J.: Lawrence Erlbaum Associates.

Bryan, T., and Pearl, R. 1979. Self-concepts and locus of control in children with learning disabilities. *Journal of Clinical Child Psychology* **8,** 223–226.

Buros, O. K. (ed.). 1978. *The eighth mental measurements yearbook,* vols. 1 and 2. Highland Park, N.J.: Gryphon.

Bush, P. J., and Iannotti, R. J. 1985. The development of children's health orientations and behaviors: Lessons for substance use prevention. In C. L. Jones, and R. J. Battjes (eds.), *Etiology of drug abuse: Implications for prevention*, pp. 45–74. NIDA Research Monograph 56. Rockville, Md.: National Institute on Drug Abuse.

Buss, D. M., Block, J. H., and Block, J. 1980. Preschool activity level: Personality correlates and developmental implications. *Child Development* **51**, 401–408.

Calhoun, J. F., Acocella, J. R., and Goodstein, L. D. 1977. *Abnormal psychology: Current perspectives*. New York: Random House.

Callner, D. A. 1975. Behavioral treatment approaches to drug abuse: A critical review of the research. *Psychological Bulletin* **82**, 143–164.

Camp, B. W. 1977. Verbal mediation in young aggressive boys. *Journal of Abnormal Psychology* **86**, 145–153.

Campbell, S. B., Breaux, A. M., Ewing, L. J., and Szumowski, E. K. 1986. Correlates and predictors of hyperactivity and aggression: A longitudinal study of parent-referred problem preschoolers. *Journal of Abnormal Child Psychology* **14**, 217–234.

Campbell, S. B., Douglas, V. I., and Morgenstern, G. 1971. Cognitive style in hyperactive children and the effect of methylphenidate. *Journal of Child Psychology and Psychiatry* **12**, 55–67.

Campbell, S. B., Endman, M. W., and Bernfeld, G. 1977. A three-year follow-up of hyperactive preschoolers into elementary school. *Journal of Child Psychology and Psychiatry* **18**, 239–249.

Campbell, S. B., and Paulauskas, S. 1979. Peer relations in hyperactive children. *Journal of Child Psychology and Psychiatry* **20**, 233–246.

Campbell, S. B., and Werry, J. S. 1986. Attention deficit disorder (hyperactivity). In H. C. Quay, and J. S. Werry (eds.), *Psychological disorders of childhood*. 3d ed., pp. 111–155. New York: Wiley.

Cantwell, D. P. 1980. The diagnostic process and diagnostic classification in child psychiatry: DSM-III. *Journal of the American Academy of Child Psychiatry* **19**, 345–355.

Carlson, C. L., Figueroa, R. G., and Lahey, B. B. 1986. Behavior therapy for childhood anxiety disorders. In R. Gittelman (ed.), *Anxiety disorders of childhood*, pp. 204–232. New York: Guilford Press.

Carlson, C. L., Lahey B. B., and Neeper, R. 1984. Peer assessment of the social behavior of accepted, rejected and neglected children. *Journal of Abnormal Child Psychology* **12**, 187–198.

Carlson, G. A., and Cantwell, D. P. 1980. A survey of depressive symptoms, syndrome, and disorder in a child psychiatric population. *Journal of Child Psychology and Psychiatry* **21**, 19–25.

Carlson, G. A., and Garber, J. 1986. Developmental issues in the classification of depression in children. In M. Rutter, C. E. Izard, and P. B. Read (eds.), *Depression in young people: Developmental and clinical perspectives*, pp. 339–434. New York: Guilford Press.

Carr, J. 1975. *Young children with Down's syndrome: Their development, upbringing and effect on their families*. London: Butterworth.

Casey, R. J., and Berman, J. S. 1985. The outcome of psychotherapy with children. *Psychological Bulletin* **98**, 388–400.

Cass, L. K., and Thomas, C. B. 1979. *Childhood pathology and later adjustment: The question of prediction*. New York: Wiley.

Ceci, S. J., and Baker, J. C. 1987. How shall we conceptualize the language problems of learning-disabled children? In S. J. Ceci (ed.), *Handbook of cognitive, social and neuropsychological aspects of learning disabilities*, vol. 2, pp. 103–114. Hillsdale, N.J.: Lawrence Erlbaum Associates.

Chadwick, O., and Rutter, M. 1983. Neuropsychological assessment. In M. Rutter (ed.), *Developmental neuropsychiatry*, pp. 181–212. New York: Guilford Press.

Chandler, M. J. 1973. Egocentrism and antisocial behavior: The assessment and training of social perspective-taking skills. *Developmental Psychology* **9**, 326–332.

Chess, S. 1971. Autism in children with congenital rubella. *Journal of Autism and Childhood Schizophrenia* **1**, 33–47.

Children and the law. 1978. *Journal of Clinical Child Psychology* **7.**

Cicchetti, D., and Schneider-Rosen, K. 1986. An organizational approach to childhood depression. In M. Rutter, C. E. Izard, and P. B. Read (eds.), *Depression in young people: Developmental and clinical perspectives,* pp. 71–134. New York: Guilford Press.

Ciminero, A. R. 1977. Behavioral assessment: An overview. In A. R. Ciminero, K. S. Calhoun, and H. E. Adams (eds.), *The handbook of behavioral assessment.* New York: Wiley.

Clarke, A. M., and Clarke, A. D. B. 1977. *Early experience: Myth and evidence.* New York: Free Press.

Cohler, B. J. 1987. Adversity, resilience, and the study of lives. In E. J. Anthony and B. J. Cohler (eds.), *The invulnerable child* (pp. 363–424). New York: Guilford Press.

Coleman, J. C. 1980. Friendship and the peer group in adolescence. In J. Adelson (ed.), *Handbook of adolescent psychology.* New York: Wiley.

Corah, N. L., Anthony, E. J., Painter, P., Stern, J. A., and Thurston, D. 1965. Effects of perinatal anoxia after seven years. *Psychological Monographs* **79** (3, whole no. 596).

Coulter, W. A., and Morrow, H. W. (eds.). 1978. *Adaptive behavior. Concepts and measurements.* New York: Grune & Stratton.

Cross, W. E. Jr. 1987. A two-factory theory of black identity: Implications for the study of identity development in minority children. In J. S. Phinney, and M. J. Rotheram (eds.), *Children's ethnic socialization. Pluralism and development,* pp. 117–133. Newbury Park, Calif.: Sage Publications.

Cummings, N. A. 1979. Funding for children's services. *American Psychologist* **34,** 1037–1039.

Davis, C. M. 1929. Self selection of diet by newly weaned infants. *American Journal of Diseases of Children* **36,** 651–679.

Davis, C. M. 1935. Choice of formulas made by three infants throughout the nursing period. *American Journal of Diseases of Children* **50,** 385–394.

de Hirsch, K., Jansky, J., and Langford, W. 1966. *Predicting reading failure: A preliminary study of reading, writing, and spelling disabilities in preschool children.* New York: Harper & Row.

Delamater, A. M. 1986. Psychological aspects of diabetes mellitus in children. In B. B. Lahey, and A. E. Kazdin (eds.), *Advances in clinical child psychology,* vol. 9, pp. 333–376. New York: Plenum Press.

de Mause, L. (ed.). 1974. *The history of childhood.* New York: Psychohistory Press.

DeMyer, M. 1976. The nature of the neuropsychological disability in autistic children. In E. Schopler and R. J. Reichler (eds.), *Psychopathology and child development.* New York: Plenum Press.

Diaz-Guerrero, R. 1987. Historical sociocultural premises and ethnic socialization. In J. S. Phinney and M. J. Rotheram (eds.), *Children's ethnic socialization: Pluralism and development,* pp. 239–250. Newbury Park, Calif.: Sage Publications.

Digdon, N., and Gotlib, I. H. 1985. Developmental considerations in the study of childhood depression. *Developmental Review* **5,** 162–199.

Doane, J. A. 1978. Family interaction and communication deviance in disturbed and normal families: A review of research. *Family Process* **17,** 357–376.

Dodge, K. A., and Frame, C. L. 1982. Social cognitive biases and deficits in aggressive boys. *Child Development* **53,** 620–635.

Doehring, D. G., and Hoshko, I. M. 1977. Classification of reading problems by the Q-technique of factor analysis. *Cortex* **13**(3), 281–294.

Doleys, D. M. 1977. Behavioral treatments for nocturnal enuresis in children: A review of the recent literature. *Psychological Bulletin* **84,** 30–54.

Dorner, G., Geier, T., Ahrens, L., Krell, L., Munx, G., Sieler, H., Kittner, E., and Muller, H. 1980. Prenatal stress and possible aetiogenetic factor homosexuality in human males. *Endokrinologie* **75,** 365–368.

Douglas, V. I. 1980. Treatment and training approaches to hyperactivity: Establishing internal or external control? In C. K. Whalen and B. Henker (eds.), *Hyperactive children: The social ecology of identification and treatment.* New York: Academic Press.

Douglas, V. I. 1983. Attention and cognitive problems. In M. Rutter (ed.), *Developmental neuropsychiatry,* pp. 280–329. New York: Guilford Press.

Douglas, V. I., and Peters, K. G. 1980. Toward a clearer definition of the attentional deficit of hyperactive children. In G. A. Hale and M. Lewis (eds.), *Attention and the development of cognitive skills.* New York: Plenum Press.

Dudley-Marling, C. C., and Edmiaston, R. 1985. Social status of learning-disabled children and adolescents: A review. *Learning Disabilities Quarterly* **8,** 189–204.

Dunn, L. M. 1965. *Expanded manual for the Peabody Picture Vocabulary Test.* Minneapolis: American Guidance Service.

Dweck, C. S., and Slaby, R. G. 1983. Achievement motivation. In P. H. Mussen (ed.), *Handbook of child psychology.* 4th ed., vol. 4, pp. 643–692. New York: Wiley.

Edelbrock, C., and Achenbach, T. M. 1980. A typology of child behavior profile patterns: Distribution and correlates for disturbed children aged 6–16. *Journal of Abnormal Child Psychology* **8,** 441–470.

Egeland, B., Sroufe, L. A., and Erickson, M. 1984. The developmental consequences of different patterns of maltreatment. *International Journal of Child Abuse* **7,** 459–469.

Eisenberg, N., and Miller, P. A. 1987. The relation of empathy to prosocial and related behaviors. *Psychological Bulletin* **101,** 91–119.

Elkind, D. 1976. Cognitive development and psychopathology: Observations on egocentrism and ego defense. In E. Schopler and R. J. Reichler (eds.), *Psychopathology and child development: Research and treatment.* New York: Plenum Press.

Ellis, A. 1970. *The essence of rational psychotherapy: A comprehensive approach to treatment.* New York: Institute for Rational Living.

Ellis, L., and Ames, M. A. 1987. Neurohormonal functioning and sexual orientation: A theory of homosexuality–heterosexuality. *Psychological Bulletin* **101,** 233–258.

Elmer, E., Evans, S., and Reinhart, J. B. *Fragile families, troubled children.* Pittsburgh: University of Pittsburgh Press.

Emde, R. N., Katz, E. L., and Thorpe, J. K. 1978. Emotional expression in infancy. Early deviation in Down's syndrome. In M. Lewis and L. A. Rosenblum (eds.), *The development of affect.* New York: Plenum Press.

Epstein, L. H., and Wing, R. R. 1987. Behavioral treatment of childhood obesity. *Psychological Bulletin* **101,** 331–342.

Erikson, E. 1950. *Childhood and society.* New York: Norton.

Erikson, E. 1968. *Identity: Youth and crisis.* New York: Norton.

Escalona, S. 1948. Some considerations regarding psychotherapy for psychotic children. *Bulletin of the Menninger Clinic* **2,** 126–134.

Essen, J., and Peckham, C. 1976. Nocturnal enuresis in childhood. *Developmental Medicine and Child Neurology* **18,** 577–589.

Etaugh, C. 1980. Effects of nonmaternal care on children: Research evidence and popular views. *American Psychologist* **35,** 309–319.

Evans, I. M., and Nelson, R. O. 1977. Assessment of child behavior problems. In A. R. Ciminero, K. S. Calhoun, and H. E. Adams (eds.), *Handbook of behavioral assessment.* New York: Wiley.

Exner, J. E. 1974. *The Rorschach: A comprehensive system,* vol. 1. New York: Wiley.

Exner, J. E. 1978. *The Rorschach: A comprehensive approach,* vol. 2. Current Research and Advanced Interpretation. New York: Wiley.

Exner, J. E., and Weiner, I. 1982. *The Rorschach: A Comprehensive System,* vol. 3. Assessment of Children and Adolescence. New York: Wiley.

Eysenck, H. J. 1952. The effects of psychotherapy: An evaluation. *Journal of Consulting Psychology* **16,** 319–324.

Eysenck, H. J. 1960. *Handbook of abnormal psychology.* London: Pittman.

Farrington, D. P. 1986. The sociocultural context of childhood disorders. In H. C. Quay and J. S. Werry (eds.), *Psychopathological disorders of childhood*, 2d ed., pp. 391–422. New York: Wiley.

Fein, D., Humes, M., Kaplan, E., Lucci, D., and Waterhouse, L. 1984. The question of left hemisphere dysfunction in infantile autism. *Psychological Bulletin* **95**, 258–281.

Ferster, C. B., and DeMyer, M. K. 1962. A method for the experimental analysis of the behavior of autistic children. *American Journal of Orthopsychiatry* **32**, 89–98.

Fincham, F. D., and Cain, K. M. 1986. Learned helplessness in humans: A developmental analysis. *Developmental Review* **6**, 301–333.

Finkelhor, D. (ed.). 1986a. *A sourcebook of child sexual abuse*. Beverly Hills: Sage Publications.

Finkelhor, D. 1986b. Prevention: A review of programs and research. In D. Finkelhor (ed.), *A sourcebook of child sexual abuse*, pp. 224–254. Beverly Hills: Sage Publications.

Finkelhor, D., and Baron, L. 1986. High-risk children. In D. Finkelhor (ed.), *A sourcebook of child sexual abuse*, pp. 60–88. Beverly Hills: Sage Publications.

Finkelhor, D., and Browne, A. 1986. Initial and long-term effects: A conceptual framework. In D. Finkelhor (ed.), *A sourcebook of child sexual abuse*, pp. 180–198. Beverly Hills: Sage Publications.

Fish, B. 1971. Contributions of developmental research to a theory of schizophrenia. In J. Hellmuth (ed.), *Exceptional infant: Studies in abnormalities*. New York: Brunner/Mazel.

Fish, B. 1976. Biological disorders in infants at risk for schizophrenia. In E. R. Ritvo, B. Freeman, E. M. Ornitz, and P. E. Tanquay (eds.), *Autism: Diagnosis, current research, and management*. New York: Spectrum.

Fish, B. 1984. Characteristics and sequelae of the neurointegrative disorder in infants at risk for schizophrenia: 1952–1982. In N. F. Watt, E. J. Anthony, L. C. Wynne, and J. E. Rolf (eds.), *Children at risk for schizophrenia: A longitudinal perspective*, pp. 423–439. Cambridge: Cambridge University Press.

Fisher, S., and Greenberg, R. P. 1977. *The scientific credibility of Freud's theories and therapy*. New York: Basic Books.

Flavell, J. H. 1977. *Cognitive development*. Englewood Cliffs, N.J.: Prentice-Hall.

Foley, M. A., Johnson, M. K., and Raye, C. L. 1983. Age-related changes in confusion between memories for thought and memories for speech. *Child Development* **54**, 51–60.

Forehand, R. 1977. Child noncompliance to parental requests: Behavioral analysis and treatment. In M. Hersen, R. M. Eisler, and P. M. Miller (eds.), *Progress in behavior modification*, vol. 5, pp. 111–148. New York: Academic Press.

Fraiberg, S. 1977. *Insights from the blind: Comparative studies of blind and sighted infants*. New York: Basic Books.

Freedman, J. L. 1986. Television violence and aggression: A rejoinder. *Psychological Bulletin* **100**, 372–378.

Freud, A. 1946. *The ego and the mechanisms of defense*. New York: International Universities Press.

Freud, A. 1965. *Normality and pathology in childhood: Assessment of development*. New York: International Universities Press.

Freud, A., and Dann, S. 1951. An experiment in group upbringing. In R. S. Eisler, A. Freud, H. Hartmann, and E. Kris (eds.), *The psychoanalytic study of the child*, vol. 6. New York: International Universities Press.

Freud, S. 1953. Three essays on the theory of sexuality (1905). In *The standard edition of the complete psychological works of Sigmund Freud*, vol. 7. London: Hogarth Press.

Friedrich, W. N., and Boriskin, J. A. 1976. The role of the child in abuse: A review of the literature. *American Journal of Orthopsychiatry*, **46**, 580–590.

Frostig, M. 1972. Visual perception, integrative functions and academic learning. *Journal of Learning Disabilities* **5**, 1–15.

Furman, R. A. 1973. A child's capacity for mourning. In E. J. Anthony and C. Koupernik (eds.), *The child in his family: The impact of disease and death*, vol. 2. New York: Wiley.

Fyffe, C., and Prior, M. 1978. Evidence for language recording in autistic, retarded and normal children: A re-examination. *British Journal of Psychology* **69,** 393–402.

Gandour, M. J. 1984. Bulimia: Clinical description, assessment, etiology and treatment. *International Journal of Eating Disorders* **3,** 3–38.

Gard, G. C., and Berry, K. K. 1986. Oppositional children: Taming tyrants. *Journal of Clinical Child Psychology* **15,** 148–158.

Garfield, S. L., and Bergin, A. (eds.). 1978. *Handbook of psychotherapy and behavior change: An empirical analysis,* 2d ed. New York: Wiley.

Garfinkel, P. E., and Garner, D. M. 1982. *Anorexia nervosa: A multidimensional perspective.* New York: Brunner/Mazel.

Garfinkel, P. E., and Garner, D. M. 1986. Anorexia nervosa and adolescent mental health. In R. A. Feldman and A. R. Stiffman (eds.), *Advances in adolescent mental health,* vol. 1, part A, pp. 163–204. Greenwich, Conn.: JAI Press.

Garmezy, N. 1974. Children at risk: The search for antecedents of schizophrenia. Part II. Ongoing research programs, issues and intervention. *Schizophrenia Bulletin,* **9,** 55–125.

Garmezy, N. 1986. Developmental aspects of children's responses to the stress of separation and loss. In M. Rutter, C. E. Izard, and P. B. Read (eds.). *Depression in young people: Developmental and clinical perspectives,* pp. 297–324. New York: Guilford Press.

Garmezy, N., and Streitman, S. 1974. Children at risk: The search for antecedents of schizophrenia. Part I. Conceptual models and research methods. *Schizophrenia Bulletin* **8,** 14–90.

Garner, D. M., Garfinkel, P. E., and O'Shaughnessy, M. 1985. The validity of the distinction between bulimia with and without anorexia nervosa. *American Journal of Psychiatry* **142,** 581–587.

Gelfand, D. M., Jenson, W. R., and Drew, C. J. 1988. *Understanding child behavior disorders,* 2d ed. New York: Holt, Rinehart and Winston.

Gelman, R., and Baillargeon, R. 1983. A review of some Piagetian concepts. In P. H. Mussen (ed.), *Handbook of child psychology,* vol. III. J. H. Flavell and E. M. Markman (eds.). pp. 167–230. New York: Wiley.

Gelman, R., and Schatz, M. 1977. Appropriate speech adjustment. The operation of conversational constraints on talk of two year olds. In M. Lewis, and L. A. Rosenbaum (eds.), *Interaction, conversation and the development of language,* pp. 27–62. New York: Wiley.

Gendreau, P., and Ross, R. 1979. Effective correctional treatment: Bibliotherapy for cynics. *Crime and Delinquency,* **25,** 463–489.

George, C., and Main, M. 1980. Abused children: Their rejection of peers and caregivers. In T. M. Field (ed.), *High-risk infants and children: Adult and peer interactions.* New York: Academic Press.

Gesell, A., and Ilg, F. L. 1949. *Child development: An introduction to the study of human growth.* New York: Harper.

Gesell, A., Ilg, F. L., Ames, L. B., and Bullis, G. E. 1946. *The child from five to ten.* New York: Harper.

Gibbs, J. C. 1987. Social processes in delinquency: The need to facilitate empathy as well as sociomoral reasoning. In W. M. Kurtines and J. L. Gewirtz (eds.), *Moral development through social interaction,* pp. 296–316. New York: Wiley.

Gibson, D. 1978. *Down's syndrome. The psychology of mongolism.* Cambridge: Cambridge University Press.

Gittelman, R. 1983a. Hyperkinetic syndrome: Treatment issues and principles. In M. Rutter (ed.), *Developmental neuropsychiatry,* pp. 437–451. New York: Guilford Press.

Gittelman, R. 1983b. Treatment of reading disorders. In M. Rutter (ed.), *Developmental neuropsychiatry,* pp. 520–539. New York: Guilford Press.

Gittelman, R., and Kanner, A. 1986. Psychopharmacotherapy. In H. C. Quay and J. S. Werry (eds.), *Psychological disorders of childhood,* 3d ed., pp. 455–495. New York: Wiley.

Glaser, K. 1968. Masked depression in children and adolescents. *Annual Progress in Child Psychiatry and Child Development* **1,** 345–355.

Gold, M., and Petronio, R. J. 1980. Delinquent

behavior in adolescence. In J. Adelson (ed.), *Handbook of adolescent psychology.* New York: Wiley.

Goldenberg, I., and Goldenberg, H. 1980. *Family therapy: An overview.* Monterey, Calif.: Brooks/Cole.

Goldfarb, W. 1970. Childhood psychoses. In P. M. Mussen (ed.), *Carmichael's manual of child psychology,* vol. 2. New York: Wiley.

Goldstein, D., and Dundon, W. D. 1987. Affect and cognition in learning disabilities. In S. J. Ceci (ed.), *Handbook of cognitive, social and neuropsychological aspects of learning disabilities,* vol. 2, pp. 233–250. Hillsdale, N.J.: Lawrence Erlbaum Associates.

Golombok, S., Spencer, A., and Rutter, M. 1983. Children in lesbian and single-parent households: Psychosexual and psychiatric appraisal. *Journal of Child Psychology and Psychiatry* **24,** 551–572.

Gottesman, I. I. 1978. Schizophrenia and genetics: Where are we? Are you sure? In L. C. Wynne, R. L. Cromwell, and S. Matthysse (eds.), *The nature of schizophrenia: New approaches to research and treatment.* New York: Wiley.

Graham, F. K., Ernhart, C. B., Thurston, D., and Craft, M. 1962. Development three years after perinatal anoxia and other potentially damaging newborn experiences. *Psychological Monographs* **76,** (3, whole no. 522).

Gray Oral Reading Tests, Revised (GORT-R). 1986. Austin, Tex.: Pro-Ed.

Graziano, A. M., DeGiovanni, I. S., and Garcia, K. A. 1979. Behavioral treatment of childhood fears: A review. *Psychological Bulletin* **86,** 804–830.

Green, R. 1987. *The "sissy boy syndrome" and the development of homosexuality.* New Haven: Yale University Press.

Gregory, I. 1966. Retrospective data concerning childhood loss of a parent. *Archives of General Psychiatry* **15,** 362–367.

Gresham, F. M. 1986. Conceptual and definitional issues in the assessment of children's social skills: Implications for classification and training. *Journal of Clinical Child Psychology* **15,** 3–15.

Group for the Advancement of Psychiatry. 1966. *Psychopathological disorders in childhood: Theoretical considerations and a proposed classification,* vol. 6, no. 62.

Guralnick, M. J. 1986. The peer relations of young handicapped and non-handicapped children. In P. S. Strain, M. J. Guralnick, and H. M. Walker (eds.), *Children's social behavior: Development, assessment and modification,* pp. 93–140. New York: Academic Press.

Hall, C. S. 1904. *Adolescence.* New York: Appleton.

Harrison, A., Serafica, F., and McAdoo, H. 1982. Ethnic families of color. In R. D. Parke (ed.), *Review of child development research, vol. 7. The Family,* pp. 329–371. Chicago: The University of Chicago Press.

Halstead Neuropsychological Test Battery for Children. 1969. Indianapolis: Reitan.

Hare, E. H. 1962. Masturbatory insanity: The history of an idea. *Journal of Mental Science* **108,** 1–25.

Harter, S. 1983. Developmental perspective on the self-system. In P. H. Mussen (ed.), *Handbook of child psychology.* New York: Wiley.

Hartley, X. Y. 1986. A summary of recent research into the development of children with Down's syndrome. *Journal of Mental Deficiency Research* **30,** 1–14.

Hartman, H. 1964. *Essays on ego psychology.* New York: International Universities Press.

Hartup, W. W. 1983. Peer relations. In P. H. Mussen (ed.), *Handbook of child psychology,* vol. 4, 4th ed., pp. 103–196. New York: Wiley.

Harvey, J. H., and Weary, G. 1981. *Perspectives on attributional processes.* Dubuque, Iowa: William C. Brown.

Haswell, K. L., Hock, E., and Wenar, C. 1982. Techniques for dealing with oppositional behavior in preschool children. *Young Children,* March, pp. 13–18.

Hawkins, J. D., Lishner, D., and Catalano, Jr., R. F. 1985. Childhood predictors and the prevention of adolescent substance abuse. In C. L. Jones and R. J. Battjes (eds.), *Etiology of drug abuse: Implications for prevention*, pp. 75–126. NIDA Research Monograph 56. Rockville, Md.: National Institute on Drug Abuse.

Hawton, K. 1986. *Suicide and attempted suicide among children and adolescents.* Beverly Hills: Sage Publications.

Hayes, M. 1979. Rights of the child. In J. D. Noshpitz (ed.), *Basic handbook of child psychiatry.* Vol. 4, *Prevention and current issues.* New York: Basic Books.

Haywood, H. C., Meyers, C. E., and Switzky, H. N. 1982. Mental retardation. In M. R. Rosenzweig and L. W. Porter (eds.), *Annual review of psychology*, vol. 33, pp. 309–342. Palo Alto, Calif.: Annual Reviews.

Hazelrigg, M. D., Cooper, H. M., and Borduin, C. M. 1987. Evaluating the effectiveness of family therapies: An integrative review and analysis. *Psychological Bulletin* **101**, 428–442.

Heinicke, C. M. 1956. Some effects of separating two-year-old children from their parents: A comparative study. *Human Relations* **9**, 105–176.

Heinstein, M. I. 1963. Behavioral correlates of breast–bottle regimes under varying parent–infant relationships. *Monographs of the Society for Research in Child Development* **28** (4, serial no. 88).

Helper, M. M. 1980. Follow-up of children with minimal brain dysfunction: Outcomes and predictors. In H. E. Rie and E. D. Rie (eds.), *Handbook of minimal brain dysfunctions: A critical view.* New York: Wiley.

Herbert, M. 1974. *Emotional problems of development in children.* New York: Academic Press.

Hermelin, B. 1976. Coding and sense modalities. In L. Wing (ed.), *Early childhood autism: Clinical, educational and social aspects.* New York: Pergamon Press.

Hersov, L. 1977. Fecal soiling. In M. Rutter and L. Hersov (eds.), *Child psychiatry: Modern approaches.* Oxford: Blackwell Scientific Publications.

Hersov, L. A. 1960. Persistent non-attendance at school. *Journal of Child Psychology and Psychiatry* **1**, 130–136.

Herzog, E., and Sudia, C. E. 1973. Children in fatherless families. In B. E. Caldwell and H. N. Ricciuti (eds.), *Review of child development research*, vol. 3. Chicago: University of Chicago Press.

Hetherington, E. M., and Camara, K. A. 1984. Families in transition: The process of dissolution and reconstitution. In R. E. Parke (ed.), *Review of child development research*, vol. 7, pp. 398–440. Chicago: University of Chicago Press.

Hetherington, E. M., and Martin, B. 1986. Family interaction. In H. C. Quay and J. S. Werry (eds.), *Psychopathological disorders of childhood*, 3d ed. New York: Wiley.

Hetherington, E. M., and Parke, R. D. 1986. *Child psychology: A contemporary viewpoint*, 3d ed. New York: McGraw-Hill.

Hilgard, J. R., Newman, M. F., and Fisk, F. 1960. Strength of adult ego following childhood bereavement. *American Journal of Orthopsychiatry* **30**, 788–798.

Hinshaw, S. P. 1987. On the distinction between attentional deficits/hyperactivity and conduct problems/aggression in child psychopathology. *Psychological Bulletin* **101**, 443–463.

Hobson, R. P. 1982. The question of childhood egocentrism: The coordination of perspectives in relation to operational thinking. *Journal of Child Psychology and Psychiatry* **23**, 43–60.

Hobson, R. P. 1984. Early childhood autism and the question of egocentrism. *Journal of Autism and Developmental Disorders* **14**, 85–104.

Hobson, R. P. 1986a. The autistic child's appraisal of expressions of emotion. *Journal of Child Psychology and Psychiatry* **27**, 321–342.

Hobson, R. P. 1986b. The autistic child's appraisal of expression of emotions: A further study. *Journal of Child Psychology and Psychiatry* **27**, 671–680.

Hoffman, M. L. 1978. Toward a theory of empathetic arousal and development. In M. Lewis and L. A. Rosenblum (eds.), *The development of affect*, vol. 1, pp. 227–256. New York: Plenum.

Huelsman, C. B. 1970. The WISC subtest syndrome for disabled readers. *Perceptual and Motor Skills* **30**, 535–550.

Huesmann, L. R., Eron, L. D., Lefkowitz, M. M., and Walder, L. O. 1984. Stability of aggression over time and generation. *Developmental Psychology* **20**, 1120–1134.

Humphreys, L., Forehand, R., McMahon, R., and Roberts, M. 1978. Parent behavior training to modify child noncompliance: Effects on untreated siblings. *Journal of Behavior Therapy and Experimental Psychiatry* **9**, 235–238.

Huon, G. F., and Brown, L. B. 1986. Body image in anorexia nervosa and bulimia nervosa. *International Journal of Eating Disorders* **5**, 421–439.

Israel, A. C., Weinstein, J. B., and Prince, R. 1985. Eating behavior, eating styles and children's weight status: Failure to find an obese eating style. *International Journal of Eating Disorders* **4**, 113–119.

Izard, C. E., and Schwartz, G. M. 1986. Patterns of emotion in depression. In M. Rutter, C. E. Izard, and P. B. Read (eds.), *Depression in young people: Developmental and clinical perspectives*, pp. 33–70. New York: Guilford Press.

Jacob, T., and Grounds, L. 1978. Confusions and conclusions: A response to Doane. *Family Process* **17**, 377–387.

Jacobs, J. 1971. *Adolescent suicide.* New York: Wiley-Interscience.

Jacobson, E. 1964. *The self and the object world.* New York: International Universities Press.

Janis, I. L. (ed.). 1969. *Personality: Dynamics, development, and assessment.* New York: Harcourt Brace & World.

Jarvie, G. J., Lahey, B., Graziano, W., and Framer, E. 1983. Childhood obesity and social stigma: What we know and what we don't know. *Developmental Review* **3**, 237–273.

Jastak, J. F., and Jastak, S. R. 1978. *The Wide-Range Achievement Test*, rev. ed. Wilmington, Del.: Guidance Associates.

Jersild, A. T., and Holmes, F. B. 1935. *Children's fears.* Child Development, monograph no. 20. New York: Teachers' College, Columbia University.

Jessor, R. 1979. Marijuana: A review of recent psychosocial research. In R. I. Dupont, A. Goldstein, and J. O'Donnell (eds.), *Handbook on drug abuse.* Washington, D.C.: National Institute on Drug Abuse.

Jessor, R. 1985. Bridging etiology and prevention in drug abuse research. In C. L. Jones and R. J. Battjes (eds.), *Etiology of drug abuse: Implications for prevention*, pp. 257–268. NIDA Research Monograph 56, Rockville, Md.: National Institute on Drug Abuse.

Jessor, R., and Jessor, S. L. 1977. *Problem behavior and psychosocial development: A longitudinal study of youth.* New York: Academic Press.

Johnson, C., and Larson, R. 1982. Bulimia: An analysis of mood and behavior. *Psychosomatic Medicine* **44**, 341–351.

Johnston, L. D. 1985. The etiology and prevention of substance use: What can we learn from recent historical changes? In C. L. Jones and R. J. Battjes (eds.), *Etiology of drug abuse: Implications for prevention*, pp. 155–177. NIDA Research Monograph 56. Rockville, Md.: National Institute on Drug Abuse.

Johnston, L. D., Bachman, J. G., and O'Malley, P. M. 1977. *Highlights from: Drug use among American high school students, 1975–1977.* Rockville, Md.: National Institute on Drug Abuse.

Johnston, L. D., O'Malley, P. M., and Jerald, G. 1987. Psychotherapeutic, licit and illicit use of drugs among adolescents: An epidemiological perspective. *Journal of Adolescent Health Care* **8**, 36–51.

Jurkovic, G. J. 1980. The juvenile deliquent as a moral philosopher: A structural-developmental perspective. *Psychological Bulletin* **88**, 709–727.

Jurkovic, G. J., and Prentice, N. M. 1977. Relation of moral and cognitive development to dimensions of juvenile delinquency. *Journal of Abnormal Psychology* **86**, 414–420.

Kaffman, M., and Elizur, E. 1977. *Infants who become enuretics: A longitudinal study of 161 Kibbutz children.* Monographs of the Society for Research in Child Development, vol. 42, no. 2.

Kail, R. 1982. *The development of memory in children*, 2d ed. New York: Freeman.

Kandel, D. B. 1978. Convergence in prospective longitudinal surveys of drug use in normal populations. In D. B. Kandel (ed.), *Longitudinal research in drug use: Empirical findings and methodological issues.* Washington, D.C.: Hemisphere.

Kandel, D. B., Kessler, R. C., and Margulies, R. Z. 1978. Antecedents of adolescent initiation into stages of drug use: A developmental analysis. In D. B. Kandel (ed.), *Longitudinal research in drug use. Empirical findings and methodological issues.* Washington, D.C.: Hemisphere.

Kandel, D. B., and Yamaguchi, K. 1985. Developmental patterns of the use of legal, illegal, and medically prescribed psychotropic drugs from adolescence to young adulthood. In C. L. Jones and R. J. Battjes (eds.), *Etiology of drug abuse: Implications for prevention,* pp. 193–235. NIDA Research Monograph 56. Rockville, Md.: National Institute on Drug Abuse.

Kanfer, R., Eyberg, S. M., and Krahn, G. L. 1983. Interviewing strategies in child assessment. In E. Walker and M. Roberts (eds.), *Handbook of clinical child psychology,* pp. 95–108. New York: Wiley.

Kanner, L. 1946–1947. Irrelevant and metaphorical language in early infantile autism. *American Journal of Psychiatry* **103,** 242–246.

Kanner, L. 1977. *Child psychiatry,* 4th ed. Springfield, Ill.: Charles C Thomas.

Kanner, L., Rodriguez, A., and Ashenden, B. 1972. How far can autistic children go in matters of social adaptation? *Journal of Autism and Childhood Schizophrenia* **2,** 9–33.

Kantor, R. E., Wallner, J. M., and Winder, C. L. 1953. Process and reactive schizophrenia. *Journal of Consulting Psychology* **17,** 157–162.

Kasik, M. M., Sabatino, D. A., and Spoentgen, P. 1987. Psychosocial aspects of learning disabilities. In S. J. Ceci (ed.), *Handbook of cognitive, social and neuropsychological aspects of learning disabilities,* vol. 2, pp. 251–272. Hillsdale, N.J.: Lawrence Erlbaum Associates.

Katz, P. A. 1987. Development of social processes in ethnic attitudes and self-identification. In J. S. Phinney and M. J. Rotheram (eds.), *Children's ethnic socialization: Pluralism and development,* pp. 92–100. Newbury Park, Calif.: Sage Publications.

Kaufman, A. S. 1979. *Intelligence Testing with WISC-R.* New York: Wiley.

Kaufman Assessment Battery for Children (K-ABC). 1983. Circle Pines, Minnesota: American Guidance Service.

Kazdin, A. E. 1980. *Behavior modification in applied settings.* Homewood, Ill.: Dorsey Press.

Kazdin, A. E. 1987. *Conduct disorders in childhood and adolescence.* Newbury Park, Calif.: Sage Publications.

Kazdin, A. E. 1989. Developmental psychopathology: Current research, issues and directions. *American Psychologist* **44,** 180–187.

Kazdin, A. E., French, N. H., Unis, A. S., Esveldt-Dawson, K., and Sherick, R. B. 1983. Hopelessness, depression and suicidal intent among psychiatrically disturbed inpatient children. *Journal of Consulting and Clinical Psychology* **51,** 504–510.

Kelley, T. L., Madden, R., Gardner, E. F., and Rudman, H. C. 1964. *The Stanford Achievement Test.* New York: Harcourt Brace Jovanovich.

Kelly, E. W. Jr. 1973. School phobia: A review of theory and treatment. *Psychology in the Schools* **10,** 33–42.

Kenny, T. J. 1980. Hyperactivity. In H. E. Rie and E. D. Rie (eds.), *Handbook of minimal brain dysfunctions. A critical view.* New York: Wiley.

Kenny, T. J., and Burka, A. 1980. Coordinating multiple interventions. In H. E. Rie and E. D. Rie (eds.), *Handbook of minimal brain dysfunctions. A critical view.* New York: Wiley.

Kent, R. N., and Foster, S. L. 1977. Direct observational procedures: Methodological issues in naturalistic settings. In A. R. Ciminero, K. S. Calhoun, and H. E. Adams (eds.), *Handbook of behavioral assessment.* New York: Wiley.

Kephart, N. 1968. *Learning disability: An educational adventure.* West Lafayette, Ind.: Kappa Delta Pi Press.

Kessler, J. W. 1966. *Psychopathology of childhood.* Englewood Cliffs, N.J.: Prentice-Hall.

Kessler, J. W. 1980. History of minimal brain dysfunctions. In H. E. Rie and E. D. Rie (eds.), *Handbook of minimal brain dysfunctions: A critical view.* New York: Wiley.

Kinsbourne, M., and Caplan, P. J. 1979. *Children's learning and attention problems.* Boston: Little, Brown.

Kinsbourne, M., and Hiscock, M. 1978. Cerebral lateralization and cognitive development. In J. S. Chall and A. F. Mirsky (eds.), *Education and the brain: The seventy-seventh yearbook of the National Society for the Study of Education* (part 2). Chicago: University of Chicago Press.

Kinsey, A. C., Pomeroy, W. B., and Martin, C. E. 1948. *Sexual behavior in the human male.* Philadelphia: Saunders.

Kirk, S., McCarthy, J., and Kirk, W. 1968. *Illinois Test of Psycholinguistic Ability,* rev. ed. Urbana, Ill.: University of Illinois Press.

Klausmeier, H., and Allen, P. S. 1978. *Cognitive development of children and youth: A longitudinal study.* New York: Academic Press.

Klopfer, W. G., and Taulbee, E. S. 1976. Projective tests. In M. R. Rosenzweig and L. W. Porter (eds.), *Annual review of psychology,* vol. 27. Palo Alto, Calif.: Annual Reviews.

Knitzer, J. E. 1976. Child advocacy: A perspective. *American Journal of Orthopsychiatry* **46,** 200–216.

Kohlberg, L. 1976. Moral stages and moralization: The cognitive-developmental approach. In T. Lickona (ed.), *Moral development and behavior. Theory, research and social issues.* New York: Holt, Rinehart & Winston.

Kohlberg, L., LaCrossee, J., and Ricks, D. 1972. The predictability of adult mental health from childhood behavior. In B. J. Wolman (ed.), *Manual of child psychopathology.* New York: McGraw-Hill.

Kohn, M. 1977. *Social competence, symptoms and underachievement in childhood: A longitudinal perspective.* Silver Spring, Md.: V. H. Winston.

Kolvin, I., Ounsted, C., Humphrey, M., and McNay, A. 1971. Studies in childhood psychoses. Part 2. The phenomenology of childhood psychoses. *British Journal of Psychiatry* **118,** 385–395.

Kolvin, I., Ounsted, C., Richardson, L. M., and Garside, R. 1971. Studies in childhood psychoses. Part 3. The family and social background in childhood psychosis. *British Journal of Psychiatry,* **118,** 396–402.

Koppitz, E. M. 1971. *Children with learning disabilities: A five-year follow-up study.* New York: Grune & Stratton.

Koppitz, E. M. 1973. *The Bender Gestalt Test for Young Children.* New York: Grune & Stratton.

Korchin, S. J. 1976. *Modern clinical psychology. Principles of intervention in the clinic and community.* New York: Basic Books.

Kovacs, M. 1986. A developmental perspective on methods and measures in the assessment of depressive disorders: The clinical interview. In M. Rutter, C. E. Izard, and P. B. Read (eds.), *Depression in young people: Developmental and clinical perspectives,* pp. 435–466. New York: Guilford Press.

Kovacs, M., and Beck, A. T. 1977. An empirical-clinical approach toward a definition of childhood depression. In J. G. Schulterbrandt and A. Raskin (eds.), *Depression in childhood: Diagnosis, treatment and conceptual models.* New York: Raven Press.

Kovacs, M., Feinberg, T. L., Crouse-Novak, M., Paulauskas, S. L., Pollock, M., and Finkelstein, R. 1984. Depressive disorders in childhood. II. A longitudinal study of the risk for a subsequent major depression. *Archives of General Psychiatry* **41,** 643–649.

Kovacs, M., Feinberg, T. L., Paulauskas, S., Finkelstein, R., Pollack, M., and Crouse-Novak, M. 1985. Initial coping responses and psychosocial characteristics of children with insulin-dependent diabetes mellitus. *Journal of Pediatrics* **106,** 827–834.

Kovacs, M., and Paulauskas, S. 1986. The traditional psychotherapies. In H. C. Quay and J. S. Werry (eds.), *Psychopathological disorders of childhood,* 3d ed., pp. 496–522. New York: Wiley.

Kraft, I. A. 1979. Group therapy. In J. D. Noshpitz (ed.), *Basic handbook of child psychiatry.* Vol. 3, *Therapeutic interventions.* New York: Basic Books.

Kubicek, L. F. 1980. Organization in two mother–infant interactions involving a normal infant and his fraternal twin brother, who was later diagnosed as autistic. In T. M. Field (ed.), *High-risk infants and children. Adult and peer interaction.* New York: Academic Press.

LaRose, L., and Wolfe, D. A. 1987. Psychological characteristics of parents who abuse or neglect their children. In B. B. Lahey and A. E. Kazdin (eds.), *Advances in clinical child psychology,* pp. 55–98. New York: Plenum.

LaVietes, R. 1978. Mental retardation: Psychological treatment. In B. J. Wolman (ed.), *Handbook of treatment of mental disorders in childhood and adolescence.* Englewood Cliffs, N.J.: Prentice-Hall.

Lazar, I., and Darlington, R. B. 1982. Lasting effects of early education. *Monographs of the Society for Research in Child Development* **47,** (2–3, serial no. 195).

Ledingham, J. E. 1981. Developmental patterns of aggressive and withdrawn behavior in childhood: a possible method for identifying pre-schizophrenics. *Journal of Abnormal Child Psychology* **9,** 1–22.

Ledwidge, B. 1978. Cognitive behavior modification: A step in the wrong direction? *Psychological Bulletin* **85,** 353–375.

Ledwidge, B. 1979. Cognitive behavior modification or new ways to change minds: Reply to Mahoney and Kazdin. *Psychological Bulletin* **86,** 1050–1053.

Lefkowitz, M. M., Eron, L. D., Walder, L. O., and Huesmann, L. R. 1977. *Growing up to be violent: A longitudinal study of the development of aggression.* New York: Pergamon.

Leon, G. R. 1979. Cognitive-behavioral therapy for eating disturbances. In P. Kendall and S. Hollon (eds.), *Cognitive-behavioral interventions: Theory, research and procedures,* pp. 357–388. New York: Academic Press.

Leon, G. R., and Dinklage, D. 1983. Childhood obesity and anorexia nervosa. In T. H. Ollendick and M. Hersen (eds.), *Handbook of child psychopathology,* pp. 253–276. New York: Plenum Press.

Leon, G. R., Lucas, A. R., Colligan, R. C., Ferdinande, R. J., and Kamp, J. 1985. Sexuality, body-image, and personality attitudes in anorexia nervosa. *Journal of Abnormal Child Psychology* **13,** 245–258.

Leon, G. R., and Phelan, P. W. 1985. Anorexia nervosa. In B. B. Lahey and A. E. Kazdin (eds.), *Advances in clinical child psychology,* vol. 8, pp. 81–113. New York: Plenum.

Levitt, E. E. 1957. The results of psychotherapy with children: An evaluation. *Journal of Consulting Psychology,* **21,** 189–196.

Levy, D. M. 1955. Oppositional syndrome and oppositional behavior. In P. H. Hoch and J. Zubin (eds.), *Psychopathology of childhood,* pp. 204–226. New York: Grune & Stratton.

Levy, F. 1980. The development of sustained attention (vigilance) and inhibition in children: Some normative data. *Journal of Child Psychology and Psychiatry* **21,** 77–84.

Lewine, R. R. J. 1984. Stalking the schizophrenia marker: Evidence for a general vulnerability model of psychopathology. In N. F. Watt, E. J. Anthony, L. C. Wynne, and J. E. Rolf (eds.), *Children at risk for schizophrenia: A longitudinal perspective,* pp. 545–550. Cambridge: Cambridge University Press.

Lewine, R. R. J., Watt, N. F., and Grubb, T. W. 1984. High-risk-for-schizophrenia research: Sampling bias and its implications. In N. F. Watt, E. J. Anthony, L. C. Wynne, and J. E. Rolf (eds.), *Children at risk for schizophrenia: A longitudinal perspective,* pp. 557–564. Cambridge: Cambridge University Press.

Lewis, M. 1986. Principles of intensive individual psychoanalytic psychotherapy with childhood anxiety disorders. In R. Gittelman (ed.), *Anxiety disorders of childhood,* pp. 233–255. New York. Guilford Press.

Lidz, T. 1973. *The origin and treatment of schizophrenic disorders.* New York: Basic Books.

Lindquist, E. F., and Hieronymus, A. M. 1955–1956. *Iowa Tests of Basic Skills manuals.* Boston: Houghton-Mifflin.

Linscheid, T. R., Tarnowski, K. J., and Richmond, D. A. 1988. Behavioral approaches to anorexia nervosa, bulimia and obesity. In D. Routh (ed.),

Handbook of pediatric psychology. New York: Guilford Press.

Lochman, J. E., and Lampron, L. B. 1986. Situational social problem-solving skills and self-esteem of aggressive and nonaggressive boys. *Journal of Abnormal Child Psychology* **14**, 605–617.

Lord, C. 1985. Autism and the comprehension of language. In E. Schopler and G. B. Mesibov (eds.), *Communication problems in autism*, pp. 257–282. New York: Plenum Press.

Lotter, V. 1978. Follow-up studies. In M. Rutter and E. Schopler (eds.), *Autism: A reappraisal of concepts and treatment.* New York: Plenum Press.

Lovaas, O. I. 1977. *The autistic child. Language development through behavior modification.* New York: Irvington.

Lovaas, O. I., Koegel, R. L., and Schreibman, L. 1979. Stimulus overselectivity in autism: A review of research. *Psychological Bulletin* **86**, 1236–1254.

Lovibond, S. H., and Coote, M. A. 1979. Enuresis. In C. G. Costello, (ed.), *Symptoms of psychopathology: A handbook.* New York: Wiley.

Maccoby, E. E., and Martin, J. A. 1983. Socialization in the context of the family: Parent child interaction. In P. H. Mussen (ed.), *Handbook of child psychology.* Vol. IV, E. M. Hetherington (ed.), pp. 1–102. New York: Wiley.

Macfarlane, J. W. 1964. Perspectives on personal consistency and change: The guidance study. *Vita Humana*, **7**, 115–126.

Macfarlane, J. W., Allen, L., and Honzik, M. P. 1954. *A developmental study of the behavior problems of normal children between 21 months and 14 years of age.* Berkeley and Los Angeles: University of California Press.

MacFarlane, K. 1986. Child sexual abuse allegations in divorce proceedings. In K. MacFarlane and J. Waterman (eds.), *Sexual abuse of young children: Evaluation and treatment*, pp. 121–150. New York: Guilford Press.

MacFarlane, K., and Krebs, S. 1986. Techniques for interviewing and evidence gathering. In K. MacFarlane and J. Waterman (eds.), *Sexual abuse*

of young children: Evaluation and treatment, pp. 67–100. New York: Guilford Press.

Maclean, M., Bryant, P., and Bradley, L. 1987. Rhymes, nursery rhymes and reading in early childhood. *Merrill Palmer Quarterly* **33**, 255–282.

McAdoo, W. G., and DeMyer, M. K. 1978. Personality characteristics of parents. In M. Rutter and E. Schopler (eds.), *Autism: A reappraisal of concepts and treatment*, pp. 251–267. New York: Plenum Press.

McArthur, D. S., and Roberts, G. E. 1984. *Roberts apperception test for children.* Los Angeles: Western Psychological Services.

McConaghy, M. J. 1979. Gender permanence and the genital basis of gender: Stages in the development of constancy of gender identity. *Child Development* **50**, 1223–1226.

McCord, J. 1978. A thirty-year follow-up of treatment effects. *American Psychologist* **33**, 284–289.

McGlothlin, W. H. 1979. Drugs and crime. In R. I. Dupont, A. Goldstein, and J. O'Donnell (eds.), *Handbook on drug abuse.* Washington, D.C.: National Institute on Drug Abuse.

Machover, K. 1949. *Personality projection in the drawing of the human figure.* Springfield, Ill.: Charles C Thomas.

Magnusson, D. 1988. *Individual development from an interactional perspective: A longitudinal study.* Hillsdale, N.J.: Lawrence Erlbaum Associates.

Magrab, P. R., and Lehr, E. 1982. Assessment techniques. In J. M. Tuma (ed.), *Handbook for the practice of pediatric psychology*, pp. 67–109. New York: Wiley.

Mahler, M. S. 1952. On childhood psychosis and schizophrenia: Autistic and symbiotic infantile psychosis. In R. S. Eissler, A. Freud, H. Hartmann, and E. Kris (eds.), *The psychoanalytic study of the child*, vol. 7, pp. 286–305. New York: International Universities Press.

Mahler, M. S. 1965. On early infantile psychosis: The symbiotic and autistic syndromes. *Journal of the American Academy of Child Psychiatry* **4**, 442–468.

Mahoney, M. J. 1974. *Cognition and behavior modification.* Cambridge, Mass.: Ballinger.

Mahoney, M. J. 1977. Reflections on the cognitive-learning trend in psychotherapy. *American Psychologist* **32**, 5–13.

Mahoney, M. J., and Kazdin, A. E. 1979. Cognitive behavior modification: Misconceptions and premature evacuation. *Psychological Bulletin* **86**, 1044–1049.

Mahoney, M. J., Kazdin, A. E., and Lesswing, N.J. 1974. Behavior modification: Delusion or deliverance? In C. M. Franks and G. T. Wilson (eds.), *Annual review of behavior therapy, theory and practice*, vol. 2. New York: Brunner/Mazel.

Malmquist, C. P. 1980. Depressive phenomena in children. In B. B. Wolman (ed.), *Manual of child psychopathology*. New York: McGraw-Hill.

Marcia, J. E. 1980. Identity in adolescence. In J. Adelson (ed.), *Handbook of adolescent psychology*. New York: Wiley.

Martin, H. P., and Breezley, P. 1977. Behavioral observations of abused children. *Developmental Medicine and Child Neurology* **19**, 373–387.

Martin, H. P., Breezley, P., Conway, E. F., and Kempe, C. H. 1974. The development of abused children, Part 1: A review of the literature. In I. Schulman (ed.), *Advances in pediatrics*, vol. 21. Chicago: Yearbook Medical Publishers.

Martin, H. P., and Kempe, C. H. 1976. *The abused child: A multidisciplinary approach to developmental issues and treatment.* Cambridge, Mass.: Ballinger.

Massie, H. N. 1980. Pathological interactions in infancy. In T. M. Field (ed.), *High-risk infants and children. Adult and peer interaction.* New York: Academic Press.

Mednick, B. R. 1973. Breakdown in high-risk subjects: Familial and early environmental factors. *Journal of Abnormal Psychology* **82**, 469–475.

Mednick, S. A., Schulsinger, H., and Schulsinger, F. 1975. Schizophrenia in children of schizophrenic mothers. In A. Davids (ed.), *Child personality and psychopathology: Current topics*, vol. 2. New York: Wiley.

Meehl, P. E. 1978. Theoretical risks and tabular asterisks: Sir Karl, Sir Ronald, and the slow progress of soft psychology. *Journal of Consulting and Clinical Psychology* **46**, 806–834.

Meichenbaum, D. H., and Goodman, J. 1971. Training impulsive children to talk to themselves: A means of developing self-control. *Journal of Abnormal Psychology* **77**, 115–126.

Meissner, W. W., Mack, J. E., and Semrad, E. V. 1975. Classical psychoanalysis. In A. M. Freedman, H. I. Kaplan, and R. J. Sadock (eds.), *Comprehensive textbook of psychiatry*, vol. 2. Baltimore: Williams & Wilkins.

Mejia, D. 1983. The development of Mexican-American children. In G. J. Powell (ed.), *The psychosocial development of minority group children*, pp. 77–114. New York: Brunner/Mazel.

Mendelson, M. 1975. Intrapersonal psychodynamics of depression. In F. F. Flach and S. C. Draghi (eds.), *The nature and treatment of depression.* New York: Wiley.

Menyuk, P. 1978. Language: What's wrong and why. In M. Rutter and E. Schopler (eds.), *Autism: A reappraisal of concepts and treatment.* New York: Plenum Press.

Menyuk, P., and Quill, K. 1985. Semantic problems in autistic children. In E. Schopler and G. B. Mesibov (eds.), *Communication problems in autism*, pp. 127–145. New York: Plenum Press.

Michelson, L., and Mannarino, A. 1986. Social skills training with children: Research and clinical application. In P. S. Strain, M. J. Guralnick, and H. M. Walker (eds.), *Children's social behavior: Development, assessment, and modification*, pp. 373–406. Orlando: Academic Press.

Millar, H. E. C. 1979. Health care for high-risk mothers. In J. D. Noshpitz (ed.), *Basic handbook for child psychiatry.* Vol. 4, pp. 30–40. *Prevention and current issues*, pp. 30–40. New York: Basic Books.

Miller, L. C. 1983. Fears and anxieties in children. In C. F. Walker and M. C. Roberts (eds.), *Handbook of clinical child psychology.* New York: Wiley.

Miller, L. C., Barrett, C. L., and Hampe, E. 1974. Phobias of childhood in a prescientific era. In A. Davids (ed.), *Child personality and psychopathology: Current topics*, vol. 1. New York: Wiley.

Miller, L. C., Barrett, C. L., Hampe, E., and Noble, H. 1972. Comparison of reciprocal inhibition, psychotherapy and waiting list control for phobic children. *Journal of Abnormal Psychology* **79**, 269–279.

Miller, N. E., and Dollard, J. 1941. *Social learning and imitation.* New Haven, Conn.: Yale University Press.

Miller, R. T. 1974. Childhood schizophrenia: A review of selected literature. *International Journal of Mental Health* **3**, 3–46.

Minuchin, P. P., and Shapiro, E. K. 1983. The school as a context for social development. In P. H. Mussen (ed.), *Handbook of child psychology,* vol. 4, 4th ed. New York: Wiley.

Minuchin, S., Baker, L., Rosman, B. L., Liebman, R., Milman, L., and Todd, T. C. 1975. A conceptual model of psychosomatic illness in children. *Archives of General Psychiatry* **32**, 1031–1038.

Minuchin, S., Montalvo, B., Guerney, B. G. Jr., Rosman, B. L., and Schumer, F. 1967. *Families of the slums.* New York: Basic Books.

Mischel, W. 1974. Processes in delay of gratification. In L. Berkowitz (ed.), *Advances in experimental social psychology,* vol. 7. New York: Academic Press.

Mischel, W. 1978. How children postpone pleasure. *Human Nature* **1**, 50–55.

Mishler, E. G., and Waxler, N. E. 1965. Family interaction and schizophrenia: A review of current theories. *Merrill-Palmer Quarterly* **11**, 269–316.

Money, J. 1970. Sexual dimorphism and homosexual gender identity. *Psychological Bulletin* **74**, 425–440.

Money, J., and Ehrhardt, A. A. 1972. *Man and woman, boy and girl. The differentiation and dimorphism of gender identity from conception to maturity.* Baltimore: Johns Hopkins University Press.

Money, J., and Higham, E. 1976. Juvenile gender identity: Differentiation and transpositions. In A. Davids (ed.), *Child personality and psychopathology: Current topics,* vol. 3. New York: Wiley.

Moore, C. L. 1985. Another psychobiological view of sexual differentiation. *Developmental Review* **5**, 18–55.

Morris, R. J., and Kratochwill, T. R. (eds.). 1983. *The practice of child therapy.* New York: Pergamon.

Mosher, L. R., and Keith, S. J. 1977. Research on the psychosocial treatment of schizophrenia: A summary report. *American Journal of Psychiatry* **136**, 623–631.

Munro, A. 1966. Parental deprivation in depressive patients. *British Journal of Psychiatry* **112**, 443–457.

Murray, D. M., and Perry, C. L. 1985. The prevention of adolescent drug abuse: Implications of etiological, developmental, behavioral, and environmental models. In C. L. Jones and R. J. Battjes (eds.), *Etiology of drug abuse: Implications for prevention,* pp. 236–256. NIDA Research Monograph 56. Rockville, Md.: National Institute on Drug Abuse.

Myers, H. F., and King, L. M. 1983. Mental health issues in the development of the black American child. In G. J. Powell (ed.), *The psychosocial development of minority group children,* pp. 275–306. New York: Brunner/Mazel.

Nagera, H. 1966. Early childhood disturbances, the infantile neurosis, and the adult disturbances: Problems of a developmental psychoanalytic psychology. *The psychoanalytic study of the child.* Monograph no. 2. New York: International Universities Press.

Naylor, H. 1980. Reading disability and lateral asymmetry: An information-processing analysis. *Psychological Bulletin* **87**, 531–545.

Neeper, R., and Greenwood, R. S. 1987. On the psychiatric importance of neurological soft signs. In B. B. Lahey and A. E. Kazdin (eds.), *Advances in clinical child psychology,* vol. 10, pp. 217–258. New York: Plenum.

Nihira, K. 1976. Dimensions of adaptive behavior in institutionalized mentally retarded children and adults: Developmental perspectives. *American Journal of Mental Deficiency* **81**, 215–226.

Nihira, K. 1978. Factorial descriptions of the AAMD Adaptive Behavior Scale. In W. A. Coulter and H. W. Morrow (eds.), *Adaptive behavior: Concepts and measurements.* New York: Grune & Stratton.

Nihira, K., Foster R., Shellhaas, M., and Leland, H. 1974. *AAMD Adaptive Behavior Scale, 1974 revision.* Washington, D.C.: American Association on Mental Deficiency.

Norton, D. G. 1983. Black family life patterns, the development of self and cognitive development of black children. In G. J. Powell (ed.), *The psychosocial development of minority group children,* pp. 181–193. New York: Brunner/Mazel.

Noshpitz, J. D. (ed.). 1979a. *Basic handbook of child psychiatry.* Vol. 3, *Therapeutic interventions.* New York: Basic Books.

Noshpitz, J. D. (ed.). 1979b. *Basic handbook of child psychiatry.* Vol. 4, *Prevention and current issues.* New York: Basic Books.

Nuechterlein, K. H. 1984. Sustained attention among children vulnerable to adult schizophrenia and among hyperactive children. In N. F. Watt, E. J. Anthony, L. C. Wynne, and J. E. Rolf (eds.), *Children at risk for schizophrenia: A longitudinal perspective,* pp. 304–311. Cambridge: Cambridge University Press.

Nuechterlein, K. H. 1986. Childhood precursors of adult schizophrenia. *Journal of Child Psychology and Psychiatry* 27, 133–144.

Nuechterlein, K. H., Edell, W. S., Norris, M., and Dawson, M. E. 1986. Attentional vulnerability indicators, thought disorders and negative symptoms. *Schizophrenia Bulletin* 12, 408–426.

Offord, D. R., and Cross, L. A. 1969. Behavioral antecedents of adult schizophrenia. A review. *Archives of General Psychiatry* 21, 267–283.

Olweus, D. 1979. Stability of aggressive reaction patterns in males: A review. *Psychological Bulletin* 86, 852–875.

Ornitz, E. M. 1976. The modulation of sensory input and motor output in autistic children. In E. Schopler and R. J. Reichler (eds.), *Psychopathology and child development.* New York: Plenum.

Ornitz, E. M., and Ritvo, E. R. 1976. The syndrome of autism: A critical review. *American Journal of Psychiatry* 133(6), 609–621.

Otis, A. S., and Lennon, R. T. 1967. *Otis-Lennon Mental Abilities Test.* New York: Harcourt Brace.

Parke, R. D., and Collmer, C. W. 1975. Child abuse: An interdisciplinary analysis. In E. M. Hetherington (ed.), *Review of child development research,* vol. 5. Chicago: University of Chicago Press.

Patterson, G. R. 1982. *Coercive family process.* Eugene, Oreg.: Castalia Publishing.

Patterson, G. R., Littman, R. A., and Bricker, W. 1967. Assertive behavior in children: A step toward a theory of aggression. *Monographs of the Society for Research in Child Development* 32 (5, serial no. 113).

Paul, G. L., and Lentz, R. J. 1977. *Psychosocial treatment of chronic mental patients.* Cambridge, Mass.: Harvard University Press.

Paulson, M. J., and Stone, D. 1974. Suicidal behavior of latency-age children. *Journal of Clinical Child Psychology* 3, 50–53.

Peller, L. E. 1964. Libidinal development as reflected in play. In M. R. Haworth (ed.), *Child psychotherapy.* New York: Basic Books.

Perlmutter, B. F. 1986. Personality variables and peer relations of children and adolescents with learning disabilities. In S. J. Ceci (ed.), *Handbook of cognitive, social and neuropsychological aspects of learning disabilities,* vol. 1, pp. 339–360. Hillsdale, N.J.: Lawrence Erlbaum Associates.

Peters, S. D., Wyatt, G. E., and Finkelhor, D. 1986. Prevalence. In D. Finkelhor (ed.), *A sourcebook of child sexual abuse,* pp. 15–59. Beverly Hills: Sage Publications.

Peterson, L., and Roberts, M. C. 1986. Community intervention and prevention. In H. C. Quay and J. S. Werry (eds.), *Psychopathological disorders of childhood,* 3d ed., pp. 622–660. New York: Wiley.

Peterson, R. C. (ed.) 1980. Marijuana research findings. *NIDA Research Monograph 31.* Washington, D.C.: National Institute of Drug Abuse.

Pfeffer, C. R., Conte, H. R., Plutchik, R., and Jerrett, M. A. 1980. Suicidal behavior in latency-age children: An outpatient population. *Journal* of the American Academy of Child Psychiatry **19,** 703–710.

Phares, E. J. 1976. *Locus of control in personality.* Morristown, N. J.: General Learning Press.

Piaget, J. 1930. *The child's conception of physical causality.* London: Kegan Paul.

Piaget, J. 1932. *The moral judgment of the child.* London: Kegan Paul.

Piaget, J. 1954. *The construction of reality in the child.* New York: Basic Books.

Piaget, J. 1967. *Six psychological studies.* New York: Random House.

Plomir, R. 1983. Childhood temperament. In B. B. Lahey and A. E. Kazdin (eds.), *Advances in clinical child psychology,* vol. 6, pp. 45–92. New York: Plenum Press.

Powell, D. G. (ed.). 1983. *The psychosocial development of minority group children.* New York: Brunner/Mazel.

Premorbid adjustment and schizophrenic heterogeneity. 1977. *Schizophrenia Bulletin* **3**(2), 180–182.

Prior, M. R. 1979. Cognitive abilities and disabilities in infantile autism: A review. *Journal of Abnormal Child Psychology* **7,** 357–380.

Prior, M. R., and Chen, C. S. 1976. Short-term and serial memory in autistic, retarded, and normal children. *Journal of Autism and Childhood Schizophrenia* **6,** 121–131.

Prior, M., and Sanson, A. 1986. Attention deficit disorder with hyperactivity: A critique. *Journal of Child Psychology and Psychiatry* **27,** 307–319.

Prior, M., and Werry, J. S. 1986. Autism, schizophrenia and allied disorders. In H. C. Quay and J. S. Werry (eds.), *Psychopathological disorders of childhood,* 3d ed., pp. 156–210. New York: Wiley.

Proctor, J. T. 1958. Hysteria in childhood. *American Journal of Orthopsychiatry* **28,** 394–407.

Provence, S., and Lipton, R. C. 1962. *Infants in institutions.* New York: International Universities Press.

Quay, H. C. 1986a. Classification. In H. C. Quay and J. S. Werry (eds.), *Psychopathological disorders of childhood,* 3d ed., pp. 1–34. New York: Wiley.

Quay, H. C. 1986b. Conduct disorders. In H. C. Quay and J. S. Werry (eds.), *Psychopathological disorders of childhood,* 3d ed., pp. 35–72. New York: Wiley.

Radke-Yarrow, M., Zahn-Waxler, C., and Chapman, M. 1983. Children's prosocial dispositions and behavior. In P. H. Mussen (ed.), *Handbook of child psychology,* vol. 4, *Socialization, Personality and Social Development.* E. M. Hetherington (ed.), pp. 469–546. New York: Wiley.

Ramsey, P. G. 1987. Young children's thinking about ethnic differences. In J. S. Phinney and M. J. Rotheram (eds.), *Children's ethnic socialization: Pluralism and development,* pp. 56–72. Newbury Park, Calif.: Sage Publications.

Rapoport, J. L. 1986. Childhood obsessive compulsive disorders. *Journal of Child Psychology and Psychiatry* **27,** 289–295.

Rapoport, J., Mikkelsen, E. J., and Werry, J. S. Antimanic, antianxiety, hallucinogenic, and miscellaneous drugs. In J. S. Werry (ed.), *Pediatric psychopharmacology.* New York: Brunner/Mazel.

Redd, W. H., Porterfield, A. L., and Andersen, B. L. 1979. Behavior modification. *Behavioral approaches to human problems.* New York: Random House.

Redl, F., and Wineman, D. 1951. *Children who hate. The disorganization and breakdown of behavior controls.* New York: Free Press.

Reese, H. W., and Lipsitt, L. P. 1970. *Experimental child psychology.* New York: Academic Press.

Reitan-Indiana Neuropsychological Test Battery. 1969. Indianapolis: Reitan.

Richardson, S. A., Goodman, N., Hastorf, A. H., and Dornbusch, S. M. 1961. Cultural uniformity in reaction to physical disabilities. *American Sociological Review* **26,** 241–247.

Rie, E. D. 1980. Effects of MBD on learning, intellectual functions and achievement. In H. E. Rie and E. D. Rie (eds.), *Handbook of minimal brain dysfunctions: A critical view.* New York: Wiley.

Rie, H. E. 1971. Historical perspective of concepts

of child psychopathology. In H. E. Rie (ed.), *Perspectives in child psychopathology.* Chicago: Aldine-Atherton.

Rie, H. E. 1980. Definitional problems. In H. E. Rie and E. D. Rie (eds.), *Handbook of minimal brain dysfunctions: A critical view.* New York: Wiley.

Rimland, B. 1971. The differentiation of childhood psychoses: An analysis of check lists for 2,218 psychotic children. *Journal of Autism and Childhood Schizophrenia* **1,** 161–174.

Risk factors for suicide attempts. *Adolinks,* vol. 4, no. 2 (undated).

Roberts, C. W., Green, R., Williams, K., and Goodman, M. 1987. Boyhood gender identity development: A statistical contrast of two family groups. *Developmental Psychology* **23,** 544–557.

Roberts, M. 1975. Persistent school refusal among children and adolescents. In R. D. Wirt, G. Winokur, and M. Roff (eds.), *Life history research in psychopathology,* vol. 4. Minneapolis: University of Minnesota Press.

Robins, L. N. 1966. *Deviant children grown up: A sociological and psychiatric study of sociopathic personality.* Baltimore: Williams & Wilkins.

Robins, L. N. 1972. Follow-up studies of behavior disorders in children. In H. C. Quay and J. S. Werry (eds.), *Psychopathological disorders of childhood.* New York: Wiley.

Robins, L. N. 1979. Addict careers. In R. I. Dupont, A. Goldstein, and J. O'Donnell (eds.), *Handbook on drug abuse.* Washington, D.C.: National Institute on Drug Abuse.

Robins, L. N. 1980. The natural history of drug abuse. In D. J. Lettieri, M. Sayers, and H. W. Pearson (eds.), *Theories on drug abuse. Selected contemporary perspectives. NIDA Research Monograph* 30. Washington, D.C.: National Institute on Drug Abuse.

Robins, L. N., Davis, D. H., and Nurco, D. N. 1974. How permanent was Vietnam drug addiction? *American Journal of Public Health* **64** (suppl.), 38–43.

Robins, L. N., and Przybeck, T. R. 1985. Age of onset of drug use as a factor in drug and other disorders. In C. L. Jones and R. J. Battjes (eds.), *Etiology of drug abuse: Implications for prevention,* pp. 178–192. NIDA Research Monograph 56. Rockville, Md.: National Institute on Drug Abuse.

Robinson, N. M., and Robinson, H. B. 1976. *The mentally retarded child: A psychological approach,* 2d ed. New York: McGraw-Hill.

Rodnick, E. H., Goldstein, M. J., Lewis, J. M., and Doane, J. A. 1984. Parental communication style, affect and role as precursors of offspring schizophrenia-spectrum disorders. In N. F. Watt, E. J. Anthony, L. C. Wynne, and J. E. Rolf (eds.), *Children at risk for schizophrenia: A longitudinal perspective,* pp. 81–92. Cambridge: Cambridge University Press.

Roff, J. D. 1974. Adolescent schizophrenia: Variables related to differences in long-term adult outcome. *Journal of Consulting and Clinical Psychology* **42,** 180–183.

Roff, M. 1966. *Some childhood and adolescent characteristics of adult homosexuals.* Report No. 66. University of Minnesota Institute of Child Development.

Rogers, C. R. 1959. A theory of therapy, personality, and interpersonal relationships as developed in the client-centered framework. In S. Koch (ed.), *Psychology: Study of a science.* Vol. 3, *Formulations of the person and the social context.* New York: McGraw-Hill.

Rosenberg, F. R., and Rosenberg, M. 1978. Self-esteem and delinquency. *Journal of Youth and Adolescence* **7,** 293–294.

Rosenberg, M. S., and Reppucci, N. D. 1985. Primary prevention of child abuse. *Journal of Consulting and Clinical Psychology* **53,** 576–585.

Rosenblith, J. F., and Sims-Knight. 1985. *In the beginning: Development in the first two years of life.* Monterey, Calif.: Brooks/Cole.

Rosenthal, D., Wender, P. H., Kety, S. S., Schulsinger, F., Welner, J., and Rieder, R. O. 1975. Parent-child relationships and psychopathological disorder in the child. *Archives of General Psychiatry* **32,** 466–476.

Rosenthal, D. A. 1987. Ethnic identity development in adolescents. In J. S. Phinney and M. J. Rotheram (eds.), *Children's ethnic socialization:*

Pluralism and development, pp. 153–155. Newbury Park, Calif.: Sage Publications.

Rosenthal, P. A., and Rosenthal, S. 1984. Suicidal behavior by preschool children. *American Journal of Psychiatry* **141,** 520–525.

Ross, A. O. 1980. *Psychological disorders of children: A behavioral approach to theory, research, and therapy,* 2d ed. New York: McGraw-Hill.

Ross, A. O. 1981. *Child behavior therapy: Principles, procedures, and empirical basis.* New York: Wiley.

Ross, A. O., and Nelson, R. O. 1979. Behavior therapy. In H. C. Quay and J. S. Werry (eds.), *Psychopathological disorders of childhood,* 2d ed. New York: Wiley.

Ross, D. C. 1964. *A classification of child psychiatry.* 4951 McKean Ave., Philadelphia.

Ross, D. M., and Ross, S. A. 1976. *Hyperactivity: Research, theory, and action.* New York: Wiley.

Rotheram, M. J., and Phinney, J. S. 1987. Ethnic behavior patterns as an aspect of identity. In J. S. Phinney and M. J. Rotheram (eds.), *Children's ethnic socialization: Pluralism and development,* pp. 180–200. Newbury Park, Calif.: Sage Publications.

Routh, D. K. 1979. Activity, attention and aggression in learning-disabled children. *Journal of Clinical Child Psychology* **8,** 183–187.

Rubin, H. T. 1977. The juvenile court's search for identity and responsibility. *Crime and Delinquency* **23,** 1–13.

Ruiz, R. A., and Padilla, A. M. 1983. Counseling Latinos. In D. R. Atkinson, G. Morten, and D. W. Sue (eds.), *Counseling American minorities: A cross-cultural perspective,* 2nd ed., pp. 213–236. Dubuque, Iowa: William C. Brown.

Ruttenberg, B. 1971. A psychoanalytic understanding of infantile autism and treatment. In D. W. Churchill, G. D. Alpern, and M. K. DeMyer (eds.), *Infantile autism.* Springfield, Ill.: Charles C Thomas.

Ruttenberg, B. A., Kalish, B., Wenar, C., and Wolf, E. G. 1978. *Behavior rating instrument for autistic and other atypical children* (BRIACC). Chicago: Stolting.

Rutter, M. 1971. Psychiatry. In J. Wortis (ed.),

Mental retardation: An annual review, vol. 3. New York: Grune & Stratton.

Rutter, M. 1972. *Maternal deprivation reassessed.* New York: Penguin.

Rutter, M. 1978. Diagnoses and definition. In M. Rutter and E. Schopler (eds.), *Autism: A reappraisal of concepts and treatment.* New York: Plenum Press.

Rutter, M. 1979a. *Changing youth in a changing society: Patterns of adolescent development and disorder.* London: Nuffield Provincial Hospitals Trust.

Rutter, M. 1979b. Maternal deprivation, 1972–1978: New findings, new concepts, new approaches. *Child Development* **50,** 283–305.

Rutter, M. 1981. Psychological sequelae of brain-damaged children. *American Journal of Psychiatry* **138,** 1533–1544.

Rutter, M. 1983. School effects on pupil progress: Research findings and policy implications. *Child Development* **54,** 1–29.

Rutter, M. 1985. Infantile autism. In D. Shaffer, A. A. Ehrhardt, and L. L. Greenhill (eds.), *The clinical guide to child psychiatry,* pp. 49–78. New York: Free Press.

Rutter, M. 1986a. The developmental psychopathology of depression: Issues and perspectives. In M. Rutter, C. E. Izard, and P. B. Read (eds.), *Depression in young people: Developmental and clinical perspectives,* pp. 3–32. New York: Guilford Press.

Rutter, M. 1986b. Depressive feelings, cognitions, and disorders: A research postscript. In M. Rutter, C. E. Izard, and P. B. Read (eds.), *Depression in young people: Developmental and clinical perspectives,* pp. 491–520. New York: Guilford Press.

Rutter, M., and Garmezy, N. 1983. Developmental psychopathology. In P. H. Mussen (ed.), *Handbook of child psychology,* vol. 4, *Socialization, Personality and Social Development.* E. M. Hetherington, ed., pp. 775–911. New York: Wiley.

Rutter, M., and Giller, H. 1983. *Juvenile delinquency: Trends and perspectives.* New York: Penguin.

Rutter, M., and Quinton, D. 1984. Long-term follow-up of women institutionalized in childhood: Factors promoting good functioning in adult life. *British Journal of Developmental Psychology* **2,** 191–204.

Rutter, M., and Shaffer, D. 1980. DSM-III—A step forward or back in terms of the classification of child psychiatric disorders? *Journal of the American Academy of Child Psychiatry* **19,** 371–394.

Sameroff, A. J., and Chandler, M. J. 1975. Reproductive risk and the continuum of caretaking casualty. In F. D. Horowitz (ed.), *Review of child development research,* vol. 4. Chicago: University of Chicago Press.

Sander, L. W. 1964. Adaptive relationships in early mother–child interaction. *Journal of the American Academy of Child Psychiatry* **3,** 231–264.

Santa, L. S. 1983. Mental health issues of Japanese-American children. In G. J. Powell (ed.), *The psychosocial development of minority group children,* pp. 362–372. New York: Brunner/Mazel.

Saposnek, D. T. 1983. *Mediating child custody disputes.* San Francisco: Jossey-Bass.

Saposnek, D. T., Hamburg, J., Delano, C. D., and Michaelsen, H. 1984. How has mandatory mediation fared? Research findings of the first year's follow-up. *Conciliation Courts Review* **22,** 7–19.

Satir, V. 1967. *Conjoint family therapy: A guide to theory and technique,* 2d ed. Palo Alto, Calif.: Science and Behavior Books.

Sattler, J. M. 1982. *Assessment of children's intelligence and special abilities.* Philadelphia: Saunders.

Schacht, T., and Nathan, P. E. 1977. But is it good for the psychologists? Appraisal and status of DSM-III. *American Psychologist* **32,** 1017–1025.

Scharfman, M. A. 1978. Psychoanalytic treatment. In B. B. Wolman, J. Egan, and A. O. Ross (eds.), *Handbook of treatment of mental disorders in childhood and adolescence.* Englewood Cliffs, N.J.: Prentice-Hall.

Schlesier-Stropp, B. 1984. Bulimia: A review of the literature. *Psychological Bulletin* **95,** 247–257.

Schneider, G. E. 1979. Is it really better to have your brain lesion early? A revision of the "Kennard principle." *Neuropsychologica* **17,** 557–583.

Schopler, E., and Mesibov, G. B. (eds.). 1985. *Communication problems in autism.* New York: Plenum Press.

Schwartz, I. M., and Levi, L. B. 1986. The juvenile justice system: The lessons of "reform." *Division of Child, Youth and Family Services Newsletter,* vol. 4, Fall, pp. 1, 10.

Schwartz, S., and Johnson, J. H. 1985. *Psychopathology of childhood: A clinical-experimental approach,* 2d ed. New York: Pergamon Press.

Sears, R. R. 1975. Your ancients revisited: A history of child development. In E. M. Hetherington (ed.), *Review of child development research,* vol. 5. Chicago: University of Chicago Press.

Segal, H. 1973. *Introduction to the work of Melanie Klein.* New York: Basic Books.

Self, P. A., and Horowitz, F. D. The behavioral assessment of the neonate: An overview. In T. D. Osofsky (ed.), *Handbook of infant development.* New York: Wiley.

Seligman, M. E. P. 1975. *Helplessness: On depression, development and death.* San Francisco: Freeman.

Seligman, M. E. P., and Peterson, C. 1986. A learned helplessness perspective on childhood depression: Theory and research. In M. Rutter, C. E. Izard, and P. B. Read (eds.), *Depression in young people: Developmental and clinical perspectives,* pp. 223–250. New York: Guilford Press.

Sells, S. B., and Simpson, D. D. 1980. The case for drug treatment effectiveness based on the DARP research program. *British Journal of Addications* **75,** 117–131.

Selman, R. L., and Byrne, D. F. 1974. A structural-developmental analysis of levels of role taking in middle childhood. *Child Development* **45,** 803–806.

Selye, H. 1956. *The stress of life.* New York: McGraw-Hill.

Senf, G. M., and Comrey, A. L. 1975. State initiative in learning disabilities. Illinois project SCREEN Report 1: The SCREEN early identification project. *Journal of Learning Disabilities* **8**, 451–457.

Serafica, F. C., and Cicchetti, D. 1976. Down's syndrome children in a strange situation: Attachment and exploration behaviors. *Merrill-Palmer Quarterly* **22**, 137–150.

Serafica, F. C., and Harway, N. I. 1979. Social relations and self-esteem of children with learning disabilities. *Journal of Clinical Child Psychology* **8**, 227–233.

Serafica, F. C., and Walsh-Hurley, M. E. 1987. Developmental considerations in research on socioemotional aspects of learning disabilities. In S. J. Ceci (ed.), *Handbook of cognitive, social and neuropsychological aspects of learning disabilities,* vol. 2, pp. 403–422. Hillsdale, N.J.: Lawrence Erlbaum Associates.

Shaffer, D. 1977. Enuresis. In M. Rutter and L. Hersov (eds.), *Child Psychiatry: Modern approaches.* Oxford: Blackwell Scientific Publications.

Shaffer, D. 1985. *Developmental psychology.* Monterey, Calif.: Brooks/Cole.

Shaffer, D., Chadwick, O., and Rutter, M. 1975. Psychiatric outcome of localized head injuries in children. Outcome of severe damage to the central nervous system. *Ciba Foundation Symposium* **34**, 191–209. (new series)

Shaffer, D., Schonfeld, I., O'Connor, P. A., Stokman, C., Trautman, P., Shafer, S., and Ng, S. 1985. Neurological soft signs: Their relation to psychiatric disorder and intelligence in childhood and adolescence. *Archives of General Psychiatry* **42**, 342–351.

Shakow, D. 1953. Experimental psychology. In R. R. Grinker (ed.), *Midcentury psychiatry.* Springfield, Ill.: Charles C Thomas.

Shantz, C. U. 1975. The development of social cognition. In E. M. Hetherington (ed.), *Review of child development research,* vol. 5. Chicago: University of Chicago Press.

Shantz, C. U. 1983. Social cognition. In P. H. Mussen (ed.), *Handbook of child psychology,* vol. 3, 4th ed., pp. 495–555. New York: Wiley.

Shapiro, S. 1973. Disturbances in development and childhood neurosis. In S. L. Copel (ed.), *Behavior pathology of childhood and adolescence.* New York: Basic Books.

Shore, M. F. 1985. Correlates and concepts: Are we chasing our tails? In D. L. Jones and R. J. Battjes (eds.), *Etiology of drug abuse: Implications for prevention,* pp. 127–135. NIDA Research Monograph 56. Rockville, Md.: National Institute on Drug Abuse.

Short, R. J., and Simeonsson, R. J. 1986. Social cognition and aggression in delinquent adolescent males. *Adolescence* **21**, 159–176.

Silber, T. J. 1986. Anorexia nervosa in blacks and Hispanics. *International Journal of Eating Disorders* **5**, 121–128.

Singer, M. T., Wynne, L. C., and Toohey, B. A. 1979. Communication disorders and the families of schizophrenics. In L. C. Wynne, R. L. Cromwell, and S. Matthysse (eds.), *The nature of schizophrenia: New approaches to research and treatment.* New York: Wiley.

Skeels, H. M. 1966. Adult status of children with contrasting early life experiences. *Monographs of the Society for Research in Child Development* **31** (3, serial no. 105).

Skinner, B. F. 1948. *Walden Two.* New York: Macmillan.

Skinner, B. F. 1953. *Science and human behavior.* New York: Macmillan.

Slaughter, D. T. 1983. Early intervention and its effects on maternal and child development. *Monographs of the Society for Research in Child Development* **48** (4, series no. 202).

Slavson, S. R, and Schiffer, M. 1975. *Group psychotherapies for children: A textbook.* New York: International Universities Press.

Sloane, R. B., Staples, F. R., Cristol, A. H., Yorkston, N. J., and Whipple, K. 1975. *Psychotherapy versus behavior therapy.* Cambridge, Mass.: Harvard University Press.

Smith, F. 1973. *Psycholinguistics and Reading.* New York: Holt, Rinehart & Winston.

Sours, J. A. 1969. Anorexia nervosa: Nosology, diagnosis, developmental patterns, and power-control dynamics. In G. Caplan and S. Lebovici (eds.), *Adolescence: Psychosocial perspectives.* New York: Basic Books.

Spencer, M. B. 1987. Black children's ethnic identity formation: Risk and resilience of castelike minorities. In J. S. Phinney and M. J. Rotheram (eds.), *Children's ethnic socialization: Pluralism and development*, pp. 103–116. Newbury Park, Calif.: Sage Publications.

Spitz, R. A. 1945. Hospitalism: An inquiry into the genesis of psychiatric conditions in early childhood. *Psychoanalytic study of the child*, vol. 1. New York: International Universities Press.

Spitz, R. A. 1946. Anaclitic depression. *Psychoanalytic study of the child*, vol. 2. New York: International Universities Press.

Spitzer, R. L., and Cantwell, D. P. 1987. The DSM-III classification of the psychiatric disorders of infancy, childhood and adolescence. *Journal of the American Academy of Child Psychiatry* **19**, 356–370.

Spivack, G., Platt, J. J., and Shure, M. 1976. *The problem-solving approach to adjustment*. San Francisco: Jossey-Bass.

Spock, B. 1963. The striving for autonomy and regressive object relations. *Psychoanalytic study and the child*, vol. 18. New York: International Universities Press.

Sroufe, L. A., Waters, F., and Matas, L. 1974. Contextual determinants of infant affective response. In M. Lewis and L. Rosenblum (eds.), *The origins of fear*, pp. 49–72. New York: Wiley.

Stanford-Binet Intelligence Scale. 1986. 4th ed. Chicago: Riverside Publishing.

Stanovich, K. E. 1987. New beginnings, old problems. In S. J. Ceci (ed.), *Handbook of cognitive, social and neuropsychological aspects of learning disabilities*, vol. 1, pp. 229–238. Hillsdale, N.J.: Lawrence Erlbaum Associates.

Starr, R. 1982. *Child abuse and prediction*. Cambridge, Mass.: Gallinger.

Steinhausen, H. C., and Glanville, K. 1983a. Retrospective and prospective follow-up studies in anorexia nervosa. *International Journal of Eating Disorders* **2**, 221–235.

Steinhausen, H. C., and Glanville, K. 1983b. Follow-up studies of anorexia nervosa: A review of research findings. *Psychological Medicine* **13**, 239–249.

Strauss, J. S., Kokes, R. F., Carpenter, W. T., Jr., and Ritzler, B. A. 1978. The course of schizophrenia as a developmental process. In L. C. Wynne, R. L. Cromwell, and S. Matthysse (eds.), *The nature of schizophrenia: New approaches to research and treatment*. New York: Wiley.

Striegel-Moore, R. H., Silberstein, L. R., and Rodin, J. 1986. Toward an understanding of risk factors in bulimia. *American Psychologist* **41**, 245–263.

Sullivan, H. S. 1953. *The interpersonal theory of psychiatry*. New York: Norton.

Sweet, A. A. 1984. The therapeutic relationship in behavioral therapy. *Clinical Psychology Review* **4**, 253–272.

Swisher, L., and Demetras, M. J. 1985. The expressive language characteristics of autistic children compared with mentally retarded or specific language-impaired children. In E. Schopler and G. B. Mesibov (eds.), *Communication problems in autism*, pp. 147–162. New York: Plenum Press.

Sykes, D. H., Douglas, V. I., and Morgenstern, G. 1973. Sustained attention in hyperactive children. *Journal of Child Psychology and Psychiatry* **14**, 213–220.

Tager-Flusberg, H. 1985. Psycholinguistic approaches to language and communication in autism. In E. Schopler and G. B. Mesibov (eds.), *Communication problems in autism*, pp. 89–92. New York: Plenum Press.

Tarnowski, K. J., Prinz, R. J., and Nay, S. M. 1986. Comparative analysis of attentional deficits in hyperactive and learning-disabled children. *Journal of Abnormal Psychology* **95**, 341–345.

Teuber, H. L. 1975. Recovery of function after brain injury in man: Outcome of severe damage to the central nervous system. *Ciba Foundation Symposium*, n.s. **34**, 159–190.

Thomas, A., and Chess, S. 1977. *Temperament and development*. New York: Brunner/Mazel.

Thomas, A., Chess, S., and Birch, H. 1968. *Temperament and behavior disorders in children*. New York: New York University Press.

Tizard, B., and Hodges, J. 1978. The effects of early institutional rearing on the development of eight-year-old children. *Journal of Child Psychology and Psychiatry* **19**, 99–118.

Tizard, B., and Rees, J. 1975. The effect of early institutional rearing on behavior problems and affectional relations of four-year-old children. *Journal of Child Psychology and Psychiatry* **16**, 61–73.

Toner, B. B., Garfinkel, P. E., and Garner, D. M. 1986. Long-term follow-up of anorexia nervosa. *Psychosomatic Medicine* **48**, 520–528.

Torgensen, J. 1975. Problems and prospects in the study of learning disabilities. In E. M. Hetherington (ed.), *Review of child development research,* vol. 5. Chicago: University of Chicago Press.

Townes, B. D., Trupin, E. W., Martin, D. C., and Goldstein, D. 1980. Neuropsychological correlates of academic success among elementary school children. *Journal of Consulting and Clinical Psychology* **48**, 675–684.

Trankina, F. J. 1983. Clinical issues and techniques in working with Hispanic children and their families. In G. J. Powell (ed.), *The psychosocial development of minority group children,* pp. 307–329. New York: Brunner/Mazel.

Trueman, D. 1984. What are the characteristics of school phobic children? *Psychological Reports* **54**, 191–202.

Tuma, J. M. 1989. Mental health services for children: The state of the art. *American Psychologist* **44**, 188–199.

U.S. Department of Commerce. 1980. Bureau of the Census. *1980 Census of population.* Vol. 1, *General population characteristics.* part 1, U.S. Summary. PC80-1-B1.

Valles, E., and Oddy, M. 1984. The influence of a return to school on the long-term adjustment of school refusers. *Journal of Adolescence* **7**, 35–44.

Vaughan, G. M. 1987. A social psychological model of ethnic identity development. In J. S. Phinney and M. J. Rotheram (eds.), *Children's ethnic socialization: Pluralism and development,* pp. 73–91. Newbury Park, Calif.: Sage Publications.

Vega, W. A., Hough, R. L., and Romero, A. 1983. Family life patterns of Mexican-Americans. In G. J. Powell (ed.), *The psychosocial development of minority group children,* pp. 194–215. New York: Brunner/Mazel.

Vellutino, F. R. 1987. Linguistic and cognitive correlates of learning disability: Review of three reviews. In S. J. Ceci (ed.), *Handbook of cognitive, social and neuropsychological aspects of learning disabilities,* vol. 1, pp. 317–335. Hillsdale, N.J.: Lawrence Erlbaum Associates.

Vellutino, F. R., and Scanlon, D. M. 1987. Phonological coding, phonological awareness and reading ability: Evidence from a longitudinal and experimental study. *Merrill Palmer Quarterly* **33**, 321–364.

Vorrath, H. H., and Brendtro, L. K. 1985. *Positive peer culture,* 2d ed. New York: Aldine.

Voss, H. L. 1963. The predictive efficiency of the Glueck Social Prediction Tables. *Journal of Criminal Law, Criminology, and Police Science* **54**, 421–430.

Vurpillot, E. 1968. The development of scanning strategies and their relation to visual differentiation. *Journal of Experimental Child Psychology* **6**, 632–650.

Wadden, T. A., Foster, G. D., Brownell, K. D., and Finley, E. 1984. Self-concept in obese and normal weight children. *Journal of Consulting and Clinical Psychology* **52**, 1104–1105.

Waelder, B. 1960. *Basic theory of psychoanalysis.* New York: International Universities Press.

Waldron, S., Jr., Shrier, D. K., Stone, B., and Tobin, F. 1975. School phobia and other childhood neuroses. A systematic study of children and their families. *American Journal of Psychiatry* **132**, 802–808.

Wallerstein, J. S. 1984. Children of divorce: Preliminary report of a 10-year follow-up of young children. *American Journal of Orthopsychiatry* **53**, 444–458.

Wallerstein, J. S. 1985. Children of divorce: Preliminary report of a ten-year follow-up of older children and adolescents. *Journal of the American Academy of Child Psychiatry* **24**(5), 545–553.

Wallerstein, J. S., and Kelly, J. B. 1974. The effects of parental divorce: The adolescent experience. In E. J. Anthony and G. Koupernik (eds)., *The child in his family: Children at psychiatric risk*, vol. 3. New York: Wiley.

Waterman, J. 1986. Developmental considerations. In K. MacFarlane and J. Waterman (eds.), *Sexual abuse of young children: Evaluation and treatment*, pp. 15–29. New York: Guilford Press.

Watson, J. B. 1913. Psychology as the behaviorist views it. *Psychological Review* **20**, 158–177.

Watson, J. B. 1919. *Psychology from the standpoint of the behaviorist*. Philadelphia: Lippincott.

Watson, J. S., and Ramey, C. T. 1972. Reactions to responsive-contingent stimulation in early infancy. *Merrill-Palmer Quarterly* **18**, 219–227.

Watson, L. R. 1985. The TEACCH communication curriculum. In E. Schopler and G. B. Mesibov (eds.), *Communication problems in autism*, pp. 187–206. New York: Plenum Press.

Watt, N. F. 1984. In a nutshell: The first two decades of high-risk research in schizophrenia. In N. F. Watt, E. J. Anthony, L. C. Wayne, and J. E. Rolf (eds.), *Children at risk for schizophrenia: A longitudinal perspective*, pp. 572–595. Cambridge: Cambridge University Press.

Watt, N. F., Anthony E. J., Wynne, L. C., and Rolf, J. E. (eds.). 1984. *Children at risk for schizophrenia: A longitudinal perspective*. Cambridge: Cambridge University Press.

Watt, N. F., and Lubensky, A. W. 1976. Childhood roots of schizophrenia. *Journal of Consulting and Clinical Psychology* **44**, 363–375.

Wechsler, D. 1974. *Manual for the Wechsler Intelligence Scale for Children-Revised*. New York: Psychological Corporation.

Wechsler Memory Scale. 1987. Rev. ed. San Antonio, Tex.: Psychological Corporation.

Weiner, I. B. 1970. *Psychological disturbances in adolescence.* New York: Wiley.

Weiner, I. B. 1980. Psychopathology in adolescence. In J. Adelson (ed.), *Handbook of adolescent psychology.* New York: Wiley.

Weiner, P. S. 1980. Developmental language disorder. In H. E. Rie and E. D. Rie (eds.), *Handbook of minimal brain dysfunctions: A critical view.* New York: Wiley.

Weiss, B., Weisz, J. R., and Bromfield, R. 1986. Performance of retarded and nonretarded persons on information-processing tasks: Further tests of the similar structure hypothesis. *Psychological Bulletin* **100**, 157–175.

Weiss, G. MBD: Critical diagnostic issues. In H. E. Rie and E. D. Rie (eds.), *Handbook of minimal brain dysfunctions. A critical view.* New York: Wiley, 1980.

Weiss, S. R., and Ebert, M. H. 1983. Psychological and behavioral characteristics of normal weight bulimics and normal weight controls. *Psychosomatic Medicine* **45**, 293–303.

Weissberg, R. P., Cowen, E. L., Lotyczewski, B. S., and Gesten, E. L. 1983. The Primary Mental Health Project: Seven consecutive years of program outcome research. *Journal of Consulting and Clinical Psychology* **51**, 100–107.

Weisz, J. R., Weiss, B., Alicke, M. D., and Klotz, M. L. 1987. Effectiveness of psychotherapy with children and adolescents: A meta-analysis. *Journal of Consulting and Clinical Psychology* **55**, 542–549.

Wenar, C. 1971. *Personality development from infancy to adulthood.* Boston: Houghton-Mifflin.

Wenar, C. 1976. Executive competence in toddlers: A prospective, observational study. *Genetic Psychology Monographs* **93**, 189–285.

Wenar, C. 1982. On negativism. *Human Development* **25**, 1–23.

Wenar, C. 1989. Phobias. In M. Lewis and S. M. Miller (eds.), *Handbook of developmental psychopathology.* New York: Plenum Press.

Wenar, C., and Ruttenberg, B. A. 1976. The use of BRIACC for evaluating therapeutic effectiveness. *Journal of Autism and Childhood Schizophrenia* **6**, 175–191.

Wenar, C., Ruttenberg, B. A., Kalish-Weiss, B., and Wolf, E. G. 1986. The development of normal and autistic children: A comparative study. *Journal of Autism and Developmental Disorders* **16**, 317–333.

Werner, E. E. 1980. Environmental interaction in minimal brain dysfunction. In H. E. Rie and E. D. Rie (eds.), *Handbook of minimal brain dysfunctions: A critical view*. New York: Wiley.

Werry, J. S. 1986a. Biological factors. In H. C. Quay and J. S. Werry (eds.), *Psychopathological disorders of childhood*, 3d ed., pp. 294–331. New York: Wiley.

Werry, J. S. 1986b. Physical illness, symptoms and allied disorders. In H. C. Quay and J. S. Werry (eds.), *Psychopathological disorders of childhood*, 3d ed., pp. 232–293. New York: Wiley.

West, D. J. 1967. *Homosexuality*. Chicago: Aldine.

White, R. W. 1959. Motivation reconsidered: The concept of competence. *Psychological Review* **66**, 297–333.

Whiteside, M. F. 1979. Family therapy. In J. D. Noshpitz (ed.), *Therapeutic interventions: Basic handbook of child psychiatry*, vol. 3. New York: Basic Books.

Wicks-Nelson, R., and Israel, A. C. 1984. *Behavior disorders of childhood*. Englewood Cliffs, N.J.: Prentice-Hall.

Wiggins, J. S. 1981. Clinical and statistical prediction: Where are we and where do we go from here? *Clinical Psychology Review* **1**, 3–18.

Wilkinson, D. A., Leigh, G. M., Cordingley, J., Martin, G. W., and Lei, H. 1987. Dimensions of multiple drug use and a typology of drug users. *British Journal of Addiction* **82**, 259–273.

Wimmer, H., Gruber, S., and Perner, J. 1984. Young children's conception of lying: Lexical realism–moral subjectivism. *Journal of Experimental Child Psychology* **37**, 1–30.

Winsberg, B. G., and Yepes, L. E. 1978. Antipsychotics (major tranquilizers, neuroleptics). In J. S. Werry (ed.), *Pediatric psychopharmacology*. New York: Brunner/Mazel.

Wirt, R. D., Lachar, D., Klinedinst, J. K., and Seat, P. D. 1977. *Personality Inventory for Children*. Los Angeles: Western Psychological Services.

Wohl, T. H. 1980. Other assessment techniques. In H. E. Rie and E. D. Rie (eds.), *Handbook of minimal brain dysfunctions*. New York: Wiley.

Wolfe, D. A. 1987. Child abuse: Implications for child development and psychopathology. *Developmental Clinical Psychology and Psychiatry* **10**, Newbury Park, Calif.: Sage Publications.

Wolpe, J. 1973. *The practice of behavior therapy*, 2d ed. New York: Pergamon Press.

Woodcock-Johnson Psycho-Educational Battery. 1977. Hingham, Mass.: Teaching Resources Corp.

Woodcock Reading Mastery Tests. 1987. Rev. ed. Circle Pines, Minn.: American Guidance Service.

Worden, P. E. 1986. Prose comprehension and recall in disabled learners. In S. J. Ceci (ed.), *Handbook of cognitive, social and neuropsychological aspects of learning disabilities*, vol. 1, pp. 241–262. Hillsdale, N.J.: Lawrence Erlbaum Associates.

Wright, J. C., and Vliestra, A. G. 1975. The development of selective attention: From perceptual exploration to logical search. In H. W. Reese (ed.), *Advances in child development and behavior*, vol. 10. New York: Academic Press.

Wynne, L. C. 1984. Communication patterns and family relations of children at risk for schizophrenia. In N. F. Watt, E. J. Anthony, L. C. Wynne, and J. E. Rolf (eds.), *Children at risk for schizophrenia: A longitudinal perspective*, pp. 572–595. Cambridge: Cambridge University Press.

Wynne, L. C., Toohey, M. L., and Doane, J. 1979 Family studies. In L. Bellak (ed.), *Disorders of the schizophrenic syndrome*. New York: Basic Books.

Yager, J. 1982. Family issues in pathogenesis of anorexia nervosa. *Psychosomatic Medicine* **44**, 43–60.

Yalom, I. D. 1975. *The theory and practice of group psychotherapy*, 2d ed. New York: Basic Books.

Yamamoto, J., and Iga, M. 1983. Emotional growth of Japanese-American children. In G. J. Powell (ed.), *The psychosocial development of minority group children*, pp. 167–180. New York: Brunner/Mazel.

Yamamoto, J., and Kubota, M. 1983. The Japanese-American family. In G. J. Powell (ed.), *The psychosocial development of minority group children*, pp. 237–246. New York: Brunner/Mazel.

Yarrow, M. R., Campbell, J. D., and Burton, R. V. 1970. Recollections of childhood: A study of the retrospective method. *Monographs of the Society for Research in Child Development* **35** (5, serial no. 138).

Yule, W., and Rutter, M. 1985. Reading and other learning difficulties. In M. Rutter and L. Hersov (eds.), *Child and adolescent psychiatry: Modern approaches*, 2d ed., pp. 444–464. Oxford: Black

well Scientific Publications.

Yuwiler, A., Geller, E., and Ritvo, E. R. 1976. Neurobiochemical research. In E. R. Ritvo, B. Freeman, E. M. Ornitz, and P. E. Tanguay (eds.), *Autism: Diagnosis, current research, and management*. New York: Spectrum.

Name Index

Subject Index